ANGLO-SAXON GLASTONBURY:

CHURCH AND ENDOWMENT

The early history of the religious community at Glastonbury has been the subject of much speculation and imaginative writing. The sources with some claim to respectability, however, which can throw light on Glastonbury Abbey in the Anglo-Saxon period, are few. The blatant spuriousness of so much of the 'history' associated with early Glastonbury has led some historians to shy away from the attempt to write seriously about it. This avoidance has resulted in the neglect of an important ecclesiastical establishment. *Anglo-Saxon Glastonbury* brings together the diverse evidence of royal and episcopal grants of land, combined with that of Domesday Book, to produce a survey of the landed endowment of Glastonbury Abbey before 1066 and an analysis of the history of its Anglo-Saxon estates.

A complete account of Glastonbury's early landholdings cannot be written on the present evidence; but, collected together here, the surviving information can at least begin to outline a history for each place named in connection with the pre-Conquest religious house. In addition, each case helps to establish an overall framework for the life-cycle of the Anglo-Saxon estate, building on our understanding of actual conditions of tenure and of the various fortunes ecclesiastical land might potentially experience. Taken together, the estate-histories offer insight into the larger issues of Anglo-Saxon landholding and raise questions about charter-production, charter-transmission, and royal and aristocratic patronage.

LESLEY ABRAMS is a Lecturer in the Department of History and Welsh History of the University of Wales, Aberystwyth, and the author of various studies on mediaeval English and Scandinavian history.

STUDIES IN ANGLO-SAXON HISTORY

General Editor: David Dumville

Editorial Advisors:

Mark Blackburn   Niels Lund
James Campbell   Roger Ray
Simon Keynes   Anton Scharer

Editorial Manager: Clare Orchard

ISSN 0950–3412

Already published

ANGLO-SAXON GLASTONBURY:

CHURCH AND ENDOWMENT

LESLEY ABRAMS

THE BOYDELL PRESS

First published 1996
The Boydell Press, Woodbridge

ISBN 0 85115 369 0

The Boydell Press is an imprint of Boydell & Brewer Ltd
PO Box 9, Woodbridge, Suffolk IP12 3DF, UK
and of Boydell & Brewer Inc.
PO Box 41026, Rochester, NY 14604-4126, USA

British Library Cataloguing-in-Publication Data
Abrams, Lesley
Anglo-Saxon Glastonbury : Church and
Endowment. – (Studies in Anglo-Saxon
History, ISSN 0950–3412 ; Vol. 8)
I. Title II. Series
942.383
ISBN 0–85115–369–0

Library of Congress Cataloging-in-Publication Data
Abrams, Lesley
Anglo-Saxon Glastonbury : church and endowment / Lesley Abrams.
p. cm.
Includes bibliographical references and indexes.
ISBN 0–85115–369–0 (alk. paper)
1. Glastonbury Abbey – History. 2. Excavations (Archaeology) –
England – Glastonbury Region. 3. Glastonbury Region (England) –
Church history. 4. Glastonbury Region (England) – Antiquities.
5. Anglo-Saxons – England – Glastonbury Region. 6. Glastonbury
Region (England) – History. 7. Domesday book. I. Title.
DA690.G45A27   1996
942.3'83–dc20   95–32343

The paper used in this publication meets the minimum requirements
of American National Standard for Information Sciences –
Permanence of Paper for Printed Library Materials, ANSI Z39.48–1984

Printed in Great Britain by the publisher

CONTENTS

LISTS

LIST OF MAPS

For My Father

GENERAL EDITOR'S FOREWORD

In this volume Lesley Abrams has made the most thorough analysis yet published of the records of the endowment of an Anglo-Saxon church. It is particularly appropriate that she should have devoted this exercise to Glastonbury Abbey, for few other ecclesiastical institutions of mediaeval Britain have gathered about themselves so much legend, romance, and wilful fantasy. Dr Abrams's analysis is a consummate historical exposition, relentlessly exposing merely apparent knowledge and showing instead how the records, both those which survive and those which were calendared in the middle ages but are now lost, can be used to draw new patterns of interpretation. Her remarkable study of the account of Glastonbury Abbey's holdings in Domesday Book contains much of more general applicability; in my opinion, it constitutes a milestone in our understanding of the nature of the evidence offered by that extraordinary record. I take great pleasure in welcoming this volume to *Studies in Anglo-Saxon History* and in commending it to its readers.

David N. Dumville
Girton College,
Cambridge

PREFACE

This is a study of the pre-Conquest estates of Glastonbury Abbey, using in particular the charter-material as an entrée into the analysis of the landed endowment of one of the most important religious houses of Anglo-Saxon England. Although revised for publication, the present work has the same shape as my Ph.D. dissertation which underlies it and is not a history of Glastonbury in the pre-Conquest period; a more or less contemporary doctoral dissertation by Matthew Blows, of the University of London, adopted that more narrative approach. Instead I have tried, in my analysis and survey of the abbey's estates, to address questions about patterns of landholding and patronage and also about the documents on which we rely to detect and assess these patterns. Focussing on Glastonbury's estates and on the charters and other evidence which informs us about their history is nevertheless one way of tracing the abbey's progress from its foundation to the Norman conquest: I hope that my research not only draws attention to Glastonbury's particular complexities but also offers the possibility of rewarding comparison with the endowments of other religious houses.

Academic debts incurred during research have been legion. In particular, James Carley and David Dumville initially encouraged me to think about Glastonbury and to appreciate its peculiar pleasures and confront its difficulties. Numerous people have generously allowed me to see work in advance of publication: Matthew Blows, Michael Costen, David Dumville, Jem Harrison, Susan Kelly, Simon Keynes, Peter Kitson, and Stephen Rippon. Others have willingly answered queries and offered opinions on specific points: Debby Banham, Paul Bibire, Michael Costen, Rosemary Cramp, Bob Croft, Sarah Foot, Harold Fox, Margaret Gelling, Kate Harris, Jem Harrison, Peter Kitson, Michael McGarvie, Stephen Morland, Andy Orchard, Oliver Padel, Warwick Rodwell, Michael Swanton, and Leslie Webster. Susan Kelly read and commented on several chapters, and Ian Agnew drew the maps. I am most grateful for all their contributions, which I hope I have acknowledged in the appropriate locations. More generally, David Dumville has been characteristically generous with his assistance. Errors, omissions, and misconstructions of the evidence are of course my own responsibility.

Personal debts are as numerous and as varied. The first stage of the project was supported by many family-members and friends: Marjorie Abrams, Karen Baclawski, Deirdre Baker, Naomi Black, Stillman and Florence Drake, Jacqueline Elton, Sarah Foot, Paul Gooch, Paul Hay, Maryanne Kowaleski, Margaret McClintock, David Needham, Nimbus, Anthea Pascaris, Bridget Penhale, Piglet, Pat Rosenbaum, Fay Sears, Dan Smith, Gary Soroka, Bill Stoneman, Matthew Strickland, Pauline Thompson, Beryl Thorburn, Pat Valentine, Susan Watkins, and Bill Zajac. Latterly, Dan Smith dedicated much time and energy to my technical problems, Ruth Johnson helped to keep the technology under control, Pru Harrison dealt expertly with a difficult set of proofs, and Alicia Corrêa, Susan Kelly, Marion Palmer, and Jan Parker offered vital moral support. Finally, I should like to acknowledge my debt to the choir of St John's College, Cambridge, whose musical artistry, liberal friendship, and *joie de boire* have soothed, resuscitated, and sustained me both during the writing of my dissertation and its subsequent transformation into a book.

L.J.A.
Cambridge, St George's Day, 1994

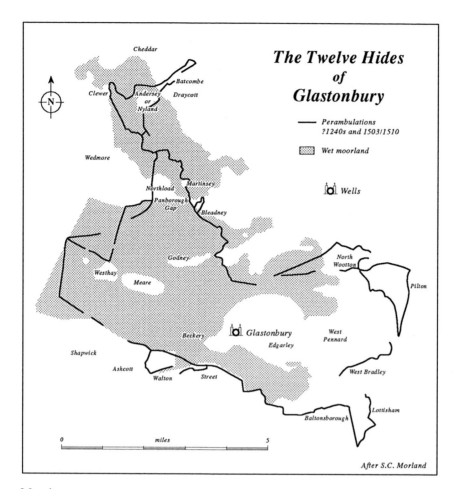

The Twelve Hides
of
Glastonbury

Perambulations
?1240s and 1503/1510

Wet moorland

Wells

After S.C. Morland

Map 1

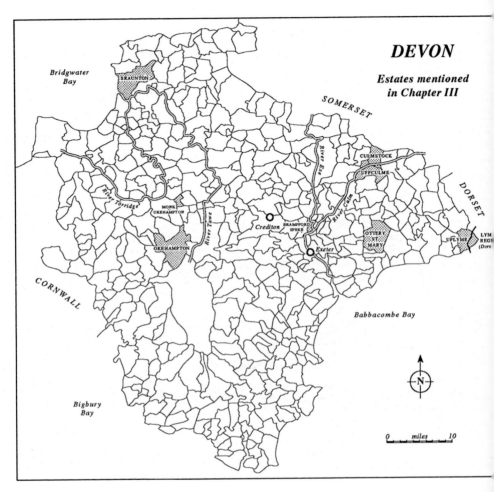

DEVON

Estates mentioned in Chapter III

Map 2

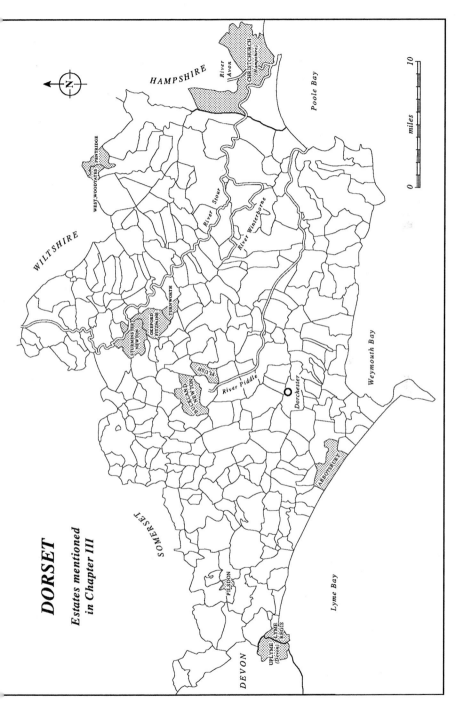

DORSET

*Estates mentioned
in Chapter III*

HAMPSHIRE

WILTSHIRE

SOMERSET

DEVON

River Avon

CHRISTCHURCH
(Hampshire)

Poole Bay

WEST WOODYATES, PENTRIDGE

River Stour

River Winterbourne

STURMINSTER
NEWTON
OKEFORD
FITZPAINE
TURNWORTH

PLUSH
MELCOMBE HORSEY

River Piddle

Dorchester

ABBOTSBURY

Weymouth Bay

PILSDON

UPLYME
(Devon)
LYME
REGIS

Lyme Bay

miles

0   10

xv

Map 3

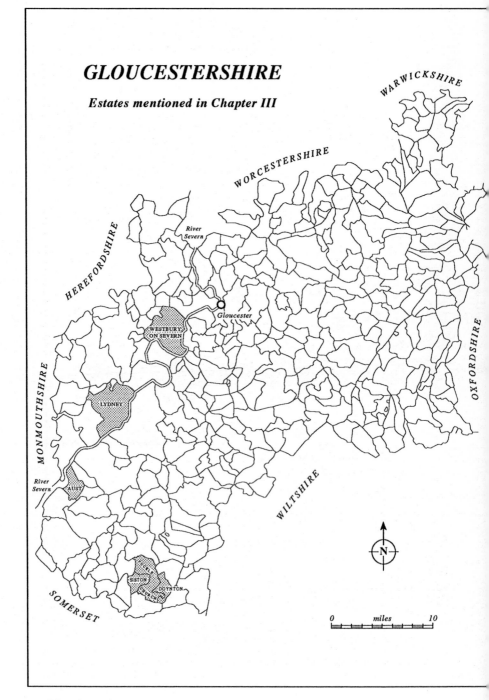

GLOUCESTERSHIRE

Estates mentioned in Chapter III

WARWICKSHIRE

WORCESTERSHIRE

HEREFORDSHIRE

River
Severn

Gloucester

WESTBURY
ON SEVERN

OXFORDSHIRE

MONMOUTHSHIRE

LYDNEY

River
Severn   AUST

WILTSHIRE

SISTON   DOYNTON

SOMERSET

0   miles   10

Map 4

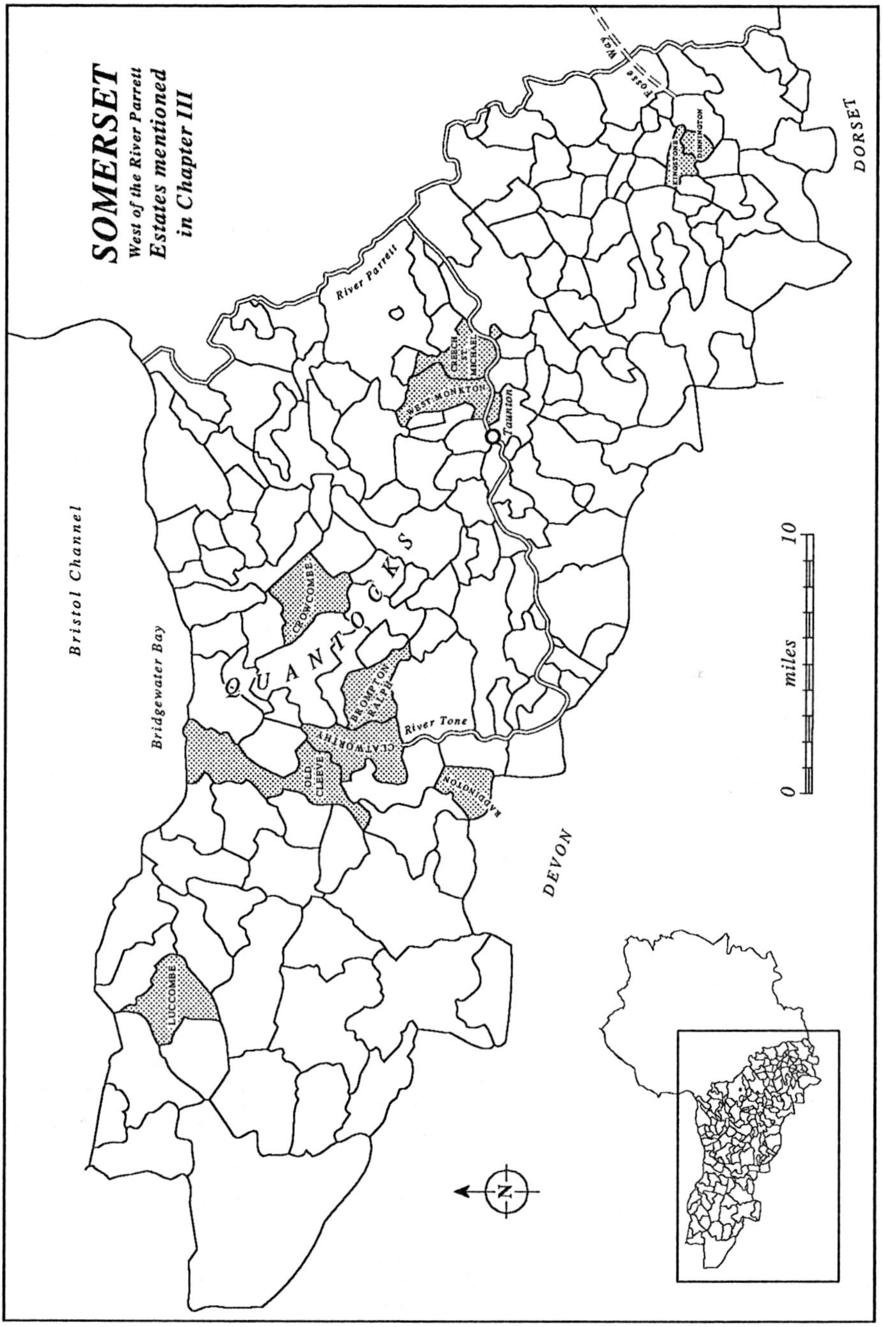

SOMERSET
West of the River Parrett
Estates mentioned
in Chapter III
Bristol Channel
Bridgewater Bay
QUANTOCKS
River Parrett
River Tone
Taunton
Fosse Way
LUCCOMBE
OLD CLEEVE
CLATWORTHY
BROMPTON RALPH
CROWCOMBE
RADDINGTON
WEST MONKTON
CREECH ST. MICHAEL
KINGSTONE
DINNINGTON
DEVON
DORSET
0
miles
10
N

Map 5

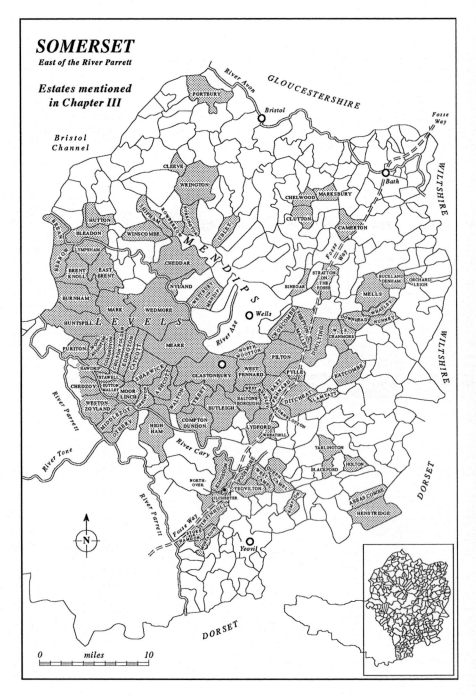

SOMERSET

East of the River Parrett

Estates mentioned in Chapter III

Bristol Channel

GLOUCESTERSHIRE

River Avon

Fosse Way

Bristol

WILTSHIRE

PORTBURY

CLEEVE

WRINGTON

Bath

CHELWOOD MARKSBURY

CLUTTON

CAMERTON

HUTTON
BLEADON
BRENT
BRANCTON
WINSCOMBE
UBLEY

CHEDDAR

STRATTON-ON-THE-FOSSE

BUCKLAND DENHAM

ORCHARD LEIGH

MELLS

CLYMPSHAM
EAST BRENT
BRENT KNOLL
NYLAND
WHETLEY

BINEGAR

DOWNHEAD
NUNNEY

WHATLEY

BURNHAM

HUNTSPILL
MARK
WEDMORE

River Axe

Wells

CRANMORE

MEARE

CROSCOMBE

DOULTING

BATCOMBE

PURITON
CATCOTT
SHAPWICK
EDINGTON
CHILTON POLDEN
ASHCOTT

NORTH WOOTTON

PILTON

WEST PENNARD

PYLLE

HAWDRIP
STAWELL
CHEDZOY
SUTTON MALLET
MOOR LINCH
WALTON
STREET

GLASTONBURY

EAST PENNARD

DITCHEAT

LAMYATT

WESTON ZOYLAND
MIDDLEZOY
OTHERY

BUTLEIGH

BALTONSBOROUGH

COMPTON DUNDON

LYDFORD

HIGH HAM

WHEATHILL

River Cary

River Tone

River Parrett

YARLINGTON

BLACKFORD

HOLTON

NORTHOVER

YEOVILTON

ILCHESTER

ABBAS COMBE

HENSTRIDGE

DORSET

River Parrett

Fosse Way

STOKE
CHARLTON

Yeovil

DORSET

WILTSHIRE

0   miles   10

N

Map 6

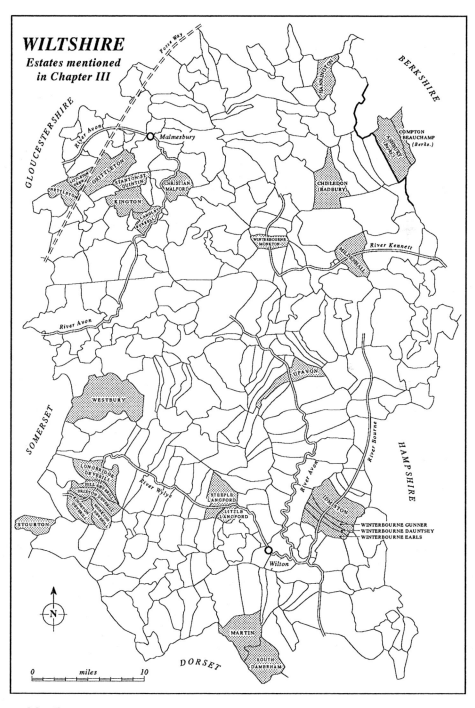

WILTSHIRE

Estates mentioned
in Chapter III

GLOUCESTERSHIRE

BERKSHIRE

Fosse Way

River Avon

Malmesbury

LITTLETON DREW
NETTLETON
GRITTLETON
STANTON-ST-
QUINTIN
CHRISTIAN
MALFORD
KINGTON
LANGLEY
BURRELL

WINTERBOURNE
MONKETON

LIDDINGTON

COMPTON
BEAUCHAMP
(Berks.)

ASHBURY
(Berks.)

CHISLEDON
(BADBURY)

River Kennett

OGBOURNE

River Avon

WESTBURY

SOMERSET

UPAVON

River Bourne

HAMPSHIRE

River Avon

River Wylye

LONGBRIDGE
DEVERILL
HILL
DEVERILL
BRIXTON
DEVERILL
MONKTON
DEVERILL

STOURTON

STEEPLE
LANGFORD
LITTLE
LANGFORD

IDMISTON

WINTERBOURNE GUNNER
WINTERBOURNE DAUNTSEY
WINTERBOURNE EARLS

Wilton

N

0   *miles*   10

MARTIN

SOUTH
DAMERHAM

DORSET

Map 7

xix

I

THE PROBLEM

Thanks to the cult of King Arthur and to a flourishing strain of local mysticism, Glastonbury Abbey's fame is not restricted to historical circles, and it is consequently one of the better known ecclesiastical sites of early mediaeval England. For the visitor, the past is uniquely present: King Arthur and his knights, Joseph of Arimathea, St Patrick, and St Brigit are not merely memorialised in the local landscape but are felt by many to be a vivid, contemporary, presence. For the Anglo-Saxon historian, Glastonbury is perhaps less glamorous, but redolent nonetheless of ancient associations. It is identified with the earliest days of monasticism, closely linked with the monastic reform of the tenth century, and frequently cited as the richest ecclesiastical house in England in 1066.[1] Yet discussions of Glastonbury are noticeably absent from general and synthetic works of Anglo-Saxon history, and no major study of the pre-Conquest community has yet been published.[2] This tendency of scholars to steer clear derives essentially from the condition of the available primary sources. There are two principal difficulties. The first is that there is so little source-material; reputable hagiographical literature which bears on the pre-Conquest community is extant only after *ca* A.D. 1000, and the narrative and annalistic material from which so much of the history of Anglo-Saxon England is derived offers only occasional fragments of information on Glastonbury. Secondly, the burgeoning there in the late middle ages of a fertile imaginative literature has cast a shadow over anything written about the house by its supporters. Glastonbury's monks clearly had historical pretensions but no qualms about invention, and stories of historical, quasi-historical, and fictional figures were happily combined to produce poetry, narratives, and even charters which upheld the status of the community not merely as the backdrop for some extraordinary tales but as the last bastion of 'Celtic' Christianity and as the *fons et origo* of the English Church. Their blatant spuriousness has led some historians not merely to reject the claims about Arthur and Joseph of Arimathea and Patrick in these sources but to shy away from the attempt to write serious

---

[1] For example, by Knowles, *The Monastic Order*, pp. 37–9 and 101–2; see also Knowles & Hadcock, *Medieval Religious Houses*, pp. 11–13.
[2] J. Armitage Robinson's excellent essays (see bibliography) on aspects of Glastonbury's early history are small but important exceptions to this statement. See also the recent dissertation by Matthew Blows, 'Studies', and two more general studies by James Carley (*Glastonbury Abbey*) and Philip Rahtz (*English Heritage Book of Glastonbury*).

history about Glastonbury.[3] This avoidance has resulted in the neglect of an important ecclesiastical establishment.

Glastonbury has been similarly ill served by archaeology.[4] Extensive excavations in the abbey-precinct by F. Bligh Bond in the early decades of the twentieth century were eventually halted after it was revealed that the excavator held his regular site-conferences with the spirits of mediaeval monks and that his excavation-strategy was dictated – literally – by automatic writing.[5] Bond's obsession with the then fashionable 'science' of numerology led him, according to some of his contemporaries, to find and record what he was determined (and inspired) to discover, rather than what was there.[6] Such eccentricities aside, Bond worked when the greatest developments in excavation-, dating-, and recording-techniques were still to come.[7] In addition, his principal interest was in the very end of the middle ages, and particularly in the Edgar and Loretto Chapels, added by Abbot Beere (A.D. 1494–1524/5?) to the east and north (respectively) of the great abbey-church;[8] Bond's work revealed little of the pre-Conquest monastery. Bond was replaced (briefly) by Theodore Fyfe and then by the trio of C.R. Peers, A.W. Clapham, and E. Thorne, who published short reports from the mid-1920s to the end of the 1930s.[9] Their work included the excavation from 1926 to 1929 of a substantial church which they identified as that reputedly built by King Ine (A.D. 688–726); they relied heavily on the late and suspect literary evidence as a guide, and this, along with disturbingly inconsistent site-plans, does not inspire confidence in their method or interpretations. In 1951 excavations were resumed by C.A. Ralegh Radford and continued until 1964; among his pre-Conquest discoveries were a large ditch, the monastic cemetery, and a glass-furnace which he dated to the ninth century. None of the results of the excavations of the mid-1920s to the 1960s has been fully published. From the interim reports, however, it appears that Radford's reconstructions of the evidence for the pre-Conquest churches which had been uncovered by his predecessors were also controlled

---

3   For examples of a new approach, see the various articles in *The Archaeology*, edd. Abrams & Carley.

4   Philip Rahtz has recently remarked that despite thirty-four seasons of digging the fundamental aims of the excavations 'have not been realised' (*English Heritage Book of Glastonbury*, p. 67).

5   Bond published a series of reports from 1908 to 1926 (see bibliography). Most of these have been collected and reprinted in the biography of Bond (Kenawell, *The Quest*, pp. 165–315). Bond's reports are reticent about his technique, but his books are more explicit: see, for example, *The Gate of Remembrance*.

6   Horne, 'The Edgar Chapel'.

7   Rahtz has praised Bond's drawings, however (*English Heritage Book of Glastonbury*, p. 77).

8   Bond's communications from 'the other side' were generally received from monks of the late fifteenth and early sixteenth centuries; when 'Awfwold ye Saxon' tried to get through with a message about the early church-buildings he was thwarted, according to Bond's regular (Dissolution-era) correspondent, because 'hee knows not ye tongue' (Kenawell, *The Quest*, p. 134).

9   Fyfe, 'Glastonbury excavations' (two reports); Peers *et al.*, 'Glastonbury Abbey excavations' (nine reports).

largely by what he found in the unreliable, post-Conquest, written sources and – for the later phases – by analogy with the better known site of Cluny; at Glaston-bury the earliest material remains were fragmentary and disturbed, and the dating evidence was singularly lacking.[10] Much has been made of all this nonetheless. In 1955, it was announced that the post-holes of a wattled building had been found, associated with Roman and sub-Roman pottery which 'indicated a date in the fifth or sixth century' for the structure: this building was taken to 'confirm the Glastonbury tradition that the first church – the *uetusta ecclesia* – which formed the cult-centre of the monastery till its destruction in the fire of 1184, was built of wattles'.[11] The discovery of this feature has since been widely used as proof of the existence of a British monastery at Glastonbury,[12] although there was nothing to indicate that the building was a church; and more specifically, there was nothing to identify it with the so-called *uetusta ecclesia*, allegedly second-century, which, later mediaeval writers emphasised, had stood for centuries some distance to the northwest of the excavated building, on the site of the present Lady Chapel (which replaced it after a fire).[13] In 1981 it was acknowledged that the pottery which had dated the wattled structure was residual, brought in with the clay used to level the area, and had 'no bearing on the origins of the monastery'.[14] Even the date of the structure, therefore, was discredited, and no physical evidence of a British monas-tery has survived the analysis of those results which are available.[15] Fifth- and

---

[10] As far as we can tell, that is, without the publication of detailed site-reports. For his summary of the excavations, published in 1981, see Radford, 'Glastonbury Abbey before 1184'. See also Robinson, 'The historical evidence', Cramp, 'Monastic sites', pp. 241–6, and Rodwell, 'Churches in the landscape', pp. 18–21. Taylor & Taylor (*Anglo-Saxon Architecture*, I.253) published a rough (but helpful) composite plan of some of the principal features described by Radford, but the lack of a reliable plan showing all the excavated pre-Conquest features at Glastonbury has been regretted (Hill, 'The Anglo-Saxons 700–1066 AD', p. 113). This has been remedied in part by Philip Rahtz, who has recently re-analysed the archaeological investigations of the site and provided a welcome (though necessarily approximate) plan of excavations (*English Heritage Book of Glastonbury*, pp. 66–100, especially p. 68). He has also reproduced Roger Leech's plan of the excavated early features and provided his own of the pre-Conquest layout (pp. 70–1). Rahtz has commented on the 'many inconsistencies and contradictions about the location of walls and features' (p. 68). Fortunately, 'excava-tions did not in most cases go as deep as the natural subsoil and there is still much undisturbed ground in other parts of the precinct' (p. 68).

[11] Radford, 'The excavations . . . 1951–4', p. 21.

[12] Taylor & Taylor, in their survey of Anglo-Saxon architecture, stated that this discovery confirmed 'the existence of a monastery of the Celtic type on the site' (*Anglo-Saxon Architecture*, I.250–7, at 254); Edwards (*The Charters*, p. 65) was led to the same conclusion by this interpretation of the archaeology.

[13] *De antiquitate*, §2 (ed. & transl. Scott, pp. 46–51); John of Glastonbury, *Cronica*, §§1 and 96 (edd. & transl. Carley & Townsend, pp. 8–11 and 178–9). The excavated wattled building was under the west walk of the later cloister. See Taylor & Taylor, *Anglo-Saxon Architecture*, I.253, or Rahtz, *English Heritage Book of Glastonbury*, p. 70.

[14] Radford, 'Glastonbury Abbey before 1184', p. 111.

[15] I am grateful to Rosemary Cramp, Michael Swanton, and Warwick Rodwell for their opinions on this point (the last-named in a letter dated 3 November, 1993).

sixth-century activity in the area is indeed attested – but on Glastonbury Tor (less than a mile to the east), not on the abbey-site.[16]

Two further seasons of excavation in the abbey-precinct – unpublished – were conducted by W.J. Wedlake in 1978 and 1979, and a few trenches have been examined in the course of road-widening and in other rescue-situations; in 1988 an archaeological evaluation of an area of the northern precinct-boundary was undertaken by Peter Leach.[17] It is to be hoped that work at the abbey, in the town, and outside Glastonbury at sites associated with it in the Anglo-Saxon period may offer more in the future, although large non-rescue excavation-projects are out of favour in the current climate.[18]

Although Glastonbury's history and archaeology bear such obvious signs of contamination – not encouraging for the investigator – it is nevertheless worth the effort to untangle the authentic from the spurious and attempt to piece together something of the history of this early and important house. The following is not, however, a narrative history of Glastonbury Abbey in the Anglo-Saxon period. It is instead one way of looking at the abbey's progress from foundation to Norman takeover, through a study of its lands. Domesday Book provides the finishing line for such a study, presenting as it does a snapshot of the endowment at the time of the Norman conquest. The bulk of the evidence – and the main source on which this study is based – is the collection of Anglo-Saxon charters in the community's archive. These documents purportedly recorded (or acted as proof of) the acquisition of the estates which made up the abbey's landed wealth before 1066. The

[16] Rahtz, 'Excavations on Glastonbury Tor', and *English Heritage Book of Glastonbury*, pp. 54–65. Rahtz has argued that the Tor was 'the pre-Saxon religious nucleus of Glastonbury', whose 'inconvenient location necessitated expansion to a new site' on flatter ground in the early Anglo-Saxon period (*ibid.*, pp. 59–60; see also his 'Pagan and Christian', pp. 23–34). As Rahtz has admitted, however, the ecclesiastical character of the fifth- and sixth-century occcupation of Glastonbury Tor has not been proved and a secular interpretation is also possible.

[17] Ellis, 'Excavations at Silver Street', where two pre-Conquest phases of the *uallum* of the north-east corner of the monastic precinct were identified, the earliest being carbon-dated A.D. 670+100/–30 and A.D. 610+50/–70; Hollinrake & Hollinrake, 'The abbey enclosure ditch', pp. 73–8, where a section of a possibly tenth-century enclosure-ditch to the west was examined. See also Leach & Ellis, 'The medieval precinct'. A copper-alloy censer of late sixth- or seventh-century date and of Eastern Mediterranean provenance was allegedly found in a service-trench near the abbey-precinct in the late 1970s or early 1980s and was purchased by the British Museum in 1986. See Cramp, *Anglo-Saxon Connections*, p. 32 (no. 49), Rahtz, 'Pagan and Christian', pp. 33–4, and Leslie Webster *apud* Webster & Backhouse, *The Making of England*, p. 94 (no. 68). I am grateful to Leslie Webster for information on the censer.

[18] Controlled excavation and survey have not stopped entirely, however. Small excavations took place on the abbey-site in advance of the construction of a visitors' centre in the late 1980s. The Shapwick Project, co-ordinated by M.A. Aston and M.D. Costen of the University of Bristol, has undertaken a detailed study of one of Glastonbury's important estates (see *The Shapwick Project*, edd. Aston *et al.*: 2nd–5th reports); and the Anglo-Saxon royal complex at Milborne Port has been surveyed by the Trust for Wessex Archaeology. I am grateful to Bob Croft, of the Planning Department of the Somerset County Council, for information on current archaeological work in the county.

archive as a whole and each charter in particular require (and will elsewhere receive)[19] diplomatic analysis: this will establish questions of authenticity. My aim here, however, has had to be more limited: to use the charters, together with Domesday Book, as evidence for the composition of Glastonbury's endowment and the abbey's relationship with the Anglo-Saxon kings and other, mainly secular, patrons. Although the charters bear indirectly on specific issues of broad, English, interest, in the following survey they have a predominantly local application, in respect of the accumulation of the vast estates upon which Glastonbury's economic wealth and political importance rested. The results, however, are not simply of local interest, although I hope that my detailed examination (in chapter III, below) of places associated with Glastonbury in the pre-Conquest period does advance our knowledge of the history of individual estates. But a comparative study – combining the results of this analysis with corresponding analyses of other establishments having different backgrounds, in different parts of the country – would offer a new contribution to the history of the Anglo-Saxon Church which would greatly enhance our understanding of the processes of growth and decline and of the complexities involved in the management of its landed wealth.

The charters, however, were not designed to answer all the questions of historians: there are many interesting points on which they fail to inform us. The difficult question of Glastonbury's origins is first on this list of silences. Glastonbury is frequently cited as a surviving 'Celtic' house,[20] a 'temple of reconciliation [which] must have played no small part in the blending of the two races'.[21] Scrutiny of the written sources, however, reveals no more evidence to support this than has so far been offered by the excavated remains.[22] A charter (once supposedly in the archive but no longer extant) purporting to be a gift of five hides at *Inesuuitrin* by a king of Dumnonia in A.D. 601 was interpreted by William of Malmesbury as a grant of land to a British house at Glastonbury, but the fragment of the text of the alleged grant which has been preserved bears no Celtic attributes and is singularly unconvincing as a document.[23] Compounding the difficulty is

---

[19] In the series of editions of Anglo-Saxon charters, archive by archive, published jointly by the British Academy and the Royal Historical Society.

[20] The word 'Celtic' in this context is ultimately derived from the now abandoned concept of the 'Celtic Church'; see Hughes, 'The Celtic Church', and Davies, 'The Celtic Church'. It is rarely defined by those who use it with reference to the early history of Glastonbury; it appears to connote anything from a subordinate relationship with the Welsh or Irish Churches to, more simply, a community run by people who spoke a Brittonic language, especially before the Anglo-Saxon conquest.

[21] Robinson, *Somerset*, p. 35.

[22] As noted above, it is nonetheless assumed to be so by many: see, for example, C.A.R. Radford ('The Church in Somerset', p. 36, and 'Glastonbury Abbey', p. 104), who considered the existence of cults of Irish saints at Glastonbury in the later Anglo-Saxon period and later middle ages to be evidence of Christian worship at a date before the Saxon conquest of the region; see also Pearce, *The Kingdom*, p. 100. Blows has discussed – and rejected – the 'Celtic' derivation of the place-name Glastonbury ('Studies', pp. 60–1). Finberg (*Lucerna*, pp. 83–5) was not convinced by references in the *De antiquitate* to British names (reputedly of abbots) on a painting in the church and on a 'pyramid' in the cemetery (§§32 and 35; ed. & transl. Scott, pp. 84 and 88).

[23] It has nonetheless been used recently to argue for the existence of a British monastery,

the fact that no Anglo-Saxon foundation-charter – authentic or spurious – survives to signal either the end of a British ecclesiastical régime or the establishment *de novo* of an English house. Perhaps such a document was suppressed when the legends of more glamorous founders such as St James's twelve disciples and SS. Phagan and Deruvian (not to mention St Patrick) were cultivated in the later middle ages.[24] It is also possible that houses of the earliest period of foundation were endowed with their lands before the habit of charter-writing had taken hold on the English side of the Channel.[25] The lack of documentation for Glastonbury's origins has allowed various claims to be made – often quite fantastic – and permitted great controversy to flourish concerning the date and context of its foundation. It is a measure of the difficulty that if we restrict ourselves to the historical (rather than legendary) sources, the evidence is so poor and so doubtful that we cannot be certain of Glastonbury's original dedication,[26] or even identify who was responsible for the initial endowment of the house. The first Anglo-Saxon king credited with a gift of land to the abbey is Cenwealh (A.D. 642–672);[27] the community may be said to begin to emerge from documentary obscurity shortly thereafter, during the reign of King Centwine (A.D. 676–?685), a man praised by Aldhelm for his benefactions to ecclesiastical houses.[28] Charters and records of charters offer information on royal and episcopal grants to the abbot of Glastonbury and his *familia* in Centwine's reign.[29] To what extent

replaced without a significant break by an Anglo-Saxon one: Edwards, *The Charters*, pp. 64–5. For the charter, see *De antiquitate*, §35 (ed. & transl. Scott, p. 88), and William of Malmesbury, *Gesta regum Anglorum*, §§27–28 (ed. Stubbs, I.28–9). For distinctive Celtic characteristics in Latin charters, see Davies, 'The Latin charter-tradition', especially pp. 262–3. For Finberg's treatment of this document, see below, chapter III, *s.n.* Glastonbury.

24 *De antiquitate*, §33 (ed. & transl. Scott, p. 86), conveniently runs through the list of (spurious) founders. On the association with St Patrick, see Abrams, 'St Patrick and Glastonbury', and the literature cited there.

25 Some attribute its introduction to Theodore, archbishop of Canterbury, A.D. 669–690. On the first use of royal diplomas in England, see Chaplais, 'Who introduced charters', and Kelly, 'Anglo-Saxon lay society', pp. 39–43.

26 Glastonbury is usually associated explicitly with Mary in pre-Conquest sources, although King Ine's church is said in the *De antiquitate* (§40; ed. & transl. Scott, p. 94) to have been dedicated to St Peter and St Paul, a dedication apparently attested in the corrupt text of S.1410 (A.D. 744) and in B's Life of St Dunstan (which, however, mentions only St Peter: *Memorials*, ed. Stubbs, p. 7). In fact, evidence of the dedication to Mary seems not to predate the tenth century; Blows has suggested that the reign of Edmund marked its beginning ('Studies', p. 333). A dedication to Christ is recorded in the dubious privilege of Pope Leo dated A.D. 798 (*De antiquitate*, §50; ed. & transl. Scott, p. 108) and in §3 of B's Life (there paired with both St Mary and St Peter: *Memorials*, ed. Stubbs, p. 7). Multiple churches could account for these dedications.

27 Assertions of gifts by this king to Sherborne and Exeter may indicate such activity by him in the newly acquired West or, alternatively, that forgers used his name to suggest great antiquity and to link their houses with the origins of institutional Christianity in Wessex.

28 *Aldhelmi Opera*, ed. Ehwald, pp. 14–15; *Aldhelm. The Poetic Works*, transl. Lapidge & Rosier, pp. 47–8.

29 S.236, S.237, S.1249, S.1666, S.1667, and S.1668. See chapter III, *s.n.* Glastonbury.

Glastonbury was then an established community or a new foundation, however, is not revealed in the charter-record. The size (or value) of its endowment at that time (or at any one time thereafter, with the exception of 1066) is impossible to determine.

Glastonbury Abbey's fate during the First Viking Age is another issue of great interest. It has been conventional to assume collapse, destruction, and discontinuity[30] – that King Alfred seems to have given no land to Glastonbury has been taken to prove the abbey's dereliction.[31] A small number of late ninth- and early tenth-century charters nevertheless apparently indicates the continued existence of a community there. Whether this consisted of monks or canons – or others less recognisable to us as professionally religious – is obscure and will probably remain so. What is more relevant for my purpose is the recognition that a suspension of monastic discipline need not have meant the dissolution of the endowment and the end of corporate landholding. The epithet *insula regalis* applied to the abbey by Dunstan's biographer, B, raises the question of the extent to which Glastonbury in the early tenth century was a royal proprietary church.[32] If it was a royal minster, the difference between royal land and abbatial land – probably crystal-clear to contemporaries, if a distinction existed – is quite obscure to us. The evidently special relationship between Glastonbury and the house of Wessex – both before and after the tenth-century reform – would have coloured the history of the community's endowment and the nature of its land-transactions (and their documentation), but again the evidence of the charters on this question is obscure.[33]

What, then, do Glastonbury's charters tell us? Diplomas are, in general, a rich mine of evidence on the authority of kings, the administration of patronage, and the political fortunes of individuals. When examined principally from the point of view of the growth of the endowment, they testify to grants made to the abbey by kings, queens, sub-kings, and bishops, as well as recording royal grants to religious or laypeople who may or may not have passed the properties in question on

---

[30] For the view that Glastonbury did not survive the ninth century, see, for example, Knowles, *The Monastic Order*, p. 33, and Costen, 'Dunstan, Glastonbury, and the economy', p. 26. The statement by William of Malmesbury in his *Gesta pontificum Anglorum* (§91; ed. Hamilton, p. 196) that the site was *desolatus* after the time of the Danes has presumably been largely responsible for the idea of total collapse.

[31] Blows, however, has proposed an alternative – political – explanation ('Studies', pp. 277–83, and below, pp. 337–8).

[32] B, *Vita S. Dunstani*, §3 (*Memorials*, ed. Stubbs, pp. 6–7). B wrote *ca* A.D. 1000 and may have known Dunstan at Glastonbury. Another biographer, Osbern of Canterbury, writing in the late eleventh century, stated that 'ea tempestate, Glestonia regalibus stipendiis addicta' ('at that time, Glastonbury belonged to the king's treasury'): Osbern, *Vita S. Dunstani*, §6 (*Memorials*, ed. Stubbs, p. 74), translated and discussed by H.P.R. Finberg in *West-Country Historical Studies*, pp. 75–6. In the English context, this might describe a house which had fallen into royal hands as a result of the difficulties of the ninth century; regardless of the existence of a religious community, the land would have been considered the king's. Such a state of affairs should not have survived the tenth-century reform. Blows, on the other hand, has argued that Glastonbury was always a royal foundation ('Studies', p. 280). See further below, pp. 337–43.

[33] See below, chapter III, *s.n.* Glastonbury, and pp. 335–50.

to the community.[34] The documents bear dates from the late seventh century to the early eleventh. A large amount of land came into Glastonbury's hands, apparently by these means, and some of it seems to have passed out of its grasp after a relatively short period, although the record is sufficiently fragmentary and equivocal to complicate most attempts at a decision on the date and means of acquisition and loss (especially the latter).[35] The evidence is unwieldy as well: the accumulation of the documentary material and its organisation by place has proved to be a necessary prerequisite of the proper analysis both of the charters and of the estates granted. An examination of the archive from the point of view of the land-transactions which it documents offers much information for the mapping of the Anglo-Saxon landscape; but it also raises fundamental questions about what it was that charters were intended to achieve and about the nature of landholding, at least in this part of Wessex. In particular, the reconstruction of estate-histories from the charter-material exposes the difficulties of interpretation which the corpus offers and reveals the weakness of our grasp of the mechanics of conveyancing and the conditions of land-tenure in Anglo-Saxon England. How, for example, are we to interpret successive charters granting ostensibly permanent possession to the abbey (or to different laypeople) of what appears to be the same land? What did the beneficiary of a solemn diploma receive? Can we detect the difference between a gift of land, a confirmation of a previous gift, or a transaction involving not necessarily real acres but something less tangible, such as commendation? What does it signify if an estate's hidage was different in the tenth century from its total in Domesday Book? To what extent does the appearance of an estate in any one of the several sources in which Glastonbury's charters are preserved validate the assumption that the abbey held the land? What does it mean if land granted to lay recipients (and recorded as such in the abbey's archive) appears as Glastonbury's in Domesday Book? And what does it mean if that land is said to belong to someone else? How did the shape of the endowment change between the seventh and the eleventh century, and to what extent can this process be detected in the charter-record? All these questions, if not answered, are at least raised and tackled in the survey and analysis which follow. Because of the bulk of the charter-material, it has been necessary to treat it more or less as a self-contained sample; but those familiar with the archives of other houses will, I hope, find parallels (and differences) worth noting.

Domesday Book, with its wealth of detail – unparalleled in the pre-Conquest sources and, indeed, unmatched in eleventh-century Europe – offers a crucial complement to the charter-material. It is the sole essentially scrupulous witness to the composition of Glastonbury's endowment at the end of the Anglo-Saxon period, and without it the history of the abbey's estates would be significantly impoverished. Domesday Book's illuminating light can dim perceptibly when analysis is taken further and awkward questions are posed, however. First among these questions must be a consideration of the conditions of tenure on Glaston-

---

[34] For fuller accounts of Glastonbury's identifiable patrons in the later Anglo-Saxon period, see Hart, 'Athelstan "Half King" ', Williams, *'Princeps Merciorum gentis'*, Loud, 'An introduction to the Somerset Domesday', pp. 14–19, and Blows, 'Studies', especially pp. 271–99 and 345–52.

[35] See below, especially pp. 321–34.

bury's estates in 1066, a subject which I have examined in detail below.[36] Despite probing, the data remain obscure in this respect and resist comparison with other (better understood) parts of the country.

Given these difficulties of interpretation, which compound the handicap imposed by the inevitably fragmentary survival of sources, a complete reconstruction of the history of Glastonbury's estates cannot be expected. But the material nonetheless comprises a bank of information which can be used at least to begin to outline a history for each place. Sometimes this is only a passing glimpse, sometimes a story of puzzling complexity. When the evidence for each estate is collected, patterns and problems emerge; although this combined evidence so often proves perplexing, it is only when it has been brought together that the larger problems which it raises can be confronted. Overall, each case helps to establish a framework for the life-cycle of the Anglo-Saxon estate, building on our awareness of the vicissitudes and upheavals to which ecclesiastical land might be subject.

Although much from pre-Conquest Glastonbury has been lost, the land itself remains as evidence; and the charter-record, though woefully incomplete, offers information on over two hundred places associated with the Anglo-Saxon abbey, places whose history this study attempts to trace.

---

[36] See pp. 289–312.

II

THE SOURCES

The documentary sources for the history of Glastonbury's pre-Conquest estates, though fragmentary, compare well in number with those available for most early English ecclesiastical communities. The relative wealth of material, however, does not necessarily simplify the task of the historian interested in studying the development of the abbey's endowment. Thanks to the complication that more information makes the picture more contradictory, it is often difficult to draw even tentative conclusions.

Diplomas – whether issued by kings, bishops, or laymen – are the fundamental source for the history of pre-Conquest estates.[1] Anglo-Saxon charters survive in two different forms: either as single sheets or as texts copied into larger collections. Within these two basic categories there are further types. Single sheets can be originals – contemporary with the grants which they document – or later copies, these latter produced with either innocent or fraudulent aims. Glastonbury's archive contains examples of all of these. Of authentic originals, S.563 (a grant by King Eadred to Ælfgyth, dated 955) appears to be the lone survivor. Of later copies, S.236 is a probably tenth-century single-sheet version of a grant (dated 681) by a King Baldred. S.248 is a difficult single sheet to classify, but I have argued elsewhere that this diploma in the name of King Ine, dated 705/6, is a facsimile-copy, perhaps of late Anglo-Saxon date.[2] S.553, ostensibly a tenth-century original in confirmation of a grant by King Eadred to Glastonbury, is an example of an eleventh- or twelfth-century forgery.[3] A single sheet of another grant by King Eadred (S.530 or S.541) was extant as late as ca 1600, when it was seen by the antiquary Francis Tate, but it has since disappeared.[4]

---

1 General studies of Anglo-Saxon diplomas include Stenton, *The Latin Charters*, Dorothy Whitelock's introduction to the subject in *English Historical Documents*, pp. 369–82, Chaplais, 'The origin', 'The Anglo-Saxon chancery', and 'Some early Anglo-Saxon diplomas', Brooks, 'Anglo-Saxon charters', Keynes, *The Diplomas of King Æthelred*, pp. 1–39, Wormald, *Bede and the Conversion*, and Kelly, 'Anglo-Saxon lay society'. Studies of particular groups of charters and individual archives will be referred to as they arise in discussion. Anglo-Saxon charters are cited by the number given by Sawyer, *Anglo-Saxon Charters* (hereafter S.).

2 See Abrams, 'A single-sheet facsimile'.

3 See Abrams, ' "Lucid intervals" '.

4 Tate compiled a glossary of technical words with very short citations (Cambridge, University Library, MS. Ff.5.15); he glossed the word *hid* with a reference to 'carta Eadredi facta Wulfrico ministro suo de 5 mansis seu hydis æt Yfemesta' nunc sunt

The four extant single sheets are the only remnants of what must have been an impressive collection. They did not come down to us together as a group. The first two, S.563 and S.236, both for land at Pennard, were preserved in the collection of Glastonbury's documents now in the library of the Marquess of Bath at Longleat House.[5] These presumably went to Longleat, together with a substantial number of other documents relating to former abbatial lands, when Sir John Thynne (*ob.* 1580), builder of Longleat House and secretary to Edward Seymour, Duke of Somerset and Protector of the Realm, was accumulating his vast estates. There appears to be no surviving record of their transfer, but at least some of the documents relating to estates previously belonging to Glastonbury were at Longleat by 1555.[6]

Not all of Glastonbury's muniments followed the same route after the Dissolution. Other landowners in addition to the Thynnes bought or were rewarded with the abbey's property. The history of the surviving single sheet of S.248 is as obscure as the date of its composition, but it may have travelled from Glastonbury to Mells, an abbatial estate bought in 1543 by its tenant, John Horner, whose family had been tenants and officials of Glastonbury Abbey for over a hundred years.[7] The first definite post-Dissolution appearance of the single sheet of S.248 occurred when it was presented as a gift to the newly formed Somerset Archaeological and Natural History Society in 1849.[8] The family of the donor, the Reverend Hill Dawe Wickham, had had a long association with the Horners and Mells, and it is possible that this connexion had provided one of the Wickhams with the opportunity to acquire the charter.[9] It is now lodged at the Somerset Record Office.[10]

uocatur Ydemeston in com' Wilt'' – one of two grants of Idmiston to the same beneficiary; Tate got his information *ex ipsa carta*, but where he got the charter from is unknown. The texts of both S.530 and S.541 survive in Glastonbury's cartulary-collections. I am indebted to Simon Keynes for directing me to Tate's glossary.

5 Longleat House, Marquess of Bath, MSS. NMR 10565 and 10564. Although both diplomas are for Pennard, they applied to East and West Pennard respectively. For S.236, see Stenton, *Anglo-Saxon England*, p. 67, n. 1, and Edwards, *The Charters*, pp. 11–15. I am grateful to Kate Harris (archivist and librarian to the Marquess of Bath) for her help through correspondence and during my visits to Longleat. The Glastonbury material at Longleat has been catalogued by Harris & Smith, *Glastonbury Abbey Records*.

6 In a letter of February 1555, William Paulet, the Lord Treasurer, requested that Sir John Thynne return 'all suche bookes, muniments, transcriptes, and writinges as you had out of the house of Glastonburie' (Longleat House, Marquess of Bath, MS. NMR 10580; Harris & Smith, *Glastonbury Abbey Records*, pp. vii and 86). The site and the church of Glastonbury had been granted to Edward Seymour in 1547. For the dispersal of monastic lands in Somerset, see Bettey, *The Suppression*, especially pp. 131–48, and Wyndham, 'In pursuit of Crown land'.

7 Cf. Bettey, *The Suppression*, pp. 36–7. I am most grateful to Michael McGarvie for his information on the Horners and the Mells archive and to Lord Oxford for allowing me access to the manuscripts at Mells.

8 See Anon., 'First annual meeting', p. 25.

9 For a fuller discussion, see Abrams, 'A single-sheet facsimile', p. 100.

10 Taunton, Somerset Record Office, MS. DD/SAS.PR.501.c/795.

The preservation of the fourth single sheet, S.553, is due in part to the hostilities which broke out between the see of Bath and Wells and the abbey of Glastonbury in the late twelfth century, when Bishop Savaric (A.D. 1191–1205) attempted to annex the monastery to the cathedral. This cause was diligently pursued by Bishop Jocelin (A.D. 1206–1242) and, although the take-over was ultimately unsuccessful, disputes over land which had been seized by Wells continued into the later thirteenth century.[11] Some manipulation of the written record may have taken place as a result. Documents associated with at least those estates retained by the see of Wells were apparently housed in the cathedral's archives. When the diploma S.553 was transcribed by T. Duffus Hardy in the 1860s or 1870s, it belonged to the Dean and Chapter of Wells Cathedral, having perhaps been transferred there in the thirteenth century when Glastonbury finally lost its fight for the land granted in the charter. For some time, S.553 was lost sight of – it was apparently no longer at Wells when Walter de Gray Birch, editor of the collected Anglo-Saxon charters, went there before 1893[12] – but it too is now lodged at the Somerset Record Office in Taunton.[13]

We can extend our knowledge of the Anglo-Saxon archive of Glastonbury Abbey beyond these four single sheets, thanks to the preservation in two later mediaeval cartularies of the texts of fifty-six pre-Conquest diplomas relating to estates (or, in some cases, confused with places with similar names) still held by the abbey in the mid-fourteenth century. Only one of the grants represented by the extant single sheets (S.236) was copied into the cartulary-collections. The Great Cartulary (Longleat House, Marquess of Bath, MS. 39) was written *ca* A.D. 1340.[14] This manuscript consists of 219 folios of charters organised in groups by estate, with the addition of material in hands of the later fourteenth to early sixteenth century (219v–244v). The editor of the cartulary, Aelred Watkin, has referred to it as 'a serviceable but unhandsome office reference-book'.[15] The

---

11 For the first 'composition' between Wells and Glastonbury in A.D. 1203, in which several manors were transferred to the cathedral, see *The Great Chartulary*, ed. Watkin, I.73–9 (no. 126); for the second composition (A.D. 1219), whereby the bishop returned a number of the manors, see *ibid.*, I.87–9 (no. 140); for the confirmation by Henry III in A.D. 1227 of Wells's possession of four of these manors which had been Glastonbury's, see [Bird], *Calendar of the Manuscripts of the Dean and Chapter of Wells*, I.359–60; for the third composition, a quitclaim of the abbot for the four manors in A.D. 1266, see *The Great Chartulary*, ed. Watkin, I.95–100 (no. 147); for the final concord in A.D. 1275 between the bishop and the abbot (and, it seems, the last word on the four manors), see [Bird], *Calendar of the Manuscripts of the Dean and Chapter of Wells*, I.168. Wells is known to have seized land at Ashbury, Badbury, Berrow, Blackford, *Bocland*, Christian Malford, Cranmore, Damerham, East Brent, *Kyngtone*, *Lim* (two manors), Meare, Pucklechurch, Sturminster Newton, and Winscombe (*q.v.*). Glastonbury apparently recovered all of these save Blackford, Cranmore, Pucklechurch, and Winscombe.

12 Birch's text was taken from Hardy's transcript: *Cartularium Saxonicum*, ed. Birch, III.43–6 (no. 887).

13 Taunton, Somerset Record Office, MS. DD/CC.111489. For a fuller discussion, see Abrams, ' "Lucid intervals" '.

14 *The Great Chartulary*, ed. Watkin; Davis, *Medieval Cartularies*, p. 49 (no. 434).

15 *The Great Chartulary*, ed. Watkin, I.xi.

Secretum abbatis or *Secretum domini* (Oxford, Bodleian Library, MS. Wood empt. 1 [*S.C.* 8589]), which Watkin has called its 'sister manuscript', is, according to him, an ornate fair copy of the Great Cartulary for the abbot's personal use, and is probably datable to *ca* A.D. 1342.[16] The Great Cartulary was presumably transferred to Longleat House, like the single sheets already mentioned, when Sir John Thynne acquired his large share of Glastonbury's lands. Its continued presence there is attested by a variety of evidence, including its use in litigation and its citation in works of antiquarian scholarship.[17] The immediately post-Dissolution history of the *Secretum domini* is unknown, but it is now bound with another Glastonbury manuscript in a leather cover which bears the Sheldon arms. Bought by Ralph Sheldon (1623–1684) 'from among other books lying in the vestry of St. Clement Danes, London', it had previously belonged to the Earl of Arundel.[18] It was acquired by Anthony Wood (1632–1695) for his collection of manuscripts, part of which – including the *Secretum domini* – went to the Bodleian Library by sale in 1690.[19] The Great Cartulary and the *Secretum domini*, though very different in form, are essentially identical in their contents.[20] However, two of the pre-Conquest grants in the *Secretum domini* (S.253 and S.871) do not appear in the Great Cartulary. This circumstance complicates – but does not, however, invalidate – Watkin's description of the former as a fair copy of the latter.[21] The charters in these two collections are listed at the end of this chapter.

A third manuscript (Longleat House, Marquess of Bath, MS. NMR 10586) provides one text (at pp. 128–9) of an Anglo-Saxon diploma (S.237, in the name of King Centwine and dated 682) which is not found in the fourteenth-century cartularies. MS. NMR 10586 is an incomplete early sixteenth-century paper

---

16 Davis, *Medieval Cartularies*, pp. 49–50 (no. 435); *The Great Chartulary*, ed. Watkin, I.xi. It was said to have been written by 'frater Thomas de Lamport' and was given the siglum 'D' by the scribe of a later Glastonbury manuscript: see *A Feodary*, ed. Weaver, p. 2.

17 It was the *magnus liber* or 'great parchment book' referred to, for example, some time after 1604 in the dispute over Sharpham Park (Longleat House, Marquess of Bath, MS. NMR 6214; Harris & Smith, *Glastonbury Abbey Records*, pp. 89–90). Humphrey Wanley consulted it for his *Catalogus Historico-criticus*. See Hickes, *Linguarum Veterum Septentrionalium Thesaurus*, II. 283–4.

18 According to a note on a loose sheet kept with Oxford, Bodleian Library, MS. Wood D.6 (*S.C.* 8528), Anthony Wood's catalogue of Sheldon's manuscripts; see *A Feodary*, ed. Weaver, pp. xvii–xix.

19 *Ibid.* MS. Wood empt. 1 is described in the 1697 catalogue of Wood's manuscripts as 'an ancient, large and very fair Leiger Book of Glastenbury Abbey, usually called *Secretum Abbatis*, as being alwaies in his own custody': [Bernard], *Catalogi*, p. 371. For the sale of Wood's manuscripts in 1690, see Macray, *Annals*, p. 157.

20 An index of the contents of MS. Wood empt. 1 has been printed: see 'Index', edd. Weaver & Mayo.

21 The position of S.871 would allow it to have been a later addition to the *Secretum*, while S.253, which heads the Shapwick section of the *Secretum*, could have been accidentally omitted from the Great Cartulary and the omission rectified when the fair copy was made.

cartulary of documents relating to a few specific estates, including West Monkton, for which S.237 has been presumed to be the earliest title-deed.[22]

These cartularies are relatively late witnesses from Glastonbury's archive and represent the state of the abbey's endowment at a time far removed from the Anglo-Saxon period. There was, however, a much earlier cartulary, which recorded Glastonbury's territorial strength before the administrative and economic changes of the later middle ages, when the ecclesiastical map of the region was significantly redrawn. This early cartulary is now lost, but its existence is known because a list of its contents was transcribed and survives in a manuscript of A.D. 1247/8, now Cambridge, Trinity College, MS. R.5.33 (724) (77r–78r), which also contains a text of the early history of the house, the *De antiquitate Glastonie ecclesie*, its continuation (the *Libellus de rebus gestis Glastoniensibus*), and many late mediaeval documentary records.[23] The *Liber terrarum* or *Landbok*, as it was called, included a far greater number of pre-Conquest documents than now survive: according to its contents-list, it contained 134 charters (plus three apparent additions, one seemingly a duplicate and one a list of Glastonbury's lands). It is not always possible to correlate the entries exactly with surviving texts, but an approximate measure of what has been lost can be made if we say that about ninety of the grants recorded in the *Liber terrarum* do not appear to be found in extant documents. The contents-list of the *Liber terrarum*, however, is minimalist in style: in general, only the names of estate, donor, and beneficiary were recorded; if Glastonbury was the direct beneficiary, the abbot of the time was occasionally also named. Without details of the terms of the grant, the transaction cannot always be identified confidently by comparison with grants recorded in other sources. But it is certain that many of the transactions cited in the *Liber terrarum* can no longer be found in other documentary witnesses; the extant contents-list therefore offers a glimpse of a quite different stage of Glastonbury's endowment and archival organisation from that portrayed in the mid-fourteenth-century cartularies. A list of the charters from the contents-list of the *Liber terrarum* is provided at the end of this chapter.

The date of this lost cartulary has proved to be difficult to establish. Joseph Armitage Robinson pointed out that the latest diplomas recorded were grants by King Æthelred the Unready (A.D. 978–1016) (LT79 and LT133) and suggested that the manuscript might have been compiled after A.D. 984 (a date given

---

22 Davis, *Medieval Cartularies*, p. 50 (no. 437). For a discussion of whether S.237 was indeed a grant of West Monkton, see below, chapter III, *s.n. Cantucuudu*.

23 James, *The Western Manuscripts in the Library of Trinity College*, II.198–202; for a description of this manuscript and an analysis of its compilation, see Crick, 'The marshalling'. The contents-list of the lost cartulary was printed by Thomas Hearne, *Johannis Confratris et Monachi Glastoniensis Chronica*, II.370–5. The contents-list has been dated to the year 1247, on the assumption that it was created and revised at the same time as the dated library-catalogue on folios 102–104 of the same manuscript (*Somerset Mediaeval Libraries*, ed. Williams, pp. 52–78). The lost cartulary itself appears in this library-catalogue: 'Liber terrarum Glastonie, uetustus sed legibilis' (MS. R.5.33, 103ra42). It was crossed off, presumably in 1248 when the list was checked and revised. I should like to thank Simon Keynes for allowing me to see his unpublished reconstruction of the contents of the *Liber terrarum*.

elsewhere for the transaction represented by LT133) and possibly before Dunstan's death in A.D. 988.[24] H.P.R. Finberg, presumably on the same grounds, ascribed the compilation of the cartulary to (in one work) the close of the tenth century or (in another) the beginning of the eleventh.[25] The absence from the *Liber terrarum* of a grant by King Æthelred of *ca* A.D. 1000 which is recorded in other sources would seem to support the late tenth-century date for the compilation of the cartulary;[26] seven further transactions by Æthelred are found in other Glastonbury sources but were apparently not in the *Liber terrarum*,[27] a fact which appears to substantiate the idea of a *terminus ante quem* for its composition some time in Æthelred's reign.[28] But the texts of six of these eight grants are lost, and any (or all) of them could have been later forgeries; further, the evidence of the two extant charter-texts (S.866 and S.871) may be problematic.[29] Arguments based on the absence of these eight grants from the *Liber terrarum* are therefore not necessarily ultimately convincing, although the fact of their omission ought not to be dismissed lightly. There is another problem: a number of seemingly authentic diplomas from the mid-tenth century were not included in the *Liber terrarum*, although if genuine they clearly predate the cartulary. *Their* omission, then, must have some explanation other than chronology. As Simon Keynes has observed, 'one would like to think that the non-inclusion of several charters of Æthelred in the *Liber terrarum* reflects on the date of its composition: the principle is perfectly sound, but its operation in this context requires confidence in the authenticity of non-existent charters and acceptance of its *non*-operation for several earlier tenth-century charters directly in favour of Glastonbury'.[30] The absence from the *Liber terrarum* of writs and of diplomas of Cnut or Edward the Confessor is paralleled in later collections of Glastonbury muniments (with one exception, there are no charters from these kings' reigns in the fourteenth-century cartularies); so their omission, too, is inconclusive for purposes of dating.[31]

---

24 Robinson, *Somerset*, p. 45; the other occurrence of LT133 (a grant of Wilton) is in the *De antiquitate Glastonie ecclesie* (on which, see below, pp. 21–7), §§63 and 69 (ed. & transl. Scott, pp. 130 and 144).

25 Finberg, *Lucerna*, p. 97, and *The Early Charters of Wessex*, p. 14.

26 A grant of a fishery or a place called *Fiswere* which is cited in the *Index chartarum* (IC A16; on which see below, pp. 16–17) and in the *De antiquitate*, §§63 and 69 (ed. & transl. Scott, pp. 130 and 144).

27 S.866 (A.D. 987) and S.871 (A.D. 988); and IC C11–14 and D22 in the *Index chartarum* (see below, pp. 16–17).

28 Like the *Liber Wigorniensis* at Worcester; see Ker, 'Hemming's cartulary', and Finberg, *The Early Charters of the West Midlands*, pp. 15–18.

29 Simon Keynes has pointed out that some suspicion must attach to S.866 simply because it is recorded only in the Great Cartulary and the *Secretum* and nowhere else in Glastonbury's archive; Keynes, 'Studies', I.172. This circumstance would be somewhat less suspicious, however, if the *Liber terrarum* predated S.866 (A.D. 987). S.871, a grant from the king to the bishop of Sherborne and a layman, may not necessarily represent land which Glastonbury itself received, in which case the charter could have been deposited at the abbey at any time after its date of 988.

30 *Ibid.*, I.174.

31 The only charter for Glastonbury in the name of Cnut (S.966, a grant of privileges) is probably post-Conquest in its current form. Keynes has pointed out that cartularies of

To test the assumption that the *Liber terrarum* was compiled in the late tenth century, Keynes compared its contents-list with an index of those pre-Conquest charters surviving in the Glastonbury archive in the mid-thirteenth century, which occurs in Trinity College, MS. R.5.33, after the contents-list of the lost *Liber terrarum*.[32] This index is the next in the series of documentary sources offering significant testimony about Glastonbury's Anglo-Saxon endowment. There are five groups of pre-Conquest *cartae*, under the headings 'Carte ueteres regum de terris datis Glastonie quas adhuc habet, et sunt sine sigillis', 'Carte ueteres regum de terris datis suis seruientibus quas adhuc Glastonie sine sigillis', 'Carte ueteres de terris datis Glastonie immediate quas non habet', 'Carte ueteres regum de terris datis suis seruientibus quas creditur habuisse Glastoniensis ecclesia sed modo non habet', and 'Antiqua priuilegia'. These five lists are collectively now referred to as the *Index chartarum* and are designated A, B, C, D, and E. They contain twenty, twelve,[33] fifteen, twenty-two, and three entries, respectively, a total of seventy-two (numbered and listed at the end of this chapter). One would expect to find the same charters in these lists as appear in the *Liber terrarum*, in addition to those acquired after that cartulary was compiled. Unfortunately, the situation is not so simple.

The charters on List A are those for lands given directly to Glastonbury which the monastery still retained, presumably in A.D. 1247 – the date of the manuscript, although the lists could of course have been compiled at an earlier stage.[34] Of these twenty documents, only eleven were to be found in the *Liber terrarum*, as far as it is possible to tell from the often cryptic entries; only one of the twenty is as late as the reign of King Æthelred.[35] List B consists of charters for lands given to the kings' *seruientes* – and presumably then passed on to the abbey – which Glastonbury still owned. Four of these had appeared in the *Liber terrarum*;[36] why the other eight were not included is unclear, as they are all in the names of earlier kings.[37] List C, of charters for lands given directly to Glastonbury but which the monks no longer held (again, presumably in A.D. 1247), exhibits a similar pattern: of the fifteen on the list, only four were in the *Liber terrarum*.[38] The logic of this list is particularly opaque, as it contradicts its rubric in two ways, by including documentation for lands which seem to have been given

---

other houses exhibit a similar scarcity of grants of the late tenth or eleventh century (*ibid.*, I.167). According to the *Secretum* (66v), Cnut's charter *scribitur in principio de Landeboc*, but there is no reference to it in the extant contents-list.

[32] MS. R.5.33, 77v–78v; Keynes, 'Studies', I.170–7.

[33] The twelfth entry is an addition.

[34] The order of estates found in §70 of the *De antiquitate Glastonie ecclesie* (see below) is identical to the order of estates in List D, suggesting that the arrangement found in the *Index chartarum* predated the writing of R.5.33, as the *De antiquitate* was begun *ca* A.D. 1129. However, I consider it likely that §70 is a later interpolation (*ca* A.D. 1129x1247): see below, pp. 24–6. Therefore the deduction may not be appropriate.

[35] IC A1–4, 7, 9, 11, 14, 18–20. IC A16 is the grant of *Fiswere* by Æthelred mentioned above.

[36] IC B4, 5, 7, and 10.

[37] If they were not later forgeries, perhaps these eight charters were passed on to Glastonbury only after the compilation of the early cartulary.

[38] IC C3, 4, 9, and 10. C10–14 are in the name of Æthelred.

not to the abbey directly but to laymen (C7, for Blackford, and C9, for Winscombe),[39] and, in one case, for land which Glastonbury seems not to have lost (C8, for Sturminster Newton).[40] The fourth group, of charters for lands given to the kings' servants and once owned by Glastonbury but no longer held, continues the pattern: only seven of twenty-two appear to have been entered in the *Liber terrarum*.[41] The three 'ancient' privileges of List E are probably post-Conquest compositions, none of which is listed as having been in the *Liber*.[42]

These lists, therefore, provide little help in determining the date of the lost *Liber terrarum*. Domesday Book should perhaps be more useful, but there is no significant pattern revealed there in the eleventh century among those estates held by the abbey during the reign of King Edward the Confessor and yet not documented in the early cartulary.[43] Keynes has consequently proposed a post-Domesday date for the *Liber terrarum*, with the composition of the *De antiquitate* ca A.D. 1129 as the *terminus ante quem*.[44] Heather Edwards and Matthew Blows, however, have preferred to see it as a pre-Conquest compilation.[45] It is especially unfortunate that a fixed date cannot be given to this lost cartulary, in order to provide a historical context for its compilation. It would also be useful to know whether the archival situation which it represents was a pre- or post-Conquest one. It is apparent from notes in the contents-list that information – possibly in the form of endorsements on the charters, copied into the cartulary – may have been provided on the means of transfer of some of the lands from their lay owners to the abbey, a question of importance about which we should like to know much more. If the information came from the charters themselves it would carry great weight; the compiler of the contents-list may, however, have supplied this information on his own initiative, a circumstance which would compromise the value

---

[39] These entries are marked '*seruienti*'. Supplementary documentation or charters which had been directly in favour of the abbey may have once existed, justifying inclusion of C7 and C9 here.

[40] Sturminster Newton appears regularly in the later mediaeval records of the abbey's estates. A temporary loss (spanning the 1240s), however, is not impossible. See below, chapter III, *s.n.* Sturminster Newton.

[41] IC D2, 4, 9, 11, 16, 17, and 18. Only D22 is in Æthelred's name.

[42] S.250, S.783 (both in the Great Cartulary as well as the *De antiquitate*), and the 'Charter of St Patrick' (*De antiquitate*, §9; ed. & transl. Scott, pp. 54–8).

[43] Keynes, 'Studies', I.177–8.

[44] *Ibid.*, I.167–8. The latter date is, however, not entirely sure, for the lines in the *De antiquitate* (in §70) on which Keynes has based his argument may be interpolated. Discrepancies between the information in the preceding section and that in the main body of the work must raise the possibility that §§69–71 – two summaries in prose and an index of abbots – represent later additions. Even if some of §70 were William's work, its list of estates, used as evidence by Keynes, bears signs of interpolation. The list is not in the equivalent chapter of John of Glastonbury's *Cronica*. See below, pp. 24–7.

[45] Edwards, *The Charters*, p. 4; Blows, 'Studies', pp. 26–31. Blows has considered other factors (such as the description in A.D. 1247 of the *Liber terrarum* as *uetustus* and the possible context of the composition of the lost cartulary) and has suggested that it was compiled during the abbacy of Æthelweard (*recte* Ælfweard) (ca A.D. 975–?1009) to establish the identity of the abbey's patrons and the antiquity of its endowment.

of these notes as evidence. Without the charter-texts, we can only speculate, and many questions remain unanswered: the principles which governed inclusion in the *Liber terrarum* are uncertain; nor is it known whether that cartulary distinguished between different types of document (and included vernacular leases, which were not preserved in the mid-fourteenth-century collections), whether it identified sales as distinct from benefactions, or whether its record favoured particular periods of acquisition. The one point which seems clear from the evidence as a whole is that neither the *Liber terrarum* nor the *Index chartarum* was a comprehensive collection.

This conclusion is confirmed by the evidence of a late mediaeval inventory of charters (Longleat House, Marquess of Bath, MS. 39a).[46] This early fifteenth-century register, of eighty-six folios, lists documents of all dates (most of them later mediaeval), grouped first by estate and then by ecclesiastical office.[47] It was not a static document: some sort of updating seems to be attested by the presence of several later hands whose owners supplied additional entries, in many cases citing the earliest charters. Although the topographical arrangement and order mirror those of the mid-fourteenth-century cartularies,[48] the addition of so many entries seems to indicate changes in record-keeping practices, if only in terms of cataloguing. Forty-seven identifiably pre-Conquest charters are listed, with two further possibly Anglo-Saxon documents cited without sufficient detail to fix their date with certainty. These charters are numbered and listed at the end of this chapter. As we should expect, some of the fifty-six Anglo-Saxon charters of the mid-fourteenth-century cartularies are missing from MS. 39a;[49] but (and by now we should not be surprised) eleven pre-Conquest documents not in those cartularies are listed as extant in the fifteenth century,[50] together with some twenty Anglo-Saxon charters not in the *Liber terrarum*;[51] likewise, an even greater number of pre-Conquest charters not in the *Index chartarum* is cited in this inventory.[52] If we assume that the charters listed in MS. 39a were genuine, its testimony indicates that

---

[46] *Olim* 38b; Davis, *Medieval Cartularies*, p. 50 (no. 439). A.J. Horwood printed an incomplete list of the pre-Conquest charters mentioned in this manuscript in Anon., *Fourth Report*, Appendix, p. 228.

[47] Most of the pre-Conquest charters appear in the topographical sections, but two (L46 and 47) are included among the muniments of the *cameraria*, and another (possibly) (L47a) among those of the *coquinarius*.

[48] The two (possibly three) charters not in the topographical sections of MS. 39a which appear in the contents-list of the *Liber terrarum* are missing from the Great Cartulary, the *Secretum domini*, and the *Index chartarum* (L46, L47, and perhaps L47a; LT51, LT8, and LT10). This might imply that they were already separated from the others in A.D. 1247 and might serve as a clue to the circumstances behind the compilation of the lists and the later cartularies. There may have been other lists, now lost (perhaps even lost by *ca* A.D. 1340, though possibly simply out of use), of estates assigned to the different monastic officers such as the *camerarius* and *coquinarius*.

[49] This includes all the grants of privileges (S.246, S.250, S.257, S.303, S.499, S.783, and S.966) as well as S.580, S.462, S.442, S.474, S.513, S.747, S.551, S.530 (or S.541), S.504, S.568(?), S.288, S.253, and S.871.

[50] L5, 12, 16, 25a, 30, 33, 43, 44, 46, 47, and 47a.

[51] L5, 9, 16, 18, 20, 21, 24, 25, 25a, 26, 28, 30, 33, 34, 35, 37, 38, 40, 43, and 44.

[52] L4, 6, 10, 13, 14, 15, 16, 22, 25a, 26, 27, 31, 32, 33, 37, 39, 43, 44, 45, 46, and 47.

a significant number of the abbey's pre-Conquest documents were not included in the *Liber terrarum* or in the lists compiled in A.D. 1247/8. It also shows that omission from the *Index chartarum* and the Great Cartulary cannot be taken to mean that the charters had disappeared from the archive.

At least eight of the Anglo-Saxon charters listed in MS. 39a are there specifically identified as copies, implying perhaps that the rest were thought to be originals.[53] If so, the survival of so many pre-Conquest documents in the fifteenth century is noteworthy. The copies may have been made from the early cartulary, as three are referred to by their number in the *Liber terrarum* and a fourth entry is more specific: 'copia carte . . . ut patet in landboke'.[54] Although there is evidence that the fourteenth-century cartularist had access to the *Liber terrarum*,[55] the citation of *Liber terrarum* numbers in MS. 39a need not signify the survival of the early cartulary in the fifteenth century; it is perhaps more likely that it reflects information given in endorsements on the original single sheets. Endorsements citing exactly that information occur on the two single sheets at Longleat.[56] It is possible, therefore, that MS. 39a was compiled not from the *Liber terrarum* but from pre-Conquest single sheets and/or from later single-sheet copies. If so, this would provide an interesting insight into Glastonbury's archival practices in the later middle ages.

Occasionally, other Anglo-Saxon archives can be drawn into the discussion to supplement the information about Glastonbury's estates which is provided by the abbey's own record. Charters belonging to other communities can illuminate the fortunes of an estate if it – or a charter for it – was held for a time by another religious house. Wills or other documents preserved elsewhere occasionally throw light on an estate or a patron associated with Glastonbury.[57] In particular, disputes between churches could give rise to documentation, some of it quite untrustworthy.[58] Diplomatic reasons, however, may lie behind the unusual and interesting

These include what appear to have been separate boundary-descriptions: 'Bunde de Wynterborne et Idemyston in uetusta cedula' (L33).

53 L4, 13, 14, 15, 22, 25a, 35, and 47a; the entries for L5, 9, 12, 34, and 35 may imply the existence of an original *and* a copy.

54 L4, 13, 14, and 15 (LT3, 91, 82, and 83).

55 The bounds of several estates were omitted from the Great Cartulary and the *Secretum* but were there said to be found 'in libro qui dicitur Landebok'. See chapter III, *s.n.* Idmiston, Little Langford, and Merton.

56 S.563 (an original dated 955) and S.236 (a seemingly tenth-century copy of a seventh-century grant) bear respectively the endorsements 'carta Edredi regis de Pennard minster et est LXVIII in landboke' and 'carta Baldredi regis de Pennard et est septima in landeboke' in the same thirteenth-century hand; the two Pennard charters are indeed in the seventh and sixty-eighth places on the contents-list of the *Liber terrarum* as found in MS. R.5.33. For the endorsements, see the reproductions given in *Facsimiles*, ed. Sanders, II, Marquess of Bath 1 and 2.

57 See, for example, S.1512 (A.D. 964x980), the will of Brihtric Grim, which was preserved at Winchester Cathedral (in London, British Library, MS. Add. 15350). The document was witnessed by the communities of Glastonbury and of the New and Old Minsters at Winchester (*Anglo-Saxon Wills*, ed. & transl. Whitelock, p. 18 [no. 7]).

58 Glastonbury's disputes are not well documented: Patrick Wormald has described Glastonbury as an 'absentee' from his list of recorded pre-Conquest disputes, citing only

case of two texts of the so-called 'Dunstan-B' type which appear in the cartularies of Abingdon and Shaftesbury respectively (S.564 and S.570) as well as in the Glastonbury record;[59] diplomas which appear to be duplicates of these were recorded in the contents-list of the *Liber terrarum*, but have since disappeared from Glastonbury's collection (LT109 and LT97).[60]

Other, non-documentary, sources occasionally throw light on Glastonbury's endowment. The Life of Dunstan by B, written between A.D. 995 and 1005 but offering knowledge of Dunstan's life only before A.D. 960,[61] tells us something of the abbey's noble patrons during the reigns of successive kings from Æthelstan to Edgar.[62] But such sources are few and their contribution to a study of the endowment is small.

The most complete and best known source for Glastonbury's pre-Conquest estates catches them at the end of their history. Domesday Book marks the close of Glastonbury Abbey's four hundred years of Anglo-Saxon life and – unlike many of the apparently pre-Conquest sources – is an essentially scrupulous witness to and largely credible record of the abbey's endowment at one moment in 1066 and again in 1086.[63] It is thus the authority for the last chapter of many estate-histories. Without it, the composition of Glastonbury's holdings at the close of the Anglo-Saxon period would be impossible to define. A relatively small number of estates with no recorded connexion with Glastonbury before 1066 appears among the abbey's properties in Domesday Book, but many of these are likely to have been parts of other estates for which there is earlier documentation.[64] Domesday Book's testimony can combine with the charter-material not only to indicate what the monks held but also – less reliably (as is always the

---

S.1705 and S.1777, lost restitutions of *Cumtone* and Pucklechurch respectively ('A handlist of Anglo-Saxon lawsuits', p. 272, n. 33).

[59] London, British Library, MS. Cotton Claudius B.vi, 40v–41r; London, British Library, MS. Harley 61, 6v–7r. For the peculiarities of the 'Dunstan B' charters, see Hart, *The Early Charters of Northern England*, pp. 19–22; and Keynes, *The Diplomas of King Æthelred*, pp. 46–8, and 'The "Dunstan B" charters'. S.563, one of Glastonbury's extant single sheets, belongs to this distinctive group which is associated with Dunstan and charter-production at Glastonbury. See also below, pp. 328 and 346–7.

[60] See chapter III below, *s.n.* Henstridge and Compton Beauchamp.

[61] Lapidge, 'B. and the *Vita S. Dunstani*', pp. 247–9. For the possible identification of B as the deacon Byrhthelm, see *ibid.*, pp. 257–8.

[62] See §§10–12 (*Memorials*, ed. Stubbs, pp. 17–21), for the noble ladies Æthelflæd and Æthelwynn, for example.

[63] The text of Domesday Book is available in *Domesday Book*, ed. Farley, and *Great Domesday. Facsimile*, gen. ed. Erskine. *Domesday Book*, gen. ed. Morris, provides convenient editions and translations of the returns by county.

[64] A list of these estates is provided below; see p. 41. Their independence in Domesday Book gives them all a separate identity which may not have pertained when they were acquired, as many of them appear to have been carved out of other estates (for which records exist). This contrasts with the situation at Christ Church, Canterbury, where there is no evidence for the acquisition of thirty-six of the church's eighty-nine manors named in Domesday Book; Brooks, *The Early History*, pp. 105–7. Without the (admittedly ambiguous) evidence of the contents-list of the *Liber terrarum*, the *Index chartarum*, and the *De antiquitate*, the number of estates at Glastonbury undocumented before Domesday Book would be far higher than it is.

case with negative evidence) – to suggest what they had lost. Further, in addition to much welcome and previously unavailable detail on the land's resources, husbandry, population, and values, Domesday Book offers the earliest evidence of how the abbey's estates were managed and of the nature of the tie between the abbot and the men and women on the community's land. Its testimony on these matters is not easy to interpret, as will be shown below.[65]

One final source remains to be introduced. The *De antiquitate Glastonie ecclesie* was begun probably in the late 1120s by William of Malmesbury, possibly in fulfilment of a commission by the monks of Glastonbury.[66] It is arranged in chronological order: an account of Glastonbury's territorial acquisitions, grouped together by reign, forms §§35–70. These chapters are based on charter-material: the name of the abbot (if known) is given, the grants made during his abbacy are described, including details such as date, donor, recipient, and hidage. Occasionally, quotations, apparently from charter-texts, appear in the narrative, but the only complete texts copied into the work are papal and royal grants of privileges. The testimony of the *De antiquitate* has generally been taken as authoritative, and its fuller details of the benefactions by pre-Conquest kings have in many cases been used to fill out the sketchy information on the substantial number of grants whose texts have been lost.[67] Yet William's reputation as a careful and sensible historian, a 'modern' writer allegedly uncontaminated by the flair for fantasy exhibited by some of his contemporaries,[68] has given the *De antiquitate* an authority which it may not deserve as a record of Glastonbury's early endowment.

The problem is fundamental and twofold. First, the many interpolations intruded into the text of the *De antiquitate* in the later twelfth and thirteenth centuries often cannot be distinguished from William's work. It has generally been accepted that those sections in the first part of the *De antiquitate* (§§1–36)

---

[65] See chapter IV.

[66] It has been edited and translated by John Scott, *The Early History*. An earlier edition was published by Thomas Hearne (*Adami de Domerham Historia*) and a translation by Lomax (*The Antiquities*). The extant version is dedicated to Henry of Blois, abbot of Glastonbury (A.D. 1126–1171) and bishop of Winchester (A.D. 1129–1171), after his consecration as bishop, although it may have originally been addressed to the monks alone: *De antiquitate*, Preface (ed. & transl. Scott, pp. 40–2); Robinson, *Somerset*, p. 4. William Stubbs, in his study of William of Malmesbury's *Gesta regum Anglorum*, placed the composition of the *De antiquitate* between the so-called first edition of the *Gesta regum* (A.D. 1125) and the third (A.D. 1135x1140): for the three editions of the *Gesta regum* and the interpolations into the *De antiquitate*, see *Willelmi Malmesbiriensis monachi de gestis regum Anglorum*, ed. Stubbs, I.xxvii and xxxi. For the *Libellus de rebus gestis Glastoniensibus* and the continuations of the narrative beyond the abbacy of Henry of Blois, see Crick, 'The marshalling', pp. 234–42.

[67] See Edwards, *The Charters*, pp. 11–77, for examples.

[68] Gransden, 'The growth', p. 346, has called his treatment 'restrained and scholarly', for example. For a study of William as a historian and of his method of composition, see Thomson, *William of Malmesbury*, especially pp. 11–38 and 164–73. For a condemnation of William's 'dangerous pages' and his status as a 'treacherous witness' in Anglo-Saxon historiography, see Dumville, *Wessex and England*, pp. 142 and 146.

which are not also found in the so-called third edition of William's *Gesta regum Anglorum* (after A.D. 1135) cannot reliably be seen as his.[69] Unfortunately, we cannot apply this method of cross-checking to the subsequent sections of the *De antiquitate*, where the pre-Conquest grants of land to Glastonbury are documented, as they were naturally not included in the *Gesta*. Some of these may be later additions, and the history of the Anglo-Saxon endowment may thus have been supplemented between the 1120s and 1247 by historians of the abbey working with spurious or corrupt sources or with the intention to mislead. For this reason, I have avoided giving William credit for sole authorship of the extant text's account of the endowment.

The second problem concerns William's (and any continuators') method of writing history. Certainly William worked in Glastonbury's archive and it has always been assumed that he obtained his information on grants directly from old charters.[70] The creation of a narrative, however, not the transcription of documents, was his goal; the charters were source-material, and their principal interest was as tools for the unfolding story of 'qui et quanti uiri fundauerunt et prouexerunt ecclesiam'.[71] This historian's first task was not to preserve the texts which documented these transactions but to focus on the abbots who had amassed Glastonbury's magnificent collection of estates and on the kings who had been so generous in their benefactions. Nevertheless, as has been mentioned, fragmentary verbatim quotations from charters appear occasionally in the narrative of the *De antiquitate* (with a shift into the first person, for example, in a record of the disposition of land or in a witness-list),[72] and the texts of a number of grants of privileges were transcribed in full. It certainly appears that original documents were being used. Thomson has praised William's 'nearly unique' realisation of how such material could be employed to discover the dates and sequence of the pre-Conquest abbots of the house.[73] He has also drawn attention to William's editorial style and his handling, in the *Gesta regum Anglorum* and *Gesta pontificum Anglorum*, of primary sources, which he abridged (to omit unnecessary information) or reworded (to achieve a better effect).[74] The *De antiquitate* was probably not composed under the same circumstances as these larger works, and

[69] *De gestis regum Anglorum*, ed. Stubbs, I.lviii–lxii. Robinson, *Somerset*, pp. 1–25, argued that what was original in the *De antiquitate* was to be found in the C-text of the *Gesta regum Anglorum* and that §§1–35 of the *De antiquitate* were largely interpolated. Newell, 'William of Malmesbury', also discussed the interpolations, as did Faral (*La légende*, II.402–9, 421–32, and 451–4) and Scott (*The Early History*, pp. 27–33). Scott also provided a hypothetical reconstruction of William's original text of §§1–36 (*ibid.*, pp. 168–72).

[70] The claim that the information on royal grants came from the original charters ('sicut per cartulas ueteres apparet') is not necessarily William's, however, for it appears in the possibly interpolated §70 (ed. & transl. Scott, p. 144).

[71] 'The number and identity of the men who founded and promoted the church'; *De antiquitate*, Preface (ed. & transl. Scott, p. 42).

[72] For example, *De antiquitate*, §§37–8 (ed. & transl. Scott, p. 90).

[73] Thomson, *William of Malmesbury*, p. 17.

[74] *Ibid.*, p. 166. Thomson (pp. 162–3) has drawn attention to a papal letter which William reproduced in the *Gesta regum*: William added to the text of his (still extant) exemplar (in London, British Library, MS. Cotton Tiberius A.xv) details which he must have

we cannot be sure how far William (and later continuators) altered and 'improved', perhaps even invented, original sources. Whether his handling of the primary documentary material conformed to our ideas of historical integrity is debatable. William's method in his other historical works allowed for 'alterations on the grounds of concision and stylistic consistency',[75] and in the *De antiquitate* he appears to have conflated and abbreviated texts and witness-lists, substituted synonyms, added his own stock-phrases, and changed the tense of verbs.[76] Motives could have been mixed. The quoted texts, for example, could have been manipulated to rationalise confusing information, to aim for greater thoroughness, or to deceive, or they could have been rearranged (or manufactured) purely for stylistic effect; whichever motivation applied, this possible manipulation means that the texts lack authority. Their doubtful evidence cannot simply be discarded, however, as it may in fact be sound. Similarly, interpretations with no basis in Anglo-Saxon reality may have been made – and inserted – by the later mediaeval historians of Glastonbury, who may have drawn spurious conclusions of which we should beware.

The question of the authority of the material in the *De antiquitate*, whether original or interpolated, is not just a theoretical one, for it bears significantly on the writing of histories of Glastonbury's pre-Conquest estates. This is because the *De antiquitate* frequently supplies otherwise unknown details – especially dates, hidage, and names of the laypeople or abbots who received the grants – which supplement the sparse information on the large number of lost texts recorded in the contents-list of the *Liber terrarum* and in the *Index chartarum*. In addition, some pre-Conquest grants by charter appear nowhere else in Glastonbury's surviving historical record, being known only from the *De antiquitate*;[77] it supplies also the only known mediaeval text of S.152, a confirmation (said to have been agreed at Glastonbury in A.D. 797) by Cenwulf, king of Mercia, of an earlier privilege.[78] The additional information most frequently offered, however, and the one with the greatest significance for our understanding of the process of the acquisition of land by the abbey, applies to the many royal grants made to laypeople which are recorded in the archive. The oft-repeated claim in the *De antiquitate* is that the lay recipients of these royal charters went on to grant the land to Glastonbury. It is not at all clear whether these statements are based on information which we now lack (possibly recorded, as mentioned above, on endorsements

found in a Glastonbury text (*Gesta regum Anglorum*, §151; ed. Stubbs, I.172–3; *Memorials*, ed. Stubbs, pp. 396–7).

[75] Thomson, *William of Malmesbury*, p. 165.

[76] See the comments of Edwards, *The Charters*, pp. 80–1, and the more detailed analysis by Blows, 'Studies', pp. 16–23 and 399–405. Blows has judged that William adapted his material, employing a stock of descriptive phrases which do not always appear in his sources (where they survive for comparison), but did not fabricate the details of the grants.

[77] For a list of grants attested only in the *De antiquitate*, see below, pp. 40–1.

[78] *De antiquitate*, §51 (ed. & transl. Scott, p. 110); the Latin text of this document is claimed in the *De antiquitate* (§49; ed. & transl. Scott, p. 106) to be a translation from Old English. Edwards, *The Charters*, pp. 52–5, has argued that William of Malmesbury found this document, and the papal privilege accompanying it, not at Glastonbury but at Winchcombe. On the Mercian connexion at Glastonbury, see below, pp. 335–7.

on the single sheets, endorsements which may have been copied into the *Liber terrarum*) or instead on assumption (perhaps based on Glastonbury's later ownership of the land) or simply on a feeling that the transfer claimed should have taken place.[79] This uncertainty affects the history of many of the two hundred and more estates discussed in chapter III, below.[80]

Some doubt, too, attaches to the status of the information in §69 and §70 of the *De antiquitate* ('De possessionibus Glastonie datis ab Anglis ad fidem conuersis' and 'Item de aliis datis Glastonie'), which provide, respectively, a summary of all the pre-Conquest grants recited in the *De antiquitate* and an additional list of lands given to Glastonbury but not mentioned in the main narrative. These sections cannot definitely be identified as part of the original text of the earlier twelfth century.[81] Information included in the summary (§69) but not in the central chapters could have been added by the original author, without a lapse of time, but the fact that it sometimes differs from the main text should at least raise some doubt about the status of the summary as part of the original composition (not to mention, additionally or alternatively, the status of the information in the main text).[82] The list of names in §70 is not found in John of Glastonbury's *Cronica*, a narrative reliant on the *De antiquitate* for its pre-Conquest material,[83] and it may be that an earlier version of the *De antiquitate*, without this list, was John's exemplar.[84] The list consists of eleven names of places which can be found (in the same order) in List D of the *Index chartarum* (including all the places in that group which were not represented in the *Liber terrarum*); it is followed by a further sixteen places, all in the *Liber terrarum* (also in the same order) but like the first eleven not in the body of the *De antiquitate*.[85] Simon Keynes has taken §70 to be William's; he therefore proposed that at the end of his narrative William

---

[79] For further discussion, see below, pp. 332–4.

[80] See, for example, *s.n.* Ham.

[81] Scott has accepted §70 as an organic part of the original *De antiquitate*, arguing that the passage which expresses awareness of the rather astonishing scale of Glastonbury's claims and explains the complications of the record 'reads like William's work' (*The Early History*, p. 208). This may be true, but it does not necessarily apply to the list of estates which it follows. The statements which Scott has cited would fit just as well at the end of §68 or §69. This last is in fact where they are found in the *Cronica* (which lacks the list); see §16 (edd. & transl. Carley & Townsend, p. 42).

[82] An example of an addition is the grant of Pennard Minster by Ælfgyth (S.563), mentioned in the summary only (*De antiquitate*, §69; ed. & transl. Scott, p. 144). Editorial alterations are illustrated by the case of twenty hides on the River *Tamer* (*recte Tan*), which in §40 are described *scilicet Linis* in the margin; in §69, *scilicet Linig* (*sic*) has been incorporated in the running text (ed. & transl. Scott, pp. 94 and 140). A ten-hide estate at *Brente* is cited in §39 as a gift of King Ine, but in §69 Ine is described as granting twenty hides at *Brentemareis* (ed. & transl. Scott, pp. 92 and 140), the hidage and name-form of the latter being in line with those of Domesday Book (I, 90vb; Somerset, 8.33). Grants omitted from the summary include Centwine's six hides at Glastonbury (*De antiquitate*, §37; ed. & transl. Scott, p. 90).

[83] See below, p. 27.

[84] Alternatively, the list could have dropped out between the copying of the *De antiquitate* and that of the *Cronica*.

[85] Keynes, 'Studies', I.168–70.

might have checked his work against the *Liber terrarum* itself and another document (on which the later lists of the *Index chartarum* also depended).[86] But if §69
and §70 (or at least the list of place-names in the latter) belong to the substantial
body of thirteenth-century interpolations, they should perhaps be seen as exten-
sions of the cataloguing activity (of A.D. 1247/8) apparent elsewhere in the
earliest manuscript of the *De antiquitate*. Perhaps the scribe of R.5.33 checked the
narrative of the *De antiquitate* against the contents-list of the *Liber* and against
the *Index* (which he went on to transcribe) and, to round out the account, supplied
the names of places which were mentioned in those two lists but which had not
been cited in the *De antiquitate*.

A place's mention in §70, then, is not necessarily proof of Glastonbury's
ownership, despite the rubric's claim, but according to this interpretation would
instead be simply an indication that a charter for that land once existed in its
archive. There is no need to assume that the recipient was the abbot or the
community.

The question of the extent to which the testimony of the *De antiquitate* clarifies our understanding of the Anglo-Saxon endowment is, for all these reasons,
not a simple one to answer. Even the relatively basic question of its sources
remains obscure.[87] The problems which this raises will be seen in operation in
chapter III in my examination of the evidence for individual estates. In summary,
however, it can be said that diplomas in the archive do seem to have been
consulted by the successive authors of the *De antiquitate*. As has been mentioned,
many of these charters no longer survive, either as single sheets or as cartulary-
texts. Single sheets which have since been lost may have been the source of
information on those grants now attested in the *De antiquitate* only. Furthermore,
some charters seem once to have existed in a form different from that of their
extant representatives.[88] The gospel-book of St Dunstan is cited in the *De antiquitate* as a source which reputedly contained a confirmation (now lost) by King
Æthelstan of gifts of land to Glastonbury by several laymen; this (or another)
gospel-book was the source of the text of a privilege of King Edmund (S.499)
which was preserved also in the fourteenth-century cartularies.[89] Other such

---

[86] *Ibid.*

[87] Scott has discussed William's sources and historical models on a more general level:
The Early History, pp. 6–14.

[88] Robinson assumed, for example, that William worked frequently from composite charters which had been created by the conflation of several originals (cf. *Somerset*, p. 41).

[89] 'In texto sancti Dunstani annotatum est' and 'scriptaque est litteris aureis in libro
euuangeliorum' (*De antiquitate*, §§54 and 56; ed. & transl. Scott, pp. 114 and 118). The
relation of this 'St Dunstan's Gospel' of §54 to the *liber Sancti Dunstani* or *liber
Domusday* referred to as a source in the mid-fourteenth-century Glastonbury feodary in
MS. Wood empt. 1 is unclear. The name of the latter was said to derive from the
existence of an ornate crucifix, thought to have been the work of Dunstan, attached to
the front board of the cover: *A Feodary*, ed. Weaver, p. 2. The gospel-book with golden
letters cited in §56 of the *De antiquitate* was said to have been a gift of King Edmund.
In the Great Cartulary, the record of S.499 makes the connexion between the two
gospel-books, with a note saying that Edmund's privilege was written *in textu Sancti
Dunstani* (*The Great Chartulary*, ed. Watkin, I.144–5 [no. 203]). For the copying of
important documents into gospel-books, see Wormald, 'The Sherborne "chartulary" ',

non-documentary manuscripts may have offered evidence to Glastonbury's medi-aeval historians. Was the early cartulary used? There is no explicit reference in the *De antiquitate* to the survival of the *Liber terrarum*, and the apparently haphazard structure of the latter cannot be traced in that of the *De antiquitate*, which is chronological. The only definite point of contact lies in the list of places in §70, as discussed above.[90] Since the status of this list in relation to the main text of the *De antiquitate* is uncertain, we can say only that the contents-list of the *Liber terrarum* and the *Index chartarum* (or a document like it) were available to the author of the version which we now have, the earliest context for this recension being the late 1120s and the latest (which I prefer) A.D. 1247. The date of the arrangement of the charters recorded in these lists is a matter of interest, for the archival structure visible in the mid-fourteenth-century cartularies clearly had not yet been introduced.[91]

Therefore, although the *De antiquitate* is in some ways the most extensive account of Glastonbury's Anglo-Saxon endowment to survive, for the reasons given its evidence is not without problems,[92] especially when details conflict with those found in other sources.[93] We must remember that the *De antiquitate* is not a contemporary source for the pre-Conquest period, even in its earliest recension; it is inevitable that confusion and error, not to mention deceptive editing and down-

---

pp. 106–7, and Dumville, *Liturgy*, pp. 119–27 (including a list of English examples). For a Welsh example, see Jenkins & Owen, 'The Welsh marginalia', pp. 52–4 and 61–6; for a Continental instance, a charter of William the Conqueror for Notre Dame at Cherbourg (now London, British Library, MS. Cotton Tiberius A.xv, 174), see Brett, 'A Breton pilgrim', p. 51.

[90] See pp. 24–5.

[91] At some time between *ca* A.D. 1129 and *ca* A.D. 1340 Glastonbury's archive was reorganised: the previous arrangement appears to have been without topographical or chronological logic. (An attempt at chronological order is detectable in the first part of the *Liber terrarum*, but the scheme soon breaks down. Most of the grants of the seventh to the ninth century do, however, appear near the beginning of the list.) By the time when the exemplar of the lists (now known as *Index chartarum*) in MS. R.5.33 was compiled, the Anglo-Saxon charters were kept separately from the post-Conquest documents (the lists of which follow them in the manuscript), and were filed by categories, according to donor (royal or lay) and present owner (Glastonbury or not). They had also been ordered chronologically within these groups. The change to an arrangement on a topographical basis, estate by estate (following a circuit of each county in which the abbey held land), generally but not always with a pre-Conquest charter at the head of the group, must have required a major reorganisation. Although the restructuring could have taken place much earlier, it is possible that the new position of *custos munimen-torum* created in A.D. 1340 by Abbot John of Breynton was instituted for this purpose. The holder was to receive one mark a year, half in payment for parchment for making records and for other things necessary for the preservation of the muniments. He was also to train a junior in the method of keeping records (*The Great Chartulary*, ed. Watkin, III.cclv–cclvi and 728 [no. 1335]).

[92] Sarah Foot has discussed the drawbacks of the *De antiquitate* as a source in 'Glaston-bury's early abbots', pp. 166–8.

[93] For example, S.237; *De antiquitate*, §37 (ed. & transl. Scott, p. 90). See below, chapter III, *s.n. Cantucuudu*.

right revisionism,[94] should have crept in. When applied to the task of constructing estate-histories, the evidence of the *De antiquitate* must be used with its weaknesses in mind.

A later history of Glastonbury, John of Glastonbury's *Cronica siue antiquitates Glastoniensis ecclesie*, provides no additional Anglo-Saxon material and does not, unfortunately, offer any assistance in evaluating the authority of the *De antiquitate*, although it does offer occasional help in assessing the development of interpolations to the original text.[95] John, according to his editor, 'showed a great reluctance to write anything in his own words, or even to paraphrase other authors'.[96] For this early period he seems to have added nothing to what he found in the *De antiquitate*. On occasion he nonetheless may to have had sources other than those represented by the extant version of the *De antiquitate*.[97]

In summary, it can be said that the sources for the history of Glastonbury Abbey's Anglo-Saxon endowment consist of sixty-one Latin charter-texts (four in single sheets, a further fifty-five – plus one repeat – in the Great Cartulary or the *Secretum domini*, one in a later cartulary, and one preserved in the *De antiquitate* alone). Many of these include a boundary clause – mainly in the vernacular, but some five with short Latin, possibly early, bounds[98] – defining the extent of the estate concerned; not all of these descriptions are contemporary with the grant. In addition, the contents-list of the lost early cartulary and the lists of charters in the archive in 1247/8 provide us with basic information on approximately 120 more grants whose documentation has been lost. Domesday Book tells us which estates Glastonbury held in 1066 and 1086 and offers a glimpse of the individuals holding the abbey's land. The *De antiquitate*, begun *ca* 1129 but added to until 1247/8, in addition to the one otherwise unattested full text which it supplies, amplifies the account of many of the lost grants and mentions over twenty more not cited elsewhere. Finally, an inventory made in the fifteenth century reveals almost fifty pre-Conquest charters and copies still in the archive, including a few of which there seems to be no record in any other extant source.[99] All this evidence – fragmentary, incomplete, and mostly put together many years after the period to which it applied – inevitably produces a flawed picture, but one in which we can dimly perceive Glastonbury Abbey at the peak of its territorial achievement.

---

[94] The most obvious example of the latter is the text of King Ine's Great Privilege (S.250): it upholds – ostensibly in A.D. 725 – Glastonbury's rights against the bishop of Wells (a see not founded until A.D. 909). See *De antiquitate*, §42 (ed. & transl. Scott, pp. 98–102).

[95] *The Chronicle*, edd. & transl. Carley & Townsend. James Carley has identified the author as John Seen (*ob.* before A.D. 1377) and dated the work to the 1340s, revising the traditional date for its compilation (of *ca* A.D. 1400); Carley, 'An identification'.

[96] *The Chronicle*, edd. & transl. Carley & Townsend, p. xxxv.

[97] See, for example, chapter III, below, *s.n.* Ashbury, Meare, and Pucklechurch.

[98] There are Latin bounds for Baltonsborough, Brent, *Cantucuudu*, Pennard, and *Pouelt* (S.1410, S.238, S.237, S.236, and S.248).

[99] L16 (a charter in Old English) and possibly L43 and L44.

CHARTERS IN THE GREAT CARTULARY
AND *SECRETUM DOMINI*

The charters are listed in the order in which they appear in the manuscripts (Longleat House, Marquess of Bath, MS. 39, and Oxford, Bodleian Library, MS. Wood empt. 1 [hereafter WE]).

1. **S.250**: Ine, king of Wessex, to Glastonbury, A.D. 725 (confirmation and 'Great Privilege') (MS. 39, 58r/v; WE, 66v–67r)

2. **S.246**: Ine, king of Wessex, A.D. 704 (privileges) (MS. 39, 58v; WE, 67r)

3. **S.257**: Cuthred, king of Wessex, A.D. 745 (privileges) (MS. 39, 58v–59r; WE, 67v)

4. **S.303**: Æthelwulf, king of Wessex, A.D. 854 (*Boclond tonn*, Pennard, *Cetenesfelde, Cerawycombe, Sowy*, Puriton, *Lodegaresberghe, Colom, Ocmund*, and *Branot*) (MS. 39, 59r; WE, 67v)

5. **S.499**: King Edmund to Glastonbury and Dunstan, A.D. 944 (privileges) (MS. 39, 59v; WE, 68r)

6. **S.783**: King Edgar to Glastonbury, A.D. 971 (privileges) (MS. 39, 60v–61r; WE, 68r/v)

7. **S.966**: King Cnut to Glastonbury, A.D. 1032 (privileges) (MS. 39, 61v; WE, 69r [A.D. 1030])

8. **S.580**: King Eadred to Wulfheah, A.D. 946x955 (Langford) (MS. 39, 86r; WE, 97v)

9. **S.626**: King Eadwig to Glastonbury, A.D. 956 (Panborough) (MS. 39, 134r/v; WE, 149v)

10. **S.1249**: Hædde, bishop of the West Saxons, to Hæmgils, abbot of Glastonbury, A.D. 680 (*Lantokal* and *Ferramere*) (MS. 39, 134v; WE, 149v–150r)

11. **S.1253**: Forthhere, bishop of Sherborne, to Ealdberht, abbot of Glastonbury, A.D. 712 (Bleadney, etc.) (MS. 39, 134v; WE, 150r)

12. **S.227**: Cenwealh, king of Wessex, to Beorhtwald, abbot of Glastonbury, A.D. 670 (*Ferramere*) (MS. 39, 135r; WE, 150r)

13. **S.253**: Æthelheard, king of Wessex, and Queen Frithugyth, to Coengisl, abbot of Glastonbury, A.D. 729 (*Pouholt*) (WE, 152r)

14. **S.270a**: Ecgberht, king of Wessex, to Eadgils, A.D. 801 (Butleigh) (MS. 39, 153r; WE, 169r)

15. **S.1410**: Lulla to Glastonbury, A.D. 744 (Baltonsborough and *Scobbanwirht*; Lottisham and Lydford) (MS. 39, 153v–154r; WE, 169v–170r)

16. **S.247**: Ine, king of Wessex, to Berwald, abbot of Glastonbury, A.D. 705 (land on the *Duluting*) (MS. 39, 155r and 161r; WE, 171r and 178v)

17. **S.509**: King Edmund to Æthelnoth, A.D. 946 (North Wootton) (MS. 39, 160v; WE, 177r)

18. **S.481**: King Edmund to Æthelstan, A.D. 942 (Mells) (MS. 39, 161v; WE, 178v–179r)

19. **S.462**: King Edmund to Ælfswith, A.D. 940 (Batcombe) (MS. 39, 167r; WE, 181v)
20. **S.292**: Æthelwulf, king of Wessex, to Eanwulf, A.D. 842 (Ditcheat and Lottisham) (MS. 39, 168r; WE, 182v–183r)
21. **S.236**: Baldred, sub-king of Wessex, to Glastonbury, A.D. 681 (Pennard) (MS. 39, 168r/v; WE, 183r/v)
22. **S.743**: King Edgar to Glastonbury, A.D. 966 (*Middilton*) (MS. 39, 169v; WE, 185r)
23. **S.791**: King Edgar to Glastonbury, A.D. 973 (exchange of *Brauncmynstre* for Ham) (MS. 39, 174r; WE, 190v–191r)
24. **S.251**: Ine, king of Wessex, to Glastonbury, A.D. 725 (*Sowy*) (MS. 39, 174r/v; WE, 191r/v)
25. **S.721**: King Edgar to Wulfhelm, A.D. 963 (*Otheri*) (MS. 39, 174v; WE, 191v)
26. **S.238**: Ine, king of Wessex, to Hæmgils, abbot of Glastonbury, A.D. 663 for ?693 (Brent) (MS. 39, 180v–181r; WE, 201r)
27. **S.498**: King Edmund to Æthelstan, A.D. 944 (*Brentefordlond*) (MS. 39, 181r; WE, 201r/v)
28. **S.793**: King Edgar to Wulfmær, A.D. 973 (Berrow) (MS. 39, 181r; WE, 201v)
29. **S.371**: King Edward the Elder to Æthelfrith, A.D. 904 (Wrington) (MS. 39, 185r/v; WE, 206v–207r)
30. **S.431**: King Æthelstan to Æthelhelm, A.D. 936 (Marksbury) (MS. 39, 186r/v; WE, 208r/v)
31. **S.442**: King Æthelstan to Æthelstan, A.D. 938 (*Lym*) (MS. 39, 188v–189r; WE, 212r/v)
32. **S.644**: King Eadwig to Huna, A.D. 957 (*Lym*) (MS. 39, 189r; WE, 212v)
33. **S.764**: King Edgar to Glastonbury, A.D. 968 (*Stour'*) (MS. 39, 192v; WE, 218r/v)
34. **S.742**: King Edgar to Ælfthryth, A.D. 966 (*Boclaunde*) (MS. 39, 195v–196r; WE, 223r/v)
35. **S.474**: King Edmund to Ælfflæd, A.D. 941 (*Boclonde* and Plush) (MS. 39, 196r; WE, 223v)
36. **S.555**: King Eadred to Ælfhere, A.D. 951 (*Boclaunde*) (MS. 39, 196r; WE, 224r)
37. **S.347**: Alfred, king of Wessex, to Berhtwulf, A.D. 891 (Plush and Raddington) (MS. 39, 199r; WE, 228r/v)
38. **S.513**: King Edmund to Æthelflæd, A.D. 944x946 (Pentridge, Damerham, and Martin) (MS. 39, 199r; WE, 228v)
39. **S.747**: King Edgar to Ælfheah and Ælfswith, A.D. 967 (Merton and Dulwich) (MS. 39, 199r/v; WE, 228v–229r)
40. **S.551**: King Eadred to Wulfric, A.D. 949 (Merton) (MS. 39, 199v; WE, 229r)

41. **S.775**: King Edgar to Ælfswith, A.D. 970 (Idmiston) (MS. 39, 202r; WE, 233v)
42. **S.530**: King Eadred to Wulfric, A.D. 947 (Idmiston) (MS. 39, 202r; WE, 233v–234r)
43. **S.541**: King Eadred to Wulfric, A.D. 948 (Idmiston) (MS. 39, 202r/v; WE, 234r)
44. **S.504**: King Edmund to Wulfric, A.D. 944 (Nettleton) (MS. 39, 202v; WE, 234r/v)
45. **S.625**: King Eadwig to *Elswy*, abbot of Glastonbury, A.D. 956 (Nettleton) (MS. 39, 202v; WE, 234v)
46. **S.472**: King Edmund to Wulfric, A.D. 940 (Grittleton) (MS. 39, 202v–203r; WE, 234v–235r)
47. **S.426**: King Æthelstan to Æthelhelm, A.D. 934 (*Kyngtone*) (MS. 39, 203r; WE, 235r/v)
48. **S.866**: King Æthelred to Glastonbury, A.D. 987 (*Kyngtone*) (MS. 39, 203r/v; WE, 235v)
49. **S.473**: King Edmund to Wulfric, A.D. 940 (*Langeleghe*) (MS. 39, 204v–205r; WE, 238r)
50. **S.466**: King Edmund to Dunstan, abbot of Glastonbury, A.D. 940 (Christian Malford) (MS. 39, 205v; WE, 239r/v)
51. **S.399**: King Æthelstan to Ælfflæd, A.D. 928 (Winterbourne) (MS. 39, 206r/v; WE, 240v)
52. **S.341**: Æthelred, king of Wessex, to Wulfhere, A.D. 869 (Winterbourne) (MS. 39, 206v; WE, 240v–241r)
53. **S.568**: King Eadred to Dunstan, abbot of Glastonbury, A.D. 955 (Badbury) (MS. 39, 207r; WE, 242r)
54. **S.288**: Æthelwulf, king of Wessex, to Duda, A.D. 840 (*Asshedoune*) (MS. 39, 209r; WE, 245r)
55. **S.524**: King Eadred to Eadric, A.D. 947 (*Aysshedune*) (MS. 39, 209r/v; WE, 245r/v)
56. **S.871**: King Æthelred to Æthelsige, bishop of Sherborne, and Æthelmær, A.D. 988 (Winchester) (WE, 253v–254r)

CONTENTS-LIST OF THE *LIBER TERRARUM*
(CAMBRIDGE, TRINITY COLLEGE, MS. R.5.33, 77r/v)

Since the entries have no numbers in the manuscript, these have been supplied;
Sawyer-numbers are also given for ease of reference. In presenting the text, I have
usually left *dat'* unexpanded, since the archivist referred to places sometimes as
masculine or neuter (*de eodem*) and sometimes as feminine (*quam*).

[Rubric]
Carte contente in libro terrarum Glastonie

[At foot of first column of entries]
Nota quod ubi apponitur .G., terre ille immediate conferebantur Glastonie; ubi .S.,
seruientibus, per quos transierunt ad Glastoniam.

LT1 (S.1666): Carta Kenwini de insula Glastonie
LT2 (?S.245): Carta Yne de libertatibus concessis ecclesie in West Saxonia
LT3 (S.227): Carta Cenuuali de Ferramere dat' Glastonie
LT4 (S.1669): Kenwinus de Elosaneg dat' .S.
LT5 (S.1249): Hedda episcopus de Lantokay .i. Leghe dat' Glastonie .ii.
LT6 (S.——):
LT7 (S.236): Baldredus de Pengred .i. Pennard dat' Glastonie
LT8 (S.237): Kenwinus de Cantucwdu .s. Munekatone .G.
LT9 (?S.247 = S.1672): Yna de Piltone dat' Glastonie
LT10 (S.1675): Wilfridus episcopus de Clifuuere .G.
LT11 (S.1253): Forthere de Bledenie .G.
LT12 (S.1673): Yna de Oram .G.
LT13 (S.1665): Baldredus de Pedrithe .G.
LT14 (S.251): Yna de Sowy .G.
LT15 (S.253): Æthelardus de Poolt .i. Poldone .G.
LT16 (S.1677): Fridogida de Brunamtone .G.
LT17 (S.1410): Lulla de Baltenesbeorg .G.
LT18 (S.1678): Cuthredus de Ure .G.
LT19 (S.1695): Æthelbaldus de Brannocmynstre .G.
LT20 (?S.238 = S.1671): Yna de Brentemarais .G.
LT21 (S.257): Cuthredus de libertatibus concessis Glastonie
LT22 (S.——): Æthebaldus de Seacesceg et Bradanleag .S.
LT23 (S.1696): Anglice de Ocemund <d'>
LT24 (S.1687): Cyniuulf de Culum .S.
LT25 (S.1683): Idem de Cumbe iuxta Culum dat' Cuthberto .S.

LT26 (S.1691): Cuthbertus de Culum dat' Sulco qui dedit Glastonie

LT27 (S.1684): Cynewlfus de .v. hidis .G.

LT28 (S.1692): Offa de Inesuuyrth iuxta Hunespulle .S. qui .G.

LT29 (S.1676): Æthelardus de Torric .G.

LT30 (S.1693): Ecgbirhtus de libertate eiusdem .G.

LT31 (S.1681): Cyneuulfus de Elenbearo dat' Æthelardo qui .G.

LT32 (S.1742): Eddredus de Dulting et Nunig .G.

LT33 (S.1703): Tumbeord episcopus de Logderesdone .i. Montagu .G.

LT34 (S.1728): Edmundus de Tintanhulle dat' Wilfrico qui .G.

LT35 (S.1753): Eadwi de Þidingete dat' Byrhtere .S. qui .G.

LT36 (S.1717): Ethelstan de Stoke dat' Ælfrico .S. qui .G.

LT37 (S.513): Edmundus de Domerham, Mertone, Pendrig .G.

LT38 (S.270a): Ecgbirhtus de Budecleghe dat' Eadgillo qui ʽuel uxorʼ .G.

LT39 (S.1685): Cyneuulf de Cumtone .G.

LT40 (S.1694): Ætheluulf de Cluttone dat' Ætheluulfo quam Ethelstanus comes filius Æthelnoti dedit .G.

LT41 (S.371): Edwardus de Þring ʽUurintoneʼ dat' Æthelfriþo quam eius filius Ethelstanus dux dedit .G.

LT42 (S.442): Ethelstanus de Lim dat' .S. Ethelstano duci qui .G.

LT43 (S.472): Edmundus de Gretelingtone dat' Uulfrico quam eius successor, Ælfþine .s., dedit Glastonie.

LT44 (S.504): Edmundus de Neteltone dat' Wlfrico quam eius successor Ælfwine commendauit Glastonie

LT45 (S.1721): Edmundus de Ceollamþirþe dat' Æthelwoldo

LT46 (S.1743): Eddred de Horutone dat' Uuilfrico quam eius successor .s. Ælþine commendauit Glastonie

LT47 (S.1689): Item Cenwlf de eodem .S.

LT48 (S.1729): Edmundus de Turnanwrthe dat' Wilfrico quam et ipse dedit Glastonie

LT49 (S.1719): Edmundus de Acford dat' Ælflede que dedit .G.

LT50 (S.474): Edmundus de Bocland dat' Ælflede que dedit .G.

LT51 (S.1714): Ethelstanus de Deuerel dat' Wlfhemo quam et ipse .G.

LT52 (S.1713): Idem de Uuerdeuerel dat' Osfriþo quam ipse .G.

LT53 (S.1757): Edwius de Blacaford G.

LT54 (S.1710): Ethelstanus de Worstone dat' Affe .S.

LT55 (S.1711): Idem de Westone uel Foxcote dat' Ethelstano quam ipse .G.

LT56 (S.1725): Edmundus de Stane dat' .G.

LT57 (S.1726): Idem de Wetheleage dat' .G.

LT58 (S.1723): Idem de Escford dat' .G.

LT59 (S.1718): Idem de Cantmel dat' Ælfgario .S.

LT60 (S.1755): Edwy de eodem dat' Cinrico .S.

LT61 (S.——): Edmundus de Langeford dat' Wlfheago .S.

LT62 (S.580): Eddredus de eodem et eidem

LT63 (S.1680): Sigebeorth de Poolt dat' .G.

LT64 (S.1700): Æthelbaldus de Wodetone dat' Heregithe .S.

LT65 (S.1722): Edmundus de Ruganbeorge dat' Ælfredo .S.

LT66 (S.1731): Idem de Gyrdlingatone dat' Þulfric quam ipse post dedit Glastonie

LT67 (S.568): Eddredus de Baddanbury dat .G.

LT68 (S.563): Idem de Pengeardmunster dat' Ælfgiþe .S.

LT69 (S.1746): Edwius de Cranemere dat' Elfheah

LT70 (S.1766): Edgarus de Cylfan dat' Ældred qui dedit .G.

LT71 (S.1767): Idem de Diranbeorge dat' Ældredo qui dedit .G.

LT72 (S.1769): Idem de Lucum dat' Glastonie

LT73 (S.1704): Elfred de Hanandone dat' Uulfhere .S.

LT74 (S.1763): Edgarus de eodem dat' Alwoldo qui dimisit .G.

LT75 (S.1741): Eddredus de Tuyneam dat' .G.

LT76 (S.626): Edwius de Pathenebeorge dat' .G.

LT77 (S.1750): Idem de Peasucmere dat' Alwoldo .S.

LT78 (S.1751): Idem de Wydancumbe dat' Æltheric .S.

LT79 (S.1779): Ethelredus de Stoke dat' Godrico .S.

LT80 (S.1765): Edgarus de Healtone dat' Byrnsige .S.

LT81 (S.1768): Idem de Blakeford dat' .G.

LT82 (S.743): Idem de Mideltone dat' .G.

LT83 (S.1773 = S.791): Idem de Hamme dat' .G.

LT84 (S.1682): Cynewlf de Mildenhealh dat' Bican .S.

LT85 (S.473): Edmundus de Langelea .i. Cunctun dat' Wlfric

LT86 (S.1770): Edgar de Wethehyl dat' Glastonie

LT87 (S.1702): Burgred de Lideneg dat' Æthelredo

LT88 (S.1756): Edwius de Lambageate dat' Cynrico

LT89 (S.1747): Idem de Westbury dat' Ælfero

LT90 (S.1760): Edgarus de eodem dat' eidem

LT91 (S.292): Æthelwlfus de Dichesgete et Lochesham datis Ænulfo principi .S.

LT92 (S.1699): Æthelbaldus de Hornblawertone dat' Ænulfo, iuxta Dichesgete .S.

LT93 (S.1701): Burhredus de Beaganhangran dat' Ænulfo

LT94 (S.1679): Æthelbaldus de Iecesig et Bradraleah dat' .G.

LT95 (S.1712): Ethelstanus de Hengesteshrege dat' Ethelredo

LT96 (S.1736): Æddredus de eodem dat' Ælfheago

LT97 (?S.570): Idem de eodem dat' Birhtrico

LT98 (S.1744): Idem de Pukelescericham dat' Wlfhel episcopo

LT99 (S.1727): Edmundus de Abbedesbury dat' Sigewlf

LT100 (S.1724): Idem de Pukeleschuriche dat' Glastonie

LT101 (S.481): Edmundus Mylne dat' Æthelstano

LT102 (S.399): Ethelstanus de Winterburna dat' Ælflede

LT103 (S.775): Edgar de Yfemestone dat' Ælfswid

LT104 (S.530): Eddred de eodem dat' Wlfrico

LT105 (S.541): Idem de eodem dat' eidem

LT106 (S.462): Edmundus de Batancumbe dat' Ælfsige .S.

LT107 (S.288): Æthelwlfus de Æssesdone dat' Dudan .S.

LT108 (S.524): Æddred de eodem dat' Ædrico .S.

LT109 (?S.564): Idem de Cumtone iuxta Æscesdone dat' Ælpheho

LT110 (S.1748): Edwius de Pendescliue dat' Ælfswithe

LT111 (S.1761): Edgarus de Ætheresig et Streton datis Ælfswid

LT112 (S.551): Eddredus de Mertone dat' Wlfhric .S.

LT113 (S.747): Edgarus de Meretone dat' Ælfheah .S.

LT114 (S.1762): Idem de Wynescumbe dat' Ælfswyd .S.

LT115 (S.341): Eddred de Winterburne dat' Wlfhere .S.

LT116 (S.1737 = S.555): Idem de Bocland dat' Ælfhere .S.

LT117 (S.1759): Edgar de Orcherleag dat' Ælfhere .S.

LT118 (S.1754): Edwius de Gilfeltone dat' Byrhrico quam idem cum suo corpore dedit Glastonie

LT119 (S.1764): Edgarus de Cantmel dat' Brichrico .S.

LT120 (S.1740): Eddredus de Ternuc dat' Ælfredo et aliis .S.

LT121 (S.1739): Idem de Camlar dat' Ælfredo .S.

LT122 (S.1738): Idem de eodem dat' Athelwoldo .S.

LT123 (S.1752): Edwy de Scyrphamme dat' Athelwoldo .S.

LT124 (S.1730): Edmundus de Pidelan dat' Wllauo .S.

LT125 (S.1709): Ethelstanus de Byrhtulfingtun becocer dat' Elfrico

LT126 (S.1745): Eddredus de Cumbe dat' Wlfrico

LT127 (S.1720): Edmundus de Uppauene dat' Ælfswid

LT128 (S.431): Ethelstanus de Merkesbyri dat' Æthelhelmo

LT129 (S.1749): Edwy de Sturtone dat' Ælwine .S.

LT130 (S.1758): Idem de Easetenetone dat' Wlfod' .S.

LT131 (S.509): Edmundus de Wdutone dat' Glastonie

LT132 (S.——): Quedam carta de Wringtone

LT133 (S.1774): Ethelredus de quodam predio in Wiltone dat' .G.

LT134 (S.1715): Ethelstanus de Hamanstane dat' Wlfhelmo

[gap of two lines]

LT135 (?S.245): Priuilegium Yne concessum generaliter omnibus ecclesiis

LT136 (S.303): Athelwlfus de decima parte terrarum suarum data ecclesiis

LT137 (S.——): Nomina diuersorum maneriorum pertinencium Glastonie

LIST OF CHARTERS: *INDEX CHARTARUM*
(CAMBRIDGE, TRINITY COLLEGE, MS. R.5.33, 77v–78v)

Since the entries are not numbered in the manuscript, letters and numbers have been supplied; Sawyer-numbers are also given for ease of reference.

Carte ueteres regum de terris datis Glastonie, quas adhuc habet, et sunt sine sigillis.

A1	(S.236): Baldredus de Pennard	
A2	(S.1665): Idem de piscaria que uocatur Pedride	Hemgillo abbati
A3	(S.1249): Hedde episcopus de Lantokay et Ferremere	
A4	(S.238 and ?S.1671): Yna rex de Brente	
A5	(?S.247/?S.248): Idem de Dulting	
A6	(S.1670): Idem terra ad pedem de Munedup	Beorwaldo abbati
A7	(S.251): Idem Sowy	
A8	(S.1705): Edwardus de Cumptone	
A9	(S.513): Edmundus de Domerham, Mertone et Pendrig	
A10	(S.466): Idem de Cristemuleford	
A11	(S.509): Idem de Wottone	Dunstano
A12	(S.——): Idem de Acford	
A13	(S.——): Eddredus de Asscesdone	
A14	(S.626): Edwyus de Pathenebeorge .ii. paria .G.	Elsio abbati
A15	(S.625): Idem de Netelingtone Pasture	
A16	(S.1775): Ethelredus de Fiswere	
A17	(S.1668): Cenewre rex de Clifwere	
A18	(S.1253): Fortherede episcopus de Bledenie	Alberto abbati
A19	(S.1410): Lulle femina de Baltenesbeorge	
A20	(S.1675): Wilferfus rex de Cliwere. inutilis	

Carte ueteres regum de terris datis suis seruientibus, quas adhuc Glastonie sine sigillis

B1	(S.1690): Cenwlfus de Mertone
B2	(S.426): Ethelstanus de Kingtone
B3	(S.1716): Idem de Ydemestone
B4	(S.399): Idem de Winterburne
B5	(S.431): Idem de Merkebury
B6	(S.721): Edgar de Odery
B7	(S.747): Idem de Mertone et Dylpirce

B8 (S.——): Eddredus de Pennard
B9 (S.644): Edwius de Lym
B10 (S.341): Ethelredus de Winterburne
B11 (?S.347): Elfleda de Plis
B12 (?S.481): Ethelstanus de Mylne [addition]

Carte ueteres de terris datis Glastonie immediate, quas non habet

C1 (S.1667): Carta Kenelmi de Wethmor facta Wilfrido episcopo
C2 (S.1674): Carta dicti Wilfridi de eodem facta Beorwaldo abbati .G.
C3 (S.1725): Edmundus de Stane
C4 (S.1741): Eddredus de Tyneam
C5 (S.——): Idem de Ternuc et Stapelpille
C6 (S.553): Idem de Pukeleschuriche
C7 (?S.1757): Edwius de Blakeford.   Seruienti.
C8 (S.764): Edgar de Sture
C9 (?S.1762): Idem de Wynescumbe.   Seruienti.
C10 (S.1774): Ethelredus de quodam predio in Wiltone
C11 (S.1777): Idem de Pukeleschuriche
C12 (S.1778): Idem de Sethebeorge
C13 (S.1780): Idem de Austancliue
C14 (S.1776): Idem de Hamandone
C15 (S.——): Quoddam memoriale de Offaculum

Carte ueteres regum de terris datis suis seruientibus, quas creditur habuisse Glastonie ecclesia, sed modo non habet.

D1 (S.1686): Cenwlf de Aldamtone et quibusdam aliis
D2 (S.1687): Idem de Culum
D3 (S.1688): Idem de Cynemersforda
D4 (S.1681): Idem de Ellenbearo
D5 (S.1698): Athelwlf de Lennucmere
D6 (S.1706): Edward de Pillesdone
D7 (S.1707): Idem de Portbrig
D8 (S.1708): Idem de Giffeltone
D9 (S.1715): Ethelstan de Hamanstane
D10 (S.1735): Edmundus de Lutramtone .ii. paria d'
D11 (S.——): Idem de Langeford
D12 (S.1732): Idem de Cluttone
D13 (S.1734): Idem de Eatumberesder
D14 (S.1733): Idem de Cympanhamme

D15 (S.498): Idem de Brenforlande
D16 (S.580): Eddredus de Langaford
D17 (S.563): Idem de Pergarminstre
D18 (S.1748): Edwius de Pendescliue
D19 (S.1771): Edgar de Hubbanlege
D20 (S.1772): Idem de Ðidamgate
D21 (S.793): Idem de Beorgon
D22 (S.1781): Ethelredus de Portbrig

Antiqua Priuilegia

E1 (S.250): Magnum priuilegium Yne regis
E2 (S.783): Priuilegium Edgari regis
E3 (S.——): Carta sancti Patricii

⎱ Haec non sunt
⎰ signata.

PRE-CONQUEST CHARTERS IN LONGLEAT HOUSE, MARQUESS OF BATH, MS. 39a

Since the entries are not numbered in the manuscript, letters and numbers have been supplied; Sawyer-numbers are also given for ease of reference. The charters are listed in the order in which they appear in the manuscript. Entries marked (†) are not in the original hand. Additions to entries are in angled brackets.

L1 (S.1249): Carta Hedde episcopi facta Hengislo abbati de Lantocay et Ferramere (MS. 39a, 12v)

L2 (S.626): Carta regis Edwy de Panneburge. dupplicatur (MS. 39a, 12v) †

L3 (S.1253): Carta Forthhere episcopi facta Aldberto abbati de Bledenye (MS. 39a, 12v) †

L4 (S.227): Copia carte Cenwalli de Ferramer et est iii in landbok (MS. 39a, 12v) †

L5 (S.1705): Carta Edwardi primi de restauracione de Cumton Dunden ante conquestum dccccxii cum copia eiusdem (MS. 39a, 17v) †

L6 (S.270a): Carta Edberti regis de Buddecleghe, fere est consumpta (MS. 39a, 22v)

L7 (S.1410): Carta Lulle Christi ancille de Baltenesbeorgh (MS. 39a, 23v) †

L8 (S.509): Carta Edmundi regis de Wottone (MS. 39a, 25r)

L9 (?S.247/S.248): Carta Ini regis de Doultyng. dupplicatur (MS. 39a, 25v)

L10 (S.481): Carta Edmundi regis de Melles (MS. 39a, 26r)

L11 (S.236): Carta Baldredi regis de manerio de Pennard (MS. 39a, 27r) †

L12 (S.563): Carta Edredi regis de manerio de Pennard <dupplicatur excepte limitibus et [?] testibus> (MS. 39a, 27r) †

L13 (S.292): Copia carte Ethelwulfi regis de Dichesyate et Lotteshame et est xci in landboke (MS. 39a, 29r) †

L14 (S.743): Copia Edgar regis de Middeltone et est lxxxii in landboke (MS. 39a, 31v) †

L15 (S.791/S.1733?): Copia carte regis Edgari de Hamme ut patet in landboke <exceptis limitibus> (MS. 39a, 33r) †

L16 (S.——): Item est una cedula in Anglico de Hamme, notabilis ualde <deficit> (MS. 39a, 33r) †

L17 (S.251): Carta regis Ine de manerio de Sowy (MS. 39a, 33r)

L18 (S.721): Carta regis Edgari facta Wulhem de Othery (MS. 39a, 33r)

L19 (S.238/S.1671): Carta regis Ine de Brente (MS. 39a, 40r)

L20 (S.498): Carta regis Edmundi facta Athelstano comiti de Brenteforlond (MS. 39a, 40r)

L21 (S.793): Carta regis Edgari facta Wolmero ministro suo de Berghes (MS. 39a, 40r)

L22 (?S.371): Copia carte Eddredi regis de prima donacio manerii <cum copiam bunde manerii> [Wrington] (MS. 39a, 42r) †

L23 (S.431): Carta regis Athelstani de Merkesbury (MS. 39a, 42v)

L24 (S.644): Carta regis Edwy de manerio de Lyme (MS. 39a, 43v)

L25 (S.764): Carta regis Edgari de Stoure (MS. 39a, 44v)

L25a (S.—): Copia bundarum manerii de Niewtone (MS. 39a, 46r)

L26 (S.742): Carta regis Edgari facta Ethelrede regine de eodem [Buckland and Plush] (MS. 39a, 46v)

L27 (S.555/S.1737): Carta Eddredi regis facta Elfere de eodem [Buckland and Plush] (MS. 39a, 46v)

L28 (S.347): Carta Elfredi regis facta Bertulpho de Pluyshe (MS. 39a, 47v)

L29 (S.747): Carta Edgari regis facta Elphean comiti et uxori eius de Mertone (MS. 39a, 48r)

L30 (S.1690): Carta Cenwulphi regis facta cuidam de eodem [Damerham and Martin] (MS. 39a, 48r)

L31 (S.775): Carta regis Edgari facta Eleswythe sanctemoniale de Idest' <deficit> (MS. 39a, 50r)

L32 (S.530 or S.541): Carta Edredi regis de eodem facta Wlfrico ministro suo [Idmiston] (MS. 39a, 50r)

L33 (S.——): Bunde de Wynterborne et Idemyston in uetusta cedula (MS. 39a, 50r)

L34 (S.625): Carta regis Edwy de Netelingtone (MS. 39a, 50r)

L35 (?S.625): Copia carte Edwik regis [Nettleton] (MS. 39a, 50r) †

L36 (S.472): Carta Edmundi regis de Lytlantone alias Grutlyngtone (MS. 39a, 50r) †

L37 (S.866): Carta Etelredi regis de Kyngton (MS. 39a, 50v)

L38 (S.426): Carta Athelstani regis facta Atellmo de eodem [Kington] (MS. 39a, 50v)

L39 (S.473): Carta regis Edmundi facta Wolfrico de Langele (MS. 39a, 50v)

L40 (S.466): Carta Edmundi regis facta sancto Dunstano de eodem [Christian Malford] (MS. 39a, 51r)

L41 (S.399): Carta Athelstani regis facta Elfethe uxori sue de Winterborne (MS. 39a, 51v)

L42 (S.341): Carta Eddredi regis facta cuidam sui principi de eodem [Winterbourne] (MS. 39a, 51v)

L43〕 (?S.568): Due antique cedule tangentes manerium de Baddebury tempore
L44〕 Edgari regis et sancti Dunstani (MS. 39a, 52r)

L45 (S.524): Carta Eddredi regis facta Eddrico de Aissdonne (MS. 39a, 53r)

L46 (S.1714): Carta regis Athelstani facta Wolphelmo de manerio de Deverel-langbrigge [cameraria] (MS. 39a, 68v)

L47 (S.237): Carta Centwyny regis de Cantucuudu manerio Westmonketon iuxta Tauntone [cameraria] (MS. 39a, 70r) †

L47a (?S.1668/?S.1675): Copia carte de Clyfwere [coquinarius] (MS. 39a, 79v)

GRANTS ATTESTED EXCLUSIVELY IN THE *DE ANTIQUITATE*

This list aims to include grants made by charter (in so far as they can be distinguished) which appear in the *De antiquitate* but in no other source (including
probably spurious charters); it does not include the many cases where the
author(s) of the *De antiquitate* claim that the recipient of a grant passed the land
on to Glastonbury. On these, see below, pp. 332–4. In some cases, the apparently
unique appearance of a grant in the *De antiquitate* can be explained as a result of
confusion, the grant appearing elsewhere under a different name (see, for example, chapter III below, *s.n. Caric*).

1. Twenty hides in *Caric* given by King Centwine, *ca* A.D. 678 (§37; ed. &
    transl. Scott, p. 90)
2. Sixteen hides at *Logworesbeorh* given by King Baldred, A.D. 681 (§38; *ibid.*,
    p. 90)
3. One half-hide at *Escford* and a fishery given by King Ine, A.D. 705 (§40;
    ibid., p. 94)
4. A fishery on the Axe given by King Ine, A.D. 719 (§40; *ibid.*, p. 94)
5. Six hides in the west of *Poholt* given by King Sigeberht, A.D. 754 (§47; *ibid.*,
    p. 104)
6. *Huneresberg* on the east of the River Parrett given by King Cynewulf, A.D.
    760 (§48; *ibid.*, p. 106)
7. One hide at *Hunespulle* given by Æthelmund, A.D. 757x796 (§48; *ibid.*, p.
    106)
8. Three hides at *Cumbe* given by Sulca or Æthelheard, A.D. 757x786 (§§48
    and 69; *ibid.*, pp. 106 and 142)
9. Part of one *cassatum* at *Brunham* sold by Abbot Guthlac, A.D. 824 (§52;
    ibid., p. 110)
10. Doulting transferred to *ius monasteriale* by Abbot Ealhmund, A.D. 851 (§53;
    ibid., p. 112)
11. Twenty hides added to Doulting by King Æthelwulf, A.D. 851 (§53; *ibid.*, p.
    112)
12. Eight hides at *Kingestan* given by King Edmund, A.D. 940 (§55; *ibid.*, p.
    114)
13. Fifteen hides at *Hamedune* given by Queen Ælfflæd, A.D. 939x946 (§55;
    ibid., p. 114)
14. Fifteen hides at *Hanandone* given by Æthelflæd, A.D. 959x975 (§62; *ibid.*, p.
    130)
15. Return of ten hides at Marksbury by King Edgar, A.D. 963 (§62; *ibid.*, p. 128)
16. Five hides at *Dundene* given by King Edgar, A.D. 965 (§62; *ibid.*, p. 128)
17. Twenty hides at Batcombe given by Ealdorman Ælfhere, A.D. 959x975 (§62;
    ibid., p. 130)

18. Five hides at Tintinhull given by 'Queen' Ælfswith, A.D. 959x975 (§62; *ibid.*, p. 130)

19. Fifteen hides at Mildenhall given by *Hedred*, A.D. 959x975 (§62; *ibid.*, p. 130)

20. Forty hides at *Essebur'* given by *Hedred*, A.D. 959x975 (§62; *ibid.*, p. 130)

21. Twenty hides at *Estun* given by Wulfwine, A.D. 1000 (§63; *ibid.*, p. 130)

22. Seventeen hides at *Newetone Kastel* given by Edmund Ironside, A.D. 1016 (§64; *ibid.*, p. 132)

ESTATES MENTIONED ONLY IN DOMESDAY BOOK

The following is a list of estates which were part of Glastonbury's endowment as recorded in Domesday Book, but for which there is no other documentation linking them (by that name) with the pre-Conquest abbey. Most may in fact have been part of other (documented) estates, from which they had split by 1066. See the individual entries in chapter III, below. The following list does not include estates owned in 1066, according to Domesday Book, for which there is no explicit evidence of their actual transfer into Glastonbury's possession: many more estates fall into that category, but as the evidence for acquisition by the abbey is so dubious and its evaluation so discretionary, no attempt has been made to compile such a list.

Bodesleghe (So)
Clatworthy (So)
Dinnington (So)
Draycott (So)
Edingworth (*Iodenwrthe*) (So)
Hetsecome (So)
Hutton (So)
Ilchester (St Andrew's) (So)
Lattiford (So)
Malmesbury (W)
Millescote (So)
Overleigh (So)
Ower (H)
Winterhead (So)

III

THE ENDOWMENT: SURVEY AND ANALYSIS

The first requirement for a consideration of Glastonbury's pre-Conquest endowment is a complete list of the community's estates which takes account of all the sources discussed in the preceding chapter.[1] Reorganised by place, the extensive evidence offered by these sources has here been analysed, criticised, and applied to the compilation of an estate-history for each of the places mentioned in connexion with Glastonbury Abbey. Inevitably, some of these 'histories' offer only a passing glimpse of the pre-Conquest estate; others tell a more detailed story – although it is never complete and rarely uncomplicated. Scholarly comment, where available, has been added to the bank of data. In this instance, the priority has been to record, and not always to reconcile, past discussion, leaving the reader to judge if it parts company with the assembled evidence.

The form of the place-name as it is found in each primary source is given when the evidence of that source is introduced. It seemed best to preserve the details of variant spellings, in case the evidence of the name-forms might prove significant in subsequent argument.[2] For this reason, a possibly disconcerting number of spellings may be employed for a single place in the course of documenting the primary evidence; thereafter, the modern name has been used. If, however, there is no definite modern identification of the place, the earliest or most reliable form of the name (in so far as this could be determined) has been preferred. Counties are identified according to the pre-1974 boundaries (if the location of the place in question is known).

Milage from Glastonbury has been given as an indication of distance between settlement-centres, but the figures are approximate and are based on the modern road-map, not on mediaeval routes of communication. Travelling distances by road were no doubt usually greater; no attempt has been made to consider transport by water, which would often have been a more convenient route.

As the exact shape of estates in the Anglo-Saxon period is often unknown, no map can accurately represent their location; maps based on later parish boundaries (and therefore unavoidably conjectural) have nonetheless been provided for the reader's convenience (see pp. xiii–xix). Some of the places which did not become parishes can be located on map 1 (The Twelve Hides of Glastonbury). A list of regnal dates (from the late seventh century, when the run of diplomas

---

1 A summary-list of these references is to be found at the end of this chapter, pp. 259–65.
2 Unfortunately, Eilert Ekwall did not incorporate in his study of English place-names much of the evidence offered by Glastonbury's early records: the name-forms in the contents-list of the *Liber terrarum*, *Index chartarum*, and MS. 39a do not appear in *The Concise Oxford Dictionary of English Place-names*.

begins) has also been supplied, below. Only the kings of Wessex are included for the period before the reign of Æthelstan; dates of kings of other kingdoms are given in the text where relevant. Dates have been taken from the *Handbook of British Chronology*, edd. Fryde *et al*.

Rulers of Wessex
Cenwealh A.D. 642–672
Q. Seaxburh A.D. 672–674
Æscwine A.D. 674–676
Centwine A.D. 676–685
Cædwalla A.D. 685–688
Ine A.D. 688–726
Æthelheard A.D. 726–?740
    Q. Frithugyth A.D. 729x739
Cuthred A.D. 740–756
Sigeberht A.D. 756–757
Cynewulf A.D. 757–786
Brihtric A.D. 786–802
Ecgberht A.D. 802–839
Æthelwulf A.D. 839–858
Æthelbald A.D. 855–860
Æthelberht A.D. 860–865
Æthelred A.D. 865–871
Alfred A.D. 871–899
Edward the Elder A.D. 899–924
Ælfweard A.D. 924

Kings of England
Æthelstan A.D. 924–939 (king of all England from 927)
Edmund I A.D. 939–946
Eadred A.D. 946–955
Eadwig A.D. 955–959
Edgar A.D. 959–975
Edward I the Martyr A.D. 975–978
Æthelred the Unready A.D. 978–1016
[Swegn Forkbeard A.D. 1013–1014]
Edmund II Ironside A.D. 1016
Cnut A.D. 1016–1035
Harold I Harefoot A.D. 1035/6–1040
Harthacnut A.D. 1040–1042
Edward II the Confessor A.D. 1042–1066
Harold II Godwinesson A.D. 1066

Abbedesbury

According to the contents-list of the *Liber terrarum*, King Edmund granted land at *Abbedesbury* to one Sigewulf (S.1727; LT99). This charter was not recorded in any of Glastonbury's later documentary lists or collections. The only additional information on this place in sources associated with Glastonbury is found in the *De antiquitate*, where it is said that Sigewulf gave five hides at *Abbedesburi* to the abbey, with the consent of King Edmund.[3] This land has commonly been identified with Abbotsbury in Dorset (*Abedesberie* in Domesday Book), where twenty-two hides were held by Abbotsbury Abbey in 1066 and twenty-one in 1086, one hide (*ad uictum monachorum*) having been lost.[4] Abbotsbury is on the south coast, about forty-five miles from Glastonbury.

Abbotsbury Abbey was founded by one of King Cnut's housecarls, Orc, and his wife Tola.[5] Between A.D. 1016 and 1035 Orc received from Cnut a charter for seventeen hides at Abbotsbury, and a diploma of King Edward the Confessor confirmed (apparently in A.D. 1044) the foundation of the abbey.[6] It seems that there was already a church with a priest on the site, but there is no reliable information on the origins of this establishment.[7] Thomas Gerard, in his survey of Dorset written in the 1620s, claimed that, after being built by 'Bertufus an holy Prest', who had been given a charter by St Peter himself, Abbotsbury became a 'retireing place' for the West Saxon kings; Simon Keynes has pointed out that this latter claim could simply indicate that the author had seen 'a charter showing that in the ninth or tenth century the place had been in a king's gift'.[8] No such single sheets granting Abbotsbury survive; nor do the transcripts made by Sir Henry Spelman in the first half of the seventeenth century from the lost cartulary of the abbey contain any charters for Abbotsbury itself earlier than that of Cnut. Gerard's account of Abbotsbury, derived from the lost cartulary, also claimed that in Orc and Tola's time the church was 'decayed and forsaken by reason the Rovers from the Sea often infested it', but his evidence for this statement is unknown.[9]

There is no particular reason to think that if Glastonbury did obtain five hides at Abbotsbury it held them for very long: as Keynes has observed, 'it is quite possible that the land in question was actually in secular hands throughout the later tenth century and into the eleventh'.[10] By the early eleventh century Abbotsbury, if indeed the surviving information relates to the same place, had expanded from five hides to seventeen; with the addition of five more hides at Rodden, which lies beside Abbotsbury, the Domesday estate-total of twenty-two was

---

3   *De antiquitate*, §§55 and 69 (ed. & transl. Scott, pp. 116 and 142); *Cronica*, §§16 and 64 (edd. & transl. Carley & Townsend, pp. 40 and 122).

4   Domesday Book, I, 78rb (Dorset, 13.1). The only other pre-Conquest form attested for the Dorset estate is *Abbodesbyrig*: see Ekwall, *The Concise Oxford Dictionary of English Place-names*, *s.n.* Abbotsbury, p. 1.

5   Knowles and Hadcock, *Medieval Religious Houses*, p. 58; see also Calthrop, 'The abbey of Abbotsbury', and Keynes, 'The lost cartulary'.

6   Keynes, 'The lost cartulary', pp. 229–31 and 222.

7   *Ibid.*, pp. 208 and 236, n. 141.

8   Coker, *A Survey*, pp. 30–1; Keynes, 'The lost cartulary', pp. 222–3.

9   Coker, *A Survey*, pp. 30–1.

10 Keynes, 'The lost cartulary', p. 208.

reached.[11] Spelman's extracts from the lost cartulary included a grant of Rodden by King Æthelred the Unready in A.D. 1014 to his thegn 'Sealwyne'; Rodden was also the subject of a fragmentary chirograph from somewhat later in the century, preserved in the Abbotsbury archive.[12] It is remotely possible that Glastonbury's five hides could be those at Rodden, but this is suggested only by the coincidence of the numbers and by Rodden's apparent inclusion in Abbotsbury's Domesday total.

The *Abbedesbury* of the contents-list of the *Liber terrarum*, however, may not necessarily refer to the Dorset estate. This name could have denoted a relationship with any monastic community, not just the one which retains the name today. Glastonbury's *Abbedesbury* or Abbotsbury may have been located elsewhere.

Abbotsbury (Dorset)
See *Abbedesbury*.

Aldamtone

According to the *Index chartarum*, Cynewulf, king of Wessex (A.D. 757–786), granted land at *Aldamtone et aliis* to a layman (S.1686; IC D1).[13] In 1066 and 1086 land at Alhampton (*Alentone*) was a part (consisting of six and a half hides) of the composite estate of Ditcheat near Glastonbury.[14] Twenty-five hides at Ditcheat were reputedly granted to Glastonbury in a charter of A.D. 842 (S.292) in the name of Æthelwulf, king of Wessex (A.D. 839–858). This could suggest that Alhampton was originally granted to Glastonbury as a separate estate in the mid- to late eighth century and was back in royal hands before A.D. 842, when it was considered to belong to the larger unit of Ditcheat and was regranted to the abbey in the guise of a component part of that estate. Confirmation of this, however, is not found in the sparse evidence for the other portions of Domesday Ditcheat: a charter for Hornblotton said to have been in the *Liber terrarum* apparently stated that the estate was given to a certain *Ænulfus* by Æthelbald (king of Wessex, A.D. 855–860) (S.1699; LT92), while Lamyatt was granted by King Eadwig (A.D. 955–959) to one Cynric (S.1756; LT88). The complications raised by the fact that these supposed transactions postdate the alleged grant of Ditcheat to the abbey will be discussed below, under Ditcheat. The appearance of *Aldamtone* on List D (of charters for lands lost to the abbey) may further suggest that the identification with Alhampton is incorrect, and that land elsewhere was involved.

The only other occurrence of *Aldamtone* by name in Glastonbury's record is in the *De antiquitate*, where it appears in §70 as the first of the *alia [maneria] data Glastonie*, a list of lands which appears to have been compiled from the same source as List D of the *Index chartarum*.[15]

---

[11] *Ibid.*, p. 230; Domesday Book, I, 78rb (Dorset, 13.1).
[12] Keynes, 'The lost cartulary', pp. 227–9.
[13] Cf. Edwards, *The Charters*, pp. 74–5.
[14] Domesday Book, I, 90vb (Somerset, 8.30). For Ditcheat, see below.
[15] *De antiquitate*, §70 (ed. & transl. Scott, p. 144); for the relationship of List D and §70, see above, pp. 24–6.

Alhampton (Somerset)

See *Aldamtone*.

Andersey (Somerset)

The earliest recorded transaction involving *Andersey* by name in Glastonbury's documentary sources occurs in the contents-list of the *Liber terrarum*, which records *Ætheresig* (along with *Streton*) as granted to Ælfswith by King Edgar (S.1761; LT111).[16] In Domesday Book, *Ederesige* consisted of two hides and was one of the 'islands' of the estate of Glastonbury itself. Its modern name is Nyland.[17]

A history of the estate beginning much earlier is offered by the *De antiquitate*: according to that source, *Andreyesie* was given to Glastonbury by King Cenwealh, along with Beckery, Godney, and Marchey.[18] This claim was repeated in the so-called Great Privilege of King Ine (S.250), which appears in the *De antiquitate* and the *Cronica*, in the fourteenth-century cartularies, and in William of Malmesbury's *Gesta regum Anglorum*.[19] In addition, the *De antiquitate* amplifies the information provided by the contents-list of the *Liber terrarum* on Ælfswith's grant by recording her gift of *Aetheredesige* to Glastonbury and a confirmation of it by King Edgar, adding that the grant was of half a hide.[20] This does not help to explain the two-hide total in 1086.

Nyland is less than eight miles from the abbey, as the crow flies. It is on the western edge of the Twelve Hides of Glastonbury, a privileged zone whose early history and original limits (before those preserved in the extant mid-thirteenth-century perambulation) are unknown.[21] A substantial hill in a low-lying, often flooded, area, for topographical reasons Nyland always had the potential to be a site of importance, part of a network of such 'islands' in the moor. But Glastonbury's extant charter in the name of King Cenwealh, for Meare (S.227), is prob-

---

16 For Ælfswith, and other transactions associated with her, see below, *s.n.* Idmiston.

17 Domesday Book, I, 90ra (Somerset, 8.1). Morland ('Some Domesday manors', p. 39) has rejected E.H. Bates's identification of *Ederesige* with Edgarley (in Baltonsborough): 'Text of the Somerset Domesday', ed. Bates, p. 460. O.S. Anderson (*The English Hundred Names*, p. 68, n. 1) agreed with the identification with Nyland. Ekwall (*The Concise Oxford Dictionary of English Place-names*, *s.n.* Nyland, p. 346) also accepted *Andersey* as the old name of Nyland.

18 *De antiquitate*, §§36 and 69 (ed. & transl. Scott, pp. 90 and 140); also in the *Cronica*, §§16 and 42 (edd. & transl. Carley & Townsend, pp. 40 and 88).

19 *De antiquitate*, §42 (ed. & transl. Scott, pp. 98–102); *Cronica*, §49 (edd. & transl. Carley & Townsend, pp. 96–100); *The Great Chartulary*, ed. Watkin, I, no. 199 (text not printed by Watkin; see p. lviii); *Gesta regum Anglorum*, §36 (ed. Stubbs, I.36–9). The privilege of King Edgar (S.783) cites its chapel as one of several exempt from the power of the bishop of Wells: *De antiquitate*, §60 (ed. & transl. Scott, p. 124), and *Cronica*, §71 (edd. & transl. Carley & Townsend, p. 134). For a fuller discussion of the core-estate of Glastonbury and the royal privileges, see below, *s.n.* Glastonbury.

20 *De antiquitate*, §§62 and 69 (ed. & transl. Scott, p. 130); *Cronica*, §§16 and 73 (edd. & transl. Carley & Townsend, pp. 42 and 138).

21 For the Twelve Hides, see the discussion below, *s.n.* Glastonbury, and map 1. For the perambulation, see *De antiquitate*, §§72–3 (ed. & transl. Scott, pp. 148–52); *Cronica*, §§2–4 (edd. & transl. Carley & Townsend, pp. 10–16).

ably a forgery,[22] and some doubt may therefore attach to other grants in the archive associated with the name of this king. There must be some significance, however, in the grouping together of the estates (Meare, Beckery, Godney, Marchey, and *Andreyesie*) attributed to Cenwealh's gift and further associated with one another (with some variation) in the forged privilege cited above. It is not the case that Domesday Book's record of the sub-units of the main Glastonbury estate provided this list, for there only Meare and *Ederesige* are mentioned by name (with the addition of Panborough).

The modern name for *Andersey*, Nyland, is found in later mediaeval but not pre-Conquest sources.[23] In the *De antiquitate* and the *Cronica* we find both names, with the explanation that *Andersey* was so called because a church dedicated to St Andrew was located there;[24] but Ekwall cited the form found in S.250 (*Ederedeseie*) to support his interpretation of the name as meaning 'Eadred's island'.[25]

Stephen Morland has suggested that a gift of *Elosaneg* to Glastonbury by King Centwine recorded only in the *Liber terrarum* might have referred to Nyland, but it could equally refer to any of the early 'island'-territories.[26]

Ashbury (Berkshire)

Two charters extant in the fourteenth-century cartularies record grants of *Asshedoune*: in S.288, dated 840, Æthelwulf, king of Wessex, granted ten hides there to his *minister* Duda; and, according to S.524, King Eadred granted twenty hides there to his *comes* Eadric in A.D. 947.[27] A note following the text of S.524 in the mid-fourteenth-century cartularies states that Eadric gave the estate and the diploma to Dunstan. Eadred's diploma for Eadric still existed in the archive in the fifteenth century (L45). According to the *Index chartarum*, there was also a charter in Eadred's name (now lost) granting *Asscesdone* directly to Abbot Dunstan (IC A13). The *De antiquitate* cites the gift of forty hides at *Essebur'* to the abbey by a certain *Hedred*, but seemingly contemporary with and confirmed by

---

[22] See the discussion by Robinson in *Somerset*, pp. 47–53, and below, *s.n.* Meare.

[23] See Robinson, 'Andresey', pp. 77–8.

[24] *De antiquitate*, §73 (ed. & transl. Scott, p. 152); *Cronica*, §2 (edd. & transl. Carley & Townsend, p. 12).

[25] Ekwall, *The Concise Oxford Dictionary of English Place-names, s.n.* Nyland, p. 346. Ekwall does not appear to have considered the spellings in the contents-list of the *Liber terrarum* (*Ætheresig*) or Domesday Book (*Ederesige*), however. Robinson ('Andresey', p. 78), who had cited all the forms, proposed the derivation 'Æthelred's island'. S.292, a diploma in the name of King Æthelwulf preserved in Glastonbury's fourteenth-century cartularies, is said to have been written 'in loco celebri qui uocatur Andredesdune'. That is the reading in MS. 39, *contra* Watkin (who printed *Andredesdime: The Great Cartulary*, II.469–70 [no. 851]). Finberg suggested that this might have been Andersey, on the basis of Birch's version (*Andredeseme*) from MS. Wood empt. 1 (Birch, *Cartularium Saxonicum*, II.13–14 [no. 438]; Finberg, *The Early Charters of Wessex*, p. 121 [no. 405]).

[26] Morland, 'Hidation', p. 75. See below, *s.n. Elosaneg*.

[27] These were in the *Liber terrarum* as LT107 and 108.

King Edgar; the earlier grant by Æthelwulf does not apppear.[28] According to Domesday Book, Glastonbury held forty hides at *Eissesberie*.[29]

A charter of A.D. 705x726 preserved in the Abingdon archive (S.1179, in the name of Hean) records an agreement with Cille, the donor's sister, and Abingdon concerning land in several places in Berkshire, including fifty-five hides at *Escesdune*. Frank Stenton rejected this charter as spurious, but Heather Edwards has argued in its favour.[30] If S.1179, S.288, and S.524 were genuine or based on genuine material, Hean's grant could suggest the existence of a large estate called Ashdown, from which Æthelwulf's ten- and Eadred's twenty-hide gifts were carved (the whole having reverted to the king between the early eighth and the mid-ninth century). The identification (by W.H. Stevenson and later by Margaret Gelling) of Ashdown as a lost name for the Berkshire Downs lends some weight to this idea,[31] although presumably (if that were so) the original estate would have been much larger than the fifty-five hides of S.1179. Control of the lands to the west of the middle Thames had long been disputed between Mercia and Wessex, and Stenton has identified Æthelwulf as the king who settled the issue, in favour of Wessex.[32] This would offer a context for Æthelwulf's grant. Thereafter, the land could have been returned to the king or stayed in secular possession. S.1504, the will of Ealdorman Æthelwold, reveals that S.524, which appears to be a straightforward royal grant to a layperson who in turn gave the estate to Glastonbury, conceals a rather more complex situation. Ashdown in the mid-940s was not a royal possession, but was held by Ealdorman Æthelwold, who in A.D. 946/7 willed it, with several other estates, to his brother Eadric.[33] Eadred's lost charter for Glastonbury, therefore, may have acted as a confirmation (not necessarily contemporary) of Eadric's gift of the estate to the abbey, after Eadric had received it from his brother. Why (if it is genuine) a grant to Eadric from the king was deemed necessary is unclear, but the destruction by fire of the charters of Ealdor-

---

28 *De antiquitate*, §§62 & 69 (ed. & transl. Scott, pp. 130 and 144); Scott did not recognise this estate as Ashbury in Berkshire. See also *Cronica*, §§16 and 73 (edd. & transl. Carley & Townsend, pp. 42 and 138). §§62 and 69 of the *De antiquitate* cite the grant by *Hedred* in a way which implies that the donor was a layman whose gift was confirmed by King Edgar. §73 of the *Cronica* duplicates the entry in the *De antiquitate*, as does John's summary (§16), but there we also find a reference to a direct grant by King Eadred. This may suggest that John had sources other than those represented by the extant version of the *De antiquitate*.

29 Domesday Book, I, 59va (Berkshire, 8.1).

30 Stenton, *The Early History*, p. 9; Edwards, *The Charters*, pp. 170–2. Stenton rejected the document (called a *testamentum* in the *Historia monasterii de Abingdon* written in the mid-twelfth century), saying that it did not conform to any of the characteristics of the Anglo-Saxon will; but as Edwards has pointed out, only the later mediaeval rubric claims that it is a will. The document has many acceptable features as a diploma.

31 *Asser's Life of King Alfred*, ed. Stevenson, pp. 235–7; Gelling, *The Place-names of Berkshire*, I.2–4.

32 *Anglo-Saxon England*, pp. 244–5, and *The Early History*, pp. 25–7. The year 840, however, is rather earlier than that proposed by Stenton for the success of Wessex (A.D. 844x850).

33 S.1504: see *Select English Historical Documents*, ed. & transl. Harmer, pp. 33, 63–4, and 117–18 (no. 20).

man Æthelfrith, Æthelwold's and Eadric's father (see S.371), may suggest that Eadric received the estate with incomplete documentation and required confirmation of his possession.

Stevenson argued that the pre-Conquest name *Asshedoune* survived in Ashdown Park in modern Ashbury, but Gelling has suggested that he was 'perhaps too positive'.[34] The note after S.524 in the cartularies makes it clear that the Ashdown of Glastonbury's tenth-century charter was called Ashbury in the mid-fourteenth century.[35] It is important, however, that we distinguish Glastonbury's Ashdown, later Ashbury, from the *Æscesbyrig* which was the subject of S.317, S.503, S.561, S.575, and S.687 and which consisted of the estates later called Uffington and Woolstone.[36] The transactions involving these estates are recorded in the archives of Abingdon and Winchester (Old Minster).

S.524 includes bounds, but Gelling has complained that modernisation by the cartularist has had such unfortunate results that the extent of the tenth-century estate could not be determined exactly. She could not discover whether the bounds described the whole of the modern parish of Ashbury (in the Vale of the White Horse, over sixty miles from Glastonbury) or only its western half, excluding Odstone (which did not belong to Glastonbury in 1066).[37]

The later name-form (Ashbury) which is found in the *De antiquitate* parallels that of Glastonbury's Domesday Book entry. In addition, the forty hides mentioned in the *De antiquitate* appear to have been based on the Domesday total for the estate, with which it agrees. This suggests that the lost charter in King Eadred's name (IC A13) for forty hides may have been a post-Conquest forgery whose information was based on Domesday Book or the *De antiquitate*.[38] It may be relevant that Ashbury was one of the manors appropriated by Wells (and one of those recovered by Glastonbury) during the protracted but ultimately unsuccessful attempt to annex the abbey to the see which was begun by Bishop Savaric (A.D. 1191–1205) and diligently pursued by Bishop Jocelin (A.D. 1206–1242).[39]

Ashcott (Somerset)

Ashcott has no documentation in its own name predating its appearance as part of Walton in Domesday Book.[40] There were in fact two sub-units of Walton called Ashcott, one of three hides and one of two, held in 1086 by different tenants. These two were probably originally one five-hide unit (characteristic of the

---

[34] *Asser's Life of King Alfred*, ed. Stevenson, p. 235; Gelling, *The Place-names of Berkshire*, I.3.

[35] 'Manerium quod nunc uocatur Aysshebury': *The Great Chartulary*, ed. Watkin, III.686–7 (no. 1272).

[36] Sawyer, *Anglo-Saxon Charters*, no. 317 (p. 149); also Gelling, *The Early Charters of the Thames Valley*, pp. 27, 28, 33, 36, 42, 49, and 52–3; Gelling, *The Place-names of Berkshire*, III.675; and the map in Hooke, 'Charters and the landscape', p. 92.

[37] Gelling, *The Early Charters of the Thames Valley*, p. 38. Odstone was held by Osgot from the king in 1066 (Domesday Book, I, 61rb [Berkshire, 28.3]). For the perambulation, see Gelling, *The Place-names of Berkshire*, III.694–6.

[38] The lost charter, however, seems to have used the early form of the name, Ashdown not Ashbury.

[39] See above, p. 12.

[40] Domesday Book, I, 90rb (Somerset, 8.11 and 8.14).

component parts of these composite Domesday estates),[41] but the date of their division is unknown. The nature and history of the Walton estate is discussed below, under *Pouelt*.

Asshedoune
See Ashbury.

Aust Cliff (Gloucestershire)
According to a charter (now lost) from the *Index chartarum*, a King Æthelred granted land at *Austancliue* to Glastonbury (S.1780; IC C13). That this was probably Æthelred the Unready, rather than Æthelred of Wessex (A.D. 865–871) or Æthelred of Mercia (A.D. 675–704),[42] is suggested by a note in the fourteenth-century cartularies following an undated papal privilege, itself sandwiched between privileges in the names of King Edgar and King Cnut. This note states that Æthelred gave Pucklechurch (also in Gloucestershire and supposedly a tenth-century royal gift) and *Austecleue* to the abbey.[43] The *De antiquitate* offers a few more details: the gift was for six hides, and Abbot Sigegar (*ca* A.D. 970–*ca* 975) was the recipient.[44] In Domesday Book, *Austre cliue* was a five-hide component of the estate of Westbury on Trym, which belonged to the church of Worcester.[45]

Charters preserved at Worcester relate to an estate at *Austan*; S.77 (A.D. 691x699) is a dubious grant of thirty hides at Aust and Henbury in the name of Æthelred, king of Mercia, in favour of Bishop Oftfor and St Peter's, Worcester. S.137 is a record of the restoration of land at Aust by Offa, king of Mercia, to Heathored, bishop of Worcester, dated A.D. 794. According to this record from a council of *Clofesho*, Æthelbald, king of Mercia (A.D. 716–757), had granted a charter for five hides at Aust to Worcester, but the land had been lost. When Bishop Heathored produced this charter at the synod, he regained the land from the ealdorman, Bynna, who was holding it. There is then a gap in the documentation until the tenth century, when, in a forged diploma dated 929, King Æthelstan is alleged to have granted a fishery at Aust to St Mary's, Worcester (S.401); this last charter includes Old English bounds which claim to define the estate.[46]

---

[41] See Bates, 'The five-hide unit', and Hollings, 'The survival'.

[42] For Mercian grants recorded at Glastonbury, see below, pp. 335–7.

[43] *The Great Chartulary*, ed. Watkin I.147 (no. 205).

[44] *De antiquitate*, §§63 and 69 (ed. & transl. Scott, pp. 130 and 145); *Cronica*, §§16 and 74 (edd. & transl. Carley & Townsend, pp. 42 and 142). Sigegar's abbacy, however, appears to predate Æthelred's reign (A.D. 978–1016).

[45] Domesday Book, I, 164vb (Gloucestershire, 3.1).

[46] Peter Kitson accepted the bounds of S.401 as contemporary with the date of Æthelstan's grant, arguing on philological and topographical grounds that if S.401 were a forgery, it was fabricated around a set of genuinely tenth-century bounds. Two sides of the estates are fixed by neighbouring surveys (S.1362, for Compton Greenfield and Marsh, and S.664, for Olveston and Long Ashton), with which Aust apparently shared a boundary; the third side was bounded by Littleton-on-Severn, but the description of its boundary in S.862 does not match that of S.401. I am most grateful to Mr Kitson for allowing me to see unpublished work on Anglo-Saxon charter-boundaries and for answering (in a letter dated September 28, 1992) my queries about S.401. Subsequent

Aust Cliff refers to the high cliff on the bank of the River Severn, half a mile from the existing settlement at Aust.[47] It is not likely that Glastonbury's *Austancliue* represents a different estate from that called *Austan* in the Worcester archive, as the Old English bounds of *Austan* clearly begin and end at the Severn. We are thus faced with contradictory documentation, with both Worcester and Glastonbury claiming that a King Æthelred gave them the estate. It may strain credulity to consider that different kings of the same name (three centuries apart) were involved; in any event, a struggle for possession between the two churches appears to be indicated, but with the limited evidence available it is impossible to judge the two claims. Worcester may win on bulk, but the spuriousness of S.77 and S.401 does not inspire confidence in the rest of their documentation. It is not impossible, in fact, that S.401 was produced to bolster Worcester's claim in the face of territorial aggression by Glastonbury.[48] Whichever church was granted Aust Cliff by (whichever) Æthelred, in 1066 at least Worcester's possession of the estate was recognised in Domesday Book.

Axe (River, Fishery on)

According to the *De antiquitate*, one hide and a fishery (*captura piscium*) on the River Axe were granted to Abbot Ecgfrith by King Ine in A.D. 719.[49] An interlineation in MS. R.5.33 has added *scilicet Scipelade*;[50] this identification, like all those in the Trinity manuscript of the *De antiquitate*, occurring as it does at such remove from the original grant, cannot be accepted as strong proof of the location of Ine's grant, although it ought not to be dismissed completely. S.606, a grant by King Eadwig to the thegn Æthelwold in A.D. 956 which is preserved in the *Codex Wintoniensis*, cites *scypeladæs pylle* as a boundary point of Bleadon. This estate, which does touch the Axe, belonged to the bishop of Winchester in 1066; at that date at least it was set aside for the monks' supplies.[51] This Shiplade in Bleadon may be a candidate for the place referred to in the interlinear note of the *De antiquitate*, which may have been the site of Ine's fishery, but there is no evidence before the thirteenth century to link the two, no confirmation in other sources of Glastonbury's pre-Conquest ownership of a hide at *Scipelade*, nor any evidence of a claim by Glastonbury on the Bleadon estate.

---

citations of his opinion refer to his unpublished material, unless otherwise specified. For the perambulation, see Grundy, *Saxon Charters and Field Names of Gloucestershire*, pp. 37–40.

[47] Where the Severn Bridge now crosses the river. In Roman times this was also an important river-crossing; the place-name may preserve some form of the name 'Augustus', from the Legio Augusta. See Smith, *The Place-names of Gloucestershire*, III.127–30.

[48] The diplomatic of S.401 would suggest a mid- or late tenth-century date for its construction; a *terminus post quem* of the early eleventh century is provided by the manuscript (London, British Library, MS. Cotton Tiberius A.xiii, 53–54).

[49] *De antiquitate*, §§40 and 69 (ed. & transl. Scott, pp. 94 and 142); *Cronica*, §§16 and 48 (edd. & transl. Carley & Townsend, pp. 40 and 94). The summary chapters omit the location on the Axe, mentioning only one hide *cum piscaria*.

[50] MS. R.5.33, 8v.

[51] Domesday Book, I, 87vb (Somerset, 2.11).

Robinson suggested another possible location for this fishery: he cited a gift by Ine of land at the foot of the Mendips in a charter now lost but recorded in the *Index chartarum* (S.1670; IC A6). Since the place to which this grant referred is also unidentified, Robinson's suggestion does not advance the effort to locate the site on the Axe; in any event it may not bear on it at all, as the charters appear to have been granted to different recipients.[52]

Badbury (Wiltshire)

According to a note which follows the Privilege of King Edmund I (S.499) in the fourteenth-century cartularies, King Eadred gave the *manerium* of Badbury to Dunstan and confirmed the gift with a charter.[1] The charter in question (S.568) was copied into the cartularies, as it had been into the *Liber terrarum* (LT67), and it may have survived into the fifteenth century.[2] According to the text of S.568, in A.D. 955 Eadred granted twenty-five hides at Badbury to Dunstan, for 150 gold *solidi*. The *De antiquitate* introduces some variation: the year was 954, the grant was of twenty-six hides (twenty-five in the summary chapter, however), and the price was fifty gold *solidi*.[3] In Domesday Book, Glastonbury held twenty hides at Badbury.[4]

G.B. Grundy considered that the bounds of S.568 indicated that the Anglo-Saxon estate of Badbury covered the whole of what is now Chiseldon, southeast of Swindon (over fifty miles from Glastonbury).[5] Rune Forsberg, however, reckoned the bounds to apply only to the eastern part of Chiseldon, that is to say, 'the one-time manor of Badbury'.[6] No other charters are extant for Badbury by name and the present evidence is insufficient to determine Badbury's relation to Chiseldon in the Anglo-Saxon period.[7] Chiseldon's history reveals no connexion with Glastonbury. Chiseldon is the subject of S.354, S.359, S.366, S.370, S.1417, and S.1507. The first, with the date 879x899, is a charter in the name of King Alfred,

---

52 Robinson, *Somerset*, p. 34. In the *De antiquitate* the abbot who received the hide on the Axe was identified as Ecgfrith, whereas in the *Index chartarum* the recipient of the grant at the foot of the Mendips appears to be Abbot Berwald. Neither of these sources, however, is so rigorous that its evidence must be accepted as irrefutable.

1 *The Great Chartulary*, ed. Watkin, I.145 (no. 203).

2 If the scribe of MS. 39a confused Eadred and Edgar in his reference to 'due antique cedule tangentes manerium de Baddebury tempore Edgari regis et sancti Dunstani' (L43 and 44); these may, however, represent later transactions.

3 *De antiquitate*, §§57 and 69 (ed. & transl. Scott, pp. 118 and 142); *Cronica*, §§16 and 66 (edd. & transl. Carley & Townsend, pp. 41 and 124) (likewise with conflicting figures of twenty-five and twenty-six). On the Anglo-Saxon land market, see Campbell, 'The sale of land'.

4 Domesday Book, I, 66va (Wiltshire, 7.6).

5 Grundy, 'The Saxon land charters of Wiltshire', pp. 205–10.

6 Forsberg, *A Contribution*, p. 7.

7 Grundy ('The Saxon land charters of Wiltshire', pp. 205–10) interpreted the bounds of S.366, a grant of Chiseldon, as defining the estate of Badbury, and the bounds of S.568, the charter for Badbury, as describing the estate of Chiseldon. No clarification of Grundy's seemingly peculiar decision can be achieved without going over the perambulations on the ground.

a complex document involving the regrant of the reversion of certain estates (including fifty hides at Chisledon); Æthelwulf had promised these lands to the bishop of Winchester after Alfred's death, but Winchester had given up its right to the reversion, in exchange for permission not to pay tribute to the *pagani*. Æthelwulf's intentions, at least, are confirmed by Alfred's will, in which the bookland at Chisledon was to be granted to Winchester 'on the terms on which my father bequeathed it'.[8] S.354 supposedly regranted Chisledon to the bishop; yet the attached bounds are for the estates which Alfred received in return. S.359 is another exchange, whereby Chisledon ostensibly returned to royal hands in A.D. 900. King Edward the Elder is then supposed to have granted fifty hides at Chisledon to the New Minster as part of its foundation-endowment (S.366 and S.370; A.D. 901 and 903). A lease of the estate by the *familia* of the New Minster to the thegn Alfred in A.D. 924x933 (S.1417, which survives in a contemporary single sheet)[9] refers to only twenty hides. The status of S.359, S.366, and S.370 is very suspect, and a history of this estate is not to be built on their evidence.

Glastonbury's twenty-five hides at Badbury therefore seem to belong to a time when Chisledon was in the hands of the New Minster, which still held forty hides there in 1066.[10] It seems most likely that Badbury was a neighbour, not a part, of Chisledon, despite Grundy's interpretation of the bounds of S.568.[11] How the number of hides at Badbury dropped by five (or six) by 1066 is another unsolved problem: a portion of the estate may have been lost after the 950s, or alternatively the assessment may have been lowered while the area remained the same; the two (lost) *cedule* of MS. 39a (L43 and 44) may have borne on this question.

Badbury belongs to a group of estates which seems to have been acquired as a result of a new eastward-looking movement in Glastonbury's pattern of land-holding in the mid-tenth century. This trend – associated with St Dunstan – has been connected with the desire to exploit chalk uplands (with better drainage than the heavy clays of the abbey's estates in the Somerset plain).[12] We may take this as a dim reflexion of the kind of manipulation of land-resources visible more clearly in Æthelwold's development of the endowment of Ely Abbey.[13]

Badbury was one of the manors appropriated by Wells (and one of those recovered by Glastonbury) during the protracted but ultimately unsuccessful attempt to annex the monastery to the see which was begun by Bishop Savaric (A.D. 1191–1205) and diligently pursued by Bishop Jocelin (A.D. 1206–1242).[14]

Baltonsborough (Somerset)

Baltonsborough, only a few miles southeast of Glastonbury, is the subject of an unusual charter, obviously corrupt but probably essentially authentic, which was

---

[8] S.1507; *English Historical Documents*, transl. Whitelock, p. 535 (no. 96).
[9] On the script of S.1417, see Dumville, 'English square minuscule', p. 174.
[10] Domesday Book, I, 67va (Wiltshire, 10.5).
[11] See above, p. 52, n. 7.
[12] Stacy, 'The estates', pp. 2–3. See map 7.
[13] *Anglo-Saxon Ely*, edd. & transl. Keynes & Kennedy, and *Liber Eliensis*, ed. Blake, pp. 63–117 and 395–9.
[14] *Cronica*, §§106 and 113 (edd. & transl. Carley & Townsend, pp. 196 and 212). See above, p. 12.

in the *Liber terrarum* and is preserved in the Glastonbury cartularies (S.1410; LT17);[15] according to this grant, Lulla, *humilis ancilla Christi*, sold ten hides there (and at *Scobbanwirht*) to the abbey, a transaction confirmed by Æthelbald, king of Mercia, in A.D. 744. The charter was still in the archive in A.D. 1247 (IC A19) and in the fifteenth century (L7). The *De antiquitate* records the transaction but dates it in the following year.[16]

According to Domesday Book, in 1066 Glastonbury held five hides at Baltonsborough.[17] The figures could suggest that Lulla's grant had consisted of five hides in each of the two places mentioned, after which *Scobbanwirht* was detached from its association with Baltonsborough, possibly becoming part of Ditcheat. The question is complicated by the virtual disappearance of *Scobbanwirht* from the record. It may, however, be found in S.292 and in Domesday Book in association with the estates of Lottisham and Lydford.[18]

Edwards has described S.1410 as 'a transfer of property between neighbouring houses',[19] basing her judgment on a clause which refers to the possibility of contention between two communities ('inter tributarios uestros nostrosque colonos'),[20] which Edwards took to imply that the lands of Lulla's community and those of Glastonbury shared a boundary. Lulla's church is not identified, however, here or in other extant documents, and the context of this grant remains obscure.

The bounds of S.1410 are characteristic of early descriptions: they are in Latin (though with vernacular names, probably modernised), short, and not very helpful.[21] The early date of these bounds (and the absence of any other record of this estate) appears, therefore, to suggest that Baltonsborough may have been in Glastonbury's possession from the mid-eighth century until 1066, although movement between those dates could have been concealed by loss of documents from the intervening years.

---

15 See Edwards, *The Charters*, pp. 41–5 and 48–52.
16 *De antiquitate*, §§46 and 69 (ed. & transl. Scott, pp. 104 and 142); *Cronica*, §§16 and 52 (edd. & transl. Carley & Townsend, pp. 40 and 104). On Glastonbury and Mercia, see below, pp. 335–7.
17 Domesday Book, I, 90va (Somerset, 8.22).
18 See below, *s.n.* Ditcheat and *Scobbanwirht*; see also Edwards, *The Charters*, p. 44.
19 *Ibid.*, p. 42.
20 'Between your rent-payers and our peasants'.
21 Costen has accepted them as original: 'The late Saxon landscape', p. 33. As Grundy put it, they were probably written 'before the Saxons had learnt the art of survey'; *The Saxon Charters*, p. 61. They offer the interesting information that 'circa quidem prata euidens fossa declarat limites' (a conspicuous ditch marks the boundary [pl.] around the meadows). Grundy expressed the view (p. 62) that the Anglo-Saxon estate probably did not include the northern and northwestern parts of the modern parish of Baltonsborough, as these were low-lying and therefore possibly unusable at that period. This explanation is less persuasive than it might be, inasmuch as Grundy employed it so often when bounds proved difficult to solve. On the nature of the landscape at this period, see Williams, *The Draining*, especially pp. 17–24, and Rippon, 'Landscape evolution'. I am grateful to Stephen Rippon for allowing me to see work in progress.

Batcombe (Somerset)

A charter of King Edmund I for twenty hides at Batcombe, dated 940, survives in the fourteenth-century cartularies (S.462). It was apparently also in the *Liber terrarum* (LT106), but is not found in the later list of single sheets. The recipient, according to the contents-list of the lost *Liber*, was Ælfsige, whereas the extant versions cite 'meo propinquo et fideli ministro uocitato Elswythe'. This *Elswythe* has been interpreted as a corruption of the female name Ælfswith, a suggestion reinforced by the will of Ælfheah, ealdorman of Hampshire, in which he left the estate of Batcombe to his wife, Ælfswith, with eventual reversion to Glastonbury (A.D. 968x971).[22] Dorothy Whitelock therefore suggested that Batcombe was originally given to Ælfheah and Ælfswith jointly, and that the copyist of S.462 simply omitted Ælfheah's name. The charter, however, employs the masculine singular and nowhere reflects a female (or more than one) recipient. It seems more likely that the charter of the *Liber terrarum* was indeed granted to Ælfsige, after which the land passed to Ælfheah, either directly or via the king. The mistake in the surviving text of S.462 may therefore be the corruption of Ælfsige to *Elswythe*, rather than the omission of Ælfheah. The charter presumably came to Glastonbury with the land when Ælfheah left it to the abbey. The *De antiquitate* preserves the record of two grants of Batcombe to Glastonbury, by Ælfsige *and* Ælfheah: it claims that *Aelsy* gave Glastonbury twenty hides with King Edmund's approval, and later records the gift of twenty hides at Batcombe by Ealdorman *Aelfare* (*recte* Ælfheah?).[23] The summary section includes both these grants. It is likely that the author of the *De antiquitate* is assuming that all the archivally documented lands granted to laypeople were handed over to Glastonbury by their recipients, an assumption which creates confusion if an earlier charter had been preserved and transferred with the land merely as a title-deed.

W. de G. Birch identified S.462 as relating to Batcombe in Nyland, near Wedmore, whereas J.M. Kemble and G.B. Grundy identified it with the Batcombe near Bruton in the east of the county, about twelve miles from Glastonbury.[24] In Domesday Book, Glastonbury held twenty hides at Batcombe, seven and a half hides of which were said to have been at Westcombe.[25] If the Batcombe of S.462 is the estate in Domesday Book (and there is no evidence that the estate which is the subject of the charter left Glastonbury's possession after A.D. 968x971), the inclusion of Westcombe (on the other side of the steep valley of the Batcombe near Bruton) makes the identification proposed by Kemble certain.

---

[22] S.1485; *Anglo-Saxon Wills*, ed. & transl. Whitelock, pp. 22–4 and 121–5 (no. 9). Ælfswith also makes an appearance in S.866; see below, *s.n. Kyngton*. For other estates associated with her and her husband, see below, *s.n.* Idmiston. On Ealdorman Ælfheah, see Williams, '*Princeps Merciorum gentis*', especially pp. 147–54.

[23] *De antiquitate*, §§55, 62, and 69 (ed. & transl. Scott, pp. 114–16, 130, and 142–4); *Cronica*, §§16, 64, and 73 (edd. & transl. Carley & Townsend, pp. 40–2, 122, and 138).

[24] *Cartularium Saxonicum*, ed. Birch, II.470–2 (no. 749); *Codex Diplomaticus*, ed. Kemble, II.224–5 (no. 383); Grundy, *The Saxon Charters*, pp. 86–91.

[25] Domesday Book, I, 90va (Somerset, 8.24).

Beckery (Somerset)

Beckery, like *Andreyesie*, appears in the forged Great Privilege of King Ine (S.250), where it is stated that the land was originally given to Glastonbury by King Cenwealh.[26] Beckery is also one of the group of chapels cited in S.783, the privilege of King Edgar, as exempt from the jurisdiction of the bishop of Wells.[27] It came to bear the name *Parua Hibernia* and was associated with St Brigit, who was supposed to have arrived there in A.D. 488, leaving behind on her return to Ireland some objects which were venerated at a much later date.[28] The *De antiquitate* also cites the grant of Beckery by King Cenwealh.[29]

Beckery is on the western edge of the 'peninsula' projecting from Glastonbury into the moors. Excavations in the 1960s revealed the existence of a Mid-Saxon settlement, with timber structures and a cemetery whose make-up suggested to the excavators that the community had been a monastic one.[30] This has led to the interpretation of Beckery as a kind of satellite of the church of Glastonbury, a pattern which might have been mirrored at other, similar, sites in the Levels nearby.[31] Beckery does not appear by name in Domesday Book and was probably assessed under Glastonbury itself; it is likely that Beckery was considered part of the core-estate of Glastonbury from a very early date, although its association with King Cenwealh must be treated with some caution, considering the doubtful nature of Glastonbury's surviving charter in the name of this king (S.227).[32] It is possible that another charter (in the name of a less impressive donor) was suppressed in favour of King Cenwealh and, later, of St Brigit.[33]

Bedul

Bedul was interpreted by Scott in his edition of the *De antiquitate* as an estate forming part of King Æthelwulf's gift of a tenth of his lands to the Church.[34] In the Great Cartulary's version (S.303; A.D. 854), however, it does not look like a

---

26 *De antiquitate*, §42 (ed. & transl. Scott, p. 98); *Cronica*, §49 (edd. & transl. Carley & Townsend, p. 96). See also above, *s.n. Andersey*.

27 *De antiquitate*, §60 (ed. & transl. Scott, p. 124); *Cronica*, §71 (edd. & transl. Carley & Townsend, p. 134). See also the privilege of Henry II: *Cronica*, §95 (edd. & transl. Carley & Townsend, p. 176).

28 *De antiquitate*, §12 (ed. & transl. Scott, p. 60); *Cronica*, §28 (edd. & transl. Carley & Townsend, p. 66). Beckery seems to be a rare example of an Irish place-name in England: *Becc-Ériu* means 'little Ireland' in Old and Middle Irish (Ekwall, *The Concise Oxford Dictionary of English Place-names, s.n. Beckery*, p. 33; also Campbell, 'The debt', p. 340). H.P.R. Finberg proposed instead an English derivation, from Old English *beocere*, 'beekeeper': see his *West-Country Historical Studies*, pp. 81–2. For St Brigit, see also Robinson, 'St Brigid and Glastonbury', pp. 97–9.

29 *De antiquitate*, §§36 and 69 (ed. & transl. Scott, pp. 90 and 140); *Cronica*, §§16 and 42 (edd. & transl. Carley & Townsend, pp. 40 and 88).

30 See Rahtz & Hirst, *Beckery Chapel*, especially pp. 24–39. For excavations in the 1880s, see Morland, 'St Bridget's Chapel', pp. 121–6.

31 Such as Godney and Marchey (*Martinsey*); Rahtz & Hirst, *Beckery Chapel*, p. 55.

32 See *s.n. Andersey* and Glastonbury.

33 Cenwealh may have replaced an episcopal donor at Meare (*q.v.*).

34 *De antiquitate*, §§53 and 69 (ed. & transl. Scott, pp. 112 and 142); *Cronica*, §§16 and 56 (edd. & transl. Carley & Townsend, pp. 40 and 108).

place-name (it is not capitalised, unlike the other names on the list) and it is probably a corruption of Old English *be dæl*, 'in the valley' or 'at the portion [of land]'.[35] The other extant list of Glastonbury's lands involved in Æthelwulf's Decimation – in the *Secretum domini* (68v) – is highly abbreviated and omits *bedul*.

Berrow (Somerset)

A diploma dated A.D. 973, and in the name of King Edgar, granted five hides at *Burgh'* to his thegn Wulfmær (S.793). This charter was not in the *Liber terrarum*, but was recorded on a single sheet still in the archive in A.D. 1247 (IC D21), was preserved in the later cartularies, and was extant in the fifteenth century (L21). Berrow lies about fifteen miles from Glastonbury between Brent and the Severn-shore, and the early bounds in a charter granting Brent to Glastonbury (S.238; A.D. ?693) appear to include it, a circumstance which would explain the exclusion of its name from Domesday Book.[36] The position of the charter for *Burgh'* in the cartularies and MS. 39a reveals that in the later middle ages it was considered to relate to part of Brent, which estate appears to have been an important element of Glastonbury's endowment from the eighth century.[37] Grundy did not analyse the bounds recorded in S.793 and they have yet to be satisfactorily 'solved'.[38] They refer to the River Axe and *Merkmere*, possibly the 'pool of Mark', Mark being an estate southeast of Brent; if this latter boundary point is correctly identified and Berrow did touch the Mark estate, Berrow would have included much territory outside its modern parish and overlapped much of Brent, as Finberg pointed out.[39] This seems very unlikely.

That Berrow appears to have been included in Brent in the eighth century and again in Domesday Book, but is apparently treated separately in this charter, does present some difficulty. If the charter is genuine, it could suggest that by the late tenth century the estate had broken into sub-units with a potentially independent tenurial (and documentary) existence. If that were the case, however, we might expect Berrow to be referred to by name in the Brent entry in Domesday Book. If the charter is spurious, it may have been produced to face a challenge to Glaston-bury's possession of Brent. One possible context might be the apparent seizure of East Brent and Berrow (*Berwes*) by Savaric, bishop of Wells (A.D. 1191–1205), at the time of his appropriation of a number of other manors belonging to Glaston-bury. His return of East Brent and Berrow in A.D. 1203 was part of the first

---

[35] MS. 39, 59r. On the different texts of Æthelwulf's Decimation charter for Glastonbury, and the interpretation of his grant, see below, *s.n. Brannocmynstre*, Monk Okehampton, and pp. 322–4.

[36] Morland concluded that it formed part of Brent's twenty hides in 1066; 'The Glaston-bury manors', p. 69.

[37] See below, *s.n.* Brent.

[38] I am grateful to Jem Harrison for the information (in a letter of 17 August, 1993) that boundary points mentioned cannot be traced in later mediaeval or modern documents and maps.

[39] Finberg, *The Early Charters of Wessex*, pp. 146–7; although (as Harrison has pointed out to me) Berrow could perhaps have had a detached portion in Mark Moor described in this way.

composition of the dispute between the cathedral and the abbey.[40] A further possibility – and perhaps the most persuasive – is that the charter referred not to Berrow but to another five hides with a similar name (since lost as an estate-name). A candidate may be found, perhaps, in Elborough (where Glastonbury held three hides in 1066), Oldbury in Cheddar, or Barrow's Hams (or even 'the Borough') in Wedmore.[41] If Edgar's grant (or the attached boundary, if they did not originate together) did not apply to Berrow, it was certainly associated with it by the time the cartularies were compiled.

Edgar's grant does not appear in the *De antiquitate* or the *Cronica*; the sole appearance of Berrow in these sources, it seems, is in a corrupt version of a charter of William the Conqueror (not found elsewhere, but possibly a reconstruction of a genuine text of A.D. 1071x1087) which confirmed Glastonbury's possession of seven estates, including *Berwes*.[42]

Binegar (Somerset)

Binegar lies approximately five miles northeast of Wells. An entry in the contents-list of the *Liber terrarum* (S.1701; LT93) records a grant of *Beaganhangran* by Burgred, king of Mercia (A.D. 852x874), to Eanwulf.[43] This charter was not recorded in the later lists, nor does its text survive. The *De antiquitate*, in its customary fashion, presented this transaction as a gift to Glastonbury by Eanwulf (who reputedly gave a number of estates to the abbey), confirmed by the king.[44]

---

[40] *The Great Chartulary*, ed Watkin, I.xli–xliii and 77 (no. 126). See above, p.12.

[41] See below, *s.n. Cedern*, Elborough, and Wedmore. I am indebted to Jem Harrison for the last suggestion.

[42] *De antiquitate*, §75 (ed. & transl. Scott, p. 154); *Cronica*, §83 (edd. & transl. Carley & Townsend, p. 154); *Regesta regum Anglo-Normannorum*, edd. Davis, *et al.*, I.71 (no. 273). According to the text of this document, the relevant charters were inspected, which would imply that the Berrow charter was extant in the archive in A.D. 1071x1087. Although the charter in William's name is a clumsy forgery, Davis suggested that it might have been an attempt to reconstruct a lost document, since a document of Henry I mentions a charter issued by his father which confirmed these places to Glastonbury. The implications of this confirmation are not clear; the significance of the grouping of the estates, however, is probably of relevance to the post-Conquest, not pre-Conquest, situation, and therefore outside the scope of this survey.

[43] The identification of this place has been established by the following sequence of forms: *Begenhangra*, *Behenhanger*, and *Benhangre* (Ekwall, *The Concise Oxford Dictionary of English Place-names*, *s.n.* Binegar, p. 44).

[44] *De antiquitate*, §§53 and 69 (ed. & transl. Scott, pp. 112 and 142); *Cronica*, §§16 and 56 (edd. & transl. Carley & Townsend, pp. 40 and 108). The king is called Æthelwulf, possibly a result of conflating several grants or, alternatively, an assumption (as Æthelwulf reputedly granted other lands to Eanwulf). It may be, however, that Æthelwulf confirmed the charter, or that it was granted jointly by Burgred and Æthelwulf. Eanwulf is also said to have given Ditcheat, Hornblotton, and Lottisham (*q.v.*), a block of estates to the southeast of Glastonbury with good access to the Fosse Way (and he may be the same man who bought or leased *Brunham*, although the date of that transaction – A.D. 824 – may be too early, as the donor of the other estates was probably the ealdorman who died in A.D. 867; *Chronicon Æthelweardi*, Book 14, §2; *The Chronicle of Æthelweard*, ed. & transl. Campbell, p. 36).

No further evidence for the possession of this estate is extant except S.1042, a charter for Wells in the name of King Edward the Confessor, which bears the date 1065. Binegar is one of a very long list of places confirmed to Wells in this document. S.1042 has generally been considered spurious, exhibiting as it does some unconventional, non-Anglo-Saxon, features, but Keynes has defended its authenticity, explaining these features as the result of continental influences.[45] Its testimony, then, would suggest that Binegar was in the possession of the church of Wells at the end of the Anglo-Saxon period; this cannot be confirmed through Domesday Book, however, as Binegar does not appear there by name. Whether it was ever in Glastonbury's hands depends on our interpretation of the grant to Eanwulf and the reference in the *De antiquitate* to his gift of the land to the abbey. The grant of land in Somerset by Burgred, a Mercian, may (if genuine) reflect the alliance between Burgred and Æthelwulf which is known from their joint venture against the West Welsh and Burgred's marriage to Æthelwulf's daughter.[46] Record of another grant by Burgred is preserved in Glastonbury's archive.[47] If the other grants associated with Eanwulf are to be credited, he – the ealdorman of Somerset – also was a beneficiary of King Æthelwulf's largesse.[48] Burgred's generosity would therefore have been in step with Wessex interests.

Blackford (Somerset)

There are two Blackfords in Somerset, one near Wedmore in the Levels and another outside Wincanton in the far southeast of the county. Two entries in the contents-list of the *Liber terrarum* refer to charters for an estate of this name: one was given by King Eadwig (S.1757; LT53) and the other by King Edgar (S.1768; LT81), both grants being made directly to Glastonbury. A charter of King Eadwig granting Blackford apparently to a layman was also in the archive in A.D. 1247 (IC C7; no Sawyer-number).[49] The texts of these charters do not survive. According to the *De antiquitate*, King Eadwig gave Glastonbury three (or six) hides at

---

[45] Keynes, 'Regenbald', especially pp. 200–5.

[46] ASC 853; Stenton, *Anglo-Saxon England*, p. 245. On Glastonbury's Mercian connexion, see below, pp. 335–7.

[47] See below, *s.n.* Lydney.

[48] See below, *s.n.* Ditcheat. An ealdorman Eanwulf defeated the Danes at the mouth of the Parrett in A.D. 845 and attested a number of West Saxon charters. That he came from near Glastonbury is suggested by the reference to him as *Eanulf penearding* (Pennard being the name of two estates adjacent to Glastonbury) in S.1445, a letter written to document a dispute in Wiltshire: *Select English Historical Documents*, ed. & transl. Harmer, pp. 62 and 115 (no. 18); see also Keynes, 'The Fonthill letter', pp. 56–7, and Blows, 'Studies', pp. 272–7. Blows has suggested (pp. 276–83) that Eanwulf's association with King Æthelwulf's son Æthelbald, and his support of the latter's rebellion against his father, affected King Alfred's attitude to Glastonbury, which had been the beneficiary of grants by Eanwulf and Æthelbald. For Eanwulf's opposition to Æthelwulf, see Asser's Life of King Alfred, §12 (ed. Stevenson, pp. 9–10 and 195–9; *Alfred the Great*, transl. Keynes & Lapidge, pp. 70 and 234–5 [no. 26]).

[49] This grant appears on the list of charters in favour of the abbey, but marked *seruienti*; see above, p. 17.

Blackford,[50] and King Edgar gave six hides (or five) there; there is no mention of a grant to a layman.[51] Glastonbury held a four-hide estate at Blackford in Domesday Book, while another Blackford holding, of one hide, was in the hands of *Aluuardus* in 1066.[52] Blackford was confirmed to Glastonbury in the corrupt charter of William the Conqueror preserved in the *De antiquitate*, but no details of its extent or original donor were documented there.[53] Further, the *De antiquitate* states that Abbot Herluin had recovered Blackford after A.D. 1101 from *Ulricus*, the brother of the bishop of Durham.[54]

It is difficult to choose between the two Blackfords in assigning locations to these charters. The relation of Eadwig's and Edgar's charters to the later estates is obscure, a condition greatly aggravated by the fact that there are two versions of the number of hides for both grants. The evidence does not allow us to decide whether the two pre-Conquest charters might have granted the same estate, or parts of it, or two different Blackfords. Even the identity of the Domesday Book holdings has not been agreed.

Morland argued that two different estates were involved. He identified the grant by Eadwig with Blackford in Wedmore and the grant by Edgar with Blackford near Wincanton.[55] Certainly the position of Edgar's charter in the *Liber terrarum*, following one for Holton (also near Wincanton), would seem to support this latter identification, if there is not more than one Holton involved.[56] Morland's argument for identifying Eadwig's grant with Blackford in Wedmore, however, has not been universally accepted. The *Liber Henrici de Soliaco*, a survey of Glastonbury's lands made in A.D. 1189, reveals that Blackford in Wedmore was at that date one of the abbey's manors, but any earlier connexion with Glastonbury is uncertain, especially as Wells held Wedmore in 1066 and 1086.[57] Morland, however, identified both Eadwig's grant and Glastonbury's four-hide Domesday estate of Blackford with this Blackford in Wedmore;[58] he

---

50 *De antiquitate*, §§58 and 69 (ed. & transl. Scott, pp. 120 and 144); *Cronica*, §§16 and 67 (edd. & transl. Carley & Townsend, pp. 42 and 126) (six hides, not three, in the summaries).

51 *De antiquitate*, §§62 and 69 (ed. & transl. Scott, pp. 128 and 144); *Cronica*, §§16 and 73 (edd. & transl. Carley & Townsend, pp. 42 and 138) (five hides in the summaries).

52 *Aluuardus* held from Thurstan son of Rolf in 1086: Domesday Book, I, 90ra and 97vb (Somerset, 8.9 and 36.8).

53 See above, *s.n.* Berrow.

54 *De antiquitate*, §79 (ed. & transl. Scott, p. 160); *Cronica*, §87 (edd. & transl. Carley & Townsend, p. 162).

55 Morland, 'Some Domesday manors', p. 45; also 'The Glastonbury manors', p. 69.

56 A place called Holton was also the subject of a charter of King Edgar. See below, *s.n.* Holton. The *Liber terrarum* was not, however, contemporary with Edgar's grant, and it is not therefore clear that the order of its contents has any standing in the argument.

57 *Liber Henrici*, ed. Jackson, pp. 81–4; proof of relationship between this Blackford and Wedmore is offered by the obligation of the former to pay hearthpenny to the church of Wedmore (p. 84). Small excavations in the 1950s at the site called the 'Bishop's Palace' at Blackford uncovered buildings of the late thirteenth and fourteenth centuries, interpreted as the episcopal hall known from Wells bishops' registers: see Rendell, 'Blackford (Wedmore)', pp. 72–8.

58 Morland, 'Some Domesday manors', p. 45; 'The Glastonbury manors', p. 69.

considered that Blackford near Wincanton (granted to Glastonbury by Edgar) was assessed in Domesday Book under Butleigh (eight hides of which, he argued, consisted of five at Blackford and three at Holton, although Domesday Book gives no names for these portions).[59] As the earliest mention of Butleigh (S.270a, ostensibly of A.D. 801) gives a figure of twenty hides, the same as the assessment in 1066,[60] Blackford and Holton must have been attached to Butleigh without altering its hidage, if Morland's identification is correct. This identification seems unlikely, given the distance of Butleigh from Wincanton, and the fact that Glastonbury's Blackford (of eight hides and still paired with Holton) is clearly distinguished from Butleigh (and its twenty hides) in a mid-fourteenth-century source.[61] The order of the entries in Domesday Book (by hundreds) also suggests Wincanton, rather than Wedmore, as the location of Glastonbury's four Blackford hides of 1066. E.H. Bates and C. and F. Thorn therefore identified Blackford in Wincanton as the estate in Glastonbury's Domesday Book entry.[62] C. and F. Thorn suggested that the post-Conquest estate there, which consisted of eight hides, was made up of the four hides of Domesday Blackford (*Somerset*, 8.9), the one hide held at Blackford by *Aluuardus* (36.8), the two hides of Holton (45.4), and one hide from Thurstan's adjacent holdings in Woolston, Maperton, Clapton, or North Cadbury. They did not attempt to relate the Blackford of 1066 to the pre-Conquest grants or to find Blackford in Wedmore in Domesday Book.

If we reject the association of Glastonbury's Domesday Blackford with Butleigh, however, we leave one piece of evidence unexplained. In Domesday Book, two hides in *Lodreford* (held in 1066 by Glastonbury but lost to the king) are said to have belonged to the manor of Butleigh.[63] Lattiford, too, is near Wincanton and was in fact later in Holton parish, and this connexion may validate the suggestion that Blackford and Holton were attached to Butleigh as well.[64] If a *Lodreford* could be found in Butleigh, however, the connexion would disappear.

Whichever Blackford is actually represented as Glastonbury's in Domesday Book, Blackford near Wedmore was one of the manors lost to Wells during the protracted but ultimately unsuccessful attempt to annex the abbey to the see which was begun by Bishop Savaric (A.D. 1191–1205) and diligently pursued by Bishop Jocelin (A.D. 1206–1242). Litigation throughout the thirteenth century involving Blackford, Cranmore, Pucklechurch, and Winscombe culminated in their surren-

---

[59] Neil Stacy, who has agreed with Morland's identification of Blackford, differed from him on this point; he considered the eight hides to have consisted of three hides at Blackford and five hides at Holton, the latter reputedly given to Glastonbury by one Beornsige (Stacy, 'The estates', p. 32).

[60] If S.270a were an eleventh-century forgery, however, it would not be a reliable witness to Butleigh's hidage in A.D. 801.

[61] Morland, 'Hidation', p. 77; *A Feodary*, ed. Weaver, pp. 58 and 62. Morland, however, cited this last source to prove his point that Blackford was in Butleigh.

[62] Bates, 'Text of the Somerset Domesday', p. 462; *Somerset*, edd. & transl. Thorn & Thorn, p. 355.

[63] Domesday Book, I, 90rb (Somerset, 8.19).

[64] Ekwall derived Lattiford from *Lodreford* (*The Concise Oxford Dictionary of English Place-names*, *s.n.* Lattiford, p. 289) but found no forms earlier than those in Domesday Book.

der to the bishop.[65] In the case of Pucklechurch, disputed lordship produced spurious documentation in Eadred's name (at least).[66] One (or both) of the royal diplomas for Blackford might merit suspicion on this account; their appearance in the *Liber terrarum* seems to provide a *terminus ante quem* predating that dispute, but Herluin's early twelfth-century restoration might be within the extreme dating limits of that lost cartulary.[67]

Bleadney (Somerset)

A charter in the name of Forthhere, bishop of Sherborne, bearing the date 712, survives in the fourteenth-century cartularies (S.1253).[68] It preserves a grant by the bishop to *Aldbertus*, abbot of Glastonbury, of three pieces of land on the River Axe: 'ad portam que dicitur Bledenythe, ad insulam paruam, et ad ecclesiam beati Martini confessoris'.[69] Forthhere's charter was preserved in the *Liber terrarum* (LT11) and listed in the *Index chartarum* (IC A18) and MS. 39a (L3). Further reference to Bleadney (*Bledeni*) occurs in the spurious Great Privilege of King Ine (S.250), where one hide there is named among the estates given by that king to Glastonbury.[70] The *De antiquitate* mentions Forthhere's gift of one hide at *Bleda-hit/Bledanhid*, but not of the other two lands.[71] If Forthhere's charter was genuine, it would indicate that the early layers of Glastonbury's endowment were built up, not just from royal patronage, but from grants of episcopal land – from the new bishopric of Sherborne – as well. An even earlier grant to Glastonbury by the bishop of Winchester may provide a parallel.[72]

Bleadney's subsequent pre-Conquest history is undocumented. Its status as a holding of Glastonbury at the end of the Anglo-Saxon period, however, is called into question by its appearance in S.1042, the confirmation charter of A.D. 1065 for Wells in the name of King Edward the Confessor.[73] Bleadney's non-appearance in

---

65 See above, p. 12. The Anglo-Saxon charter for Pucklechurch (S.553), another of these manors (*q.v.*), was apparently transferred to Wells with the estate; Blackford's pre-Conquest documentation presumably made the same trip. The absence of the Blackford in Wedmore from the Glastonbury feodary of A.D. 1342 (and Blackford in Wincanton's inclusion therein) indicates that it was the Wedmore Blackford that was lost to Wells (*A Feodary*, ed. Weaver).

66 See Abrams, ' "Lucid intervals" '.

67 For the date of the *Liber terrarum*, see above, pp. 14–17.

68 The indiction (the first) suggests the date 718.

69 Goodchild, misunderstanding the syntax, interpreted this charter as revealing the existence of a monastery at Bleadon (of which Ealdberht was abbot) and identified this as the house at which Boniface was educated; 'St Boniface and Somerset', pp. 172–3.

70 *De antiquitate*, §42 (ed. & transl. Scott, p. 98); *Cronica*, §49 (edd. & transl. Carley & Townsend, p. 96).

71 *De antiquitate*, §§40 and 69 (ed. & transl. Scott, pp. 94 and 142); *Cronica*, §§16 and 47 (edd. & transl. Carley & Townsend, pp. 40 and 92).

72 See below, *s.n. Lantokay*, Marchey, and Meare; it may be noteworthy that the place-names of two of the four estates attributed to these early bishops' gift apparently refer to saints: Kay and Martin.

73 As mentioned above (*s.n.* Binegar) Keynes has argued in favour of the authenticity of this charter.

Domesday Book as a possession of either Glastonbury or Wells suggests that it was counted as part of another estate: that it was later included in the Twelve Hides of Glastonbury may indicate that Bleadney formed part of the abbey's core-estate, at least by 1066. It certainly shows that, even if Wells did claim Bleadney, the bishop did not succeed in detaching it from the abbey.[74] Five miles from both Wells and Glastonbury (the three places form a triangle), Bleadney's position on the river (which has since moved its course) would have made it desirable to both churches. Its designation (*porta*) in Forthhere's charter presumably indicates its strategic importance in the early eighth century, providing access to markets and transportation routes.[75]

Bocland

A charter dated 951, in the name of King Eadred and granting twenty hides at *Bocland* to his kinsman Ælfhere, was copied into the *Liber terrarum* (on the evidence of the contents-list) and the extant cartularies and was still in the archive in the fifteenth century (S.555 and S.1737; LT116; L27).[76] In the cartularies and MS. 39a it was filed with the charters for Buckland Newton, in Dorset. The bounds of S.555, however, including as they do a reference to Kilmersdon (outside Radstock), identify the Buckland of the charter as an estate half-way between Radstock and Frome, now called Buckland Denham or Dinham.[77] The grant by Eadred does not appear in the *Index chartarum* or the *De antiquitate*. In 1066, a twelve-hide estate at Buckland Denham belonged to Donno, a king's thegn.[78] If this is the same estate as the one granted in S.555, it had lost eight hides of land – or been reassessed – by 1066.

It is possible that Buckland Denham never came into Glastonbury's possession, the charter (and others) being deposited there by its owner, Ealdorman Ælfhere, who was buried at Glastonbury.[79] It is also possible that the bounds for Buckland Denham were attached at a later date to a charter for another Buckland;

---

[74] *De antiquitate*, §72 (ed. & transl. Scott, p. 150); *Cronica*, §3 (edd. & transl. Carley & Townsend, p. 14). For the Twelve Hides, see below, *s.n.* Glastonbury.

[75] Blows has identified Forthhere's grant not with Bleadney but with Bleadon, an estate on the Axe near its mouth. Bleadon was the subject of two grants with Winchester associations: S.606 (A.D. 956), by King Eadwig to a layman, and S.804 (A.D. 975) by King Edgar to the Old Minster. The name-forms in the latter are *Bleodun* and *Bledone*. Bleadon in 1066 belonged to the bishop of Winchester (Domesday Book, I, 87rb; Somerset, 2.11). Ekwall has no entry for Bleadney (*Bleadon* is on p. 48). But see Gelling, *Place-names in the Landscape*, pp. 77–8 ('Bledda's landing-place').

[76] Sawyer's no. 1737 is the same as no. 555.

[77] Ekwall, *The Concise Oxford Dictionary of English Place-names*, *s.n.* Buckland, p. 72; Finberg, *The Early Charters of Wessex*, p. 137.

[78] Domesday Book, I, 99ra (Somerset, 47.19).

[79] If he was the *dux Alfari* whose tomb, according to the *De antiquitate*, was still to be seen in the church (*De antiquitate*, §31 [ed. & transl. Scott, p. 84]). Scott seems to be mistaken in rendering this name 'Ælfheah'; see Blows, 'A Glastonbury obit-list', pp. 262 (n. 30) and 267. Ælfhere also appears on an obit-list in a thirteenth-century manuscript from Glastonbury (London, British Library, Add. MS. 17450, 5v). On his career, see Williams, '*Princeps Merciorum gentis*'; for his possible role in the murder of King Edward the Martyr in A.D. 978, see Fisher, 'The anti-monastic reaction', pp.

but this is unlikely to have been the only other Buckland that is known to have belonged to Glastonbury – Buckland Newton – as that estate was the subject of grants of fifteen hides by Edmund I and Edgar, which would be difficult to reconcile with the twenty hides of Eadred's charter.

Several charters are extant for this other Buckland, Buckland Newton in Dorset, about twenty-five miles from Glastonbury, mid-way between Sherborne and Dorchester. S.303 (A.D. 854), Æthelwulf's Decimation charter,[80] may have applied to Buckland Newton, or part of it: it includes five hides at *Boclond toun* among a list of estates granted to Glastonbury. S.474 is a gift by King Edmund in A.D. 941 of fifteen hides at *Boclonde* and Plush to the *religiosa femina* Ælfflæd, who, according to the rubric in the cartulary, subsequently sold the land and the charter to Glastonbury;[81] finally, S.742 is a grant by King Edgar to his wife Ælfthryth of fifteen hides at *Boclaunde* in A.D. 966. Edmund's grant is known also from the contents-list of the *Liber terrarum* (LT50) and Edgar's from MS. 39a (L26). The *De antiquitate* cites Æthelwulf's Decimation charter (S.303) and a gift by Queen Ælfflæd (Edward the Elder's widow) of twenty-seven hides at three places (Okeford Fitzpaine, Buckland Newton, and Plush).[82]

Glastonbury held fifteen hides at Buckland Newton in Domesday Book, in addition to land for eight ploughs which had never paid tax; two sub-units (of seven hides, one and a half virgates, and of two hides, respectively) were held by tenants in 1086.[83] Plush is not named.

If we accept all the charters as genuine, it appears that Æthelwulf's benefaction (if relating to Buckland Newton) applied to only part of the estate, all of which was back in royal hands by Edmund's reign.[84] Although Edmund gave Buckland to Ælfflæd, who sold it to the abbey, the land was nonetheless back in the king's

---

269–70, and Keynes, *The Diplomas of King Æthelred*, pp. 169 and 172–3. Keynes has described him as 'the most powerful layman in the kingdom' (p. 170). He is also associated with grants at Orchardleigh and Westbury (*q.v.*), where the subsequent fate of the lands is similarly difficult to determine.

80 For a fuller discussion of this charter, see below, *s.n. Brannocmynstre*, Monk Okehampton, and pp. 322–4.

81 For a discussion of the mid-tenth-century series of grants to religious women, see *The 'Historia Brittonum'*, ed. Dumville, III.14–15, and Dumville, *Wessex and England*, pp. 177–8.

82 *De antiquitate*, §§53, 55, and 69 (ed. & transl. Scott, pp. 112, 114, 142); *Cronica*, §§16, 56, and 64 (edd. & transl. Carley & Townsend, pp. 40, 108, and 122). Ælfflæd also gave land at *Hammedone*, Okeford Fitzpaine, and Winterbourne (*q.v.*). In the extant text of this charter for *Bocland*, Ælfflæd is simply called *religiosa femina*; William of Malmesbury (in his *Gesta regum Anglorum*) is the sole source of details concerning the family of Edward the Elder, including the status of Ælfflæd, the daughter of Ealdorman Æthelhelm, as the king's second wife (§126; ed. Stubbs, I.136–7). Meyer, 'Women and the tenth century English monastic reform', pp. 46–7, discussed the confusion about Edward's marriages and Ælfflæd's supposed interest in the reform movement.

83 Domesday Book, I, 77va (Dorset, 8.3).

84 For the possible appropriation of monastic lands by Alfred and Edward the Elder, see Fleming, 'Monastic lands', especially pp. 261–4, and Dumville, *Wessex and England*, pp. 29–54.

gift shortly thereafter, when granted by King Edgar to his wife. However briefly it actually stayed in Glastonbury's possession in the ninth century and the mid-tenth, it was clearly the abbey's again in 1066.

The evidence for Plush (which lies southwest of Buckland Newton and was part of the later parish of that name) complicates this history. S.347 (A.D. 891) is the record of an exchange by which King Alfred received *Suttone* in Dorset in return for twelve hides at Plush and two (*recte* five?)[85] in Raddington, which he gave to his *comes* Berhtwulf; this charter of Alfred was listed in the *Index chartarum* and MS. 39a (IC B11,[86] L28), but was not mentioned in the *De antiquitate*. Plush was, with *Boclonde*, back in the king's gift by A.D. 941, the date of Edmund's grant of the two estates to Ælfflæd. Although Plush is said in S.347 to have consisted of twelve hides, perhaps its addition to the five hides of Æthelwulf's *Boclond toun* was what raised the assessment of Edmund's combined grant in S.474 to fifteen hides. According to Grundy, Plush – which the bounds of S.347 described – was the old name of a detached part of Buckland Newton. Grundy was puzzled by the hidage of Plush in S.347, pointing out that it was difficult to credit that there were twelve hides in the comparatively small area of the detached part.[87] Plush is not named in Domesday Book, but C. and F. Thorn, too, identified it as a detached portion of Buckland Newton, consisting of only two and a half virgates. Perhaps S.347 is not to be trusted; or perhaps the identification of Plush with the small detached portion is incorrect. Something has clearly gone wrong with the hidage (twelve hides at Plush and two hides at Raddington do not make up the seventeen-hide total claimed in S.347). Perhaps Plush should have been fifteen hides (which, adding two at Raddington, would make the sum work), in which case it may be suspected that 'Plush' in S.347 was the same as 'Buckland and Plush' in S.474 and S.742. The other charters provide no clear help here: Grundy thought that the bounds of S.474 excluded Plush and defined the main part of Buckland Newton only, although he judged them to be post-Conquest; S.742 has no bounds which might help to clarify the situation.

Boclond was one of the manors appropriated by Wells (and one of those recovered by Glastonbury) during the protracted but ultimately unsuccessful attempt to annex the monastery to the see which was begun by Bishop Savaric (A.D. 1191–1205) and diligently pursued by Bishop Jocelin (A.D. 1206–1242).[88]

Bodeslege (Somerset)

A priest held three virgates from the abbot in 1066 at this unidentified estate. Arguments have been made connecting it with Butleigh (as it appears in the same hundred and its name may be a corruption of Butleigh) or with Panborough (as the part of Panborough later called Bagley is unaccounted for in Domesday Book).[89] Neither argument is conclusive.

---

[85] The total grant is of seventeen hides. Raddington – unless it is the place many miles away in Somerset (*q.v.*) – is unidentified.

[86] Although *Elfleda de Plis* could be a misfiled reference to Ælfflæd's charter.

[87] Grundy, 'Saxon charters of Dorset', pp. 254–68, especially 263.

[88] See above, p. 12.

[89] Domesday Book, I, 90rb (Somerset, 8.12 [note]), and Morland, 'Glaston Twelve Hides', p. 39. See below, *s.n.* Butleigh and Panborough.

Bradanleag

According to the contents-list of the *Liber terrarum*, Æthelbald, king of Mercia (A.D. 716–757), granted land at *Seacesceg* and *Bradanleag* to a layman (LT22; no Sawyer-number). In another charter from the contents-list, Æthelbald apparently granted these estates directly to the abbey (S.1679; LT94).[90] Both these charters are now lost. The first is unattested elsewhere; the second is quoted in the *De antiquitate*, which provides the additional information that Æthelbald sold four hides in these two places in A.D. 746 to Abbot Tunberht for four hundred *solidi*.[91] This is not necessarily the earliest reference to a purchase of land by Glastonbury but it is apparently the earliest extant charter from its archive to specify the price paid.[92]

Bradley is a common name. Its absence from Domesday Book's entries for the region hinders the attempt to locate the land acquired from Æthelbald. As Finberg pointed out, however, West Bradley, four miles east of Glastonbury, is a likely candidate.[93] Grundy considered that the bounds of S.292 (A.D. 842), for Ditcheat and Lottisham, included the northern part of West Bradley; another part of West Bradley may have been included in the bounds of S.563 (A.D. 955), Glastonbury's charter for Pennard.[94] How these transactions relate to the earlier one involving Æthelbald is not clear. West Bradley was part of East Pennard in Domesday Book.[95] *Seacesceg* is unidentified.

Bradley (West) (Somerset)

See *Bradanleag*.

Brampford Speke (Devon)

See *Brentefordlond*.

Brannocmynstre (Devon)

Half a *hiwisc* at *Branuc* is mentioned in S.303 (A.D. 854), Glastonbury's copy of the so-called Decimation charter of Æthelwulf, king of Wessex, among the list of lands included in the king's grant.[96] In the *Liber terrarum* there was apparently a

---

90 See Edwards, *The Charters*, p. 71; she considered the two entries to be the same, and accepted the lost original as a probably genuine charter. On Glastonbury and Mercia, see below, pp. 335–7.

91 *De antiquitate*, §§46 and 69 (ed. & transl. Scott, pp. 104 and 142); *Cronica*, §§16 and 52 (edd. & transl. Carley & Townsend, pp. 40 and 104).

92 On the Anglo-Saxon land market, see Campbell, 'The sale of land'; for some comparative prices, see below, *s.n.* Brompton Ralph.

93 Finberg, *The Early Charters of Wessex*, p. 179.

94 See below, *s.n.* Ditcheat and Pennard. Grundy, *The Saxon Charters*, pp. 72–4; Morland, 'The Glastonbury manors', p. 76. The date of the bounds of S.292 has not been determined; those of S.563 are contemporary with the grant.

95 Morland, 'Further notes', p. 97.

96 This grant was recorded in the *Liber terrarum* (LT 136: 'Athelwlfus de decima parte terrarum suarum dat' ecclesiis'). The text printed by Birch (*Cartularium Saxonicum*, II.68–70 [no. 472], from MS. Wood empt. 1) is incomplete (it carries only five names

charter in the name of Æthelbald,[97] granting land at *Brannocmynstre* to Glastonbury (S.1695; LT19). No confirmation of the existence of this grant occurs in any other source apart from the *De antiquitate*, which names the recipient (Abbot Hereferth), the date (A.D. 867, which must be adjusted to 855x860), and the number of hides (ten), and states that there was a salmon fishery (*ad captura isiciorum*) attached to the estate.[98] By a charter of A.D. 973, Glastonbury exchanged *Brauncmynstre* with King Edgar for land at High Ham (S.791). This grant is preserved in the existing cartularies,[99] with bounds for High Ham attached.

The names *Branoc* and *Brannocmynstre* are obsolete. Finberg identified two modern place-names which contained the same first element: Branscombe (on the south coast of Devon, fewer than ten miles from the Dorset border) and Braunton (at the mouth of the River Taw on the north coast of Devon). These Finberg explained as deriving from Brannoc, a British saint (although the word *bran* also means 'raven' in the British language).[100] Branscombe (*Branecescumbe*) was granted by King Alfred to his younger son in his will (S.1507) and five hides were held there in 1066 by the bishop of Exeter, according to Domesday Book.[101] Finberg ruled out this estate as a candidate for *Brannocmynstre* and chose Braunton instead on the grounds that the fishery of Æthelbald's grant was for freshwater fish, a well documented local industry at the mouth of the River Taw.[102] Two hides at Braunton were in the king's possession in 1066 and 1086.[103] Ekwall,

---

[*Boklond toun, Pennard, Cotenesfelda, Cerawicombe,* and *Branok*] and lacks *Sowy, Piriton, Lodegaresbergh, Colom,* and *Ocmund*; for the fuller text, see *The Great Chartulary*, ed. Watkin, I.143–4 [no. 202]). A third text (*De antiquitate*, §§53 and 69 [ed. & transl. Scott, pp. 112 and 142], followed by the *Cronica*, §§16 and 56 [edd. & transl. Carley & Townsend, pp. 40 and 108]) adds *Duneafd* and apparently substitutes *Offaculum* for *Colom* (which it omits). This last text gives no hidage for *Occenefeld/Cetenesfelda, Pirinton, Lodegaresbergh, Occemund, Branuc,* and *Duneafd*. The somewhat ambiguous wording in the Great Cartulary and the *De antiquitate* (*be Ocmund et be del healf hwysc'* in the former) has led Scott – probably incorrectly – to add another estate, *Bedul*, to the list. See above, *s.n. Bedul*. More than one copy of each community's Decimation charter (and more than one list of lands) could have existed – compare the situation at Winchester. The contemporaneity and authenticity of the lists of estates is probably more doubtful than the genuineness of the charter-texts, which have been treated with some favour in recent studies. See below, pp. 322–4.

97 Presumably Æthelwulf's successor, rather than the eighth-century Æthelbald of Mercia. (Other grants to Glastonbury are attributed to the Mercian king, however; see below, pp. 335–7.) Sawyer incorrectly included this charter among those of Æthelwulf.

98 *De antiquitate*, §§53 and 69 (ed. & transl. Scott, pp. 112 and 142); *Cronica*, §§16 and 57 (edd. & transl. Carley & Townsend, pp. 40 and 108).

99 But it is not cited in the *De antiquitate*.

100 Finberg, *Lucerna*, pp. 107–8; Ekwall, *The Concise Oxford Dictionary of English Place-names, s.n.* Branscombe, pp. 60–1. Also Turner, 'A selection', pp. 154–5, and Fleuriot, *Dictionnaire, s.n. bran*, I.89.

101 Domesday Book, I, 102ra (Devon, 2.22).

102 Finberg, *Lucerna*, p. 108.

103 Domesday Book, I, 100rb and 104rb (Devon, 1.5 and 13a.3). The second hide was held by a priest, Algar. Pearce has suggested that this hide represented the land which

although he derived Branscombe from *Branoc,* did not cite *Brannocmynstre* as an early form of Braunton and appeared instead to explain it as Old English *Bromtun,* 'the *tun* where broom grows'.[104] Despite this, Braunton's association with St Brannoc (to whom the parish church is dedicated and who was said to have been buried there),[105] probably clinches the identification with the *Branoc* and *Brannocmynstre* of the Glastonbury documents.[106]

It seems probable that Glastonbury held this estate from the king in the mid-ninth century, if not before; Æthelwulf's Decimation grant of half a *hiwisc*[107] – compared with the putative ten hides of Æthelbald's charter – is difficult to interpret, however.[108] In particular, a number of the estates which it lists may already have been in Glastonbury's hands in A.D. 854,[109] and the Decimation may not have been a conveyance of land but rather a grant of different terms of tenure on land already held by the recipient – an exemption from certain onerous secular dues, for example. An additional problem is caused by the circumstance that several of the places listed in Glastonbury's Decimation charter seem to represent fractions of estates which were apparently much larger,[110] but the significance of this is unclear. It may be that the immunities which were granted were applied to only part of the estate: this would mean that at the time of Æthelwulf's Decimation Glastonbury held more of *Brannocmynstre* than this half-hide, perhaps, in fact, the ten hides attributed to Æthelbald's grant (itself presumably a confirmation, not a conveyance?). In any event, *Brannocmynstre* subsequently returned to royal hands in a documented exchange in the later tenth century. Possibly by the ninth century (certainly by the time when the contents-list of the *Liber terrarum* was compiled) it had acquired the *-mynstre* termination, indicating that it may have been the site of a religious community before it was granted to Glastonbury, or that a community came to be founded there.[111] The later difference in hides

supported the 'necessary religious provision' made when Glastonbury surrendered the estate to the king in A.D. 973: 'The early Church in the landscape', p. 270. Radford, on the other hand, interpreted the priest-holder of the one hide as the head of a still functioning minster community: 'The pre-Conquest Church and the old minsters', p. 4.

104 Ekwall, *The Concise Oxford Dictionary of English Place-names, s.n.* Braunton, p. 61.

105 See Baring-Gould & Fisher, *Lives of the British Saints,* I.321–7.

106 See also Rose-Troup, 'The Anglo-Saxon charter of Brentford', p. 273.

107 The small size of *Branuc* is worth noting: half a *hiwisc.* Michael Costen has interpreted a *hiwisc* as a discrete unit, usually within a larger estate, probably equivalent to a hide; it represented, he has argued, a portion of a former multiple estate and a survival from an earlier system of organisation of the landscape, before the advent of open-field farming. See Costen, 'Huish and Worth', and *The Origins,* pp. 94–5.

108 On the Decimation charter in general, see *Councils,* edd. Haddan & Stubbs, III.636–45, Finberg, *The Early Charters of Wessex,* pp. 187–213, and *Alfred the Great,* transl. Keynes & Lapidge, pp. 232–4. The charter raises difficulties of interpretation as yet unsolved. See the discussion below, pp. 322–4.

109 See, for example, Pennard, *Sowy,* and Uffculme, below.

110 See below, *s.n. Culum, Lodegaresberghe,* and Monk Okehampton.

111 Pearce ('The early Church in the landscape', pp. 269–70) has proposed that a monastery had been founded there *ca* A.D. 550 by the eponymous Brannoc, and that Glastonbury had received this ten-hide estate 'about 857', 'as part of the process by which large, successful, monasteries acquired the endowments of smaller houses'. She took

(reputedly ten in the mid-ninth century, two in Domesday Book) is explained by Susan Pearce as caused by the break-up after A.D. 973 of the original estate, much of the land being thegns' holdings by 1066. The impressive income of the king's remaining hide (£16) and its forty ploughlands, however, as well as the small size of those identifiable holdings which Pearce proposed had been separated from Braunton,[112] may perhaps suggest instead a substantial reduction in assessment.

The exchange in the late tenth century may represent a policy by the abbey of divestment of distant properties in favour of land closer to home.[113]

Braunton (Devon)
See *Brannocmynstre*.

Brean (Somerset)
See Brent.

Brent (Somerset)
According to S.238, King Baldred and King Ine granted ten hides at Brent to Abbot Hæmgils;[114] Æthelbald *rex* is listed among the witnesses, presumably of a subsequent confirmation of the transaction (if genuine). A grant by King Ine was listed among the contents of the *Liber terrarum* (*Yna de Brentemarais*; S.1671; LT20),[115] in the *Index chartarum* (*Yne rex de Brente*; IC A4), and in MS. 39a (*Carta regis Ine de Brente*; L19). S.250, the spurious Great Privilege of King Ine, lists ten hides at Brent among Ine's gifts to Glastonbury. Elsewhere in the *De antiquitate*, Ine is said to have given ten hides at *Brente* to Abbot Hæmgils in A.D. 690; the summary of grants, however, describes the gift as one of twenty hides at *Brentemareis*.[116] Glastonbury held twenty hides at *Brentemerse* in 1066, according to Domesday Book.[117] To judge from the documents cited here, *Brente* and *Brentemarais* appear to refer to the same place. The discrepancy in hidage between the two, however, is difficult to explain, although the twenty hides of §69 of the *De antiquitate* and §16 of the *Cronica* are presumably linked to the twenty hides of Domesday Book.

---

no account of Æthelwulf's Decimation grant. See also Radford, 'The pre-Conquest Church and the old minsters', p. 4. Alternatively, the -*mynstre* element could perhaps indicate merely that the land belonged to a church.

112 Pearce, 'The early Church in the landscape', p. 270.
113 Stacy, 'The estates', p. 16.
114 The date given, A.D. 663, should presumably be corrected to 693 (the sixth indiction). See Edwards, *The Charters*, p. 23.
115 Sawyer (influenced perhaps by Domesday Book) represented this as a grant of twenty hides, although the entry in the *Liber terrarum* gives no figure; he interpreted this entry as representing a transaction additional to that recorded in S.238, because he considered the hidage to be different, as was the form of the name. He therefore gave it its own number (S.1671). In the *De antiquitate*, however, the references to Ine's grant of Brent seem to treat it as a single transaction (see next note).
116 *De antiquitate*, §§39 and 69 (ed. & transl. Scott, pp. 92 and 140); *Cronica*, §§16 and 45 (edd. & transl. Carley & Townsend, pp. 40 and 92).
117 Domesday Book, I, 90vb (Somerset, 8.33).

References to Brent in the *De antiquitate* show that the estate was considered to be one of the most ancient properties of the church of Glastonbury. The place-name ('Brentacnolle qui nunc Brentamirse dicitur') was said to have derived from *Bregden*, whose name appeared on one of the pyramids which William of Malmesbury reported seeing in the monks' cemetery.[118] Brent Knoll was identified as the site of an Arthurian adventure in an interpolation within the narrative of the *De antiquitate*, and the story is elaborated in the summary section to include the gift of the estate of *Brentmareis* to Glastonbury by King Arthur.[119] Less literary but possibly equally credible is the comment attached to the record of Ine's grant in the *De antiquitate*: that Abbot Berwald abandoned Brent (and subsequently deserted his monastery).[120] No reasons are given for Berwald's abandonment of the land, and no details offered as to how – or when – the estate was regained by the abbey. This remark seems to have been detached so comprehensively from its context that it can only remain mysterious.

Brent Knoll is a striking hill just inland from the Severn shore, about thirteen miles from Glastonbury. Churches at East Brent and South Brent (the latter now called Brent Knoll) appear in the later mediaeval records of the abbey, and there are two focuses of settlement today. Mick Aston has drawn attention to a possible correlation between the theoretical territory attached to the Iron Age hillfort on Brent Knoll and the early mediaeval estate.[121] The latter is identified by the bounds of S.238, which are in Latin and of the most basic sort, citing the hill and four surrounding rivers: 'in monte et circa montem qui dicitur Brente, habens ab occidente Sabrinam, ab aquilonem Axam, ab oriente Ternuc, ab austro Siger'.[122] The simplicity of the description has been taken as a confirmation of its age. The estate thus delineated included the two (later?) settlement-sites and, according to Grundy, an area larger than the later parish of Brent – including Lympsham, Brean, Berrow, and Burnham-on Sea.[123] Aston, however, identified the last element in the boundary description, the (now lost) River Siger, as running east from the Severn north of Burnham-on-Sea, excluding the latter from the original estate;[124] in view of the shifting nature of the watercourses in this area, however, Jem Harrison has raised the possibility that the Siger referred to in S.238 may have been the river later called the Brue, not far to the south of Aston's projected course.[125] By this reckoning, Burnham would have been within the bounds of the

---

[118] *De antiquitate*, §32 (ed. & transl. Scott, p. 84); *Gesta regum Anglorum*, §21 (ed. Stubbs, I.25–6). Ekwall offered instead two possibilities: a derivative of Old English *brant*, 'steep', or identical with the British name *Brigantia*, 'high place' (*The Concise Oxford Dictionary of English Place-names*, p. 63, *s.n.* Brent).

[119] *De antiquitate*, §§34 and 69 (ed. & transl. Scott, pp. 86 and 140); the gift by King Arthur is also found in the *Cronica*, §§16 and 33 (edd. & transl. Carley & Townsend, pp. 38 and 74).

[120] *De antiquitate*, §39 (ed. & transl. Scott, p. 92); not in the *Cronica*.

[121] Aston, *Interpreting*, p. 34.

[122] 'On and around the hill which is called Brent, having on the west the Severn, on the north the Axe, on the east the *Ternuc*, and the *Siger* on the south'.

[123] Grundy, *The Saxon Charters*, pp. 149–53.

[124] Aston, *Interpreting*, pp. 34 and 97. See also Costen, *The Origins*, p. 62.

[125] This suggestion was made in a letter to the author (dated 21 March, 1993). Harrison

estate. It was presumably independent of Brent when it (*Burnhamme*) was granted to Edward the Elder by King Alfred in his will (S.1507) (or earlier, if the transaction in A.D. 824 involving part of one *cassatum* at *Brunham*, sold by Abbot Guthlac to Eanwulf, related to this estate).[126] The southern boundary of Brent from the seventh century is, therefore, still conjectural. Some doubt, too, has been cast on the northern boundary. Although it is without doubt the River Axe which is referred to, what is less clear is where exactly it ran when it was cited in the boundary description: there has been so much change in the landscape that the existence of outflows other than the present one is accepted, without their location being known. One possible earlier course of the Axe may have been the sinuous boundary between Berrow and Brean;[127] if so, it would exclude the latter from the description of Brent. Neither Brean to the north nor Burnham to the south was apparently part of the estate in 1066 as they were held separately by laymen,[128] and this circumstance – together with Burnham's appearance in Alfred's will – may help to exclude them from the early boundary description as well. It may be that these two never belonged to Brent or to Glastonbury, although what was true in the 880s and 1066 was not necessarily the case in 693. Brent's hidage should perhaps offer some assistance in deciding if and when these other estates were included in it, but such help is not forthcoming.

The original grant of Brent – if S.238 is to be credited – seems to have been of ten hides, but whether this indicates a smaller area than Domesday Book's twenty or simply a smaller assessment is uncertain. Berrow, seemingly safely included within the early bounds of S.238 and therefore part of the first known Brent estate, was catalogued under Brent in the Great Cartulary, and was probably part of Brent in Domesday Book; it nonetheless may have been the subject in its own right of a grant by King Edgar to a layman (S.793, of five hides), although the identification is not certain.[129] Lympsham was not mentioned by name in Domesday Book but was part of Brent in A.D. 1189.[130] Given their location and their absence from Domesday Book, it seems likely that Berrow and Lympsham were assessed under Brent at both ends of the Anglo-Saxon period as well and were always included within its ten (later twenty) hides. The doubling of Brent's hidage cannot therefore be explained by their addition to Brent, nor by the attachment of

---

has acknowledged that the antiquity of the Brue's name (see Ekwall, *The Concise Oxford Dictionary of English Place-names*, p. 70, *s.n.* Brue) may count against this argument.

[126] For the will and a map of the estates, see *Alfred the Great*, transl. Keynes & Lapidge, especially pp. 175–7 and 317; for Guthlac's transaction, see *De antiquitate*, §52 (ed. & transl. Scott, p. 110), and below, *s.n.* Brompton Ralph.

[127] *Brean Down Excavations*, ed. Bell, pp. 256 and 258. I am indebted to Jem Harrison for this suggestion.

[128] Domesday Book, I, 95rb (Somerset, 24.29 and 24.27). They were held, respectively, by Merleswein and Brictsi.

[129] See above, *s.n.* Berrow. S.793, however – if authentic – may have referred to land elsewhere.

[130] In the late twelfth-century *Liber Henrici*, Brentmarsh included East and South Brent, Berrow, and Lympsham (ed. Jackson, pp. 64–79).

the adjacent estates of Brean and Burnham-on-Sea, as these were clearly *not* part of Brent in 1066.

East Brent and Berrow had apparently been seized by Savaric, bishop of Wells (A.D. 1191–1205), at the time of his appropriation of a number of other manors belonging to Glastonbury. His return of East Brent and Berrow in A.D. 1203 was part of the first composition of the dispute between the cathedral and the abbey.[131]

Brentefordlond

Another place thought to have been part of Brent is the estate called *Brentefordlond*. This is the subject of S.498, an extant charter in the name of King Edmund I, granting two hides there to the *comes* Æthelstan in A.D. 944 in return for eighty mancuses of gold.[132] This text was apparently not in the *Liber terrarum* but is listed in the *Index chartarum* (IC D15) and in MS. 39a (L20) where (as in the cartularies) it is grouped with the charters for Brent. Edmund's grant does not appear in the *De antiquitate*; *Brentefordlond*'s only appearance there is in §70, among the *alia [maneria] data Glastonie* for which no details are offered.[133] Finberg (followed by Cyril Hart) improved on the evidence and listed this latter reference as evidence of the gift of *Brentefordlond* by Æthelstan to Glastonbury.[134]

S.498 has Old English bounds attached. Grundy pointed out that the appearance of the (Devon) Rivers Exe and Creedy ruled out any connexion between *Brentefordlond* and Glastonbury's Somerset estate at Brent.[135] Frances Rose-Troup analysed the bounds and, although she admitted their difficulty, concluded that they were for Brampford Speke, Brampford Pyne, and Brampford Steven, on the Exe about five miles north of Exeter.[136] Forsberg offered further refinements of the analysis and proposed the rather startling conclusion that the present Brampford Speke had not formed part of the Anglo-Saxon estate, although part of the adjoining parish of Upton Pyne (previously called Brampford Pyne)[137] had been included.[138] According to Domesday Book, four places called *Brenford*, adding up to three hides, were held in 1066 by four different lay tenants. C. and F. Thorn interpreted these Domesday *Brenford*s as including the later parishes of Brampford Speke and Upton Pyne, which they equated with the two hides of Edmund's grant while not attempting to explain the discrepancy in the hidage.[139]

131 *The Great Chartulary*, ed Watkin, I.xli–xliii and 77 (no. 126). See above, p. 12.
132 On the Anglo-Saxon land market, see Campbell, 'The sale of land'. Money could be paid for temporary alienations as well: see below, *s.n.* Uffculme, for example.
133 *De antiquitate*, §70 (ed. & transl. Scott, p. 144).
134 Finberg, *The Early Charters of Devon and Cornwall*, pp. 11–12; Hart, 'Athelstan "Half King" ', p. 125, n. 5. For the unreliability of this list in the *De antiquitate* as evidence of Glastonbury's ownership of an estate, see above, pp. 24–6.
135 Grundy, *The Saxon Charters*, pp. 150–1.
136 Rose-Troup, 'The Anglo-Saxon charter of Brentford'. Brampford Pyne is now called Upton Pyne and Brampford Steven is Stevenstone (p. 262).
137 *Ibid.*
138 Forsberg, *A Contribution*, pp. 205–6.
139 Domesday Book, I, 103ra, 107vb, and 112ra (Devon, 3.67 [and notes], 16.123, 16.129, and 24.2).

A charter for *Brentefordlond*, therefore, was evidently in the Glastonbury archive when the *Index chartarum* was compiled and the source for §70 of the *De antiquitate* was written (whichever came first). The estate may have taken its name from a stream called Brent,[140] but it never had any connexion with the Somerset Brent, among whose documents its charter came to be filed. In fact, there is no incontrovertible evidence that Glastonbury ever possessed *Brenteford-lond*. S.498 is in favour of Æthelstan *comes*; perhaps he deposited the charter in the archive when he retired to Glastonbury in A.D. 957.[141] No other evidence for the early history of Brampford Speke exists to help provide a context for a possible grant to Glastonbury.[142]

Bristol

A charter of possibly Anglo-Saxon date appears on a long list of post-Conquest charters in MS. R.5.33 under the heading 'Cartae de diuersis redditibus uel rebus datis ecclesiae Glaston.'.[143] The entry in question reads 'Carta Elfere de quadam domo in Bristollia'.[144] Matthew Blows has drawn attention to a possible link between this document and Ealdorman Ælfhere, some of whose charters are indeed recorded as extant at Glastonbury in A.D. 1247.[145] This identification (or a

---

[140] Ekwall, *The Concise Oxford Dictionary of English Place-names*, *s.n.* Brampford Speke, p. 60.

[141] On Æthelstan, see Hart, 'Athelstan "Half King" ', especially pp. 125–8. The pre-eminent layman of his time, he retired from Eadwig's court to Glastonbury, where he became a monk, probably in A.D. 957 after the division of the kingdom. (I should like to thank Simon Keynes, who derived this new date from his *Atlas of Attestations in Anglo-Saxon Charters*. See also Keynes, 'The "Dunstan B" charters', p. 191, n. 108.) Dunstan's exile from Glastonbury had probably begun in January of the previous year of upheaval. See Keynes, *The Diplomas of King Æthelred*, p. 49. For other grants to Æthelstan Half-King associated with Glastonbury, see below, *s.n.* Foxcote, *Lim*, Mells, *Westone*, and Wrington. He is said – in the contents-list of the *Liber terrarum*, the fourteenth-century cartularies, or the (even less reliable) *De antiquitate* – to have granted all these estates to Glastonbury; it is not always possible to support this conclusion, which could have been drawn simply from the presence of Æthelstan's title-deeds in the archive. Only *Lim*, Mells, and Wrington were in the abbey's hands in 1066.

[142] Rose-Troup ('The Anglo-Saxon charter of Brentford', pp. 260–1) imagined the following history for the estate: it was part (the eastern portion) of the land granted in A.D. 739 to Forthhere, bishop of Sherborne, by Æthelheard, king of Wessex, for the foundation of a monastery at Crediton (i.e., in S.255); when the see of Sherborne was divided, Brampford was taken from Crediton and conferred on the new bishop, al-though, as we find it in royal possession again in King Edmund's time, it must have been confiscated and retained by King Æthelstan, after which Edmund granted it to Æthelstan Half-King. There is no direct evidence to support this hypothetical sequence of events. See also *The Crawford Collection*, edd. Napier & Stevenson, pp. 41–4, and Hooke, 'Charters and the landscape', pp. 86–8 (and map, p. 95).

[143] MS. R.5.33, 81rv. The list was printed by Hearne: *Johannis Confratris et Monachi Glastoniensis Chronica*, I.389–92.

[144] MS. R.5.33, 81v; *ibid.*, p. 392.

[145] Blows, 'A Glastonbury obit-list', p. 267. For Ælfhere's charters, see *s.n.* Bocland, Orchardleigh, and Westbury.

connexion with another pre-Conquest Ælfhere) would require the charter to have been displaced and/or misfiled, as pre-Conquest documents are otherwise strictly separate from post-Conquest ones in these series of lists. If that were the case, the entry could indicate that a holding in Bristol had been received by (or from) Ælfhere. No other evidence for this holding exists in the archive, and no contemporary connexion between Glastonbury and Bristol is known.

Brompton Ralph (Somerset)

A charter in the *Liber terrarum* whose text has not been preserved referred to a grant by Queen Frithugyth, probably the wife of King Æthelheard (A.D. 726–740), of *Brunamtone* to Glastonbury (S.1677; LT16). No documentary confirmation of this grant has survived, but the *De antiquitate* informs us that it consisted of five hides.[146] In 1066, Glastonbury held three and a half hides at *Burnetone* (Brompton Ralph) and one and a half in Clatworthy, a neighbouring estate.[147] No other information survives for Clatworthy in its own name, and it is possible that these estates west of Taunton at the foot of the Brendon Hills were once a single unit, which had broken into two sub-units by 1066. Another ten hides at *Brunetone/Burnetone* (now Brompton Regis, a further ten miles to the west) had been held in 1066 by Gytha.[148] Whether Glastonbury once held these hides as well as those that it possessed in 1066 cannot be ascertained.[149]

One other transaction may relate to Brompton Ralph. No trace survives in the cartularies or lists of charters but, according to the *De antiquitate*, in A.D. 824 Abbot Guthlac gave part of one *cassatum in Brunham* to *Eanulf*,[150] for five hundred *solidi* (two hundred for the abbot and three hundred for the monks).[151] This could be interpreted as a sale,[152] or perhaps as a payment in settlement of a dispute.[153] It might, too, indicate a need for ready cash.[154] It is perhaps most reminiscent of a lease, earmarking as it does the use of the income in this way; the figures, however, are strikingly high, especially for a piece of land with such a

---

146 *De antiquitate*, §§44 and 69 (ed. & transl. Scott, pp. 102 and 142); *Cronica*, §§16 and 52 (edd. & transl. Carley & Townsend, pp. 40 and 104).

147 Domesday Book, I, 95va and 95vb (Somerset, 25.7 and 25.8).

148 Domesday Book, I, 86vb and 92rb (Somerset, 1.11 and 19.35).

149 No pre-Conquest documentation survives for Brompton Regis.

150 Blows ('Studies', pp. 274–6) has identified this man with the ealdorman of Somerset who acquired a block of estates southeast of Glastonbury (see below, *s.n.* Ditcheat) and reputedly gave them to the abbey. The ealdorman died in A.D. 867, however, and the transaction at *Brunham* may not have been his.

151 *De antiquitate*, §52 (ed. & transl. Scott, p. 110) (this information was omitted from §69 and from the *Cronica*); Finberg, *The Early Charters of Wessex*, p. 121 (no. 404). There is no Sawyer-number for this transaction.

152 On the land market in Anglo-Saxon England, see Campbell, 'The sale of land'. For an example of an early sale by an abbot, see S.1256 (A.D. 759). Ecclesiastical land was apparently not inalienable.

153 See S.155 (A.D. 799) for such a payment (of one hundred mancuses) by Christ Church, Canterbury.

154 It can perhaps be compared with S.1278, a charter of A.D. 872, which records that Abbot Wærferth (of Worcester) leased land belonging to the community of Stratford for money to pay the Danes (for a price of twenty mancuses).

low assessment.[155] A parallel may be found in S.1412, which records a lease (but of ten hides of land) by the abbot of Medehamstede to a *princeps* between A.D. 786 and 796 for one thousand *solidi* and an annual payment;[156] the land was to return to the abbey after the death of the grantee's heirs. The possible status of Abbot Guthlac's transaction as a temporary alienation (if it was not a sale) may explain its exclusion from all the extant documentary sources.[157]

Eilert Ekwall derived Brompton Ralph and Brompton Regis from Old English *Brunantun*, the '*tun* by the Brendon Hills';[158] whether Glastonbury's *Brunham* and *Brunamtone* could have been one and the same place is unclear, but the half-hide at *Brunham*, if not part of the abbey's five-hide estate of *Brunamtone*, was perhaps in the same vicinity, near the Brendons (although the appearance of two separate estates of the same name in Domesday Book shows that the Brendon Hills influenced place-names over a fairly wide area). Brompton Ralph is approximately thirty miles from Glastonbury to the west. The abbey's ability to acquire (and retain) land at this distance is worth noting. A number of alternative locations for the lands documented in the charters could probably be proposed, however, as *Burnham/Brunham* are not uncommon forms: Blows has suggested Burnham-on-Sea, about fifteen miles northwest of Glastonbury on the Severn.[159]

Brunham / Brunamtone
See Brompton Ralph.

Buckland Denham (Somerset)
See *Bocland*.

Buckland Newton (Dorset)
See *Bocland*.

Burnham-on-Sea (Somerset)
See Brent.

---

[155] In Mercia in A.D. 675x692 (according to S.1804), five hundred *solidi* were the equivalent of twelve beds, namely feather mattresses with elaborate pillows together with muslin and linen sheets as is customary in Britain; also a slave and a slave-girl, and a gold brooch and two horses with two wagons: see Campbell, 'The sale of land', p. 27.

[156] Compare, too (from the Worcester archive), S.210 (A.D. 864) a grant which records an initial payment (of a precious wine ladle worth four hundred *solidi* and one hundred *sicli*), made when the land changed hands, also followed by an annual payment.

[157] If Guthlac's transaction was a lease, it might have been recorded in Old English, and as no vernacular documents for Glastonbury have been preserved, that, too, might explain its omission from the cartularies and its subsequent disappearance. Why it survived and was recorded by the author(s) of the *De antiquitate* is a mystery. A probable lease of the mid-tenth century is preserved (in Latin) for North Wootton (*q.v.*).

[158] Ekwall, *The Concise Oxford Dictionary of English Place-names*, *s.n.* Brompton Ralph, p. 68.

[159] 'Studies', p. 275. See also above, *s.n.* Brent.

Burrington

Burrington makes but a brief appearance in the Glastonbury archive. Its possession is confirmed to Glastonbury in the much altered charter of William the Conqueror quoted in the *De antiquitate*.[160] There are two Burringtons – one in Somerset and one in Devon – which may be the estate to which William's confirmation was intended to refer. The Somerset Burrington (in the Mendips, over fifteen miles from Glastonbury) is not in Domesday Book; the Devon manor (near Chulmleigh) consisted of an estate of three hides held by the church of Tavistock.[161] The Somerset estate is perhaps the more likely location, surrounded as it is by land owned by Glastonbury and Wells.

According to Grundy, this Burrington was a sub-unit of Wrington, another estate owned by Glastonbury, and was included in its twenty hides, though the bounds which indicate Burrington's attachment to Wrington are probably post-Conquest.[162] Its omission from Domesday Book by name, however, might suggest that Burrington's inclusion in Wrington's twenty hides was already established by 1066, and thus, by implication, at the time of the tenth-century charters for Wrington (unless the hidage remained unaltered despite the addition of territory). If this is the Burrington of William's charter, some post-Conquest threat to the sub-unit (Burrington) but not the whole estate (Wrington) may lie behind its confirmation.

Butleigh (Somerset)

Butleigh was the subject of a charter which was written in the *Liber terrarum* (on the evidence of the contents-list), listed in MS. 39a, and preserved in a corrupt form in the extant cartularies (S.270a; LT38; L6). According to the surviving text, *Edbirtus* granted twenty *mansiones* at *Buddekauleghe* to his thegn Eadgils in A.D. 801.[163] According to the *De antiquitate*, Eadgils gave twenty hides at Butleigh to Glastonbury with the assent of King Ecgberht.[164] Butleigh (*Budecalech*) also appears in the spurious Great Privilege of King Ine (S.250) and (as *Budeclega*) in the privilege of King Edgar (S.783) as one of the churches exempt from episcopal interference. Ac-

160 *De antiquitate*, §75 (ed. & transl. Scott, p. 154); *Cronica*, §83 (edd. & transl. Carley & Townsend, p. 154); *Regesta regum Anglo-Normannorum*, edd. Davis *et al.*, I.71 (no. 273). On the charter, see above, *s.n.* Berrow.

161 Domesday Book, I, 103vb (Devon, 5.8). Another Devon Burrington, consisting of one furlong held by *Aluuinus* in 1066, is too small to be an appropriate candidate (Domesday Book, I, 109vb [Devon, 17.74]).

162 Grundy, *The Saxon Charters*, pp. 171–8. See below, *s.n.* Wrington.

163 Kemble (*Codex Diplomaticus*, I.215–16 [no. 178], followed by Edwards [*The Charters*, pp. 56–9]), suggested that the donor was Queen Eadburh, the wife of Beorhtric, king of Wessex (A.D. 786–802). The form of the name (*Ecgbirhtus*) in the contents-list of the *Liber terrarum*, however, seems to support the identification with Ecgberht, king of Wessex (A.D. 802–839). A note following the charter in the cartularies ('Hanc cartulam reddidit Eadburth ad ecclesiam Glastingensem') may have been the source of Kemble's speculation. Eadburh was presumably either a mistake for Eadgils or the name of a later (female) owner of the estate (or perhaps even a corruption of Ecgberht).

164 *De antiquitate*, §§52 and 69 (ed. & transl. Scott, pp. 110 and 142); *Cronica*, §§16 and 55, edd. & transl. Carley & Townsend, pp. 40 and 108).

cording to Domesday Book, Glastonbury held twenty hides at *Boduchelei*; two hides at *Lodreford* (Lattiford), which were lost to the king by 1086, were said to have belonged to Butleigh.[165] As no other documentation survives for Lattiford in its own name, we should have assumed that it was an original part of the Butleigh estate which by 1066 had acquired some identity as a sub-unit. Lattiford's location, however, approximately twenty miles from Butleigh and over twenty-five from Glastonbury, makes this an unlikely interpretation.[166] It is more plausible that tenurial or economic considerations which we can no longer discern lay behind the attachment of Lattiford (if Lattiford *is Lodreford*) to Butleigh. The date of Lattiford's putative attachment to Butleigh is uncertain; it may have been part of an immediately post-Conquest reorganisation. The boundary clause of S.270a, which might help to resolve some of these difficulties, was not analysed by Grundy. Michael Costen has dated it to the second half of the tenth century.[167]

Morland's argument, that Blackford (near Wincanton) and Holton were assessed in Domesday Book under Butleigh, has been discussed above.[168] If his interpretation is correct, Blackford was accommodated within Butleigh's twenty hides without changing the latter's assessment. Not all the evidence, however, supports this postulated connexion between Butleigh and Blackford.

A further three virgates assessed at *Bodeslege* in Domesday Book may have belonged to Butleigh.[169] Morland, however, identified them with Bagley in Wedmore, once part of Panborough.[170]

Butleigh is only a few miles southeast of Glastonbury, bordering on the Twelve Hides.[171] The charter of Ecgberht may mark Butleigh as an early and secure element of Glastonbury's endowment; but it must be remembered that the silence of the ensuing record until 1066 does not necessarily indicate permanent possession by the abbey throughout the ninth, tenth, and eleventh centuries.

Byrhtulfington becocer

This unidentified estate is the subject of an entry in the contents-list of the *Liber terrarum* (S.1709; LT125), where King Æthelstan is said to have given an estate of that name to one Ælfric (who may have been the recipient of land at Stoke also).[172] Æthelstan's gift of *Byrhtulfington becocer* does not appear in any of the other documentary sources, or in the *De antiquitate*, except in the unauthoritative list of *alia [maneria] data Glastonie* added after the summary chapter.[173] Burton – near North, East, and West Coker (south of Yeovil) – has been suggested as a

---

[165] Domesday Book, I, 90rb (Somerset, 8.18 and 8.19); the abbot also had woodland in Butleigh, which C. and F. Thorn identified as that of Clapton manor, adjacent to a detached portion of Butleigh (Domesday Book, I, 91ra [Somerset, 8.40 and p. 357]).

[166] See below, *s.n.* Lattiford.

[167] 'Dunstan, Glastonbury, and the economy', p. 43.

[168] See above, *s.n.* Blackford.

[169] Domesday Book, I, 90rb (Somerset, 8.12 and p. 355).

[170] Morland, 'Glaston Twelve Hides', p. 37. See below, *s.n.* Panborough.

[171] *De antiquitate*, §73 (ed. & transl. Scott, p. 152); *Cronica*, §4 (edd. & transl. Carley & Townsend, p. 16); on the Twelve Hides, see below, *s.n.* Glastonbury.

[172] See below, *s.n. Stoke*.

[173] *De antiquitate*, §70 (ed. & transl. Scott, p. 144); see above, pp. 24–6.

possible location for the estate of Æthelstan's grant. In Domesday Book, Coker was a fifteen-hide estate (which paid tax for seven hides) held by Gytha in 1066 and the king in 1086.[174] I have discovered no link between Coker or Burton and Glastonbury. If Ælfric did pass the estate on to Glastonbury, it appears that the abbey did not hold it for long, as *Byrhtulfington* left little impression on the archive. Alternatively, Glastonbury may never have acquired the estate, as Ælfric or one of his heirs simply could have deposited the charter in the archive. It is also possible that the land may have changed its name after Æthelstan's grant.

Camel (Somerset)

Three entries on the contents-list of the *Liber terrarum* relate to *Cantmel*. King Edmund granted land there to a layman, Ælfgar (S.1718; LT59), as did King Eadwig to another layman, Cynric (S.1755; LT60); although different pieces of land may be involved, there is no hint of such a distinction (*Edwy de eodem*). These transactions may simply be examples of repeated (temporary) grants to laymen by the king (although booked land was theoretically a permanent grant), but they may also reveal other circumstances of tenure: the need of laypeople with booked land to have the permanent possession of their estates confirmed by the king, perhaps, maybe even each succeeding king if possible, or perhaps on the occasion when the land changed hands.[1] These 'grants' may in fact represent the expression of the relationship of commendation. Our knowledge of charters is necessarily biased towards ecclesiastical ownership, and the conditions of the booking of land to laypeople are more obscure. Alternatively, the political circumstances of Eadwig's reign may lie behind the second grant. A third entry in the *Liber terrarum*, however, reveals that *Cantmel* passed to yet another layman, Brihtric, not long after, by gift of King Edgar (S.1764; LT119). This sequence of grants might suggest that Brihtric owned LT59 and LT60 as title-deeds, and that he deposited them, with his own charter, at Glastonbury. Support for this hypothesis may be found in the text of a bequest in the *Codex Wintoniensis*: there Brihtric expresses his intention to grant the estate of Rimpton (given to him by King Eadred) to the Old Minster, Winchester, after his death and declares that he has presented to the church both Eadred's *boc* and the old charter which King Æthelstan had previously granted.[2] In the light of the case of Rimpton, then, the presence of charters for Camel might suggest that Brihtric gave the land at *Cantmel* to Glastonbury. It is also possible that the documents were handed over as a token of an intention which was never fulfilled.[3]

---

174 Domesday Book, I, 87ra (Somerset, 1.23).

1 Cases such as Horton, however, which seems to have come to Glastonbury with an eighth-century title-deed and a charter of King Eadred (but nothing in between), may indicate that if reconfirmations were indeed required, this was a development of the second half of the tenth century.

2 *Anglo-Saxon Wills*, ed. & transl. Whitelock, pp. 18 and 117–18 (no. 7). The document is dated A.D. 964x980.

3 Title-deeds belonging to Brihtric for land at Henstridge and Yeovilton (neither of which was held by Glastonbury in 1066) were also to be found in Glastonbury's archive. Brihtric reputedly gave Yeovilton to Glastonbury. See below, *s.n.* Henstridge and Yeovil-

Cantmel has been identified as Camel, in Somerset.[4] Charter-evidence is available for the next stage of Camel's history. S.884, an extant single sheet dated 995, preserves the record of the confirmation by King Æthelred the Unready of land at Camel and Ilminster to the *monasteriolum* of Muchelney. The charter states that Leofric, abbot of Muchelney, had previously purchased land at *Cantmæl*, to which was added four neighbouring hides presented to the abbey by Æthelmær, the *satrapa* of the king. There are two Camels in Domesday Book (now Queen Camel and West Camel): the king held fifteen hides at the former in 1086 (held TRE by Gytha) and Muchelney held ten hides at the latter.[5] It does not necessarily follow that West Camel only was the subject of S.884; but it seems a likely suggestion unless the division of the estate occurred after A.D. 995, in which case Æthelred's confirmation would have been of the two portions, one of which then passed out of Muchelney's hands and back into royal ownership before the Conquest.

Queen Camel and West Camel are over ten miles southeast of Glastonbury, midway between Yeovil and Castle Cary. There are few Glastonbury estates in the immediate area and, indeed, there is no certainty that the land in question was ever in the abbey's possession. In the *De antiquitate*, Camel appears only in the list of *alia [maneria] data Glastonie* in §70; in its narrative, none of the three charters for Camel which were once to be found in the *Liber terrarum* was cited, a fact which might suggest that Camel was recognised as having remained in lay ownership. The compiler of the list of places in §70, on the other hand, was faced with a group of charters which, he could see, had not appeared in the main body of the work, and he listed them in an attempt at comprehensiveness.[6]

Camerton (Somerset)

On the evidence of the contents-list, two entries in the *Liber terrarum* recorded gifts of *Camlar* to laymen: King Eadred to Alfred, and Eadred, again, to Æthelwold (S.1739 and S.1738; LT121 and LT122).[7] Only the first of these grants appears in any other source. In the *De antiquitate*, Alfred is said to have given five hides at *Camelarton* to Glastonbury, with the assent of King Eadred; this presumably was the interpretation put on the charter of Eadred for Alfred by the author of the relevant section of the *De antiquitate*, based either on lost information or on assumption, as discussed above.[8] This is not necessarily sufficient evidence to

---

ton. Charters for Brihtric preserved at Shaftesbury and Winchester (S.570 and S.571) have diplomatic links with the Glastonbury archive, and one (S.571) was witnessed there. Brihtric's charter for Henstridge seems to have been preserved at Shaftesbury and Glastonbury. See above, pp. 19–20, and below, *s.n.* Henstridge.

4   The identification of this place is established by the following sequence of place-name forms: *Cantmæl, Camelle*. See Ekwall, *The Concise Oxford Dictionary of English Place-names, s.n.* Camel, p. 84.

5   Domesday Book, I, 87ra and 91ra (Somerset, 1.22 and 9.7).

6   *De antiquitate*, §70 (ed. & transl. Scott, p. 144); see above, pp. 24–6.

7   Hart ('Athelstan "Half King" ', p. 119, n. 3) has identified Æthelwold as the brother of Æthelstan Half-King.

8   *De antiquitate*, §§57 and 69 (ed. & transl. Scott, pp. 118 and 144); *Cronica*, §§16 and 66 (edd. & transl. Carley & Townsend, pp. 42 and 126). See the discussion above, pp. 23–5.

prove Glastonbury's ownership of the estate, however. Glastonbury did hold ten hides at Camerton in 1086, but apparently not in 1066: the abbey exchanged it for Tintinhull with the count of Mortain before 1086.[9] The pre-Conquest documentation could therefore have been authentic, or alternatively it may have been forged (as proof of title) after the Conquest; a possible interpretation is that Glastonbury obtained the charters for Camerton from the count of Mortain when the land came into the abbey's possession.[10]

Other charters for an Alfred, perhaps the same man, for land at Rowberrow and Tarnock (LT65 and LT120) are as inconclusive on the question of whether Glastonbury ever received the land involved. There is no record of Rowberrow being given to Glastonbury, and its status in 1066 is unknown as it is not named in Domesday Book. Tarnock may have been held by Wells in the mid-eleventh century but was in lay hands in 1066.[11]

Camerton is situated in the Mendips, not far north of Radstock, about seventeen miles from Glastonbury.

Cantucuudu (Somerset)

According to a charter in the name of King Centwine, in A.D. 682 the king granted to Abbot Hæmgils twenty-three *mansiones* 'in loco iuxta siluam famosam qui dicitur Cantucuudu' and three hides at *Cructan* south of the River Tone (S.237). Relatively detailed Latin bounds are given. This charter was copied into the *Liber terrarum*, whose contents-list provides an updated (or simply more specific) place-name, *Munekatone* (LT8). The charter does not appear in the *Index chartarum* or the fourteenth-century cartularies, but is the sole Anglo-Saxon document in a late mediaeval collection of charters relating to West Monkton.[12] The rubric declares that the charter is for 'Cantucuudu nunc Westmonketon iuxta Tantoniam', a similar description appearing in MS. 39a, where the charter is listed among the documents of the *camerarius* (L47). The *De antiquitate* preserves a slightly different version of this grant, mentioning twenty-three *hidas* 'iuxta siluam que uocatur Cantucdun', but adding a reference to twenty hides at *Caric* as well as the three hides at *Crucan* (*sic*).[13]

Cantuc is the British name for the hills north of the Tone (now the Quantocks),

---

9   Edmer Ator had held the estate TRE: Domesday Book, I, 90vb (Somerset, 8.31). Some difficulty with the exchange or a seizure by an unnamed culprit not too long thereafter necessitated action on the part of Abbot Henry of Blois (A.D. 1126–1171), who recovered and restored (*recuperauit et restituit*) a number of manors, including Camerton: *Cronica*, §88 (edd. & transl. Carley & Townsend, p. 164).

10 The question of the attitude of the new Norman lords to the title-deeds for their English lands could profitably be pursued.

11 See below, *s.n.* Rowberrow and Tarnock.

12 Longleat House, Marquess of Bath, MS. NMR 10586; see above, pp. 13–14.

13 *De antiquitate*, §§37 and 69 (ed. & transl. Scott, pp. 90 and 140); *Cronica*, §§16 and 43 (edd. & transl. Carley & Townsend, pp. 40 and 90) (the summary chapters of both texts use the name *Munekatone* only; §37 of the *De antiquitate* has simply *Cantucdun* and §43 of the *Cronica* has 'iuxta siluam de Cantocdune manerium de Westmunkaton'). See below, *s.n.* Caric and Cructan.

and Old English *wudu* obviously refers to the *silua* mentioned in the grant.[14] The lack of a specific place-name in S.237 has not deterred scholars from identifying this grant without hesitation with West Monkton,[15] but the late provision of a place-name for an early document without one should always be viewed with some scepticism. However, Grundy's solution of the bounds (in two attempts) pointed to all of the later estate of West Monkton, as well as part of Creech St Michael (north of the Tone) comprising the land in question; if the bounds were indeed contemporary with the grant, this would confirm the identification with West Monkton.[16] Glastonbury held fifteen hides at *Monechetone* in 1066.[17] As there is no explicit record of West Monkton between Centwine's grant and Domesday Book, there are no clues to its intervening history, in particular no indication of whether it lost any territory, or simply reduced its assessment, in that time. Perhaps the eastern portion was removed to Creech St Michael before 1066.[18]

An attempt has been made to link West Monkton with a grant slightly later than that of Centwine. Twenty hides 'iuxta flumen quod appellatur Tan' were part of a multiple grant to Glastonbury by King Ine, preserved in S.248, a single-sheet copy of uncertain date.[19] West Monkton can indeed be described as on the Tone (as well as next to Quantock Wood), and the charters *may* be successive grants of the same land, but the identification of the two places as one is not entirely convincing.[20] Centwine's grant was of twenty-three hides, Ine's of twenty.[21] The former is dated 682, the latter 705/6; it is indeed possible that the estate could have reverted to the king in the short period between grants, but the link would be more credible if in both charters the land had the same hidage, not to mention the same topographical description. Davidson described Ine's charter as a confirmation of Centwine's, a suggestion unsupported by any evidence.[22] Obscure political conflicts could lie behind the grants, but there is no conclusive evidence to direct enquiry along those lines. The identification of Centwine's and Ine's grants as the same was probably occasioned by the circumstance that no known estate of

---

[14] Ekwall, *The Concise Oxford Dictionary of English Place-names*, *s.n.* Quantock Hills, p. 376.

[15] See, for example, Dickinson, 'West Monkton charter'.

[16] Grundy, *The Saxon Charters*, pp. 51–4, and 'West Monkton. Revised notes', pp. 104–6. Edwards (*The Charters*, pp. 15–17) considered the bounds to be a mixture of original and later (but pre-tenth-century) additions. Costen has agreed that they look too detailed to be seventh-century but offered no conjectural date of composition ('Dunstan, Glastonbury, and the economy', p. 28). Blows ('Studies', pp. 233–4) has argued in favour of a rewriting of the charter in the late eighth or the ninth century, with the bounds added at that time.

[17] Domesday Book, I, 90vb (Somerset, 8.28).

[18] Ten and a half hides at Creech St Michael were held by Gunhild in 1066: Domesday Book, I, 86vb (Somerset, 1.18).

[19] See above, p. 11, and Abrams, ' "Lucid intervals" '.

[20] Dickinson, 'West Monkton charter', p. 92, n. 3; Davidson, 'On the charters', p. 11.

[21] There is a possibility that Centwine's hides north of the river totalled only twenty, however. See below, *s.n. Caric*.

[22] Davidson, 'On the charters', p. 11.

Glastonbury's other than West Monkton lay directly on the Tone. Ine's grant, however, may have referred to land which was later lost for which no other record has survived.

On the other hand, if the charters are not for the same land, and if Ine's charter (S.248) *did* refer to West Monkton, Centwine's grant (S.237) may have originally applied to land elsewhere on the Quantocks. In that case, when it was rewritten S.237 was seriously tampered with, specifically to relate it to West Monkton (including the addition of Latin bounds). As the discussion of *Caric* below reveals, the ambiguity in the wording of the dispositive section of S.237 in the *De antiquitate* might indicate that its original subject was twenty hides at *Caric* in Quantock Wood – a place not yet conclusively identified, and not necessarily West Monkton. The evidence is so slim and so corrupt, however, that all interpretations are no more than speculations.

Caric (Somerset)

The claim is made in the *De antiquitate* – unattested by any other independent source – that Centwine, king of Wessex, gave twenty hides at *Caric* to Glastonbury.[23] The manner of presentation of this grant causes more than the usual difficulties raised by the *De antiquitate*. The account in that text appears to be quoted directly from the dispositive section, in the first-person singular, of a document granting land in three places: *Cantucdun*, *Caric*, and *Crucan*. The charter from which this quotation was taken survives as the lone pre-Conquest document (S.237, dated 682) in an early sixteenth-century cartulary at Longleat.[24] But in that copy, only *Cantucuudu* and *Cructan* (*sic*) are mentioned. S.237 is a text which has suffered from some meddling,[25] and, if the version in the *De antiquitate* has not added *Caric* by error or by deliberate conflation with another charter, now lost, we might assume that the third estate was dropped out, either purposely or by accident, before the extant text was copied. As we have seen, the Latin bounds, which were considered by Edwards to be a combination of original elements and later (but pre-tenth-century) additions, include the whole of West Monkton and part of Creech St Michael – that is, the land described as belonging to *Cantucuudu* (*nunc Westmonketon*)[26] – and seem thus to date from a time when *Caric* was not part of the grant. This could mean that *Caric* was intruded into a charter with existing bounds, or that the bounds were only attached to the text after *Caric* had dropped out of it. The entry in the *Liber terrarum* for S.237 (LT8) mentions only *Cantucwdu*, showing that the excision of *Caric*, if it had ever been part of that charter, might have occurred by the time when the *Liber terrarum* (or at least its contents-list) was written.

Edwards's account of S.237, in which she pointed out the patchwork-quality of the extant text (composed as it is of parts dating from various periods), nevertheless insisted that its substance remained unchanged. In that case, we might ask

---

23 *De antiquitate*, §§37 and 69 (ed. & transl. Scott, pp. 90 and 140); *Cronica*, §§16 and 43 (edd. & transl. Carley & Townsend, pp. 40 and 90).

24 Longleat House, Marquess of Bath, MS. NMR 10586. See above, pp. 13–14.

25 Edwards, *The Charters*, pp. 15–17; Davidson, 'On the charters', p. 7.

26 See *s.n. Cantucuudu* and *Cructan*.

why it was necessary to redraft the charter; innocuous answers can be offered (the decay of the original document, the desire to bring all charters into line diplomatically). The omission of one of the estates granted might also be a motive for rewriting, but this would be unusual, as lands are generally written in, not out, of charters being altered or 'improved'. What this might mean about the ownership-history of the lands involved is unclear.

The Cary is a river that runs from its source near Sparkford in southeastern Somerset to the River Parrett, now channelled in its course through the Levels via the King's Sedgemoor Drain. Various settlements in the area take their name from the river. In Domesday Book there are four places called *Cari*, of one hide (minus one furlong), fifteen hides, one hide (plus one furlong), and two hides, respectively. These have been identified with Cary Fitzpaine, Castle Cary, Lytes Cary, and Lower Lytes Cary (or Cooks Cary).[27] Finberg assumed that the *Caric* of the *De antiquitate* was in this area.[28] No other pre-Conquest charters survive to assist in the identification. One other possibility, however, is worth considering. The phrasing in the *De antiquitate* is as follows: 'et iuxta siluam que uocatur Cantuc-dun .xxiii. hidas in Caric .xx. hidas et in Crucan .iii. hidas'.[29] Could this not be read as twenty-three hides next to Quantock Wood, that is, twenty hides at *Caric* and three hides at *Crucan*? If so, we should look for a site for *Caric* in the Quantocks rather than by the River Cary.[30] A *Caric* in that vicinity (possibly West Monkton or Creech St Michael) would resolve the difficulty of the absence of any of the known Cary estates from the dispositive section and the bounds of S.237.[31]

Catcott (Somerset)
Catcott was a five-hide sub-unit of Shapwick in Domesday Book.[32] No earlier documentation survives for Catcott by name, but its history is probably to be seen in the context of the large estate of *Pouelt*, discussed in detail below.

Cecce
See *Cetenesfelda.*

Cedern
According to the *De antiquitate*, Æthelheard, a thegn of Cynewulf, king of

---

[27] Domesday Book, I, 94vb, 95rb, and 98ra (Somerset, 22.18, 24.17, 45.1, 45.2, and pp. 362 and 367).

[28] Finberg, *The Early Charters of Wessex*, p. 110.

[29] See note 23. The cartulary-version which omits Cary has, seemingly unambiguously, twenty-three hides at Quantock Wood and three hides at *Cructan*. In the margin of the manuscript, *xxiii* had been added beside this grant, but the *iii* was subsequently crossed out.

[30] See *s.n. Cantucuudu* and *Crycbeorh.*

[31] Blows ('Studies', p. 232) came to the same conclusion independently; he has cited Padel's observation that *cruc-* is often corrupted or changed by folk etymology to *car-*, and he made the connexion with *Crycbeorh* and Creech St Michael. See below, *s.n. Crycbeorh*. For Padel, see *Cornish Place-name Elements*, pp. 73–4, *s.n. cruc.*

[32] Domesday Book, I, 90ra (Somerset, 8.5).

Wessex (A.D. 757–786), gave three hides at *Cedern* to Glastonbury.[33] In MS. R.5.33, both references to this grant bear the marginal note, 'id est Elenbeorge'; John's *Cronica* incorporates this addition into the narrative. *Cedern* may be identified with Cheddar, although there is no other record of a transaction involving Glastonbury with the nearby royal estate at the foot of the Mendips, which in 1066 was in the king's hands and reputedly had never paid tax; in addition, a small independent holding there of two hides and one virgate was in the hands of Roger of Courseulles in 1086 (*Adulfus* in 1066).[34] *Elenbearo*, on the other hand, is on the contents-list of the *Liber terrarum*, where King Cynewulf is said to have granted land there to one Æthelheard, who granted it to Glastonbury (S.1681; LT31). This charter was also listed in the *Index chartarum* (IC D4). Further, the *De antiquitate* (unsupported elsewhere) reports that King Eadred gave part of *Elenberwe* (one hide) to Glastonbury.[35] The abbey held three hides at *Eleberie* (Elborough) in 1066, losing them by 1086 to the bishop of Coutances.[36]

Finberg identified the *Cedern id est Eleanbeorge* of the *De antiquitate* with Domesday Book's Elborough (later in the parish of Hutton), north of the Axe near the Severn-shore.[37] This has led to some misunderstanding. Scott, in his translation of the *De antiquitate*, proceeded to substitute Elborough for all occurrences of the name *Cedern* or *Ceddre*, not only with reference to the gift by Æthelheard, but also in the perambulation of the Twelve Hides of Glastonbury, a substitution which ignored the fact that the Twelve Hides bordered for some distance on the royal manor of Cheddar, with which Elborough has no connexion.[38] It is possible, too, that Finberg also was mistaken, and that the purported grant by Cynewulf was actually in Cheddar (as the original statement in the *De antiquitate* implies), and that *Elenbeorge* was not Elborough, but the area to the east of Cheddar now called Oldbury.[39] If Glastonbury did hold land in Cheddar, it left no other trace but this ambiguous reference. The charter of King Edgar for five hides at *Burgh'* which he granted to his thegn Wulfmær in A.D. 973 (S.793), which has been taken to refer to Berrow, may instead apply to a place with a similar name.[40] Elborough and Oldbury may be possible candidates.

---

[33] *De antiquitate*, §§48 and 69 (ed. & transl. Scott, pp. 106 and 142); *Cronica*, §§16 and 54 (edd. & transl. Carley & Townsend, pp. 40 and 106).

[34] Domesday Book, I, 86rb and 94rb (Somerset, 1.2 and 21.78). On Cheddar, see Rahtz *et al.*, *The Saxon and Medieval Palaces*.

[35] *De antiquitate*, §§57 and 69 (ed. & transl. Scott, pp. 118 and 142); *Cronica*, §§16 and 66 (edd. & transl. Carley & Townsend, pp. 42 and 124). The hidage is given in the summaries only.

[36] Domesday Book, I, 88ra and 91ra (Somerset, 5.11 and 8.38).

[37] Finberg, *The Early Charters of Wessex*, p. 117.

[38] *De antiquitate*, §72 (ed. & transl. Scott, pp. 150–1); corrected to Cheddar in the translation of the *Cronica*, §3 (edd. & transl. Carley & Townsend, p. 15).

[39] An identification suggested by Frances Neale and Hazel Hudson, quoted in *Cronica*, edd. & transl. Carley & Townsend, p. 288 (n. 188).

[40] See above, *s.n.* Berrow. The bounds attached to S.793 have so far foiled attempts to identify them with Berrow. See also below, *s.n.* Elborough.

Ceollamwirthe

A charter of King Edmund for *Ceollamwirthe*, in favour of one Æthelwold, is recorded in the contents-list of the *Liber terrarum* (S.1721; LT45). Reference to Glastonbury's possession of this land is found nowhere else but in §70 of the *De antiquitate*, which, as we have seen, appears to have been compiled from those charters which had not been used in the main part of that narrative.[41] The presence of *Ceollamwirthe* on this list alone may suggest that the estate never came into Glastonbury's possession or, alternatively, that the land was soon lost, perhaps before the Conquest. An Æthelwold was the recipient of two other charters for estates of which one, at least, did not necessarily become part of the abbey's endowment.[42] Hart identified this Æthelwold with the ealdorman who was the brother of Æthelstan Half-King, and stated that he gave *Ceollamwirthe* to Glastonbury during his lifetime, an unsupported assumption derived from the *Liber terrarum* reference and the absence of *Ceollamwirthe* from Æthelwold's will (S.1504; A.D. 946x947).[43]

Sawyer has identified the *Ceollamwirthe* of the contents-list of the *Liber terrarum* with Chelworth, in Wiltshire. This estate, according to S.356 (A.D. 871x899), was leased by King Alfred, with the consent of the church of Malmesbury, to the thegn Dudig. In A.D. 901, Malmesbury arranged an exchange with Ordlaf, who received Chelworth for five lives in return for Mannington (S.1205 and S.1797). Chelworth reappears *ca* A.D. 968x971 in the will of Ealdorman Ælfheah who bequeathed it to King Edgar (S.1485). Chelworth is also to be found in a confirmation to Malmesbury in the name of Edward the Confessor of various lands, including four hides at *Chellewrtha*, which had been given to that church by King Cædwalla (S.1038; A.D. 1065).[44] According to Domesday Book, Malmesbury held a thirty-hide estate there, while another two hides were held by one of the 'king's servants', *Warinus* (TRE by Eadric).[45]

Although we need not credit that Chelworth was given to Malmesbury by King Cædwalla, it does seem nonetheless to have formed part of that church's endowment in the late ninth and early tenth centuries. Robin Fleming has cited Chelworth's appearance in Ealdorman Ælfheah's will as an indication that Malmesbury had lost the estate – an example of the confiscation of monastic land by the Wessex kings in the First Viking Age[46] – but the evidence may be misleading. Might the ealdorman have held the abbey's land on lease from the king, to whom he 'willed' it to ensure its return? Or, alternatively, might the Chelworth in lay hands – that of the *Liber terrarum* and/or Ælfheah's will – be the smaller estate of that name which was held in 1066 by the layman Eadric?

---

[41] See above, pp. 24–6.

[42] LT122 and LT123; see *s.n.* Camerton and Sharpham.

[43] Hart, 'Athelstan "Half King" ', p. 119.

[44] Keynes has described this confirmation as 'seemingly disreputable' but has raised the possibility that it might have been a genuine *pancarta*: 'Regenbald', p. 214, n. 174.

[45] Domesday Book, I, 67ra and 74vb (Wiltshire, 8.7 and 68.30). For a detailed discussion of Chelworth's pre-Conquest history, see Dumville, *Wessex and England*, pp. 43–4.

[46] Fleming, 'Monastic lands', p. 252.

Whatever interpretation we put on the evidence for Chelworth, Glastonbury seems to have had no role beyond that of custodian of one of its documents. It is possible, too, that even this connexion is imaginary, and that the charter in the *Liber terrarum* was not for Chelworth, but for another place altogether. Morland has pointed out that *Ceollamwirthe* could be identified with Chelwood, in Somerset, a neighbour of Glastonbury's Marksbury.[47] Two estates of this name were in secular hands in 1066 and 1086,[48] but no evidence survives for their earlier history.

Cerawycombe

According to King Æthelwulf's Decimation charter (S.303; A.D. 854), the king granted six hides at *Cerawycombe* to Glastonbury. In the *De antiquitate*, which preserves a slightly different list of estates from those of the cartulary-texts of Æthelwulf's donation, this place seems to be represented by the name *Scearamtone*.[49] The identification of *Scearamtone* as *Cerawycombe* is based on their positions in the sequence of names in the two lists and the fact that both lands were assessed at six hides. Finberg suggested that *Scearamtone* might have been Shirehampton, in Gloucestershire.[50] Shirehampton is not recorded by name in Domesday Book, nor does it appear (in identifiable form) in an Anglo-Saxon charter; in consequence, its pre-Conquest history cannot be written and a link with Glastonbury cannot be either established or dismissed.

Different versions of Æthelwulf's Decimation charter – with different estates named – may have existed, and *Scearamtone* and *Cerawycombe* are therefore not necessarily the same place.[51] The latter has alternatively been identified as Crowcombe,[52] to which some pre-Conquest documentation does attach; it points to a connexion with the Old Minster, Winchester, however, rather than with Glastonbury. King Edward the Elder was reputed (in S.373) to have exchanged ten hides at *Crawancumbe* and land elsewhere with the bishop of Winchester in return for a grant of privileges at Taunton in A.D. 904; a confirmation by King Edgar of the grants of his predecessors (S.825) repeated the claim. These charters probably have been modified,[53] but they may at least indicate Winchester's previous possession of the estates named. If that was the case, Winchester regained its land,

---

47 Morland, 'The Glastonbury manors', p. 91. Ekwall gave the form *Celeworde* (from Domesday Book) for Chelwood and *Cellanwurd, Cellewird, Ceolæs wyr, Celeorde,* and *Celewrde* for Chelworth: *The Concise Oxford Dictionary of English Place-names*, pp. 99–100.

48 Domesday Book, I, 91va and 97ra (Somerset, 17.5 and 34.1 [three hides and five hides]).

49 *De antiquitate*, §§53 and 69 (ed. & transl. Scott, pp. 112 and 142); *Cronica*, §§16 and 56 (edd. & transl. Carley & Townsend, pp. 40 and 108). On the Decimation charter, see above, *s.n. Brannocmynstre*, and below, *s.n.* Monk Okehampton and pp. 322–4.

50 Finberg, *The Early Charters of the West Midlands*, p. 47; in 'Some early Gloucestershire estates', p. 3, Finberg envisaged an alliance between Mercia and Wessex as the context for such a grant to Glastonbury.

51 The lists may also have been tampered with.

52 Finberg, *The Early Charters of Wessex*, p. 122.

53 *Anglo-Saxon Writs*, ed. & transl. Harmer, pp. 524–5.

albeit briefly, when in A.D. 1053 Gytha granted four hides at *Crawecumban* to that church, which still held it in 1066 but not 1086.[54]

Crowcombe is in the Quantocks, about ten miles north of Taunton and not far from Glastonbury's estates of Brompton Ralph and Clatworthy. The evidence could suggest that Æthelwulf's grant may have conferred immunities from secular burdens rather than ownership.[55] Whatever the relationship, it was apparently not long-lasting, in that the estate soon passed to the Old Minster, and from its hands to the king's. Alternatively, Glastonbury's copy of Æthelwulf's Decimation charter could have had the name interpolated in an attempt to claim the estate from Winchester. It is also possible that *Cerawycombe* in S.303 does not refer to Crowcombe at all (the other forms of the name all lack the *e* before the *r*),[56] but to another (unidentified) estate.

Cetenesfelda

One *hywysce* at *Cetenesfelda* is cited in S.303, Glastonbury's copy of King Æthelwulf's Decimation charter of A.D. 854.[57] The account of the king's gifts to Glastonbury which appears in the *De antiquitate*, as opposed to the slightly different lists in the cartularies' version of this grant, seems to spell this place-name *Occenefeld*.[58] This identification, as with the preceding case of *Cerawy-combe*, is based on the order of names in the two lists as well as their similarity in form.[59] If more than one version of Æthelwulf's charter – with different names – existed, or if the lists of estates have been altered, this identification may be spurious. In any case, whether one or two places were involved, the location is unidentified, and no other reference is known.

The summary of grants in the Trinity manuscript of the *De antiquitate* (§69) adds the interlinear identification *uel Cecce* above *Cetenesfelda*.[60] Apart from being late, this information is not very useful, as *Cecce*, like *Cetenesfelda*, is obsolete and unidentified.

---

[54] Finberg, *The Early Charters of Wessex*, p. 150. Domesday Book, I, 91vb (Somerset, 19.7). The bishop of Winchester lost Crowcombe to the count of Mortain. It may be a coincidence that the assessment in Domesday Book is the remainder of ten hides (S.373 and S.825) minus six hides (S.303); this arithmetic might suggest the existence of two estates. If so, the six hides are invisible in 1066, and where the other four were in A.D. 854 is another, difficult, question.

[55] See below, pp. 322–4.

[56] Ekwall, *The Concise Oxford Dictionary of English Place-names*, p. 133, *s.n.* Crow-combe (*Crauuancumb, Crawancumb, Crawecumbe*).

[57] On this charter, see above, *s.n. Brannocmynstre*, and below, *s.n.* Monk Okehampton, and pp. 322–4. On the *hiwisc*, a unit which has been interpreted as equivalent to a hide, see Costen, 'Huish and Worth' and *The Origins*, pp. 94–5. Costen has argued that the *hiwisc* represents a survival of the component land-units of early multiple estates.

[58] *De antiquitate*, §§53 and 69 (ed. & transl. Scott, pp. 112 and 142); *Cronica*, §§16 and 56 (edd. & transl. Carley & Townsend, pp. 40 and 108).

[59] The first four letters (*Occenefelda*) may have been picked up by the scribe from a later name on the list (*Occemund*) and written in by mistake.

[60] MS. R.5.33, 15v; *De antiquitate*, §69 (ed. & transl. Scott, p. 142).

Charlton (Somerset)
Charlton was a sub-unit of Doulting consisting of three hides and one virgate TRE and TRW.[61] It does not appear by name in any source before Domesday Book. For the history of Doulting, see below.

Cheddar (Somerset)
See *Cedern.*

Chelwood (Somerset) / Chelworth (Wiltshire)
See *Ceollamwirthe.*

Chilton Polden (Somerset)
Chilton Polden (*Cepton* in Domesday Book) was a sub-unit of Shapwick consisting of five hides TRE and TRW.[62] It, too, does not occur by name before 1086. Its relationship with Shapwick and Glastonbury should be seen in the context of the history of the large estate of *Pouelt*, discussed in detail below.

Christian Malford (Wiltshire)
A diploma in the name of King Edmund which granted twenty hides at Christian Malford to Abbot Dunstan survives in the mid-fourteenth-century cartularies (S.466; A.D. 940). This charter, which includes Old English bounds, was not in the *Liber terrarum* (or, at least, the surviving contents-list does not record it), but does appear in the *Index chartarum* (IC A10) and MS. 39a (L40). The *De antiquitate* also records the grant.[63] In Domesday Book, Glastonbury held twenty hides at *Cristemelforde*.[64] Six acres of meadow which in 1086 were considered to be in Stanton St Quintin and four more in Littleton Drew had belonged to Christian Malford when they were leased to laymen in 1066.[65]

Christian Malford lies almost five miles northeast of Chippenham, approximately forty miles from Glastonbury, in an area of northern Wiltshire in which there was a concentration of estates owned by the abbey. These lands seems to have been acquired in the mid- to later tenth century and to represent expansion into a new region – with new, better-draining soils – possibly specifically at the time of Dunstan's abbacy.[66] We may take this as a dim reflexion of the kind of

---

61 Domesday Book, I, 90va (Somerset, 8.23).
62 Domesday Book, I, 90ra (Somerset, 8.5). The identification of this place is established by the following sequence of forms: *Ceptone, Cahalton, Chauton, Cheltone.* See Ekwall, *The Concise Oxford Dictionary of English Place-names,* p. 105, *s.n.* Chilton upon Polden.
63 *De antiquitate,* §§55 and 69 (ed. & transl. Scott, pp. 114 and 142); *Cronica,* §§16 and 64 (edd. & transl. Carley & Townsend, pp. 40 and 120). Brooks ('The career', p. 4) has suggested that this charter may originally have had a lay beneficiary, Dunstan's name being substituted at a later date (after the compilation of the *Liber terrarum*). It is the only evidence for Dunstan's abbacy as early as A.D. 940.
64 Domesday Book, I, 66va (Wiltshire, 7.4).
65 Domesday Book, I, 66va (Wiltshire, 7.5).
66 Stacy, 'The estates', pp. 2–3. See map 7 and below, *s.n.* Grittleton, *Kyngton,* and Nettleton.

manipulation of land resources visible more clearly in Æthelwold's development of the endowment of Ely Abbey.[67]

Christian Malford was one of the abbey's manors seized by Wells (and one of those recovered) during the protracted but ultimately unsuccessful attempt to annex Glastonbury to the see which was begun by Bishop Savaric (A.D. 1191–1205) and diligently pursued by Bishop Jocelin (A.D. 1206–1242).[68]

Clatworthy (Somerset)

Clatworthy was adjacent to the abbatial estate of Brompton Ralph, over ten miles west of Taunton, at the junction of six combes whose streams form the headwaters of the River Tone.[69] No separate documentation for Clatworthy survives before Domesday Book, where one and a half hides there were recorded as having been Glastonbury's in 1066, though held by William de Mohun in 1086.[70] Clatworthy's one and a half hides would seem to combine naturally with the adjacent Brompton Ralph's three and a half hides to form a five-hide unit, which may have been the estate originally granted (under the name *Brunamton*) to Glastonbury by Frithugyth, probably the wife of King Æthelheard, in the first half of the eighth century.[71] At some time before 1066, then, Glastonbury's *Brunamton* may have been divided, the smaller of the two portions bearing the name Clatworthy.

Cleeve

According to the contents-list of the *Liber terrarum*, King Edgar gave *Cylfan* to one Ealdred, who gave it to Glastonbury (S.1766; LT70). This charter has failed to survive and no reference to it appears in any of the other documentary collections. The *De antiquitate*, which seems to quote from the charter, adds the information that the gift by Ealdred, of eleven hides, was confirmed by King Edgar.[72] Cleeve does not appear in Domesday Book as a Glastonbury holding.

There are two Cleeves in Somerset. One, now called Old Cleeve, was held by Earl Harold TRE and by the king TRW. It has many attributes of a royal estate and a strategic position on the coast, between Watchet and Minehead.[73] The other Cleeve is near Congresbury, southwest of Bristol; it does not appear in Domesday Book by name. The place-name, deriving as it does from Old English *clif*, 'cliff', 'hill',[74] is a common one and could have been applied to a number of places, some of which we may no longer be able to identify. The location of Ealdred's

---

[67] See *Anglo-Saxon Ely*, edd. & transl Keynes & Kennedy, and *Liber Eliensis*, ed. Blake, pp. 63–117 and 395–9.

[68] See above, p. 12.

[69] Bush, 'Clatworthy', p. 31.

[70] Domesday Book, I, 95vb (Somerset, 25.8). No reference to Glastonbury's recent loss of Clatworthy, however, occurs in the expected places in Domesday Book or its associated texts, such as in the list of lost estates at the end of Glastonbury's main entry or under the *Terrae occupatae* heading in the *Liber Exoniensis*.

[71] See above, *s.n.* Brompton Ralph.

[72] *De antiquitate*, §§62 and 69 (ed. & transl. Scott, pp. 130 and 144); *Cronica*, §§16 and 73 (edd. & transl. Carley & Townsend, pp. 42 and 138).

[73] Domesday Book, I, 86vb (Somerset, 1.13).

[74] Ekwall, *The Concise Oxford Dictionary of English Place-names, s.n.* Cleeve, p. 111.

eleven hides therefore remains uncertain. As Ealdred reputedly also gave land at nearby Durborough to Glastonbury, however, there may be a connexion with Old Cleeve,[75] though the transfer of neither of these estates to the abbey can be demonstrated. Monkleigh, later in the parish of Monk Okehampton in Devon (originally *Monkeclyue*, 'monk's cliff'),[76] may be another possible candidate.

Clewer (Somerset)

According to a charter once in the *Liber terrarum*, Bishop Wilfrid (d. A.D. 709/710) granted land at *Clifuuere* to Glastonbury (S.1675; LT10). This has been identified as Clewer, north of Wedmore, about ten miles northwest of Glastonbury. The text of Wilfrid's charter was not written into the later cartularies; however, its existence was noted in the *Index chartarum*, assuming that it is the document described as 'Wilferfus rex de Cliwere, inutilis' (IC A20). The *Index chartarum* cites another document for this estate: 'Cenewre rex de Clifwere' (S.1668; IC A17). This was presumably a charter in the name of Centwine, king of Wessex, but no further details concerning it are available, as it is not preserved in any of the other documentary sources. If genuine, it could have been, as Finberg assumed, a diploma granting the land to Wilfrid,[77] before Wilfrid granted it to Glastonbury.

The *De antiquitate* makes this connexion explicit: Centwine gave Clewer to the Northumbrian bishop, who, apparently in the time of King Ine, gave Abbot Berwald one hide at *uillam de Cliwere* and seventy hides at Wedmore, its neighbour.[78] The *Index chartarum* records two grants involving Wilfrid and the estate of Wedmore, both of which parallel the Clewer grants. Preserved in the list of charters for lands no longer held by the abbey are a charter of *Kenelm* (*recte* Centwine, presumably) granting Wedmore to Bishop Wilfrid (S.1667; IC C1) and a charter of Wilfrid, granting the estate to Abbot Berwald (S.1674; IC C2). The existence of separate pairs of charters – IC A17 and A20 for Clewer and IC C1 and C2 for Wedmore – tends to suggest that from the start the two estates were distinct; but if those charters were not genuine, Clewer could have originally been part of Wedmore, and the charters possibly produced to supply separate title-deeds when Clewer became a detached sub-unit (which Glastonbury retained, Wedmore having been lost);[79] or perhaps Glastonbury never held Wedmore but once laid claim to it (unsuccessfully). There is apparently no proof elsewhere that Wedmore was ever in Glastonbury's hands.

One of Wilfrid's charters for Clewer may have been copied and its text preserved in the archive in the fifteenth century: MS. 39a records the presence of a 'copia carte de Clyfwere' among the records of the *coquinarius* (L47a) but, since

---

[75] Stacy, 'The estates', p. 14, n. 9.

[76] Gover *et al.*, *The Place-names of Devon*, I.154.

[77] Finberg, *The Early Charters of Wessex*, p. 111.

[78] *De antiquitate*, §§40 and 69 (ed. & transl. Scott, pp. 94 and 142); *Cronica*, §§16 and 47 (edd. & transl. Carley & Townsend, pp. 40 and 92).

[79] Hazel Hudson has suggested that a substantial boundary bank south of Clewer could mark an ancient division between the Clewer and Wedmore estates; no date for this bank has been proposed, however ('Wedmore').

the donor's name is not given, we have no context – pre- or post-Conquest – for this document.[80]

Edwards accepted all four lost charters as representing genuine transactions.[81] She considered that the inclusion of the Clewer charters on List A, of lands still owned by Glastonbury (unlike Wedmore, on List C, of lands no longer belonging to the abbey), was 'almost certainly erroneous'.[82] The evidence of Domesday Book appears to suggest that Clewer was lost by 1066: three virgates (less one furlong) there were held by the bishop of Coutances in 1086, and by Thorkell TRE, with no evident connexion with Glastonbury.[83] This may be misleading, however, as Clewer was held by the abbey in the late twelfth and thirteenth centuries.[84] It may be that an unrecorded agreement between Thorkell and the abbot lay behind the seemingly independent tenure in 1066, and that the monks were able to assert their lordship over the Norman tenant on the basis of this relationship.[85] Or perhaps Clewer was indeed seized, but retrieved by Glastonbury.

Wilfrid's was a name readily available to forgers of a later age, and the credibility of his grants of Clewer and Wedmore to Glastonbury must be assessed with his renown in mind. A link between Wilfrid and Glastonbury is questionable, but not impossible. Aelred Watkin has suggested that his presence there had been commemorated on a sculpture in the monastic cemetery, described in the early twelfth century by William of Malmesbury; this 'pyramid' bore, among others, the name *Wulfred*.[86] Even if we decline to credit Watkin's hypothetical delegation to Glastonbury – composed of Wilfrid, Queen Eanfled, and Ætla, bishop of Dorchester (A.D. ?660–?) – with the aim of Romanising a 'Celtic' establishment, a grant to Wilfrid by Centwine is not inconceivable, given that in the early 680s the exiled bishop had been received by the king, although the queen (who was sister-in-law to Ecgfrith, king of Northumbria) was not friendly and Wilfrid stayed but a short time;[87] Wilfrid's visit to Glastonbury is, however, unconfirmed by other sources. The alleged beneficiary of Wilfrid's grant, Abbot Berwald, is of questionable reality himself: Sarah Foot has rejected the supposition that there was an abbot of this name at Glastonbury in the 670s or 680s.[88]

If, however, we accept the possibility of grants to Glastonbury by Wilfrid, we must ask whether Centwine might have been sufficiently well disposed to grant

---

[80] No doubt Clewer had been assigned to the *coquinarius* because it rendered a substantial number of eels, at least in the late twelfth century (*Liber Henrici*, ed. Jackson, p. 9).

[81] Edwards, *The Charters*, pp. 67–8.

[82] *Ibid.*, p. 68.

[83] Domesday Book, I, 88rb (Somerset, 5.19).

[84] Morland, 'The Glastonbury manors', p. 70.

[85] For silences in the evidence of Domesday Book, see below, p. 308.

[86] *De antiquitate*, §32 (ed. & transl. Scott, p. 84); Watkin, 'The Glastonbury "pyramids" ', especially p. 41.

[87] Stephanus, *Vita S. Wilfridi*, §40 (*The Life of Bishop Wilfrid*, ed. & transl. Colgrave, p. 80). Patrick Sims-Williams tentatively has placed these charters (if genuine) in late 680 or early in 681 ('St Wilfrid and two charters', p. 179).

[88] 'Glastonbury's early abbots', pp. 171–4. A Glastonbury forger could have found notice of a supposedly seventh-century Berhtwald in the *De antiquitate* (§36; ed. & transl.

him such a substantial estate as Wedmore. In his Life of Wilfrid, Stephen described how King Cædwalla had given the exiled bishop 'innumerable' tracts of land.[89] A grant of the same magnitude was indeed made by Cædwalla to Wilfrid for the foundation of the monastery of Selsey (S.232). Centwine's generosity, though praised by Aldhelm, is badly recorded.[90] Wedmore was a royal estate in the ninth century, as we know from Asser and from Alfred's will (S.1507), and if Wilfrid had received it from Centwine and granted it to Glastonbury it must somehow have returned to the king.[91] Fleming considered Wedmore to have been an example of land confiscated by the house of Wessex in its struggle against the Viking invaders;[92] if this were the case, the seizure must have already taken place by *ca* A.D. 880 when Alfred wrote his will. Wedmore left royal hands at the end of the Anglo-Saxon period: S.1115, a writ of Edward the Confessor, effected its transfer from the king to Giso, bishop of Wells, in A.D. 1061x1066.[93] In 1066 and 1086 the bishop of Wells held ten hides there, although Wedmore was considered a *membrum* of the royal manor of Cheddar, held by the bishop from the king.[94] S.1042, the confirmation charter in the name of King Edward already discussed in relation to Binegar (*q.v.*), confirmed four hides at Wedmore to the bishop, along with its appurtenances (Tarnock, *Heawycan*, and Mark).[95]

The sources, therefore, confirm Wedmore's royal connexion from the late ninth century. Before that, we have only the testimony of lost charters whose reliability cannot be judged. This circumstance – and the absence of other evidence – likewise limits our knowledge of Clewer and of its relationship with Wedmore; the extent to which Clewer's history ran parallel to that of its important neighbour and the point at which it diverged cannot be identified. The relationship of both of these estates with Glastonbury is also necessarily uncertain.

Clutton (Somerset)

According to an unusually detailed entry in the contents-list of the *Liber terrarum*, Æthelwulf (king of Wessex) gave land at *Cluttone* to another Æthelwulf, and Æthelstan *comes*, son of Æthelnoth, gave it to Glastonbury (S.1694; LT40). This information was presumably copied from an endorsement on the charter. According to the *De antiquitate*, Æthelstan *comes* gave ten hides at Clutton

Scott, p. 90) and S.227 (A.D. 670). He may have been derived from a confused memory of the Berwald or Berhtwald who was abbot from *ca* A.D. 705 to 709x731.

89 Stephanus, *Vita S. Wilfridi*, §42 (ed. & transl. Colgrave, p. 84); Robinson, *Somerset*, p. 32.

90 See below, p. 125.

91 Asser, *Life of King Alfred*, §56 (ed. Stephenson, p. 47; *Alfred the Great*, transl. Keynes & Lapidge, pp. 85 and 175).

92 Fleming, 'Monastic lands', p. 252; but see Dumville, *Wessex and England*, especially p. 41, n. 56.

93 See *Anglo-Saxon Writs*, ed. & transl. Harmer, pp. 273–4 and 489, on Wedmore and its royal connexions; see also Bishop Giso's *Historiola de primordiis epicopatus Somersetensis* (*Ecclesiastical Documents*, ed. Hunter, especially pp. 16–17).

94 Domesday Book, I, 86rb and 89va (Somerset, 1.2, 6.15, and notes).

95 Tarnock was also claimed by Glastonbury (as a grant by King Eadred). See below, *s.n.* Tarnock.

(which lies in the hills fifteen miles north of Glastonbury) to the abbey with the consent of King Æthelwulf, committing the *cartula hereditatis* to the church with his body.[96] The identities of the layman Æthelwulf and of Æthelstan *comes* are uncertain; but Hart has identified the latter as Æthelstan Half-King and the former as his paternal grandfather.[97] According to Hart, however, Æthelstan Half-King's father was called Æthelfrith (not Æthelnoth, the father of the Æthelstan *comes* noted in the entry in the *Liber terrarum*).[98] If the *De antiquitate* is to be trusted, the chronology likewise makes the identification impossible, as the text implies that Æthelstan *comes* and King Æthelwulf were contemporaries.

One other charter for Clutton is recorded, in the *Index chartarum*. This was a grant by King Edmund which appears on the list of charters in favour of laymen for land not held by the abbey in A.D. 1247 (S.1732; IC D12). Edmund's grant appears nowhere else in the Glastonbury archive, a circumstance which may lend some support to Stacy's suggestion that it was a lease.[99] Glastonbury appears to have lost Clutton before the Conquest, as it was held by Thorkell in 1066, but the example of Clewer, also held TRE by Thorkell, may remind us that some unrecorded agreement with the abbey might have underlain his (seemingly independent) tenure.[100] Clutton, like Clewer, was held by the bishop of Coutances in 1086, but, unlike Clewer, Clutton does not appear to have returned to Glastonbury thereafter.

Compton Beauchamp (Berkshire)

Preserved in the contents-list of the *Liber terrarum* was the record of a charter of King Eadred for *Cumtone iuxta Æscesdone dat' Ælpheho* (LT109). This grant is grouped in the contents-list with the two charters for Glastonbury's estate at Ashbury (Berkshire), to which the land it grants is adjacent.[101] Ealdorman Ælfheah, the recipient of *Cumtone*, had given Batcombe to Glastonbury in his will (S.1485; *ca* A.D. 970) and had close links with the abbey.[102] Eadred's diploma, however, does not appear in any of the other cartularies or lists of charters, nor is it or the transfer of *Cumtone iuxta Æscesdone* (now called Compton Beauchamp) to Glastonbury mentioned in the *De antiquitate*. Earlier grants of a place called *Cumton* do appear in all these sources, but these have generally been interpreted as relating to another Compton – Compton Dundon in Somerset – discussed below.

It may be, in fact, that despite the abbey's ownership of neighbouring Ashbury, Compton Beauchamp was never Glastonbury's land. This is one interpretation

---

[96] *De antiquitate*, §§53 and 69 (ed. & transl. Scott, pp. 112 and 142); *Cronica*, §§16 and 56 (edd. & transl. Carley & Townsend, pp. 40 and 108).

[97] Hart, 'Athelstan "Half King" ', p. 125.

[98] *Ibid.*, pp. 116–17.

[99] Stacy, 'The estates', pp. 24–5.

[100] Domesday Book, I, 88ra and 88rb (Somerset, 5.14 and 5.19); Stacy, 'The estates', p. 15. For Clewer, see above.

[101] LT107 and LT108; see above, *s.n.* Ashbury. For a map, see Hooke, 'Charters and the landscape', p. 92.

[102] See above, *s.n.* Batcombe. On his career and family connexions, see Williams, '*Princeps Merciorum gentis*', especially pp. 147–54. On grants to his wife which were claimed by Glastonbury, see below, *s.n.* Idmiston.

which can be derived simply from the omission of Eadred's charter from the later mediaeval cartularies and lists; it is strengthened by the survival of the text of a charter from the Abingdon archive (S.564; A.D. 955) in the name of King Eadred, for Ælfheah, for land at Compton Beauchamp – in other words, presumably a duplicate of the grant in Glastonbury's *Liber terrarum*. There is, unfortunately, no way of determining why there were apparently two copies of this charter (unless two different estates were involved). Abingdon did not hold Compton Beauchamp in 1066 (it was in secular hands),[103] and the history of the estate after Ælfheah obtained it is unrecorded. He did not bequeath it in his will. There is no later evidence to connect Compton Beauchamp with either Glastonbury or Abingdon.[104] Ælfheah's charter may have accompanied the gift of the estate to either of these houses; an intended gift to one or the other may have failed to take place; or Ælfheah may simply have been using both depositories for his documents. Alternatively, the particular circumstances of the charter's production – it belongs to a group associated with Glastonbury – may account for its survival there.[105]

Compton Dundon (Somerset)

The other *Cumtone*, in Somerset, was clearly a possession of the Glastonbury community. It was reputedly a gift to the abbey by Cynewulf, king of Wessex, according to the contents-list of the *Liber terrarum* (S.1685; LT39). In the *De antiquitate* we are told that the gift was of five hides and took place in A.D. 762.[106] Further transactions followed. King Edward the Elder, according to a charter listed in the *Index chartarum* and MS. 39a, restored *Cumton Dunden* to Abbot *Aldrinus* in A.D. 912 (S.1705; IC A8; L5). Like that of Cynewulf, this charter's text was not preserved in the later cartularies, although a reference to it does occur there in a historical note on the kings of Wessex, with the additional statement that it was *Aldrinus*'s predecessor who had lost the estate through *inpotencia*.[107] The *De antiquitate* says only that Edward returned *Cumtone* to Abbot *Aldhunus*, giving the obviously incorrect date of A.D. 992.[108]

One further reference in the *De antiquitate* may apply to Compton Dundon. It is said there that King Edgar gave Abbot Sigegar five hides at *Dundene*.[109] Finberg identified this as a gift of the estate of Compton Dundon,[110] but it is also

---

103 Held by *Almar* 'in alod' de rege' in 1066: Domesday Book, I, 61ra (Berkshire, 22.11).
104 Garbett & Alexander, 'Compton Beauchamp', p. 524.
105 Keynes, 'The "Dunstan B" charters', especially p. 188; see also below, *s.n.* Henstridge.
106 *De antiquitate*, §§48 and 69 (ed. & transl. Scott, pp. 106 and 142); *Cronica*, §§16 and 54 (edd. & transl. Carley & Townsend, pp. 40 and 106).
107 The note follows Æthelwulf's Decimation charter: *The Great Chartulary*, ed. Watkin, I.144 (no. 202).
108 *De antiquitate*, §54 (ed. & transl. Scott, p. 114); Scott corrected 992 to 922 but, in view of the reference in MS. 39a, 912 might be substituted. Edward's restoration of Compton Dundon does not appear in the *Cronica*.
109 *De antiquitate*, §§62 and 69 (ed. & transl. Scott, pp. 128 and 144); *Cronica*, §§16 and 73 (edd. & transl. Carley & Townsend, pp. 42 and 138).
110 Finberg, *The Early Charters of Wessex*, p. 144.

possible that it related to its neighbour, Dundon.[111] *Cumtone* and *Dundene* were assessed at the same number of hides, and the possibility must be considered that the two names once referred to the same land-unit, now with the composite name of Compton Dundon. The appearance of separate estates called *Contone* and *Dondeme* in Domesday Book, however, argues against this idea; although both were of five hides and held from the abbot by Roger of Courseulles (which could suggest that only one estate – cited twice – was actually involved) the details given (acres of meadow and furlongs of woodland) are not the same, and *Contone* and *Dondeme* appear to be two different estates.[112]

Compton Dundon, only a few miles directly south of Glastonbury, was recorded as a five-hide sub-unit of Walton in Domesday Book. The history of Walton – and the adjoining estate of Shapwick – may go back to the earliest period of Glastonbury's endowment.[113] The evidence for the composition of the original estate of *Pouelt* (of which Walton, and therefore Compton Dundon, may have been a part) is so slight, however, that it is not possible to say whether it might have acquired additional territory over time – such as the five-hide unit of *Cumtone* – or whether *Pouelt* from the beginning included within it all the land which is visible in later records as separate sub-units of Shapwick and Walton. The first known charter for *Cumtone*, in the name of Cynewulf, could be interpreted as the continuation of the granting, in portions, of the large *Pouelt* estate which his predecessors, Kings Ine and Æthelheard, had begun to transfer to the abbey in the first half of the eighth century. Glastonbury seems to have lost *Cumtone*, however, apparently in the late ninth century (if Edward the Elder's restoration is to be credited), but the king returned it to the abbey in the early tenth. Whether Edgar's grant of *Dundene* was a repetition of this process in the later tenth century depends on the identity of that estate. By 1066 *Cumtone* was part of Walton, but *Dondeme*, it seems, was not.[114]

The problems of identification do not end here. There are Comptons distributed throughout Somerset, some of them associated with charters from other pre-Conquest archives and some without documentary history.[115] There is always

---

[111] See below, *s.n.* Dundon.
[112] Domesday Book, I, 90rb (Somerset, 8.11 and 8.13).
[113] See below, *s.n. Pouelt*.
[114] Domesday Book, I, 90rb (Somerset, 8.11 and 8.13). One hide at *Cumpton* was retrieved by Abbot Herluin in the early years of the twelfth century, along with several other estates and portions of estates; but the *De antiquitate* does not report the identity of the person who had appropriated it. It had presumably been seized after the Conquest: *De antiquitate*, §79 (ed. & transl. Scott, p. 160); *Cronica*, §87 (edd. & transl. Carley & Townsend, p. 162).
[115] King Edward the Elder granted the bishop of Winchester privileges for the minster at Taunton in return for twenty hides at Compton (S.373; A.D. 904); Edward then gave Compton to the community at Cheddar in exchange for Carhampton (A.D. 904x925, according to S.806; A.D. 978 for ?968). Finberg (*The Early Charters of Wessex*, pp. 128–9) suggested that this might be Compton Bishop, and its pairing here and in S.373 with Banwell would support the connexion, as the two are close to one another, just north of the Axe near Axbridge. S.777 records the grant of land at Clifton by King Edgar in A.D. 970 to St Peter's, Bath, in exchange for ten *mansae* at *Cumtun*, this time

the chance that Glastonbury's charters in the name of Cynewulf and Edward the Elder for *Cumtone* applied to one or another of these places; likewise, some of the places called *Cumton* mentioned in pre-Conquest wills may have been Compton Dundon or Compton Beauchamp.[116] It seems fair to say, however, that the identifications so far made are sensible interpretations of the available evidence.

Contone (Somerset)
See Compton Dundon.

Corregescumb (Somerset)
In A.D. 705 or 706, King Ine gave to Glastonbury four estates, including five hides in the valley called *Corregescumb*, according to a single-sheet copy of uncertain date of a probably authentic charter (S.248). This grant is not recorded elsewhere in the archive, except in the *De antiquitate*, which alters the number of hides to six in an interlinear note.[117] Because the formulation of location is so vague in early diplomas, and because no Old English bounds were subsequently added to it, the attempt to identify the places granted in this charter has met with some difficulty.[118]

The testimony of S.248 was apparently found to be inadequate by the tenth century, and up-to-date versions of charters for the four estates granted in it may have been produced at that time. Only one of these survives, S.247, for 'uiginti cassatos . . . ex utraque parte fluminis cuius uocabulum est Doultynge', in the cartulary under the rubric for the manor of Pilton.[119] The vernacular bounds attached to this charter, however, show that Pilton, at least at the time of the composition of the bounds, included the land now called Croscombe as well as Shepton Mallet west of the Fosse Way.[120] We can therefore say that when the bounds were written Croscombe was included in Pilton's twenty hides on the River *Doultynge* (now the Sheppey). Whether Croscombe was included in those twenty hides at the time of the original grant, however, is uncertain. Whether it is related to the possible grant of *Korstone* to a layman by King Æthelstan is also unclear.[121]

---

identified by Finberg (p. 145) as Chilcompton (in the Mendips) or Compton Dando, closer to Bath. There is also a Compton Martin in the Mendips.

[116] S.1507 (in King Alfred's will, associated with several places of that name in Sussex, Surrey, and Hampshire; *Alfred the Great*, transl. Keynes & Lapidge, pp. 177 and 321–2, n. 68); S.1538 (A.D. 984x1016, associated with Compton Dando or Chilcompton; *Anglo-Saxon Wills*, ed. & transl. Whitelock, p. 174 [no. 21]); S.1503 (A.D. 1015, associated with a Compton in Sussex; *ibid.*, p. 171 [no. 20]).

[117] *De antiquitate*, §40 (ed. & transl. Scott, p. 94) (omitted from the summary chapter); *Cronica*, §47 (edd. & transl. Carley & Townsend, p. 92) (five hides, not six).

[118] See Abrams, 'A single-sheet facsimile', pp. 122–32.

[119] And also under Doulting; but see below, *s.n.* Doulting.

[120] Davidson, 'On the charters', pp. 19–23 (and map).

[121] The form of the place-name for Croscombe in Domesday Book is *Coristone*; a *Korstone* is among the list of *alia* [*maneria*] *data Glastonie* in the *De antiquitate* (§70; ed. & transl. Scott, p. 144), possibly the same as *Worstone* which Æthelstan gave to *Affe* (LT54). *Korstone* and *Worstone* are so far unidentified.

A complication arises when we compare S.247 with Ine's original gift in S.248, and note in the latter the grant of five hides 'ex occidentali uero plaga eiusdem uallis [*Corregescumb*]'. If Croscombe was part of the twenty hides on the Sheppey, it cannot also be the land referred to in this additional grant of five hides in the valley, as Morland has seemed to conclude.[122] Davidson had instead identified the *Corregescumb* of Ine's grant with the estate of North Wootton, which lies between Glastonbury and Shepton Mallet, adjacent to Pilton on the west.[123] According to the *De antiquitate*, King Cynewulf gave five hides at *Wudeton* to Abbot Guba in A.D. 760; an incomplete statement in the contents-list of the *Liber terrarum* may refer to this transaction (S.1684; LT27).[124] Another entry in the contents-list records a grant of *Wodetone* to Heregyth by King Æthelwulf in A.D. 855x860 (S.1700; LT64). Finally, a charter of A.D. 946 in the name of King Edmund appears to represent a lease of a five-hide estate there (S.509; LT131). The identification of North Wootton with the five *Corregescumb* hides, however, is not definite. It appears to be based on the agreement in hidage and on the fact that North Wootton lies beside the tenth-century Pilton estate, which (as we have seen) has been identified, thanks to the vernacular bounds of S.247, as the twenty hides on the river which were granted in the same charter by Ine. Davidson and Grundy found some coincidences in the bounds of S.509 (for North Wootton) and S.247 (for Pilton) which confirmed a shared boundary, but this proved only that those two estates were adjacent, which did not need proving. It did nothing to locate eighth-century *Corregescumb* or identify it as the estate subsequently called North Wootton.

To complicate matters further, in Domesday Book (though not when the bounds were written, if Davidson's analysis of S.247 was sound) North Wootton was a component of Pilton, assessed at five hides. The bounds, however, may not necessarily have been written before 1066.[125] Croscombe, also part of Pilton in Domesday Book, was only three hides.[126] These circumstances illustrate the mobility of land within estates and should remind us of the possible changes – in hidage, in tenurial status, in name – which can lie behind the silence of the documents. Frequently the documentary record casts no light at all on the gaps between the (perhaps initial) grants of land, in the eighth century in this case, and the first appearance of descriptions of the territory or details about its nature (in the late Anglo-Saxon bounds or Domesday Book). Without more contemporary help than we have, we can go no further in attempting to locate the *Corregescumb* hides or proving them to be either Croscombe, North Wootton, or somewhere else altogether.

---

[122] Morland, 'The Glastonbury manors', p. 71.

[123] Davidson, 'On the charters', pp. 19–23. See also below, *s.n.* North Wootton.

[124] 'Cynewlfus de .u. hidis G.'

[125] See Grundy, *The Saxon Charters*, pp. 79–80. Among language-experts there is disagreement on the date of these bounds: Peter Kitson and Margaret Gelling have placed them in the second half of the tenth century (the former in his unpublished work on charter-bounds, the latter in a letter of 16 July, 1989), but Paul Bibire (in a note written in June 1991) has judged them to be twelfth- and thirteenth-century, revealing no evidence of an Old English exemplar. See below, *s.n.* Doulting and Pilton.

[126] Domesday Book, I, 90rb–va (Somerset, 8.20).

Cossington (Somerset)

Cossington first appears by name in Domesday Book, which records that three hides there had been held TRE from the abbot by *Aluuinus* (and by Walter of Douai in 1086).[127] Though undocumented before 1066, Cossington may have belonged to the earliest phase of Glastonbury's endowment, and its acquisition by the abbey can arguably be seen in the context of the break-up of an early large estate, *Pouelt*, which may have covered the whole of the Polden Hills.[128] Cossington is one of a series of rectangular estates running north from the Roman road on the ridge of the Poldens and extending into the moor. Not just the boundaries between estates but the settlements, too, show signs of planning, a reorganisation of resources which Michael Costen has associated (though without conclusive evidence of date) with the tenth century.[129] The estates to the north of the Roman road, with the exception of Puriton and Cossington, were all sub-units of Shapwick in Domesday Book, and it seems very likely from the layout of the landscape that Cossington itself was originally part of the larger unit. How it achieved the degree of tenurial independence attested to by Domesday Book is uncertain; perhaps part of Shapwick was leased out and thereby removed from the original estate, though not from Glastonbury's lordship.[130]

Cranmore (Somerset)

According to a charter from the contents-list of the *Liber terrarum*, King Eadwig gave land at *Cranemere* to his *minister* Ælfheah (S.1746; LT69). This text was not preserved in the later cartularies or recorded on any of the other lists of charters. The *De antiquitate* mentions only Cranmore's being granted by Ælfheah to Glastonbury and specifies that it was of twelve hides, given with King Eadwig's consent.[131] A subsequent reference to a grant by Ælfheah to Glastonbury of ten hides at Cranmore, confirmed by King Edgar, may be a case of scribal confusion. The first citation of Ælfheah's gift of Cranmore had been omitted from what was apparently its proper place, in the account of Eadwig's reign, and was added there in the margin of R.5.33.[132] Although the second reference is not identical (ten hides instead of twelve, Edgar instead of Eadwig) it could be that it was the same

---

[127] Domesday Book, I, 90ra (Somerset, 8.7).

[128] See below, *s.n. Pouelt*.

[129] See Costen, 'Some evidence for new settlements', and 'Dunstan, Glastonbury, and the economy'.

[130] By the time when the bounds were written for S.253 (Æthelheard's grant of *Pouelt* to Glastonbury dated 729) Cossington appears not to have been included in the estate they described, for 'territoria que pertinent ad Cosingtone' is said to lie to the west. These bounds, although typical of the earliest type (short and in Latin) are not found in the expected place in the body of the charter but have been added after the witness-list. The date of the bounds is, therefore, uncertain, but they do at least confirm Cossington's separateness.

[131] *De antiquitate*, §§58 and 69 (ed. & transl. Scott, pp. 120 and 144); *Cronica*, §§16 and 67 (edd. & transl. Carley & Townsend, pp. 42 and 126).

[132] *De antiquitate*, §§62 and 69 (ed. & transl. Scott, pp. 130 and 144); *Cronica*, §§16 and 73 (edd. & transl. Carley & Townsend, pp. 42 and 138). For the marginal insertion, see Scott, p. 120.

charter, copied in the wrong place, an error corrected by the marginal insertion (but not by deletion of the misplaced reference). Alternatively, the first charter cited could represent Eadwig's grant to Ælfheah, which (with additional information or by assumption) was extrapolated in the *De antiquitate* into a gift to Glastonbury, and the second charter could have been the real record of this gift, actually made during the reign of Edgar.[133] Several other estates granted to Ælfheah were passed on to Glastonbury, directly or through his heirs.[134] In 1066 the abbey held twelve hides at Cranmore, according to Domesday Book.[135] This may have included the current East and West Cranmore, to the east of Shepton Mallet, approximately twelve miles northeast of Glastonbury. Morland, however, disagreed with C. and F. Thorn, who interpreted the split into two parts as a post-Conquest phenomenon, and instead proposed that Glastonbury's Cranmore was West Cranmore only, East Cranmore being identifiable with the five hides in the king's demesne in Frome Hundred in the Geld Roll.[136]

Cranmore was one of the four manors lost to Wells following the protracted but ultimately unsuccessful attempt to annex the abbey to the see which was begun by Bishop Savaric (A.D. 1191–1205) and diligently pursued by Bishop Jocelin (A.D. 1206–1242).[137] Cranmore's pre-Conquest charters may have gone to Wells when Glastonbury finally lost its fight for the land in the late thirteenth century.

Creech St Michael (Somerset)
See *Crycbeorh*.

Croscombe (Somerset)
See *Corregescumb*.

Crowcombe (Somerset)
See *Cerawycombe*.

Cructan
Cructan was the British name for *Crycbeorh*, the subject of a charter of King Centwine (S.237) treated below.

Crycbeorh (Somerset)
In a charter dated 682 and preserved only in an early sixteenth-century cartulary-copy, King Centwine is said to have granted twenty-three hides in *Cantucuudu*

---

133 Grants by both Eadwig and Edgar of Westbury to Ælfheah's brother, Ealdorman Ælfhere, are similarly attested in the *Liber terrarum* (LT89 and LT90). See below, *s.n.* Westbury.

134 On Ælfheah's career, see Williams, '*Princeps Merciorum gentis*', pp. 147–54. See also below, *s.n.* Idmiston, for Ælfheah and for those estates granted to his wife, Ælfswith, which Glastonbury later held (or claimed).

135 Domesday Book, I, 90vb (Somerset, 8.32 and notes).

136 *Ibid.*; Morland, 'Some Domesday manors', p. 46. These five hides do not appear among the *terrae regis* in Domesday Book but are noted at the end of the *Liber Exoniensis* (E 527a).

137 See above, p. 12.

with three hides 'in australi parte amnis Tan ad insulam iuxta collem qui dicitur brettannica lingua Cructan, apud nos Crycbeorh' (S.237).[138] This land is described as having 'ab austro Blacanbroc, ab aquilone Tan'. The grant of *Cantucuudu* appears in the contents-list of the *Liber terrarum* (LT8), but *Crycbeorh* is not mentioned there or in the reference to this charter of Centwine in MS. 39a (L47).

There is some difficulty in establishing exactly what was disposed of in S.237; differences between the version of the grant in the late cartulary and in the text of the *De antiquitate* raise doubts about how many places (one, two, or three) and how many hides (twenty, twenty-three, or twenty-six) were involved;[139] the wording could suggest that the hidage total included the three hides south of the river, or alternatively that those three – at *Crycbeorh* – were additional to the total. The latter interpretation could, too, suggest further that the grant of *Crycbeorh* (which comes after the bounds of *Cantucuudu* and before the dating clause and has its own brief boundary description) was an addition to the text; two charters of Centwine could have been conflated, or *Crycbeorh* simply interpolated. The *De antiquitate* does not help to clarify the situation, but rather adds its own complication by citing yet a third name (*Caric*), which may or may not represent another place.[140] The *De antiquitate* also omits the English name, *Crycbeorh*, referring simply to its British predecessor, *Crucan* (sic).[141]

These three hides at *Crycbeorh*, like *Cantucuudu*, have been identified as part of West Monkton, near Taunton. According to Grundy, unlike the first description (of the twenty hides), these three hides south of the river 'present no difficulty', and consisted of the part of West Monkton south of the Tone, including Creechbarrow Hill.[142] In Domesday Book, West Monkton was an estate of fifteen hides belonging to Glastonbury.[143] This offers no help in deciding what happened to *Crycbeorh* after the seventh century. By 1066 it could have been absorbed into West Monkton or detached from it – perhaps added to the estate of Creech St Michael, as suggested by Dickinson,[144] or incorporated into Taunton, in which the area around Creechbarrow Hill now lies. It is almost twenty-five miles to the west of Glastonbury.

---

[138] 'On the southern side of the River Tone at the island at the hill which is called *Cructan* in the British tongue, *Crycbeorh* by us'; on the cartulary, see above, pp. 13–14.

[139] Robinson suggested that the author of the *De antiquitate* had used a composite charter: *Somerset*, p. 29, n. 5. Dickinson ('West Monkton charter', p. 97) concluded that the three hides were additional; Morland ('The Glastonbury manors', p. 76) seems to have included them in the twenty-three. See above, *s.n. Cantucuudu* and *Caric*.

[140] See above, *s.n. Cantucuudu* and *Caric*.

[141] *De antiquitate*, §§37 and 69 (ed. & transl. Scott, pp. 90 and 140); *Cronica*, §§16 and 43 (edd. & transl. Carley & Townsend, pp. 40 and 90).

[142] Grundy, *The Saxon Charters*, pp. 51–4, especially p. 52; see also Morland, 'The Glastonbury manors', p. 76, and Robinson, ' "Crucan" or "Cructan" '.

[143] Domesday Book, I, 90vb (Somerset, 8.28).

[144] Dickinson, 'West Monkton charter', p. 98; Creech St Michael (ten and a half hides) was held by Gunhild in 1066 (Domesday Book, I, 86vb [Somerset, 1.18]). Fleming ('Monastic lands', pp. 252 and 256) has cited Creech St Michael as a Glastonbury estate on the basis of S.237, but Grundy's solution apparently shows that the

Culm Davy (Devon)
See *Cumbe.*

Culmstock (Devon)
See *Culum.*

Culum (Devon)

Two entries in the contents-list of the *Liber terrarum* relate to land at *Culum*. One says only that Cynewulf (king of Wessex, A.D. 757–786), granted land there to a layman (S.1687; LT24). The other states that Cuthberht gave *Culum* to Sulca, who gave it to Glastonbury (S.1691; LT26). The texts of both of these charters are no longer extant. The first appeared on the list in the *Index chartarum* of grants to laymen of lands since lost (IC D2), but is not mentioned in the *De antiquitate*; we might assume that it was the means by which Cuthberht received the land. His grant to Sulca (*Christi ancilla*) likewise does not appear in the *De antiquitate*, which simply notes her gift of eleven hides at *Culum* to Glastonbury.[145] One and a half *hiwiscs* at *Colom* were included in Glastonbury's copy of King Æthelwulf's Decimation charter (S.303; A.D. 854).[146] Thereafter, there is a gap in the documentation until five hides at *Culumstocc* were claimed as the gift of King Æthelstan in ?A.D. 938 to the church of Exeter (S.386). In 1066, five hides at *Culmestoche* were held by the bishop of Exeter.[147]

C. and F. Thorn have suggested that the fifteen ploughlands at *Culmestoche* in Domesday Book indicate a holding larger than the five taxed hides; they have equated the estate held by the bishop of Exeter in 1066 with Glastonbury's eleven hides at *Culum* granted in the eighth century, with the addition of three hides at

---

Crycbeorh granted in that charter was not necessarily ever part of the estate which came to be known as Creech St Michael, although *Cantucuudu* may have included part of Creech. Blows, by deriving *Caric* from *cryc*, identified Centwine's grant with Creech St Michael, however ('Studies', p. 232). Although the place-name of the fifteen hides granted to a layman by King Alfred at *Cyricestun* in A.D. 882 (S.345) is derived from the same natural feature as in *Crycbeorh* (Mawer & Stenton, *The Place-names of Worcestershire*, p. 107, and Ekwall, *The Concise Oxford Dictionary of English Place-names*, s.n. Creech, p. 129), Alfred's charter may not necessarily have applied to the land granted by King Centwine at *Crycbeorh* and *Cantucuudu*, as Fleming has assumed; Grundy associated the bounds of Alfred's *Cyricestun* with Norton Fitzwarren (*The Saxon Charters*, pp. 142–9).

[145] *De antiquitate*, §§48 and 69 (ed. & transl. Scott, pp. 106 and 142); *Cronica*, §§16 and 54 (edd. & transl. Carley & Townsend, pp. 40 and 106).

[146] Finberg (*The Early Charters of Devon and Cornwall*, p. 19) incorrectly translated the amount, *opþer healf hiwisc*, 'half the other, or second, hide' (i.e., one and a half), as half a hide. For this idiom, see Campbell, *Old English Grammar*, p. 285 (no. 690), and Mitchell, *Old English Syntax*, I.226 (no. 579). On the *hiwisc* as a land-unit equivalent to a hide and possibly representing a survival from an earlier system of organisation of the landscape, see Costen, 'Huish and Worth' and *The Origins*, pp. 94–5. On the Decimation charter, see above, *s.n. Brannocmynstre*, and below, *s.n.* Monk Okehampton, and pp. 322–4.

[147] Domesday Book, I, 101vb (Devon, 2.12).

Cumbe (also given to Glastonbury by Sulca).[148] Finberg, too, identified the *Culum* of Cynewulf's and Æthelwulf's grants as Culmstock, in the Culm Valley in Devon, over thirty miles from Glastonbury and a few miles upriver from the abbey's estate at Uffculme.[149] Stacy, however, has pointed out that Uffculme's fourteen hides in Domesday Book were the same as the combined total of *Cumbe* and *Culum*, and wondered whether *Culum-Cumbe* and Uffculme were the same estate.[150] This seems, too, to be the significance of the omission of *Culum* and the insertion of *Offaculum xxiiii hidas* (*recte* xiiii?) in the version of Æthelwulf's Decimation in the *De antiquitate*.[151]

If Glastonbury did acquire *Culum* from Cuthberht and Sulca in the eighth century,[152] how long it held the estate is unclear; the doubts about its identity make its subsequent history impossible to decide with certainty.[153] Æthelwulf's Decimation charter may show that *Culum* – wherever it was – was within the abbey's endowment before the date of that grant (A.D. 854). If Æthelwulf's Decimation granted not land but exemptions from dues or services which burdened land already held by the recipient, it might indicate that Glastonbury retained the property after Cuthberht's and Sulca's grants in the second half of the eighth century; *Culum*'s modest hidage in S.303 (one and a half hides as opposed to *Culum-Cumbe*'s fourteen or Culmstock's five) may not be a problem, as several places in the Decimation charter seem to represent only a portion of a larger estate.[154] If we were to accept the identification with Culmstock, there is no evidence of who owned the land thereafter until the mid-eleventh century: S.386, the charter of Æthelstan's grant of the estate to Exeter, is a forgery of that date;[155] Leofric, bishop of Exeter (A.D. 1050–1072), claimed (in the list of his gifts to the cathedral which is to be found at the beginning of the Exeter Book) to have 'recovered' Culmstock.[156] These two records, therefore, provide only a *terminus ante quem* of the second half of the eleventh century for Exeter's acquisition of the property. If Culmstock was Glastonbury's *Culum*, therefore, the abbey could

---

148 *Ibid.*, 2.12 (note). At least one of the *Cumbe* hides in Domesday Book, however, was assessed separately and belonged to a layman. See below, *s.n. Cumbe*.

149 Finberg, *The Early Charters of Devon and Cornwall*, p. 8. He equated *Cumbe* with Culm Davy.

150 Stacy, 'The estates', p. 12, n. 3. See below, *s.n.* Uffculme.

151 *De antiquitate*, §§53 and 69 (ed. & transl. Scott, pp. 112 and 142); *Cronica*, §§16 and 56 (edd. & transl. Carley & Townsend, pp. 40 and 108). On the different versions of the charter, see above, *s.n. Brannocmynstre*.

152 Edwards, *The Charters*, pp. 73–4, considered it likely.

153 If there was a relationship between *Culum* and the later Culmstock, it would be interesting to note that *Culum* was given first to a nun, who then gave it to Glastonbury. It has long been suggested by place-name scholars that the Old English element *-stoc* (which has several meanings) can denote a religious establishment. Was there perhaps a community of religious women at *Culum* in the second half of the eighth century? See Ekwall, *The Concise Oxford Dictionary of English Place-names*, *s.n. stoc*, p. 443.

154 See above, *s.n. Brannocmynstre*, or below, *s.n.* Monk Okehampton, and pp. 322–4.

155 Chaplais, 'The authenticity', pp. 5–7.

156 *Ibid.*, p. 7; the text of this list is in *Anglo-Saxon Charters*, ed. & transl. Robertson, p. 226 (Appendix I, no. 1).

perhaps have held it till then or, alternatively, could have lost it any time after the mid-ninth century. If, however, the *Culum* and *Cumbe* granted in the eighth century (and possibly exempted from some secular burdens in the ninth) represent not Culmstock but the estate later called Uffculme, which Glastonbury held until the Conquest,[157] a more enduring relationship appears to be signalled. The difficulty of ascertaining where exactly in the Culm Valley *Culum*, *Cumbe*, *Culumstocc*, and *Offaculum* lay – and how they related to one another and to the modern settlements bearing associated names – prevents us from drawing firm conclusions about their history.

Cumbe (Devon)

According to the contents-list of the *Liber terrarum*, Cynewulf, king of Wessex, also gave land at *Cumbe iuxta Culum* to the layman Cuthberht (S.1683; LT25). Land at *Cumbe* which was granted by King Eadred to Wulfric (S.1745; LT126) may have been the same estate. In the *De antiquitate* Cuthberht's grant is not recorded, but we find it said there that (apparently during Cynewulf's reign) Sulca (*Christi ancilla*) gave three hides at *Cumbe* along with eleven at *Culum*, although the summary of grants presents the three hides at *Cumbe* as the gift of Cynewulf's *minister* Æthelheard.[158] Eadred's charter for Wulfric is not mentioned in the *De antiquitate*, and no other evidence of transactions relating to *Cumbe* survives. One hide at *Cumbe*, identified as Culm Davy in Hemyock parish in Devon, was held in Domesday Book by a layman.[159] If this was part of Glastonbury's eighth-century *Cumbe*, the other two hides must have been transferred elsewhere or the assessment lowered. However, the possibility that *Cumbe*'s three hides were combined with the eleven at *Culum* to form the estate later called Uffculme (which Glastonbury still held in the mid-eleventh century) has been raised above.[160] The lone hide at *Cumbe* in lay hands in Domesday Book may therefore be unconnected with Glastonbury (*Cumbe* is, after all, a very common name, especially in the region) or, perhaps, may be related to the *Cumbe* granted by Eadred to Wulfric.

Cumtone

See Compton Beauchamp and Compton Dundon.

Cympanhamme

A charter on the *Index chartarum* recorded the grant by King Edmund to a layman of land at *Cympanhamme* (S.1733; IC D14), on the list of lands lost. This transaction appears nowhere else in Glastonbury's archive, except among the *alia* [*maneria*] *data Glastonie* of §70 of the *De antiquitate* (as *Scippamhame*).[161]

---

157 See below, *s.n.* Uffculme.

158 *De antiquitate*, §§48 and 69 (ed. & transl. Scott, pp. 106 and 142); *Cronica*, §§16 and 54 (edd. & transl. Carley & Townsend, pp. 40 and 106). The text of the *De antiquitate* may be corrupt here; confusion between *Culum* (given by Sulca, according to the *Liber terrarum*) and *Cumbe iuxta Culum* could account for the possibly erroneous attribution of the latter to Sulca's gift. See above, *s.n.* Culum.

159 Domesday Book, I, 115va (Devon, 36.18 and notes).

160 See above, *s.n.* Culum, and below, *s.n.* Uffculme.

161 *De antiquitate*, §70 (ed. & transl. Scott, p. 144). See above, pp. 24–6.

Finberg suggested that this otherwise unidentified place might be Shipham (in the Mendips north of Axbridge), where four hides were in secular hands in the later eleventh century, according to Domesday Book.[162] There is no evidence to connect Glastonbury with Shipham, and no other pre-Conquest sources survive to offer information on the estate. A range of possibilities exists: perhaps the grant was never meant for the abbey; alternatively, an intended transfer may never have taken effect; or, Glastonbury may have received the land from Edmund but lost it before 1066; *Cympanhamme* may also have changed its name, appearing in the record thereafter in another guise. The same effect would be achieved if it had been incorporated into another estate and its name lost.

Cynemersforda

Another charter on the list of grants to laymen of lands subsequently lost was for land at *Cynemersforda*, given by Cynewulf, king of Wessex (S.1688; IC D3). In common with ten other places on this list, *Cynemersforda* also appears on the list of *alia [maneria] data Glastonie* in §70 of the *De antiquitate*.[163] It appears nowhere else in the pre-Conquest archive and remains unidentified. Finberg suggested Quemerford (in Calne, Wiltshire) or Kempsford (Gloucestershire) as possible identifications.[164] According to Domesday Book, Calne was held in 1066 by the king as unhidated land; twenty-one hides at Kempsford were in lay hands.[165] The same range of options applies to *Cynemersforda* as to the other estates which appear only on List D and in §70: that the grant was never intended for the abbey; that the transfer was somehow blocked; that the land was lost between the time of the original grant and 1066; or that it changed its name and appears in the record in another guise.

Damerham (Wiltshire / Hampshire)

A diploma is extant in the name of King Edmund to his second wife, Æthelflæd, granting one hundred hides of land at three places, Damerham and Martin (now in Hampshire but in Wiltshire until 1895)[1] and Pentridge (in Dorset) in A.D. 944x946 (S.513). The grant was for Æthelflæd's lifetime only, with reversion to Glastonbury. A diploma of Edmund for these three estates – which is listed among the contents of the *Liber terrarum* – named Glastonbury, not the queen, as the recipient (LT37); a notice of the charter appears (with all three estates named) in List A of the *Index chartarum*, the list of lands granted directly to the abbey (IC A9).[2] In the *De antiquitate* the circumstances are interpreted slightly differently, with the statement that Æthelflæd gave the hundred hides at Edmund's command;

---

162 Finberg, *The Early Charters of Wessex*, p. 134; Domesday Book, I, 94rb (Somerset, 21.79).

163 *De antiquitate*, §70 (ed. & transl. Scott, p. 144). See above, pp. 24–6.

164 Finberg, *The Early Charters of Wessex*, p. 179.

165 Domesday Book, I, 64vb and 169ra (Wiltshire, 1.1, and Gloucestershire, 60.1).

1 Darlington, 'Text and translation of the Wiltshire geld rolls', p. 202.

2 It is at least possible that there was a charter other than S.513, also in Edmund's name and a direct grant to Glastonbury, which these references represent. For a possibly comparable situation, see below, *s.n. Stane*.

in the summary, however, the grant is simply presented as a gift to the abbey by King Edmund.[3] Damerham – at least in King Alfred's reign – appears to have been the site of a religious community which held land in its own right,[4] possibly a royal establishment which was transferred to Glastonbury only after Æthelflæd died. It might not be fanciful to attribute this transfer to the influence of the new ideals of monastic reform. More practically, E.H. Lane Poole described Damerham as 'the principal endowment of the refounded convent' of Glastonbury, by which Edmund financed Glastonbury's revival;[5] as in fact we know very little about the way reform was effected at Glastonbury (or, indeed, when), this speculation may not be useful. But the transfer of such a large and wealthy estate must, whatever the context, have been a significant act. Glastonbury still held Damerham in 1066, assessed then at fifty-two hides, but experiencing some *confusio terrae* in 1086, with a greatly increased value, still in the course of adjustment; one hide at Damerham also belonged to the church of Cranborne.[6] Martin is thought to have been included in Damerham's assessment in Domesday Book.[7] Pentridge was separately assessed (for six hides) and recorded in the Dorset return. In 1066 it was held from Glastonbury by Wulfweard, who may have been a thegn of Queen Edith (and Queen Emma before her).[8]

The conditions imposed in S.513, requiring Æthelflæd to return the estates to the abbey, were apparently fulfilled in her will, which included the bequest of Damerham to Glastonbury (S.1494; A.D. 962x991, probably after 975).[9] A complication arises when we consider the evidence of another will, that of King Eadred, in which Damerham was also bequeathed, but to the Old Minster, Winchester (S.1515; A.D. 951x955). How was it that Eadred granted to Winchester an estate which Æthelflæd had held by a royal diploma since the 940s and which was earmarked for Glastonbury after her death? And why does the Winchester archive know nothing of Damerham? The logical answer to the second question would appear to be that Eadred's bequest to Winchester never took place; it seems very

---

[3] *De antiquitate*, §§55 and 69 (ed. & transl. Scott, pp. 114 and 142); *Cronica*, §§16 and 64 (edd. & transl. Carley & Townsend, pp. 40 and 122). All three estates are named in these references.

[4] See King Alfred's will (S.1507; *Alfred the Great*, transl. Keynes & Lapidge, pp. 178 and 326).

[5] Lane Poole, *Damerham and Martin*, p. 51.

[6] Domesday Book, I, 66va and 67va (Wiltshire, 7.1 and 11.2).

[7] Darlington, 'Text and translation of the Wiltshire geld rolls', p. 202; the three holdings in *Mertone* held by *seruientes regis* were identified by Darlington ('Translation of the text of the Wiltshire Domesday', pp. 164 and 166) as in Marten, near Great Bedwyn, rather than Martin, near Damerham, which was a *membrum* of the manor of Damerham in A.D. 1171; Stacy, 'The estates', p. 243. See below, *s.n.* Martin.

[8] Domesday Book, I, 77va (Dorset, 8.5). Glastonbury had lost it to the king by 1086. The holder in 1066 may have been Wulfweard the White, and if so Pentridge may have been taken with Wulfweard's other lands (which he had perhaps held from Queen Edith) when they were returned to the royal demesne. On Wulfweard and the descent of his property, see Loud, 'An introduction to the Somerset Domesday', p. 17.

[9] *Anglo-Saxon Wills*, ed. & transl. Whitelock, pp. 34–7 and 137–41 (no. 14).

unlikely that Æthelflæd gave up Damerham in her lifetime.[10] The first question is less easy to address, due to our ignorance of the peculiar political circumstances which must have lain behind Eadred's will – both its composition and its status after his death.[11]

The bounds of S.513 are described in the fourteenth-century cartularies as 'per copiam in landbok'. Grundy analysed them and concluded that they applied to South Damerham, Martin, and the district of Allenford and Toyd. This land lies south of Salisbury, where Wiltshire, Dorset, and Hampshire meet. Although *Pentringtone* is named in the dispositive section of S.513, Grundy decided that no part of Pentridge was included in the bounds, which he judged to be late in date.[12] Reanalysis of the bounds might alter this conclusion but, if Grundy's solution is correct, the omission of Pentridge may indicate that it had been separated from Damerham – though not lost by Glastonbury – before the bounds were written; the evidence of Domesday Book suggests that this separation had taken place by 1066. Martin, not mentioned by name in Domesday Book or the bounds, may conversely have lost its independent identity and been absorbed into Damerham by the late Anglo-Saxon period. R.R. Darlington, in attempting to identify the estate granted by Edmund, acknowledged that the area covered was difficult to determine and that the discrepancy in hidage between Æthelflæd's one hundred hides and Domesday Book's fifty-two was not easy to explain.[13] Damerham must have lost a substantial proportion of its territory or experienced a very favourable reassessment in value.

The land granted covers a very large area and is over fifty miles from Glastonbury. At some distance from most of the abbey's other Wiltshire estates (which are in the north of the county), it nevertheless belongs to the eastward-looking movement of the endowment which seems to have begun in the 940s and to have been associated with Dunstan and the exploitation of new types of landscape.[14] We may take this as a dim reflexion of the kind of manipulation of land resources visible more clearly in Æthelwold's well documented development of the endowment of Ely Abbey.[15]

Edmund's grant to Æthelflæd, a specifically temporary alienation with reversion to Glastonbury, has important implications for the question of what exactly

---

10 The D-text of the Anglo-Saxon Chronicle shows that (some time before the late eleventh century) Æthelflæd was referred to as 'Æthelflæd of Damerham' (*s.a.* 946).

11 I am grateful to David Dumville for pointing out to me in detail the peculiarities of King Eadred's will.

12 Grundy, 'The Saxon land charters of Hampshire', pp. 65–6; he gave no more specific opinion on the date. Forsberg considered that part of Alderholt was also included (*A Contribution*, pp. 206–7), and Darlington suggested that Compton Chamberlayne, though (like Pentridge) assessed separately in 1066, may have been included in Edmund's grant.

13 Darlington, 'Introduction to the Wiltshire Domesday', p. 96.

14 Stacy, 'The estates', pp. 2–3. See above, map 7, and also *s.n.* Badbury, Christian Malford, Grittleton, Idmiston, *Kyngton*, and Nettleton.

15 See *Anglo-Saxon Ely*, edd. & transl. Keynes & Kennedy, and *Liber Eliensis*, ed. Blake, pp. 63–117 and 395–9.

charters were intended to achieve.[16] Edmund's charter in effect adopted the royal diploma's form in order to create, not bookland, but loanland or temporary tenure,[17] although it seems that more permanent possession was envisaged for the next holder after Æthelflæd (that is, Glastonbury). The formulation is unique among Glastonbury's charters, but it is impossible, unfortunately, to assess to what extent it represented abnormal circumstances. In any event, the tenure thus instituted for Æthelflæd did not loosen Glastonbury's hold on Damerham, which remained an important part of its endowment in the post-Conquest period.[18] The probable identification of the mid-eleventh-century tenant of Pentridge as Wulfweard the White, however, seems to reveal some sort of continuing connexion between that estate and the queen, more than a century after the grant recorded in S.513 – a connexion which may have been a contributing cause of Glastonbury's loss of the estate.[19]

Deuerel (Wiltshire)

A charter apparently in the *Liber terrarum* recorded the grant by King Æthelstan of *Deuerel* to one Wulfhelm, who gave it to Glastonbury (S.1714; LT51). The text of this charter does not survive; it was presumably the document listed in MS. 39a (L46, among the possessions of the *camerarius*) described as the grant of *Deuerellangbrigg* to Wulfhelm by Æthelstan. In the *De antiquitate* Wulfhelm is described as the archbishop of Canterbury (*ca* A.D. 926–941) and it is specified there that the grant of *Deuerel* was made with Æthelstan's consent and that the estate was of twenty hides.[20] Glastonbury held two estates called *Deurel* in 1066, each of ten hides. These have been identified as Longbridge Deverill and Monkton Deverill (the latter also known as Over Deverill).[21] The obvious interpretation – a twenty-hide estate of Deverill, granted by Æthelstan, split into two and

---

16 See below, pp. 321–5.

17 As has been pointed out by Simon Keynes, *The Diplomas of King Æthelred*, pp. 32–3. Loanland, however, may not have been simply land held by lease; examples from Worcester show that land covered by a formal ecclesiastical lease could be categorised as bookland (in S.1347, for example, a Latin lease by Bishop Oswald is followed by a vernacular note which implies that the lease converted the estate concerned from loanland to bookland). Loanland as such was presumably a temporary alienation of a different kind. On Glastonbury's leases see below, pp. 305–9.

18 Recorded as Glastonbury's in Domesday Book, Damerham was evidently seized (by an unnamed predator) not long thereafter, as its recovery in the early twelfth century by Abbot Henry of Blois was recorded in the *Cronica* (§88 [edd. & transl. Carley & Townsend, p. 164]). Stacy has attributed some difficulties to appropriations by the canons there; they were ejected by Abbot Henry of Blois ('The estates', p. 105). Damerham was also apparently seized by Wells at some point during Glastonbury's later struggles with the cathedral, as its return is recorded in the third composition between the two churches (A.D. 1266; *The Great Chartulary*, ed. Watkin, I.96 [no. 147]). On these disputes, see above, p. 12.

19 See above, p. 105, n. 8.

20 *De antiquitate*, §§54 and 69 (ed. & transl. Scott, pp. 112 and 142); *Cronica*, §§16 and 60 (edd. & transl. Carley & Townsend, pp. 40 and 112). The *Cronica* adds that the gift was *pro uestimentis monachorum*.

21 Domesday Book, I, 66va and 66vb (Wiltshire, 7.3 [and note] and 7.16).

tenurially separate by 1066, with later epithets added to distinguish the two parts – is called into question by the fact that the later estates bearing these names are not contiguous, and by the item which follows Æthelstan's grant in the contents-list of the *Liber terrarum*: a grant by King Æthelstan, this time to the layman Osfrith, of land at *Uuerdeuerel*, which land Osfrith gave to Glastonbury (S.1713; LT52). The only other record of this grant occurs in the *De antiquitate*, where it is said that Osfrith's gift was confirmed by King Æthelstan and consisted of ten hides at *Uuerdeuerel, hoc est Munecaton*.[22] If Osfrith gave Monkton Deverill's ten hides to the abbey, they cannot have been included in Wulfhelm's twenty-hide gift, unless Osfrith antedated Wulfhelm and his gift had returned to the king. If Osfrith's grant did not precede that of Wulfhelm, the argument which has been used elsewhere to explain the presence of a seemingly extraneous charter to a layman – that it was simply kept by the holder of the estate as a title-deed and was not the means of transfer of the land in question into the hands of the church which preserved the charter – would not necessarily apply, for it is not the *De antiquitate* alone (frequently unreliable on just this point) but also the contents-list of the *Liber terrarum* which records that both Wulfric *and* Osfrith gave their estates to the abbey. Perhaps this was an error made by the copyist of the cartulary or the contents-list. Or perhaps the error was in the *De antiquitate*, and Wulfhelm received not twenty hides but ten, which would fit the ten hides of Longbridge Deverill. Or perhaps Osfrith's gift was short-lived. Without more information we can only speculate.

In A.D. 968 King Edgar supposedly confirmed Wilton Abbey's possession of a twenty-hide estate at a place called *Defereal* which previously had been granted to Wilton by *Wulsrythe* (S.766). Richard Colt Hoare thought that the bounds of this charter applied to Kingston Deverill, but Grundy rejected the identification of its (very vague) landmarks as 'obviously wrong'; he could not himself offer a location, however.[23] If this estate was the same as Glastonbury's *Deuerel*, it would indicate that the abbey lost the land in the middle of the tenth century but had regained it by 1066.

Other Deverills also appear in Domesday Book; four estates of this name, totalling twenty-one hides and half a virgate, were in lay hands in 1066. These were the later Brixton Deverill, Kingston Deverill, and Hill Deverill (two holdings), with no discernible connexion with Glastonbury (or Wilton) in the eleventh century.[24] It is possible that all the estates of this name had formed part of a large land-unit called Deverill, south of Warminster (some twenty-five miles east of Glastonbury), which had fragmented before the mid-tenth century. They could, however, have simply taken their names from the nearby river (the Wylye, also

---

22 *De antiquitate*, §§54 and 69 (ed. & transl. Scott, pp. 112 and 142); *Cronica*, §§16 and 60 (edd. & transl. Carley & Townsend, pp. 40 and 112). The *Cronica* has *Ouerdeuerel, id est Estmunkatun* in §60.

23 Hoare, *Registrum Wiltunense*, p. 14; Grundy, 'Saxon land charters of Wiltshire', *Archaeological Journal* 77 (1920), pp. 109–10. (Grundy misrepresented Hoare as having identified the bounds with Longbridge Deverill.) Darlington, too, considered *Defereal* unidentified: 'Introduction to the Wiltshire Domesday', p. 93.

24 Domesday Book, I, 68va, 69va, and 72vb (Wiltshire, 17.1, 19.1, 24.18, 48.8, and notes).

known as the Deverill),[25] and have had no early tenurial connexion with each other or with Glastonbury's lands of the same name.

Dinnington (Somerset)

A modest holding of three virgates in the independent estate of Dinnington, outside Ilminster in the south of Somerset, over twenty miles from Glastonbury, was held from the abbey TRE by Eadmer Ator and TRW by Siward, according to Domesday Book.[26] As Stacy has pointed out, these three virgates may comprise the three missing from the eight-hide total of neighbouring Kingstone, a Glastonbury estate.[27] Dinnington itself consisted of three hides in the hands of first Eadmer and then Siward, apparently independent of any connexion with Glastonbury in 1066.[28] It is not clear whether Glastonbury's three virgates escaped from Kingstone into Dinnington, or whether Dinnington, perhaps originally an estate held by the abbey, had lost them in gaining its independence. Robert Dunning has suggested that Kingstone and Dinnington formed a single unit, held by Glastonbury, in the tenth and eleventh centuries.[29] No documentation for Dinnington survives before Domesday Book, but notice of a lost charter in the *De antiquitate* for *Kingestan*, in which eight hides were granted to Abbot Dunstan by King Edmund, may suggest that the three virgates at Dinnington – if they were then attached to Kingstone – came by this means into Glastonbury's hands.[30] They maintained a separate identity from the remainder of the Dinnington estate until the fourteenth century.[31]

The presence of the three virgates in the list of *Terrae occupatae* of the *Liber Exoniensis* – generally land which had been lost but including also land re-organised after 1066 – may suggest that their dislocation can be dated 1066x1086.

Ditcheat (Somerset)

A grant of twenty-five hides at Ditcheat and five at Lottisham, in the name of Æthelwulf, king of Wessex, to his *princeps* Eanwulf,[32] dated 842, survives in the mid-fourteenth-century cartularies (S.292). Separate boundary descriptions of the

---

25 Darlington, 'Introduction to the Wiltshire Domesday', p. 49.

26 Domesday Book, I, 90vb (Somerset, 8.36).

27 Stacy, 'The estates', p. 49. Kingstone was lost to the Count of Mortain in 1086, and the three virgates at Dinnington appear at the head of the list of Glastonbury's lost land which ends its main entry in Domesday Book. Kingstone's own entry is at Domesday Book, I, 92ra (Somerset, 19.10).

28 Domesday Book, I, 99ra (Somerset, 47.10).

29 Dunning, 'Kingstone', pp. 203–4.

30 *De antiquitate*, §§55 and 69 (ed. & transl. Scott, pp. 114 and 142); *Cronica*, §§16 and 64 (edd. & transl. Carley & Townsend, pp. 40 and 120).

31 Dunning, 'Dinnington', pp. 147–8.

32 This was presumably the ealdorman who led the men of Somerset to victory against a Danish army at the mouth of the River Parrett (ASC 845). His local associations are presumably revealed by the reference to him as *Eanulf penearding* (Pennard being the name of two estates adjacent to Glastonbury) in S.1445, a letter written to document a dispute over an estate in Wiltshire: *Select English Historical Documents*, ed. & transl.

two estates are given. This charter was apparently entered in the *Liber terrarum* (LT91), and a copy is listed in MS. 39a (L13). The *De antiquitate* records only the gift of the estates to Glastonbury by Eanwulf, with the consent of and confirmation by King Æthelwulf.[33] Glastonbury held thirty hides at Ditcheat in 1066, according to Domesday Book; sub-units at Hornblotton, Alhampton, and Lamyatt are named (but Lottisham is not).[34] Eight hides (unnamed) were lost from Ditcheat between 1066 and 1086. Seven of these may have been at Yarlington or at Stone (now in East Pennard).[35]

The village of Ditcheat is less than eight miles east of Glastonbury; Lamyatt lies just beyond it to the east, with Alhampton and Hornblotton to the southwest, bordering the Fosse Way. Lottisham is farther west still, closer to Glastonbury on the western side of the Fosse, next to Baltonsborough and south of Lydford. The nature of the relationships between these places and the chronology of their development is very obscure. Lottisham (then paired with Lydford) had appeared in an allegedly earlier grant by Lulla, *ancilla Christi*, by which she is said to have given Baltonsborough and *Scobbanwirht* to Glastonbury in A.D. 744 (S.1410) and to have left ten hides at Lottisham and Lydford to the *arbitrium* of Æthelbald, king of Mercia. Exactly what this meant is unclear, but Lottisham was evidently in the hands of the king of Wessex – with Ditcheat this time – in the mid-ninth century, if S.292 is genuine. Lottisham's subsequent disappearance from the pre-Conquest record and its omission (by name) from Domesday Book may indicate that it was no longer distinguished as a separate unit, having by 1066 been totally absorbed into Ditcheat: that the sum of Ditcheat and Lottisham in S.292 offers the same total as Ditcheat's in 1066 may support this conclusion.[36] Edwards's suggestion – that the appearance of *Scobbanwirht* in the bounds of S.292 could indicate that it too had been incorporated into Ditcheat by the mid-eighth century – did not face the difficulty that in that description *Scobbanwirht* occurs in the second set of bounds (for Lottisham).[37] Costen has proposed

---

Harmer, pp. 62 and 115 (no. 118); see also Keynes, 'The Fonthill letter', pp. 56–7. Eanwulf is also associated with the grant of Binegar and (perhaps) the transaction involving *Brunham* (*q.v.*). On Eanwulf's support for King Æthelbald's rebellion against his father *ca* A.D. 855, the rebels' associations with Glastonbury, and Blows's suggestion that this may have affected King Alfred's attitude to the abbey, see Asser's Life of King Alfred, §12 (ed. Stevenson, pp. 9–10 and 195–9; *Alfred the Great*, transl. Keynes & Lapidge, pp. 70 and 234–5, n. 26), and Blows, 'Studies', pp. 276–83.

33 *De antiquitate*, §§53 and 69 (ed. & transl. Scott, pp. 112 and 142); *Cronica*, §§16 and 56 (edd. & transl. Carley & Townsend, pp. 40 and 108) (twenty hides, not thirty, in the *Cronica*).

34 Domesday Book, I, 90vb (Somerset, 8.30). The sum of the parts is actually half a hide more than the thirty in the statement of assessment. For a map of the parts of Ditcheat, see Costen, 'The late Saxon landscape', p. 47.

35 For the former identification, see Stacy, 'The estates', p. 31, and *Somerset*, edd. & transl. Thorn & Thorn, p. 356; see below, *s.n.* Yarlington. Morland ('The Glastonbury manors', pp. 72 and 79–80) found the hides at Stone (*q.v*) instead.

36 Somerset, 8.30 (edd. & transl. Thorn & Thorn, p. 356) (although Domesday Ditcheat is actually one half-hide larger); Edwards, *The Charters*, p. 44.

37 *Ibid.* See below, *s.n. Scobbanwirht*, for a possible later connexion with Lydford.

that the thirty hides of Ditcheat granted to Eanwulf in A.D. 842 had until then been part of the royal multiple estate of Bruton.[38]

It has been assumed that the thirty hides which were the subject of S.292, allegedly in A.D. 842, comprised the same parts which made up Ditcheat's thirty hides in 1066.[39] If that were the case, however, we should not expect to find any of these latter lands being granted separately to the abbey, but this is what we do in fact discover. Alhampton, Hornblotton, Lamyatt, and Lottisham appear all to have been the subject of grants distinct from that of Ditcheat itself: Alhampton and Lottisham ostensibly before, but Hornblotton and Lamyatt *after*, Æthelwulf's grant. Alhampton may have been a gift by King Cynewulf to a layman in the eighth century (IC D1);[40] Lottisham, as we have seen, was left by Lulla to Æthelbald of Mercia to dispose of (S.1410); Hornblotton (said to be *iuxta Diches-gete*) was given to Eanwulf by King Æthelbald, according to the contents-list of the *Liber terrarum* (S.1699; LT92);[41] in the *De antiquitate* it is claimed that Eanwulf (who had given Ditcheat) gave Hornblotton to Glastonbury.[42] Lastly, Lamyatt was recorded as a gift of King Eadwig to Cynric (LT88) (although no source, not even the *De antiquitate*, mentions a subsequent gift by Cynric to Glastonbury).[43] If these charters can be accepted as reflecting real transactions, the bonds holding the parts of Ditcheat together seem to have been very fluid, especially in the ninth century.

It is possible, however, to interpret the situation quite differently. There is no documentary evidence for the inclusion of Hornblotton and Lamyatt in Ditcheat until Domesday Book. It might, therefore, be preferable to envisage, not an early multiple estate fragmenting and reassembling, but small estates, held by laymen, which came into Glastonbury's hands and were combined together in or after the ninth century. Stacy, who has suggested that Ditcheat and Hornblotton might have gone to Glastonbury as Eanwulf's soul-scot, has interpreted Ditcheat's pre-Conquest history as a sequence of attachments of properties to an estate-centre.[44] If this model is apposite, however, one might expect Ditcheat's assessment to

---

[38] Costen, *The Origins*, p. 113.

[39] *Somerset*, 8.30 (edd. & transl. Thorn & Thorn, p. 356).

[40] Its presence on List D, however, a list of charters for lands lost, must at least raise the question of mistaken identity, for Alhampton was still in Ditcheat – and therefore a possession of the abbey – in the fourteenth century (*A Feodary*, ed. Weaver, p. xxxvii). See above, *s.n. Aldamtone*.

[41] The place-name Hornblotton has been explained as the *tun* of the hornblower or hornblowers (Ekwall, *The Concise Oxford Dictionary of English Place-names*, *s.n.* Hornblotton, p. 250). The royal forest of Selwood is only a few miles to the east.

[42] *De antiquitate*, §§53 and 69 (ed. & transl. Scott, pp. 112 and 142); *Cronica*, §§16 and 56 (edd. & transl. Carley & Townsend, pp. 40 and 108). Eanwulf is also said to have given Binegar (*q.v.*).

[43] Lamyatt does appear in §70, however (ed. & transl. Scott, p. 144). On the significance of this, see above, pp. 24–6.

[44] Stacy, 'The estates', pp. 31–2. Eanwulf was buried at Glastonbury (*Chronicon Æthelweardi*, Book IV, §2: *The Chronicle of Æthelweard*, ed. & transl. Campbell, p. 36). Costen, on the other hand, has suggested that Glastonbury may not have received Ditcheat until after A.D. 940 ('Dunstan, Glastonbury, and the economy', p. 43).

reflect its growth. But the first record of Ditcheat (S.292) described it as comprising thirty hides, an assessment which apparently stayed the same (unless altered in the extant text in the cartulary) during this process of expansion.

The bounds of S.292 might help to clarify this question. Grundy concluded that the first set of bounds in the charter covered Ditcheat itself and Alhampton, while the second set (labelled *Lottesham*) referred to the whole of West Bradley, which he suggested had originally been called Lottisham.[45] Hornblotton and Lamyatt were not included. Grundy admitted, however, that the determination of the landmarks was very difficult, although to the west they seem to have had some relationship with the boundary of Baltonsborough in S.1410.[46] Morland disagreed with Grundy's identification of Lottisham with West Bradley, insisting on its (Lottisham's) status as a detached part of Ditcheat.[47] He agreed that Hornblotton and Lamyatt (and possibly Stone) were outside the bounds, and went one step further, in the same direction as Stacy, claiming that they had not been included in Æthelwulf's grant in the first place and were outside the original thirty hides. When they were added to Ditcheat (at an unspecified date) the hidage was not altered, this being a case of 'hide reduction by boundary extension'.[48] This argument ignores the crucial complicating factor of a likely discrepancy between the date of the grant and that of the description of the bounds: what stage of Ditcheat's development do the bounds really represent?[49] Morland's proposal of territorial expansion without raised hidage offers a convenient solution to an awkward problem, here and elsewhere, but its resolution of the difficulties may be excessively neat; the sources offer us insufficient information for a solution.

In any event, it seems that Ditcheat may exhibit a different pattern in comparison with Shapwick and Walton, two other manors in Domesday Book where the sub-units are named;[50] these latter seem to be relics of a fragmented multiple estate of the earliest period of the endowment. Whether this model has any relevance for Ditcheat is more uncertain.

Doulting (Somerset)

Doulting presents problems of a different sort.[51] There was apparently a charter in the name of King Eadred in the *Liber terrarum* for *Dulting* and *Nunig* (S.1742;

---

45 Grundy, *The Saxon Charters*, pp. 55–8 and 72–4. For a more recent survey of the first set only, see Costen, 'The late Saxon landscape', p. 47.

46 *Whatleighe* and *Nimede* appear in both the bounds of S.1410 and of S.292, and *Scobbanwirht*, granted in the former, is in the latter mentioned as the site of twelve acres of meadow belonging to Lottisham.

47 Morland, 'The Glastonbury manors', pp. 71–2.

48 Morland, 'Hidation', p. 77.

49 Peter Kitson has dated the boundary description to the tenth or eleventh century (in his unpublished work on charter-bounds); Grundy thought that it was probably twelfth-century in date (*The Saxon Charters*, p. 72). Costen has taken it to be tenth-century, but representing the mid-ninth-century boundary of the estate (*The Origins*, p. 122).

50 Separate sub-units are noted for several more estates in Domesday Book, but, lacking place-names, they cannot be traced in the documents.

51 See also the discussion of Pilton below.

LT32). Its text does not survive but, according to the *De antiquitate*, it involved a restoration to Glastonbury.[52] Although no evidence exists to confirm this, the record of a genuine transfer of twenty hides there to the abbey may be preserved in the *De antiquitate* in the mention of an earlier transaction involving Doulting and King Æthelwulf in A.D. 851, although the form in which it is couched is rather dubious. It too is called a restoration.[53] Looking still further back, we come to an entry in the *Index chartarum*, '[Yna rex] de Dulting', which implies an even earlier grant to Glastonbury (IC A5). In the *De antiquitate*, too, Doulting is listed as a gift of King Ine, and in the spurious Great Privilege in Ine's name (S.250) it is likewise cited as one of his gifts.[54] A charter of King Ine was entered in the Doulting section of the mid-fourteenth-century cartularies (S.247), and duplicate charters in his name for Doulting were listed in MS. 39a (L9). According to Domesday Book, Glastonbury held twenty hides at Doulting.[55]

From this evidence, it would appear that Ine granted Doulting to Glastonbury, following which several restorations or confirmations by the king were necessary. Unfortunately, close examination of the early documents raises questions about this interpretation. The charter (S.247) in Ine's name in the Doulting section of the cartularies, for a start, does not claim to dispose of Doulting, but rather of land on the River *Duluting* – not necessarily the same thing. This charter is not an authentic text, but an updated version, written possibly in the tenth century, of S.248, a multiple grant by King Ine which is probably authentic (though extant only in a later copy).[56] S.248 disposes of lands in the vaguest of terms, and it is here, probably, that the confusion began which obscures Doulting's history.

S.248 included a grant of twenty hides on the River *Duluting*; S.247, its 'modernised' version, kept this wording but attached Old English bounds to the grant, bounds which reveal that it was not Doulting but Pilton (with Croscombe and part of Shepton Mallet, west of the Fosse) which was granted – or at least, was at issue when the bounds were written.[57] S.247 was entered in the cartularies

---

[52] *De antiquitate*, §§57 and 69 (ed. & transl. Scott, pp. 118 and 144); omitted from the *Cronica*.

[53] *De antiquitate*, §§53 and 69 (ed. & transl. Scott, pp. 112 and 142); in §53, Doulting was said to have been transferred to the church *in ius monasteriale* by Abbot *Elmund*, with the consent of Bishop *Alhstan* and King Æthelwulf, who added twenty hides *ad supplementum uite regularis*, while in §69 Æthelwulf is said to have given twenty-five hides (*sic*) and returned (*reddidit*) Doulting. The *Cronica* (§§16 and 56, edd. & transl. Carley & Townsend, pp. 40 and 108) follows the *De antiquitate*.

[54] *De antiquitate*, §§40 and 69 (ed. & transl. Scott, pp. 94 and 140); *Cronica*, §§16 and 47 (edd. & transl. Carley & Townsend, pp. 40 and 92); *De antiquitate*, §42 (ed. & transl. Scott, p. 98) (ten hides only), and *Cronica*, §49 (edd. & transl. Carley & Townsend, p. 96) (twenty hides), for the Great Privilege.

[55] Domesday Book, I, 90va (Somerset, 8.23). Doulting included three hides and one virgate at *Cerletone*, which Morland identified as Charlton, now in Shepton Mallet ('The Glastonbury manors', p. 72).

[56] See Abrams, 'A single-sheet facsimile'.

[57] Among language-experts there is disagreement on the date of these bounds: Peter Kitson and Margaret Gelling have placed them in the second half of the tenth century

under Pilton as well as Doulting; in the contents-list of the *Liber terrarum* a grant of Pilton by Ine is noted (LT9).[58] It was probably S.247.[59] Were the *Index chartarum* and MS. 39a references to a charter of Ine for Doulting citing this document as well? The presence of S.247 in the Doulting section could be explained either as an error (confusion of the name of the river, *Duluting*, now the Sheppey, and the name of the estate in which the source of the river is to be found) or as a deliberate attempt to provide a pre-Conquest title-deed for an estate which lacked one. Glastonbury held twenty hides at Pilton in 1066, in addition to the estate at Doulting.[60]

This confusion over the name necessarily calls into question all the references to Doulting cited above. We cannot be certain whether they referred to Doulting, the estate, or to the hides on the *Duluting*, which at least in S.247 meant neighbouring Pilton. The endorsements of S.248 show that its *Duluting* hides were thought to apply to Doulting, not Pilton, in the later middle ages.[61] Unfortunately, exactly what was granted in the eighth century remains obscure.

In his *Gesta pontificum Anglorum*, William of Malmesbury stated that the *uilla* of *Dulting* had been given to Glastonbury by Aldhelm,[62] but no claim of this sort survives in Glastonbury's archive. It was at Doulting that Aldhelm died in A.D. 709 or 710; Glastonbury reputedly built a stone church there in commemoration.[63] Was it this Doulting, or the estate which came to be called Pilton, which was restored to the abbey in A.D. 851? Should we interpret rigorously the comment in the *De antiquitate* that *Dulting* was restored at that time and twenty hides added to it? We might then have a glimpse of a pair of estates, one (the gift of Ine?) appropriated and then returned by Æthelwulf with the gift of the other. The source may not, however, bear such close interpretation.[64] Eadred's subsequent restoration could have applied to either – or both – estates. And an extra twenty ploughlands in Domesday Pilton which did not pay tax may be relevant here.

These problems raised by S.247 and S.248 not only obscure the origins of the estates of Doulting and Pilton, but should serve as a warning: the more material we have, especially from the earlier period, the more complex – and confusing – the picture. It is worth remembering this in other cases where the record is less full and the story seemingly more simple.

(the former in his unpublished work on charter-bounds, the latter in a letter of 16 July, 1989), but Paul Bibire (in notes written in June 1991) has judged the two versions to be twelfth- and thirteenth-century, lacking any evidence of an Old English exemplar. I am grateful to them for their help on this question. For a map of the bounds, see Davidson, 'On the charters'.

58 Sawyer gave this a number (S.1672) though he raised the possibility (probably correct) that LT9 (S.1672) might have been S.247.
59 Although it may have been S.248.
60 Domesday Book, I, 90rb (Somerset, 8.20).
61 Abrams, 'A single-sheet facsimile', pp. 104 and 128, n. 142.
62 *Gesta pontificum Anglorum*, §228; ed. Hamilton, pp. 382–3.
63 *Ibid*.
64 One which Morland seems to have accepted ('The Glastonbury manors', p. 72).

Downhead (Somerset)

The record of King Æthelwulf's Decimation of A.D. 854 in the *De antiquitate* cites *Duneafd* among the list of lands attached to the king's grant.[65] *Duneafd* does not appear in the texts of S.303 in the mid-fourteenth-century cartularies, but more than one of these documents may have existed, or their lists may have been manipulated. It is unclear whether this land relates to the three hides at Downhead held by Glastonbury in 1066.[66] Of the two places of this name in Somerset, the estate recorded in Domesday Book may perhaps be identified with the Downhead midway between Shepton Mallet and Mells, about fifteen miles from Glastonbury.[67] No pre-Conquest evidence seems to survive for the other Downhead, which is located between Glastonbury's estate of Podimore Milton and the Camels, about ten miles south of Glastonbury.

Draycott (Somerset)

According to Domesday Book, Glastonbury had held an estate of two hides at Draycott in 1066; by 1086 it had lost it to the count of Mortain.[68] No pre-Conquest source records its earlier history.[69]

Draycott is about eight miles north of Glastonbury, to the south of Cheddar. It is mentioned as a landmark-point in the perambulation of the Twelve Hides of Glastonbury.[70]

Dulwich (Surrey)

A charter dated 967 in the name of King Edgar, granting land to the *comes* Ælfheah and his wife Ælfswith,[71] survives in the mid-fourteenth-century cartularies (S.747). The grant disposed of an unnamed piece of land on the Thames, twenty hides at *Mertone*, and five hides at *Dilwyhs*, the last two identified as Merton and Dulwich in Surrey, estates with no known connexion with Glastonbury; the Old English bounds are of Merton.[72] This charter was probably in the *Liber terrarum*, although the contents-list mentions only Merton, omitting Dulwich and the land on the Thames in the relevant entry (LT113).[73] In the cartularies

---

[65] *De antiquitate*, §§53 and 69 (ed. & transl. Scott, pp. 112 and 142); *Cronica*, §§16 and 56 (edd. & transl. Carley & Townsend, pp. 40 and 108). On this charter, see below, *s.n.* Monk Okehampton and pp. 322–4.

[66] Domesday Book, I, 90vb (Somerset, 8.35).

[67] Neighbouring Whatley was held from the abbot by the same Anglo-Saxon tenant (Wulfgar *monachus*).

[68] Domesday Book, I, 91ra and 92ra (Somerset, 8.39 and 19.12); see also the entry in the list of *Terrae occupatae* in the *Liber Exoniensis* (E 524a7).

[69] Morland ('The Glastonbury manors', p. 92) considered that it might be identified with *Easetenetone* (*q.v.*), presumably because Draycott adjoined Ashington (*Essentone* in Domesday Book) and lacked pre-Conquest documentation.

[70] *De antiquitate*, §72 (ed. & transl. Scott, p. 150); see below, *s.n.* Glastonbury.

[71] On Ælfheah, see Williams, '*Princeps Merciorum gentis*', especially pp. 147–54. On grants to Ælfheah and Ælfswith, see below, *s.n.* Idmiston.

[72] Gover *et al.*, *The Place-names of Surrey*, p. 25, n. 1.

[73] 'Edgarus de Meretone dat' Ælfheah. S.'

Edgar's charter (and S.551, also for Merton) was placed in the Damerham section, on the assumption that it related to Martin, in Wiltshire, which was part of the large estate of Damerham held by Glastonbury from the tenth century.[74] The compiler of the *Index chartarum* seems to have made the same mistake, for he entered the charter on List B, charters for estates given to laymen which Glaston-bury still held in A.D. 1247 (IC B7). The original author of the *De antiquitate*, however, seems to have known better, for no gift of Merton or Dulwich is men-tioned in the text. Dulwich makes a predictable appearance in §70, among the *alia* [*maneria*] *data Glastonie*, but (interestingly) without Merton – the compiler of this list may have thought that the latter had already been covered in the narra-tive.[75] Alternatively, he may have been noting a separate charter for Dulwich which has since been lost. Dulwich is not in Domesday Book by name, but Merton is recorded as being held by Earl Harold in 1066 and by the king in 1086.[76] It need not be assumed that Dulwich was absorbed into Merton before 1066; Merton is assessed in Domesday Book at the same number of hides (twenty) as it was in A.D. 967, *without* Dulwich. Their histories may not have run in tandem at all, but may have coincided only briefly in the grant by Edgar to Ælfheah. Dulwich, however, cannot be traced more closely, as no other charter for it survives.

Merton has a slightly more complex archival record. In addition to S.747, the extant charter of King Edgar to Ælfheah and Ælfswith, the text of an earlier grant by King Eadred, of twenty hides at *Mertone* to the layman Wulfric (probably Dunstan's brother),[77] also survives (S.551; A.D. 949).[78] This charter was in the *Liber terrarum* (LT112). The text reveals that the land at Merton had for a long time been held by Wulfric's family, and that the king had ordered a new charter to be written; the transaction is not mentioned in the *De antiquitate*. An even earlier charter may have applied to this estate. At the head of List B in the *Index chartarum* is an entry, *Cenwlfus de Mertone*, which preserves notice of a charter recorded nowhere else but in MS. 39a (S.1690; IC B1; L30). This could have been a grant by Cynewulf of Wessex or Cenwulf of Mercia, of Martin or Merton, being an earlier title-deed for either place.[79] It was kept (as indicated in MS. 39a) with the Damerham documents, but this could be another example of the same confu-sion which caused S.551 and S.747 to be misfiled.

No relationship between Merton or Dulwich and Glastonbury is visible in the pre-Conquest record, apart from the existence of these charters in the abbey's archive. However, other estates granted to Wulfric were subsequently acquired by

---

[74] See above, *s.n.* Damerham, and below, *s.n.* Martin.

[75] *De antiquitate*, §70 (ed. & transl. Scott, p. 144); on this list, see above, pp. 24–6.

[76] Domesday Book, I, 30va (Surrey, 1.5).

[77] See below, *s.n.* Grittleton.

[78] No bounds are attached to S.551 in the extant cartularies, but a marginal note refers the reader to the bounds to be found at the end of the *Liber terrarum* and also *in prima carta*, a reference to S.747 which precedes it in the manuscript; *The Great Chartulary*, ed. Watkin, III.628 (no. 1168).

[79] Or elsewhere; Finberg (*The Early Charters of Wessex*, p. 179) suggested Compton Martin in Somerset. Cenwulf ruled Mercia from A.D. 796 to 821.

Ælfswith, and by Glastonbury thereafter.[80] We cannot therefore do more than consider the usual options: that Glastonbury received, but lost, the land before 1066; that a grant was made but never took effect; or that Glastonbury never had any claim on Dulwich or Merton, their charters being deposited there solely for safe-keeping or for other (no longer discernible) reasons.

Dundon (Somerset)

According to the *De antiquitate*, five hides at *Dundene* were given by King Edgar to Abbot Sigegar.[81] No other record of this transaction survives. In 1066, *Dondeme* was a five-hide estate held from the abbot by a tenant.[82] The relationship of this estate to its neighbour, Compton Dundon, and to Walton, the large estate of which Compton Dundon was a part, is unclear.[83] It seems, however, that Dundon and *Contone* were not two names for the same place (now called Compton Dundon), at least, to judge from the existence of two different estates in Domesday Book.[84] The evidence for the period before 1066 is inconclusive, however, and Edgar's grant of *Dundene* (if genuine) could have been either a restoration of Compton Dundon or a grant of another five (neighbouring) hides.

Durborough (Somerset)

According to the contents-list, there was in the *Liber terrarum* a charter in the name of King Edgar to *Ældred* for land at *Diranbeorge* (S.1767; LT71). The text of the charter does not survive and no other evidence for this grant exists outside the *De antiquitate*, where it is said that Ælfhelm (*sic*) gave Glastonbury two hides there, confirmed by King Edgar.[85] Stacy has cited Durborough as a possible example of the gift by a layman of a food-rent to the church (rather than the transfer of land);[86] there is unfortunately no evidence to support this, as Glastonbury's two hides at Durborough cited in Domesday Book look no different from the entries for all the other abbatial estates held by tenants.[87] Presumably it was Durborough's distance from Glastonbury which suggested this idea to Stacy: the estate is near Stogursey in the eastern Quantocks, over twenty-five miles away and somewhat isolated from the abbey's nearest known pre-Conquest holding.

Easetenetone

A charter for this unidentified estate, granted by King Eadwig to *Wlfod*, is noted on the contents-list of the *Liber terrarum* (S.1758; LT130). It appears nowhere else in the archive, except in §70 of the *De antiquitate*, among the *alia [maneria] data Glastonie*, places with charters which had not been mentioned in the body of

---

[80] See below, *s.n.* Idmiston, *Kyngton*, and Tintinhull.
[81] *De antiquitate*, §§62 and 69 (ed. & transl. Scott, pp. 128 and 144); *Cronica*, §§16 and 73 (edd. & transl. Carley & Townsend, pp. 42 and 138).
[82] Domesday Book, I, 90rb (Somerset, 8.13).
[83] See above, *s.n.* Compton Dundon.
[84] *Contone*: Domesday Book, I, 90rb (Somerset, 8.11).
[85] *De antiquitate*, §§62 and 69 (ed. & transl. Scott, pp. 130 and 144); *Cronica*, §§16 and 73 (edd. & transl. Carley & Townsend, pp. 42 and 138).
[86] Stacy, 'The estates', p. 30.
[87] Domesday Book, I, 90ra (Somerset, 8.8).

that work.[1] This circumstance may suggest that the estate had never been Glaston-bury's property, or that it had been held only briefly; as *Easetenetone* is unidenti-fied, however, no conclusions can be drawn about its status or history.[2]

Eatumberesder

A charter of King Edmund for *Eatumberesder*, another unidentified location, is cited in the *Index chartarum* (S.1734; IC D13); it, too, appears nowhere else in the archival record except in §70 of the *De antiquitate* (as *Eatumberg*).[3] Wherever it may have been, the land – if it ever came into Glastonbury's hands – was apparently lost by A.D. 1247, as the charter appears on List D; the estate's absence from Glastonbury's entry in Domesday Book could suggest that it was not part of the church's endowment in 1066, but the failure of an estate of that name to appear as the holding of any other lord prevents us from drawing any conclusions about its status in 1066.

Edington (Somerset)

Edington was a five-hide sub-unit of Shapwick, according to Domesday Book.[4] No pre-Conquest documentation survives for it by name, but its history should probably be seen in the context of the break-up of the large early estate of *Pouelt* which may have extended across the whole of the Polden Hills; *Pouelt* is dis-cussed in detail below.

Edingworth (Somerset)

Glastonbury held two hides at Edingworth (*Iodenwrde*) in 1066.[5] No pre-Conquest charter granting land with this name exists; Edingworth, just north of Brent, appears to have been included in the original grant of that estate to Glas-tonbury in the late seventh century, as it lies within the (apparently contemporary) bounds of Brent as described in S.238.[6] The circumstances which detached it from Brent's twenty Domesday hides – and the date of this development – can only be guessed at.

    The derivation of the place-name has caused some difficulty: Old English

---

1   *De antiquitate*, §70 (ed. & transl. Scott, p. 144). See above, pp. 24–6.
2   Morland, attempting to match estates from Domesday Book which lack Anglo-Saxon documentation with Anglo-Saxon charters for estates not named in Domesday Book (a perilous exercise), has suggested ('The Glastonbury manors', p. 92) that this was Draycott (*q.v.*), which adjoined Ashington (*Essentone*, held by Godwine TRE and Vitalis TRW: Domesday Book, I, 94rb [Somerset, 21.94]).
3   *De antiquitate*, §70 (ed. & transl. Scott, p. 144). See above, pp. 24–6.
4   Domesday Book, I, 90ra (Somerset, 8.5).
5   Domesday Book, I, 90vb (Somerset, 8.34). Turner ('A selection', p. 155) and Morland ('The Glastonbury manors', p. 73, and review of *Domesday Book: Somerset*, p. 137) corrected the reading *Lodenwrde* of Farley's diplomatic edition of Domesday Book to *Iodenwrde*. This agrees with the form in the *Liber Exoniensis* (*Iodena Wirda*; E 171a1) as well as the later spellings. Ekwall listed the forms *Lodenwrde, Iodena Wirda, Hedeneworth, Edenworth, Edenewrthy*: *The Concise Oxford Dictionary of English Place-names*, pp. 160–1, *s.n.* Edingworth.
6   See above, *s.n.* Brent.

*Eow-denu, 'yew valley', does not suit the topography, and A.G.C. Turner's suggestion, deriving the first element from the Celtic *Ituna*, later **Idona*, a river-name, is problematical (according to Turner) because of the location of Edingworth on the old course of the River Axe.[7] Turner suggested that the name might have applied to a locality, rather than a stream, and might have borne the more appropriate meaning 'water' or 'wet place'.

Elborough (Somerset)

According to the contents-list of the *Liber terrarum*, Cynewulf, king of Wessex, gave *Elenbearo* to Æthelheard, who gave it to Glastonbury (S.1681; LT31). This charter was extant in A.D. 1247 (IC D4), but is not found in the later cartularies. The transaction may be represented by the statement in the *De antiquitate* that Æthelheard gave three hides at *Cedern*, which a marginal note identifies as *Elenbeorge*.[8] A gift of Elborough (or part of it) in its own name by King Eadred is also mentioned (with the additional information in the summary that it consisted of one hide).[9] Glastonbury held three hides at Elborough in 1066, which it lost before 1086 to the bishop of Coutances.[10]

The routine *caveat* against the evidence of marginal identifications in the Trinity manuscript of the *De antiquitate* applies here. Elborough may have been the thirteenth-century name of *Cedern* but, if so, why does the *Liber terrarum* appear to have used the name Elborough? Unless the writer of the contents-list substituted the contemporary name and suppressed the original one, the appearance of *Elenbearo* there could be evidence of a charter for Elborough for which no other record has survived, and which the author of the *De antiquitate* equated with the extant grant of a different estate – *Cedern* – to the same recipient.

Hazel Hudson and Frances Neale have also suggested that *Cedern id est Elenbeorge* is not to be identified as Elborough (which is near Hutton,[11] north of the Axe near the Severn and over twenty miles from Glastonbury), but as Oldbury near Cheddar.[12] If so, there is no evidence of when Elborough itself became Glastonbury's, although Eadred's restoration of one hide there provides a *terminus ante quem*. A charter which records the grant of five hides at *Burgh'* by King Edgar to his thegn Wulfmær (S.793; A.D. 973), generally taken to refer to Berrow, may perhaps be profitably considered here. Its attached boundary description – which mentions the River Axe – has so far eluded solution at Berrow. If indeed it

---

[7] Ekwall, *The Concise Oxford Dictionary of English Place-names*, pp. 160–1, *s.n.* Edingworth; Turner, 'A selection', pp. 155–6.

[8] *De antiquitate*, §§48 and 69 (ed. & transl. Scott, pp. 106 and 142); *Cronica*, §§16 and 54 (edd. & transl. Carley & Townsend, pp. 40 and 106). See above, *s.n. Cedern*.

[9] *De antiquitate*, §§57 and 69 (ed. & transl. Scott, pp. 118 and 142); *Cronica*, §§16 and 66 (edd. & transl. Carley & Townsend, pp. 42 and 124).

[10] Domesday Book, I, 91ra and 88ra (Somerset, 8.38 and 5.11).

[11] Finberg, *The Early Charters of Wessex*, pp. 117 and 137.

[12] Cited by Carley in *Cronica*, edd. & transl. Carley & Townsend, p. 288, n. 188. Carley has stated there that *Esenberge* in the *Cronica*'s version of Cynewulf's grant was distinct from the grant of *Cedern*, but the form of the phrasing ('tres hidas in Cedern id est Esenberge') seems to argue that the two were synonymous – at least in the view of the writer.

(or the grant alone, if the bounds are independent of the grant) did originally apply to Elborough, by the time the cartularies were compiled the charter had been misfiled.[13]

Elosaneg

According to the *Liber terrarum*, Centwine, king of Wessex, gave land at *Elosaneg* to an unnamed layman (S.1669; LT4). No other witness to this transaction exists in the archive, although *Elonsanige* appears among the *alia* [*maneria*] *data Glastonie* of §70 of the *De antiquitate*.[14] Since it is unidentified, there is no evidence to determine whether or not this land came into Glastonbury's hands. The *-eg* element (Old English for 'island') could suggest that the place concerned was one of the areas of raised ground in the Levels (such as Godney and Marchey), which one would expect to have belonged to the earliest stratum of endowments of the community of Glastonbury and with which Centwine is elsewhere associated.[15] 'Islands' elsewhere, however, are not unknown.

Escford

An entry in the contents-list of the *Liber terrarum* records a grant of *Escford* by King Edmund to Glastonbury (S.1723; LT58). This information is repeated only in the *De antiquitate*, where we are told further that the land consisted of half a hide *cum captura piscium*.[16] Elsewhere in the *De antiquitate*, a grant by King Ine to Abbot Berwald of half a hide at *Escford* with a fishery had been recorded.[17] Without further details, little can be made of this information, especially as *Escford* is unidentified. Finberg suggested that Ine's grant was probably of a ford on the River Axe, a judgment presumably based on the place-name. Ine also granted one hide and a fishery on that river to Abbot *Echfrid* in A.D. 719, according to the *De antiquitate*,[18] but there is no need to think that this was the same place – in fact, the difference in hidage suggests that it was not. The repetition by Edmund of Ine's grant of *Escford* could indicate that the land had been lost at some time, and that Glastonbury succeeded in retrieving it in the

---

[13] See above, *s.n.* Berrow. There is the difficulty, however, of different hidages. The place-names may also argue against this identification, but the absence of early forms hinders the interpretation. For Berrow, Ekwall cited only *at Burgh'* of S.793 (from the mid-fourteenth-century cartulary) (from Old English *beorg*, 'hill'), while for Elborough the earliest forms were *Illebera* and *Eleberie* from Domesday Book (Old English *bearu*, 'grove', with the personal name Ella): see *The Concise Oxford Dictionary of English Place-names*, pp. 39 and 162, *s.n.* Berrow and Elborough.

[14] *De antiquitate*, §70 (ed. & transl. Scott, p. 144); see above, pp. 24–6.

[15] Morland ('Hidation', p. 75) has suggested *Andersey* as a candidate for *Elosaneg*. See above, *s.n.* Andersey. On these 'islands', see below, *s.n.* Glastonbury. Centwine may have been the donor of at least part of the core-estate of Glastonbury.

[16] *De antiquitate*, §§55 and 69 (ed. & transl. Scott, pp. 114 and 142); *Cronica*, §§16 and 64 (edd. & transl. Carley & Townsend, pp. 40 and 122).

[17] *De antiquitate*, §40 (ed. & transl. Scott, p. 94); *Cronica*, §47 (edd. & transl. Carley & Townsend, p. 92). *De antiquitate*, §69 (ed. & transl. Scott, p. 142), and *Cronica*, §16 (edd. & transl. Carley & Townsend, p. 40) omit *Escford* and the fishery.

[18] Finberg, *The Early Charters of Wessex*, p. 113. See above, *s.n.* Axe (River, Fishery on).

mid-tenth century; or perhaps Edmund's diploma was only a confirmation. Alternatively, the existence of grants by Ine and Edmund might point instead to some manipulation of the documents, but as both charters are lost no conclusions can be drawn about their authenticity or their possible relationship.

Estun

A grant to Glastonbury of twenty hides at *Estun* or *Esctun* by *Wlfwin*, confirmed by King Æthelred the Unready, is attested in the *De antiquitate* but in none of the documentary sources.[19] This may represent the existence in the archive of a royal charter (now lost) granting the estate to the abbey or, equally possible (given the way grants are described in that work), to Wulfwine. As we have seen elsewhere, the possession of charters to lay recipients does not necessarily mean that Glastonbury in its turn received the estates involved. Wulfwine may never have transferred the land in question to Glastonbury, despite the interpretation in the *De antiquitate*; alternatively, Wulfwine or his heirs may indeed have bequeathed the estate to the monks, but Glastonbury is not recorded in Domesday Book as holding land of this name. The bishop of Coutances, however, held twenty hides at *Estune* which three thegns (unnamed) had held in 1066.[20] This *Estune* (now Long Ashton, a suburb of Bristol) may have been Wulfwine's twenty hides. If so, and if Glastonbury did receive them, it apparently did not hold them for long. On the other hand, it may be that, like *Escford*, *Esctun* was on the Axe. If that were the case, it was either omitted from Domesday Book or appeared there under another name.

Eswirht

See *Inesuuyrth*.

Ferramere (Somerset)

See Meare.

Fiswere

A charter of King Æthelred *de Fiswere* is listed on the *Index chartarum* (S.1775; IC A16). The *De antiquitate* preserves the only other record of this grant; we are told there that the transaction took place in A.D. 1000 and that the recipient was Abbot Beorhtred (who, however, did not become abbot until A.D. 1009).[1] Although Finberg interpreted *Fiswere* as a fishery rather than the name of a place,[2] it is perhaps more likely to have been a place-name, if the grant did indeed date to the reign of Æthelred the Unready.[3] On the *Index chartarum*, however, the grant of

---

[19] *De antiquitate*, §§63 and 69 (ed. & transl. Scott, pp. 130 and 144); *Cronica*, §§16 and 75 (edd. & transl. Carley & Townsend, pp. 42 and 142). In §75 of the *Cronica* the gift is said to have been made by Æthelred himself.

[20] Domesday Book, I, 88va (Somerset, 5.34).

[1] *De antiquitate*, §§63 and 69 (ed. & transl. Scott, pp. 130 and 144); *Cronica*, §§16 and 75 (edd. & transl. Carley & Townsend, pp. 42 and 142).

[2] Finberg, *The Early Charters of Wessex*, p. 183.

[3] Descriptive epithets rather than actual place-names tend to be a feature of the earliest charters only.

Fiswere is associated with a group of grants to Abbot Ealdberht, apparently an abbot of Glastonbury in the early eighth century.[4] Might the donor therefore have been Æthelred, king of Mercia (A.D. 675–?716)? Ealdberht was reputedly given land *iuxta fluuium Aesce*, at Bleadney, Marchey, and another small island by the bishop of Sherborne in A.D. 712 (S.1253). In this context (if S.1253 is genuine), the likelihood of the acquisition of another fishery by royal gift is therefore not remote.

It is difficult to choose between the two possibilities: the attribution to Abbot Ealdberht rests on the authority of the thirteenth-century copyist of the *Index chartarum*, while that to Abbot Beorhtred depends on the statement in the thirteenth-century manuscript of the *De antiquitate*. The ambiguity of the name keeps both options open: if it were denoting a fishery,[5] it would suit an eighth-century better than an eleventh-century context. If *Fiswere* were a place-name, the opposite would apply. Whether the series of grants to Glastonbury by Mercian kings could have begun this early is debatable.[6] The absence of a place called *Fiswere* from Domesday Book might perhaps weight the case slightly in favour of the first, early, option, but the evidence is hardly conclusive.

The location of this grant is unidentified, although the compiler of the *Index chartarum* apparently thought Glastonbury still to be in possession of it, as he placed it on List A.

Foxcote

According to a charter recorded on the contents-list of the *Liber terrarum*, King Æthelstan gave land at *Westone uel Foxcote* to Æthelstan, who gave it to Glastonbury (S.1711; LT55). Further information is supplied in the *De antiquitate*: the grant was apparently of five hides and the recipient-donor was the ealdorman who became a monk at Glastonbury (in A.D. 957).[7]

---

4 According to the *De antiquitate* (§40, ed. & transl. Scott, p. 94), he ruled Glastonbury A.D. 712–719 (in the equivalent chapter of the *Cronica*, no dates are given for Ealdberht). This is a very late and doubtful authority, compared with the earliest list of Glastonbury's abbots in London, British Library, MS. Cotton Tiberius B.v, part 1, at 23va, on which Ealdberht does not appear (see Foot, 'Glastonbury's early abbots'). A possible witness to Ealdberht's existence is S.1253, however, a grant to him from the bishop of Sherborne, dated 712.

5 On fisheries in late Anglo-Saxon England, see Loyn, *Anglo-Saxon England and the Norman Conquest*, pp. 373–5, and Salisbury, 'Primitive British fishweirs'.

6 On these grants, see below, pp. 335–7.

7 *De antiquitate*, §§54 and 69 (ed. & transl. Scott, pp. 112 and 142); *Cronica*, §§16 and 60 (edd. & transl. Carley & Townsend, pp. 40 and 112). On Æthelstan, see Hart, 'Athelstan "Half King" ', especially p. 128. Hart has accepted the identification in the *De antiquitate* of the Æthelstan in LT55 with Æthelstan Half-King, the pre-eminent layman in the kingdom, who retired to Glastonbury from Eadwig's court in A.D. 957. (I should like to thank Simon Keynes, who derived this new date from his *Atlas of Attestations in Anglo-Saxon Charters*. See also Keynes, 'The "Dunstan B" charters', p. 191, n. 108.) Dunstan's exile from Glastonbury probably began in January of the previous year of political (and ecclesiastical) upheaval. See Keynes, *The Diplomas of King Æthelred*, p. 49. For other grants to Æthelstan Half-King which were associated with Glastonbury, see above, *s.n. Brentefordlond*, and below *s.n. Lim*, Mells, *Westone*,

In 1066, an estate of five hides at *Fuscote* was in lay hands.[8] This was Forscote (also spelled Foxcote), east of Radstock, about twenty miles northeast of Glastonbury. We cannot be certain that this is the same estate as that of Æthelstan's grant, nor, indeed, that Glastonbury received any land of this name from Æthelstan (despite the statement to that effect in the contents-list of the *Liber terrarum*). If *Foxcote* did come into the abbey's possession, it seems to have been lost before the Conquest, unless it changed its name.[9]

Fulebroc

An estate of this name may have belonged to Glastonbury before 1066, but the evidence is very dubious. It consists of a single occurrence of the name in a corrupt version of a charter in the name of William the Conqueror confirming Glastonbury's possession of a number of estates, the unique text of which is found in the *De antiquitate* (though repeated in the *Cronica*).[10] This charter may be a reconstruction of a genuine text of A.D. 1071x1087,[11] but in the course of reconstruction any number of names could have been added.

A *fulan broc* is cited as a landmark in the bounds of S.563 (for East Pennard) but natural features of this sort cannot have been so unusual that the Pennard muddy brook can be equated with the place of that description ostensibly confirmed by King William.[12] Without further evidence, the land must remain unidentified.

Gassig

See *Iecesig*.

Glastonbury (Somerset)

As discussed in chapter I, great controversy attaches to the issue of the date and context of Glastonbury's foundation. The historical problems caused by the rich growth of legend grafted onto Glastonbury's house-tradition have been outlined there. For my immediate purpose – a reconstruction of the abbey's landholdings – the question of a possible British antecedent to the Anglo-Saxon community is only relevant to the issue of the endowment of the latter in its earliest days. If there had been a 'Celtic' establishment on the site – and the hard evidence is lacking –

---

and Wrington. Æthelstan is said – in the contents-list of the *Liber terrarum*, the fourteenth-century cartularies, or the (even less reliable) *De antiquitate* – to have granted all these (except *Brentefordlond*) to Glastonbury; it is not always possible to support this conclusion, which could have been drawn simply from the presence of Æthelstan's title-deeds in the archive (only *Lim*, Mells, and Wrington were in the abbey's hands in 1066).

8   Domesday Book, I, 88va (Somerset, 5.42).
9   See below, *s.n. Westone*.
10 *De antiquitate*, §75 (ed. & transl. Scott, p. 154); *Cronica*, §83 (edd. & transl. Carley & Townsend, p. 154).
11 *Regesta regum Anglo-Normannorum*, edd. Davis *et al.*, I.71 (no. 273). See above, *s.n.* Berrow.
12 Grundy identified the Pennard *fulan broc* as the small stream on the boundary of East Pennard near Evercreech junction (*The Saxon Charters*, p. 70; see also p. 234).

we can only speculate about the details of its economic base, its fortunes in the sixth and seventh centuries, and its relationship to its English successor.[1]

As we have seen, the evidence for the early history of the Anglo-Saxon community on the site is so poor and so doubtful that it cannot even be suggested with confidence which king – if it was a king – was responsible for its foundation. The extent of the original gift of territory is, not surprisingly, consequently obscure. The first royal benefactor to be cited in extant documents is Cenwealh, king of Wessex (A.D. 642–672) and the founder of the Old Minster, Winchester.[2] The estates which in the *De antiquitate* and in S.250 (the spurious Great Privilege of King Ine) he is said to have given to Glastonbury (Meare, Beckery, Godney, Marchey, and Nyland) all apparently formed part of the core-estate of the abbey by 1066 at least; Meare and Nyland are explicitly named in Domesday Book as parts of Glastonbury itself, and it is likely that the other three were its sub-units as well.[3] The one surviving text of a diploma of Cenwealh for Glastonbury – S.227, for Meare – appears to be a forgery, a circumstance which might throw suspicion on the lost charters in his name (on the assumption that a bogus job-lot might have been manufactured). S.227, however, contains authentically seventh-century elements, and genuine diplomas of Cenwealh in the archive may therefore have served as its model.[4] We should also remember that the dubiousness of S.227 does not prove the falseness of Glastonbury's claim to the land in question, or even of its attribution to Cenwealh (or, by association, the other lands ascribed to

---

[1] The charter (no longer extant) purporting to be a gift by a king of Dumnonia of five hides at *Inesuuitrin* to the *ecclesia uetusta* of Glastonbury in A.D. 601 was interpreted by William of Malmesbury as a grant of land at Glastonbury to a 'Celtic' house there, but the evidence is quite unconvincing (*De antiquitate*, §35 [ed. & transl. Scott, p. 88]; *Gesta regum Anglorum*, §§27–8 [ed. Stubbs, I.28–9]). Finberg discussed (and accepted) this charter, but rewrote the evidence in the process, claiming that the charter had been issued by King Gerent *ca* A.D. 700, for land granted to Glastonbury in Cornwall: *Lucerna*, pp. 83–94. Edwards, while acknowledging that the charter corresponds with Anglo-Saxon, rather than 'Celtic', charter-conventions, could imagine no motive for its forgery and therefore has accepted it as genuine (*The Charters*, pp. 64–5). She then proceeded to argue for continuity between a British house and the Anglo-Saxon community on the basis of the document's survival (and the archaeological evidence; but on this, see above, pp. 2–4).

[2] On Cenwealh's reign and his conversion to Christianity, see Bede, *Historia ecclesiastica*, Book III, §7 (*Bede's Ecclesiastical History*, edd. & transl. Colgrave & Mynors, pp. 232–6), and the entries in the Anglo-Saxon Chronicle (*s.a.* 641–672).

[3] Along with Panborough: Domesday Book, I, 90ra (Somerset, 8.1). Beckery, Godney, and Marchey are nowhere named in Domesday Book but this omission probably indicates their inclusion in another estate, and their location and later history would argue that it was Glastonbury to which they belonged.

[4] See Robinson, *Somerset*, pp. 47–53, and Edwards, *The Charters*, pp. 20–3. Compare the complex situation at Exeter, where charters in Æthelstan's name, but bearing the date 670 (the same date as S.227), were produced in the eleventh century (S.386, S.387, S.388, S.389, and S.390), perhaps with the help of charters of Cenwealh; the extant charters in his name (S.228 for Sherborne and S.229 for Winchester) are universally judged to be spurious. On the Exeter charters, see Davidson ('On some Anglo-Saxon charters at Exeter', pp. 263–9), who offered a different explanation of the date.

his gift), but suspicions once raised should not be forgotten.[5] It is noteworthy, too, that no grant of land at Glastonbury itself – that is to say, the actual site of the community – is linked with Cenwealh.

Centwine, who reigned in Wessex in obscure political circumstances in the period 676–685,[6] is the next king whose gifts are cited in the archive. This king – who ended his career in an unidentified monastic house – was praised by Aldhelm for granting many estates to recently established monastic churches; unfortunately, none of these was named.[7] The first entry on the contents-list of the *Liber terrarum*, in fact, is a record of a charter for the *insula Glastonie* in Centwine's name (S.1666; LT1). The authenticity of this charter cannot be ascertained, as it was not copied into the later cartularies.[8] It was not listed in the *Index chartarum*. It was seen by the author of the *De antiquitate*, however, who added the information that Centwine's grant was of six hides at Glastonbury *liberae ab omni seruicio*, and that Abbot Hæmgils was the recipient.[9] This statement is followed by an account of Centwine's appointment of Hæmgils as abbot and the subsequent arrangements for abbatial election according to the Benedictine Rule. These obviously anachronistic details should make us uneasy about the reliability of the charter, but the very modesty of the gift – six hides – could perhaps assuage some

---

[5] Although Cenwealh appears as the donor of five estates in S.250, he is absent from the lists of Glastonbury's benefactors in the other royal privileges: S.257 (A.D. 744/5, a privilege in the name of King Cuthred), S.499 (A.D. 944, in Edmund's name), and S.966 (A.D. 1032, in Cnut's name). (Edgar's privilege [S.783] omits the list of kings altogether.) This non-appearance is suggestive, implying perhaps that Cenwealh's charters as well as the text of Ine's privilege (as we have it) were produced after these other privileges (or their base-texts) were written. Cenwealh is absent from the privilege of Henry I, but appears in that of Henry II. See below, p. 128, n. 26.

[6] For Bede's account of the period, see *Historia ecclesiastica*, Book IV, §12 (*Bede's Ecclesiastical History*, edd. & transl. Colgrave & Mynors, p. 369). On the evidence for these years and the complexities of the political situation, see Sawyer, *From Roman Britain*, pp. 43–8, and Kirby, 'Problems of early West Saxon history', especially pp. 17–22.

[7] *Aldhelmi Opera*, ed. Ehwald, pp. 14–15; *Aldhelm. The Poetic Works*, transl. Lapidge & Rosier, pp. 47–8. According to the *De antiquitate* (§31; ed. & transl. Scott, p. 83; *Cronica*, §43; edd. & transl. Carley & Townsend, p. 90), Centwine was buried at Glastonbury, and William of Malmesbury in his *Gesta regum Anglorum* (but not in the *De antiquitate*) claimed that his name could be read on a 'pyramid' in the cemetery (*Gesta regum Anglorum*, §21; ed. Stubbs, I.25–6); see also Watkin, 'The Glastonbury "pyramids" ', pp. 35–6. John of Glastonbury identified Centwine as the abbey's first royal Anglo-Saxon benefactor (*Cronica*, §14; edd. & transl. Carley & Townsend, p. 30). The construction of a church by Centwine's daughter Bugga was the occasion for Aldhelm's poem. Was she the abbess who was recorded as granting land at *Ora* (*q.v.*) to Glastonbury?

[8] It would be interesting to know the circumstances of its non-inclusion in these later collections.

[9] *De antiquitate*, §37 (ed. & transl. Scott, p. 90); *Cronica*, §43 (edd. & transl. Carley & Townsend, p. 90). Omitted from the summaries. Blows was inclined to accept that this notice was based on an authentic foundation-charter ('Studies', pp. 122–5).

of our doubts, at least about the disposal of the land. The same exemplar was apparently used by the forger of S.250, who repeated the provisions for abbatial election.[10] It is interesting (though perhaps not significant) that S.250 does not associate Centwine with any gift of land, but offers the information that he 'Glastingeie matrem sanctorum uocare solitus fuerat et ab omni seculari et ecclesiastico obsequio immunem statuit'.[11] Might this have come from the charter (now lost) granting the *insula Glastonie*? Other purported gifts to Glastonbury by Centwine (of land at *Cantucuudu* and *Crycbeorh*) are better documented;[12] by the ostensible date (A.D. 678) of the extant text of Glastonbury's charter recording those grants, the house is beginning to emerge from documentary obscurity. But the surviving sources do not reveal the extent to which it was an established community at that time.

Another glimpse of the grant of Glastonbury may be provided by the text of a diploma, in the name of a King Baldred, granting land at *Pengerd* in A.D. 681 to Abbot Hæmgils (S.236; LT7). This charter survives as a single sheet, possibly written in the tenth century, which specifies that the land granted comprised twelve hides *ad supplementum honorabilis ecclesie*.[13] The cartulary-text, however (and the *De antiquitate*), gives six hides as the total. Baldred was a sub-king who was contemporary with Centwine, and these six hides (if we prefer that reading) may be the six hides of Centwine's grant. Political circumstances might offer an explanation for the doubling-up of documentation: competitive grants may have been one result of the troubled times.[14] Baldred may have been the local ruler and may have lost out to Centwine; or Baldred may later have been written out of the documentation in the light of the West Saxon regnal list, on which he does not appear.[15] There is no difficulty in describing (West) Pennard, an intrinsic part of the Glastonbury estate, as *in insula Glastonie*. It could be, on the other hand, that Pennard's six hides and the six hides granted by Centwine combined to make up a twelve-hide unit, which is what we find Glastonbury assessed at in 1066.[16] Perhaps we have here the origin of the so-called Glastonbury Twelve Hides, a territorial unit of uncertain origin and flexible extent. (See map 1.)

The Twelve Hides do not make an explicit appearance in the documentary record until the thirteenth century, well beyond the chronological framework of this study, but in as much as they may reflect earlier circumstances they merit

---

10 On S.250, see further below, pp. 127–30.
11 'He was accustomed to call Glastonbury the mother of saints and granted her immunity from every secular and ecclesiastical burden.'
12 S.237; see above, *s.n. Cantucuudu* and *Crycbeorh*.
13 Longleat House, Marquess of Bath, MS. NMR 10564. Does the phrase *ad supplementum ecclesie* suggest a foundation-context? Even if it might be interpreted that way, it could simply represent a tenth-century opinion, not a seventh-century fact.
14 Blows has argued that soon thereafter Ine confirmed Centwine's grants as a demonstration of his (Ine's) dominance ('Studies', p. 173).
15 On the regnal list, see Dumville, 'The West Saxon genealogical regnal list and the chronology of early Wessex'.
16 Morland, 'Hidation', p. 75. The twelve hides in the single-sheet copy may thus have been a 'corrected' total inserted by the tenth-century scribe.

some discussion here. Morland's analysis has summarised the evidence.[17] The earliest useful sources, the two texts entitled 'Bunde duodecim hidarum' and 'Loca principalia infra .xii. hidas', were interpolated into the *De antiquitate*;[18] their date of composition is unknown.[19] The testimony of these texts may bear little relation to the original extent of the Twelve Hides, for it is clear that its area was subject to change. For example, the thirteenth-century bounds – as mapped by Morland from these descriptions – appear to have included the southwestern corner of North Wootton; a sixteenth-century perambulation of the Twelve Hides by Abbot Beere shows that even more of North Wootton and parts of Pilton had been incorporated.[20] This creeping expansion of the Twelve Hides provides a late illustration of the changing nature of the (tenurial) landscape; earlier examples are less obvious, due to the paucity of sources.

The account of the *loca principalia* ends with the following claim: 'Hec omnia loca infra bundas duodecim hidarum contenta et ad Glastoniam pertinencia omni immunitate gaudent regie dignitatis a temporibus antiquis, confirmatumque est ecclesie Glastonie tam a regibus Britonum quam Anglorum et Normannorum.'[21] It is clear from this and from the subsequent history of the Twelve Hides that the concept of a core-estate, an especially privileged ancient zone, was consciously developed in the post-Conquest period. What is less certain is the extent to which this idea had taken hold in the Anglo-Saxon period, and to what degree it was a representation of reality.

S.250, the spurious Great Privilege of King Ine (who is elsewhere identified as the founder of Glastonbury Abbey)[22] has something to tell us about the develop-

---

[17] Morland, 'Glaston Twelve Hides'. See also Robinson, 'Memories of St Dunstan', pp. 13–23, and Morland, 'The Brue', pp. 78–86.

[18] *De antiquitate*, §§72 and 73 (ed. & transl. Scott, pp. 148–52); *Cronica*, §§3 and 4 (with slightly different rubrics) (edd. & transl. Carley & Townsend, pp. 12–16).

[19] From internal evidence, Morland ascribed them to *ca* A.D. 1263, failing to consider the date of the manuscript (A.D. 1247/8) ('Glaston Twelve Hides', p. 39). Hazel Hudson and Frances Neale adopted a general date of 'early thirteenth century' for convenience: 'The Panborough Saxon charter', p. 68, n. 16. For the date of MS. R.5.33, see James, *The Western Manuscripts in the Library of Trinity College*, II.198–202, Scott, *The Early History*, p. 36, and Crick, 'The marshalling', especially pp. 235–43. Morland did not raise the interesting question of why there are two very similar texts of the perambulation. It may be that one is earlier than the other.

[20] Morland, 'Glaston Twelve Hides', facing p. 34.

[21] 'All these places, which are contained within the boundaries of the Twelve Hides and belong to Glastonbury, have enjoyed every immunity of a royal dignity from ancient times and this has been confirmed for the church of Glastonbury by the kings of the Britons as well as the kings of the English and the Normans' (Scott's translation): *De antiquitate*, §73 (ed. & transl. Scott, pp. 152–3); *Cronica*, §4 (edd. & transl. Carley & Townsend, p. 16).

[22] Ine is identified as Glastonbury's founder only in later sources. William of Malmesbury attributed Glastonbury's foundation to Ine in his *Gesta pontificum Anglorum* (§91; ed. Hamilton, p. 196), but had apparently changed his mind by the time he began the *De antiquitate*. The A-text of the Anglo-Saxon Chronicle offered the information as a marginal addition *s.a.* 688 (which was there by A.D. 1001x1013 when G was copied

ment of the concept of a core-estate and privileged zone, but the context of its message is difficult to discern. No specific date has been assigned to this forgery, although its appearance in William of Malmesbury's *Gesta regum Anglorum* supplies a *terminus ante quem* of the early twelfth century.[23] In S.250 and (with some variation) in those texts connected with it, such as the privileges of King Cuthred (S.257; A.D. 744/5),[24] King Edmund, King Edgar, and King Cnut (S.499, S.783, and S.966; A.D. 944, 971, and 1032)[25], and those of Henry I and Henry II,[26] several layers of grants of land and immunity are found. In S.250, which is the most explicit of the supposedly pre-Conquest texts, Ine's gifts are listed first (Brent, *Sowy*, Pilton, Doulting, and Bleadney), followed by those of Cenwealh (Meare, Beckery, Godney, Marchey, and *Andersey*), Centwine (freedom from secular and ecclesiastical burdens), and Bishop Hædde, Baldred, and (anachronistically) Æthelheard (*Lantocai*, Pennard, and *Pouelt*, respectively).[27] 'With the approval of Pope Gregory', the immunity from secular dues granted by previous kings (Cenwealh, Centwine, Cædwalla, and Baldred) was confirmed ('ab omni-

from A; see *The Anglo-Saxon Chronicle. MS A*, ed. Bately, pp. xxxviii and 32). See also the West Saxon genealogies in London, British Library, MS. Cotton Tiberius B.v, part 1 (23r), and the *Textus Roffensis* (Rochester, Cathedral Library, MS. A.3.5, 104r). Dumville has dated the addition of Ine to the exemplar of the genealogies of Tiberius B.v to activity at Glastonbury *ca* A.D. 969. See 'The Anglian collection', pp. 42–3. In the entry in the Annals of St Neots *s.a.* 726 Ine is said to have *monasterium constructum atque dedicatum apud Glastoniam* (*The Annals of St Neots*, edd. Dumville & Lapidge, pp. xviii, xxxvi–xxxvii, lxix, and 29). J.M. Wallace-Hadrill commented that Ine had been to Glastonbury what Dagobert had been to S. Denis (*Early Germanic Kingship*, p. 90). A dedicatory epigram from Ine's church was preserved in the *De antiquitate* (§40; ed. & transl. Scott, pp. 94–6); see Lapidge in Hunt, 'Manuscript evidence', pp. 290–1.

23 *Gesta regum Anglorum*, §36 (ed. Stubbs, I.36–9). Scott has suggested (and Blows has tentatively agreed) that William of Malmesbury may have been responsible for the forgery: *The Early History*, p. 32, and 'Studies', pp. 389–92.

24 Cuthred's privilege lists no lands, only royal donors, whose gifts – including the *pristina urbs Glastingei* – he confirmed. The list of kings (Centwine, Baldred, Cædwalla, Ine, Æthelheard, and Æthelbald of Mercia [A.D. 716–757]) could, unlike the comparable list in S.250, have been compiled at the purported date of the charter. Unlike Glastonbury's other royal privileges, Cuthred's was apparently in the *Liber terrarum* (LT21) (as was Ine's more general grant to all West Saxon churches, S.245 [LT2]; a duplicate of S.245 was apparently included at the end [LT135]).

25 Edgar's privilege omits the names of his predecessors and their gifts; Edmund's and Cnut's – like Cuthred's – list the royal donors but not their benefactions.

26 The privilege of Henry I is in the Great Cartulary (ed. Watkin, I.185–6 [no. 301]), dated by Watkin '?April 1121'. The privilege of Henry II is in the *Cronica* (§95; edd. & transl. Carley & Townsend, pp. 174–6) (datable A.D. 1184x1189). They both preserve lists of benefactors and lands.

27 Cædwalla (king of Wessex A.D. 685–689) also makes the list, not as a donor but as the king who confirmed Bishop Hædde's grant. By the time when the summary of grants was added to the *De antiquitate*, Cædwalla and Cenwealh had become confused: the grants of Meare *et al.* were said to have been made by *Kenewalchius siue Cedwald* (*De antiquitate*, §69 [ed. & transl. Scott, p. 141]; the *Cronica*, §16 [edd. & transl. Carley & Townsend, p. 38], has *Kenewalchius siue Cenwalli*).

bus regiis exactionibus et operibus que indici solent, uidelicet expedicione et pontis arcisue constructione'),[28] and sole legal jurisdiction (ecclesiastical and secular) proclaimed. Exemption from subordination to the bishop, ostensibly granted by Ine's predecessors, is claimed, first for Glastonbury itself, then for all its landed possessions ('omnes terre et loca et possessiones beate Marie Glastonie'),[29] and then more specifically for a network of churches: *Sowy*, Brent, Moorlinch, Shapwick, Street, Butleigh, and Pilton, and their chapels.[30] In Edgar's privilege these are called the *ecclesiae parochiales* of the monastery, and it is specified there that no other authority should be allowed within, not just the *termini Glastonie*, but also the *parochiae* mentioned.[31] This restriction is repeated in the confirmation of lands by Henry II.[32] Edgar's privilege affirmed the exemption from secular dues ('ab omni tributo fiscalium negociorum') and added a detailed list of jurisdictional rights, repeating those elaborated in King Edmund's (but not Ine's) charter. Cnut's privilege (S.966) reaffirmed the exemptions and the jurisdictional rights, but in less detail.[33]

Ine's privilege imposes its conditions on all of Glastonbury's endowment, listing the estates by name.[34] The implication is that the circumstances apply simply because it is ecclesiastical land. But in other documents we find a concept of a special, more restricted, zone, the *insula* of Glastonbury, a precursor of the Twelve Hides. Edmund's privilege states, 'sed precipue ipsa uilla Glastonie . . .

---

[28] 'From all royal exactions and works which have been appointed, such as army-service and the construction of bridges and fortifications.'

[29] 'All the lands and places and possessions of the [church of] the Blessed Mary at Glastonbury.'

[30] This same list was interpolated into a late tenth-century letter from a Pope John to the layman Ælfric which was reproduced in the *Gesta regum Anglorum* (§151; ed. Stubbs, I.172–3; *Papsturkunden*, ed. Zimmermann, I.550–1 [no. 282]). On this letter see further below, p. 330.

[31] The list in S.783 (Edgar's privilege) is slightly different from that in S.250: *Sowy*, Moorlinch, Shapwick, Street, and Butleigh, with the addition of the chapels of Beckery, Godney, Marchey, Meare, Panborough and Nyland. Pilton and Brent have been omitted: *De antiquitate*, §60 (ed. & transl. Scott, pp. 122–6); *Cronica*, §71 (edd. & transl. Carley & Townsend, pp. 132–6).

[32] Street, Pilton, Ditcheat, Butleigh, Shapwick, Moorlinch, *Sowy, cum capellis suis*. This list is the same as in S.250, save for the substitution of Ditcheat for Brent: *Cronica*, §95 (edd. & transl. Carley & Townsend, p. 176).

[33] Blows has discussed these privileges in detail; see 'Studies', pp. 379–98.

[34] Whoever concocted this forgery was apparently not as thorough as he might have been: he seems to have failed to include the names of all the places for which charters were extant predating the purported year of Ine's privilege (A.D. 725). No grants of land in Centwine's name are cited, for example, although elsewhere Centwine is said to have given land at Glastonbury, *Cantucuudu*, and *Crycbeorh* (*q.v.*). Charters for reputedly earlier grants – of Clewer, *Elosaneg, Lodegaresberghe*, Wedmore, and a fishery on the River Parrett (*q.v.*) – were noted in A.D. 1247 on the contents-list of the *Liber terrarum* and the lists of the *Index chartarum* but were not used in the construction of S.250. If this occurred in the twelfth century, the charters apparently had not yet been lost: was it simply pointless to lay claim to certain estates at this time?

pre ceteris suis sit liberior cum terminis suis'.[35] The charter of Henry I refers explicitly to the church of Glastonbury *cum suis insulis*, which it lists as Beckery, Godney, Marchey, Meare, Panborough, and Nyland. We have seen this list before; it may encompass all the elements of the core-estate of Glastonbury in 1066, assessed at twelve hides. The date of the establishment of this special zone is of great interest, but at this stage of the analysis it is not possible to do more than question whether it is a pre- or post-Conquest development. There are a number of possible contexts. The creation of a bishopric at neighbouring Wells in A.D. 909 might have been perceived as a threat, to be faced with the manufacture of propaganda. Perhaps the reform of Glastonbury in the mid-tenth century – whatever exactly it entailed – was the occasion for the development of a new self-image, including a new concept of the abbey's physical identity in relation to the world immediately outside its gates. An anecdote of inter-abbatial wrangling in the late eleventh century preserved in the *De antiquitate* shows the abbot of Glastonbury (Thurstan) standing up to the authority of the bishop of Wells (Giso) on a matter of ecclesiastical jurisdiction involving the abbots of neighbouring Muchelney and Athelney Abbeys.[36] Perhaps Glastonbury felt the need to bolster its status and emphasise its uniqueness at this date. Certainly the late twelfth century – when Bishop Savaric (A.D. 1191–1205) began the protracted but ultimately unsuccessful attempt to annex Glastonbury to the see of Wells – provides a context for an attempt to establish special powers in defence against an aggressive bishop and offers a reason for the forgery of retroactive documentation to support this cause.[37] There is also the possibility that an actual tenth-century immunity, paralleling the documented grants of hundredal jurisdiction at Winchester and Worcester, lay behind this concept of the exempt *insula* of Glastonbury with its *termini*, an immunity which Edmund's privilege, copied in golden letters in a gospel-book (according to the *De antiquitate*), may have implemented in the early stages of reform.[38] Alternatively, Edgar may have been the first to establish such conditions at Glastonbury. The abbey's entry in Domesday Book, however, unlike that of Worcester, offers no hint of such an immunity and no details to support a possible parallel.

Whatever its status, the estate of Glastonbury proper was apparently not a static entity from the seventh to the eleventh century. As far as we can tell from the fragmentary evidence, the places recorded as 'parts' of Glastonbury in Domesday Book were not necessarily all originally members of the ancient estate. Panborough, a sub-unit of sixty acres in Domesday Book, may have come to the

---

[35] 'But especially let the *uilla* of Glastonbury with its bounds . . . be freer than the rest': *De antiquitate*, §56 (ed. & transl. Scott, pp. 116–17). (The text in *Cartularium Saxonicum*, ed. Birch, I.544–6 [no. 794] omits the *suis* after *ceteris* and reads *terris* for *terminis*.)

[36] *De antiquitate*, §76 (ed. & transl. Scott, pp. 154–6); *Cronica*, §84 (edd. & transl. Carley & Townsend, p. 156).

[37] See above, p. 12.

[38] For the liberty of Oswaldslow at Worcester, see John, *Land Tenure*, pp. 113–61; on Winchester, see *idem*, 'The church of Worcester', especially pp. 423–4; for the development of these liberties more generally, see *idem*, *Orbis Britanniae*, pp. 175–6.

abbey in A.D. 956, according to a diploma of King Eadwig (S.626), although the sixty acres of Panborough 'in' Glastonbury in 1066 appear to have been only a fraction of the tenth-century estate which was the subject of this grant.[39] The evidence for Godney, Marchey, and Meare is so corrupt that no definite conclusions can be drawn about their incorporation into 'greater Glastonbury', although there is some evidence that Marchey and Meare were early episcopal grants (from Sherborne and Winchester respectively).[40] Nyland (or *Andersey*) (also claimed as a gift of Cenwealh), a sub-unit of two hides in Domesday Book, was apparently the subject of another grant (but of half a hide only) by King Edgar to Ælfswith (who reputedly then gave it to Glastonbury).[41] The apparent grant of land such as this – which might have been deemed a permanent member of the core-estate – raises questions about the cohesion of this putative early unit. That we cannot begin to discern a context for the transaction involving Ælfswith – a grant of a portion of what may or may not have been ancient abbatial land to a laywoman by the royal champion of monastic reform – simply underlines the inadequacy of the extant sources; they fail to provide us with the means of addressing the particular question of what constituted Glastonbury proper at any time in the Anglo-Saxon period, not to mention what conditions pertained on the so-called *insula regalis*.[42] The nature of (and changes in) the abbey's relationship with the king before, during, and after the First Viking Age – which should obviously affect our interpretation of the status of the house and its endowment – is another large, crucial, but unanswered question.[43]

Godney (Somerset)

Godney was one of the 'islands' of Glastonbury, claimed in the *De antiquitate* to have been the gift of King Cenwealh (A.D. 642–672).[44] In the *Cronica* it is stated explicitly that the two small islands granted in Cenwealh's charter for Meare were Godney and Westhay, although neither the extant (apparently spurious) text of the charter for Meare (S.227) nor the *De antiquitate* makes this association, grouping Godney instead with the other islands (Beckery, Marchey, and *Andreyesie*) and not mentioning Westhay. In the Great Privilege of King Ine (S.250), Cenwealh is cited as the donor of Godney,[45] and the privilege of King Edgar (S.783) lists its church among those exempt from episcopal interference.[46] 'Insula de Godenye

---

[39] It is uncertain whether Eadwig's diploma marked the abbey's acquisition of this land. See below, *s.n.* Panborough.

[40] See below, *s.n.* Marchey and Meare.

[41] See above, *s.n. Andersey*.

[42] Dunstan's biographer B applied this term to Glastonbury: *Vita S. Dunstani*, §3 (*Memorials*, ed. Stubbs, pp. 6–7). See above, p. 7.

[43] See further discussion below, especially pp. 335–50.

[44] *De antiquitate*, §§36 and 69 (ed. & transl. Scott, pp. 90 and 140); *Cronica*, §§16 and 42 (edd. & transl. Carley & Townsend, pp. 40 and 88).

[45] *De antiquitate*, §42 (ed. & transl. Scott, p. 98); *Cronica*, §49 (edd. & transl. Carley & Townsend, p. 96).

[46] *De antiquitate*, §60 (ed. & transl. Scott, p. 124); *Cronica*, §71 (edd. & transl. Carley & Townsend, p. 134). The charter of confirmation of Henry II (*Cronica*, §95 [p. 176])

cum suis terris et moris largissimis' was included within the *loca principalia* of the Twelve Hides; its name was there explained as deriving from a chapel of the Holy Trinity.[47] Godney lies fewer than three miles northwest of Glastonbury and, given the limited amount of useful land so close to the abbey before the moors were extensively drained, it would be logical for it to have belonged to the monks from a very early period, even if the documentation of the seventh- and eighth-century grants is suspect.[48]

Greinton (Somerset)

Greinton was a small property of two and a half hides held by Glastonbury in 1066 and 1086.[49] Some sort of subordination of Greinton to the neighbouring *manerium* of Ashcott in 1086 appears in the entry in the *Liber Exoniensis*; Ashcott itself was recorded as part of Walton in Domesday Book.[50] Greinton's history, therefore, like that of Ashcott and Walton, should probably be seen in the context of the break-up of the large early estate of *Pouelt* which may have extended across the whole of the Polden Hills.[51] This association is evoked by the marginal note in a thirteenth-century hand in the text of Ine's Great Privilege in the *De antiquitate*, where *Poelt*, one of only two places among Glastonbury's estates at which the bishop of Wells was allowed to stay overnight, was glossed *id est Grenton*.[52] The huge estate of *Pouelt* cannot have been co-terminous with Greinton, but this note at least suggests that at one time Greinton belonged – or was thought to belong – to that large unit.

Grittleton (Wiltshire)

A charter of King Edmund for his *minister* Wulfric, for twenty-five hides at *Grutelintone*, dated 940, survives in the fourteenth-century cartularies (S.472). A note following the text states that Wulfric (called *minister regis Eddredi*) gave (*commendauit*) the land to Glastonbury after his wife's death, and that *Elswyne* carried out the bequest. The contents-list of the *Liber terrarum* clarifies this statement, identifying Ælfwine as Wulfric's *successor* (LT43).[53] The same infor-

---

repeats this information. Henry I's charter exempted Godney, as one of Glastonbury's islands, from outside control but does not mention a church there (*The Great Chartulary*, ed. Watkin, I.185 [no. 301]).

47 *De antiquitate*, §73 (ed. & transl. Scott, p. 152); *Cronica*, §4 (edd. & transl. Carley & Townsend, p. 16). Ekwall offered instead the derivation, '*Goda*'s island': *The Concise Oxford Dictionary of English Place-names, s.n.* Godney, p. 200.

48 See above, *s.n.* Glastonbury.

49 Domesday Book, I, 90rb (Somerset, 8.15).

50 'De eadem mansione [Ashcott] tenet Girardus unum mansionem quem uocatur Graintona': E 164b2. For Ashcott, see Domesday Book, I, 90rb (Somerset, 8.11 and 8.14).

51 See below, *s.n. Pouelt.*

52 *De antiquitate*, §42 (ed. & transl. Scott, p. 100); the *Cronica* does not include this identification.

53 LT44 and LT46 (for Nettleton and Horton, *q.v.*) were similar transactions. The exact significance of *commendauit* in this context is unknown. Wulfric was probably Dunstan's brother. He received grants of Tintinhull (LT34), Turnworth (LT48), Yarlington (LT66), Kington Langley (S.473), and Nettleton (S.504) from Edmund and land at

mation is offered in the *De antiquitate*, where the transaction is cited twice, among both King Edmund's and King Edgar's grants; in the summary it is stated that the gift by Ælfwine was confirmed by King Edgar.[54] In 1066 Glastonbury held an estate of thirty hides at *Gretelintone*, according to Domesday Book;[55] this represents an increase of five hides over the total of the grant by Edmund.

We may be able to find a hint of these hides. References to a charter of King Edmund for *Lytlantone alias Grutlyngtone* in MS. 39a (L36) and another *de Lutramtone* (S.1735; IC D10) could refer to S.472, Edmund's charter for Grittleton, or they could, alternatively, indicate the addition of an estate of five hides – Littleton – to Grittleton.[56] The author of §70 of the *De antiquitate* included *Litlantone* on his list of *alia [maneria] data Glastonie*, apparently on the grounds that no other charter already discussed had dealt with this land.[57] There was an unnamed five-hide sub-unit at Grittleton in Domesday Book, said to have been held from the abbot by the bishop of Coutances in 1086, which Morland and Stacy identified with Grittleton's neighbour, Littleton Drew;[58] Littleton Drew appears by name, however, among the bishop's own holdings, where it is said to have been taken from Glastonbury.[59] The value of the bishop's *Liteltone* in Domesday Book is the same as that of his sub-unit of Grittleton, but it is odd that the thirty-hide estate of *Gretelintone* appears to be intact in 1086, no mention being made in that entry of a loss of territory. Perhaps there was some difference of opinion about who owned these five hides, a difference which had not achieved the status of a dispute (and was therefore not recorded as such).[60]

Grittleton is in northern Wiltshire, over forty miles from Glastonbury, in an area where there was a concentration of estates owned by the abbey. This land

Horton (LT46), Idmiston (S.530 and S.541), and Merton (S.551) from Eadred. He is said to have granted some of these directly to Glastonbury (Tintinhull, Turnworth, and Yarlington), while others (Grittleton, Horton, and Nettleton) were first acquired by Ælfwine, who then gave them to Glastonbury. One of these (Tintinhull) and three others (Idmiston, Kington Langley, and Merton) were acquired by Ælfswith, probably the wife of Ealdorman Ælfheah, who reputedly gave Idmiston and Kington Langley to Glastonbury. The abbey held at least five of these nine in 1066 (Horton is unidentified; Merton, Turnworth, and Yarlington were held by laymen). On Wulfric, see Brooks, 'The career', pp. 8–11, and Hart, *The Early Charters of Northern England*, pp. 370–2; on Ælfwine, see Keynes, 'The "Dunstan B" charters', pp. 192–3.

54 *De antiquitate*, §§55, 62, and 69 (ed. & transl. Scott, pp. 114, 130, and 144); *Cronica*, §§16, 64, and 73 (edd. & transl. Carley & Townsend, pp. 42, 122, and 138); §55 of the *De antiquitate* (*Cronica*, §64) gives the total as thirty, but the other references agree with the extant text's total of twenty-five.
55 Domesday Book, I, 66va–b (Wiltshire, 7.10).
56 Although, as Finberg pointed out (*The Early Charters of Wessex*, p. 182), *Lutramtone*/Littleton in the *Index chartarum* could represent any number of places in Somerset, Dorset, or Wiltshire.
57 *De antiquitate*, §70 (ed. & transl. Scott, p. 144). See above, pp. 24–6.
58 Morland, 'The Glastonbury manors', pp. 85 and 87; Stacy, 'The estates', p. 21; also (Wiltshire, 5.6 [note]).
59 Domesday Book, I, 66rb (Wiltshire, 5.6). In this entry, the bishop is the tenant-in-chief.
60 This has been suggested by Stacy ('The estates', p. 49, n. 3).

seems to have been acquired in the mid- to later tenth century and to represent concerted expansion into a new region – with new, better draining soils – perhaps specifically at the time of Dunstan's abbacy.[61] This may be taken as a dim reflexion of the kind of manipulation of land resources more clearly visible in the well documented development by Æthelwold of the endowment of Ely Abbey.[62] Wulfric may have been instrumental in implementing this new policy during his brother's time in office (possibly before A.D. 951).[63]

Grundy's analysis of the bounds of S.472 seems to indicate that they covered Grittleton only, not crossing the Fosse Way into Littleton Drew. This could be taken to prove that originally Littleton Drew formed no part of Grittleton. The language of the bounds, however, appears to be of post-Conquest date; Littleton's omission could therefore support the idea that it was the portion of Grittleton lost to the bishop of Coutances.[64]

Four acres of meadow in Littleton Drew were leased to a tenant by the abbot of Glastonbury in 1066 and 1086; together with six acres in Stanton St Quintin, these should have belonged to Christian Malford.[65]

Ham (Somerset)

According to a charter whose text is preserved in the fourteenth-century cartularies, seven hides at *Hamme* were granted to Glastonbury in A.D. 973 by King Edgar, in exchange for *Brauncmynstre* (S.791).[1] A charter of Edgar for Ham had apparently been in the *Liber terrarum* (LT83); a copy of it (*exceptis limitibus*, without its bounds) was listed in MS. 39a (L15). According to Domesday Book, Glastonbury held seventeen hides at Ham.[2] The discrepancy in hides (seven in S.791, seventeen in Domesday Book) could have arisen from a copying error, or, alternatively, the estate could have been granted in two portions or the hidage changed. An examination of the rather different account of Ham in the *De antiquitate* further obscures the picture. Although the summary of grants records a gift of seven hides,[3] according to the main narrative account seventeen hides at *Hamme* were given by King Edgar to Abbot Sigegar of Glastonbury in the year 965. This transaction is recorded by means of what appears to be a quotation, in the first person, from the charter.[4] The extant cartulary-text, however, is quite

---

[61] Stacy, 'The estates', pp. 2–3. See also *s.n.* Christian Malford, *Kyngton*, and Nettleton, and map 7.

[62] See *Anglo-Saxon Ely*, edd. & transl. Keynes & Kennedy, and *Liber Eliensis*, ed. Blake, pp. 63–117 and 395–9.

[63] The date of Wulfric's death is uncertain; see Brooks, 'The career', p. 10.

[64] Grundy, 'The Saxon land charters of Wiltshire', *Archaeological Journal* 76 (1919), pp. 251–3.

[65] Domesday Book, I, 66va (Wiltshire, 7.5).

[1] Braunton, in Devon; see above, *s.n. Brannocmynstre*.

[2] Domesday Book, I, 90rb (Somerset, 8.17).

[3] *De antiquitate*, §69 (ed. & transl. Scott, p. 144); *Cronica*, §16 (edd. & transl. Carley & Townsend, p. 42).

[4] *De antiquitate*, §62 (ed. & transl. Scott, p. 128); *Cronica*, §73 (edd. & transl. Carley & Townsend, p. 138), retains the date and the name of the abbot but omits the prose and alters the number of hides to seven, perhaps to make it agree with the summary.

different: apart from the discrepancy in hidage already mentioned, the date there is 973 (not 965), the recipient is simply the church of Glastonbury (without Sigegar), and the phrases quoted by the *De antiquitate* (*iure perpetuo, ad ecclesiam uetustam honorabilem*, and *pro remedio anime mee et pro patris mei*) are not to be found. It is possible that the author of this passage in the *De antiquitate* was quoting from another of Edgar's charters, as his account goes on to name two other estates, which presumably had their own documentation. But it could also be the case that a second charter of Edgar for Ham existed.[5] (Neither document need, of course, have been genuine.) No clues survive to help us interpret the evidence further. The indication in MS. 39a that 'una cedula in Anglico de Hamme notabilis ualde' was in the archive can only add to the obscurity (L16). Perhaps this was the vernacular boundary-description missing from the copy of Edgar's charter (L15).[6]

High Ham is about seven miles across the moor southwest of Glastonbury. The bounds attached to S.791 caused Grundy some difficulty, although he confidently identified them as belonging to High Ham; they seemed to him, however, to enclose an area rather different from the later parish of that name, omitting especially the northern, probably marshy, area.[7]

We can only speculate about Glastonbury's reasons for wishing to divest itself of the distant estate of *Brauncmynstre* at this time; certainly the acquisition of lands in the mid- and later tenth century seems to have been an eastward-looking process, which may also have involved deliberate removal from some of the more westerly properties. Perhaps also there was a policy of intensified land-exploitation in the area of the abbey itself, and Ham linked up well with the neighbouring estates which were already part of Glastonbury's endowment. Indeed, given Ham's position, it is surprising that no evidence exists of any interest there before this rather late date; other, earlier, charters linking Ham to Glastonbury may have been lost. Ham may reveal the same kind of development in the tenth century as Nicholas Corcos and Michael Costen have proposed for the estates on the Poldens.[8]

Hamandone / Hamedune

See Hannington.

Hamanstane

According to the contents-list of the *Liber terrarum*, King Æthelstan granted a charter for *Hamanstane* to one Wulfhelm (S.1715; LT134). It appears in the list of charters for lands lost (IC D9), but in no other Glastonbury source. As *Haman-*

---

[5] Finberg distinguished between the two grants (*The Early Charters of Wessex*, pp. 142 and 147) and was followed by Sawyer, who gave the grant attested in the *De antiquitate* a separate number (S.1773). For the difficulties of interpreting the use of charters in the *De antiquitate*, see above, pp. 21–6.
[6] The separate transmission of bounds is interesting. Separate bounds for Idmiston, Sturminster Newton, *Winterborne*, and Wrington are also recorded in MS. 39a.
[7] Grundy, *The Saxon Charters*, pp. 118–23.
[8] Corcos, 'Early estates on the Poldens'; Costen, 'Some evidence for new settlements', and 'Dunstan, Glastonbury, and the economy'. See below, *s.n. Pouelt*.

stane has not been identified, no help exists to decide the question of whether Glastonbury ever actually held this land. Another grant of land by King Æthelstan to a Wulfhelm (at *Deuerel*) was apparently passed on to Glastonbury, according to the contents-list of the *Liber terrarum*,[9] but no such comment is made there about *Hamanstane*.

Hanandone
See Hannington.

Hannington (Wiltshire)
No texts survive, but there were apparently two charters relating to *Hanandone* in the *Liber terrarum*: King Alfred granted land there to the layman Wulfhere (S.1704; LT73), and King Edgar made a grant to *Alwoldus, qui dimisit G.* (S.1763; LT74). A charter in the name of King Æthelred, granting land at *Hamandone* to Glastonbury, was recorded in the *Index chartarum* (S.1776; IC C14). According to Domesday Book, Glastonbury held fifteen hides at *Hanindone* (Hannington in Wiltshire); three of these hides had been leased for three lives, but had returned *ad dominium* by 1086.[10]

This history is both corroborated and complicated by the account of the *De antiquitate*. The earliest record there is that of a grant to the abbey of fifteen hides at *Hammedone* or *Hamedune* by Ælfflæd, Edward the Elder's widow, with King Edmund's approval.[11] Next is a grant to Glastonbury by *Aedelfleda* of fifteen hides at *Hanandone*, seemingly during the reign of King Edgar; Finberg suggested that this Æthelflæd may have been the widow of the Ælfwold who had received Edgar's grant.[12] Lastly, a grant of *Hanandune* to Glastonbury by King Æthelred the Unready is cited, without the number of hides being specified.[13]

It is not certain that all these grants refer to the same place,[14] but they will be treated as a group in the absence of better data. The evidence tends to suggest that the earliest recorded grant, that of King Alfred, may have come to Glastonbury simply as a title-deed and did not represent a transfer of the land to the abbey. This transfer may have been effected during the reign of King Edgar, when the estate was granted first to the layman Ælfwold, and then perhaps by his widow to the church. If we leave aside the untestable hypothesis that an earlier grant to Glastonbury by Ælfflæd, Edward the Elder's widow, was spurious, *her* charter could

---

9 S.1714; LT51. See above, *s.n. Deuerel*.

10 Domesday Book, I, 66va (Wiltshire, 7.2).

11 *De antiquitate*, §§55 and 69 (ed. & transl. Scott, pp. 114 and 142); *Cronica*, §§16 and 64 (edd. & transl. Carley & Townsend, pp. 40 and 122). For Ælfflæd, see below, *s.n.* Okeford Fitzpaine.

12 *De antiquitate*, §§62 and 69 (ed. & transl. Scott, pp. 130 and 144); *Cronica*, §§16 and 73 (edd. & transl. Carley & Townsend, pp. 42 and 138). Finberg, *The Early Charters of Wessex*, p. 96.

13 *De antiquitate*, §§63 and 69 (ed. & transl. Scott, pp. 130 and 144); *Cronica*, §§16 and 75 (edd. & transl. Carley & Townsend, pp. 42 and 142).

14 The sequence of forms for Hannington provided by Ekwall includes none with an *m* after the *a*: *Hanindone, Hanedone, Hanendon*. See Ekwall, *The Concise Oxford Dictionary of English Place-names*, p. 217, *s.n.* Hannington.

be interpreted in (at least) three ways: she had granted the land to Glastonbury but it had been retrieved by the king before (or during) Edgar's reign; she had received the land from King Edmund with a charter seen by the author of the *De antiquitate*, who assumed, incorrectly, that she had passed it on to the church; or she had received a grant of another estate altogether, possibly at Ham (*q.v.*) or in the area of Ham Hill, where several names still preserve an element ('Hamdon') which might be identifiable with *Hamandone* – for example, Glastonbury held land at Stoke sub Hamdon in 1066.[15] The fact that the hidage of Ælfflæd's *Hammedone* and Æthelflæd's *Hanandone* is the same, however, tends to weaken the last suggestion, which may perhaps more appropriately be applied to King Æthelred's grant. But King Æthelred made a separate grant of *Stoke* (reputedly Stoke sub Hamdon) to a layman.[16] If Æthelred's grant of *Hanandune* is not a grant of another estate, and not a forgery designed to provide a more impressive title than might have been offered by the (now lost) charter of Edgar (S.1763), it seems that possession of the estate passed back and forth from the king to Glastonbury several times in the tenth century, although it came to rest in the latter's hands.

Hannington lies a few miles north of Swindon, over fifty miles from Glastonbury, well beyond the concentration of Glastonbury's estates in north Wiltshire (around Christian Malford). Hannington's acquisition may have formed part of the eastward-looking movement of the endowment – associated with Dunstan – which seems to have begun in the mid-tenth century. This apparent trend may be a dim reflection of the kind of manipulation of land-resources visible more clearly in Æthelwold's development of the endowment of Ely Abbey.[17]

Henstridge (Somerset)

Three charters known from the contents-list of the *Liber terrarum* applied to the estate of *Hengesteshrege*: one granted by King Æthelstan to the layman Æthelred (S.1712; LT95) and two grants to laymen, Ælfheah (S.1736; LT96) and Brihtric (LT97), by King Eadred. No further record of these charters survives in the Glastonbury archive; Henstridge is listed among the *alia* [*maneria*] *data Glastonie* of §70 of the *De antiquitate*, but as we have seen this need not necessarily imply that the land was transferred to the abbey.[18]

The survival outside Glastonbury of the charter seemingly represented by LT97, the text of which is to be found in the Shaftesbury cartulary (S.570), may strengthen the suggestion that Glastonbury never held the land concerned. The diploma, a grant of five hides at *Hengstesrig* by Eadred to Brihtric, has much in common with S.571 (also for Brihtric); both belong to a group of charters which may have been written at Glastonbury.[19] Unfortunately, the land described by the

---

[15] Domesday Book, I, 91ra (Somerset, 8.39). See below, *s.n. Stoke.*
[16] See below, *s.n. Stoke.*
[17] See Stacy, 'The estates', pp. 2–3, and above, *s.n.* Grittleton; on Æthelwold, see *Anglo-Saxon Ely*, edd. & transl. Keynes & Kennedy, and *Liber Eliensis*, ed. Blake, pp. 63–117 and 395–9.
[18] *De antiquitate*, §70 (ed. & transl. Scott, p. 144). See above, pp. 24–6.
[19] Abrams, ' "Lucid intervals" ', p. 52, and Keynes, 'The "Dunstan B" charters'. S.570 and S.571 are dated 956 (for 953x955).

bounds has proved difficult to identify, thereby complicating the question of who later possessed the estate granted by S.570. Grundy located it with some uncertainty at Henstridge itself, where four hides were held in 1066 by Eadnoth and ten hides by Earl Harold (but by the king in 1086).[20] Forsberg preferred the identification with Abbas Combe, a neighbour (and, he assumed, once a part) of Henstridge, where five hides were held by Shaftesbury at the time of Domesday Book.[21] Certainly the latter identification is tempting, given the hidage and the connexion with Shaftesbury. Assigning Shaftesbury's Henstridge charter (S.570) to Abbas Combe leaves open the possibility that the Henstridge charter once lodged at Glastonbury (LT97) was for the neighbouring estate and was not a duplicate. Abbas Combe and Henstridge are fewer than ten miles west of Shaftesbury in the southernmost part of Somerset, about twenty-five miles from Glastonbury.

A similar group of three charters for land at Camel, with Brihtric also apparently the latest of the lay recipients, existed in the Glastonbury archive, similarly without convincing evidence that the church ever acquired the estate.[22] Two charters for Yeovilton (the second granting it to Brihtric), were also preserved among the abbey's documents; in this last case, the uncertainty about Glastonbury's relationship to the estate is complicated by the evidence of the contents-list of the *Liber terrarum*. We find there the information that Brihtric gave Yeovilton to Glastonbury 'with his body'.[23] This may have been the message of an endorsement on the charter or, alternatively, simply an embellishment by the copyist of the list. Without the charters to evaluate, we cannot tell. Yeovilton was in lay hands in 1066. It is impossible to determine whether this explanation – if we accepted it – might apply to all of Brihtric's charters and estates associated with Glastonbury, or to Yeovilton and its documents alone. The record of a bequest by Brihtric to the Old Minster, Winchester, which follows the text of S.571 in the Winchester cartulary, offers a suggestive parallel.[24] There Brihtric is said to intend to grant Rimpton to the Old Minster after his death and in the meantime to have presented to the church both the charter of King Eadred for Rimpton and the old charter which King Æthelstan had previously granted. This would support the deposition of Brihtric's title-deeds at Glastonbury, whether the abbey received Henstridge (or Abbas Combe) or merely a promise of a benefaction; it does not, however, explain the apparent duplication of the grant (if both references are to the same estate), unless Brihtric promised it to both churches and gave each a copy of his charter in token of his intention.[25] Brihtric's bequest to the Old

---

20 Grundy, *The Saxon Charters*, pp. 109–12. Domesday Book, I, 87ra and 91vb (Somerset, 1.25 and 18.4).

21 Forsberg, 'Topographical notes', p. 158; Domesday Book, I, 91rb (Somerset, 14.1).

22 See above, *s.n.* Camel.

23 See below, *s.n.* Yeovilton.

24 *Anglo-Saxon Wills*, ed. & transl. Whitelock, pp. 18 and 117–18 (no. 7) (S.1512). The document is dated A.D. 964x980.

25 The key to the puzzle may instead lie with Ælfheah (the recipient of LT96 for Henstridge); his charter for *Cumtone* (S.564; A.D. 955), like Brihtric's for Henstridge, was preserved in two archives – Glastonbury and Abingdon. See above, *s.n.* Compton Beauchamp.

Minster was witnessed not just by the two Winchester communities but by the community of Glastonbury as well. This may support the alternative suggestion that the particular circumstances of the charter's production – possibly at Glastonbury – may account for its preservation there.

Hetsecome (Somerset)

An estate of this name, now unidentified, was held by Glastonbury in 1066, but was lost to the bishop of Coutances, who in 1086 held two hides and three virgates at *Hasecumbe* which had previously been held by four thegns.[26] *Hetsecome* belonged to a group of four Somerset estates which had been seized from Glastonbury and transferred to the bishop, and, according to the *Terrae occupatae* of the *Liber Exoniensis*, one hide and one virgate had been added to the estate by 1086.[27]

A tithing of Hesecombe was recorded in the nineteenth century, probably part of West Coker (in Tintinhull Hundred), southwest of Yeovil. Morland believed this to be the *Hetsecome* of Domesday Book, which he identified with the two hides and three virgates 'missing' from Tintinhull in 1086.[28] If this identification were correct, the history of *Hetsecome* would probably belong to that of Tintinhull.

Holton (Somerset)

According to an entry in the contents-list of the *Liber terrarum*, King Edgar gave an estate at *Healtone* to the layman Byrnsige (S.1765; LT80). No confirmation of this grant appears in the documentary sources, but in the *De antiquitate* a grant of five hides at Holton to Glastonbury by Byrnsige, confirmed by King Edgar, is mentioned.[29] Since it may have been a feature of the *De antiquitate* to present all charters in the archive in favour of laymen as leading to subsequent gifts to the abbey, we cannot necessarily accept its evidence without question. That this hesitation may be justified seems to be confirmed by the appearance in lay hands in the later tenth century of Holton, identified by W. Hunt as near Blackford: it was part of the bequest of Wulfwaru to her younger son, described in her will which was written some time between A.D. 984 and 1016.[30] As Byrnsige's grant for *Healtone* was apparently placed in the *Liber terrarum* next to a charter for Blackford, it has seemed reasonable to identify it with the Holton near Blackford and Wincanton in the far southeast of Somerset. There is some circularity here, however, as Blackford has been identified as the Blackford near Wincanton on the basis of its placing after the Holton grant in the *Liber terrarum*.[31] It should also be remembered that the order of entries in the contents-list may have no significance of this sort. Holton is not an uncommon name, and Wulfwaru's estate so called may not have been the same as Byrnsige's.

---

[26] Domesday Book, I, 91ra and 87vb (Somerset, 8.38 and 5.3).

[27] E 510b7.

[28] Morland, 'Some Domesday manors', p. 47; see below, *s.n.* Tintinhull.

[29] *De antiquitate*, §§62 and 69 (ed. & transl. Scott, pp. 130 and 144); *Cronica*, §§16 and 73 (edd. & transl. Carley & Townsend, pp. 42 and 138).

[30] S.1538; *Two Chartularies*, ed. Hunt, pp. 32–2, and *Anglo-Saxon Wills*, ed. & transl. Whitelock, pp. 62–5 and 174–5 (no. 21).

[31] See above, *s.n.* Blackford.

Two hides at *Altone* were held in 1066 by *Alnod* and in 1086 by a layman;[32] Holton, however (whether these hides or some others is unclear), was later in Glastonbury's possession, together with Blackford, where Glastonbury had held four hides in 1066 and 1086. Blackford reputedly had been the subject of a grant by King Edgar directly to the abbey (S.1768; LT81), although as we have seen its history is complicated by the possibility of confusion with another Blackford, also a Glastonbury holding.[33] Further complication is offered by uncertainty over the number of hides at pre-Conquest Blackford. Morland argued that three hides at Holton, along with five at Blackford near Wincanton, were assessed in Domesday Book under Glastonbury's estate of Butleigh.[34] He did not offer an explanation for the supposed attachment of land to an estate-centre so far away, and his suggestion was not accepted by C. and F. Thorn.[35] It would, however, account for the three remaining hides of Holton which seem to be missing from the account in Domesday Book. C. and F. Thorn's suggestion that the two hides at Holton held by *Alnod* in 1066 were part of post-Conquest Blackford also leaves three of the five hides mentioned in the *De antiquitate* unaccounted for. Stacy's interpretation avoided that difficulty: he suggested that all five of Byrnsige's hides at Holton were in Butleigh, and that Domesday Book's two hides at *Altone* were the same as two hides at Lattiford cited separately.[36]

The evidence for Holton is particularly difficult to interpret without qualification. Edgar's charter may not have been genuine – or its transmission in the *De antiquitate* may have been garbled, in which case the three hides which I have been chasing may be imaginary. Byrnsige may not have given the land to Glastonbury. Wulfwaru's Holton may not have been the one associated with Glastonbury (either in King Edgar's charter or in Domesday Book). The holder of two hides at Holton in 1066 may have been either the abbot of Glastonbury or a thegn with no connexion with the abbey. All this leaves a number of question-marks over the status of pre-Conquest Holton. What *is* clear is that Holton, paired with Blackford, was a possession of the Glastonbury community in A.D. 1189, held from the abbot *in antiquis*.[37] The evidence does not help us to determine whether this meant from the time of King Edgar, from the late eleventh century, or from the early twelfth century when Blackford, having been seized from the abbey, was recovered.

---

[32] Domesday Book, I, 99rb (Somerset, 45.4 [and 8.9 and 36.8, notes]). It should be noted that the holder in 1066 had the same name as the then abbot of Glastonbury (*Alnod*), although he is not identified as such. At Blackford (Somerset, 8.9), however, *Alnoth*, probably the same man, is said to hold from the abbot, making the identification unlikely.

[33] See above, *s.n.* Blackford.

[34] Morland, 'Some Domesday manors', p. 45. Stacy, however, has calculated the eight hides differently: three at Blackford and five at Holton ('The estates', p. 32).

[35] Somerset, 8.9 (note).

[36] Stacy, 'The estates', p. 32. See *s.n.* Butleigh and *Lodreford*.

[37] *A Feodary*, ed. Weaver, p. 58.

Hornblotton (Somerset)

Hornblotton was in 1066 a sub-unit of Glastonbury's estate of Ditcheat, assessed at five and a half hides in Domesday Book.[38] Its pre-Conquest history and the question of its relationship with Ditcheat are considered above in the discussion of that estate.

Horton

According to the contents-list of the *Liber terrarum*, *Horutone* had been the subject of two pre-Conquest grants. First, King *Cenwlf* gave it to a layman (S.1689; LT47);[39] approximately one hundred and fifty to two hundred years later it (with two others) had been commended to Glastonbury by Ælfwine, the *successor* of Wulfric, Wulfric having received the estate from King Eadred (S.1743; LT46).[40] This latter information – the same as offered for Grittleton and Nettleton – may have come from an endorsement on the charter, which is now lost and which was not recorded in the *Index chartarum* or copied into the fourteenth-century cartularies. It (or the text in the *Liber terrarum*) was presumably seen by the author of the *De antiquitate*, who added the information that the estate consisted of ten hides, and that the grant, like those of Grittleton and Nettleton, was confirmed by King Edgar.[41]

The first charter, that of *Cenwlf*, is cited nowhere else in the archive, and may have been a title-deed for the estate, passed on with the land when Ælfwine joined the community at Glastonbury. If so, it is worth noting the substantial time-span over which charters to laymen could be preserved; it is also noteworthy that no more charters for the estate were attached, suggesting at least the possibility that no others had been granted in the interval.

Glastonbury's Horton has not been identified; Finberg proposed the settlement outside Ilminster as one possible candidate.[42] No holder of this Horton, nor of that in Wiltshire (near Devizes), is recorded in Domesday Book; ten hides at Horton (Gloucestershire), about ten miles northeast of Bristol, however, were held by laymen in 1066 and 1086,[43] and seven hides at Horton in Dorset by Horton Abbey.[44] If the hidage is a reliable indicator, Horton near Bristol might be the most reasonable place to identify with the estate held by Glastonbury. Whatever the location of Glastonbury's Horton, however, it seems likely that, unlike Grittleton and Nettleton, the abbey did not hold it for long (at least, by that name), as it quickly disappeared from the archival record.

---

[38] Domesday Book, I, 90vb (Somerset, 8.30).

[39] Edwards (*The Charters*, p. 75) has pointed out that the donor could have been either Cynewulf, king of Wessex (A.D. 757–786), or Cenwulf, king of Mercia (A.D. 796–821).

[40] On Wulfric (probably Dunstan's brother) and Ælfwine (possibly another relative), see above, *s.n.* Grittleton. The significance of *commendauit* in this context is unclear.

[41] *De antiquitate*, §§57 and (for Edgar's confirmation) 69 (ed. & transl. Scott, pp. 118 and 144); *Cronica*, §§16 and 66 (edd. & transl. Carley & Townsend, pp. 42 and 124–6).

[42] Finberg, *The Early Charters of Wessex*, p. 180.

[43] Domesday Book, I, 168rb (Gloucestershire, 46.2).

[44] Domesday Book, I, 78va (Dorset, 14.1).

Houndsborough (Somerset)

No charters are extant for Houndsborough which, according to John Collinson, was the ancient name of a hundred, now represented by Houndston, just west of Yeovil, itself about eighteen miles from Glastonbury.[45] The reference in the *De antiquitate* to a grant to Glastonbury in A.D. 760 by King Cynewulf of 'Huneresberg in orientali ripa Petride' (no hidage specified) is therefore unsupported elsewhere.[46] One hide at *Hundestone* was held by a layman in 1066, without any visible connexion with Glastonbury, while Haselbury and North Perrott, included in Houndsborough Hundred, were also in lay hands.[47] We can therefore only choose from among the usual options: that Glastonbury received the land in the eighth century but lost it at a later date; that an intended grant never took effect; that the document from which this information was taken was not a reliable record of transfer; or that the land was recorded elsewhere among Glastonbury's documents under another name.

Hunespulle

One hide at *Hunespulle* was granted to Glastonbury by a certain Æthelmund, with the consent of Offa (king of Mercia, A.D. 757–796), according to the unsupported testimony of the *De antiquitate*.[48] This may have been the same hide as that recorded in Domesday Book at Huntspill in Somerset (*Honspil*), held by a layman without any evident link with Glastonbury; another three virgates there were assessed separately and held by a different layman.[49] Land at *Inesuuyrth iuxta Hunespulle*, which remains unidentified, was reputedly granted to Glastonbury by an unnamed layman who had received it from King Offa (S.1692; LT28).[50] Finberg proposed that *Inesuuyrth* was Innsworth, near Gloucester, and that the grants of *Inesuuyrth* and of *Hunespulle* had been conflated by mistake, *Hunespulle* being the estate in Somerset.[51] If Æthelmund was the ealdorman of the Hwicce, grants of land in Gloucestershire would not be surprising; but if *Inesuuyrth* and *Hunespulle* were rightly paired and were both in that county, an

---

45 Collinson, *The History and Antiquities of the County of Somerset*, II.323.

46 '*Huneresberg* on the eastern bank of the River Parrett': *De antiquitate*, §§48 and 69 (ed. & transl. Scott, pp. 106 and 142); *Cronica*, §§16 and 54 (edd. & transl. Carley & Townsend, pp. 40 and 106). It may, however, be the 'Cynewlfus de .u. hidis G.' in the contents-list of the *Liber terrarum* (LT27); another candidate for this unidentified entry is North Wootton (*q.v.*) which, unlike Houndsborough, is known to have comprised five hides.

47 Domesday Book, I, 93ra, 99ra, and 92va (Somerset, 19.81, 47.17, and 19.45).

48 *De antiquitate*, §§48 and 69 (ed. & transl. Scott, pp. 106 and 142); *Cronica*, §§16 and 55 (edd. & transl. Carley & Townsend, pp. 40 and 106). This Æthelmund may have been the ealdorman of the Hwicce who was killed in A.D. 802 at Kempsford; see Sims-Williams, *Religion and Literature*, pp. 38–9 (on Offa's ecclesiastical politics, see pp. 155–76). On the Mercian connexion, see below, *s.n. Inesuuyrth*, and pp. 335–7.

49 Domesday Book, I, 95rb and 95va (Somerset, 24.28 and 24.34).

50 See below, *s.n. Inesuuyrth*. In the *De antiquitate*, *Inesuuyrth/Eswirht* is described as a gift by King Offa directly to the abbot of Glastonbury.

51 'Some early Gloucestershire estates', p. 2, n. 3.

unidentified *Hunespulle*, also near Gloucester, must be sought. Alternatively, an *Inesuuyrth* in Somerset near Huntspill might have been at issue. In any event, if Glastonbury did hold Huntspill in Somerset (on the River Brue at the Severn, about ten miles northwest of the abbey), it appears to have lost it by 1066, unless the land had been incorporated into an estate of another name or had changed its name before the mid-eleventh century. If *Hunespulle* and *Inesuuyrth* were in Gloucestershire, they do not appear to have remained in Glastonbury's possession, and their history after Offa's grant is unknown.

Huntspill (Somerset)
See *Hunespulle*.

Hutton (Somerset)
The earliest definite record of Hutton is of its loss before 1086 to the bishop of Coutances, together with Elborough, Stratton, and *Hetsecome*; according to Domesday Book, before 1066 it had been held as two manors, assessed together at five hides.[52] No charter documents Glastonbury's acquisition of this estate by name, nor does it appear in the *De antiquitate*. This circumstance could indicate that Hutton was an early acquisition, with a different name, now lost. Alternatively, it could have come into Glastonbury's hands as part of the grant of a larger (named) land-unit (of neighbouring Elborough, for example [S.1681; LT31]), without being separately identified in the documentation; or it could have been transferred to Glastonbury in a very early charter with only a vague locational description (such as Ine's charter for land at the foot of the Mendips [S.1670; IC A6]).[53] These speculative identifications cannot, however, be supported by any evidence. It is also possible that Hutton was a late acquisition: no record is preserved of gifts to Glastonbury after Æthelred's reign.

Hutton lies north of the River Axe, near its mouth, over twenty miles northwest of Glastonbury.

Idmiston (Wiltshire)
Texts of three charters (and record of a fourth) relating to Idmiston are extant. The earliest was a grant by King Æthelstan to an unnamed layman, a document now lost but listed in A.D. 1247 on the *Index chartarum* (S.1716; IC B3); it is mentioned in no other Glastonbury source. The surviving charter-texts are in the name of Eadred and Edgar. The first is a grant of five hides at *Idemestone* by King Eadred to his *minister* Wulfric in A.D. 947 (S.530); the second, dated in the following year, granted five hides in the same place to the same recipient (S.541);[1] the last is a grant of ten hides at Idmiston by King Edgar to the widow and nun Ælfswith in A.D. 970 (S.775). According to a note in the fourteenth-century cartularies, three sets of bounds, one for each of these texts, were in the *Liber terrarum*, but the later cartularist saw fit to copy bounds at the end of S.541

---

[52] Domesday Book, I, 91ra and 88ra (Somerset, 8.38 and 5.10).
[53] Morland, 'The Glastonbury manors', p. 74.

[1] One of these was still extant as a single sheet *ca* 1600; see above, pp. 10–11.

only.[2] All three charters were apparently in the *Liber terrarum* (LT105, LT104, and LT103) and Edgar's and one of Eadred's were listed in MS. 39a, along with a *uetusta cedula* of the bounds (L31, L32, and L33).[3] The *De antiquitate*, for once, offers less information than the documentary sources, mentioning only a grant of ten hides at Idmiston to Glastonbury by 'Queen' Ælfswith, confirmed by King Edgar.[4] In 1066 Glastonbury held ten hides at Idmiston, according to Domesday Book.[5]

Ælfswith was apparently the donor of several other estates to the abbey.[6] She may have given the three earlier charters for Idmiston (the grants by Æthelstan and Eadred) to Glastonbury as title-deeds along with the land and her own charter. The two charters of King Eadred illustrate an interesting phenomenon. Since, apart from their dates, the dispositive sections of the two charters appear to be identical (five hides at *Idemeston* to Wulfric), we might have interpreted the second grant as a copy, or redundant, or as possible evidence that the first charter had failed to take effect. Instead, the hidage of the two grants (two times five) and that of the later estate (ten) seems clearly to indicate that Idmiston, originally of ten hides, was divided and granted to the same man (probably Dunstan's brother, the *praepositus* of the abbey)[7] in two equal portions in succeeding years. Once reunited in Wulfric's possession, they preserved their unity and were still treated

---

2   *The Great Chartulary*, ed. Watkin, III.644 (no. 1197).
3   The separate transmission of the bounds is worth noting. Separate bounds for Ham, Sturminster Newton, *Winterborne*, and Wrington are also recorded in MS. 39a.
4   *De antiquitate*, §§62 and 69 (ed. & transl. Scott, pp. 130 and 144); *Cronica*, §§16 and 73 (edd. & transl. Carley & Townsend, pp. 42 and 138). Ælfswith's claim to the title of queen given to her by the *De antiquitate* is unknown. She was probably the wife of Ealdorman Ælfheah. On his career and family connexions, see Williams, '*Princeps Merciorum gentis*', especially pp. 147–54; on grants which he is said to have made to Glastonbury, see Compton Beauchamp and Cranmore and (with his wife) Batcombe, Dulwich, and Merton. He appears on the witness-list of S.784, apparently in A.D. 972, but otherwise his attestations cease in A.D. 970 (the year of S.775, where Ælfswith is referred to as a widow). Ælfheah may have been buried at Glastonbury and Ælfswith is said to have retired there (see below, p. 345). Unless there was more than one person of this name involved, she is associated with a number of other grants of land which were recorded in Glastonbury's archive: see *s.n. Andersey*, Batcombe, Dulwich, *Kyngton*, Merton, *Pendescliue*, *Streton*, Tintinhull, Winscombe, and Upavon. Several (if not all) of these estates were acquired by Glastonbury: with the exception of Dulwich, Merton, and Upavon, and possibly *Pendescliue* and *Streton*, they were still held by the abbey in 1066. In most cases, the unreliable testimony of the *De antiquitate* comprises the only evidence that it was Ælfswith who was responsible for passing the lands on to Glastonbury. Her documents may have come to the abbey as a group, whether or not the community received all the land in question.
5   Domesday Book, I, 66vb (Wiltshire, 7.14).
6   See above, n. 4.
7   Wulfric received a substantial number of grants from Kings Edmund and Eadred, most of which lands were acquired – directly or indirectly – by Glastonbury. See above, *s.n.* Grittleton, for a list of his recorded holdings. See further, Brooks, 'The career', pp. 8–11, and Hart, *The Early Charters of Northern England*, pp. 370–2. Of the grants to Wulfric, Kington Langley, Merton, and Tintinhull as well as Idmiston seem to have been acquired by Ælfswith; all but Merton were held by Glastonbury in 1066.

as a single estate in 1066 and 1086.[8] It is interesting to consider whether the estate was first divided under Eadred, or whether it had been split and reassembled before. Æthelstan's charter, which would have helped to answer this question, unfortunately does not survive. The bounds of S.541, according to Grundy, described the whole, ten-hide, estate, but they are late in date.[9]

Grundy experienced great difficulty with the landmarks of the bounds, tentatively concluding that they excluded Porton (subsequently part of Idmiston) and in fact included only a fraction of the later large parish of Idmiston, which was perhaps a later mediaeval creation.[10] Idmiston lies on the River Bourne, over five miles northeast of Salisbury and almost sixty miles east of Glastonbury. Its acquisition appears to be connected with the eastward-looking movement of the endowment which seems to have begun in the mid-tenth century. This expansion into new regions – associated with Dunstan – may have been motivated in part by the search for better-draining soils on the chalk uplands.[11] We may be seeing here a dim reflexion of the kind of manipulation of land resources visible more clearly in Æthelwold's development of the endowment of Ely Abbey.[12] Wulfric may have been instrumental in implementing this new policy during his brother's abbacy.[13]

Iecesig

According to the contents-list of the *Liber terrarum*, King Æthelbald gave *Iecesig* and *Bradraleah* to Glastonbury (S.1679; LT94).[14] The *De antiquitate* offers the information that Abbot Tunberht paid the king (of Mercia) four hundred *solidi* for four hides at these places in A.D. 746; this is not necessarily the first mention of a sale to Glastonbury but is apparently the earliest extant charter from its archive to specify the price paid for land.[15] A grant of *Bradanleag* and *Seacesceg* – presumably another form of the name represented by *Iecesig* – by King Æthelbald to an unnamed layman was recorded in the contents-list of the *Liber terrarum* (LT22;

---

[8] Darlington ('Introduction to the Wiltshire Domesday', p. 96), on the other hand, thought that Eadred's and Edgar's charters were not for the same place and concluded that in the tenth century Idmiston consisted of twenty hides; Domesday Book's entry (ten hides) was thus for only part of Idmiston. But Darlington did not attempt to account for the other ten hides in 1066.

[9] Grundy, 'The Saxon land charters of Wiltshire', *Archaeological Journal* 77 (1920), pp. 16–19. Grundy gave no hint of a date; by 'late' he seems to have meant simply not contemporary with the grant.

[10] *Ibid.*, p. 16.

[11] Stacy, 'The estates', pp. 2–3. See above, map 7.

[12] See *Anglo-Saxon Ely*, edd. & transl. Keynes & Kennedy, and *Liber Eliensis*, ed. Blake, pp. 63–117 and 395–9.

[13] The date of Wulfric's death (possibly before A.D. 951) is uncertain; see Brooks, 'The career', p. 10.

[14] This was presumably the king of Mercia (A.D. 716–757) rather than that of Wessex (A.D. 855–860) (in view of the date given in the *De antiquitate*); see below, pp. 335–7.

[15] *De antiquitate*, §§46 and 69 (ed. & transl. Scott, pp. 104 and 142); *Cronica*, §§16 and 52 (edd. & transl. Carley & Townsend, pp. 40 and 104). S.1410 for Baltonsborough, dated 744, implies a sale but does not give the price. On the Anglo-Saxon land market, see Campbell, 'The sale of land', and above, *s.n.* Brompton Ralph, for some comparative figures.

no Sawyer-number) but in none of the other documentary sources nor the *De antiquitate*. How this charter relates to the one cited above, apparently issued by the same king for the same estates but directly in favour of the abbey, is unclear;[16] Æthelbald may have granted the estates to a layman, retrieved them, and then sold them to Glastonbury, but if so, it seems odd that the layman's charters should have accompanied the land into Glastonbury's possession. Perhaps this circumstance should cast suspicion on Æthelbald's charter to the abbey, which may have been fabricated to provide a better title than LT22 was thought to offer, after the unknown layman or his heir had given the estates – and his charter for them – to the abbey. Whether this invalidates the interesting information that four hundred *solidi* were paid for the land is unclear.[17] Criticism is hampered by the fact that the text of neither charter survives; nor were the single sheets recorded as extant in A.D. 1247.

Iecesig is glossed *uel Gassig* in the *De antiquitate*,[18] but neither of these versions of the name – nor *Seacesceg* – has been associated with an extant place-name. No later record of *Iecesig* survives to help locate it; the land concerned remains unidentified and its history unknown.

Ilchester (St Andrew's Church) (Somerset)

According to Domesday Book, in 1066 a tenant had held St Andrew's church (at Ilchester) from Glastonbury with three hides, but the holding had been lost to the possession of the bishop of Coutances by 1086.[19] How Glastonbury came to hold this church is unknown, as this is the only record of the abbey's relationship with Ilchester. Ilchester (and Northover – across the River Yeo – which is where St Andrew's is actually located), according to Robert Dunning, was probably held by the West Saxon kings as part of the royal estate of Somerton,[20] although neither Ilchester proper nor Northover is assessed by name in Domesday Book.

Dunning has proposed that the minster at Northover originated as an extramural church adjacent to the Roman town of *Lendinis* (Ilchester).[21] He suggested that Glastonbury may have obtained the minster at the same time as it acquired the nearby estates of Podimore Milton, Tintinhull, and Brearly (then part of Tintinhull).[22] The evidence, however, is too slight to offer more than the odd clue for speculation as to how (or when) Glastonbury acquired this important church. The grant of three hides at *Ure* by King Cuthred to Glastonbury, for example, or King Ine's (or Abbess Bugu's) grant of three hides at *Ora*, have been proposed as possible grants of Northover,[23] but they could equally refer to any number of

---

16 Edwards (*The Charters*, p. 71) quite ignored the problem by referring to LT22 and LT94 as 'two versions of the same document'.

17 This information may have been lifted from the layman's charter. Robinson (*Somerset*, p. 37) took it as possibly 'the sign of a genuine document'.

18 But reversed in §69, which reads *Gassic*, with *uel Iecesig* added interlineally. The *Cronica* reads *Gassic* and *Glassing*.

19 Domesday Book, I, 91ra and 91rb (Somerset, 8.37 and 15.1).

20 Dunning, 'Ilchester: a study', p. 44; *idem*, 'Northover', p. 224, and 'Ilchester', p. 179.

21 Dunning, 'Ilchester: a study', p. 46.

22 *Ibid.*

23 Morland, 'The Glastonbury manors', p. 76.

unidentified places.[24] No pre-Conquest documentation for Northover survives to support or condemn any of these identifications.

Inesuuyrth

A reference in the *De antiquitate* to a grant by Offa, king of Mercia, of ten hides at *Eswirht* to Abbot Beaduwulf is unattested in the documentary sources.[25] In the summary of grants in the *De antiquitate*, we find a different form of the place-name: *Ineswurth*.[26] A place called *Inesuuyrth*, described as *iuxta Hunespulle*, was on the contents-list of the *Liber terrarum* as the subject of a grant by King Offa to a layman who gave it to Glastonbury (S.1692; LT28). The text of this charter does not survive. An identification with Huntspill, on the River Brue near the Severn shore, about ten miles northwest of Glastonbury, has been proposed.[27] The description *iuxta* need have been provided only to suggest location, not to indicate that *Ineswurth* was part of Huntspill proper, although one hide there was itself granted to Glastonbury by a certain Æthelmund with the consent of King Offa, according to the unconfirmed evidence of the *De antiquitate*.[28]

One hide at Huntspill and another holding of three virgates were held by laymen in Domesday Book.[29] Perhaps the one hide was the same as Æthelmund's land at *Hunespulle*, which may or may not have been in Glastonbury's hands before 1066.[30] As for *Ineswurth*, no name deriving from it survives in the area of Huntspill, and it remains unidentified. Finberg considered it to be Innsworth,[31] near Gloucester, but this identification seems unlikely, if the supposed relationship with Huntspill is legitimate.[32] Finberg dismissed the difficulty of the distance between Huntspill and Innsworth by suggesting that the description *iuxta Hunespulle* had been mistakenly associated with *Inesuuyrth* by the scribe(s) of the *Liber terrarum*, who had conflated Offa's grant of the latter estate with the grant of Huntspill also made in his reign. If this also seems unlikely, perhaps we should look instead for an unidentified *Inesuuyrth* near Huntspill. No other pre-Conquest record of Innsworth is extant to provide assistance with the identification, nor does *Inesuuyrth* or Innsworth appear by name in Domesday Book. If it was in

---

24 See below, *s.n. Ora* and *Ure*.
25 *De antiquitate*, §48 (ed. & transl. Scott, p. 106); *Cronica*, §55 (edd. & transl. Carley & Townsend, p. 106).
26 Did the scribe of §48 read his exemplar as *in eswurth*, interpreting *in* as a preposition and omitting it from the name? *De antiquitate*, §69 (ed. & transl. Scott, p. 142); *Cronica*, §16 (edd. & transl. Carley & Townsend, p. 40, as *Inelworth*).
27 See above, *s.n. Hunespulle*.
28 *De antiquitate*, §§48 and 69 (ed. & transl. Scott, pp. 106 and 142); *Cronica*, §§16 and 55 (edd. & transl. Carley & Townsend, pp. 40 and 106).
29 Domesday Book, I, 95rb and 95va (Somerset, 24.28 and 24.34).
30 See above, *s.n. Hunespulle*.
31 Finberg, *The Early Charters of the West Midlands*, p. 42, and 'Some early Gloucestershire estates', pp. 1–2.
32 On the other hand, if Æthelmund, the reputed donor of *Hunespulle*, was the ealdorman of the Hwicce who died in A.D. 802, a location in Gloucestershire (at least for *Hunespulle*) might be expected. See Sims-Williams, *Religion and Literature*, pp. 38–9.

Gloucestershire, like *Hunespulle* it does not seem to have remained in the abbey's possession.

Stacy has accepted Finberg's identification and has seen in Offa's grant the beginning of a reorientation of the community's interests, part of an attempt to 'move' Glastonbury from Wessex to Mercia.[33] The retraction of Mercian power after A.D. 802 would, he argued, provide a context for Glastonbury's subsequent loss of *Inesuuyrth*. It is unclear whether the evidence for *Inesuuyrth* can really bear this interpretation, which Stacy supported with dubious documentation.[34]

Iodenwrde
See Edingworth.

Kingstone (Somerset)
Glastonbury held eight hides at *Chingestone* in 1066, although it had lost them to the count of Mortain by 1086.[1] This estate can be identified as Kingstone, a few miles southeast of Ilminster, over twenty miles south of Glastonbury. It is dealt with more fully below, in the discussion of *Stane*.

Kington Langley (Wiltshire)
Kington Langley was a hamlet of Kington St Michael and is discussed together with that estate, below, under *Kyngton*.

Kington St Michael (Wiltshire)
See *Kyngton*.

Korston
See Worston.

Kulmeton
According to the *Historiola de primordiis episcopatus Somersetensis*, which contains an account of transactions reputedly made by Giso, bishop of Wells (A.D. 1060–1088), in order to build up the endowment of his church and that of his canons, an estate of this name was given to Wells by Æthelnoth, abbot of Glastonbury.[2] It is said in the *Historiola* that this estate had descended to Æthelnoth by hereditary right on the death of his mother. This would suggest that the land belonged to the abbot in his private capacity; but the appearance of his mother as a tenant of Glastonbury (at Batcombe, for example), at least raises the possibility that she may have held *Kulmeton* on similar terms. 'Owing to the

---

33 Stacy, 'The estates', p. 11. See below, pp. 335–7.
34 See S.152 and *Cartularium Saxonicum*, ed. Birch, I.392–4 (no. 284) for a confirmation of Glastonbury to his successors by Cenwulf, king of Mercia, and for Pope Leo's supporting privilege (also in *De antiquitate*, §§50 and 51; ed. & transl. Scott, pp. 108–10); both of these the author of the *De antiquitate* claimed to have translated into Latin from vernacular translations of the originals.
1 Domesday Book, I, 92ra (Somerset, 19.10).
2 *Ecclesiastical Documents*, ed. Hunter, p. 19.

diabolical interference of a certain powerful person', Wells did not hold the estate for long.[3] The identity of this *potens* is unknown, and the location of *Kulmeton* is unidentified. The form of the name may suggest an identification with Kilmington (*Chelmetone/Kelmetone*), now in Wiltshire; if so, its entry in Domesday Book betrays nothing of this association with Wells and Glastonbury.[4]

Kyngton

A charter in the name of King Æthelstan granting fifteen hides *at Kyngtone* to one Æthelhelm survives in the fourteenth-century cartularies (S.426; A.D. 934). This charter was listed in the *Index chartarum* (IC B2) and in MS. 39a (L38), but was apparently not in the *Liber terrarum* and is not mentioned in the *De antiquitate*. Although Æthelstan's charter could originally have referred to one of any number of Kingtons or Kingstons in the Southwest, its appearance in the cartularies among documents for Glastonbury's estate at Kington St Michael may mean that it represented a title-deed for that land. Problems of identification arise, however, when comparison is made with the other pre-Conquest charter in that section of the cartulary, a diploma of King Æthelred the Unready granting forty hides at *Kyngtone* to Glastonbury (S.866; A.D. 987). There the background information – that Ælfswith, the wife of the ealdorman Ælfheah, had paid King Edgar forty mancuses of gold for the estate[5] – is offered. Æthelred's charter was listed in MS. 39a (L37), but no confirmation of the transaction is to be found in any other Glastonbury source, even the *De antiquitate*; as a result, Simon Keynes has doubted the authenticity of the charter.[6] Another grant may apply to this estate and complicate the issue further: according to the *De antiquitate*, 'Wilfrid', one of King Edmund's thegns, gave thirty hides at *Kington* to Glastonbury, confirmed by the king.[7] This grant seems to relate to the one referred to in the contents-list of the *Liber terrarum* as a gift by King Edmund to Wulfric (*sic*) of *Langelea id est Cunctun* (LT85).[8] We therefore apparently have four grants, possibly of land in the same place, two of them to Glastonbury, but three of the four for differing numbers of hides: fifteen, thirty, or forty.

Domesday Book does not dispel the confusion, for only one and a half hides at Kington St Michael were held by Glastonbury in 1066, and no other land with this name is cited as the holding of another lord.[9] To the question of the extent of *Kyngton* in the Anglo-Saxon period is therefore added that of its whereabouts in Domesday Book.

---

3   *Ibid.* (Hunter's translation).
4   Ekwall, *The Concise Oxford Dictionary of English Place-names*, p. 276, *s.n.* Kilmington; Domesday Book, I, 98ra (Somerset, 37.7). Five hides there were held TRE by Alfsi.
5   On the Anglo-Saxon land market, see Campbell, 'The sale of land'.
6   'Studies', I.172.
7   *De antiquitate*, §§55 and 69 (ed. & transl. Scott, pp. 114 and 142); *Cronica*, §§16 and 64 (edd. & transl. Carley & Townsend, pp. 40 and 122).
8   It was also in the later cartularies (S.473, see below) and MS. 39a (L39).
9   Domesday Book, I, 72va (Wiltshire, 41.8). Glastonbury lost the land to Ralph of Mortimer before 1086.

Assuming that Glastonbury did not lose most of Kington before 1066 (an assumption derived from the presence of Kington St Michael among the abbey's post-Conquest manors), it may be possible to locate the land in Domesday Book under another name. The reference in the contents-list of the *Liber terrarum* to *Langelea id est Cunctun* leads us to a place called *Langhelei* (later Kington Langley), a hamlet adjacent to Kington St Michael: twenty-nine hides at *Langhelei* were recorded in Domesday Book as held by Glastonbury.[10] Could these, combined with the hide and a half, be the pre-Conquest estate of *Kyngton* granted in S.426 and (perhaps) S.866? This interpretation seems sensible, but the existence of S.473, a charter of A.D. 940 specifically for Langley, makes the situation less straightforward, though not impenetrable. One of the 'alliterative' charters and generally accepted as authentic,[11] it granted to Wulfric thirty hides at *Langeleghe*, which Kemble and Birch identified as Langley Burrell,[12] although the description in the contents-list of the *Liber terrarum* makes it clear that – at least in A.D. 1247 – the charter was thought to refer to Kington. J.E. Jackson accepted this connexion with Kington, and Grundy's examination of the (admittedly difficult) bounds of S.473 confirmed the association with Kington Langley, as did Forsberg's.[13] Jackson, Darlington, and Forsberg identified the Anglo-Saxon estate of S.473 with Glastonbury's Domesday Langley, apparently comprising Kington Langley and Kington St Michael (excluding Easton Piercy).[14] The most recent study of the bounds of the charter – by Avice Wilson and John Tucker – has upheld this identification.[15] None of these analyses, however, has taken into account the problems raised by Æthelred's charter and its forty hides at *Kyngtone*.

If all the charters for *Kyngton* and *Langhelei* were genuine, one interpretation of their seemingly conflicting information could be that they did not apply to the same place. Leaving aside this possibility of Kingstons and Langleys elsewhere, perhaps there may have been some connexion between Edmund's grants of Langley and the neighbouring estate later called Langley Burrell (*Langefel* in Domesday Book), which was in lay hands in 1066 and 1086.[16] The assessment of

---

10 Domesday Book, I, 66vb (Wiltshire, 7.11 and notes).

11 *English Historical Documents*, transl. Whitelock, pp. 372–3; Keynes, *The Diplomas of King Æthelred*, p. 82, n. 165.

12 *Cartularium Saxonicum*, ed. Birch, II.473–5 (no. 751), and *Codex Diplomaticus*, ed. Kemble, VI.308 (no. 382).

13 Jackson, 'Kington St Michael', pp. 38 and 47; Grundy, 'The Saxon land charters of Wiltshire', *Archaeological Journal* 76 (1919), pp. 253–5; Forsberg, *A Contribution*, p. 204.

14 Jackson, 'Kington St Michael', pp. 38 and 47; Darlington, 'Introduction to the Wiltshire Domesday', p. 96; Forsberg, *A Contribution*, p. 204: the bounds included Peckingell, now in Langley Burrell, but formerly an outlying portion of Kington St Michael. Weaver too identified Domesday Langley with the later Kington St Michael (*A Feodary*, ed. Weaver, pp. xxiii and 13–16).

15 Wilson & Tucker, 'The Langley charter'.

16 Domesday Book, I, 69vb (Wiltshire, 24.31). Although the bounds attached to Edmund's extant charter (S.473) do not describe Langley Burrell, they were added to the text at a date well after its composition and do not necessarily represent the estate granted in A.D. 940.

this Langley at only seven hides in Domesday Book discourages the association, however, and the absence of other pre-Conquest evidence means that its relationship to Kington Langley and Kington St Michael remains obscure.

Despite the problems raised by the charters for *Kyngton* and *Langhelei*, it is nonetheless possible to use these documents to construct a relatively coherent history, although more information would no doubt alter the interpretation. To begin with, the grant by Æthelstan of fifteen hides at Kington to the layman Æthelhelm could have been preserved as the title-deed of a portion of the estate which later came to Glastonbury, possibly during the reign of King Edmund. We have seen (at Idmiston, for example) that estates could be granted in portions which were subsequently reunited, and so there is no difficulty in seeing Æthelhelm's fifteen hides as half of the later Kington. The appearance of two grants by Edmund – one to a layman who was probably Dunstan's brother[17] and one directly to the abbey – may cast doubt on the latter. The probably reliable surviving text of S.473 and the reference in the contents-list of the *Liber terrarum* indicate a grant of the entire thirty hides to Wulfric, presumably after Æthelhelm's land had reverted to the king. Only in the comparatively unreliable *De antiquitate* are we told of Wulfric's gift of the estate to Glastonbury, and, as we have seen, its author may have drawn such a conclusion without warrant on other occasions.[18] It is perhaps possible, however, that one of Edmund's two grants did not take effect. In any case, if S.866 is genuine, the estate was back in royal hands in Edgar's reign, as it was said to have been purchased from the king at that time by a laywoman, the wife of the ealdorman of central Wessex whose family had close connexions with Glastonbury;[19] by A.D. 987 *Kyngton* was again in the hands of the king, whence it came to Glastonbury. As noted above, however, suspicion attaches to this diploma, and its forty hides are difficult to reconcile with the thirty of King Edmund's charters and of Domesday Book. Perhaps Æthelred's charter was concocted to replace a less impressive title-deed – Edmund's for Wulfric, for example – or to validate a grant of land at Kington Langley to Glastonbury by Ælfswith.[20] Or perhaps the land had indeed been seized by the king and bought by the ealdorman's wife before Glastonbury successfully retrieved it (but without the benefit of documentation). In any event, *Kyngton* and *Langhelei* appear to have been securely in the abbey's hands in 1066, perhaps after a period of some instability from the reign of Edmund (or perhaps just Edgar) to that of Æthelred.

Kington St Michael and Kington Langley lie a few miles north of Chippenham, approximately forty-five miles northeast of Glastonbury among a concentration of the abbey's estates acquired in the mid-tenth century.[21] Langley Burrell is closer to Chippenham, to the south of Kington Langley. The acquisition of these

---

[17] On Wulfric and the grants he received, see above, *s.n.* Grittleton.

[18] See above, pp. 23–4. Most of Wulfric's estates did pass to Glastonbury, although not all of them directly. See above, *s.n.* Grittleton.

[19] On Ealdorman Ælfheah and his brother, Ealdorman Ælfhere, see Williams, '*Princeps Merciorum gentis*', and above, *s.n. Bocland.*

[20] Idmiston, Merton, and Tintinhull were also grants to Wulfric which passed first into Ælfswith's hands and, at least in the case of Idmiston and Tintinhull, into Glastonbury's thereafter. On Ælfswith, see above, *s.n.* Idmiston.

[21] See also Christian Malford, Grittleton, and Nettleton.

estates in Wiltshire appears to be connected with the eastward-looking movement of the endowment which apparently began in the mid-tenth century. This expansion into new regions – associated with Dunstan – may have been motivated by the search for better-draining soils.[22] We may be seeing here a dim reflection of the kind of manipulation of land resources visible more clearly in Æthelwold's development of the endowment of Ely Abbey. Dunstan's brother Wulfric may have played an important role in implementing this new policy.[23]

Kington was one of several manors appropriated by Wells (and one of those recovered by Glastonbury) during the protracted but ultimately unsuccessful attempt to annex the abbey to the see which was begun by Bishop Savaric (A.D. 1191–1205) and pursued by Bishop Jocelin (A.D. 1206–1242).[24] This post-Conquest threat to Glastonbury's ownership – here and elsewhere – could have provided the motive for the manufacture of retroactive documentation.

Lamyatt (Somerset)

Lamyatt was a sub-unit of Ditcheat (itself held by Glastonbury) which was assessed at five and a half hides in Domesday Book; according to the *Liber Exoniensis*, Lamyatt was held by its tenant from the king in 1086.[1] The only other pre-Conquest documentation for Lamyatt is a charter of King Eadwig granting land there to Cynric, a layman, which was recorded in the *Liber terrarum* (S.1756; LT88); its text does not survive, nor was it listed in the *Index chartarum* or MS. 39a. Lamyatt is not mentioned in the *De antiquitate* either, except in §70 among the unreliable list of *alia* [*maneria*] *data Glastonie*.[2]

In the case of the Domesday estates of Shapwick and Walton, the sub-units recorded in 1066 appear to represent the secondary divisions of an ancient single unit. The evidence for Ditcheat in 1066, although complicated by problems of hidage, could indicate conversely that its parts came together over time, amalgamating rather than fragmenting. Twenty-five hides at Ditcheat appear to have been in Glastonbury's hands in the mid-ninth century, thanks to the patronage of Ealdorman Eanwulf,[3] but the make-up of these hides is uncertain. The grant of Lamyatt to a layman in the mid-tenth century might suggest that it was not yet attached to Ditcheat, unless the king was in the habit of granting out portions of abbatial estates;[4] we are too short of information to draw any save the most tentative conclusions. The charter for Cynric might possibly provide a *terminus post quem* for Lamyatt's incorporation into Ditcheat; there is no certain evidence for this relationship before the time of Domesday Book.

---

22 Stacy, 'The estates', pp. 2–3.
23 See *Anglo-Saxon Ely*, edd. & transl. Keynes & Kennedy, and *Liber Eliensis*; ed. Blake, pp. 63–117 and 395–9. On Wulfric, see Brooks, 'The career', pp. 8–11.
24 See above, p. 12.
1 Domesday Book, I, 90vb (Somerset, 8.30); E 170a1–2.
2 *De antiquitate*, §70 (ed. & transl. Scott, p. 144); see above, pp. 24–6.
3 See above, *s.n.* Ditcheat.
4 A charter in the king's name granting abbatial land is not inconceivable: compare, for example, S.513 and S.509 (*s.n.* Damerham and North Wootton).

Langford
See Little Langford.

Langley
See *Kyngton*.

Lantokay (Somerset)

The text of a charter (dated 680) in the name of Hædde, bishop of the West Saxons (A.D. 676–705/6), granting three hides at *Lantocal* (*sic*) and two hides at *Ferramere* (Meare) to Abbot Hæmgils survives in the fourteenth-century cartularies (S.1249). The contents-list of the *Liber terrarum* provides an identification for the first of these places, the name of which is now obsolete: *Lantokay id est Leghe* (LT5 and LT6).[5] A charter for *Lantokay* and *Ferremere* was listed in the *Index chartarum* and in MS. 39a (IC A3; L1, under Meare and Godney). There is a different version in the *De antiquitate*, where a grant of *six* hides at *Lantocay* (also called *Leghe*) by the bishop in A.D. 681, with the consent of Centwine and Baldred and confirmation by Cædwalla, is described.[6] The gift of *Lantocai* is also mentioned in the spurious Great Privilege of King Ine (S.250).

J.A. Robinson identified this charter as relating to Leigh (later in the parish of Street), two miles south of Glastonbury.[7] Finberg interpreted the name *Lantokay* as deriving from a chapel of St Kay,[8] although there is no evidence for this dedication at Street (apart from the name in this charter). Although the association of Hædde's gift of *Lantokay* with Leigh is generally accepted, it should not be forgotten that it is hardly contemporary with Hædde's grant, the earliest evidence for the identification being the contents-list of the *Liber terrarum* and the *De antiquitate*. S.1249 could possibly refer to another, unidentified, estate. Glastonbury nevertheless held four hides at *Lega* in 1066 (perhaps Lower Leigh, Middle Leigh, and Overleigh, all later in Street parish),[9] for which there is no pre-Conquest documentation. Several more places called *Lege* and one and a half

---

5   There appear to have been two charters in the *Liber terrarum* representing this transaction: these may have been two copies of the charter we now have (S.1249), or perhaps two separate charters, one for *Lantokay* and the other for Meare. Robinson (*Somerset*, pp. 48–9) accepted S.1249 as a charter with 'very primitive' features but observed that the *De antiquitate* seems to have had a different source for its information on this grant.

6   *De antiquitate*, §§38 and 69 (ed. & transl. Scott, pp. 92 and 140); *Cronica*, §§16 and 43 (edd. & transl. Carley & Townsend, pp. 40 and 90).

7   Robinson, *Somerset*, p. 48.

8   From the British element *llan*, 'enclosure, church' (Smith, *English Place-name Elements*, II.16, *s.n. lann*), followed by the element *te*, 'thy', an endearment added before the personal name. For a parallel construction, see Landkey, Devon (Gover *et al.*, *The Place-names of Devon*, II.341). See also Finberg, *The Early Charters of Wessex*, pp. 109–10; Turner, 'Some Somerset place-names', p. 113, and 'A selection', p. 152; and Morland, 'Glaston Twelve Hides', p. 36. On St Kay or Kea, see Doble, *Four Saints*, pp. 7–34, Porter, *The Celtic Church*, pp. 60–1, and Carley, *Glastonbury Abbey*, pp. 96–8. From the place-name Costen extrapolated that in this place a small church had survived 'from the Old Welsh period' (*The Origins*, p. 107).

9   Domesday Book, I, 90rb (Somerset, 8.16).

hides at *Strate* were in other hands in 1066, according to Domesday Book; but C. and F. Thorn have identified these as settlements elsewhere in the county, near Chard.[10] If the identifications by the Thorns are correct, Street itself (the one just south of Glastonbury) does not appear in Domesday Book by name. Given the likely possibility that the extant charter of Hædde which we have has been rewritten,[11] and considering the disagreement in the extant sources about the number of hides at *Lantokay* in the seventh century – not to mention the length of time between the original grant and the appearance of Glastonbury's *Lege* in Domesday Book – it seems unprofitable to attempt to relate *Lantokay* to *Lege* exactly and to speculate on exact locations. No bounds were later attached to the text of S.1249 to facilitate identification.

Street's church is cited in S.250 and S.783, the spurious privileges of King Ine and King Edgar, among those exempt from episcopal interference, implying a longstanding special status. There has been some suggestion that Street was (topographically) part of ancient *Pouelt*, though the extant bounds (of uncertain date) seem to exclude it from at least a portion of that estate.[12] Situated so close to Glastonbury and occupying an important area of raised ground, Street has the appearance of an estate which should have been part of the endowment of the community from the earliest period. For this reason, the evidence of the rather questionable charter S.1249 has been accepted, despite its drawbacks. Even if the documentation has been tampered with, the association of *Lantokay* with the foundation-period may be legitimate.[13] If so, it would indicate that the early layers of Glastonbury's endowment were built up, not just from royal patronage, but from grants of episcopal land as well. A slightly later grant by the bishop of Sherborne may provide a parallel.[14]

Lattiford (Somerset)
See *Lodreford*.

Leigh-in-Street (Somerset)
See *Lantokay*.

Lennucmere
The *Index chartarum* records a charter, now lost, of King Æthelwulf for *Lennucmere* (S.1698 IC D5). This estate appears nowhere else in the Glastonbury

---

[10] Domesday Book, I, 87va, 91va, 95va, 96rb, and 97va (Somerset, 2.9, 16.9, 25.5, 25.6 [and note], 25.47, and 35.14). Names formed with Old English *stret* are quite common in Somerset, particularly near the Fosse Way. See also *Streton*.
[11] Robinson, *Somerset*, pp. 47–53.
[12] See below, *s.n. Pouelt*.
[13] Street is not included within the Twelve Hides of Glastonbury, however, at least in their earliest extant definition (from the mid-thirteenth century). See above, *s.n.* Glastonbury.
[14] See also above, *s.n.* Bleadney, and below, *s.n.* Marchey and Meare. It may be noteworthy that the place-names of two of the four estates attributed to these bishops' gift apparently refer to saints: Kay and Martin.

archive, except in the questionable list of *alia* [*maneria*] *data Glastonie* of §70 of the *De antiquitate*.[15] Since the diploma of Æthelwulf appears on a list of charters for laymen, it is possible that the estate remained in lay hands and was never transferred to Glastonbury. Alternatively, it could have been held, but later lost, or held and incorporated into another unit and thereafter recorded under another name; its appearance on List D (of charters for lands lost) indicates at least that it was not recognised as a possession of Glastonbury's in A.D. 1247. No help is offered by other charters or Domesday Book, in which *Lennucmere* does not appear, and it remains unidentified.

Lim (Devon and Dorset)

Two grants of *Lim* survive in the fourteenth-century cartularies. The first is a charter dated 938 in the name of King Æthelstan for Ealdorman Æthelstan Half-King, for six hides (S.442). The information – perhaps taken from an endorsement on the single sheet (now lost) – that Æthelstan Half-King had given the land to Glastonbury on his entry there as a monk is found in the fourteenth-century cartularies, at the end of the charter's text. The contents-list of the *Liber terrarum* also specifies that the ealdorman gave to the abbey this land which he had received from the king (LT42). In the *De antiquitate*, only the ealdorman's gift to Glastonbury is recorded (but confirmed, it is said, by King Æthelstan).[16]

The second grant of *Lim*, dated 957, is recorded in an extant charter in the name of King Eadwig in which the king gave four hides there to Huna (S.644). This charter is not found on the contents-list of the *Liber terrarum*, but does appear on the lists of the *Index chartarum* and MS. 39a (IC B9; L24). It is not mentioned in the *De antiquitate*. Unlike S.442, there are no bounds attached to this charter.

In 1066 Glastonbury held two estates called *Lim*, according to Domesday Book, one (in Devon) of six hides, and the other (contiguous, but across the border in Dorset) assessed at three hides.[17] We can therefore reasonably set aside the possibility that Eadwig's charter was a regrant of the land granted by

---

[15] *De antiquitate*, §70 (ed. & transl. Scott, p. 144) (as *Leimucmere*); see above, pp. 24–6.

[16] *De antiquitate*, §§54 and 69 (ed. & transl. Scott, pp. 112 and 142); *Cronica*, §§16 and 60 (edd. & transl. Carley & Townsend, pp. 40 and 112). On Æthelstan, see Hart, 'Athelstan "Half King" '. The pre-eminent layman of his time, he retired from Eadwig's court in A.D. 957, probably at the division of the kingdom. (I should like to thank Simon Keynes, who derived this new date from his *Atlas of Attestations in Anglo-Saxon Charters*. See also Keynes, 'The "Dunstan B" charters', p. 191, n. 108.) Dunstan's exile from Glastonbury had probably begun in January of the previous year of upheaval; see Keynes, *The Diplomas of King Æthelred*, p. 49. For other grants to Æthelstan Half-King which are associated with Glastonbury, see above, *s.n. Brentefordlond* and *Foxcote*, and below, *s.n.* Mells, *Westone*, and Wrington. Æthelstan is said – in the contents-list of the *Liber terrarum*, the fourteenth-century cartularies, or the (even less reliable) *De antiquitate* – to have granted all these (except *Brentefordlond*) to Glastonbury; it is not always possible to support this conclusion, which could have been drawn simply from the presence of Æthelstan's title-deeds in the archive. Only *Lim*, Mells, and Wrington were in the abbey's hands in 1066.

[17] Domesday Book, I, 103ra and 77ra (Devon, 4.1, and Dorset, 8.6).

Æthelstan and instead assume the existence of two estates as early as the mid-tenth century. Thanks to the bounds attached to S.442, Æthelstan Half-King's bequest can be identified as the Devon *Lim*, later to be called *Owerlym*, now Uplyme.[18] The Dorset *Lim*, later *Netherlim*, and later still Colway in the parish of Lyme Regis,[19] can probably be safely associated with Eadwig's grant to Huna, although if so one hide seems to have been lost between the years 957 and 1066. It is possible, however, to suggest where this hide might have gone, as two further portions of the estate are to be found in Domesday Book: one hide was held in 1066 by a woman called Ælfgifu, and land for one plough which had never paid tax was held by the bishop of Salisbury.[20] The bishop's land was probably identical with the hide at *Lim* reputedly granted to Sherborne (the episcopal predecessor of Salisbury) by King Cynewulf in A.D. 774 (S.263),[21] and is unlikely, therefore, to be the hide once held by Glastonbury. Ælfgifu's, rather, looks like the missing hide. Perhaps it had been held by a sub-tenant who had managed to detach it from Glastonbury's endowment in the later tenth or the eleventh century.[22]

It appears, therefore, that a ten-hide estate at *Lim* was in royal hands in the early tenth century, when a portion was granted to Ealdorman Æthelstan who gave it to Glastonbury (well before his profession as a monk in A.D. 957, if King Æthelstan's confirmation is to be credited). The second portion of *Lim* may have been granted to a different recipient at the same time; that a record survives of its gift to a layperson in Eadwig's reign is perhaps because that charter (if genuine) was given to Glastonbury with the land at some subsequent date. If the grant to Huna represents a real transaction and he did acquire the land, Glastonbury presumably received the second *Lim* between A.D. 957 and 1066. Once in Glastonbury's hands, the two portions appear to have remained separate, the first (Uplyme) being held – according to Domesday Book – directly by the church and the second (Lyme Regis) by a sub-tenant of the abbey. As we have seen, the latter estate lost one hide before 1066. If the two *Lim*s had once been one, the original estate had straddled (or predated) the Devon-Dorset border, which became the dividing line between the two portions.[23] The Devon land was, at least in the late

---

[18] Hart ('Some Dorset charter boundaries', pp. 160–1) mistakenly related the bounds to Lyme Regis, although he later reversed his opinion ('Athelstan "Half King" ', p. 125, n. 4). Fox (in 'The boundary of Uplyme') made the identification with Uplyme after the discovery of a description of its boundary made for Glastonbury Abbey in A.D. 1516. Fox has provided a map of the bounds of Uplyme (p. 40). See also Barker, 'The early history of Sherborne', p. 88.

[19] Williams, 'Introduction to the Dorset Domesday', p. 56.

[20] Domesday Book, I, 85ra and 75vb (Dorset, 57.14 and 2.5).

[21] See *Charters of Sherborne*, ed. O'Donovan, pp. 4–5 and 81, and Barker, 'The early history of Sherborne', pp. 90–1.

[22] For a map of all four portions of *Lim*, and for their pre-Conquest development, see *ibid.*, pp. 88–9 (and notes).

[23] It seems unlikely that a county boundary would bisect a single estate; yet putting one half of *Lim* in Devon and the other half in Dorset at a time when the two halves were held (albeit separately) by the same house seems odd as well. Perhaps it was done at a time when Æthelstan Half-King held Uplyme, before the transfer of both parts to Glastonbury. (I should like to thank Harold Fox for this suggestion and for discussing the history of *Lim* with me.)

eleventh century, essentially agricultural, but Lyme Regis – both Glastonbury's holding and the other hide – yielded salt and fish as well as agricultural produce. The specialised and essential industry of salt-production doubtless explains at least in part the attachment of this distant estate – on the south coast, over thirty-five miles away – to Glastonbury.

A *Lim* was confirmed to Glastonbury in the corrupt charter of William the Conqueror preserved in the *De antiquitate*.[24] Its appearance there may have some connexion with the statement in the *De antiquitate* that after A.D. 1101 Abbot Herluin *extorsit* Mells and *Lim* from Harding, a powerful layman.[25] It seems that both of the estates of this name were the object of Wells's territorial ambitions in the late twelfth and early thirteenth centuries. A *Lim* was appropriated by the bishop of Wells but was returned to the monks before A.D. 1205, in partial compensation for the seizure of ten abbatial manors (including the other *Lim*).[26] The retrieved *Lim* was identified by Watkin as Uplyme,[27] but perhaps the fact that it was earmarked as belonging to Glastonbury's kitchen, where salt – and fish – would have been essential, points to Lyme Regis instead.[28] The (rare) information identifying this estate with the kitchen was presumably included to distinguish it from the other *Lim*, which Wells (temporarily) retained: logically this latter would have been Uplyme, taken from Glastonbury when Lyme Regis was returned.

Linig
See Tone (River, Land on).

Litlantone
See Grittleton.

Litlenye (Somerset)
A charter dated 712 survives in which Forthhere, bishop of Sherborne (A.D. 709/10–?737), granted to Glastonbury one hide at Bleadney, at St Martin's church (probably Marchey), and at a small island (S.1253). Hazel Hudson and Frances Neale have suggested that this small island is to be identified with *Litlenye*, which appears between Bleadney and Marchey in the Perambulation of the Twelve Hides.[29] *Litlenye* appears nowhere else by name in pre-Conquest sources. In

---

[24] *De antiquitate*, §75 (ed. & transl. Scott, p. 154); *Cronica*, §83 (edd. & transl. Carley & Townsend, p. 154); *Regesta regum Anglo-Normannorum*, edd. Davis *et al.*, I.71 (no. 273). See above, *s.n.* Berrow. Scott rendered this *Lim* as Lyme Regis; Davis *et al.* opted for Uplyme.

[25] *De antiquitate*, §79 (ed. & transl. Scott, p. 160); *Cronica*, §87 (edd. & transl. Carley & Townsend, p. 162).

[26] See above, p. 12; *The Great Chartulary*, ed. Watkin, I.77 (no. 126). A *Lim* had been confirmed to Glastonbury in A.D. 1168 by Pope Alexander III's privilege (*ibid.*, I.128 [no. 173]). These disputes may have encouraged charter-doctoring.

[27] *Ibid.*, I.xli.

[28] According to Harold Fox, the abbey bought and transported fish from there in the thirteenth century (letter of 29 April, 1993).

[29] Hudson and Neale, quoted by Morland in 'Glaston Twelve Hides', p. 37; *De antiqui-*

157

general, uncorroborated post-mediaeval place-names attached to otherwise un-identified places should be treated with caution. On topographical grounds, the derivation of the name, 'little island', from Old English *litle eg*, could suggest an association with a number of places in the Somerset Levels; but the location of *Litlenye*, adjacent to Bleadney and Marchey, does recommend that identification.

Little Langford (Wiltshire)

An abbreviated charter of King Eadred survives in the fourteenth-century cartularies, granting one hide *atte Langeforth* to *meus homo* Wulfheah (S.580; A.D. 946x955). A note refers the reader to the *Liber terrarum* for the bounds. Eadred's diploma for Wulfheah was apparently preceded in the *Liber terrarum* by another charter for Langford (whose text does not survive) in the name of King Edmund and for the same recipient (LT61 and LT62).[30] Both of these documents appear in the *Index chartarum* on List D, and this suggests that Glastonbury had lost the land by A.D. 1247 (IC D11 and D16). We have seen successive grants such as this, of parts of the same estate, elsewhere.[31] Neither of these royal grants to Wulfheah is mentioned in the *De antiquitate*, but we find there the information that he himself gave two hides at Langford to Glastonbury.[32] This could mean that Eadred's lost grant was of two hides or that the grants by Edmund and Eadred to Wulfheah totalled two hides. In Domesday Book, Glastonbury is recorded as holding two hides at Langford in 1066 and 1086, but a further hide held *in eadem uilla* by Edward of Salisbury in 1086 belonged by right (*iure pertinet*) to the abbey.[33] If the two recorded grants by Edmund and Eadred totalled only two hides, a third pre-Conquest charter granting one hide to Glastonbury may therefore have been lost.

Further documentation for Langford in the Anglo-Saxon period survives in the archive of Wilton Abbey. S.1811 is an incomplete diploma of King Edmund granting three hides (according to the bounds) at *Langanforda* to an unknown recipient; it is preserved in the Wilton Cartulary.[34] The bounds of this charter, according to Grundy, described the western part of Little Langford, over four miles northwest of Wilton.[35] A second charter in the same cartulary, S.612, records the grant by King Eadwig of six hides at Langford to the thegn Beornric

---

tate, §72 (ed. & transl. Scott, p. 150); *Cronica*, §3 (edd. & transl. Carley & Townsend, p. 14) (as *Liteline*). On the Twelve Hides, see above, *s.n.* Glastonbury, and map 1.

30 There is no Sawyer-number for Edmund's charter.

31 See above, *s.n.* Idmiston.

32 *De antiquitate*, §§55 and 69 (ed. & transl. Scott, pp. 116 and 142); *Cronica*, §§16 and 64 (edd. & transl. Carley & Townsend, pp. 40 and 122). The summaries state that King Edmund confirmed Wulfheah's gift of the two hides; this is unlikely if, as is suggested by the contents-list of the *Liber terrarum*, Wulfheah received one of the hides from King Eadred.

33 Domesday Book, I, 66vb and 69vb (Wiltshire, 7.12, 7.13, and 24.42).

34 A.D. 963 for 943. The folio with the invocation, proem, and most of the dispositive section of the diploma is missing from the manuscript (London, British Library, MS. Harley 436).

35 Grundy, 'The Saxon land charters of Wiltshire', *Archaeological Journal* 76 (1919), pp. 278–82.

in A.D. 956, and Grundy identified its 'sketchy' bounds as those of the whole of Little Langford.[36] In addition to Glastonbury's three hides at Little Langford recorded in Domesday Book, another three hides there were held by Wilton in 1066 and 1086.[37] It seems accordingly that there was initially an estate of at least six hides which at some point (certainly by the reign of King Edmund) was divided into several portions and granted to laymen, after which these portions were themselves granted by the laymen (not necessarily immediately) to the communities at Glastonbury and Wilton.[38] Eadwig's grant of six hides at Langford complicates the question of what happened in his reign. If we were to ignore the unreliable statement in the *De antiquitate* that Wulfheah gave two hides at Langford to Glastonbury, and assume instead that the author incorrectly based this conclusion on the existence of a charter of King Edmund (or Eadred) for Wulfheah in the *Liber terrarum*, we could perhaps postulate that the gifts of all the portions of Langford made by Edmund to laymen were of short duration and soon reverted to the king; Eadwig then granted the six hides together to one layman, after which a two-fold division may have been re-established and the portions returned (via laymen) to Glastonbury and Wilton, who proved to be more successful in keeping the land until (and in most cases, beyond) 1086. Alternatively, the political circumstances of the year 956 might offer a more simple solution: they could certainly have provided the context for a grant by Eadwig of an estate already held by another (church or lay) to his own man. Regardless of the preservation of this diploma, the grant it represented may never have taken place, and Glastonbury and Wilton may have retained their portions of Langford without interruption from Eadwig and Beornric.

There are other places in Wiltshire which in Domesday Book bear the name Langford (now Hanging Langford and Steeple Langford), where laymen had holdings of five, ten, and five hides in 1066 and 1086.[39] As R.R. Darlington observed, it is difficult to equate Eadwig's charter with any of these places.[40] Although they are neighbours of Little Langford in the Wylye Valley and originally may have belonged with it to one large unit called Langford, the parts would seem to have achieved independence by the mid-tenth century, when Little Langford begins to appear in the records of Glastonbury and Wilton.

Little Langford is about forty miles from Glastonbury in the Wylye Valley, midway between the abbey's other holdings in southern Wiltshire. Its acquisition would appear to form part of the eastward-looking movement of Glastonbury's endowment – possibly associated with Dunstan – which apparently began in the

---

[36] *Ibid.*
[37] Domesday Book, I, 68ra (Wiltshire, 13.13 [and note, which refers, probably incorrectly, to S.612]).
[38] If this interpretation is correct, S.1811 (Edmund's grant recorded at Wilton) and LT61 (Edmund's grant recorded at Glastonbury) were therefore different charters for different land, not duplicate copies of the same grant, as was assumed by Finberg (*The Early Charters of Wessex*, pp. 87–8).
[39] Domesday Book, I, 68vb and 72ra (Wiltshire, 20.5 [Hanging Langford], 37.7 [Steeple Langford], and 37.8 [Hanging Langford], and notes).
[40] Darlington, 'Introduction to the Wiltshire Domesday', p. 93.

mid-tenth century.[41] We may take this as a dim reflection of the kind of manipulation of land resources visible more clearly in Æthelwold's development of the endowment of Ely Abbey.[42]

Littleton Drew (Wiltshire)
See Grittleton.

Lodegaresberghe/Logderesdone **(Somerset)**
The contents-list of the *Liber terrarum* preserves a notice of the otherwise unrecorded grant to Glastonbury by Tunberht, bishop of Winchester (A.D. 871x879), of land at *Logderesdone id est Montagu* (S.1703; LT33). In the *De antiquitate*, information is provided – also unsubstantiated – relating to an earlier grant of sixteen hides at *Logworesbeorh* to Glastonbury by King Baldred.[43] According to the *De antiquitate*, *Logderesbeorgu* was included in King Æthelwulf's Decimation of A.D. 854.[44] The extant text of the Decimation charter (S.303) in the Great Cartulary does indeed list one and a half *hywyscs* (one and a half hides) at *Lodegaresberghe*.[45] No documents survive relating to this estate in the tenth century or the first half of the eleventh, but according to the *Cronica*, William the Conqueror seized *Lodgaresburgh* from Glastonbury.[46] In Domesday Book, the estate was called *Biscopestone* and the count of Mortain was recorded as holding nine hides there in 1086 (which the abbey of Athelney had held in 1066); the count of Mortain had obtained this land in exchange for the manor of *Candel* (Purse Caundle).[47] The Norman name for the estate was *Montaigu*, from which the modern form, Montacute, developed.[48]

---

41 Stacy, 'The estates', pp. 2–3. See above, *s.n.* Grittleton, and map 7.
42 See *Anglo-Saxon Ely*, edd. & transl. Keynes & Kennedy, and *Liber Eliensis* (ed. Blake, pp. 63–117 and 395–9).
43 *De antiquitate*, §§38 and 69 (ed. & transl. Scott, pp. 90 and 140); *Cronica*, §§16 and 43 (edd. & transl. Carley & Townsend, pp. 40 and 90).
44 *De antiquitate*, §§53 and 69 (ed. & transl. Scott, pp. 112 and 142); *Cronica*, §§16 and 56 (edd. & transl. Carley & Townsend, pp. 40 and 108).
45 The text in the *Secretum domini* omits half of the estates, including *Lodegaresberghe*. (For the different texts of the Decimation, see above, *s.n. Brannocmynstre*.) Finberg (followed by many scholars: see, for instance, Dunning, 'Montacute', pp. 213 and 220) interpreted the grant as half a hide (*The Early Charters of Wessex*, p. 122), mistranslating *oþþer healf* ('half the other, or second, hide'); for this idiom, see Campbell, *Old English Grammar*, p. 285 (no. 690), and Mitchell, *Old English Syntax*, I.226 (no. 579). On *hiwisces*, which he has interpreted as a discrete unit within an estate, equivalent to one hide, see Costen, 'Huish and Worth', and *The Origins*, pp. 94–5. Costen has interpreted these units as survivals of an earlier form of organisation of the landscape.
46 *Cronica*, §82 (edd. & transl. Carley & Townsend, p. 154).
47 Domesday Book, I, 93ra (Somerset, 19.86).
48 Ekwall, *The Concise Oxford Dictionary of English Place-names*, p. 330, *s.n.* Montacute; Turner, 'Notes on some Somerset place-names', pp. 120–1. The only evidence for the connexion of the *Lodegaresbergh*-type forms with Bishopstone comes indirectly: Bishopstone is clearly equated with Montacute in Domesday Book ('ibi [in *Biscopestone*] est castellum eius quod uocatur Montagud'; Domesday Book, I, 93ra [Somerset, 19.86]), as is *Lodegaresbergh* in the contents-list of the *Liber terrarum* and

The evidence that Glastonbury held this estate is questionable: Baldred's alleged grant receives no direct support outside the unreliable *De antiquitate*; and the authenticity of the bishop's charter in the *Liber terrarum* cannot be evaluated, as it too does not survive. The Decimation charter, although it is difficult to assess, nonetheless may tilt the balance in favour of the abbey's possession of the land, if the lists preserve genuine information. If the Decimation charter granted not territory but exemption from certain dues and services on land which the recipient already possessed, it might be reasonable evidence that Glastonbury did indeed hold *Logderesdone*, at least in A.D. 854.[49] The connotation of the later Old English place-name, Bishopstone, might in turn argue against Glastonbury's lordship; but the name could have been derived from its episcopal donor, if Tunberht did indeed grant the land to the abbey as claimed.[50] Robert Dunning has speculated that the transaction represented by Tunberht's lost charter may have been not an accretion of property but a confirmation by the bishop – possibly previously an abbot of the house – of land which Glastonbury already held; why the bishop of Winchester would have done such a thing is unexplained.[51] Independent, but dubious, evidence survives which seems to suggest that during Cnut's reign Montacute was in the hands of Tofig the sheriff.[52] In 1066 the estate appears to have been held by Athelney Abbey, but nothing survives to suggest how it might have come into the possession of that community. The accusation in the *Cronica* – that King William seized the estate from Glastonbury – is noticeably absent from the *De antiquitate*. Such an appropriation could have provided the occasion for the forgery of a document claiming (rightly *or* falsely) ancient ownership (Baldred's or Tunberht's). Alternatively, the accusation could have derived from an attempt on Glastonbury's part to lay claim to the estate for the first time. If so, the estate's name (in its oldest form) would have to have been added fraudulently to

in the *De antiquitate* and the *Gesta regum Anglorum* (see Turner, p. 120). But nowhere are *Lodegaresbergh* and Bishopstone directly connected. William of Malmesbury associated *Logweresbeorh* with *Logwor*, one of the names commemorated on the stone pyramids which he had seen in the monks' cemetery at Glastonbury (*Gesta regum Anglorum*, §21 [ed. Stubbs, I.25–6]; *De antiquitate*, §32 [ed. & transl. Scott, p. 84]). When *Logderesdone/Lodegaresberghe* became *Biscopestone* is unclear.

49 The small total mentioned in Æthelwulf's charter (one and a half hides) as opposed to Baldred's sixteen hides (or indeed Domesday Book's nine) may not be an obstacle to this interpretation. It may be that the immunities which were granted in the charter applied to only a portion of the property: if so, at the time of Æthelwulf's Decimation Glastonbury could have held the entire estate. On the Decimation charter, see above, *s.n. Brannocmynstre*, or below, *s.n.* Monk Okehampton, and pp. 322–4.

50 As pointed out by Turner, 'Notes on some Somerset place-names', p. 121. An episcopal charter could have been concocted to match the place-name, however.

51 Dunning, 'Montacute', p. 213. Dunning has also suggested that Glastonbury lost the land by reason of its 'virtual collapse . . . during the Danish invasions', an unproved assumption as far as its endowment is concerned. For Tunberht, see Foot, 'Glastonbury's early abbots', pp. 177–8.

52 'Tractatus de inuentione sanctae crucis nostrae', §§6–7 (*The Foundation of Waltham Abbey*, ed. Stubbs, pp. 5–8). Tofig was the lucky man who was said to have found the Holy Cross on his land at Montacute in A.D. 1034.

the lists attached to Æthelwuf's Decimation charter. Although it is clear that the Glastonbury community felt that it had some claim over *Lodegaresberghe*, the legitimacy of that claim – and the extent of the abbey's success in enforcing it – is obscure.

Montacute is in the southeast of Somerset, between fifteen and twenty miles from Glastonbury.

Lodreford (Somerset)

Lodreford, assessed at two hides, belonged to Glastonbury's *manerium* of Butleigh in 1066 but was lost to the king by 1086.[53] Butleigh was reputed to have entered Glastonbury's holdings in A.D. 801; as no documentation survives for Lattiford in its own name before 1066, we might perhaps have concluded that it was at first an intrinsic part of Butleigh and had acquired an identity of its own only towards the end of the pre-Conquest period.[54] Lattiford's location, however – near Wincanton in the far southeast of Somerset and about fifteen miles from Butleigh – makes this an unlikely interpretation. It is maybe more plausible that Lattiford was deliberately attached to Butleigh for tenurial or economic reasons which we can no longer determine. If a *Lodreford* could be found near Butleigh, however, the connexion with Lattiford – and this particular problem – would disappear.

There appears to be no evidence to hint at the date at which *Lodreford* came into Glastonbury's hands, nor to suggest the circumstances and date of its putative association with Butleigh, or indeed with Holton, in which parish Lattiford later lay.[55] Morland and Stacy, however, have identified these two hides at *Lodreford* with the two hides at *Altone* (Holton) which Glastonbury had held in 1066 and lost in 1086. How these two hides related to the five hides at Holton which were the subject of a grant by King Edgar to Byrnsige is uncertain.[56]

Lottisham (Somerset)

The history of Lottisham is considered above in the discussion of Ditcheat.

Luccombe (Somerset)

According to the contents-list of the *Liber terrarum*, King Edgar gave *Lucum* to Glastonbury (S.1769; LT72). This is the only surviving reference in the documentary sources to Glastonbury's ownership of Luccombe, although a grant of two hides there by Edgar (possibly in A.D. 963) was recorded in the *De*

---

53 Domesday Book, I, 90rb (Somerset, 8.19). The identification of this place is established by the following sequence of forms: *Lodreford*, *Lodereforda*, *Loderford* (Ekwall, *The Concise Oxford Dictionary of English Place-names*, p. 289, *s.n.* Lattiford).

54 See above, *s.n.* Butleigh.

55 *Lodreford* may not have been joined to Butleigh until after 1066: Holton, for example, comprised two estates in 1066 which became one by 1086 (E 139 b2).

56 Morland, 'Some Domesday manors', p. 45, and Stacy, 'The estates', p. 32. The two hides of Lattiford were held from the king in 1086 by Humphrey the Chamberlain, who also held *Altone* (neighbouring Holton) (Domesday Book, I, 99rb [Somerset, 45.4]). The tenants of these two estates in 1066 were different, however, as was the value in 1086. See above, *s.n.* Holton.

antiquitate.[57] According to Domesday Book, two hides at *Locumbe* were held by Queen Edith in 1066; another hide there was also in lay hands.[58] If Glastonbury did receive this distant property in the tenth century, it had apparently lost it by the mid-eleventh.

Luccombe is in Exmoor, not far from the coast, ten miles farther west than Glastonbury's estates in the Brendon Hills, and over forty miles from the abbey.

Lutramtone
See Grittleton.

Lydford (Somerset)

In a charter dated 744 in which Lulla granted the estates of Baltonsborough and *Scobbanwirht* to Glastonbury, ten hides at Lottisham and *Ledenford* – adjacent to Baltonsborough to the east and south – were said to have been left to the *arbitrium* of Æthelbald, king of Mercia (S.1410).[59] The meaning of this statement is obscure, but Lottisham at least appears to have been in the hands of the king of Wessex in the following century, when it was granted by King Æthelwulf in A.D. 842 to Ealdorman Eanwulf, who reputedly gave it to Glastonbury (S.292).[60] Lydford's fate between 744 and 1066 is undocumented. In the Domesday returns for Somerset there are two estates called *Lideford*, one of four hides (later called East Lydford) held by Glastonbury and one of nine hides (West Lydford) held by a layman.[61] The two portions were separated by the Fosse Way. Michael Costen has deduced from the layout of East and West Lydford (on the basis of detached portions of each estate contained within the other) that the two once formed a single unit and that the planning evident in the arrangement of resources and the shape of both settlements was the 'work of a single authority', which he has identified as the community at Glastonbury.[62] It is impossible to say whether Lulla's *Ledenford* in S.1410 (perhaps five hides, since Lottisham, the other half of the ten hides mentioned, was said to have consisted of five hides when granted in the following century) represented the whole of the later estate of *Lideford* (totalling thirteen hides in Domesday Book). If it did, the hidage of the two parts must have been reassessed – perhaps when the estate was divided. The date of this division cannot be determined, but Costen would place it after a widespread reorganisation of the landscape which he saw as having occurred in the second half of the tenth century.[63]

Scobbanwirht (possibly five hides), now unidentified, was also said to have been granted to Glastonbury in A.D. 744 by Lulla (S.1410). The name disappeared from the archive as an estate-name, but was preserved in a single reference

---

[57] *De antiquitate*, §§62 and 69 (ed. & transl. Scott, pp. 128 and 144); *Cronica*, §§16 and 73 (edd. & transl. Carley & Townsend, pp. 42 and 138). The date given may apply to only one or to all of the grants by Edgar described there.

[58] Domesday Book, I, 97ra and 98ra (Somerset, 32.2 and 38.1).

[59] See above, *s.n.* Baltonsborough.

[60] See above, *s.n.* Ditcheat.

[61] Domesday Book, I, 90ra and 99ra (Somerset, 8.4 and 47.21).

[62] Costen, 'Some evidence', pp. 46–8 (with map).

[63] *Ibid.*

(in the bounds of S.292) to meadow acres in the southwestern part of Baltonsborough, adjacent to West Lydford.[64] It is possible that some of Lydford's hides in Domesday Book which are extraneous to the five hides of the known grant of that place included *Scobbanwirht*, which seems to have lost its name and separate identity at an early period. One half-hide at *Scepeworde* which is recorded in Domesday Book, probably near West Lydford,[65] may preserve the memory of this formerly independent entity.

East and West Lydford straddle the Fosse Way where it crosses the River Brue, between five and ten miles southeast of Glastonbury.

Lydney (Gloucestershire)

The contents-list of the *Liber terrarum* records the gift of *Lideneg* by Burgred (king of Mercia, A.D. ?852–873/4), to one Æthelred (S.1702; LT87). No other documentary source in Glastonbury's archive confirms this grant, and *Lidenige* appears in the *De antiquitate* only among the *alia [maneria] data Glastonie* of §70; this suggests either that the land did not in fact come into the abbey's possession,[66] or that it was not held for long. The situation in Domesday Book is complicated by the fact that at the time of that record the new Norman lord was in the process of amalgamating several *terrae* into the new *manerium* of Lydney, but it seems that in 1066 eighteen and a half hides bore the name Lydney and were held in four portions by the bishop of Hereford, the monks of Pershore, two unnamed thegns, and Ælfhere, respectively.[67] It is not possible to ascertain with the present evidence how much of this was the land granted by Burgred in the ninth century; what happened to it between then and 1066 (and whether any of it was ever Glastonbury's territory) is likewise obscure.

Finberg had no doubts about Glastonbury's possession of Lydney.[68] He identified the recipient of Burgred's grant as Æthelred (the son of Æthelwulf, king of Wessex, Burgred's ally against the Welsh), who went on to become king of Wessex in A.D. 865. To Finberg, the grant of Lydney was indicative of the alliance between the royal houses of Mercia and Wessex which is known from their joint enterprise against the West Welsh and Burgred's marriage to Æthelwulf's daughter.[69] Burgred's apparent freedom to grant land in Somerset is shown by a record of a grant at Binegar (*q.v.*). This grant of Lydney, if genuine, may illustrate the

---

64 See below, *s.n. Scobbanwirht*.

65 Domesday Book, I, 99ra (Somerset, 47.22 and note).

66 *De antiquitate*, §70 (ed. & transl. Scott, p. 144). Finberg, however, assumed that Æthelred gave it to Glastonbury ('Some early Gloucestershire estates', p. 3). On this unreliable list, see above, pp. 24–6.

67 Domesday Book, I, 164ra and 167ra (Gloucestershire, 1.55 and 32.11). Six hides at *Lidanege* were confirmed to Pershore in S.786, one of the 'Orthodoxorum' charters in the name of King Edgar, dated 972 but probably a forgery composed after A.D. 993 (Keynes, *The Diplomas of King Æthelred*, p. 99).

68 Finberg, 'Some early Gloucestershire estates', p. 3. Stacy ('The estates', p. 16) has also accepted the identification and suggested a possible policy of deliberate withdrawal as an explanation of Glastonbury's loss of the estate, due to its great distance from the community. Politics might be a more likely explanation.

69 ASC 853. On Glastonbury's Mercian connexion, see further below, pp. 335–7.

disposal of Mercian land to Wessex, as Finberg suggested; Blows, alternatively, has proposed a possible identification of the recipient as the ealdorman of Mercia.[70] This would alter the significance of the grant with respect to Mercian-Wessex relations, not to mention Glastonbury's possession of the estate.

Glastonbury's interest in Lydney, Finberg suggested, was not only in the fisheries of the Severn but in the nearby iron-works of the Forest of Dean. Glastonbury did indeed hold territory at a great distance in order to obtain both fish and iron.[71] But especially if the land in question did relate to the abbey, it is also possible that the 'island' of Lydney was somewhat closer to home than the Gloucestershire estate, which is situated across the Severn from Glastonbury, about fifty miles away. Perhaps another *Lidenige*, now unidentified, was instead to be found in the Somerset Levels, where place-names of this type are common. The association of the grant with a Mercian donor, however, may argue against this suggestion, although the other land apparently granted by Burgred (Binegar) lay near Wells.

Lyme Regis (Dorset)
See *Lim*.

Malmesbury (Wiltshire)
According to Domesday Book, the abbot of Glastonbury had two dwellings (*mansurae*) in the borough of Malmesbury.[1] No evidence is extant to indicate how these properties were acquired. Glastonbury is not known to have had holdings of this sort in other boroughs in 1086, but as Domesday Book's coverage of boroughs is far from complete, the community may have had other, unrecorded, 'urban' properties before the Conquest.[2] Holders of such property benefited from advantageous trading rights.[3]

Marchey (Somerset)
Marchey may be referred to in a very early charter whose text survives in the fourteenth-century cartularies (S.1253). Land at Bleadney, at a small island (*Litlenye?*), and 'ad ecclesiam beati Martini confessoris' was reputedly granted to Ealdberht, abbot of Glastonbury,[4] by Forthhere, bishop of Sherborne, in A.D.

---

[70] 'Studies', p. 213, where he suggested that the charter came to Glastonbury through one of Æthelred's heirs or successors.

[71] See *s.n. Brannocmynstre* and Pucklechurch.

[1] Domesday Book, I, 64va (Wiltshire, M 4).

[2] See below, *s.n.* Wilton and Winchester.

[3] See Maitland, *Domesday Book and Beyond*, pp. 172–8; Galbraith, *Domesday Book*, pp. 151–4; Darby, *Domesday England*, pp. 31–12; and MacDonald & Snooks, *Domesday Economy*, pp. 17–21.

[4] Ealdberht is not recorded in the earliest extant list of abbots in London, British Library, MS. Cotton Tiberius B.v., part 1, at 23a (see Foot, 'Glastonbury's early abbots'), but he is named in the *Liber terrarum* as the recipient of a substantial number of estates and is said in the *De antiquitate* to have ruled Glastonbury A.D. 712–*ca* 719 (*De antiquitate*, §40; ed. & transl. Scott, p. 94). Ealdberht's dates are omitted from the relevant part of the *Cronica* (§47; edd. & transl. Carley & Townsend, p. 92).

712.[5] Given that the earliest surviving form of the place-name Marchey is *Martin-sye*,[6] a connexion between Marchey and a church of St Martin seems likely and is in fact made explicit in the description of the Twelve Hides interpolated into the *De antiquitate*.[7] No form of the name predating the thirteenth-century manuscript of this text survives, however, to indicate whether or not this is an example of late mediaeval creative etymology. It does not appear (by name) in Domesday Book.

In the *De antiquitate*, Marchey was claimed to have been a gift to Glastonbury by King Cenwealh, and Forthhere's grant is restricted to Bleadney.[8] Like the other 'island' estates in the Somerset Levels with an implied ancient relationship with the community of Glastonbury, Marchey is cited as a gift of Cenwealh in the spurious Great Privilege of King Ine (S.250), and its church was awarded special status in S.783, the privilege of King Edgar.[9] It is situated fewer than five miles north of Glastonbury and probably formed part of the abbey's core-estate. If S.1253 represents a genuine transaction, it might demonstrate that the earliest stratum of Glastonbury's endowment was put together not just from royal lands but included at least one holding of the new bishopric of Sherborne. An even earlier grant to Glastonbury from the bishop of Winchester may provide a parallel.[10]

Marksbury (Somerset)

According to the extant text of a charter in the name of King Æthelstan, that king granted (*pro placabili pecunia*) ten hides at *Merkesbury* to his thegn Æthelhelm in A.D. 936 (S.431). This charter was apparently copied into the *Liber terrarum* (LT128) and was recorded on the lists of the *Index chartarum* and MS. 39a (IC B5; L23). We find in the *De antiquitate* a reference to a grant by Æthelstan to Æthelhelm in A.D. 926 (*sic*), with the comment that Æthelhelm had subsequently granted the land to Glastonbury (a gift confirmed by the king).[11] Æthelstan's grant of Marksbury to his *dux Athellinus* is also mentioned in a historical note on the kings of Wessex which follows the text of Æthelwulf's Decimation charter in the fourteenth-century cartularies.[12] The *De antiquitate* provides the additional

---

5 It may be noteworthy that one of the other estates attributed to the gift of an early bishop apparently also refers to a dedication: see above, *s.n. Lantokay*. Costen (*The Origins*, p. 107) has stated that the church of St Martin had survived from 'the old Welsh period', but there is no evidence that it was not of seventh- or early eighth-century date.

6 *De antiquitate*, §§36, 42, 60, 69, 72, and 73 (ed. & transl. Scott, pp. 90, 98, 124, 140, 150, and 152).

7 'Martenesie a sancto Martino cuius ibidem est capella' ('[called] *Marteneseie* after St Martin whose chapel is there'): *De antiquitate*, §73 (ed. & transl. Scott, p. 152).

8 *De antiquitate*, §§36 and 69 (ed. & transl. Scott, pp. 90 and 140); *Cronica*, §§16 and 42 (edd. & transl. Carley & Townsend, pp. 40 and 88). *De antiquitate*, §§40 and 69 (ed. & transl. Scott, pp. 92 and 142); *Cronica*, §§16 and 47 (edd. & transl. Carley & Townsend, pp. 40 and 92).

9 For a more detailed discussion of these 'islands' and the royal privileges, see above, *s.n.* Glastonbury.

10 S.1249 (A.D. 680). See above, *s.n. Lantokay*, and below, *s.n.* Meare.

11 *De antiquitate*, §§54 and 69 (ed. & transl. Scott, pp. 112 and 142); *Cronica*, §§16 and 60 (edd. & transl. Carley & Townsend, pp. 40 and 112).

12 *The Great Chartulary*, ed. Watkin, I.144 (no. 202).

information – unconfirmed in other sources – that King Edgar returned ten hides at Marksbury to the abbey.[13] According to Domesday Book, Glastonbury held ten hides at *Mercesberie*.[14]

Æthelhelm had been the recipient of another grant by King Æthelstan (S.426 for *Kyngton*) which found its way into the Glastonbury archive, but possibly not until the reign of King Edmund, and possibly through the agency of another layman, Wulfric, who may have given the land and the charters to Glastonbury.[15] Might the charter for Marksbury have followed this route? As elsewhere, the value of the statement in the *De antiquitate* that Æthelhelm gave the land to the church remains debatable; Marksbury may not have come to Glastonbury until later – perhaps the restitution by King Edgar was actually the means of transfer of the land (and charters) to Glastonbury, although no charter in Edgar's name survives. If there was such a document, it may have been a forgery, however, designed to provide a better title to the land than S.431 was considered to offer.

Marksbury is more than twenty miles north of Glastonbury, southwest of Bath. It is said to have derived its name (possibly meaning 'boundary fortress') from the ancient fortification on Stantonbury Hill through which the Somerset Wansdyke passes.[16] This must have been a strategic site in Wessex-Mercian relations, but there is no evidence of any interest on Glastonbury's (or anyone else's) part until the mid-tenth century. The bounds appear to be post-Conquest.[17]

Martin (Wiltshire / Hampshire)

Martin (now in Hampshire but in Wiltshire until 1895) was part of a large grant made in A.D. 944x946 (S.513). One hundred hides 'at Domerham cum Mertone et Pentryngtone' were granted by King Edmund to his second wife, Æthelflæd, with reversion to Glastonbury at her death.[18] Martin, but not Pentridge, is thought to have been described with Damerham in the bounds attached to this charter.[19] In Domesday Book, Pentridge is separately assessed and recorded in the Dorset return. Three holdings at *Mertone* (Wiltshire) were in lay hands in 1066 and 1086, but these have been identified as land at Marten, near Great Bedwyn,[20] and the absence of any entry for Martin has led to the assumption that in 1066 it was included in the assessment of neighbouring Damerham.[21] Martin was indeed a

---

13 *De antiquitate*, §§62 and 69 (ed. & transl. Scott, pp. 128 and 144); *Cronica*, §§16 and 73 (edd. & transl. Carley & Townsend, pp. 42 and 138) (no hides mentioned in the summaries).

14 Domesday Book, I, 90vb (Somerset, 8.29).

15 See above, *s.n. Kyngton*.

16 Grundy, *The Saxon Charters*, p. 202; Turner, 'A selection', p. 157; Ekwall, *The Concise Oxford Dictionary of English Place-names*, p. 315, *s.n.* Marksbury.

17 Grundy, *The Saxon Charters*, pp. 186–90.

18 For a full discussion of this grant, see above, *s.n.* Damerham.

19 Grundy, 'The Saxon land charters of Hampshire', pp. 65–6. See above, *s.n.* Damerham.

20 Domesday Book, I, 74rb and 74va (Wiltshire, 67.83, 68.10, and 68.13). Darlington, 'Text of the Wiltshire Domesday', pp. 164 and 166.

21 Domesday Book, I, 66va (Wiltshire, 7.1). Darlington, 'Introduction to the Wiltshire geld rolls', p. 202.

membrum of the manor of Damerham in A.D. 1171,[22] and its subordinate status may have been of very long standing. It was not mentioned by name in Æthelflæd's will (S.1494; A.D. 975x991),[23] but it seems likely that when Damerham passed to Glastonbury (as commanded both in the will and in Edmund's charter) Martin went with it. Due to the nature of the grant in S.513 and the omission of Martin (as a separate entity) from Domesday Book, the size of the estate is impossible to determine.

One record may apply to Martin on its own, without Damerham. The *Index chartarum* lists a charter of *Cenwlfus* concerning the grant of *Mertone* to an unidentified layman (S.1690; IC B1). Appearing as it does on List B, lands still held by Glastonbury, the charter (now lost) was apparently considered by the compiler of the lists to apply to this Martin, rather than Merton (Surrey), for which Glastonbury held pre-Conquest charters but in which it had no post-Conquest interests.[24] In MS. 39a, a *carta Cenwulphi regis*, presumably the same document, appears in the section for Damerham, Martin, and Tidpit (L30). If the thirteenth- and fifteenth-century archivists were not mistaken in their identification of the land involved, this charter could have been an earlier title-deed – granted by Cenwulf, king of Mercia, or Cynewulf, king of Wessex – for the land which later was granted to Æthelflæd. If so, how it came into the Glastonbury archive is a nice point; if it was genuine, its presence would imply that charters for land which reverted to royal ownership themselves went back to the king and were handed over to later holders of the land, as much as one hundred and fifty or more years after the first charters had been written. It is perhaps more likely, however, that S.1690 was a record of the grant of Merton (in Surrey) which was deposited at Glastonbury along with the other charters for that estate. Merton was the subject of two extant tenth-century grants to laymen (S.551 and S.747),[25] the first of which claimed already longstanding ownership by the recipient's family.[26] These charters were mistakenly filed under Damerham by the fourteenth-century cartularist, whose lead was followed by the compiler of MS. 39a (L29). If S.1690 was a grant of Merton, not Martin, it is probably more likely (given its location) that the grantor of the land was the Mercian king.[27] Alternatively, another estate of similar name – admittedly common – could have been involved. Finberg offered Compton Martin as a third candidate.[28] Again, if S.1690 was genuine, its presence in the archive is noteworthy, indicating as it does the length of time over which charters could survive in lay hands, being issued in the eighth or early ninth century and possibly deposited as part of a package in the late tenth.

---

[22] Stacy, 'The estates', p. 243.

[23] *Anglo-Saxon Wills*, ed. & transl. Whitelock, pp. 34–7 and 137–41 (no. 14).

[24] See below, *s.n.* Merton.

[25] The beneficiary of S.551, Wulfric, was probably Dunstan's brother. He received a large number of lands from King Edmund and King Eadred; see above, *s.n.* Grittleton. Three estates which he was given (Idmiston, Kington Langley, and Tintinhull) apparently came to Glastonbury through Ælfswith, probably the wife of Ealdorman Ælfheah (the recipient of S.747, for Merton). See below, *s.n.* Merton.

[26] See below, *s.n.* Merton.

[27] Edwards, *The Charters*, p. 75.

[28] Finberg, *The Early Charters of Wessex*, p. 179.

Meare (Somerset)

Two very early charters claim to be records of the grant of Meare to Glastonbury. S.227, dated 670, a doubtful diploma in the name of King Cenwealh, purports to grant one hide (*cassatum*) at *Ferramere* and two *paruae insulae* to Abbot Berwald. S.1249, dated 680, is the abbreviated text of a charter of Hædde, bishop of the West Saxons, granting three hides at *Lantocal* (*sic*) and two hides (*manentes*) at *Ferramere* to Abbot Hæmgils.[29] Cenwealh's charter was apparently in the *Liber terrarum* (LT3) and a copy was listed in MS. 39a (L4). There may have been two charters from Hædde: the contents-list of the *Liber terrarum* allows two numbers for its entry 'Hedda episcopus de Lantokay id est Leghe dat' Glastonie' (LT5 and LT6). Perhaps one charter was for *Lantokay* and the other for *Ferramere*, the two being combined in S.1249 as we have it now.[30] Reference to *Lantocay* and *Ferramere* together occurs in the single entry for a charter of Hædde in MS. 39a (L1).

As is often the case, the testimony of the *De antiquitate* complicates the picture. It seems to combine the evidence of both charters: although it preserves in essence the version of the grant found in one of the charters (S.227) – with 'Beorhtwald' receiving Meare from Cenwealh in A.D. 670 – the hidage (two) is that found in the other charter (S.1249), as is the form of the one quoted attestation.[31] Hædde's grant of *Lantokay* in A.D. 681 (*sic*), without reference to Meare, appears in a subsequent chapter.[32] The account in the *Cronica* follows that of the *De antiquitate* in naming 'Beorhtwald' as the recipient of Meare from Cenwealh, but it omits the number of hides and the witnesses while adding a detailed description seemingly taken from the dispositive section of S.227.[33] The *Cronica* names the two *paruae insulae* as Westhay and Godney.[34]

The conclusions to be drawn from this complex evidence are far from obvious. One possibility – if S.1249 represents a recast and combined version of two genuine documents – is that *Lantokay* and Meare were indeed episcopal grants of the late seventh century, part of the earliest stratum of Glastonbury's endowment; this would suggest, therefore, that the original endowment was not assembled just

---

[29] Robinson (*Somerset*, pp. 47–53) made a detailed comparison of these two texts. See also Edwards, *The Charters*, pp. 18–22.

[30] Robinson (*Somerset*, p. 49) first made this suggestion. But Edwards (*The Charters*, pp. 22–3) has accepted S.1249 as a genuine and original text.

[31] Compare 'ego Eddi episcopus subscripsi' (S.1249), 'signum manus Theodori archiepiscopi' (S.227), and 'ego Theodorus subscripsi' (*De antiquitate*, §36 [ed. & transl. Scott, p. 90]). For the problems raised by 'Beorhtwald', see Foot, 'Glastonbury's early abbots', pp. 171–3.

[32] *De antiquitate*, §§38 and 69 (ed. & transl. Scott, pp. 92 and 140); *Cronica*, §§16 and 43 (edd. & transl. Carley & Townsend, pp. 40 and 90).

[33] Compare 'terram qui dicitur Ferramere et duas paruas insulas scilicet Westhei et Godeneie ex utraque parte stagni cum captura piscium, paladibus [*sic*], siluis et moris largissimis eidem terre pertinentibus' (*Cronica*, §42; edd. & transl. Carley & Townsend, p. 88) with 'terram qui dicitur Ferramere . . . nec non duas paruas insulas hoc est cum captura piscium in utraque parte stagni cum paludibus, siluis, pascuis apium, et omnibus ad se pertinentibus' (S.227).

[34] *Cronica*, §§16 and 42 (edd. & transl. Carley & Townsend, pp. 38–40 and 88).

from the king's but also from the bishop of Winchester's lands.[35] Cenwealh's charter was probably fabricated at a much later date,[36] perhaps to replace the original charter of Hædde for Meare (LT6?), hypothetically lost, or perhaps to provide a more impressive title, royal rather than episcopal. There is no evidence to suggest why either of these documents would have been required. Once S.227 had been forged, Cenwealh's association with Meare was established and Hædde's forgotten.

Meare receives the same treatment as the other 'islands' with which Glastonbury claimed an ancient relationship in its series of forged privileges, appearing (as *Ferlingmere*) as a gift from Cenwealh in the spurious Great Privilege of King Ine and as one of the special churches in Edgar's privilege (S.250 and S.783).[37] It is provided with an even earlier ancestry, however, in an interpolated chapter of the *De antiquitate* which recounts how the *aqua largissima* there was a direct result of the prayers of St Benignus,[38] who arrived from Ireland to become Patrick's successor as abbot of Glastonbury around A.D. 460 and lived and was buried at Meare until his translation to the abbey in A.D. 1091.[39] This story was presumably created to bolster cult-activity involving Benignus, perhaps in the early post-Conquest period.[40] Despite the spuriousness of this Irish pedigree, like that of Beckery it seems to have been applied to land which (appearances suggest) had indeed been part of the core-endowment of Glastonbury from its earliest years.

Until the draining of the Levels, Meare was aptly described as an island. Westhay and Godney (one mile west and one and a half miles northeast, respectively), identified by name in the *Cronica* only, were likewise distinguished from most of the surrounding land by their greater height above sea-level.[41] The wording of S.227 (admittedly of uncertain date) may indicate that the estate had always

---

[35] Compare with the evidence for an early grant from the new bishop of Sherborne's endowment; see *s.n.* Bleadney and Marchey. It may be noteworthy that the place-names of two of the four estates attributed to this episcopal patronage apparently refer to dedications (to Kay and to Martin); see above, *s.n.* Lantokay and Marchey.

[36] Edwards (*The Charters*, p. 22) has suggested a tenth-century date for the fabrication of S.227. See also above, *s.n.* Glastonbury.

[37] *De antiquitate*, §§42 and 60 (ed. & transl. Scott, pp. 98 and 124); *Cronica*, §§49 and 71 (edd. & transl. Carley & Townsend, pp. 96 and 134). See above, *s.n.* Glastonbury, for a discussion of the 'islands' and the grants of privileges. The reading *Ferlingmere* is in the Great Cartulary's text of Ine's privilege (on 58r) which was not printed by Watkin.

[38] Meare Pool was an impressively large expanse of water before drainage-works transformed the landscape. See Williams, *The Draining*, pp. 17 and 105–7.

[39] *De antiquitate*, §§13 and 33 (ed. & transl. Scott, pp. 62 and 86); elaborated in the *Cronica*, §§29 and 30 (edd. & transl. Carley & Townsend, pp. 68–70), but with the place-name omitted.

[40] On Benignus, see Finberg, *West-Country Historical Studies*, pp. 82–3, and *The Chronicle*, edd. & transl. Carley & Townsend, pp. xxxviii–ix. On the cult of Irish saints at Glastonbury, see Lapidge, 'The cult of St Indract', and Abrams, 'St Patrick and Glastonbury'.

[41] While it is generally unwise to accept fourteenth-century identifications of unnamed early places, in this case Westhay and Godney alone seem to qualify as 'islands' in the region of Meare.

been thought to include not just the raised land (including the two small islands) but the surrounding fisheries, swamps, and moors.[42] In Domesday Book Meare is treated as a component of the *uilla* of Glastonbury; no hides, but sixty acres of land, are mentioned.[43] Three fisheries, a vineyard, and arable and pastoral resources emphasise the contributions of this 'island' only a few miles west of Glastonbury to the community's economy in 1066. It potentially had served this important function for many centuries before those statistics were first recorded.

Meare was one of the manors appropriated by the bishop of Wells (and one of those recovered by Glastonbury) during the protracted but ultimately unsuccessful attempt to annex the abbey to the see which was begun by Bishop Savaric (A.D. 1191–1205) and pursued by Bishop Jocelin (A.D. 1206–1242).[44]

Mells (Somerset)

A charter of King Edmund granting twenty hides *at Milne* to Æthelstan *comes* in A.D. 942 survives in the fourteenth-century cartularies (S.481). This charter was apparently in the *Liber terrarum* (LT101) but was not on the lists of the *Index chartarum*, although it was recorded in MS. 39a as still extant (L10). In the *De antiquitate* we are told that Æthelstan *comes* (identified by Hart as Æthelstan Half-King)[45] gave the land to Glastonbury, a transaction confirmed by King Edmund.[46] Glastonbury held twenty hides at Mells in 1066, according to Domesday Book; five and a half of these, however, were held by the bishop of Coutances from the king in 1086.[47] Perhaps it was these hides only, rather than the whole estate, which some time after A.D. 1101 Abbot Herluin wrested from the hands of a powerful layman, Harding, who may also have appropriated another of Æthelstan's gifts to Glastonbury, *Lim*.[48] Some problem persisted, moreover, as it is

---

[42] Turner, 'Notes on some Somerset place-names', p. 119.

[43] Domesday Book, I, 90ra (Somerset, 8.1).

[44] See above, p. 12.

[45] Hart, 'Athelstan "Half King" ', especially pp. 125–8. The pre-eminent layman of his time, he retired from Eadwig's court to Glastonbury, where he became a monk, probably in A.D. 957 after the division of the kingdom. (I should like to thank Simon Keynes, who derived this new date from his *Atlas of Attestations in Anglo-Saxon Charters*. See also Keynes, 'The "Dunstan B" charters', p. 191, n. 108.) For other grants to Æthelstan Half-King which are associated with Glastonbury, see above *s.n. Brentefordlond, Foxcote,* and *Lim,* and below, *s.n. Westone* and Wrington. Æthelstan is said – in the contents-list of the *Liber terrarum,* the fourteenth-century cartularies, or the (even less reliable) *De antiquitate* – to have granted all these (except *Brentefordlond*) to Glastonbury; it is not always possible to support this conclusion, which could have been drawn simply from the presence of Æthelstan's title-deeds in the archive (only *Lim*, Mells, and Wrington were in the abbey's hands in 1066).

[46] *De antiquitate*, §§55 and 69 (ed. & transl. Scott, pp. 116 and 142); *Cronica*, §§16 and 64 (edd. & transl. Carley & Townsend, pp. 40 and 122).

[47] Domesday Book, I, 90va (Somerset, 8.25). The lost hides of Mells may have their own entry among the holdings of the bishop of Coutances, under the name *Millescote*: Domesday Book, I, 88vb (Somerset, 5.50). See Morland, 'Some Domesday manors', p. 47; but see also below, *s.n. Millescote*.

[48] *De antiquitate*, §79 (ed. & transl. Scott, p. 160); *Cronica*, §87 (edd. & transl. Carley & Townsend, p. 162).

reported in the *Cronica* that Abbot Henry of Blois restored Mells to Glastonbury, although who had appropriated it is not revealed.[49]

A record of another grant of Mells was added to List B of the *Index chartarum* (royal diplomas to lay recipients) as *Ethelstanus de Mylne* (IC B12; no Sawyer-number). This may have been a diploma issued by King Æthelstan, kept by the beneficiary and left at Glastonbury by Æthelstan Half-King when he granted the estate. Alternatively, the charter was perhaps one issued by Æthelstan Half-King himself, granting the land to Glastonbury (in which case it was incorrectly placed on List B). Perhaps this notice is most likely, however, to be a garbled reference to the extant charter of Edmund for Æthelstan Half-King, with the name of the king left out by mistake and that of the recipient confused with the donor. No other record exists of a transaction in King Æthelstan's name involving Mells.

Mells seems therefore to have stayed firmly in Glastonbury's hands from the mid-tenth to the mid-eleventh century (and, apart from one portion, beyond). It is, for once, a straightforward history. But we must not forget that a similar picture of apparent stability would be produced if transactions (leases, appropriations, restorations) in that intervening century had simply not been recorded.

Mells is less than twenty miles northeast of Glastonbury, near the estates of Whatley, Nunney, and Downhead, all possibly pre-Conquest holdings of the abbey.

Mendip (Land at the foot of) (Somerset)

A grant to Abbot Berwald by King Ine of 'terra ad pedem de Munedup' appears on the *Index chartarum* among the charters for lands still held by Glastonbury (S.1670; IC A6). No other record of a grant of land of this description survives in the documentary sources or the *De antiquitate*. This sort of vague definition of location would have been characteristic of an authentic early charter; its weakness in dispositive terms possibly provided the impetus for the recasting of early grants like that of S.248, with the addition of current place-names.[50] The original charter for the land in the Mendip-foothills may therefore have been rewritten, the replacement-charter subsequently being either lost or its connexion with this grant unrecognisable. Alternatively, Ine's original charter may have been omitted from the *Liber terrarum* because the land concerned had been lost from Glastonbury's endowment by the time when that cartulary was compiled (although, as we have seen, otiose charters do not seem to have been weeded out); that Ine's charter appears on List A of the *Index chartarum*, however, should mean that the land was held by the monks in A.D. 1247.

Morland, in an attempt to match estates which appear in Domesday Book (and yet lack pre-Conquest documentation) with Anglo-Saxon charters for unidentified places, has suggested that the land granted by Ine might have been Hutton,[51] north of the Axe near Bleadon. Edwards has preferred a possible identification with Batcombe, which was cited among the *loca principalia* of the Twelve Hides

---

49 *Cronica*, §88 (edd. & transl. Carley & Townsend, p. 164).
50 Abrams, 'A single-sheet facsimile', especially pp. 121–2. See also above, *s.n.* Doulting, and below, *s.n.* Pilton.
51 Morland, 'The Glastonbury manors', p. 74. For Hutton, see above.

in the *De antiquitate* as 'Badecumbe iuxta montem de Munidop'. This description is hardly contemporary with Ine's grant, and the connexion with S.1670, though possible, is no more likely at Batcombe than at a number of other estates later held by Glastonbury in the region – or held, even, by other landlords. The Mendips cover a substantial area north of Glastonbury and a number of abbatial estates were to be found there; but the location of Ine's grant remains unidentified.

According to a fourteenth-century list of donations of land to the church of Sherborne by kings from Cenwealh to Cnut (in London, British Library, MS. Faustina A.ii, at 25rv), twenty-five hides *aput mendip* were given to Sherborne by Cuthred.[52] There is no evidence to support or disprove a connexion with the gift by King Ine to Glastonbury. If Cuthred did grant to Sherborne land which had belonged to Glastonbury, it could indicate a hostility to the abbey and a preference for the bishop's church.[53] None of this, however, is more than speculation.

Merton (Surrey)

As we have seen above (under Dulwich and Martin), two charters in the Glastonbury archive appear to record grants of land at Merton in Surrey to laypeople. S.551 (in the name of King Eadred and dated 949) booked twenty hides there to one Wulfric, probably Dunstan's brother.[54] S.747 (in the name of King Edgar, dated 967) granted twenty hides there, as well as five hides at Dulwich and a piece of land on the Thames, to a certain Ælfheah (probably the ealdorman of that name) and his wife, Ælfswith.[55] These charters were apparently in the *Liber terrarum* (LT112 and LT113) and the latter was listed in the *Index chartarum* (IC B7) and in MS. 39a (L29). Neither makes an appearance in the *De antiquitate*. It is Edgar's charter, with its reference to Dulwich and the Thames and its detailed boundary clause, which clarifies the location of the *Mertone* granted.[56] S.551, which does not include these other places and whose bounds (although apparently included in the *Liber terrarum*) are not extant in the later cartularies, could represent a grant of another place altogether; but the agreement of the hidage at least suggests that the same land could have been involved. The text of S.551 states that King Eadred had ordered a fresh charter to be written, because Wulfric's family had possessed the land for a long time. As we have seen, record of yet another transaction involving *Mertone* and either Cynewulf of Wessex or Cenwulf of Mercia survives in the *Index chartarum* (S.1690; IC B1).[57] If genuine, this record could have been preserved since the eighth or ninth century as proof of title for Merton in Surrey (or, admittedly, Martin in Wiltshire, or somewhere else altogether).

[52] *Charters of Sherborne*, ed. O'Donovan, pp. xxxvii, xli, xlvi, and 81.
[53] Cuthred's privilege for Glastonbury (S.257; A.D. 745) is not genuine as it stands, but may contain authentic elements and reflect good, not bad, relations.
[54] On Wulfric, see Brooks, 'The career', pp. 8–11, and Hart, *The Early Charters of Northern England*, pp. 370–2; for a list of Wulfric's holdings associated with Glastonbury, see above, *s.n.* Grittleton.
[55] On Ælfheah's career and connexions, see Williams, '*Princeps Merciorum gentis*', especially pp. 147–54; on grants to Ælfswith, see above, *s.n.* Idmiston.
[56] Gover *et al.*, *The Place-names of Surrey*, p. 25, n. 1. See above, *s.n.* Dulwich.
[57] See above, *s.n.* Martin.

According to Domesday Book, twenty hides at Merton in Surrey belonged to the king in 1086, having been held by Earl Harold in 1066.[58] There is no hint anywhere of a connexion with Glastonbury, and it is possible that the abbey held the charters but not the land. It is nevertheless also possible that a transfer to the abbey did take place, after which the land returned to lay hands and the relevant documentation of the abbey's ownership (if there was any) was lost. The examples of Idmiston, Kington Langley, and Tintinhull, themselves also granted first to Wulfric and then acquired by Ælfswith (probably Ealdorman Ælheah's wife) and thereafter by Glastonbury, suggest that Merton may have followed a similar path, although those three estates were still held by Glastonbury in 1066. The absence from the *De antiquitate* of the transactions involving Merton might be used to argue that the compiler recognised that the estate was not a Glastonbury holding; against this, however, is the presence of the two charters on List B of the *Index chartarum*, implying continued ownership by the abbey in A.D. 1247. Perhaps the compiler of that list (like that of the fourteenth-century cartularies and MS. 39a) had confused Merton in Surrey with Martin in Hampshire. His confusion would be all too understandable.

Middeltone (Somerset)

The text of a diploma in King Edgar's name granting two hides at *Middeltone* to Glastonbury survives in the fourteenth-century cartularies (S.743; A.D. 966). According to the contents-list, this charter was in the *Liber terrarum* (LT82); and a copy of it was listed in MS. 39a (L14). In the *De antiquitate Mideltone* is included among a group of Edgar's grants to Glastonbury, although it seems that there the grant is dated A.D. 963.[59] In 1066 Glastonbury held six hides at *Mideltone*, according to Domesday Book.[60] The estate is mentioned in the doubtful confirmation-charter of William the Conqueror, which might indicate that Glastonbury's immediately post-Conquest (or later) possession was less than secure.[61]

The text of the charter in the cartularies specifies the location as 'in loco qui dicitur Middilton ad boriam paludestris fluminis qui dicitur Cary'. The bounds attached to S.743 have not been solved.[62] However, their reference to the River Cary and the *bradan strete* locate them somewhere to the north of Ilchester, to the east of the Fosse, and (apparently) north of the Cary. Edgar's charter comes first in the section of the cartularies under the heading *Middiltone*, a section which contains many documents for *Middiltone iuxta Iuelcestre*, apparently confirming the general location (near Ilchester) of the bounds attached to Edgar's grant. Podimore Milton is the name given to this place by Aelred Watkin and H.P.R.

---

58 Domesday Book, I, 30rb (Surrey, 1.5).
59 *De antiquitate*, §§62 and 69 (ed. & transl. Scott, pp. 128 and 144); *Cronica*, §§16 and 73 (edd. & transl. Carley & Townsend, pp. 42 and 138).
60 Domesday Book, I, 90ra (Somerset, 8.3).
61 *De antiquitate*, §75 (ed. & transl. Scott, p. 154); *Cronica*, §83 (edd. & transl. Carley & Townsend, p. 154); *Regesta regum Anglo-Normannorum*, edd. Davis *et al.*, I.71 (no. 273). See above, *s.n.* Berrow.
62 Finberg, *The Early Charters of Wessex*, p. 142.

Finberg, that on modern maps being simply Podimore.[63] Podimore, however, is south of the Cary.[64] It is about ten miles southeast of Glastonbury.

James Carley has drawn attention to the bounds of S.727 (for *Aystone*, viz Steeple Ashton in Wiltshire) to which were appended bounds (dated 968) of a *Mideltone*, with the implication that they might relate to the bounds of S.743 and/or to Podimore Milton.[65] Finberg, however, classed the bounds of S.727 as unidentified,[66] and they seem in fact to relate to a quite different place.

As no other grant of *Middeltone* to Glastonbury has been recorded, Aelred Watkin has assumed that S.743 represents the original grant of the estate of Podimore Milton to Glastonbury.[67] He did not raise the question, however, of the difference between Edgar's grant (two hides) and Glastonbury's holding at *Mideltone* in 1066 (six hides). Perhaps the extant charter granted only part of the estate; a subsequent grant of the remainder may have been made and the record lost. Or perhaps the land was reassessed. Perhaps, too, Edgar's charter related to a different place bearing this common name; the bounds may have been attached at a later date. There is no evidence for any *Mideltone* before A.D. 966.

Mildenhall (Wiltshire)

According to an entry on the contents-list of the *Liber terrarum*, Cynewulf, king of Wessex, gave land at *Mildenhealh* to the layman Bica (S.1682; LT84).[68] This transaction receives no confirmation in the other documentary sources, or in the *De antiquitate*. The latter text, however, offers its own unconfirmed information concerning Mildenhall, that *Hedred* (apparently also the donor of *Essebure*) gave fifteen hides there to Glastonbury, a grant confirmed by King Edgar.[69] Glaston-

---

63   *The Great Chartulary*, ed. Watkin, II.clxiii; Finberg, *The Early Charters of Wessex*, p. 142. C. and F. Thorn cited it as Milton Podimore (Somerset, 8.3 [note]). The name derives from the marsh in the southwest of the estate before it was drained in the later middle ages (Middle English *pode*, 'frog', and Old English *mor*, 'moor' or 'fen': Ekwall, *The Concise Oxford Dictionary of English Place-names*, pp. 330 and 369, *s.n. mor* and Podimore). See also Fox, 'The alleged transformation', p. 544.

64   Morland ('The Glastonbury manors', p. 78) has suggested that the course of the river may have changed. It is possible instead that the bounds applied to the land north of the river but were nevertheless attached to Edgar's charter. Alternatively, *Middeltone* may have been the name of that land at the time when the bounds were added to the charter-text. The specification in the charter-text itself that *Middeltone* lay north of the river is perhaps unusually helpful and not contemporary with the grant. It could have been added any time before the charter was copied into the cartulary.

65   *Cronica*, edd. & transl. Carley & Townsend, p. 294 (n. 303).

66   Finberg, *The Early Charters of Wessex*, p. 95.

67   *The Great Chartulary*, ed. Watkin, II.clxiii.

68   Bica was the recipient of another charter of King Cynewulf, the extant single sheet S.264 for land at Little Bedwyn (A.D. 778). If his charter for Mildenhall had a similar history to that of S.264 (an entirely unprovable hypothesis), it might help to associate that charter – whose provenance is unknown – with Glastonbury. See Edwards, *The Charters*, pp. 59–62, and Dumville, *Wessex and England*, pp. 82–3 and 107–12.

69   *De antiquitate*, §§62 and 69 (ed. & transl. Scott, pp. 130 and 144); *Cronica*, §§16 and 73 (edd. & transl. Carley & Townsend, pp. 42 and 138). Finberg (*The Early Charters of*

bury held ten hides at Mildenhall in Domesday Book.[70] If the charters recording these grants were genuine, they could be interpreted as representing an ancient title-deed and a document of transfer, received by Glastonbury with the land during the reign of Edgar.[71] Five hides of land at Mildenhall may have been lost between its acquisition and 1066, or the estate's hidage may simply have been reassessed.

One further document relating to Mildenhall survives – from the archive of the Old Minster at Winchester. S.1263, in the *Codex Wintoniensis* (Winchester's twelfth-century cartulary), is a grant by Ealhmund, bishop of Winchester, in which the bishop in A.D. 801x805 exchanged with Byrhthelm land at Farnham for thirty-three hides at *Wdutun*, Mildenhall, Froxfield, and Bedwyn. If this charter is genuine, it reveals that Mildenhall (or part of it) was in lay hands not long after Bica received it from Cynewulf: if the exchange did go through, the estate was apparently transferred to the bishop. Perhaps Byrhthelm was Bica's heir, holding as he did another of Bica's estates (Little Bedwyn). Byrhthelm may have resumed possession of Mildenhall after the exchange, or the bishop may have lost it to the king; by the later tenth century it was evidently back in royal hands, if the evidence of the *De antiquitate* can be trusted. By 1066 it was certainly in Glastonbury's. On present evidence it is difficult to say how ancient – or how consistent – this relationship had been.

Mildenhall is just outside Marlborough, about fifty miles northeast of Glastonbury and adjacent to Little Bedwyn.

Millescote (Somerset)

Five and a half hides at *Millescote* were held in 1066 by Glastonbury and in 1086 by the bishop of Coutances, according to Domesday Book; elsewhere in the returns for Somerset, in the main entry for Mells (*Mulle*), five and a half hides of Glastonbury's twenty-hide estate there are said to have been held in 1086 by that bishop from the king.[72] This latter portion has been identified with the north-western part of Mells.[73] But was it *Millescote*? Although the hidage is the same, different values are given for the two holdings in the list of *Terrae occupatae* of the *Liber Exoniensis*,[74] and the appearance of two distinct entries in that text should indicate that two separate pieces of land were involved. The values and the dual entries could, however, simply represent confusion in the record. No other documentation for *Millescote* survives to help to decipher its history; if it was not

---

Wessex, p. 90) identified *Hedred* as King Eadred, which is unlikely but not impossible; if he was the man who gave *Essebure* (Ashbury), however, the name may need to be corrected to Eadric. See above, *s.n.* Ashbury.

70 Domesday Book, I, 66va (Wiltshire, 7.7).

71 Finberg (*The Early Charters of Wessex*, p. 71) assumed that Bica 'or his heirs' gave Mildenhall to Glastonbury, but the estate could have reverted to the king a number of times before Glastonbury received it.

72 Domesday Book, I, 88vb and 90va (Somerset, 5.50 and 8.25).

73 *Ibid.*, notes; also Morland, 'Some Domesday manors', p. 47.

74 E 520 a1 (the lost portion of Mells): 25s. TRE and TRW; E 519b3 (*Millescote*): 40s. TRE and £4 TRW.

part of Mells when Glastonbury received that estate, its acquisition by the abbey is unrecorded.

Monk Okehampton (Devon)

The contents-list of the *Liber terrarum* preserves the record of a vernacular document (now lost) concerning this estate (*Anglice de Ocmund*; LT23; S.1696). No charter of this description appears in any of the extant cartularies or lists. Indeed, the Glastonbury archive preserves no pre-Conquest charters in Old English (boundary clauses aside). The Decimation charter of King Æthelwulf, however, refers to (among others) an uncertain amount of land at *Ocmund* (S.303; A.D. 854).[75] *Occemund* also appears among the *alia* [*maneria*] *data Glastonie* of §70 of the *De antiquitate*.[76] The compiler of that list clearly had evidence of some transaction concerning *Ocmund* (the vernacular charter represented by LT23? its text in the *Liber terrarum*?) which had not been included in the main body of the narrative.

According to Domesday Book, half a hide at *Monuchemtone* was held by one Wulfnoth in 1066 and by Baldwin the Sheriff in 1086.[77] Although J.E.B. Gover *et al.* did not associate it with any particular monastic landlord, Ekwall linked this place-name with the *Ocmund* of the Glastonbury documents, interpreting the

---

[75] The text in the Great Cartulary reads 'be Ocmund et be del healf hywysc'; this could mean 'half a hide at *Ocmund* and at the valley (or portion of land)', or, alternatively, the half-hide could refer exclusively to the *del*, a figure having been omitted after *Ocmund*. Scott understood *be del* to be a reference to a place called *Bedul* (*q.v.*) (for his text, see further this note). On the *hiwisc*, which Michael Costen has interpreted as the equivalent of a hide and representing a relic of an earlier organisation of the landscape, see Costen, 'Huish and Worth', and *The Origins*, pp. 94–5. Birch's text of the charter (from MS. Wood empt. 1) is incomplete (it carries only five names [*Boklond toun*, *Pennard*, *Cotenesfelda*, *Cerawicombe*, and *Branok*] and lacks *Ocmund*, *Sowy*, *Piriton*, *Lodegaresbergh*, and *Colom*) (*Cartularium Saxonicum*, ed. Birch, II.68–70 [no. 472]). For the fuller text in MS. 39, see *The Great Chartulary*, ed. Watkin, I.143 (no. 202). A third text of Æthelwulf's charter (in the *De antiquitate*, §§53 and 69 [ed. & transl. Scott, pp. 112 and 142]; *Cronica*, §§16 and 56 [edd. & transl. Carley and Townsend, pp. 40 and 108]) includes all the names on the Great Cartulary's list except *Culum* (for which it apparently substitutes *Offaculum*) and adds *Duneafd*. (Scott added *Bedul* to this list.) The text in the *De antiquitate* gives no hides for *Occenefeld*, *Pirinton*, *Logderesbeorgu*, *Occemund*, *Branuc*, and *Duneafd*. More than one copy of each community's Decimation charter (and more than one list of lands) could have existed – compare the situation at Winchester. The contemporaneity and authenticity of the lists of estates are probably more doubtful than the genuineness of the charter's texts, which have been treated with some favour by recent studies. See below, pp. 322–4. For a discussion of the Decimation, see Finberg, *The Early Charters of Wessex*, pp. 187–213. See also above, *s.n.* *Brannocmynstre*. Finberg postulated the existence of a lost charter of Æthelwulf for *Ocmund* and identified it with the vernacular document in the *Liber terrarum* (*The Early Charters of Devon and Cornwall*, pp. 9 and 19). Sawyer, too, thought that *Anglice de Ocmund* referred to a grant of this estate by King Æthelwulf, although I can find no evidence to support (or, admittedly, contradict) the association with that king.

[76] Ed. & transl. Scott, p. 144; on this list's lack of authority, see above, pp. 24–6.

[77] Domesday Book, I, 106ra (Devon, 16.17).

latter as Okehampton, the '*tun* on the River Okement'.[78] *Ocmundtune* (Okehampton), named as the site of a manumission (*ca* A.D. 970) in the Leofric Missal, was also held at the time of Domesday Book by Baldwin the Sheriff (by one Osferth in 1066).[79] The place-name suggests that the half-hide at *Monuchemtone* might have had some connexion with this larger estate, perhaps originally being included in it. When the monastic holder commemorated in the first part of the name had lost it and it had reverted to lay possession, Monk Okehampton nonetheless preserved the memory of the association; but by then (at least in Domesday Book) it was tenurially independent from *Ocmund* proper.

Several of the grants in Æthelwulf's Decimation are for fractions of estates known to have been much larger,[80] although others appear to represent the total hidage of the estate. The significance of this is difficult to determine. Æthelwulf's Decimation charter claimed to bestow one-tenth of his lands on the Church; however, it may have been intended to grant, not land, but exemptions from dues and services on land already held. This might suggest that the fractions were notional rather than real, with Glastonbury relieved of one-tenth, say, of the services which it would have rendered from the estate and representing this concession by one-tenth of the estate's hidage. If so, why such a fractional assessment should be applied to some but not all of the estates involved is obscure (although the lists as they stand may differ significantly from their original form). The appearance of *Ocmund*'s half-*hiwisc* in Æthelwulf's Decimation charter might nonetheless suggest that the larger estate of *Ocmundtune* was also Glastonbury's in the ninth century.[81] Æthelwulf's half-hide may, on the other hand, have been real rather than notional, as we have an identifiable piece of land to equate it with (two hundred years later) – the half-hide at *Monuchemtone* recorded in Domesday Book. No document before the time of Domesday Book survives to help to resolve this difficulty.

The modern village of Monk Okehampton lies about seven miles downriver from Okehampton itself, over sixty-five miles southwest of Glastonbury.

Monkton Deverill (Wiltshire)
See *Deuerel.*

Montacute (Somerset)
See *Lodegaresberghe.*

---

[78] Gover *et al.*, *The Place-names of Devon*, I.154; Ekwall, *The Concise Oxford Dictionary of English Place-names*, p. 349, *s.n.* Okehampton.

[79] *Cartularium Saxonicum*, ed. Birch, III.536 (no. 1245); Domesday Book, I, 105vb (Devon, 16.3). Assessed in 1066 at only three virgates and one furlong for tax purposes, this was nonetheless clearly a large estate, with land for thirty ploughs.

[80] Half a hide at *Branoc*, for example. See above, *s.n. Brannocmynstre*. On the difficulties of interpretation presented by the Decimation charter, see further below, pp. 322–4.

[81] A case can be made for this interpretation of other places in the charter with small hidages: see, for example, above, *s.n. Lodegaresberghe.*

Moorlinch (Somerset)

No authentic pre-Conquest documentation exists for Moorlinch, which also fails to appear by name in Domesday Book. It is cited, however (as *Merlinch, Merlinge,* or *Mirieling*), in the spurious Anglo-Saxon royal privileges (S.250 and S.783), where its church is named as one of those in Glastonbury's special zone which were exempt from subordination to the bishop of Wells.[82] Clearly, Glastonbury experienced some difficulties with this estate, possibly at the time of the Conquest, for the *Cronica* reports that Abbot Henry of Blois retrieved three and a half hides there which had been lost.[83]

Grundy suggested that Moorlinch, on the south side of the Polden Hills less than ten miles west of Glastonbury, may have been included in the grant of *Pouelt* to the abbey by King Æthelheard in A.D. 729 (S.253).[84] Because of its location, Morland has taken Moorlinch to be the geld-free land at Shapwick recorded in Domesday Book.[85] Although there is no documentary evidence that Glastonbury held Moorlinch before the Conquest, on topographical grounds alone it seems very likely that it belonged to *Pouelt* and that its history is best considered in the context of Glastonbury's acquisition of that estate, discussed below.

Nettleton (Wiltshire)

Two charter-texts are extant for Nettleton. S.504 is a grant of twenty hides there by King Edmund to one Wulfric in A.D. 944. S.625, in Eadwig's name and dated A.D. 956, also recorded a grant of twenty hides, the recipient apparently being Abbot *Elswius*. According to the contents-list, Edmund's charter for Wulfric was in the *Liber terrarum*, probably with a note (reproduced in the contents-list) specifying that Wulfric's *successor* Ælfwine gave (*commendauit*) it to Glastonbury (LT44).[1] This, as we have seen, was also the case with Edmund's and Eadred's grants of Grittleton and Horton to Wulfric, who was probably Dunstan's brother (S.472 and S.1743; LT43 and LT46).[2] Eadwig's charter was not, it seems, in the *Liber terrarum*, but was listed in the *Index chartarum* and in MS. 39a (IC A15; L34).[3] The details of Ælfwine's fulfilment of Wulfric's grants of Grittleton, Nettleton, and Horton are recorded in the *De antiquitate*, where it is said that Ælfwine brought the lands with him when he became a monk at Glastonbury, and

---

[82] *De antiquitate*, §§42 and 60 (ed. & transl. Scott, pp. 100 and 124); *Cronica*, §§49 and 71 (edd. & transl. Carley & Townsend, pp. 98 and 134). For this zone and the privileges attached to it, see above, *s.n.* Glastonbury.

[83] *Cronica*, §88 (edd. & transl. Carley & Townsend, p. 164).

[84] Grundy, *The Saxon Charters*, p. 115.

[85] Morland, 'The Glastonbury manors', p. 78; Domesday Book, I, 90ra (Somerset, 8.5).

[1] The exact significance of *commendauit* in this context is unknown.

[2] On Wulfric, see Brooks, 'The career', pp. 8–11, and Hart, *The Early Charters of Northern England*, pp. 370–2; for a list of Wulfric's acquisitions which were associated with Glastonbury, see above, *s.n.* Grittleton.

[3] L35 ('copia carte Edwik regis cons[. . .]'), also in the Nettleton section, was probably a copy of S.625 (L34).

that the transfer was confirmed by King Edgar.[4] Eadwig's charter is not mentioned in the *De antiquitate*. Glastonbury held twenty hides at *Niteletone* in 1066.[5]

The detailed information from the contents-list of the *Liber terrarum* may allow us to assume that Nettleton came into Glastonbury's hands when Ælfwine entered the community. The grant by Eadwig is less easy to interpret. If Wulfric and his *successor* held Nettleton from the reign of Edmund to that of Edgar, and Ælfwine's transfer of Nettleton took place during the latter (as claimed in the *De antiquitate*), a royal grant of the land directly to the abbey in the *preceding* reign makes little sense. Neither does a forgery, if there was good evidence of Edgar having confirmed the transaction. Watkin proposed that Eadwig's charter was originally a grant to a layman and that the phrase *uidelicet abbati Glastingens'* had been interpolated.[6] Perhaps Eadwig had seized the estate from its holder (whose connexions with Dunstan would not have recommended him to the king) and awarded it to one of his own men with this document, which was subsequently doctored to look like a grant to Glastonbury. Or perhaps Eadwig had seized the estate and, on Dunstan's departure from Glastonbury, granted it to Abbot Ælfsige, who is described elsewhere in the *De antiquitate* as *pseudo-abbas*, thrust upon the community by the king.[7] Perhaps, if S.625 is spurious, the fabrication was an even later act, designed to overturn or oppose an otherwise undocumented seizure of the land. Whatever the solution to this puzzle, by 1066 the land was in Glastonbury's hands.

The bounds attached to S.504 are, according to Grundy, difficult to solve, but probably included the whole of the later parish of Nettleton.[8] There are no bounds attached to Eadwig's charter. Nettleton is located in Wiltshire near Grittleton and Kington Michael, about forty miles northeast of Glastonbury in an area of concentration of properties which it appears were acquired in the mid- to late tenth century.[9] This eastward-looking movement of the endowment – associated with Dunstan – may have been motivated at least in part by the search for better-draining soils.[10] We may take this as a dim reflexion of the kind of manipulation of land resources more visible in the well documented development by Æthelwold

---

[4] *De antiquitate*, §§55, 57, 62, and 69 (ed. & transl. Scott, pp. 114, 118, 130, and 144); *Cronica*, §§16, 64, and 73 (edd. & transl. Carley & Townsend, pp. 42, 122, and 138). Ælfwine's transfer of the land to Glastonbury is mentioned in the accounts of both Edmund's and Edgar's reigns as well as in the summaries. On Ælfwine, see Keynes, 'The "Dunstan B" charters', pp. 192–3.

[5] Domesday Book, I, 66va (Wiltshire, 7.9).

[6] *The Great Chartulary*, ed. Watkin, III.ccxvi.

[7] *De antiquitate*, §58 (ed. & transl. Scott, p. 120); *Cronica*, §67 (edd. & transl. Carley & Townsend, p. 126). This Ælfsige is not otherwise known. It is not at all clear what happened when Dunstan was expelled from Glastonbury, but the presumption is that another abbot – whether a layman intruded by the king or a religious elected by the community – was chosen. B's Life gives no information on Dunstan's temporary replacement.

[8] Grundy, 'The Saxon land charters of Wiltshire', *Archaeological Journal* 76 (1919), p. 295.

[9] See above, *s.n.* Christian Malford, Grittleton, and *Kyngton*, and map 7.

[10] Stacy, 'The estates', pp. 2–3.

of the endowment of Ely Abbey.[11] Wulfric may have played an important role in implementing Glastonbury's new policy during his brother's abbacy.[12]

Newetone Kastel (Wiltshire)

See Sturminster Newton.

Northover (Somerset)

See Ilchester (St Andrew's Church).

North Wootton (Somerset)

An unusual charter in the name of King Edmund, for *Wodeton*, is preserved in the fourteenth-century cartularies (S.509; A.D. 946). This document granted five hides to Æthelnoth, with details – unique in the Glastonbury archive – of food-renders and other obligations which were required, not just of Æthelnoth, but of the households on the estate.[13] *Wodeton*'s yearly food-renders (payable to the church at Glastonbury) consisted of five *congii* of ale, one of mead, thirty loaves with accompanying *pulmentarius* (pottage), and five *congii* of corn. Every household of the estate (*terra*) had to render *munus ecclesiasticum*, *opus ecclesiasticum*, and *munus rogificum*. If these were not paid, double payment would be required; if they were defaulted on two years in a row, triple payment. If Æthelnoth failed to pay three years in a row, the monks were to take the charter and show it to the king, the bishop, and the powerful laymen of the region, who would deprive him of the land and return it to Glastonbury. Should Æthelnoth lose the land due to some legal transgression, it should not be forfeit to the king but to Glastonbury, because it belonged to that church ('quia eterne hereditatis est prefate sancte ecclesie').[14]

Thus, although the grant was made to Æthelnoth *in eternam hereditatem*, S.509 has more the appearance of a lease than a conferral of book-right. No leases from Glastonbury are known to exist which can parallel the collection at Worcester, and this document (if genuine) provides a unique insight into the conditions of

---

[11] See *Anglo-Saxon Ely*, edd. & transl. Keynes & Kennedy, and *Liber Eliensis*, ed. Blake, pp. 63–117 and 395–9.

[12] The date of Wulfric's death is uncertain (possibly before A.D. 951); see Brooks, 'The career', p. 10.

[13] For a comparison from the late seventh century, see the food-rents owed on ten hides according to King Ine's laws (§70.1; *Die Gesetze*, ed. Liebermann, I.118–21; *English Historical Documents*, transl. Whitelock, p. 406 [no. 32]). For a later comparison, see S.1493 (A.D. 978x1016), which specifies the food-rents owed to Ramsey Abbey from an estate at Hickling. See also below, pp. 267–8.

[14] Æthelwold, in his vernacular account of King Edgar's establishment of the monasteries during the reform, expressly forbade secular lords (including the king) to profit by confiscating ecclesiastical lands where a crime had been committed by the lay holder: *Councils and Synods*, edd. Whitelock *et al.*, I.142–54 (no. 33). This nonetheless continued to take place. See, for example, the lease granted *ca* A.D. 1022 by Eadric, abbot of St Peter's, Gloucester, to *Stamarcotus* for one life (S.1424): 'quare si forisfecerit ille qui terram tenet, de se et de suo emendet. Terra autem sit libera et iterum monasterio reddatur post mortem eius.' ('so that if the one who holds the land should forfeit it, he shall make amends; and afterwards let the land again be free and return to the monas-

the abbey's sub-tenancies in the mid-tenth century.[15] It is important to note that, although the renders were due to Glastonbury, the king seems to have had some kind of administrative role to play in the creation of the tenure – or was it merely the record of the tenure? The significance of Dunstan's apparent unwillingness to sanction this transaction (his attestation reads 'Dunstan abbas nolens sed regalibus obediens uerbis') can only be guessed at. Was the king endowing one of his thegns with Glastonbury's land?

The interpretation of the dues is also uncertain. *Munus ecclesiasticum* presumably refers to church-scot;[16] *opus ecclesiasticum* provides interesting evidence that ecclesiastical lords were able to command building-work from their tenants just as kings commanded from bookland the common dues of bridge-building and fortification-work;[17] *munus rogificum* is an obscure term, possibly connected with alms-giving.

It seems unlikely that *Wottone* was the only one of Glastonbury's estates held in this way; we might in fact profitably consider that such conditions lay behind the bulk of tenth-century grants to laypeople. Perhaps the regular refrain in the *De antiquitate* – that the lay recipient of a charter from the king gave the land to Glastonbury – merely represents the kind of routine reversion to the church of its own land documented in S.509. Without further evidence, this suggestion cannot be tested. Its implications are important, however, as they would significantly alter our ability to draw conclusions from the extant documents: a charter from a king to a layman who is said to have given it to Glastonbury might not so readily be open to interpretation as evidence of the departure of that land from the *terra regis* and its arrival in Glastonbury's hands, but might, conversely, be proof that the monks already held it securely but – with the king's sanction – granted it out with expectation of return. That, certainly, is the implication of Edmund's charter to Æthelnoth under discussion.

The rubric of S.509 in the fourteenth-century cartularies reads 'Carta Edmundi regis de Wottone data ecclesie Glastonie'.[18] This may indicate that the charter described in the contents-list of the *Liber terrarum* as 'Edmundus de Wduton' dat' Glastonie' (LT131) may have been this charter for Æthelnoth (S.509), rather than another charter of Edmund granting the estate to Glastonbury.[19] The listing in the *Index chartarum* among the grants directly to the abbey ([*Edmundus*] *de Wottone*) and a similar note in MS. 39a may perhaps also be references to S.509 (IC A11;

---

tery after his death.') (*Historia*, ed. Hart, I.9). For a case of Glastonbury's leased land which got away (for other reasons), see below, *s.n.* Uffculme.

15 There is always the possibility that the provision of such detail should raise doubts about the authenticity of the text.

16 For examples of ecclesiastical dues in leases granted by the church of Worcester, see *Anglo-Saxon Charters*, ed. & transl. Robertson, pp. 116–20 (nos 56–8).

17 Compare the services spelled out by Oswald in his letter to King Edgar, which included building-work (*Hemingi Chartularium*, ed. Hearne, I.292–6; *The Origins*, transl. Brown, pp. 133–4).

18 *The Great Chartulary*, ed. Watkin, II.447 (no. 814). A marginal note declares 'hec cartula est sub titulo pitancerie Glaston.' ('This charter is under the heading of the pittancer's office of Glastonbury.')

19 Finberg and Sawyer both treated this notice as a reference to S.509.

L8), although strictly speaking it is not a grant by the king to Glastonbury at all. On the other hand, there is a reference in the *De antiquitate* to a grant by Edmund of five hides at *Wudetune* to Abbot Dunstan in A.D. 940 (as opposed to A.D. 946 in S.509).[20] Just how much weight should be given to this is unclear. The format of the *De antiquitate* – where grants are listed in a group – encourages conflation of information, and the declared date and recipient may strictly apply to some of, but not all, the grants. This grant by Edmund to Dunstan may therefore be an invention of the *De antiquitate*, although other options (that it is a reference to S.509, or perhaps a forgery, now lost) may apply.

Record of at least two earlier transactions involving *Wodetone* survives which bears on the question of Glastonbury's first acquisition of the estate. An incomplete statement in the contents-list of the *Liber terrarum* ('Cynewulfus de .u. hidis. G.'; S.1684; LT27) probably refers to a grant described in the *De antiquitate*, where King Cynewulf is said to have given five hides at *Wudeton* to Abbot Guba in A.D. 760.[21] Another entry in the contents-list cites a grant of *Wodetone* by Æthelbald, king of Wessex (A.D. 855-860), to the layman Heregyth (S.1700; LT64). This is not mentioned in the *De antiquitate* and, as neither of these documents attributed to the *Liber terrarum* appears in the *Index chartarum* or the fourteenth-century cartularies, the single sheets seem to have been lost before A.D. 1247. If genuine, Cynewulf's grant could represent Glastonbury's acquisition of Wootton and Æthelbald's a lease of the same sort as S.509, but this is pure speculation and there are other options. For example, after Cynewulf's grant, Glastonbury could have lost possession of the estate, which could have been seized by the king; or perhaps the grant simply failed to take effect. It is also possible that Cynewulf's grant to Glastonbury and/or Æthelbald's to Heregyth were intended to be limited alienations, with automatic reversion to the king. Conditions parallel to those described in S.509 could have applied, but with the renders paid to the king, not the abbey. When exactly the land became Glastonbury's to grant is unclear: the specification in Edmund's diploma that the estate revert to the use of the monks if Æthelnoth should default on his renders could be interpreted either as introducing an innovation or as reinforcing an existing situation. Certainly the peculiarities of the charter (when compared with the surviving documents) seem to preserve a hint of a tenurial background different from the estates for which other charters are extant, but there is, unfortunately, no way of determining how unusual or how ordinary its conditions – if genuine – were.

An attempt has been made to push Glastonbury's acquisition of North Wootton back even further, beyond the reign of Cynewulf. In his analysis of S.248 (Ine's grant to Glastonbury in A.D. 705/6), James Davidson identified North Wootton as one of the four estates granted in that charter, an estate described simply as consisting of five hides on the side of the valley called *Corregescumb*.[22] The

---

20 *De antiquitate*, §§55 and 69 (ed. & transl. Scott, pp. 114 and 142); *Cronica*, §§16 and 64 (edd. & transl. Carley & Townsend, pp. 40 and 120). This reference too was not given separate consideration by Finberg or Sawyer.

21 *De antiquitate*, §§48 and 69 (ed. & transl. Scott, pp. 106 and 142); *Cronica*, §§16 and 54 (edd. & transl. Carley & Townsend, pp. 40 and 106).

22 Davidson, 'On the charters', pp. 12–13.

evidence for this is the coincidence in hidage and North Wootton's location next to Pilton and Croscombe (possibly also granted in S.248).[23] This is not really enough firmly to identify North Wootton's five hides with Ine's grant, although the possibility remains open. Croscombe might be a better candidate.[24]

The bounds attached to S.509 were analysed by Davidson and later by Grundy.[25] Comparing them with the bounds of S.247, for neighbouring Pilton, Davidson concluded that, at the time when the latter bounds were written, North Wootton lay outside Pilton, which included Croscombe and Shepton Mallet.[26] North Wootton in 1066 and 1086, however, was a sub-unit of Pilton.[27] The date of the bounds of S.247 is therefore of greater interest, providing as they may an indication of when North Wootton was independent. Davidson did not consider this point, on which there is now some disagreement, but the state of the language may allow one to argue against a pre-Conquest date for the bounds, which survive in two slightly different versions.[28] North Wootton, therefore, possibly separate from Pilton in A.D. 946, subordinate to it in 1066, was perhaps separate again in the post-Conquest period. Might it have been attached to Pilton for the purposes of Domesday Book alone, for administrative reasons which we cannot recover? If we knew more about the methods of the assessors we might know how to interpret their work for evidence of tenurial structure.

What interpretation is to be made of the appearance of *Witone* (possibly Wootton) in the charter of William the Conqueror, preserved only in the *De antiquitate* and possibly based on an authentic document, is also unclear.[29]

North Wootton is fewer than five miles northeast of Glastonbury. The south-western corner of North Wootton parish appears to have been included in the thirteenth-century description of the Twelve Hides of Glastonbury, as mapped by Morland; in Abbot Beere's sixteenth-century perambulation, even more of North Wootton and Pilton has been incorporated.[30] This creeping expansion of the Twelve Hides provides a late illustration of the changing make-up of the land-

---

23 See Abrams, 'A single-sheet facsimile', pp. 127–30; see also above, *s.n. Corregescumb*, and below, *s.n.* Pilton.

24 See above, *s.n. Corregescumb*.

25 Davidson, 'On the charters', pp. 18–23, with map (n.p.); Grundy, *The Saxon Charters*, pp. 94–8.

26 Davidson, 'On the charters', pp. 12 and 18–23. Grundy (*The Saxon Charters*, pp. 79 and 83) pointed out that the portion of Shepton Mallett east of the Fosse Way (Charlton) was not included, however.

27 Domesday Book, I, 90rb–va (Somerset, 8.20).

28 Davidson seems to have assumed that they were contemporary with the grant; Grundy (*The Saxon Charters*, pp. 79–80) considered that the first version of the bounds (*The Great Chartulary*, ed. Watkin, II.433 [no. 774]) was twelfth- or early thirteenth-century, and that the second (II.450 [no. 818]) was probably much later, *ca* 1300–50. Paul Bibire (in unpublished notes written in June 1991) similarly has judged that there was nothing in either version earlier than Middle English. Peter Kitson, however (in his unpublished work on charter-bounds), has dated them to the second half of the tenth century.

29 *De antiquitate*, §75 (ed. & transl. Scott, p. 154); *Cronica*, §83 (edd. & transl. Carley & Townsend, p. 154); *Regesta regum Anglo-Normannorum*, edd. Davis *et al.*, I.71 (no. 273). See above, *s.n.* Berrow.

30 Morland, 'Glaston Twelve Hides', opposite p. 54; see also above, *s.n.* Glastonbury.

scape; earlier examples of what must have been a common phenomenon are less easy to find because of the paucity of source-material.

Nunney (Somerset)

A notice in the contents-list of the *Liber terrarum* preserves a record of a grant by King Eadred of *Dulting et Nunig* to Glastonbury (S.1742; LT32). The only other source to mention this grant is the *De antiquitate*, in which it is said that Eadred gave part of Nunney (two hides) and part of Elborough (one hide) and restored land at Doulting.[31] This – if we credit the evidence of the *De antiquitate* – may provide interesting evidence that the grant of part of an estate can look the same (at least in the contents-list) as a grant of the whole, an observation which makes the task of writing estate-histories more difficult but which ought not to be forgotten.

If Glastonbury also held another part of Nunney, there is no surviving record of this in the documents. In fact, how long the two hides remained with the monks after the reign of Eadred is unknown; according to Domesday Book five hides at Nunney were in lay hands in 1066 and 1086.[32]

Nunney is about twenty miles northwest of Glastonbury, near Whatley, Down-head, and Mells (*q.v.*).

Nyland (Somerset)

See *Andersey*.

Ocmund

See Monk Okehampton.

Occenefeld

See *Cetenesfelda*.

Odiete (Dorset)

See Woodyates.

Okeford Fitzpaine (Dorset)

An entry on the contents-list of the *Liber terrarum* records that King Edmund gave land at *Acford* to Ælfflæd (who gave it to Glastonbury) (S.1719; LT49). The text of this grant does not survive, nor was it cited on the surviving lists of single-sheet documents. An entry in the *Index chartarum* (IC A12), '[Edmundus] de Acford (Dunstano)', may be a reference to this charter, although it could of course indicate instead the previous existence of a lost grant directly to the abbot. This same difficulty faced us at North Wootton with S.509 and LT131. In the *De antiquitate* we find the information that Ælfflæd, Edward the Elder's widow, gave to Glastonbury twenty-seven hides at *Acford*, Buckland, and Plush, confirmed by

---

[31] *De antiquitate*, §§57 and 69 (ed. & transl. Scott, pp. 118 and 142); *Cronica*, §§16 and 66 (edd. & transl. Carley & Townsend, pp. 40 and 124) (§57 of the *De antiquitate* does not specify the number of hides; the *Cronica* omits the reference to Doulting).

[32] Domesday Book, I, 96va (Somerset, 25.54).

her (step-)son King Edmund.[1] *Acford* was not Ælfflæd's only grant from the king.[2] Thanks to the survival in the fourteenth-century cartularies of a charter in his name for fifteen hides at Buckland and Plush (to the *religiosa femina Ælfflæd* [S.474]), we can surmise that the land at Okeford consisted of twelve hides. At the time of Domesday Book, however, Glastonbury's holding at Okeford consisted of only eight hides, held by four sub-tenants; it is possible that this land was detached from neighbouring Sturminster Newton in the reign of Eadwig.[3] A further two and a half hides in the same hundred which did not pay geld, according to the Geld Roll, may have been part of the earlier hide-count at Okeford.[4] Some kind of re-organisation may have taken place before 1066 which involved the other portions of land called *Acford*; these estates, unfortunately, are unattested before Domesday Book, but at least some of their hides may have been temporarily in Glastonbury's hands, which would account for the difference between the probable twelve hides of LT49 and the eight hides held by the abbey in 1066. This difference may be imaginary, however, as the figure twelve (reconstructed from the *De antiquitate* alone) may not be reliable. Three other Okefords, now called Child Okeford (two entries) and Shillingstone (earlier Shilling Okeford), were assessed at five hides, five hides, and sixteen hides, respectively; the first and the last were in Earl Harold's hands in 1066, the other also in lay possession.[5] If the *Acford* granted to Ælfflæd by Edmund was the same as the *Acford* held by Glastonbury in 1066 – which may have formed part of the abbatial estate later called Sturminster Newton – the *Acford* portion would have to have reverted to the king in order to have been included in Edgar's grant of the entire Sturminster estate to the abbey in A.D. 968 (if the extant charter is genuine). This portion may itself have been appropriated again by the king, if it was the *pars de Sturtone* granted by Eadwig to a layman, as suggested below.[6] Alternatively, Edmund's and/or Ælfflæd's *Acford* may have been located in one of these other places called Okeford. The hidage, however, remains unexplained by this latter suggestion. All the Okefords appear from their location and shared name to have originally been a single unit, but the date of the break-up of this putative unit is not known, nor is it known whether Glastonbury held only part or rather all of the land, which lies

1   *De antiquitate*, §§55 and 69 (ed. & transl. Scott, pp. 114 and 142); *Cronica*, §§16 and 64 (edd. & transl. Carley & Townsend, pp. 40 and 122).

2   She apparently also received land at *Bocland*, *Hammedone* (Hannington?), and *Winterborne*, q.v. A grant to her from King Æthelstan of *Winterborne* (S.399; A.D. 928) is extant in the abbey's archive. In that charter Ælfflæd is called *amabilis femina*; in the charter for Buckland (S.474; A.D. 941), *religiosa femina*. William of Malmesbury (in his *Gesta regum Anglorum*) is the sole source of details concerning Edward the Elder's family, including the identity of Ælfflæd, the daughter of Ealdorman Æthelhelm, as his second wife (§126; ed. Stubbs, I.136–7). There is a chance that Ælfflæd has been wrongly identified, a common problem in a variety of contexts. Nor were all the grants to Ælfflæd which were recorded at Glastonbury necessarily made to the same woman.

3   Domesday Book, I, 77va (Dorset, 8.2). See below, and *s.n.* Sturminster Newton.

4   Williams, 'Introduction to the Dorset geld rolls', p. 122, and 'Text and translation of the Dorset geld rolls', p. 139.

5   Domesday Book, I, 75rb, 79rb, and 83rb (Dorset, 1.7, 26.4, and 54.6 [and notes]).

6   See below, *s.n.* Sturminster Newton.

approximately thirty-five to forty miles southeast of the abbey, next to Sturminster Newton.

Ora

According to the contents-list of the *Liber terrarum*, King Ine granted *Ora* to Glastonbury (S.1673; LT12). No other record of this grant survives in the documentary sources. In the *De antiquitate*, however, additional, but conflicting, information is provided by the statement that Abbess *Bugu* gave three hides at *Ora* to Abbot Ecgfrith; in the summary, the grant is said to have been confirmed by King Ine.[7] *Bugu*'s community has not been identified, but she may have been the woman of that name associated with a minster at Withington in Gloucestershire,[8] or alternatively Bugge, the daughter of King Centwine, a correspondent of Boniface and a member of Aldhelm's circle.[9] If LT12 was actually a charter in Ine's name directly to Glastonbury, as is implied, rather than Bugge's charter with Ine's confirmation, the information offered by the *De antiquitate* might make us suspicious about its authenticity.[10]

Finberg counted *Ora* among the abbey's unidentified estates.[11] Morland, however, has suggested that it may have been the estate of Ower in Hampshire, where Glastonbury held one hide, according to Domesday Book.[12] A hide at Ower was claimed by Milton Abbey in a charter in King Æthelstan's name which is possibly of post-Conquest manufacture (S.391).[13] Some confusion attaches to Ower, as there are two modern places of this name, both in Hampshire, both in Redbridge Hundred; one is just a few miles northeast of Southampton, while the other is at the entrance to Southampton Water.[14] The description of Ower's location (at the mouth of the River Frome) in Æthelstan's charter for Milton (S.391), however, appears to indicate the existence of yet another estate of this name. This is hardly surprising, given Ower's derivation, from Old English *ora*, 'bank', 'shore'.[15] Any land on a river or coast could have been so described, especially in charters of the earliest period, where, as we have seen, a topographical epithet was often pre-

---

[7] *De antiquitate*, §§40 and 69 (ed. & transl. Scott, pp. 94 and 142); *Cronica*, §§16 and 48 (edd. & transl. Carley & Townsend, pp. 40 and 94).

[8] This was Davidson's suggestion ('On the charters', p. 17, n. 6). The community at Withington was apparently established by Æthelred, king of Mercia (A.D. 674–704), for the lady Dunne and her daughter Bugge. See Finberg, *Lucerna*, pp. 21–65. Finberg did not connect this Bugge with Glastonbury.

[9] *Aldhelm*, transl. Lapidge & Rosier, pp. 40–1 and 47–9; *Aldhelmi Opera*, ed. Ehwald, pp. 14–18; *Die Briefe*, ed. Tangl, pp. 21–8, 47–9, 214–15, 229–31, and 252–3 (nos 14, 15, 27, 94, 105, and 117).

[10] Edwards has considered it doubtful: *The Charters*, p. 68.

[11] Finberg, *The Early Charters of Wessex*, p. 179.

[12] Morland, 'The Glastonbury manors', pp. 76 and 89; Domesday Book, I, 43va (Hampshire, 11.1).

[13] On S.391, see *Anglo-Saxon Charters*, ed. & transl. Robertson, pp. 45–9 and 300–4 (no. 23).

[14] The map in the edition by C. and F. Thorn of the Domesday Book returns for Dorset identifies Glastonbury's holding at Ower with the former estate.

[15] Ekwall, *The Concise Oxford Dictionary of English Place-names*, p. 355, *s.n.* Ower.

ferred to a place-name. The identification of any of the later Owers with Bugge's or Ine's *Ora* accordingly seems perilous.

Morland has suggested yet another identification, with Northover, where Glastonbury held three hides (and St Andrew's church) in 1066.[16] The hidage at least of Bugge's *Ora* is the same, but no pre-Conquest documentation survives to support or condemn this identification. The early history of the minster at Northover is unknown; it is impossible, therefore, to assess whether it might stretch back to the early eighth century and thus connect with Abbess Bugge.

One other reference may relate to *Ora*. A charter apparently in the *Liber terrarum* recorded a grant of *Ure* to Glastonbury by King Cuthred (S.1678; LT18). This transaction is dated 745 in the *De antiquitate*; the grant apparently consisted of three hides, the recipient being Abbot Tunberht.[17] This land is unidentified, and the similarity of its name to *Ora* (and its identical hidage) has allowed the same identifications to be suggested.[18] If the charters were genuine, Cuthred's diploma for *Ure* could have been a regrant or a confirmation of the same hides as were given to Glastonbury in Ine's name, or it could have transferred a completely different estate to the community. Whichever interpretation is correct, without more evidence the claims of Northover, Ower, or another, unidentified, place (or two) to be the location of *Ora* and/or *Ure* remain equal.

Orchardleigh (Somerset)

According to the contents-list of the *Liber terrarum*, King Edgar gave *Orcherleag* to one Ælfhere (S.1759; LT117).[19] In the *De antiquitate*, a grant of five hides at *Othelee* or *Otherlee* made to Ealdorman Ælfhere is described,[20] with the additional information – quoted in the first person, as if from the dispositive section of a charter or an endorsement – that Ælfhere gave the land to Glastonbury for his

---

16 Morland, 'The Glastonbury manors', p. 76. See above, *s.n.* Ilchester (St Andrew's Church). Ekwall (*The Concise Oxford Dictionary of English Place-names*, p. 344, *s.n.* Northover) gave the following sequence of names: *Nordoure, Northovere*.

17 *De antiquitate*, §§46 and 69 (ed. & transl. Scott, pp. 104 and 142); *Cronica*, §§16 and 52 (edd. & transl. Carley & Townsend, pp. 40 and 104).

18 Morland, 'The Glastonbury manors', pp. 64 and 76.

19 This Ælfhere was apparently the ealdorman of that name: on his relations with Glastonbury, see Williams, '*Princeps Merciorum gentis*', p. 167. Ælfhere is also connected with the estates of *Bocland* (Buckland Denham) and Westbury (*q.v.*). He was apparently buried at Glastonbury – if he was the *dux Alfari* whose tomb, according to the *De antiquitate*, was still to be seen in the church (§31 [ed. & transl. Scott, p. 84]); Scott seems to be mistaken in rendering this name 'Ælfheah'. Ælfhere appears on an obit-list in a thirteenth-century manuscript from Glastonbury (London, British Library, Add. MS. 17450, at 5v). See Blows, 'A Glastonbury obit-list', pp. 262 (n. 30) and 267. Keynes has described him as 'the most powerful layman in the kingdom' (*The Diplomas of King Æthelred*, p. 170). For his role in the troubles of Æthelred's reign, see Fisher, 'The anti-monastic reaction', pp. 269–70.

20 The form of the place-name here (*Othelee/Otherlee*) seems to be corrupt; Ekwall (*The Concise Oxford Dictionary of English Place-names*, *s.n.* Orchardleigh, p. 350) did not note the evidence from Glastonbury and gave only the following forms: *Orcerdleia, Orchardesleg*.

soul and that of King Edgar.[21] *Orcirleage* appears in §70 of the *De antiquitate* among the *alia [maneria] data Glastonie*, places whose transfer to Glastonbury was apparently not covered in the main narrative.[22] This suggests that the connexion between *Othelee* and *Orcirleage* was lost on the compiler of that list; it seems nevertheless most likely that there was only one place involved.

Even if we were to trust the *De antiquitate* and accept that Ælfhere granted Orchardleigh to Glastonbury, we could nonetheless observe that the abbey did not maintain its hold on the land; five hides at *Horcerlei* were in lay hands in 1066,[23] but when Glastonbury gave them up – if it had ever had them – is not known. Orchardleigh lies a few miles north of Frome, about twenty-five miles northeast of Glastonbury and near Buckland Denham, an estate which was also held by Ælfhere. Glastonbury's archive preserves a charter apparently for this latter estate (S.555, given to Ælfhere by King Eadred) which may have been stored at the abbey or deposited there at Ælfhere's death;[24] and Ælfhere's charter for Orchardleigh could have accompanied it. As at Buckland Denham, the evidence that Glastonbury actually acquired the estate granted in the charter is debatable, although in Orchardleigh's case the claim in the *De antiquitate*, possibly quoted from a charter, may be stronger.[25] Another alleged gift by Ælfhere (of land at Westbury) raises similar problems.[26]

Otheri

The text of a grant by King Edgar to his *minister* Wulfhelm for two hides at *Otheri* in A.D. 963 survives in the fourteenth-century cartularies (S.721). This charter was apparently not in the *Liber terrarum* but was listed in the *Index chartarum* and MS. 39a (IB B6; L18). The grant does not appear in the *De antiquitate*.

The identification of the land granted in S.721 has been obscured by the confusion between two places with similar names, one – Othery – being abbatial land near *Sowy* in the Somerset Levels and the other – Ottery St Mary, in Devon, fewer than ten miles east of Exeter – having no discernible link with Glastonbury. The bounds attached to S.721 nevertheless led Finberg to reject the Somerset location and conclude that Edgar's grant to Wulfhelm had applied to the estate in Devon;[27] this argument depended on the bounds being roughly contemporary with the grant, but Finberg did not address this question, nor did he consider the possibility of duplicity.[28] The boundary defined in S.721 can be compared with a

---

[21] *De antiquitate*, §§62 and 69 (ed. & transl. Scott, pp. 130 and 144); *Cronica*, §§16 and 73 (edd. & transl. Carley & Townsend, pp. 42 and 138). The account of the grant in §62 of the *De antiquitate* pairs Ælfhere's grant of *Othelee* with his gift of Westbury, however, and the diploma that provided the quotation (if genuine) may have been for the latter estate. It is no longer extant.

[22] Ed. & transl. Scott, p. 144; see above, pp. 24–6.

[23] Domesday Book, I, 88vb (Somerset, 5.52).

[24] See above, *s.n. Bocland*.

[25] It must be said that no charter-texts of this type (granted by laymen) survive in Glastonbury's archive; similarly, the extant single sheets bear no endorsements with this message (but only one of the four was granted to a recipient other than Glastonbury).

[26] See below, *s.n.* Westbury.

[27] Finberg, *The Early Charters of Devon and Cornwall*, p. 12; 'Supplement', pp. 25–6.

later charter for Ottery St Mary (S.1033; A.D. 1061) by which King Edward granted twenty-five hides at *Otregia* to the church of St Mary, Rouen.[29] St Mary's held twenty-five hides at *Otrei* at the time of Domesday Book.[30] If S.721 granted two hides and S.1033 twenty-five hides, they cannot have covered the same area, unless the assessment had been radically altered in the interval between the two grants. The descriptions of the estate do, however, seem at least to follow the same line (the River Otter) in the east.[31]

The bounds of S.1033 end by defining the division between *wicginland* and *otrigland*, the former probably being identical with the southern part of the modern parish of Ottery St Mary.[32] Rose-Troup concluded that the inclusion of this defined division in S.1033 indicated that before A.D. 1061 Ottery had consisted of two separate estates of two nearly equal parts.[33] Unfortunately this does not further the cause of providing a context for Glastonbury's two hides.

Despite bearing the bounds of Ottery St Mary, S.721 was placed among documents for *Sowy* in Glastonbury's fourteenth-century cartularies[34] and in MS. 39a, as if it applied to the Somerset estate, Othery, about a mile from the settlement now called Middlezoy, approximately ten miles southeast of the abbey. Othery lacks Anglo-Saxon documentation and is not named in Domesday Book. Perhaps this was because, as Morland has suggested, it had been granted to Glastonbury by Ine in A.D. 725 as part of the estate of *Sowy* (S.251).[35] This may have been the case, as there is evidence of Othery's attachment to *Sowy* in the vernacular bounds attached to Ine's charter. But the date of these bounds is uncertain and Othery need not have been part of Ine's original grant. Even once included in *Sowy*, the relationship need not have been permanent. For example, parts of *Sowy* may have been leased or seized and then granted to a layman by the king.[36] Edgar's grant to Wulfhelm could represent such a development. The attachment of bounds for another estate with a similar name therefore need not completely disallow the possibility (especially given the small number of hides) that Othery, not Ottery, was indeed the subject of Edgar's grant.[37] Whoever added

---

[28] The monks could have attached a survey of one to a grant of the other if they were mounting a claim, for example.

[29] The bounds of S.1033 were printed and analysed in detail by Rose-Troup, in 'The Anglo-Saxon charter of Ottery St. Mary', pp. 201–20. Rose-Troup did not bring S.721 into her discussion. S.1033 has been discussed in detail by Keynes ('Regenbald', pp. 200–3).

[30] Domesday Book, I, 104rb (Devon, 10.1).

[31] I have found no detailed comparison of the two charters' bounds: Grundy did not study Devonshire boundaries, Finberg's analysis of the bounds of S.721 did not include a comparison with S.1033, and Rose-Troup's study of the bounds of S.1033 in turn ignored those of S.721.

[32] Gover *et al.*, *The Place-names of Devon*, II.603, n. 1.

[33] Rose-Troup, 'The Anglo-Saxon charter of Ottery St. Mary', p. 205.

[34] *The Great Chartulary*, ed. Watkin, II.496 (no. 904).

[35] Morland, 'The Saxon charters for Sowy and Pouholt', p. 233. Bates, 'Text of the Somerset Domesday', p. 461, named Othery as part of *Sowy* in Domesday Book. See below, *s.n. Sowy*.

[36] See below, *s.n. Sowy*. See above, *s.n.* North Wootton, for leased abbatial land.

the bounds of Ottery may have had ulterior motives which we can no longer perceive.

In the face of this obscurity, it must also be remembered that the question of whether or not the land was transferred to Glastonbury by the charter's recipient (or his heirs) remains open.[38]

Othery (Somerset)
See *Otheri*.

Ottery St Mary (Devon)
See *Otheri*.

Overleigh (Somerset)
See *Lantokay*.

Ower (Hampshire)
See *Ora*.

Panborough (Somerset)
According to a charter in the name of King Eadwig which is preserved in the fourteenth-century cartularies, a vineyard and two *mansiunculae* of land at *Patheneberghe* were granted to the church of Glastonbury in A.D. 956 (S.626). A rider attached to the text after the witness-list declares that the hides were free from all service ('rus omni terrene seruitutis iugo liberum'), including the three common dues. This charter was apparently in the *Liber terrarum* (LT76) and was listed in the *Index chartarum* and MS. 39a; the latter two lists record the existence of two copies (IC A14; L2). This grant also appears in the *De antiquitate*, where the recipient is named as the pseudo-abbot Ælfsige; no such person features in the text of the extant charter. The exemption from service is repeated in the *De antiquitate*, but with a different wording ('.ii. hidae ab omni seruicio liberae').[1]

No earlier charter for Panborough survives, and Eadwig's diploma has been taken to represent the acquisition of the land by Glastonbury.[2] It is possible that Panborough had been in Glastonbury's hands before the grant recorded in S.626, however. The dispositive section of the diploma seems to state that the land in

---

[37] See below (*s.n. Sowy*) for the slight suggestion that Edgar's two hides could serve to solve an inconsistency in *Sowy*'s hidage.

[38] This too depends on the identification: although Othery was clearly Glastonbury's land in the late Anglo-Saxon period, there is apparently no discernible connexion at that (or any other) time between Ottery St Mary and Glastonbury, apart from the existence of these bounds in the abbey's archive.

[1] *De antiquitate*, §§58 and 69 (ed. & transl. Scott, pp. 120 and 144); *Cronica*, §§16 and 67 (edd. & transl. Carley & Townsend, pp. 42 and 126). Only §58 of the *De antiquitate* makes explicit the connexion between Ælfsige and Panborough. The summaries of grants in both narratives exclude him completely; in §67 of the *Cronica* his existence is mentioned but he is not associated with any land-grants. See also above, *s.n.* Nettleton, for which a charter survives containing a (possibly interpolated) reference to Ælfsige.

[2] See Hudson & Neale, 'The Panborough Saxon charter', p. 57.

question had previously been set aside for or given to the church (*olim dicata*). If genuine, was S.626 restoring land which had been appropriated? Or was it merely changing the conditions of tenure, by granting permanent possession (*eterna hereditas*) and exemption from service (if the added note is genuine)? No further evidence exists to support or negate either of these suggestions, but some effort to give Panborough the status of an ancient possession was clearly made at a later date. The exemption from service added on to S.626 may reflect one stage in this process. Though not included among Glastonbury's earliest acquisitions in the Great Privilege of King Ine,[3] Panborough is nonetheless on the list of those churches whose chapels were granted special exemptions in the privilege of King Edgar, which names many of the same places with ostensibly antique associations with the community.[4] Panborough was cited also among the *loca principalia* of the Twelve Hides: 'insula de Padenbeorge et Norhthilade cum terris, pratis, pascuis, et moris, et boscis amplis ad eas spectantibus'.[5] This inclusion within the reputedly ancient unit is reflected in Panborough's appearance in Domesday Book as part of Glastonbury itself (*pertinet ibi*); six acres of land and a vineyard of three *arpents* were there in 1066.[6]

As S.626 was included in a section of the fourteenth-century cartularies entitled *Mere*, W. de G. Birch mistakenly identified the land in question as Mere, 'at the point of union of cos. Somerset, Dorset, and Wiltshire',[7] but the charter itself, naming Panborough as it does, shows that the cartularies' reference was to Meare, which lies to the south of Panborough across the moor, a few miles northwest of Glastonbury. In the fourteenth century, Panborough was included in the manor of Meare.[8] Attached to the charter are bounds which have been assumed by their latest analysts to be contemporary with Eadwig's grant.[9] Hazel Hudson and Frances Neale have rejected Grundy's solution of the bounds, which defined a small area of land around Barrow Hill.[10] Instead they have mapped a larger area, including all of Panborough and neighbouring Northload and extending north and

---

3 S.250; on this privilege, see above, *s.n.* Glastonbury.
4 S.783; *De antiquitate*, §60 (ed. & transl. Scott, p. 124); *Cronica*, §71 (edd. & transl. Carley & Townsend, p. 134). See above, *s.n.* Glastonbury.
5 'The island of Panborough and Northload with the lands, meadows, pastures, marshes, and moors belonging to them': *De antiquitate*, §73 (ed. & transl. Scott, p. 152); *Cronica*, §4 (edd. & transl. Carley & Townsend, p. 16). On the Twelve Hides, see above, *s.n.* Glastonbury, and map 1.
6 Domesday Book, I, 90ra (Somerset, 8.1).
7 *Cartularium Saxonicum*, ed. Birch, III.89 (no. 920).
8 Hudson & Neale, 'The Panborough Saxon charter', p. 66.
9 Watkin's misleading marginal note ('[early xvi cent.]' attached to the manuscript's note *perambulacio manerii ibidem*; *The Great Chartulary*, ed. Watkin, II.362 [no. 638]) was presumably meant to refer to the existence of another perambulation, included in Abbot Beere's terrier of A.D. 1507–1510 (London, British Library, MS. Egerton 3034, 3–8, on which see Hudson & Neale, 'The Panborough Saxon charter', pp. 57 ff.). Grundy (*The Saxon Charters*, p. 114) judged the bounds of S.626 to be 'probably of the Saxon age'; Kitson likewise (in his unpublished work on Anglo-Saxon charter-bounds) considered them to be contemporary with the grant.
10 Hudson & Neale, 'The Panborough Saxon charter', p. 56.

south into the moor. Hudson and Neale have emphasised the strategic importance of the Panborough Gap, 'a gap in the chain of hills linking the Axe and Brue river systems and crossed by a causeway, [which] may well have been important for both land and river communications long before the Saxon period [and] was certainly vital to the medieval transport network of Glastonbury Abbey'.[11] The place-name, derived perhaps from Old English **patha*, 'wayfarer' (with Old English *beorg*, 'hill'), may reflect this function.[12] A site of such topographical importance could have been sought after – and obtained – by Glastonbury well before Eadwig's grant.

Hudson and Neale have concluded that the small abbatial holding at Panborough recorded in Domesday Book did not include the full estate as encircled by the bounds of S.626, but referred rather to the restricted area around Barrow Hill. The association of this part of Panborough with Meare, they have argued, was already established by 1066.[13] This leaves unanswered the question of when Northload and the rest of Panborough were detached from Barrow Hill, and where they are to be found in Domesday Book (where they are not mentioned by name). Morland has suggested that Bagley (possibly Glastonbury's unidentified holding of *Bodeslege* in Domesday Book) was to be identified with Northload.[14] Alternatively, the land may already have been seized by the bishop of Wells and incorporated into his estate of Wedmore, to which parish it later belonged.[15] This conclusion, however, does not agree with the presence of Northload and Panborough among Glastonbury's estates surveyed in the *Liber Henrici* of A.D. 1189 and, with listed appurtenances, in the thirteenth- and sixteenth-century perambulations of the Twelve Hides, as cited above. It appears that the connexion with Wedmore was a later development.

Parrett (River, Fishery on)

The contents-list of the *Liber terrarum* records a grant by King Baldred *de Pedrithe* (S.1665; LT13). According to the *Index chartarum* (IC A2) and the *De antiquitate*, Baldred granted *captura piscium in Pedride* to Abbot Hæmgils.[16] In the summary – but not the main entry – this grant seems to be associated with a place, *Westwere*. As we have seen, very early charters frequently lacked place-names, mentioning instead a natural feature; the notice of this grant may therefore authentically represent an early gift to Glastonbury. The grant appears nowhere else in the archive, however, unless disguised (and unrecognised) in a recast, updated form. Morland has suggested that the fishery might have been located in

---

[11] *Ibid.*

[12] Ekwall, *The Concise Oxford Dictionary of English Place-names*, p. 357, *s.n.* Panborough.

[13] Hudson & Neale, 'The Panborough Saxon charter', p. 66.

[14] Morland, 'Glaston Twelve Hides', p. 37. A priest held three virgates at *Bodeslege* from the abbot in 1066: Domesday Book, I, 90rb (Somerset, 8.12).

[15] Hudson & Neale, 'The Panborough Saxon charter', p. 66.

[16] *De antiquitate*, §§38 and 69 (ed. & transl. Scott, pp. 90 and 140); *Cronica*, §§16 and 43 (edd. & transl. Carley & Townsend, pp. 40 and 90).

Othery or Westonzoyland, on the basis of a late mediaeval reference to a *Westwere* there, but the name is so simply descriptive that this connexion should not be forced.[17] Also it should not be forgotten that the earliest association of *Westwere* with the grant of *Pedrithe* by Baldred is in the thirteenth-century manuscript of the *De antiquitate*. There must have been many fisheries on the Parrett; for example, two early charters, one in Ine's name and one in the name of Bealdhun (S.244 and S.1176; A.D. 702 and 708), granted fisheries on that river to members of the community of Muchelney.[18]

Peasucmere

An entry in the contents-list of the *Liber terrarum* records a grant of *Peasucmere* by King Eadwig to a layman, Ælfwold (S.1750; LT77). There is no other record of this grant, except for the appearance of *Peasucmere* on the unauthoritative list of *alia [maneria] data Glastonie* in §70 of the *De antiquitate*.[19] The estate remains unidentified and its history unknown. A range of options can be proposed: that the grant was never intended for the abbey; that the transfer was somehow blocked; that the land was lost after transfer to Glastonbury and before 1066; that it was incorporated into another estate and its name lost; or that it changed its name and appears in the record (unrecognised) under another guise.

Pedrithe

See Parrett (River, Fishery on).

Pedwell (Somerset)

Glastonbury held three hides in Pedwell in 1066 as part of its estate at Walton.[20] The acquisition of Pedwell is probably to be seen in the context of the history of the large early estate of *Pouelt* and is discussed under that heading.

Pendescliue

According to the contents-list of the *Liber terrarum*, King Eadwig granted land at *Pendescliue* to Ælfswith (S.1748; LT110). This charter is listed in the *Index chartarum* among those documents for lands Glastonbury no longer held (IC D18). No other record of this grant appears in the archive; §70 of the *De antiquitate* lists *Pendescliue* among the *alia [maneria] data Glastonie*, but it does not appear in the main narrative.[21] It remains unidentified and its history unknown. A range of options can be proposed: that the grant was never intended for the abbey; that the transfer never took place; that the land was lost after transfer to Glastonbury and before 1066; that it was incorporated into another estate and its name

---

17 Morland, 'The Glastonbury manors', p. 81.
18 The first of these charters attaches a place-name to the fishery (*Swynwere*); neither charter is free from suspicion (*Two Cartularies*, ed. Bates [& Stevenson], pp. 95–6).
19 *De antiquitate*, §70 (ed. & transl. Scott, p. 144); on this list, see above, pp. 24–6.
20 Domesday Book, I, 90rb (Somerset, 8.11).
21 *De antiquitate*, §70 (ed. & transl. Scott, p. 144); on this list, see above, pp. 24–6.

lost; or that it changed its name and appears in the record (unrecognised) under another guise.[22]

Pennard (East and West) (Somerset)

Two charters survive which relate to land at Pennard. The first, S.236, in the name of Baldred and dated 681, is extant both as a single-sheet copy (possibly tenth-century)[23] and a cartulary-text. It granted twelve hides (six in the cartulary-text) 'super uerticem montis cuius uocabulum est Pengerd' to Abbot Hæmgils, with brief bounds attached. The second, S.563 (A.D. 955), records the sale of twenty hides at *Pengeardmynster* by King Eadred to the Wilton nun Ælfgyth for the sum of one hundred and twenty gold *solidi*.[24] Two hides of the twenty, according to the charter, were to be set aside for prayers in her *monasterium, prout antiquitatus*.[25] This second single sheet, which includes bounds, is the only text of Eadred's grant to survive;[26] it was not copied into the fourteenth-century cartularies.

Though preserved together, the two grants of Pennard apparently did not refer to the same land. Two estates at Pennard were later distinguished as East and West Pennard, the former being *Pennardminster* and the latter plain *Pennard* in the earlier documents. S.236 for *Pengerd* has been identified with West Pennard – immediately to the east of Glastonbury – as the bounds essentially run round most of Pennard Hill (presumably the *mons* referred to in the charter),[27] which extends eastwards for several miles. East Pennard lies beyond the hill. Birch thought that the bounds of Eadred's charter, S.563, included East and West Pennard, but Grundy demonstrated that they applied to the former only.[28] Morland has supported Grundy's conclusion, against the statement by C. and F. Thorn that *Pennarminstre* in Domesday Book included both modern Pennards.[29]

Baldred's charter was in the *Liber terrarum*, according to the entry on the contents-list: 'Baldredus de Pengred id est Pennard d' Glastonie' (LT7). It heads

---

[22] For other grants to Ælfswith associated with Glastonbury (and the subsequent history of the estates), see above, *s.n.* Idmiston.

[23] Longleat House, Marquess of Bath, MS. NMR 10564; see above, pp. 10–11.

[24] On the Anglo-Saxon land market, see Campbell, 'The sale of land'.

[25] This transaction belongs to an interesting group of grants to holy women beginning in Æthelstan's reign and continuing through Edmund's and Eadred's. This grant is the only one whose recipient is explicitly associated with a nunnery (Wilton). See Dumville, *Wessex and England*, pp. 177–8, and Brooks, 'The career', pp. 7–8. Two recently discovered charters preserved at Barking (S.517a and S.517b), to be published by C.R. Hart in his edition of the Barking archive for the British Academy and the Royal Historical Society, can be added to the group.

[26] Longleat House, Marquess of Bath, MS. NMR 10565. See above, p. 11.

[27] Grundy, *The Saxon Charters*, pp. 74–7, and Rands, 'West Pennard's Saxon charter', which maps the bounds; see also Havinden, *The Somerset Landscape*, p. 87.

[28] *Cartularium Saxonicum*, ed. Birch, III.63–4 (no. 903); Grundy, *The Saxon Charters*, pp. 65–71, at p. 65 and n. 2. On pp. 233–4 Grundy revised his account of the northern boundary-line of East Pennard to include parts of Pylle. Morland (in a letter to the author dated 5 September, 1990) has also specified that the bounds of S.563 included Pylle; the latter was nevertheless part of Pilton (*q.v.*) in 1066.

[29] Morland, review of *Domesday Book: Somerset*, p. 139; *Somerset*, edd. & transl. Thorn & Thorn, p. 356.

List A in the *Index chartarum* and is also listed in MS. 39a (IC A1; L11). The slightly different version of the grant – consisting of six hides, not twelve – which is found in the later cartularies is also preserved in the *De antiquitate*.[30] Six hides are mentioned as well in Ine's Great Privilege.[31] No entry for *Pengerd* or *Pennard* (*tout court*) is found in Domesday Book.

As has been mentioned, Eadred's charter for Ælfgyth for twenty hides at *Pengeardmynster* was not included in the fourteenth-century cartularies, although there was apparently a copy in the *Liber terrarum* (*de Pengeardmunster*: LT68); and a charter for *Pergarminstre* was listed in the *Index chartarum* among charters for lands lost (IC D17). There is no reference to this grant in the main narrative of the *De antiquitate*, but its summary of grants mentions one by Ælfgyth to Glastonbury of *ten* hides at *Pengeardmunster*.[32] Glastonbury held twenty hides at *Pennarminstre*, according to Domesday Book, but it is stated there that before 1066 the abbey paid tax for only ten.[33]

One further document must be considered. An entry in the *Index chartarum* (*Eddredus de Pennard*; IC B8) and in MS. 39a ('carta Edredi regis de manerio de Pennard dupplicatur excepte limitibus et <. . .> testibus'; L12) may have referred to S.563, Eadred's charter for Ælfgyth for *Pengeardmynster*; but, if it did, what was [*Eddredus*] *de Pergarminstre*, on the list of charters, and for land *lost* (IC D17)? Someone may have made a mistake (or two): Eadred's charter for East Pennard may have been entered on the *Index* twice by accident, once without its distinguishing *mynstre*-element and once on the wrong list. Alternatively, there may have been another charter issued by King Eadred, for West Pennard, and East Pennard may not have been in Glastonbury's hands when the *Index* was compiled.[34] The evidence provides no definite clues either way, although the fact that three of the four non-contemporary endorsements of S.563 (eleventh- to thirteenth-century) use *Pennard*, without the *mynstre*, implies that the simple form could be used for East Pennard as well as West. In MS. 39a, a charter of Eadred for *Pennard* follows that of Baldred in the section headed 'West Pennard', implying perhaps that Eadred had issued one for West as well as East Pennard. But, as there is no charter listed for *Pengeardmynster*, the reference may be to S.563 and East Pennard after all. Later documents for East Pennard are included in this section without a separate contemporary heading in the manuscript; so the suggestion of identification with West Pennard cannot bear too much weight.

Pennard also appears in the cartulary-texts of King Æthelwulf's Decimation

---

[30] *De antiquitate*, §§38 and 69 (ed. & transl. Scott, pp. 90 and 140); *Cronica*, §§16 and 43 (edd. & transl. Carley & Townsend, pp. 40 and 90). In §38 of the *De antiquitate* the form of the place-name is similar to that on the contents-list (*Penger*), with the interlinear gloss *id est Pennard*. In the summary and in the *Cronica* only the form *Pennard* is used.

[31] S.250; *De antiquitate*, §42 (ed. & transl. Scott, p. 98); *Cronica*, §49 (edd. & transl. Carley & Townsend, p. 96).

[32] *De antiquitate*, §69 (ed. & transl. Scott, p. 144); *Cronica*, §16 (edd. & transl. Carley & Townsend, p. 42).

[33] Domesday Book, I, 90va (Somerset, 8.21).

[34] Both Pennards were part of Glastonbury's post-Conquest endowment; temporary losses could, however, be undocumented.

charter for Glastonbury (S.303; A.D. 854), as a grant of six hides. The list of Æthelwulf's gifts in the *De antiquitate*, however, records nine hides at Pennard.[35] The significance of the appearance of lands in this charter (or charters) of Æthelwulf is open to interpretation;[36] in particular, the estates which it lists may already have been in Glastonbury's hands in A.D. 854, and the Decimation may have been not a grant of land but one of relief from burdens on land already held by the recipient of the charter. Pennard's appearance in Æthelwulf's Decimation, therefore, may not signal that the abbey had lost the estate after Baldred's grant, but rather that it had retained it, and could now hold it on more advantageous terms.

Given the discrepancies in hidage in the records of Baldred's grant of West Pennard, the size of the estate is open to question. Normally, a single sheet would take preference over the evidence of a cartulary-text or a narrative account but, as the single sheet of S.236 is not contemporary with the date claimed for the grant but is a later copy, its testimony may not be reliable. The hidage could have been increased to twelve for various reasons which can no longer be ascertained (including of course the intent to deceive);[37] or it could have been a scribal error. As has been mentioned above, Baldred's grant of West Pennard (if genuine) may have formed half of the primary core-estate of Glastonbury itself, combining with six hides given by King Centwine to make up an original endowment of twelve hides, a much smaller area than the later territory so called (in which West Pennard was indeed included).[38] West Pennard's non-appearance in Domesday Book is certainly logically attributable to its inclusion in Glastonbury proper; but the corrupt nature of the surviving documentation can only suggest (and not prove) that this may have been the case from the earliest period of the community's existence.

The subsequent history of West Pennard is obscured by the ambiguous nature of the reference to the charter of Eadred discussed above: if it did apply to West, not East, Pennard, there would be important implications to be considered about the relationship of the king and the community to this ostensibly ancient holding. As for East Pennard, if Eadred granted it twice, reasons would have to be sought,[39] complicating the otherwise fairly simple picture of the acquisition of the estate by Ælfgyth in A.D. 955, followed by her gift (or that of her heir) of the land to Glastonbury. But, as stated above, this second grant by Eadred might simply be a phantom-charter. And, as we shall now see, the simple picture may possibly be equally imaginary.

The question of East Pennard's history before its grant by the king and its

---

[35] *De antiquitate*, §§53 and 69 (ed. & transl. Scott, pp. 112 and 142); *Cronica*, §§16 and 56 (edd. & transl. Carley & Townsend, pp. 40 and 108).

[36] See above, *s.n. Brannocmynstre* and Monk Okehampton, and below, pp. 322–4. The lists may have been altered: the extant texts are late mediaeval copies.

[37] Perhaps the transfer of East Pennard to Glastonbury – or at least the production of records for it on its own – motivated the doctoring of documents referring to its namesake.

[38] The *loca principalia* of the Twelve Hides included *totus Westpennard*: *De antiquitate*, §73 (ed. & transl. Scott, p. 150); *Cronica*, §4 (edd. & transl. Carley & Townsend, p. 14). For the Twelve Hides, see above, *s.n.* Glastonbury.

[39] Similar to those advanced for Camel, Idmiston, or Nunney (*q.v.*), for example? Forgery is naturally another option.

consequent appearance in Glastonbury's records in the mid-tenth century must be considered. The sharing of a single name between two parts could denote an original unity, but East and West Pennard appear to have been separated already by the late seventh century (if the modest hidage of Baldred's grant to Glastonbury is a reliable indicator). The place-name (Welsh *pen ardd*, 'high hill'),[40] however, is descriptive of a natural feature and need not imply a tenurial unit or unity. East Pennard is apparently undocumented before A.D. 955, but its association, already at the time of Eadred's charter, with the *mynstre*-element suggests not necessarily the existence of a minster-church there but at least ownership by such a community (and therefore not by the king, whom we should otherwise have imagined to have been the holder of the land); Wilton, where the donor Ælfgyth was said to live, could be a candidate for this minster, but so perhaps could Glastonbury. Eadred's charter may not have been a permanent alienation (despite its rhetoric) but could perhaps be interpreted instead as a lease, not of royal land, but of the abbey's own property, with reversion to Glastonbury. This, after all, is what S.513 accomplished at Damerham; and S.509 also shows the king administering an abbatial tenure.[41] If this interpretation were accepted, it could mean that Glastonbury had held all of Pennard from the earliest times (documented simply as Pennard) and that only when East Pennard began to have a separate tenurial existence did it acquire a distinguishing name; the low hidage in Baldred's and Æthelwulf's charters is a worrisome, but not fatal, objection to this suggestion, given the non-contemporaneity of their texts (and the instability of hidage assessments).

Propositions such as these cannot be tested. They help to illustrate, however, the possibilities of interpretation which even the most apparently simple Anglo-Saxon diploma can raise when it is seen in the context of the history of the place it purports to grant. The real import of the documents is not always apparent, and close study of estate-histories reveals more and more potential interpretations.[42]

Pentridge (Dorset)

This estate was granted by King Edmund to his second wife, Æthelflæd, along with Damerham and Martin, and was held by Glastonbury in 1066.[43] It has been discussed above, under Damerham.

Pidelan

According to an entry on the contents-list of the *Liber terrarum*, King Edmund granted land at *Pidelan* to a layman, Wulflaf (S.1730; LT124). The only other appearance of *Pidelan* in Glastonbury's records is in §70 of the *De antiquitate*, among the *alia* [*maneria*] *data Glastonie*.[44] As we have seen, this is not conclusive evidence of Glastonbury's ownership of the land in question.

---

[40] Ekwall, *The Concise Oxford Dictionary of English Place-names*, p. 362, *s.n.* Pennard.

[41] See above, *s.n.* Damerham and North Wootton.

[42] For example, Costen has suggested that West Pennard was lost after its original grant and only restored after A.D. 943 ('Dunstan, Glastonbury and the economy', p. 40).

[43] Domesday Book, I, 77va (Dorset, 8.5).

[44] *De antiquitate*, §70 (ed. & transl. Scott, p. 144); see above, pp. 24–6.

According to Domesday Book, eight estates called *Pidele* belonged in 1066 to various lay owners, another was said to have been taken by Earl Harold from the church of Shaftesbury, and four were held by the bishop of Salisbury, Milton Abbey, Abbotsbury Abbey, and St Peter's, Winchester (the New Minster), respectively.[45] Further Piddles with an epithet attached (*Litelpidele, Affapidele*) are also named.[46] These lands, to one of which the charter in the *Liber terrarum* may have referred, were all on the River Piddle in Dorset. A river-name of Germanic origin, *Pidele* can be found elsewhere, however – in Piddle Brook (Worcestershire), for example;[47] without more information, therefore, Glastonbury's *Pidele* cannot be identified, and its history is unknown.[48]

Pilsdon (Dorset)

A charter of Edward the Elder for *Pillesdone* was recorded on List D of the *Index chartarum*, of charters for lay beneficiaries for lands which were no longer held by the abbey (S.1706; IC D6). No other notice of this grant survives in the Glastonbury archive, apart from that in the unauthoritative §70 of the *De antiquitate*, where Pilsdon is listed among the *alia [maneria] data Glastonie*.[49] Three hides at *Pilesdone* appear in lay hands in Domesday Book.[50] Glastonbury may never have received this land from the recipient of Edward's charter, or the monks may have lost it before 1066. Alternatively, Glastonbury's right to the land may simply be invisible in Domesday Book. Neil Stacy has pointed out that, as Pilsdon was a knight's fee of the abbey early in the twelfth century, it may not have (officially) left Glastonbury's lordship in the eleventh; he has proposed an analogy with the case of Uffculme, likewise not recorded as Glastonbury's in Domesday Book. This latter estate was leased in the eleventh century and appropriated by its tenant but later restored to the abbey by the king.[51] No documentation, however, survives to test this possibility for Pilsdon. Possession of the estate was evidently at issue in the early twelfth century, when a dispute over Pilsdon took place between the abbot of Glastonbury and the bishop of Salisbury.[52] It is even possible that this contention provided the context for the forgery of a charter in Edward's name, concocted to provide a title-deed for use in the courts. The pre-Conquest history of this estate therefore remains obscure.

---

[45] Domesday Book, I, 77rb, 79rb–va, 82vb, 83va, 84va, 78vb, 77rb, 78rb, 78va, 77vb (Dorset, 3.15, 26.20 [two estates TRE], 26.21, 26.22, 48.1, 55.16, 56.48, 19.14, 3.16 [and note], 12.5, 13.2, and 9.1). Shaftesbury's confiscated estate at Piddle may have been that granted by King Edgar in A.D. 966 (S.744). O'Donovan (*Charters of Sherborne*, pp. xlii and xliv) has suggested that the bishop of Salisbury's estate may have been the land at *Pidel* claimed to have been given to Sherborne by King Cynewulf in London, British Library, MS. Cotton Faustina A.ii, 25r/v.

[46] Domesday Book, I, 75va, 77vb (Dorset, 1.14, 11.2, 11.5).

[47] Ekwall, *The Concise Oxford Dictionary of English Place-names*, pp. 365–6, *s.n.* Piddle.

[48] Stacy has suggested that Glastonbury's estate at *Pidele* was 'conceivably' the later Tolpuddle, which took its name from Tola, one of the founders of Abbotsbury Abbey ('The estates', p. 15).

[49] *De antiquitate*, §70 (ed. & transl. Scott, p. 144); see above, pp. 24–6.

[50] Domesday Book, I, 84va (Dorset, 56.46).

[51] Stacy, 'The estates', p. 28; for Uffculme, see below.

[52] For the dispute see *Adami de Domerham Historia*, ed. Hearne, II.312–13.

Pilsdon is over thirty miles south of Glastonbury but not far (about five miles inland) from its estate at *Lim*, now Lyme Regis.

Pilton (Somerset)

An entry in the contents-list of the *Liber terrarum* records the gift of Pilton to Glastonbury by King Ine (S.1672; LT9). This is repeated in the *De antiquitate*, where twenty hides at Pilton are included in a list of Ine's grants dated 705.[53] In the Great Privilege of King Ine this gift is mentioned also, and Pilton's church is cited there among those subject to Glastonbury alone.[54] By the time of the extant (thirteenth-century) perambulation of the Twelve Hides, 'magna pars de parco de Piltone' was included in that ostensibly ancient territory.[55] In 1066 and 1086 Glastonbury held twenty hides at Pilton, according to Domesday Book.[56]

From this evidence, it would seem that in A.D. 705 King Ine granted a twenty-hide estate at Pilton – about five miles northeast of Glastonbury – which the community still held in 1066. However, although this may have been the case, a closer examination of the evidence puts paid to any certainties. The history of the estate of Pilton may have been straightforward, but the history of its documentation is complex indeed.

The first document to be considered is S.248, the multiple grant in Ine's name which survives as a single-sheet copy.[57] Four estates were granted in this diploma, one of which was described as twenty hides 'ex utroque margine fluminis cuius uocabulum est Duluting'. No name and no further information were given to help anyone to locate these hides. At a later date, a revised version of S.248 was constructed – omitting the other three pieces of land – and vernacular bounds were added. S.247, this revised version of S.248, was copied into the fourteenth-century cartularies at the head of the Pilton section. It appears again, however, among the documents for another manor, Doulting, although the two texts are essentially the same in content.[58] In spite of the continued absence of a specific place-name from the dispositive section, the bounds – which are identical, apart from orthographic variants – allowed Davidson (and later Grundy) to identify the land involved as Pilton, Croscombe, and Shepton Mallet (west of the Fosse Way).[59] Croscombe and Shepton Mallet are treated as part of Pilton in Domesday Book. Doulting itself (across the Fosse from Pilton and a twenty-hide estate held by Glastonbury in 1066)[60] was not included in the bounds of S.247.

[53] *De antiquitate*, §§40 and 69 (ed. & transl. Scott, pp. 94 and 140); *Cronica*, §§16 and 47 (edd. & transl. Carley & Townsend, pp. 40 and 92).

[54] S.250; *De antiquitate*, §42 (ed. & transl. Scott, pp. 98–100); *Cronica*, §49 (edd. & transl. Carley & Townsend, pp. 96–8).

[55] *De antiquitate*, §§72 and 73 (ed. & transl. Scott, p. 150); *Cronica*, §§3 and 4 (edd. & transl. Carley & Townsend, p. 14). For the Twelve Hides, see above, *s.n.* Glastonbury.

[56] Domesday Book, I, 90rb (Somerset, 8.20).

[57] See above, pp. 10–11; see also Abrams, 'A single-sheet facsimile', especially pp. 127–9.

[58] *The Great Chartulary*, ed Watkin, II.433 and II.450 (nos 774 and 818).

[59] Davidson, 'On the charters', pp. 12 and 18–23 (and map); Grundy, *The Saxon Charters*, pp. 79–84.

[60] Domesday Book, I, 90va (Somerset, 8.23).

Why, then, was a charter for Pilton attached to Doulting in the cartularies? Its presence there implied that it represented a separate grant of Doulting by Ine, but the boundaries are those of Pilton. The association with Doulting (due perhaps to deliberate deception or, possibly, to ignorance) was possible because of potential confusion between the river-name, *Duluting* (now the Sheppey), and the name of the estate, Doulting (where the source of the river is located). Could it be that by the fourteenth century all pre-Conquest documentation for Doulting had been lost, and that this charter, for land on the *Duluting*, was considered a suitable substitute? That there may have been documentation for Doulting is indicated by two entries in the *Index chartarum* and the contents-list of the *Liber terrarum*: '[Yna rex] de Dulting' and 'Eddredus de Dulting et Nunig .G.' (IC A5 [no Sawyer-number] and LT32 [S.1742]). The former charter may be the one cited in MS. 39a ('Carta Ini regis de Doultyng dupplicatur'; L9). Gifts of both Pilton and Doulting by Ine are recorded in the *De antiquitate*.[61] Although no such claim is preserved in the Glastonbury archive, William of Malmesbury in his *Gesta pontificum Anglorum* stated that the *uilla* of *Dulting* had been given to Glastonbury by Aldhelm.[62] In the *De antiquitate* we find the unconfirmed statement that in A.D. 851 Abbot Ealhmund transferred *Dultig in ius monasteriale*, with the consent of King Æthelwulf, who added twenty hides *ad supplementum uite regularis*; the summary of grants says only that Æthelwulf restored (*reddidit*) *Dultig* to Glastonbury.[63] One other transaction is cited in the *De antiquitate* alone (omitted from the *Cronica*): King Eadred, it is said there, also restored *Dultig* to Glastonbury.[64] This may be an interpolation.[65]

There is a serious difficulty with all these references to Pilton and Doulting. Apart from S.247, there is in fact no way of ascertaining to which land these documents originally applied. At what date the two estate-names Pilton and Doulting were first in regular use is unknown. Before that, the vague description 'land on the *Duluting*' could have applied to either place and could indeed have continued to do so even after the development of separate names. Davidson's recognition of the bounds of S.247 as those of Pilton led him to assume that Ine's original grant (in S.248) had been of that estate, an assumption which the reference in the contents-list of the *Liber terrarum* (*Yna de Pilton*) supported.[66] Davidson, however, did not confront in turn what *Yna de Dulting* (IC A5) might have meant. Nor did he question the date of the creation of the bounds of S.247, nor consider that their description of Pilton's boundary related to the time of their

---

[61] *De antiquitate*, §§40, 42 and 69 (ed. & transl. Scott, pp. 94, 98, and 140); *Cronica*, §§16, 47, and 49 (edd. & transl. Carley & Townsend, pp. 40, 92, and 96). The middle reference is to the Great Privilege of King Ine. In the text of this document in the *De antiquitate* (but nowhere else) the grant of Doulting is of ten hides, not twenty.
[62] *Gesta pontificum Anglorum*, §228 (ed. Hamilton, p. 382).
[63] *De antiquitate*, §§53 and 69 (ed. & transl. Scott, pp. 112 and 142); *Cronica*, §§16 and 49 (edd. & transl. Carley & Townsend, pp. 40 and 108).
[64] *De antiquitate*, §§57 and 69 (ed. & transl. Scott, pp. 118 and 142–4).
[65] See below, *s.n.* Pucklechurch.
[66] This reference (LT9; S.1672) is probably to S.247, in which case Sawyer's number is redundant.

composition, rather than the early eighth century.[67] The text of Ine's multiple grant (S.248) was certainly used at a later date to provide a charter with bounds for Pilton, but there is no guarantee that its original reference was to that land.

We are left with extreme uncertainty. Ine granted land on the *Duluting*, which may have been either the land which became Pilton (as S.247 and LT9 would suggest) or that later known as Doulting (the name cited in IC A5 and MS. 39a [L9]).[68] Alternatively, Ine could have granted both Pilton and Doulting, either as one unit (although the hidage does not fit) or in two separate transactions. *Yna de Pilton* and *Yna de Dulting* may therefore have been two different charters or one and the same document (the two copies of S.247? or one of S.247 and one of S.248?). The statement in the *De antiquitate* – that Ine did indeed grant both places – could reveal either superior knowledge, or confusion, ignorance, and a desire to tidy the record; its testimony is consequently not enlightening. Perhaps King Æthelwulf's actions can make better sense of things. Two pieces of land are visible in the (unconfirmed) transaction associated with him: when he restored *Dultig* to the monks, he added twenty hides to it. Perhaps here we have Pilton and Doulting together in Glastonbury's hands for the first time, leaving only the (unanswerable) question of which one constituted the original twenty hides of S.248. Eadred's restoration of *Dultig*, if it took place, seems to indicate that some part at least of the land had been lost during the intervening years, but whether this was Pilton, or Doulting, or both, is uncertain. According to Domesday Book, they were distinct twenty-hide estates (both held by Glastonbury) in 1066. At Pilton, however, there was additional land for twenty ploughs which did not pay tax. Perhaps *this* was the land added by Æthelwulf.[69] Without better evidence, the problem may be insoluble.

In the account in Domesday Book, Pilton included four named sub-units: six and a half hides at *Sepetone* (now Shepton Mallet), three hides at *Coristone* (Croscombe), five hides at *Vtone* (North Wootton), and five hides at Pylle. The first two, according to Davidson, were part of the estate described in the bounds of S.247. The latter two were not. The history of these sub-units is difficult to trace. No pre-Conquest record exists for Shepton Mallet, which makes its first appearance by name in Domesday Book.[70] Croscombe's acquisition by Glastonbury may have been recorded in S.248, in the early eighth-century grant of five hides at *Corregescumb*, but the identification is not straightforward and no more

---

67 Among language-experts there is disagreement on the date of these bounds; Peter Kitson and Margaret Gelling have placed them in the second half of the tenth century (the former in his unpublished work on charter-bounds, the latter in a letter of 16 July, 1989), but Paul Bibire (in unpublished notes written in June 1991) has judged the two versions to be twelfth- and thirteenth-century, without any evidence of an Old English exemplar. See also Grundy, *The Saxon Charters*, p. 80.

68 And the name written on the back of S.248 in later mediaeval hands; see Abrams, 'A single-sheet facsimile', p. 104.

69 For another explanation, see below, p. 203.

70 Three hides which were later in Shepton Mallet (*Cerletone*, east of the Fosse) were in Doulting in 1066: Domesday Book, I, 90va (Somerset, 8.23). Morland, 'The Glastonbury manors', p. 72; cf. Grundy, *The Saxon Charters*, p. 79.

information relating to this place survives from before 1066.[71] North Wootton seems to have had its own documentary history as an independent entity, with charters from the later eighth to the mid-tenth century, as we have seen.[72] In 1066, however, it was attached to – and assessed under – Pilton. When this relationship developed is uncertain. Pylle, according to Grundy, was in the later middle ages made up of parts which had once been in East Pennard and Shepton Mallet,[73] but the details of its Anglo-Saxon history are unknown, as Domesday Book is the earliest source to record it by name. Morland proposed that it was included in the bounds of East Pennard in S.563 (A.D. 955).[74] The evidence of the bounds of S.247 is therefore crucial here, as they show Pilton excluding North Wootton and Pylle, but until there is agreement on their date their testimony is ambiguous: if pre-Conquest, they would indicate that North Wootton and Pylle joined Pilton after the bounds were written but before 1066; if post-Conquest, the subordination of the two estates to Pilton may have been a feature of the later eleventh century only, after which they regained their original independence. The former possibility, especially, has implications for the stability or instability of Anglo-Saxon estates and the 'timelessness' of their boundaries; but both apparently illustrate the potential of estates to increase in area but not assessment, for the original twenty hides seem to have absorbed at least North Wootton's five without becoming twenty-five. The land which did not pay tax may hold the key. Morland – who argued that the bounds only made sense if they were pre-Conquest – proposed that when Pilton, Croscombe, and Shepton Mallet (originally totalling twenty hides) were extended before 1086 to include the ten hides at North Wootton and Pylle, Pilton's own ten hides were freed of geld, with the result that the assessment stayed the same: a case of hidage-reduction by boundary-extension.[75]

The date at and means by which Glastonbury acquired Pilton and the course of its pre-Domesday history are, as we have seen, obscured by problems of identification (with the attendant difficulty of making sense of the extant references) and the scarcity of allusions in the archival record before 1066 to the parts recorded in Domesday Book. Pilton's proximity to Glastonbury makes it a likely candidate as a member of the earliest endowment. The (admittedly dubious) record of restorations of *Dultig* by Æthelwulf and Eadred, however, whether they applied to Pilton or Doulting proper, or both, or parts of either, may indicate that early possession was not inviolate. The visible difference between Pilton in the bounds of S.247 and Pilton in Domesday Book may also indicate that Anglo-Saxon Pilton was not

---

[71] See above, *s.n. Corregescumb*. In Domesday Book Croscombe (*Coristone*) is assessed at only three hides.

[72] See above, *s.n.* North Wootton.

[73] Grundy, *The Saxon Charters*, pp. 233–4.

[74] In a letter to the author (5 September, 1990).

[75] 'Hidation', pp. 77–8. His evaluation of Pilton as 'originally ten hides' was reached by the subtraction of Croscombe and Shepton Mallet's nine and a half hides (in Domesday Book) from Pilton's twenty hides (as in S.247). I am grateful to Stephen Morland for his correspondence on this subject (letters of 7 August and 23 September, 1991). That the land freed from tax consisted of twenty ploughlands (not ten) is not an obstacle to this interpretation, as assessments of hides and ploughlands often do not match.

a static entity. This is worth remembering, as elsewhere the blankness of the record may blind us to the possibility of change.

Plush (Dorset)
Plush was granted with Buckland in a charter of King Edmund for Ælfflæd (S.474). It has been discussed above in the account of that estate.[76]

Podimore Milton (Somerset)
See *Middeltone*.

Portbury (Somerset)
Two entries on List D of the *Index chartarum* refer to land at *Portbrig*. One cites a grant by King Edward (presumably Edward the Elder) (S.1707; IC D7) and the other a grant by King Æthelred (S.1781; IC D22). Both of these grants were to laymen, and neither of them is recorded elsewhere. Portbury appears in the *De antiquitate*, but only in its unauthoritative §70, among the *alia [maneria] data Glastonie*,[77] which may suggest that the compiler of the main text had omitted the two charters from his account because he knew that the land had never come to Glastonbury. If the recipient of either of these charters (or his heirs) had intended to give the land to Glastonbury, and did indeed do so, the monks failed to hold it securely or for long, as the land was apparently back in the king's gift during Æthelred's reign and in lay hands in 1066. According to Domesday Book, eight hides at *Porberie* were held by one Godwine.[78]

Portbury is near the mouth of the Avon, over thirty-five miles north of Glastonbury.

Pouelt (Somerset)
Record survives of at least three (probably four) eighth-century transactions involving *Pouelt*. The earliest date claimed is A.D. 705/6, in S.248, the multiple grant by Ine which survives as a non-contemporary single-sheet copy, which included twenty hides at *Pouelt* granted to Abbot Berwald.[79] S.253 is a charter in the name of King Æthelheard, dated 729, which granted sixty hides at *Poholt* to Abbot Coengils. King Sigeberht is said to have sold twenty-two hides at *Poholt* to Abbot Tyccea in A.D. 754 for fifty *solidi* (S.1680); the sale for another fifty *solidi* of a further six hides *in occidentali parte illius* by Sigeberht presumably referred to land at *Poholt* as well (no Sawyer-number).[80]

The evidence for these grants is fragmentary and is scattered throughout the extant sources. Ine's is preserved only in the single-sheet copy and in the *De antiquitate*.[81] Æthelheard's survives as a cartulary-text, with bounds, but only in

---

[76] See above, *s.n. Bocland*.

[77] *De antiquitate*, §70 (ed. & transl. Scott, p. 144); see above, pp. 24–6.

[78] Domesday Book, I, 88va (Somerset, 5.33).

[79] See above, pp. 10–11, and Abrams, 'A single-sheet facsimile'.

[80] On the Anglo-Saxon land market, see Campbell, 'The sale of land'; for some comparative prices, see above, *s.n.* Brompton Ralph.

[81] *De antiquitate*, §§40 and 69 (ed. & transl. Scott, pp. 94 and 140–2); *Cronica*, §§16 and 47 (edd. & transl. Carley & Townsend, pp. 40 and 92).

the *Secretum domini*, not in the Great Cartulary;[82] it was apparently in the *Liber terrarum* (LT15) – and also mentioned in the *De antiquitate* and the Great Privilege of King Ine.[83] The entry in the contents-list of the *Liber terrarum* ('Sigeberth de Poolt dat' G.'; LT63 [S.1680]) may refer to either or both of Sigeberht's sales to Glastonbury: the dates, cost, and number of hides of these sales are recorded only in the *De antiquitate*, but the second transaction is omitted from its summary of grants.[84] None of these grants of *Pouelt* was noted in the *Index chartarum* or in the Great Cartulary.

Four eighth-century grants in fifty years constitutes an unusually plentiful record, but greater bafflement, rather than clarity, seems to result from this relative wealth of early sources. The four transactions involving *Pouelt* are not easy to reconcile with one other. Successive grants in A.D. 705/6, 729, and 754/6 are difficult to account for. The hidages of the grants do not agree, thus arguing against repeated grants of the same land, either appropriated or returned regularly to the king for unknown reasons. Even the exact location of the lands to which they referred is far from clear, as the name *Pouelt/Poholt* seems to have disappeared from Glastonbury's documents at an early date. The marginal note (*id est Grenton*) above the name *Poelt* in Ine's Great Privilege in the Trinity manuscript of the *De antiquitate* cannot reliably be used to identify eighth-century *Pouelt*: first, because the note postdates the supposed date of the grant by over five hundred years, and secondly because Greinton's small size makes it an inappropriate location for a sixty-hide grant.[85] Similarly, the appearance of a *Pouholt* as a landmark in the bounds of S.251 for *Sowy* – apparently at a point on the King's Sedge Drain in the Somerset Levels – does not solve the problem of the location of Ine's or Æthelheard's or Sigeberht's hides.[86] The short Latin bounds of Æthelheard's charter – the only extant description of the estate of *Pouelt* – are very basic, possibly not contemporary, and have spawned two different solutions.[87]

---

82 Watkin printed S.253 in his edition of the Great Cartulary (*The Great Chartulary*, ed Watkin, II.372 [no. 648]), but my examination of that manuscript has not located the charter there.

83 *De antiquitate*, §§44 and 69 (ed. & transl. Scott, pp. 102 and 142); *Cronica*, §§16 and 52 (edd. & transl. Carley & Townsend, pp. 40 and 104). For the Great Privilege (S.250), see *De antiquitate*, §42 (ed. & transl. Scott, p. 98); *Cronica*, §49 (edd. & transl. Carley & Townsend, p. 96).

84 *De antiquitate*, §§47 and 69 (ed. & transl. Scott, pp. 104 and 142); *Cronica*, §§16 and 53 (edd. & transl. Carley & Townsend, pp. 40 and 104–6). The date supplied in the *De antiquitate* for the first sale by Sigeberht (A.D. 754) contradicts the information (derived from other sources) that he reigned for one year after his accession in A.D. 756. The error may be traced back to a dislocation of chronology for the years between 754 and 845 in the Anglo-Saxon Chronicle. Information at Glastonbury on Sigeberht's reign may thus have come from a source which relied on this chronology.

85 Greinton is first reliably attested in Domesday Book and there assessed at two and a half hides; see above, *s.n.* Greinton. It was probably *within* the old estate of *Pouelt*, however.

86 Davidson, 'On the charters', p. 11. This point was at the northeastern corner of *Sowy*. The date of these bounds is uncertain but they are clearly not contemporary with Ine's grant.

87 Grundy (*The Saxon Charters*, pp. 114–16) was worried by the late forms of the

There is further evidence, however, which bears on the identification of *Pouelt*. A related place-name, apparently derived from it, occurs in the perambulation of the Twelve Hides and the description of their *loca principalia*.[88] This name (spelt *Poldune* and *Poldone*) is evidently the precursor of the modern name (Polden) for the hills to the southwest of Glastonbury. However, it is clear that *Poldune* is an estate, not a range of hills, in these references.[89] Could *Poldune* be the *Pouelt* of the early grants? The earliest attestation of the form *Poldune*, as a sub-heading for Æthelheard's grant in the Trinity manuscript of the *De antiquitate*,[90] seems to support the identity of the two, as does the entry in the contents-list of the *Liber terrarum*, 'Poolt, id est Poldone' (LT15), although there are linguistic problems involved in accepting one name as simply a development of the other.[91] It seems, nevertheless, that at least in the thirteenth century *Poldone* could be used to refer both to the *Pouelt* of Æthelheard's grant and to a contemporary estate on the Poldens, probably Shapwick (to judge from the perambulation of the Twelve Hides).

This connexion is borne out by the appearance of Æthelheard's charter in the *Secretum domini* under the heading 'Shapwik'. As a result, that charter's sixty hides have been taken to represent the Domesday manors of Shapwick and Walton (its neighbour), each assessed at thirty hides in 1066.[92] If we accept the eighth-century charters as genuine,[93] we must consider the question of how the twenty, sixty, and twenty-two (plus six) hides which they granted related to these later estates with which they have been identified.

place-names, which he judged to be thirteenth-century. But he accepted that they had been modernised in copying and that the bounds might be contemporary with the date of the charter. Morland ('The Saxon charters for Sowy and Pouholt', p. 234) has considered them to be genuinely eighth-century. He supplied an identification for a landmark (*Chalkbrok*) which Grundy had missed and criticised Grundy for not looking for the first boundary-point in the right place. According to Morland, the bounds show that Cossington and Street lay outside Æthelheard's sixty hides ('Hidation', p. 78). This conclusion is convincing, especially as far as Cossington is concerned. However, I would be more cautious than Morland about the date of these bounds, which may have been written to adapt to the changes in the landscape effected by Glastonbury's drainage-works in the thirteenth century; see Morland, 'The Saxon charters for Sowy and Pouholt', pp. 234–5, and Williams, *The Draining*, pp. 47–55, 62–71, and 74. Michael Costen has also considered the bounds to be eighth-century: 'The late Saxon landscape', p. 33.

88 *De antiquitate*, §§72 and 73 (ed. & transl. Scott, pp. 150 and 152); *Cronica*, §§3 and 4 (edd. & transl. Carley & Townsend, pp. 14 and 16). On the Twelve Hides, see above, *s.n.* Glastonbury.

89 As, probably, in the interpolated reference in the *De antiquitate* to King Arthur's gift of *Poweldone* to Glastonbury (§69 [ed. & transl. Scott, p. 142]; *Cronica*, §16 [edd. & transl. Carley & Townsend, p. 38]) and in other later mediaeval occurrences of the name (Abrams, 'A single-sheet facsimile', p. 126, n. 130).

90 MS. R.5.33, 9v; *De antiquitate*, §44 (ed. & transl. Scott, p. 102), omits the heading.

91 See Abrams, 'A single-sheet facsimile', pp. 111–12 and 126–7.

92 Morland, 'The Glastonbury manors', pp. 78–9, and 'Hidation', pp. 78–9; Domesday Book, I, 90ra (Shapwick) and 90rb (Walton) (Somerset, 8.5 and 8.11).

93 On this subject, see Edwards, *The Charters*, pp. 27–33, 40–1, and 72; Abrams, 'A single-sheet facsimile', especially pp. 125–6.

If the charters do not represent repeat-grants of the same land, they may instead have related to different parts of a large land-unit, parts which only later acquired individual names; this would explain the discrepancy in the number of hides while the name remained the same. Nicholas Corcos, basing his conclusions on the model developed by G.R.J. Jones,[94] has suggested that *Pouelt* was an early 'multiple estate': in the early Anglo-Saxon period it was an estate of sixty hides, possibly of Roman origin, made up of specialised constituent parts, including the pastoral unit of Shapwick.[95] Corcos has suggested that this multiple estate fragmented and disappeared, probably in the mid- to late tenth century, when a conversion to open-field farming and the development of nuclear settlement altered the face of the landscape.[96] According to Corcos, the original *Pouelt* covered approximately the area of the Polden Hills – a very considerable amount of land. Once the estate had broken up, the monks were faced with the problem of how to classify its documentation, and S.253, the surviving charter of Æthelheard for *Pouelt*, was filed in the cartulary under Shapwick, because that manor may have been remembered as the centre of the ancient estate.

Corcos's theory is attractive as far as it goes; but it omits the fact that the earliest record which we have of *Pouelt*, if it is genuine, is Ine's, which speaks of an estate of twenty hides. The sixty hides appear only in the second charter, ostensibly about twenty-five years later, and cannot, therefore (it would seem), represent the original estate before it broke into smaller parts. This failure by Corcos to consider S.248 need not scupper his theory, however. The dismantling of *Pouelt* may have originated with Ine, whose twenty hides set things in motion, after which Æthelheard's grant of sixty hides continued – and Sigeberht's sales of twenty-eight hides possibly completed – the process of transferring the whole of this hypothetical estate to Glastonbury in portions.

Michael Costen has supported Corcos's interpretation that deliberate planning characterised the later Anglo-Saxon landscape at Shapwick and elsewhere on the Poldens.[97] Certainly the layout of the mediaeval parishes (which are generally assumed to have been co-extensive with earlier estates) does not have the look of a random arrangement. On the north side of the Poldens, west of Shapwick, five rectangular estates in a row (Catcott, Edington, Chilton Polden, Cossington, and Woolavington) run north in a regular ladder-pattern from the east-west Roman road on the ridge of the hill, each having a settlement sited below the crest of the hill and the rest of the estate extending north into the moor.[98] Puriton, off the slope to the west, was not held by Glastonbury at the time of Domesday Book,[99] but three hides there were mentioned in Glastonbury's text of King Æthelwulf's Decimation charter.[100] On the south side of the ridge of hills the pattern is less

---

[94] See Jones, 'The multiple estate as a model framework', 'Multiple estates and early settlement', 'Continuity despite calamity', and 'Multiple estates perceived'.

[95] Corcos, 'Early estates on the Poldens', pp. 47–54.

[96] On the development of the open-field system, see Fox, 'Approaches to the adoption'.

[97] Costen, 'Some evidence for new settlements', pp. 48–50.

[98] See the map given by Costen, *ibid.*, p. 49, and (less detailed) above, map 6.

[99] Queen Edith held six hides at *Peritone* (only five of which paid tax) in 1066: Domesday Book, I, 91rb (Somerset, 11.1).

[100] S.303; *De antiquitate*, §§53 and 69 (ed. & transl. Scott, pp. 112 and 142); *Cronica*,

geometric, but Bawdrip, Stawell, Sutton Mallet, Moorlinch, and Greinton all share the same Roman road as their northern boundary and run south from it into yet another moor. Ashcott and Pedwell, the next estates (to the east), look very much as though they had been carved out of neighbouring Walton, as does Sharpham to its north, and these sixteen places – on the map at least – have the appearance of a single unit, systematically divided. The eastern boundary is less clear-cut. Street and Compton Dundon arguably may have been part of this original unit as well.

It is interesting that, of the five estates immediately to the west of Shapwick (those with the most artificial shape), four have place-names which are compounds of personal names with *tun* or *cot* (three of personal names and *-ingtun*).[101] These might reflect the existence of what Gelling called a 'manorial relationship': the place-names could preserve the personal names of thegns granted estates by a higher authority, in this case presumably sub-tenants of the ecclesiastical owner, Glastonbury.[102] We have no evidence for any of these five places before the time of Domesday Book,[103] so we can only speculate about when these 'manorial' names replaced the general name *Pouelt*; but they do seem to tie in with some kind of restructuring of the landscape after the eighth-century grants and before 1066. Four of the five are also five-hide units,[104] defined elsewhere as a holding suitable for a thegn.[105] No archaeological evidence has yet helped to date these developments on the land more precisely.[106]

A few pre-Conquest references to some of the other members of this putative estate survive to fill out (and in some cases to complicate) the picture. Æthelwulf's three hides at Puriton have already been mentioned; Puriton's six hides (taxed for five), were back in royal hands in 1066, held by Queen Edith.[107] Robin Fleming has mentioned this estate in her discussion of monastic lands appropri-

---

§§16 and 56 (edd. & transl. Carley & Townsend, pp. 40 and 108). Unlike the Great Cartulary's version (ed. Watkin, I.143 [no. 202]), the narrative references omit the hidage. The *Secretum domini* omits *Pirinton* altogether. On the Decimation charter, its texts, and especially its possible representation of only part of an estate, see above, *s.n.* Brannocmynstre and Monk Okehampton, and below, pp. 322–4.

101 Ekwall, *The Concise Oxford Dictionary of English Place-names*, pp. 90, 105, 123, 160, and 532, *s.n.* Catcott, Chilton Polden, Cossington, Edington, and Woolavington. The exception is Chilton, meaning '*tun* on the limestone hill'.

102 Gelling, *Signposts*, pp. 181–5; Costen, 'The late Saxon landscape', p. 39.

103 Cossington is mentioned in the bounds of S.253, but, as noted above, the date of these bounds is uncertain.

104 The exception is Cossington, with three hides.

105 *Geþyncþo*, par. 2: '7 gif ceorl geþeah, þæt he hæfde v hida fullice agenes landes, bellan 7 burhgeat, setl 7 sundornote on cynges healle, þonne wæs he þanon forð þegenrihtes wyrðe' ('and if a *ceorl* prospered, that he possessed fully five hides of land of his own, a bell and a castle-gate, a seat and special office in the king's hall, then was he henceforth entitled to the rights of a thegn'): *Die Gesetze*, ed. Liebermann, I.456, and *English Historical Documents*, transl. Whitelock, p. 468 (no. 51).

106 But see the ongoing work of the Shapwick project: *The Shapwick Project*, edd. Aston et al.

107 Domesday Book, I, 91rb (Somerset, 11.1).

ated by the house of Wessex in the late ninth and early tenth century.[108] Its site – where the Polden Hills join the River Parrett – would have linked the communication route with the river. Stawell (elsewhere paired with *Ternuc*) may have been the subject of a grant by King Eadred to the layman Alfred ('Eddredus de Ternuc dat' Ælfredo. et al. S.' in the contents-list of the *Liber terrarum* [S.1740; LT 120]). In the *Index chartarum* and the *De antiquitate* this grant by Eadred is presented as a gift directly to Glastonbury (no Sawyer-number; IC C5).[109] If either of these lost charters were authentic, it might indicate that Stawell, hypothetically a portion of *Pouelt*, had reverted to the king between the eighth century and the mid-tenth. Alternatively, it might have stayed in royal hands all that time. It seems that *Stawelle* by 1066 had achieved some independence, as its two and a half hides were separately assessed in Glastonbury's entries in Domesday Book and not treated, as were most of the other Polden estates, as a sub-unit of either Shapwick or Walton.[110] Stawell's western neighbour, Bawdrip, had been lost completely, if it had ever belonged to Glastonbury and *Pouelt*; in Domesday Book (the earliest source to mention it) two hides there were recorded in lay hands.[111]

Of the remaining places suggested as possible component parts of *Pouelt*, Shapwick itself, Sutton Mallet, Greinton, Pedwell, and Ashcott also make their first documentary appearance (by name) in Domesday Book, all (save Shapwick) as sub-units of Walton.[112] Moorlinch first occurs even later, named only in the spurious privileges of King Ine and King Edgar.[113] Like Moorlinch, Shapwick and Street are given a retroactive ancient and special status in those post-Conquest forgeries. The three easternmost candidates for membership of *Pouelt* (and the most uncertain, on topographical grounds) – Sharpham, Street, and Compton Dundon – have meagre Anglo-Saxon notices. According to the contents-list of the *Liber terrarum*, King Eadwig granted *Scyrphamme* to the layman Æthelwold (S.1752; LT123), a grant cited nowhere else in the archive. Sharpham does not even appear in Domesday Book by name, although it has been thought (presumably because of its location) to have been included in Walton.[114] Street has been associated with the very early grant to Glastonbury by Hædde, bishop of the West Saxons, of three hides at *Lantokay*, identified as Leigh-in-Street (S.1249; A.D.

---

[108] Fleming, 'Monastic lands', p. 256. But see the arguments by Dumville (*Wessex and England*, pp. 29–54).

[109] *De antiquitate*, §§57 and 69 (ed. & transl. Scott, pp. 118 and 142); *Cronica*, §§16 and 66 (edd. & transl. Carley & Townsend, pp. 42 and 124). See also below, *s.n.* Tarnock.

[110] Domesday Book, I, 90ra (Somerset, 8.10).

[111] Domesday Book, I, 95rb (Somerset, 24.23).

[112] Greinton seems to be separate in the Exchequer's text; but in the *Liber Exoniensis* (E 164b2) it is linked with Ashcott, itself connected with Walton.

[113] S.250 and S.783. *De antiquitate*, §§42 and 60 (ed. & transl. Scott, pp. 100 and 124); *Cronica*, §§49 and 71 (edd. & transl. Carley & Townsend, pp. 98 and 134). See above, *s.n.* Glastonbury.

[114] Morland, 'The Glastonbury manors', p. 79. Part of Sharpham later came to be included in the Twelve Hides; see Morland, 'Glaston Twelve Hides', pp. 38, 49, 53, and map (opposite p. 54), and the texts in *De antiquitate*, §§72 and 73 (ed. & transl. Scott, pp. 150 and 152); *Cronica*, §§3 and 4 (edd. & transl. Carley & Townsend, pp. 14–16).

680). In 1066, Glastonbury held four hides at *Lega*.[115] Compton Dundon, unlike Sharpham and Street, was classified as a sub-unit of Walton in Domesday Book; it may have been the *Cumtone* reputedly given to Glastonbury by King Cynewulf in A.D. 762 and restored by King Edward the Elder.[116] *Cumtone* may have been the last portion of *Pouelt* to be transferred to Glastonbury, joining the others in some connexion with Walton, but if so it was the only one documented with its own name, so to speak. Possibly Cynewulf's charter referred to another *Cumtone*. In any event it was Compton Dundon which Edward the Elder apparently restored.

All these places, then, may have been part of a large and early multiple estate called *Pouelt*.[117] If it is not misguided to consider the four eighth-century grants of *Pouelt* as transferring portions of this large estate from the king's hands to that of the monastic house, can any of these early grants be specifically identified with later estates on the Poldens? Assuming the hidage has not changed, Puriton, the westernmost estate, assessed at six hides in 1066, could be a candidate for Sigeberht's second sale of six hides *in occidentali parte illius*.[118] Might Shapwick's land for twenty ploughs which, according to Domesday Book, did not pay tax (and which Morland has proposed was sited at Shapwick and Moorlinch)[119] be Ine's twenty hides, and the rest of Shapwick's sub-units (with the addition of Cossington, clearly topographically part of this whole, though separate by 1066), and Walton with its sub-units, be Æthelheard's sixty hides?[120] The sums work, with only a little fiddling.[121] This still leaves the twenty-two hides of Sigeberht's first sale unaccounted for, but Bawdrip and Stawell may be considered here; and there is always the possibility that some land became detached from Shapwick and Walton and the nature of an original link with *Pouelt* thereby obscured. Hidages, too, could have changed.[122] Additions to the estate may also have been

---

115 Domesday Book, I, 90rb (Somerset, 8.16). C. and F. Thorn have identified this as Overleigh. Another three hides at *Lege*, plus one and a half at *Strate*, were in secular hands in 1066, but C. and F. Thorn have identified these as settlements in the south of Somerset, near Chard. See above, *s.n. Lantokay*.

116 See above, *s.n.* Compton Dundon.

117 The name, it has been suggested by Oliver Padel, derived from Celtic elements, possibly *pow* (Old Cornish *pou*), meaning 'region', and **elt*, the plural of **alt* (Welsh *allt*, Middle Welsh plural *eillt*), meaning 'cliff' or 'hill-slope'. See Abrams, 'A single-sheet facsimile', p. 111. I should like to thank Oliver Padel for his help with this place-name.

118 As has been suggested by Morland ('The Glastonbury manors', p. 79).

119 *Ibid.*

120 The bounds attached to Æthelheard's grant clearly exclude Cossington, and probably Compton Dundon as well (Grundy, *The Saxon Charters*, p. 114; Morland, 'Hidation', p. 78); but, as mentioned above, their evidence may not be contemporary.

121 Cossington, for example, is assessed at only three hides, not the expected five, in Domesday Book.

122 Morland, for example, has proposed a slightly different process, whereby the addition of thirteen hides at Compton Dundon, Cossington, and Woolavington (which he believed to have been outside Æthelheard's sixty hides because of their exclusion from the bounds of S.253) did not change Shapwick's assessment but did apparently free it from geld ('Hidation', pp. 78–9).

made: some of Walton's sub-units in Domesday Book, for example, may have been relatively new arrivals which had never belonged to ancient *Pouelt*.

Reconstructing the hypothetical multiple estate of *Pouelt*, based on the incomplete information of four eighth-century grants, on enigmatic and late data from Domesday Book, on place-names, and on topography may be a dangerous exercise in speculation. It is not offered here as a proven case. The evidence is so incomplete that, once the few (relatively) certain pieces of the puzzle have been laid out, we cannot do more than guess at the nature of the relationship and development of the large number of places involved in the analysis. This should only be done with caution. Hidages are notoriously unreliable, as they could be altered. Even names, as we have seen, were not permanent. In fact, we should not assume that anything remained unchanged from the earliest stage of the endowment until the Conquest and beyond. This was not a static landscape. Nor should we assume that developments were always in the same direction: an estate breaking into smaller parts may also have had new land added to it. Given the passage of time, and given the sparse nature of the evidence, it is not surprising that a neat description of *Pouelt*'s history cannot be written; but the complexity of the discussion should serve as a reminder that the more ancient the holding, the more potentially complicated its history.

Pouldone / Poweldune
See *Pouelt*.

Pucklechurch (Gloucestershire)
Four grants of Pucklechurch provide the ostensibly Anglo-Saxon material for its history. S.553 is a single-sheet diploma dated 950 in the name of King Eadred, granting twenty-five hides at Pucklechurch to Glastonbury.[123] This was probably the charter of Eadred listed in the *Index chartarum* among royal grants to the abbey (IC C6). Record (but no texts) of three other transactions involving this estate survives. The first two are in the contents-list of the *Liber terrarum*, where grants of Pucklechurch by King Edmund to Glastonbury (S.1724; LT100) and by King Eadred to Wulfhelm, the bishop of Wells (A.D. 937/8–956) (S.1744; LT98), are cited. Lastly, a charter listed in the *Index chartarum* (S.1777; IC C11) apparently testified that King Æthelred had given Pucklechurch to Glastonbury.[124] The information on the grants by Edmund and Æthelred is amplified in the *De antiquitate*, where it is specified that both gifts were of thirty hides; the latter is there described as a restitution.[125] Eadred's grant to Glastonbury is also cited, likewise as a restoration,[126] but (not surprisingly) no mention is made of any grant by Eadred to Wells.

---

[123] See above, pp. 10–12, and Abrams, ' "Lucid intervals" '.
[124] Æthelred is also cited as the donor of Pucklechurch in a note in the cartularies which follows a papal privilege (*The Great Chartulary*, ed. Watkin, I.147 [no. 205]).
[125] *De antiquitate*, §§55, 63, and 69 (ed. & transl. Scott, pp. 114, 130, and 142–4); *Cronica*, §§16, 64, and 74 (edd. & transl. Carley & Townsend, pp. 40, 42, 120–2, and 142).
[126] *De antiquitate*, §57 (ed. & transl. Scott, p. 118). It is not in the summary chapter or in the *Cronica*.

S.553, the diploma of Eadred for Glastonbury, claims to be a confirmation of Edmund's gift of Pucklechurch to the community. There is no certainty, however, that Edmund's grant ever took place: according to both Dunstan's biographer, B, and John of Worcester, Pucklechurch was still a royal vill in A.D. 946 when Edmund was murdered there.[127] In any event, S.553 is itself not a genuine document,[128] and its overt information is therefore unacceptable. The account in the *De antiquitate* gives even more detail about this grant of Pucklechurch by Eadred to Glastonbury. Eadred is said to have *restored* it (and Doulting) to the abbey, because it had been alienated in the past, either through some tyranny or the carelessness of the abbots.[129] Now if Pucklechurch had indeed been given to Glastonbury only ten or fifteen years before by Edmund, and to the same abbot as received it in turn from Eadred, this seems a curiously inappropriate remark, especially as that abbot would have to have been Dunstan. It could therefore be a comment from some other context applied here for effect. It certainly has the appearance of a later interpolation: such a description would make more sense if Pucklechurch had been lost for a longer period, or if a spurious authority were being created, perhaps for the forged charter. The omission from the summary of grants in the *De antiquitate* of any reference to Eadred's restoration of Pucklechurch – and, more damningly, its complete omission from the *Cronica*[130] – should cast further doubt on the genuineness of the information.

These doubts may be supported by the existence of the diploma in favour of Bishop Wulfhelm (LT98). If genuine, this charter (now lost) could have been the original instrument alienating the estate from royal possession; how and when Glastonbury acquired the documentation of this transaction is an intriguing (but probably unanswerable) question. If we accept its evidence at face-value and assume that Eadred granted Pucklechurch to Wells, Glastonbury seems to have obtained the estate, and probably the bishop's diploma with it, not long thereafter, possibly during Æthelred's reign. The existence of a charter in Æthelred's name (and in Glastonbury's favour) (IC C11), also now lost, may suggest that this transaction was a legal one, but, if Æthelred's charter had indeed effected a legitimate transfer of Pucklechurch into Glastonbury's possession, why did the monks feel the need to concoct a diploma (S.553) in the name of his predecessor? It is difficult to see the point of forged restitutions by both Eadred and Æthelred. The earliest extant reference to Æthelred's grant is that in the *De antiquitate*, which also provides the first witness to the existence of S.553. This latter diploma could have been based in part on the bishop's charter (LT98), which could have provided the witness-list and bounds.

It is difficult to determine on the basis of this evidence when exactly Pucklechurch became an abbatial holding. The hidage of the four grants, however, may

---

[127] B, *Vita S. Dunstani*, §§31–3 (*Memorials*, ed. Stubbs, pp. 44–6); *Florentii Wigorniensis Chronicon, s.a.* 946 (*Monumenta Historica Britannica*, edd. Petrie & Sharpe, p. 574).

[128] See Abrams, ' "Lucid intervals" '.

[129] *De antiquitate*, §57 (ed. & transl. Scott, p. 118): 'pridem alienatas aut aliqua tirannide seu incuria prelatorum'.

[130] This may indicate that John of Glastonbury based his text on a version of the *De antiquitate* without this interpolation.

offer some assistance. Edmund's gift was reputed to have been of thirty hides. We know nothing about the grant to the bishop of Wells, but the forged charter in Eadred's name is for twenty-five hides. Æthelred reputedly gave or restored thirty hides. Yet according to Domesday Book, Pucklechurch consisted of only twenty hides.[131] Grundy explained the difference between the sums of twenty-five and thirty by suggesting that at the time of Eadred's grant (which he thought to be genuine), waterlogged areas which were subsequently drained and brought back into use had been omitted from the total.[132] This explanation is unnecessarily imaginative and omits consideration of the total in Domesday Book. Although the Anglo-Saxon estate of Pucklechurch adjoined two other estates with extant vernacular boundaries (S.786, for Dyrham, and S.414, for Cold Ashton),[133] the bounds of S.553 have nevertheless raised difficulties for those attempting to solve them.[134] The key to the mystery of Pucklechurch's extent, however, may be found in two neighbouring estates, Siston and Doynton, each consisting of five hides, which appear in Domesday Book among the lands of different owners, with no obvious tenurial links with Glastonbury in 1066 or 1086.[135] According to the most recent analysis of the bounds both of these estates formed part of Pucklechurch in the mid-tenth century.[136] We can therefore consider the possibility that Pucklechurch was indeed originally thirty hides, but that it shrank when Glastonbury lost Siston and Doynton, some time before 1066. These two sub-units of the estate may have been granted out on leases, and their tenants may have managed to escape from the control of the community; or the land may have been appropriated by the king. After the Conquest, however, Glastonbury's ownership over Siston was reasserted.[137] The post-Conquest history of Pucklechurch is outside

---

[131] Domesday Book, I, 165rb (Gloucestershire, 8.1).

[132] Grundy, *The Saxon Charters and Field Names of Gloucestershire*, II.200 and 212.

[133] S.786 (A.D. 972) is a confirmation and restoration by King Edgar of lands belonging to Pershore Abbey; S.414 (A.D. 931) is a questionable diploma of Æthelstan for St Peter's, Bath. The dates of the bounds of both charters are uncertain; Kitson (in his unpublished work on charter-bounds) places the former in the 990s, the latter in the second half of the tenth century.

[134] Grundy began his perambulation with the following remark: 'This charter has caused me more trouble and difficulty than any I have had to deal with in recent years' (*The Saxon Charters and Field Names of Gloucestershire*, II.201, n. 181).

[135] Domesday Book I, 165rb and 168ra (Gloucestershire, 6.5 and 42.3).

[136] This was the opinion of Stephen Morland (in letters of 9 and 30 December, 1988) and Neil Stacy ('The estates', p. 74, and in a letter of 30 July, 1990). Peter Kitson, however, has included Doynton only (according to a letter of 15 February, 1989). I am grateful to them all for informing me of their analyses and conclusions.

[137] A charter of King Stephen of A.D. 1138 confirmed the sale of Siston to Glastonbury (for forty silver marks) and referred to Glastonbury's ancient ownership of the estate: *Adami de Domerham Historia*, ed. Hearne, II.328; *Regesta regum Anglo-Normannorum*, edd. Davis *et al*, III.130 (no. 342). The restoration of Siston by Abbot Henry of Blois, presumably by means of this purchase, is mentioned in the *Cronica* (§88; edd. & transl. Carley & Townsend, p. 164). The previous abbot, Herluin (A.D. 1101–*ca* 1120), had also regained six hides at Pucklechurch, according to the *De antiquitate* (§79; ed. & transl. Scott, p. 160). It is unclear whether these hides had been lost before or after the Conquest, however.

the frame of reference of this study, but the forged Anglo-Saxon documentation which we have been considering can probably only be understood in terms of Glastonbury's loss and retrieval of parts of the estate. Most specifically, we may seek here a clue to the puzzle of why Eadred's charter for Glastonbury (S.553) was for only twenty-five hides. Presumably, at the time when the single sheet was created, Glastonbury had either retrieved only one of Pucklechurch's lost parts, or had recovered both but held one portion securely in its own name, and so manufactured a claim for an ancient total of only twenty-five hides. We can conclude, therefore, that when Pucklechurch first left royal hands it consisted of thirty hides, two five-hide units of which had escaped by 1066. But whether Glastonbury acquired the estate in Edmund's, Eadred's, or Æthelred's reign (and how stable its possession was) is still unclear.

Pucklechurch was one of those manors appropriated by Wells (and one of the four which the bishop retained) during the protracted but eventually unsuccessful attempt to annex the monastery to the see which was begun by Bishop Savaric (A.D. 1191–1205) and pursued by Bishop Jocelin (A.D. 1206–1242).[138] This dispute, which continued into the later thirteenth century, not only provides a possible context for the production of spurious Anglo-Saxon documents for the estates at issue, but its resolution (with the loss of Pucklechurch to Wells) explains the presence of Eadred's charter for Glastonbury in the archive of the dean and chapter of Wells Cathedral.[139]

Puriton (Somerset)

Three hides at *Piriton* were cited in the cartulary-text (in the Great Cartulary but not the *Secretum domini*) of King Æthelwulf's Decimation charter for Glastonbury.[140] Six hides at *Peritone* were held by Queen Edith in 1066.[141] The pre-Conquest history of Puriton (almost fifteen miles west of Glastonbury at the edge of the Polden Hills) has been discussed above in connexion with that of the estate of *Pouelt*.

Pylle (Somerset)

Pylle was assessed as a five-hide unit of Pilton in Domesday Book.[142] It has been discussed above in the analysis of that estate.

---

138 See above, p. 12.
139 The script suggests an earlier date than that of this dispute for the forgery of S.553, however, either in the late eleventh or the twelfth century; see Abrams, ' "Lucid intervals" ', p. 49.
140 S.303 (A.D. 854); *The Great Chartulary*, ed. Watkin, I.143 (no. 202). The texts of the charter in the *De antiquitate* and *Cronica* omit the hidage; *De antiquitate*, §§53 and 69 (ed. & transl. Scott, pp. 112 and 142); *Cronica*, §§16 and 56 (edd. & transl. Carley & Townsend, pp. 40 and 108). On the charter, its texts, and its interpretation, see above, *s.n. Brannocmynstre* and Monk Okehampton, and below, pp. 322–4.
141 Domesday Book, I, 91rb (Somerset, 11.1).
142 Domesday Book, I, 90va (Somerset, 8.20).

Quantock Wood (Land near)

See *Cantucuudu.*

Raddington (Somerset)

S.347 is a charter of King Alfred for his *comes* Berhtwulf, granting in A.D. 891 twelve hides at Plush in Dorset and two hides at *Radingtone* in exchange for land at *Suttone*.[1] It was copied into the fourteenth-century cartularies, but no other record of the grant survives in Glastonbury's archive. Finberg queried the number of hides, suggesting that Raddington should perhaps have been five, not two, to make up the cited total of seventeen for the grant.[2] It seems, rather, that the mistake may have been in the hides at Plush, which should perhaps have read fifteen.[3] Two hides at Raddington were in lay hands in 1066.[4]

The bounds attached to S.347 are concerned with the Dorset estate only; no description of Raddington is given. It seems odd that two estates so far apart (Raddington is on the Devon-Somerset border, about fifteen miles west of Taunton and perhaps fifty from Plush) were paired in this way, but the evidence offers no clues to a reason. Berhtwulf's *Radingtone* may have been located elsewhere.

Nothing definitive can be said for or against Glastonbury's possession of the land. It may have come to the community from Berhtwulf or his heir, although its absence from the *De antiquitate* might count against that, as much as negative evidence *can* count in this context. Perhaps it is more likely that the charter was in the Glastonbury archive in connexion with the monks' acquisition of Plush in the mid-tenth century, by which time the connexion between Plush and *Radingtone*, whatever it had been, had been severed.

Rowberrow (Somerset)

An entry in the contents-list of the *Liber terrarum* refers to the grant of *Ruganbeorge* by King Edmund to a layman, Alfred (S.1722; LT65). No other record of this transaction survives in the archive; but *Ruthanbeorge* does appear among the unauthoritative list of *alia [maneria] data Glastonie* of §70 of the *De antiquitate*.[5] An Alfred (perhaps the same man) received at least two other charters noticed in the Glastonbury records, both for lands which the community may have held at some time in the Anglo-Saxon period (though the evidence is inconclusive),[6] but whether this argues for the abbey's possession of Rowberrow or not is impossible to say. Rowberrow does not appear in Domesday Book by name, so its status in 1066 is unknown. It may have been incorporated into another estate, held by Glastonbury or by another owner. It is in the Mendips north of Cheddar, about twenty miles northeast of Glastonbury.[7]

---

[1] Dorothy Whitelock discussed the diplomatic of this charter (which she judged to be authentic) in 'Some charters in the name of King Alfred', pp. 85–6.

[2] Finberg, *The Early Charters of Wessex*, p. 127.

[3] See above, *s.n.* Plush.

[4] Domesday Book, I, 94va (Somerset, 22.13).

[5] *De antiquitate*, §70 (ed. & transl. Scott, p. 144); see above, pp. 24–6.

[6] LT120 and LT121; see *s.n.* Camerton and Tarnock.

[7] See Foster, 'A gazetteer', p. 77, for the fragment of Anglo-Saxon scuplture preserved in the church.

Scearamtone
See *Cerawycombe*.

Scobbanwirht (Somerset)

Ten hides at Baltonsborough and *Scobbanwirht* are said to have been granted to Glastonbury in a charter in the name of Lulla (*ancilla Christi*), dated 744, which is preserved in the fourteenth-century cartularies (S.1410). Lulla's charter for Baltonsborough appears in the contents-list of the *Liber terrarum*, in the *Index chartarum*, and in MS. 39a (LT17, IC A19, and L7), but only Baltonsborough is named in those entries. *Scobbanwirht* is cited additionally only in the *De antiquitate* (spelled *Scrobbamurht*), where the date 745 is given to Lulla's grant, and the interlinear identification *uel Sabewrche* (*Scrobanmurth uel Sabewrtha* in the summary) is added; in the *Cronica* the name is given as *Scabworthe* (*Schabbesworth* in the summary chapter).[1] The obsolescence of the place-name has meant that the land in question has not been securely identified. Even its original size is uncertain, as Lulla's charter recorded only a total figure (ten hides) for both places granted. Since Baltonsborough comprised five hides in A.D. 1066, it may be reasonable to assume that it and *Scobbanwirht* each consisted of five hides in A.D. 744.[2] This assumption – based on the questionable principle of stable area and static hidage – is not without drawbacks.

Twelfmede acres on Scheobanwerzche also appear in S.292, a charter of King Æthelwulf for twenty-five hides at Ditcheat and five at Lottisham, dated 842. It occurs in the second of two sets of bounds, those for Lottisham. This provides some assistance in the identification of *Scobbanwirht*'s location, but the difficulty of identifying the landmarks hampers the process. According to Grundy, the bounds seem nevertheless to indicate that – in S.292 – *Scobbanwirht* was a detached meadow in the southwestern part of Baltonsborough which had on its north the *Olan* (a tributary of the River Brue, possibly Southwood Brook) and the Brue itself to the south, extending across the river.[3] According to S.292, the meadow consisted of twelve acres, ten south and two north of the Brue, and appears to have been attached to Lottisham. How this twelve acres of meadow is to be related to the land granted in Lulla's charter remains an unsolved problem.

Heather Edwards has suggested that five hides at *Scobbanwirht* had been incorporated into Ditcheat by the mid-eighth century, citing their appearance in the bounds of S.292 as evidence.[4] This argument, however, ignored the fact that *Scobbanwirht* was mentioned in the Lottisham, not Ditcheat, bounds of that charter; it also avoided the issue of their date.[5]

---

1 *De antiquitate*, §§46 and 69 (ed. & transl. Scott, pp. 104 and 142); *Cronica*, §§16 and 52 (edd. & transl. Carley & Townsend, pp. 40 and 104).

2 Edwards, *The Charters*, p. 44.

3 Grundy, *The Saxon Charters*, pp. 61–4 and 74. Grundy's two discussions varied slightly on the question of the position of the land in relation to the Brue.

4 Edwards, *The Charters*, p. 44.

5 See above, *s.n.* Ditcheat. Lottisham's five hides in S.292 could not include *Scobbanwirht*'s five hides, unless they were the same place, or the hidage had not been altered by the doubling of the property. The former seems impossible, as both Lottisham and *Scobbanwirht* occur as separate places in S.1410, and the latter seems unlikely.

All we can say, I think, is that Baltonsborough and *Scobbanwirht* seem to have been paired in Lulla's time, but not thereafter. *Scobbanwirht's* hypothetical five hides of A.D. 744/5 seem to have disappeared by the time of S.292, whose bounds (of uncertain date) describe land in the vicinity, including some meadow which seems to have borne this name. If these five hides existed, they must have been incorporated into some other territorial unit, as they do not seem to reappear in the Anglo-Saxon record. This may have been Ditcheat, as suggested by Edwards, but there is no documentary evidence to support it. On the ground, an association with Baltonsborough or West Lydford (adjacent to the meadow to the west) seems more likely; and, as we have seen, although West Lydford was in lay hands in 1066, it is thought once to have been part of a larger estate (with East Lydford) in Glastonbury's possession.[6] The *Scobbanwirht* of Lulla's grant may perhaps have been absorbed into Lydford: in S.1410, Lydford may have consisted of five hides, while the total of the two Lydfords in Domesday Book is thirteen hides.

Scobbanwirht itself does not appear in Domesday Book by name; but Morland has proposed to identify it with *Scepeworde*, probably adjacent to West Lydford, where half a hide was in lay hands.[7] This slight clue may preserve a memory of the *Scobbanwirht* of Lulla's grant or the twelve acres of the later bounds: it may indicate that *Scobbanwirht* was incorporated into the western part of the early *Ledenford* estate. But the evidence is inconclusive.

East and West Lydford straddle the Fosse Way where it crosses the River Brue, between five and ten miles southeast of Glastonbury.

Scyrphamme
See *Pouelt*.

Seacesceg
See *Iecesig*.

Sethebeorge
An entry in the contents-list of the *Liber terrarum* noted the grant of *Sethebeorge* to Glastonbury by King Æthelred (S.1778; IC C12). The only other record of this grant occurs in the *De antiquitate*, where a gift by Æthelred the Unready of one hide at *Siteberge* is cited.[8] Sawyer's suggestion that the name was possibly a corruption of Panborough seems unnecessary and unlikely.[9] Morland has instead recommended identification with *Sedeborge* (Sedborough) in North Devon, approximately eighty-five miles from Glastonbury, where a layman held one virgate in 1066;[10] but there may be a more appropriate candidate nearer home – not yet identified – for this stray hide.

---

[6] See above, *s.n.* Lydford.
[7] Domesday Book, I, 99ra (Somerset, 47.22); Morland, review of *Domesday Book: Somerset*, p. 139. He described *Scobbanwirht* as 'at or near Lydford'; see also 'The Glastonbury manors', p. 68. C. and F. Thorn have proposed locations in Bruton or adjacent to West Lydford (*Somerset*, edd. & transl. Thorn & Thorn, p. 368).
[8] *De antiquitate*, §§63 and 69 (ed. & transl. Scott, pp. 130 and 144); *Cronica*, §§16 and 74 (edd. & transl. Carley & Townsend, pp. 42 and 142).
[9] As pointed out in *Cronica*, edd. & transl. Carley & Townsend, p. 295 (n. 332).
[10] Domesday Book, I, 118rb (Devon, 52.33).

Shapwick (Somerset)
Glastonbury held a thirty-hide estate at Shapwick in 1066.[11] Its history has been discussed above in the context of *Pouelt*, the early holding of the abbey which may have had its centre at Shapwick.[12]

Sharpham (Somerset)
Sharpham, too, may have been part of the large *Pouelt* estate and has been discussed above under that heading.

Shepton Mallet (Somerset)
Shepton Mallet was a sub-unit of Pilton assessed at six and a half hides at the time of Domesday Book.[13] For a detailed discussion of Pilton's history, see above, under Pilton.

Shipham (Somerset)
See *Cympanhamme*.

***Sowy* (Somerset)**
The text of a charter in the name of King Ine and of his wife, Æthelburh, granting twelve hides at *Sowy* to Glastonbury in A.D. 725 survives in the fourteenth-century cartularies (S.251). The charter is noted on the contents-list of the *Liber terrarum* (LT14) and in the *Index chartarum* and MS. 39a (IC A7 and L17). The grant of *Soei* is mentioned in the *De antiquitate*, seemingly in connexion with other grants made in A.D. 705.[14] The Great Privilege (S.250) includes the twelve hides at *Sowy* among its litany of Ine's grants and names the church there as one of those with special privileges.[15] Ten hides at *Sowy* were reputedly the object of a grant to Glastonbury by King Æthelwulf in his Decimation charter (S.303; A.D. 854).[16] In 1066, Glastonbury held twelve hides at *Sowi*.[17]

Grundy analysed the bounds of S.251 and identified them as defining only the modern parish of Middlezoy.[18] Earlier, however, Davidson had expressed the view that Anglo-Saxon *Sowy* had encompassed a wider area, including Othery to the

---

11 Domesday Book, I, 90ra (Somerset, 8.5).
12 See above, *s.n. Pouelt*.
13 Domesday Book, I, 90rb (Somerset, 8.20).
14 *De antiquitate*, §§40 and 69 (ed. & transl. Scott, pp. 94 and 140); *Cronica*, §§16 and 47 (edd. & transl. Carley & Townsend, pp. 40 and 92).
15 *De antiquitate*, §42 (ed. & transl. Scott, pp. 98–100); *Cronica*, §49 (edd. & transl. Carley & Townsend, pp. 96–8). The privilege of King Edgar (S.703) includes *Sowy* in the same list of what it calls *ecclesiae parochiales*: *De antiquitate*, §60 (ed. & transl. Scott, p. 124); *Cronica*, §71 (edd. & transl. Carley & Townsend, p. 134). On these privileges, see above, *s.n.* Glastonbury.
16 *De antiquitate*, §§53 and 69 (ed. & transl. Scott, pp. 112 and 142); *Cronica*, §§16 and 56 (edd. & transl. Carley & Townsend, pp. 40 and 108); omitted from the list in the *Secretum domini*'s text, but included in that of the Great Cartulary. On the texts of this charter, see above, *s.n. Brannocmynstre* or Monk Okehampton.
17 Domesday Book, I, 90ra (Somerset, 8.6).
18 Grundy, *The Saxon Charters*, pp. 116–18.

east and Westonzoyland to the west.[19] Morland has followed this lead and redefined the bounds to include the lands of all three places.[20] These lay ten miles and more southwest of Glastonbury, immediately south of the Polden estates, divided from them by the River Cary (now carried by the King's Sedge Drain).

Edwards has very correctly raised a possibility which Davidson and Morland had not considered, that the bounds of S.251 were not contemporary with the date of the grant.[21] If that were the case, the exact extent of the land granted by Ine would be unknown – a familiar circumstance, which does indeed characterise most of the grants to Glastonbury by this king. Edwards's suggestion that whoever added the vernacular bounds had modernised the 'description of the land' (presumably meaning the hidage and the place-name) was based on the exact resemblance of the details in question in S.251 to those in the entry for *Sowy* in Domesday Book.[22] Equally, Othery, Middlezoy, and Westonzoyland are absent (by name) from both sources. Edwards's argument is compelling; unfortunately, it leaves us uncertain about Ine's *Sowy*, and we can only say that it was somewhere in this vicinity. The place-names, however, may offer slightly more evidence.

According to Ekwall, *Sowy* contains a stream-name, *sow*, with the addition of Old English *eg*, 'island'. *Zoy-* from *Sowy* is the old name of a district, and 'Zoyland' (as in Westonzoyland) means 'land belonging to *Sowy*'.[23] That Ine granted this 'district' to Glastonbury is not improbable, and that the monks rewrote his charter to update (but not necessarily falsify) the identification is also conceivable. Topographically, Othery, Middlezoy, and Westonzoyland do form a unit, clearly limited on the north and south by the Cary and the Parrett Rivers; how far east and west *Sowy* might have extended, however, is uncertain.[24]

The significance of the grant of *Sowy* in the Decimation charter depends on one's interpretation of that enigmatic document. If it represents actual grants of land, Glastonbury must have lost its possession of *Sowy* some time between A.D.

---

[19] Davidson, 'On the charters', p. 11.

[20] Morland, 'The Saxon charters for Sowy and Pouholt', pp. 233–4.

[21] Edwards, *The Charters*, pp. 38–40. Costen has suggested that they belong to the tenth century ('The late Saxon landscape', p. 35).

[22] *Ibid. Sowy*'s ten hides in S.303 rather than the twelve in S.251 and Domesday Book may preserve a clue to an earlier hidage; or it might simply be a scribal error. A charter for two hides at *Otheri* from King Edgar to one Wulfhelm, which has been identified by its bounds as relating to Ottery St Mary, was nevertheless filed in the fourteenth-century cartularies under Othery in *Sowy*. Is it a coincidence that its two hides, added to Æthelwulf's ten, make up the twelve-hide total found in S.251 and Domesday Book?

[23] Ekwall, *The Concise Oxford Dictionary of English Place-names*, pp. 325 and 509, *s.n.* Middlezoy and Westonzoyland. The earlier form of Westonzoyland was *Westsowi*.

[24] Chedzoy, beyond Westonzoyland to the northwest, is excluded from the bounds of *Pouelt* in S.253 and therefore may have been part of *Sowy*, although Ekwall (*The Concise Oxford Dictionary of English Place-names*, p. 99, *s.n.* Chedzoy) derived it from a personal name (*Cedd* + *eg*) rather than from the *Sowy* element. The early course of the Cary is relevant to the question, as it may have cut Chedzoy off from *Sowy*; but its course is uncertain (Morland, 'The Saxon charters for Sowy and Pouholt', pp. 234–5; Williams, *The Draining*, pp. 47–55, 62–71, and 74). On the east, the landmark *hamelondsmere* in the bounds of S.251 probably indicates that, at least when they were written, *Sowy* bordered on the estate at *Hamme*.

705/6 and the grant (A.D. 854); it is possible, however, that Æthelwulf's Decimation granted not land but exemption from dues or some other kind of benefit on land already held by the recipient.[25] If so, Glastonbury could have possessed *Sowy* before the Decimation grant of Æthelwulf, possibly since the time of Ine. Apart from the Decimation charter, there are few clues to *Sowy*'s history from the time of King Ine to that of King Edward the Confessor. This silence may represent an unchallenged possession by Glastonbury of a stable land-unit – but the questions raised about the bounds, and the inconsistent hidage-totals, should remind us that change could take place without documentation.

St Andrew's Church (Ilchester)
See Ilchester.

Stane
According to an entry on the contents-list of the *Liber terrarum*, King Edmund granted *Stane* to Glastonbury (S.1725; LT56). The charter was listed in the *Index chartarum* (IC C3) but its text has not survived. In the *De antiquitate* we find a slightly different story: that Æthelflæd, King Edmund's second wife, gave eight hides at *Stane* to Glastonbury.[26] Edmund's gift of Damerham to Æthelflæd (on condition that she grant it to Glastonbury on her death) is preserved in S.513; perhaps *Stane* followed the same route, even though (unlike Damerham) it is not mentioned in Æthelflæd's will.[27] Some confusion is apparent, however, as it is also said in the *De antiquitate* that Edmund gave eight hides at *Kingestan* directly to the abbey.[28] It is unclear (since the place-names could easily be variants of one another) whether two different estates were involved here, or whether one grant has been doubled by mistake.[29] Perhaps confusion was produced because there were two documents in the archive, one being the king's grant of *Stane* to Æthelflæd and another her subsequent bequest to Glastonbury. The contents-list of the *Liber terrarum* and the *Index chartarum*, however, do not signal the existence of more than one charter for *Stane* (and none for *Kingestan*). It is perhaps more credible that *Stane* parallels the situation at Damerham, which reveals similar ambiguities of documentation. Because a charter for the latter survives, we can see that (according to that document) the king granted the estate to Æthelflæd, with reversion to Glastonbury. Glastonbury's archival records (the *Liber terrarum* and *Index chartarum* and §69 of the *De antiquitate*), on the other hand, indicate a gift directly to the abbey.[30]

Finberg nevertheless assumed that two different gifts were indicated,

---

[25] See above, *s.n. Brannocmynstre* and Monk Okehampton, and below, pp. 322–4.

[26] *De antiquitate*, §§55 and 69 (ed. & transl. Scott, pp. 114 and 142); *Cronica*, §§16 and 64 (edd. & transl. Carley & Townsend, pp. 40 and 122).

[27] See above, *s.n.* Damerham.

[28] *De antiquitate*, §§55 and 69 (ed. & transl. Scott, pp. 114 and 142); *Cronica*, §§16 and 64 (edd. & transl. Carley & Townsend, pp. 40 and 120).

[29] Ekwall cited no names from these texts; the first documentary appearance of Kingstone (Somerset) is in Domesday Book (as *Chingestone*: Ekwall, *The Concise Oxford Dictionary of English Place-names*, p. 278, *s.n.* Kingstone).

[30] See above, *s.n.* Damerham.

Kingestan being modern Kingston, and *Stane* (probably) Stone, in the parish of East Pennard.[31] Sawyer has followed the identification of *Stane* with Stone, as has Morland, who in turn identified the *De antiquitate*'s *Kingestan* with the place called *Chingestone* in Domesday Book,[32] where Glastonbury had held eight hides, although it had lost the estate to the count of Mortain between 1066 and 1086.[33] At the end of the entries for Glastonbury in Domesday Book, a list of four manors lost to the count occurs, headed by *Stane*.[34] Is this *Stane* the same as *Chingestone*? Were two estates appropriated by the count, or only one? The difficulty is the same as we faced with the testimony of the *De antiquitate*. Unfortunately there is no conclusive evidence to decide the issue in either case. On the assumption that two separate estates were involved, *Stane* and *Kingestane* have been identified with two different modern places, Stone and Kingstone. We can at least ask whether grants by Edmund of either or both of these places make sense in the light of other evidence for their history.

Kingston is perhaps the most straightforward, although the name is a common one and identification therefore perilous. The eight-hide total of *Chingestone* in Domesday Book makes it likely that this estate is the same as Edmund's eight hides (at *Kingstane*). Thanks to the topographical order in which manors were assessed in Domesday Book, it is possible to identify its *Chingestone* as Kingstone, a few miles southeast of Ilminster, over twenty miles south of Glastonbury; three virgates missing from its eight-hide total in Domesday Book in 1066 were probably located at neighbouring Dinnington, where three virgates were held by Glastonbury in 1066.[35] No earlier (or later) documentation is extant to confirm (or contradict) a gift of this place to Glastonbury by Edmund.

Stane is more difficult to deal with, as its Anglo-Saxon whereabouts are more difficult to pin down. If it was a different estate from *Chingestone*, it was not (unlike the latter) recorded in its own right among the count of Mortain's entries in Domesday Book, so we know nothing of its size or location. The only possible testimony which may be of relevance – that of the vernacular bounds – is not very helpful, but will be examined.

If, as proposed by Morland, the estate called *Stane* in Domesday Book was Stone, in East Pennard, does a grant of this estate by Edmund make sense? What, for instance, was the history of its relationship with East Pennard? If Glastonbury received *Stane* from Edmund, presumably the land could have been added to East Pennard only after A.D. 955, when Glastonbury apparently acquired the latter

---

31 Finberg, *The Early Charters of Wessex*, pp. 133–4; he did not indicate where this Kingston was to be located; there is now a Kingsdon near Ilchester and a Kingstone near Ilminster.

32 Morland, 'The Glastonbury manors', pp. 79–80.

33 Domesday Book, I, 92ra (Somerset, 19.10).

34 Domesday Book, I, 91ra (Somerset, 8.39).

35 Domesday Book, I, 90vb (Somerset, 8.36). Robert Dunning has suggested that Kingstone and Dinnington formed a single unit under Glastonbury's lordship in the tenth and eleventh centuries; Dunning, 'Kingstone', pp. 203–4. The only evidence for this is Glastonbury's possession of the three virgates, the remainder of Dinnington being in lay hands in 1066. There is no earlier Anglo-Saxon evidence for Dinnington, which is not included with *Kingstane* in the abbreviated reference to Edmund's lost charter.

estate;[36] it would have had to absorb *Stane*'s eight hides without increasing its own assessment, for there were twenty hides at East Pennard in 1066, as there had been in A.D. 955.[37] Yet Grundy's solution of the bounds of S.563 for East Pennard seems to indicate that Stone (now in the south of the parish of East Pennard) was already included in East Pennard when it was granted to Glastonbury by Eadred.[38] If so, how had land granted to Glastonbury by Edmund or Æthelflæd become part of an estate not yet held (apparently) by the abbey? Perhaps this evidence rules out a grant of Stone by Edmund.

Morland has raised another possibility: that *Stane*/Stone was identical with the seven (unnamed) hides in Ditcheat which Glastonbury had lost to the count of Mortain after 1066.[39] According to this argument, therefore, Stone may have belonged in 1066 not to East Pennard but to Ditcheat – across the Fosse Way; Stone was apparently not included in the bounds of Ditcheat in Æthelwulf's grant of that estate in A.D. 842 but, Morland has argued, by 1066 it had been incorporated into Ditcheat (by means of Edmund's grant) without any change in the latter's hidage.[40] Lottisham (later part of Ditcheat), south of East Pennard, may have included Stone in A.D. 842, however; the evidence for Grundy's solution of the bounds of S.292 is not entirely convincing.[41] Nor, in any event, is their date certain. Perhaps, then, Stone was acquired when Glastonbury was granted Lottisham. This may also cast doubt on a separate grant of Stone by Edmund, although it does not rule out a temporary alienation, such as a lease.

The evidence is tricky and difficult to assess. It may nevertheless indicate that it is unnecessary to multiply estates called *Stane*; in the *De antiquitate* and in Domesday Book *Stane* may be the same as *Kingstane*, that is to say, modern Kingstone, acquired by a grant from King Edmund or his wife. The history of Stone may be unrelated and may have been drawn into the picture simply because of the resemblance of its name. On the other hand, the odd circumstance that both the *De antiquitate and* Domesday Book cite a *Stane* and a *Kingestane* might be significant. The case remains open.

Stanton St Quintin (Wiltshire)

According to Domesday Book, six acres of meadow at *Stantone* (Stanton St Quintin) had belonged to the abbot of Glastonbury's estate of Christian Malford.[42] The abbot had leased these acres to a layman; but they appear to have been appropriated into Stanton St Quintin by 1086.[43] This small example reminds us that estates were not immutable.

---

[36] Note, however (above, *s.n.* Pennard), that there is some doubt about whether A.D. 955 did indeed mark Glastonbury's first possession of East Pennard.

[37] See above, *s.n.* Pennard.

[38] Grundy, *The Saxon Charters*, p. 66. The bounds are contemporary with the grant.

[39] Domesday Book, I, 90vb (Somerset, 8.30). Morland, 'The Glastonbury manors', pp. 20–1 and 74.

[40] *Ibid.*, p. 72; Morland, 'Hidation', p. 77. See above, *s.n.* Ditcheat.

[41] That Grundy felt the need to emend *est* to *west* in the brief boundary-description (*The Saxon Charters*, p. 74) could suggest that the text was corrupt and a portion of the description missing.

[42] See above, *s.n.* Christian Malford.

[43] Domesday Book, I, 66va and 72vb (Wiltshire, 7.5 and 48.4).

Stawell (Somerset)

Stawell was an estate of two and a half hides which Glastonbury held in 1066.[44] Although independent at that time, it may earlier have been attached to *Pouelt*, and it has been discussed above in the context of that estate's history.

Stoke (Somerset)

Two entries on the contents-list of the *Liber terrarum* record grants of *Stoke*. The first, by King Æthelstan, was to a layman, Ælfric, who is said to have granted the land to Glastonbury (S.1717; LT36). The second entry records a grant by King Æthelred to another layman, Godric (S.1779; LT79). Neither of these charters was included in any of the later documentary collections. The first of these grants may relate to that described in the *De antiquitate*, where five hides at *Stoka* are mentioned as the gift to Glastonbury by the widow Uffa during the reign of King Æthelstan and the abbacy of Abbot Ælfric.[45] Uffa may have been the widow or heir of the Ælfric who received the land in the lost charter; or there may have been some conflation of detail in the contents-list, with the abbot's name being mistaken for that of the recipient. The second grant of *Stoke*, by Æthelred to Godric, is not mentioned in the *De antiquitate*. It would seem that these lands, once granted to lay recipients, were indeed turned over to the abbey, as Glastonbury held two estates called *Stoca* in 1066, both of which it lost to the count of Mortain before 1086.[46]

The identification of places having common, even generic, names is fraught with peril.[47] Even determining the location of the two estates which the count of Mortain had taken from Glastonbury is not simple, as (according to Domesday Book) he held three manors of that name, or at least, two places called *Stochet* and one *Stoche*. None of these three consisted of exactly five hides (as were in Uffa's *Stoka*).[48] Fortunately, the two that had been Glastonbury's can probably be identi-

---

44 Domesday Book, I, 90ra (Somerset, 8.10).

45 *De antiquitate*, §§54 and 69 (ed. & transl. Scott, pp. 112 and 142); *Cronica*, §§16 and 60 (edd. & transl. Carley & Townsend, pp. 40 and 112). This abbot is said in the *De antiquitate* to have ruled for fourteen years (beginning in A.D. 927); William of Malmesbury in his Life of St Dunstan named him as Dunstan's predecessor. But the earliest extant list of Glastonbury's abbots places him after Dunstan (and, therefore, not contemporary with King Æthelstan); see Foot, 'Glastonbury's early abbots', pp. 180–3.

46 Domesday Book, I, 91ra (Somerset, 8.39).

47 The dangers were illustrated, unfortunately, by Scott in his English text of the boundaries of the Twelve Hides, where *Stoke* (from the context clearly north of Marchey, near Rodney Stoke) was 'translated' Stoke-under-Ham, that is, Stoke sub Hamdon, which is many miles to the south; *De antiquitate*, §72 (ed. & transl. Scott, pp. 150–1).

48 Domesday Book, I, 92ra (Somerset, 19.11, 19.13, and 19.14 [two hides and one and a half virgates, five and a half hides, and one hide and three virgates, respectively]). Finberg read the list in Domesday Book of Glastonbury's manors lost to the count (*Stane Stoca Stoca Dreicote*; Domesday Book, I, 91ra [Somerset, 8.39]) as if there were only three places involved: Kingston, Stoke under Ham, and Stoke Draycott (*The Early Charters of Wessex*, p. 148). But the count of Mortain's entries elsewhere in Domesday Book show that the second Stoke and Draycott are separate places. There is, however, an apparently unrelated Stoke near Draycott (as seen in the perambulation of the Twelve Hides: Morland, 'Glaston Twelve Hides', p. 51).

fied by their values;[49] they total only four hides and one virgate, however. Without epithets to distinguish them, it is difficult to relate these three places of the same (or more or less the same) name to the modern map. C. and F. Thorn have identified both of the count's *Stochets* as East Stoke (a hamlet of Stoke sub Hamdon) and did not locate the third portion more specifically; these two are those which by their values seem to have been Glastonbury's lost estates.[50] Dunning, however, has proposed that one of the count's estates called *Stochet* was combined with this third portion, *Stoche*, to form Stoke sub Hamdon proper.[51] According to Dunning, there are two distinct settlement-centres at Stoke sub Hamdon, one (the smaller) being formerly the centre of Stokett parish and the site of the church.[52] This latter, at least, may have been Glastonbury's land.

A probable, but not proved, relationship exists between the two Stokes held by Glastonbury at Stoke sub Hamdon in 1066 and those granted to laymen in Æthelstan's and Æthelred's reigns, although the possibility increases with the commonness of the place-name that land elsewhere may have been involved.[53] All that is clear is that in 1066 Glastonbury had two holdings in the vicinity of Stoke sub Hamdon, about seventeen miles to the south of the abbey. How long – or how consistently – the abbey had held this land is unclear. It is not possible to decide whether the two charters apparently in the *Liber terrarum* were repeat-grants of the same land or grants of two different estates (especially as the hidage of only one is noted). Glastonbury may have acquired its two holdings together through the agency of a lay benefactor; or the community may have received two (or more) portions in succession from different laypeople, one granted during Æthelstan's reign, one during Æthelred's, and perhaps one more (the count's third *Stoke* in Domesday Book) being lost. The suggestion that some of this land called *Stoke* may have already been granted to Glastonbury in earlier days under the name *Hammedone* or *Hamedune* merely adds to the complexity of the picture.[54]

Stourton (Wiltshire)
See Sturminster Newton.

Stratton-on-the-Fosse (Somerset)
See *Streton*.

---

[49] Glastonbury's lost estates are said in the list of *Terrae occupatae* to have been worth 40s. (E 524a4); the count's three manors were assessed (in his returns) at 40s. (*Stochet*), £7 (*Stoke*), and 40s. (*Stochet*).

[50] Somerset, 19.11 and 19.14 (note).

[51] Dunning, 'Stoke sub Hamdon', p. 241. His proposal did not take account of their values.

[52] *Ibid.*, p. 237.

[53] There are other Stokes, even in Glastonbury's territory, for example. Two are cited in the bounds of the Twelve Hides, one near West Bradley and the other (near Rodney Stoke) near Nyland (Morland, 'Glaston Twelve Hides', pp. 47 and 50–1); *De antiquitate*, §72 (ed. & transl. Scott, pp. 148–50); *Cronica*, §3 (edd. & transl. Carley & Townsend, p. 14); and there are many other Stokes, in Somerset alone.

[54] See above, *s.n.* Hannington.

Street (Somerset)
See *Lantokay*.

Streton

The contents-list of the *Liber terrarum* records a gift by King Edgar of *Ætheresig et Streton* to Ælfswith (S.1761; LT111). No notice or text of this charter is preserved in the other documentary sources. In the *De antiquitate*, however, there is a long list of estates granted to Glastonbury by Ælfswith (who is identified as queen), including Winscombe, Idmiston, *Strettune* (six hides), Tintinhull, and *Aetheredesie*.[55] Three hides at *Stratone* were listed in Domesday Book as land lost by Glastonbury to the bishop of Coutances between 1066 and 1086.[56]

Variations on Street and Stratton are not uncommon in Somerset, especially in the vicinity of the Fosse Way. The topographical arrangement of the Domesday returns helps to identify Glastonbury's hides at *Stratone* as Stratton-on-the-Fosse, in the Mendips, about fifteen miles northeast of the abbey.[57] If Ælfswith's transfer of *Streton* to Glastonbury did take place, there is no guarantee that her land was connected with Glastonbury's later estate of that name. But if it was, and if we credit the unsubstantiated total (six hides) given in the *De antiquitate*, the land seems to have been split in two between A.D. 959x975 and 1066; the hypothetical other half, however, has left no trace in the charters or in Domesday Book, although it may be disguised by a change of name; it is perhaps preferable to suppose that the area of the estate remained the same but the hidage was reduced. The evidence is inconclusive.

Sturminster Newton (Dorset)

The text of a charter of King Edgar for Glastonbury in A.D. 968, reputedly granting thirty hides at *Stoure*, survives in the fourteenth-century cartularies (S.764). The *Index chartarum* and MS. 39a both list this document (IC C8; L25 and 25a). In the fourteenth-century cartularies and MS. 39a, it is the first of the records filed under the heading *Nywetone*. The place in question is called *Sturmunstre iuxta Newton Castel* in later documents, later still Sturminster Newton;[58]

---

55 *De antiquitate*, §§62 and 69 (ed. & transl. Scott, pp. 130 and 144); *Cronica*, §§16 and 73 (edd. & transl. Carley & Townsend, pp. 42 and 138). It is likely that this is the same Ælfswith who had bought land at *Kyngton* (*q.v.*) from King Edgar, according to S.866, and who is identified in that charter as the wife of Ealdorman Ælfheah. No mid-tenth-century queen of this name is listed in *The Handbook of British Chronology* (edd. Fryde *et al.*). For other grants in Glastonbury's archive which were associated with Ælfswith, see above, *s.n.* Idmiston. Although many of the estates which she was granted were acquired by Glastonbury, the unreliable testimony of the *De antiquitate* comprises (in most cases) the only evidence that it was Ælfswith who was responsible for passing the lands on to the community.

56 Domesday Book, I, 88va–b and 91ra (Somerset, 5.43 and 8.38).

57 *Somerset*, edd. & transl. Thorn & Thorn, p. 353.

58 Its name, including as it does the place-name element *mynster*, has suggested to some that there was an ancient minster church there (Pearce, *The Kingdom*, p. 119). The early forms of the name, however, do not include the element *mynster*, which does not appear until the later middle ages; the author of §73 of the *Cronica* felt compelled to explain

it is on the River Stour about thirty-five miles southeast of Glastonbury. The account of Edgar's grants (including *Sture*) in the *De antiquitate* begins with a quotation from a charter which is not S.764, giving the date A.D. 963 and naming the recipient of all the estates as Abbot Æthelweard.[59] At least one other transaction, poorly attested, purports to relate to this estate. In the *De antiquitate*, we find the claim that on his deathbed King Edmund Ironside (A.D. 1016) granted seventeen hides at *Newetone Kastel* to the church, and that the land went to the community with his body at his death.[60] The only other notice of Edmund Ironside's grant occurs in a historical note in the fourteenth-century cartularies (following a papal privilege), which may have had the *De antiquitate* as its source.[61] According to Domesday Book, in 1066 Glastonbury held twenty-two hides at *Newentone*, as well as untaxed land in demesne for fourteen ploughs.[62]

It is difficult to credit the grant by Edmund Ironside: the late form of the place-name and the absence of the grant from the documentary sources do not inspire confidence, although the suspicions they raise may be unfounded. If the bequest did take place, either a part of Sturminster Newton had been lost by Glastonbury after Edgar's grant and was returned to the monks by Edmund Ironside, or an additional portion of seventeen hides was bequeathed to them by the latter king in A.D. 1016. If the record was forged, it must be assumed that Glastonbury's ownership of the land came under threat and a document was produced to bolster the community's title – the appearance of Edgar's diploma on List C of the *Index chartarum* may support the idea that the land (or some of it) was lost at some time, although the abbey is recorded as holding thirty hides there in the later middle ages.[63] The total of seventeen hides may indicate that docu-

---

that it *nunc Stouremister* [*sic*] *dicitur*. Sturminster Marshall, about fifteen miles downriver, is nonetheless *Stureminster* as early as the 880s (S.1507; the will of King Alfred). See Ekwall, *The Concise Oxford Dictionary of English Place-names*, p. 451, *s.n.* Sturminster Marshall and Sturminster Newton.

[59] *De antiquitate*, §§62 and 69 (ed. & transl. Scott, pp. 128 and 144); *Cronica*, §§16 and 73 (edd. & transl. Carley & Townsend, pp. 42 and 138). This feature of the *De antiquitate*, where references to several grants by the same king are conflated into one summary sentence frequently citing only one date (and/or recipient), calls into question the accuracy of the information for each place mentioned; here, for example, the date 963 was perhaps that of a grant of one or more of the other places said to have been given by Edgar to Æthelweard, but not Sturminster Newton. Robinson interpreted this feature of the *De antiquitate* as indicating that the author took his information from composite charters (*Somerset*, p. 41). On the use of charters in the *De antiquitate*, see above, pp. 21–7. Æthelweard does not appear on the earliest extant list of Glastonbury's abbots in London, British Library, MS. Cotton Tiberius B.v, part 1 (23va); but he is cited in the *De antiquitate* as ruling A.D. 962–972 (§71; ed. & transl. Scott, p. 146). See Foot, 'Glastonbury's early abbots', p. 182, and Robinson, *Somerset*, p. 41.

[60] *De antiquitate*, §§64 and 69 (ed. & transl. Scott, pp. 132 and 144); *Cronica*, §§16 and 77 (edd. & transl. Carley & Townsend, pp. 42 and 148) (no Sawyer-number).

[61] *The Great Chartulary*, ed. Watkin, I.247 (no. 205).

[62] Domesday Book, I, 77va (Dorset, 8.1). Four hides had been lost by 1086.

[63] *A Feodary*, ed. Weaver, p. 30; that the estate was in Glastonbury's hands in the late twelfth, late thirteenth, and the fourteenth centuries is shown by the *Liber Henrici* of A.D. 1189 (ed. Jackson, pp. 134–6) and the inclusion of a number of late thirteenth- and

mentation was required at a time when the estate was not assessed at thirty hides (and Edgar's charter therefore perhaps not so useful as a title-deed). It might reflect the loss of four hides after 1066 which is attested by Domesday Book, but the sums do not fit this explanation exactly.[64]

Eight hides at *Acford* (neighbouring Okeford Fitzpaine) which Glastonbury held in 1066 may have been the eight hides 'missing' from Sturminster Newton's assessment in Domesday Book; added to Sturminster Newton's twenty-two, Glastonbury's eight hides at *Acford* would make up the thirty-hide total of Edgar's grant.[65] This may solve the problem of the make-up of Sturminster Newton in 1066, but it may create another, as *twelve* hides at *Acford* were reputedly granted to Glastonbury during the reign of King Edmund (although the figure twelve is only a calculation from incomplete evidence). This (if genuine) could have been a grant of one of the other estates called *Acford* in the region;[66] or it could represent an earlier grant (perhaps intentionally temporary) of the same eight hides at *Acford*, hypothetically given to Glastonbury by Edgar as part of Sturminster Newton; according to Grundy, the bounds attached to Edgar's diploma include Sturminster Newton alone, without Okeford Fitzpaine (*Acford*). This may have little significance for the question of Sturminster Newton's make-up before 1066, however, as the description may not be contemporary with the supposed grant.[67]

The fragmentary evidence of another transaction may help to clarify the problem (or may instead simply add to the confusion). According to an entry on the contents-list of the *Liber terrarum*, King Eadwig gave land at *Sturtone* to a layman, Ælfwine (S.1749; LT129). There is no other record of this grant among the documentary sources, but the gift of *una pars de Sturtone* by Ælfwine to Glastonbury is mentioned in the *De antiquitate*; the summary of grants adds that this gift consisted of eight hides and that King Eadwig confirmed it.[68] Peter Sawyer has identifed the object of this lost charter as Stourton, in Wiltshire. In 1066 Glastonbury did not hold any land there; according to Domesday Book, the eight hides at *Stortone* were in lay hands.[69]

---

fourteenth-century documents in the cartularies. A temporary loss *ca* A.D. 1247, however, is supported by the third composition between the abbot of Glastonbury and the bishop of Wells in A.D. 1266, where land at *Nywtone* is said to have been returned to the abbey (*The Great Chartulary*, ed. Watkin, I.96 [no. 147]). On the disputes with Wells at this time, see above, p. 12.

64 Four from Domesday Book's total of twenty-two hides would give eighteen, not seventeen. According to the fourteenth-century feodary (*A Feodary*, ed. Weaver, p. 30), Sturminster Newton's demesne consisted of five hides; perhaps the abbey's hold on this (but not on the other seventeen of Domesday Book's twenty-two hides) was secure, and a charter was therefore required only for the rest of the land. The four hides lost before 1086 were tenant-land.

65 See above, *s.n.* Okeford Fitzpaine.

66 See above, *s.n.* Okeford Fitzpaine.

67 Grundy, 'Saxon charters of Dorset', *Proceedings of the Dorset Natural History and Archaeological Society* 60 (1938), pp. 77–81. Eight hides at *Acford* were part of Sturminster Newton in the later middle ages, however: *A Feodary*, ed. Weaver, p. 30.

68 *De antiquitate*, §§58 and 69 (ed. & transl. Scott, pp. 120 and 144); *Cronica*, §§16 and 67 (edd. & transl. Carley & Townsend, pp. 42 and 126).

69 Domesday Book, I, 72ra (Wiltshire, 36.2).

In the face of this sparse evidence, we might conclude (if Eadwig's charter was genuine) that Glastonbury could have received the estate from Ælfwine or his heirs, but lost it before 1066, or that the land was never intended to be transferred to the community, which nevertheless (for a time) held its title-deed. It is, however, possible that the cited transaction applied not to Stourton but to Sturminster Newton.

Stourton is about twenty miles east of Glastonbury, just across the border into Wiltshire, in Selwood. It took its name from the River Stour, as did a number of other settlements, including Sturminster Newton (which is over ten miles farther downstream to the south). Eadwig's grant of *Sturtone* may have comprised land anywhere on this river, but in view of Sturminster Newton's 'missing' eight hides (the difference between its reputed grant to Glastonbury by King Edgar as a thirty-hide estate and its appearance as a twenty-two-hide holding in Domesday Book), Ælfwine's gift of *pars de Sturtone* may be relevant. If the hides apparently 'missing' from Sturminster Newton in 1066 can be equated with those granted to Ælfwine by Eadwig (assuming both Edgar's and Eadwig's charters are genuine), this would appear to indicate that a portion of the larger estate granted by Edgar was detached by Eadwig and given to one of his men. Although Ælfwine reputedly gave this *pars de Sturtone* to Glastonbury, no *Sturtone* is recorded in Glastonbury's hands in Domesday Book and it is difficult to be certain whether the abbey lost or retained it; Sturminster Newton's later mediaeval assessment of thirty hides suggests the latter, however,[70] (as does the disappearance of *Sturtone per se* from the abbey's record), and the eight hides at *Acford* which Glastonbury held in 1066 could have been Ælfwine's *pars de Sturtone*, returned to Glastonbury's possession, separately assessed in 1066, and recorded in Domesday Book under the name *Acford*, which it retained throughout the middle ages.

It is impossible to say without more evidence where the land for fourteen ploughs at Sturminster Newton which did not pay tax in 1066 fitted into this picture.

Sturtone
See Sturminster Newton.

Sutton Mallet (Somerset)
Sutone was a sub-unit of Shapwick assessed at five hides in 1066.[71] The history of Sutton Mallet, in the Polden Hills, belongs to that of the ancient estate of *Pouelt* (*q.v.*) which has been discussed in detail above.

Tarnock (Somerset)
The contents-list of the *Liber terrarum* contains a notice of a grant of *Ternuc* by King Eadred to a layman, Alfred (S.1740; LT120). A grant of *Ternuc et Stapelwille* by King Eadred appears on List C of the *Index chartarum*, a circumstance which implies that it was a grant directly to the community, rather than to a layman (IC C5; no Sawyer-number); it might, however, be Alfred's charter, put on the wrong list by mistake. In the *De antiquitate* the grants of *Ternuc* and *Staple-*

---

[70] *A Feodary*, ed. Weaver, p. 30.
[71] Domesday Book, I, 90ra (Somerset, 8.5).

wille are said to have been made by Eadred directly to the church; nothing is mentioned about a previous grant to Alfred.[1] Whether the *De antiquitate* can be trusted here is a matter of opinion. Alfred may have held the land on a short, temporary, tenure, after which it reverted to the king. Or Eadred may have repossessed it and then given it to Glastonbury; in either case, Glastonbury's possession of Alfred's charter (if genuine) is noteworthy. Did it come to the abbey from Alfred (if so, why?) or from the king (ditto)? Alternatively, Alfred's charter for *Ternuc* may have resembled S.509, granted to a lay recipient in the king's name, but actually consisting of a lease of Glastonbury's property.[2] Or perhaps one of the two grants (the king's, more likely) was not genuine. Forgeries may have been produced to act as evidence in disputes; the appearance of 'Biddesham quod Tarnuc proprie appellatur' in a long list of estates confirmed to Wells in A.D. 1065 in a charter (S.1042) issued by King Edward the Confessor may identify the other party, if there was a dispute over this land.[3] *Tarnuc* is described in S.1042 as an appurtenant hamlet of Wedmore (which was held by the bishop of Wells in 1066).[4] It was not the bishop, however, but two laymen who held one hide each at Tarnock in 1066, according to Domesday Book.[5] No Biddisham appears in Domesday Book by name.

If Alfred or his heirs did pass *Ternuc* on to Glastonbury, or even if King Eadred himself granted it directly to the abbey, it seems that the monks did not keep hold of the land (unless a relationship between the church and the lay holders is disguised in Domesday Book); equally, if the document in the *Index chartarum* had been forged to support a claim by Glastonbury, it appears to have been unsuccessful.

Tarnock lies south of the River Axe a few miles from its mouth; Biddisham is the name of the neighbouring village. These settlements are approximately fifteen miles northwest of Glastonbury, east of Brent. Tarnock preserves the name *Termic*, probably a river-name, which appears as the eastern limit of Brent in the apparently contemporary bounds of Ine's grant of that estate (S.238; A.D. ?693).[6]

Tintinhull (Somerset)

According to the contents-list of the *Liber terrarum*, King Edmund granted *Tintanhulle* to one Wulfric – probably Dunstan's brother –[7] who granted it to Glas-

---

[1] *De antiquitate*, §§57 and 69 (ed. & transl. Scott, pp. 118 and 142); *Cronica*, §§16 and 66 (edd. & transl. Carley & Townsend, pp. 42 and 124).

[2] See above, *s.n.* North Wootton. Alfred is also said to have received grants of Camerton and Rowberrow (*q.v.*).

[3] Simon Keynes has discussed this charter and recommended that it no longer be rejected as a forgery ('Regenbald', pp. 200–5); see also above, *s.n.* Binegar. Tarnock is not the only estate claimed by Glastonbury which appears in S.1042. Binegar, Bleadney, and Wedmore (*q.v.*) are also listed there.

[4] Domesday Book, I, 89va (Somerset, 6.15).

[5] Domesday Book, I, 95ra (Somerset, 24.12 and 24.13).

[6] Greswell, 'King Ina's grant', p. 255; Turner, 'Notes on some Somerset place-names', p. 122; Grundy, *The Saxon Charters*, p. 150. See above, *s.n.* Brent.

[7] On Wulfric, see Brooks, 'The career', pp. 8–11, and Hart, *The Early Charters of Northern England*, pp. 371–2.

tonbury (S.1728; LT34).[8] There is no other documentary record of this grant, which is, however, mentioned in the *De antiquitate*, with the same information provided;[9] later in that account we are told that 'Queen' Ælfswith gave five hides at Tintinhull during the reign of King Edgar (although Tintinhull is not on the list of Ælfswith's grants in the summary section).[10] No other record of Ælfswith's grant of Tintinhull is extant. Glastonbury held seven hides and one virgate (assessed at five hides) at Tintinhull in 1066, but had exchanged them for Camerton with the count of Mortain by 1086.[11] This transaction is presented rather differently in the *Cronica*, where it is claimed that William the Conqueror seized Tintinhull for the endowment of his foundation at Montacute Priory.[12] Tintinhull was certainly the more valuable land and the exchange was not advantageous to the abbey.[13] The marginal cross beside the entry in Domesday Book – which usually marks an estate belonging to Glastonbury which had been lost to another holder between 1066 and 1086 and was presumably the subject of a dispute – reinforces the suggestion that Glastonbury may have parted unwillingly with the land.

Tintinhull – over fifteen miles south of Glastonbury – is divided in two by the Fosse Way,[14] and it is therefore feasible that Wulfric's and Ælfswith's grants represent two separate five-hide units, rather than successive grants of the same five hides which had returned to the king in the succeeding interval. The ambiguity of Tintinhull's hidage in Domesday Book does not help to decide the case; either two hides and three virgates are missing from the putative combination of

8 Similar statements are made about grants to Wulfric at Turnworth and Yarlington, and Wulfric's *successor* Ælfwine allegedly gave his estates of Grittleton, Nettleton, and Horton (*q.v.*) to Glastonbury. See above, *s.n.* Grittleton.

9 *De antiquitate*, §§55 and 69 (ed. & transl. Scott, pp. 114 and 142); *Cronica*, §§16 and 64 (edd. & transl. Carley & Townsend, pp. 40 and 122).

10 *De antiquitate*, §62 (ed. & transl. Scott, p. 130); *Cronica*, §73 (edd. & transl. Carley & Townsend, p. 138). Ælfswith's other grants were at *Andersey*, Idmiston, Merton and Dulwich, *Pendescliue*, *Streton*, Upavon, and Winscombe, *q.v.* Her status as queen is not attested elsewhere. It is likely that she is to be identified with Ælfswith, the wife of Ealdorman Ælfheah, who bought *Kyngton* from King Edgar, according to S.866. This estate had been given to Wulfric in A.D. 940 by King Edmund (see above, *s.n.* *Kyngton*). Similar links between lands granted to Wulfric and later held by Ælfswith (and then Glastonbury) are to be found at Idmiston and Merton. At Idmiston, Wulfric received land from King Eadred in A.D. 947 and 948 but it was Ælfswith who gave it to Glastonbury in A.D. 970. Merton, another estate held by Wulfric as a gift of King Eadred, also was in the hands of Ealdorman Ælfheah and his wife during Edgar's reign, but there is no evidence that it became Glastonbury's (see above, *s.n.* Merton). On Ealdorman Ælfheah's career and family connexions, see Williams, 'Princeps Merciorum gentis', especially pp. 147–54.

11 Domesday Book, I, 90vb and 91vb (Somerset, 8.31 and 19.9). I have suggested above (*s.n.* Camerton) that Glastonbury may have obtained Camerton's single-sheet charters when the abbey acquired the land 1066x1086. If that were so, Glastonbury did not hand over its Anglo-Saxon documentation for Tintinhull to the count of Mortain in return.

12 *Cronica*, §82 (edd. & transl. Carley & Townsend, p. 154).

13 See below, p. 282.

14 Dunning, 'Tintinhull', pp. 255 and 257.

two five-hide units, or Domesday Book's five-hide assessment was already established in Edgar's day and only one piece of land was involved. Morland has offered the two hides and three virgates at *Hesecumbe*, otherwise unidentified, as the missing complement to Tintinhull, but this cannot be definitely accepted without more evidence.[15] Robert Dunning likewise has assumed that two estates existed at Tintinhull in the second half of the tenth century and suggested that Wulfric's land might have been Bearley, that part of Tintinhull northwest of the Fosse.[16] The history of Idmiston, Kington Langley, and Merton probably argues against such a separation, however. Like Tintinhull, those estates were first granted to Wulfric and were later acquired by Ælfswith before (in at least two of the three cases) passing to Glastonbury, possibly by her gift.[17]

Tone (River, Land on) (Somerset)

A multiple grant preserved in a single-sheet copy of uncertain date records the gift of four pieces of land, including twenty hides 'iuxta flumen quod appellatur Tan', by King Ine to Abbot Berwald in A.D. 705/6 (S.248).[18] The description of land by reference to natural features, rather than by place-names, is, as we have seen, characteristic of early charters, especially those of Ine; it poses difficulties of identification which may be insurmountable.

Such doubts did not strike earlier scholars, however. Dickinson and Davidson both identified Ine's twenty hides on the River Tone as West Monkton; twenty (or twenty-three) hides at *Cantucuudu* (in later records defined as West Monkton) had reputedly been granted to Glastonbury by King Centwine in A.D. 682 (S.237), and Ine's charter was deemed to have represented a regrant of this land.[19] As we have seen, however, the exact location even of the hides granted by Centwine cannot be determined,[20] and there is nothing to prove (or disprove) their identity with those granted by Ine; the subsequent assumption – that Ine's grant, like Centwine's, was of West Monkton – relies on a potentially dangerous faith in a static landscape. Glastonbury held fifteen hides there in 1066.[21]

Finberg made a different identification altogether. The only other record of Ine's multiple grant occurs in the *De antiquitate*, and there the text differs from that of the single sheet. Instead of the *Tan*, a gift of twenty hides *iuxta Tamer* is cited, with the interlinear comment *scilicet Linis* (or *Linig*).[22] This substitution of the River Tamar for the Tone led Finberg to search for *Linig* in Cornwall, and he

---

[15] Morland, 'Some Domesday manors', p. 47; 'Hidation', p. 76; 'The Glastonbury manors', pp. 74 and 80.

[16] Dunning, 'Tintinhull', p. 257, 'Ilchester: a study', p. 48. Why he identified this as Wulfric's rather than Ælfswith's portion is unclear.

[17] See above, *s.n.* Grittleton.

[18] See above, pp. 10–11, and Abrams, 'A single-sheet facsimile'.

[19] Dickinson, 'West Monkton charter', p. 92, n. 3; Davidson, 'On the charters', p. 11.

[20] The link with West Monkton is far from contemporary; see above, *s.n. Cantucuudu* and *Crycbeorh*.

[21] Domesday Book, I, 90vb (Somerset, 8.28).

[22] *De antiquitate*, §§40 and 69 (ed. & transl. Scott, pp. 94 and 140); *Cronica*, §§16 and 47 (edd. & transl. Carley & Townsend, pp. 40 and 92). What was an interlinear note in §40 of the *De antiquitate* has been embedded in the summary, which reads *iuxta Tamer*

found there a site between the Tamar and the River Lynher in the parish of St Dominick, where a fourteenth-century source attested to the existence of a chapel dedicated to St Indract, a saint with Glastonbury connexions.[23] Finberg therefore concluded that this was the site of Ine's grant of twenty hides. This identification is unquestionably mistaken, as the single sheet shows clearly that the *Tan*, not *Tamar*, was intended. Secondly, as Oliver Padel has shown, Finberg's linguistic argument – associating the manuscript's *Linig* with the Lynher – is not tenable.[24] A third objection is one of principle: a thirteenth-century annotator's identification of the location of an eighth-century place without a place-name invites scepticism: it may accurately represent where the ancient territory was thought to lie in the later middle ages, but without contemporary confirmation – and after over five hundred years had passed – the soundness of the identification must be open to question. This is a problem which we have encountered before.[25]

As *Linig* is not to be found in Cornwall, it should be sought on the Tone, as Padel has done. He has drawn attention to the unidentified territory called *Lini* in which Glastonbury had an interest during the middle ages, in the manor of *Sowy* and near the junction of the Tone and the Parrett.[26] It is possible that the glossator of the *De antiquitate* thought that the land on the Tone granted by Ine was located there. This may be an unlikely identification, as *Sowy* was itself apparently the subject of a separate grant by King Ine (S.251), although the exact area of land granted is (as ever) obscure.[27] The example of S.247 – a charter derived from Ine's multiple grant but later recast with an updated place-name and attached bounds – may suggest that something similar (though harder to detect) was done for the hides on the Tone.[28] Certainly the status of S.251 as a genuine text of King Ine is not free from suspicion. This may be a red herring, however, and Ine may indeed have granted two separate tracts of land in the region: it may have been simply the association of Ine with *Sowy*, and of *Lini* with the Tone, which led the glossator to make the connexion. The mistaken reference to the Tamar, on the other hand, may have been a straightforward copying error or may represent a reviser's attempt to rewrite history.[29]

In the absence of contemporary place-names and boundaries, no certain identification of Ine's hides on the Tone can be offered. The land may even have been attached to another owner and lost from Glastonbury's endowment. Without more evidence, its history remains a matter for speculation.

Torridge (River, Land on) (Devon)

Two entries on the contents-list of the *Liber terrarum* apply to land on the River Torridge, in northwestern Devon. A charter of King Æthelheard for Glastonbury

---

scilicet Linig (incorrectly printed as *Lining* by Scott, pp. 139–40); §47 of the *Cronica* cites the Tamar but omits *Linig*, which nevertheless appears in §16.

23 Finberg, *Lucerna*, pp. 100–4. On Indract, see Lapidge, 'The cult of St Indract'.
24 Padel, 'Glastonbury's Cornish connections', p. 251.
25 See, for example, *s.n. Pouelt* (*id est Grentone*).
26 *Ibid.*, p. 252.
27 See above, *s.n. Sowy*.
28 See above, *s.n. Pilton*.
29 *Ibid.*, p. 252.

de Torric and one of King Ecgberht *de libertate eiusdem* were apparently preserved in the *Liber terrarum* but in no other documentary source (S.1676 and S.1693; LT29 and LT30). Some confirmation of the existence of these charters is offered by the *De antiquitate*. The date 729 is given there for Æthelheard's grant, and the land is said to have consisted of ten hides *in Torric*.[30] In the account of Ecgberht's grant in the *De antiquitate* (which seems to be quoted directly from a charter) five hides 'secus flumen quod dicitur Toric' are said to have been given to Abbot Muca *ad usum monachorum* in A.D. 802.[31] A note in the fourteenth-century cartularies after the text of the privilege of King Cuthred (S.257; A.D. 744/5) claims that Ecgberht confirmed (*confirmauit*) five hides on the River Torridge.[32]

As with all early grants without place-names, the description of this land only in relation to a natural feature makes its location obscure. It is not certain moreover whether a single unit of territory is concerned; nor is it clear what each grant entailed. If both charters were genuine, they could have represented two separate land-units, or the regrant by Ecgberht of (perhaps only half of) the estate granted by Æthelheard. Finberg assumed that the second transaction represented an enlargement by Ecgberht of Æthelheard's gift.[33] Edwards has suggested that Ecgberht's grant, with its reference to *libertas*, was perhaps the conferral of an immunity or, alternatively, the restoration of land which the community had lost.[34] The apparent grant of *libertas*, and the specification that the land was *ad usum monachorum*, does seem to speak of a more specialised form of tenure than we find in Glastonbury's other grants, but the contemporary sample is so small that comparisons are not particularly profitable.

Finberg sought to identify Æthelheard's hides near the Torridge and proposed Hatherleigh and Jacobstowe, on the grounds that their later connexion with Tavistock Abbey might hint at an earlier link with Glastonbury;[35] he tentatively located Ecgberht's grant at Petrockstowe, which Buckfast Abbey held in 1066.[36] These

---

[30] *De antiquitate*, §§44 and 69 (ed. & transl. Scott, pp. 102 and 142); *Cronica*, §§16 and 52 (edd. & transl. Carley & Townsend, pp.40 and 104).

[31] *De antiquitate*, §§52 and 69 (ed. & transl. Scott, pp. 110 and 142); *Cronica*, §§16 and 55 (edd. & transl. Carley & Townsend, pp. 40 and 106).

[32] *The Great Chartulary*, ed. Watkin, I.142 (no. 201).

[33] Finberg, *Lucerna*, p. 104. He also described Ecgberht's grant as an 'enfranchisement' of the property acquired in A.D. 729.

[34] Edwards, *The Charters*, p. 70.

[35] Finberg, *The Early Charters of Devon and Cornwall*, p. 7. Tavistock was alleged to have been founded during the monastic reform as a daughter-house of Glastonbury, but the evidence for this is very slight. It consists of the possibility that the second and third abbots of the house (Ælfmær and Lyfing) may have been monks of Glastonbury (Finberg, 'The abbots of Tavistock', p. 160; see also *The Heads of Religious Houses,* edd. Knowles *et al.*, pp. 71–2). Finberg's suggestion nonetheless raises the question of the relations between reformed houses – especially houses belonging (perhaps) to some sort of circuit, or a group of communities (like those of Æthelwold) held together by a relationship with their founder or founding church. It is not certain that, even if a house had been founded from Glastonbury, the estates of the two establishments would reveal any contemporary or subsequent connexion.

[36] Finberg, *The Early Charters of Devon and Cornwall*, p. 8; Domesday Book, I, 103vb (Devon, 6.1). See also Pearce, 'The early Church in the landscape', p. 273.

identifications are speculative, however, without sufficient supporting evidence, and Glastonbury's land on the Torridge may have been elsewhere.[37]

Turnworth (Dorset)

The contents-list of the *Liber terrarum* records the existence of another lost charter, one in Edmund's name; this was for land at *Turnanwrthe*, granted to one Wulfric who gave it to Glastonbury (S.1729; LT48). A substantial number of charters in the archive appear to have had some association with this Wulfric, probably Dunstan's brother,[38] although texts of his bequests to Glastonbury fail to survive. In the *De antiquitate* we find the same information as in the contents-list, with the additional fact that Turnworth consisted of five hides.[39] No other record of Turnworth survives in the archive. In 1066 five hides there were in lay hands.[40] Although a substantial proportion of Wulfric's holdings can be shown to have passed to Glastonbury,[41] in the case of Turnworth the land either failed to be transferred to the abbey or was lost by 1066. Alternatively, an otherwise unattested agreement with Glastonbury may have underlain the layman's tenure recorded in Domesday Book. This, at least, has been suggested by Neil Stacy, on the principle that the man recorded in Domesday Book as holding Turnworth in 1066 held other properties from the abbey.[42] This would imply that the same person could not hold land in his own right *and* be a tenant of the abbey – a questionable conclusion.[43] Stacy's suggestion nonetheless reminds us that Domesday Book – so ostentatiously informative – may not actually reveal all that we should like to know, especially about the circumstances of tenure.

Turnworth is adjacent to Glastonbury's other Dorset holdings at Sturminster Newton and Okeford Fitzpaine, over forty miles southeast of the abbey; land at the latter is, like Turnworth, said to have been granted to patrons of the community by King Edmund.[44]

Twynham (Hampshire)

According to the contents-list of the *Liber terrarum*, King Eadred granted land at *Tuyneam* to Glastonbury (S.1741; LT75). This charter was on the *Index chartarum* (IC C4) but was recorded in no other documentary source. According to the *De antiquitate*, Eadred gave two hides *et captura piscium* 'iuxta opidum Twinam,

---

[37] There is evidence that Glastonbury may have held land in that part of Devon (at Monk Okehampton, *q.v.*), but it lay on the Okement, not the Torridge.

[38] Unless more than one man is involved. On Wulfric, see Brooks, 'The career', pp. 8–11, and Hart, *The Early Charters of Northern England*, pp. 371–2. On Wulfric's extensive holdings, see above, *s.n.* Grittleton.

[39] *De antiquitate*, §§55 and 69 (ed. & transl. Scott, pp. 114 and 142); *Cronica*, §§16 and 64 (edd. & transl. Carley & Townsend, pp. 40 and 122). The *Cronica*'s 'Wilfrid' should be Wulfric.

[40] Domesday Book, I, 82va (Dorset, 45.1).

[41] See above, *s.n.* Grittleton.

[42] Stacy, 'The estates', p. 15.

[43] Stacy was not unaware of the dangers of a 'witchhunt for hidden leaseholders': *ibid.*, p. 28.

[44] See above, *s.n.* Okeford Fitzpaine and Sturminster Newton.

id est Cristescirce'.[45] Ekwall confirmed that *Twinham* was indeed the old name of Christchurch,[46] which is on the south coast at the mouths of the Rivers Stour and Avon. Eadred's grant there (if genuine) seems thus to fit in with Glastonbury's other acquisitions of territory related to the necessary resource of fish.

A grant by Æthelstan to Milton Abbey of a weir on the River Avon at *Twynham* in A.D. 934 (S.391) may indicate – if it referred to the same fishery – that Glastonbury had assumed control of this resource from an earlier ecclesiastical holder. The charter, however, is to be treated with suspicion, and its claims – especially this one – may not be representative of pre-Conquest circumstances.[47] In any event, there must have been many fisheries in the Avon. In Domesday Book, the king and the canons of Holy Trinity, Twynham, were listed as holders of land at Twynham, but no details relating to fish or fishermen were recorded in the entries.[48] After a period of tenure in the late tenth century and before 1066, Glastonbury's two hides at *Tuyneam* may have been incorporated into one of these holdings, perhaps the most logical hypothesis being that they were absorbed back into the *terra regis*. The lost charter of King Eadred for Glastonbury may not have been genuine, however, or its bequest may have been aborted in some way for which we have no evidence. In any event, Glastonbury appears not to have held the land and fishery in 1066.

Ubley (Somerset)

A charter in Edgar's name granting land at *Hubbanlege* to a layman is recorded on List D of the *Index chartarum*, the list of charters for lay beneficiaries for lands which were no longer held by the abbey (S.1771; IC D19). No other notice of this grant survives in the documentary or narrative sources, apart from that in the unauthoritative §70 of the *De antiquitate*, where *Hubbanleghe* is listed among the *alia [maneria] data Glastonie*.[1] According to Domesday Book, five hides at *Tumbeli* were in lay hands in 1066 and 1086.[2] The land, which is in the Mendips about fifteen miles north of Glastonbury, may never have come into the possession of the community. If it did, it had apparently been lost by 1066.

Uffculme (Devon)

The final entry on List C of the *Index chartarum* reads 'quoddam memoriale de

---

[45] *De antiquitate*, §§57 and 69 (ed. & transl. Scott, pp. 118 and 142) (*Cristeschurche* only in the summary); *Cronica*, §§16 and 66 (edd. & transl. Carley & Townsend, pp. 40 and 124).

[46] Ekwall, *The Concise Oxford Dictionary of English Place-names*, p. 483, *s.n.* Twineham.

[47] *Twineham* appears in the vernacular version of this charter only (in Middle English, and thus post-Conquest), not the Latin text: *Anglo-Saxon Charters*, ed. & transl. Robertson, pp. 44–9 and 300–4 (no. 23); Finberg, *The Early Charters of Wessex*, p. 167.

[48] Domesday Book, I, 38vb and 44rb (Hampshire, 1.28 and 17.1). The king's estate was presumably the royal residence mentioned in the Anglo-Saxon Chronicle (*s.a.* 901).

[1] *De antiquitate*, §70 (ed. & transl. Scott, p. 144); see above, pp. 24–6.

[2] Domesday Book, I, 98rb (Somerset, 42.2). Bates ('Text of the Somerset Domesday', p. 519, n. 1) explained that the place-name in Domesday Book had a phonetic affix (*t*) attached. Ekwall offered the sequence *Tumbeli, Ubbele, Ubbeleia*, all post-Conquest forms (*The Concise Oxford Dictionary of English Place-names*, p. 485, *s.n.* Ubley).

Offaculum' (IC C15; no Sawyer-number).[3] No charter for Uffculme by name is extant, nor is one noticed in Glastonbury's lists. It is implied in the *De antiquitate* that King Æthelwulf's Decimation grant to Glastonbury included twenty-four hides at *Offaculum*, but the extant text of the charter (S.303; A.D. 854) omits this information.[4] In Domesday Book the holder of fourteen hides at *Offecome* in 1066 was a laywoman, Eadgifu.[5]

From this sparse information we should have had to postulate the following: a possible grant to Glastonbury by King Æthelwulf and loss of the land by the time of Domesday Book. A unique survival alerts us to the insecurity of such a judgment. In the fourteenth-century cartularies, among the papal privileges, there appears a document with the rubric 'memoriale terre alienate de Offeculum et post quomodo restituta est patebit subsequenter'.[6] This is presumably the *memoriale* cited in the *Index chartarum*, and its contents are extraordinary.[7]

According to this detailed account, Abbot Æthelweard (*ca* A.D. 1024–1053), with the permission of King Edward the Confessor and his queen, gave a certain widow, Eadgifu, the *uilla* of *Uffaculma* for the length of her life, on payment of seven gold marks. Eadgifu's son was made to swear that he would return the land to Glastonbury after his mother's death. Eadgifu had to provide sixteen sureties to this effect, and a tripartite charter recording the agreement was written, one copy for her, one for Glastonbury, and one for the bishop of Exeter. This transaction took place some time between A.D. 1050 and 1053.[8] Eadgifu then married again, this time a Norman called Walter, who was made to swear that he understood the

---

3   Sawyer (*Anglo-Saxon Charters*, p. 460) brought together this entry in the *Index charta-rum* and the description in the *De antiquitate* of a grant of Uffculme by King Æthelwulf (see below) and gave them one number (S.1697). Two different documents are probably involved, however, and I have taken 'S.1697' to refer only to the supposed grant by Æthelwulf and not the *memoriale*.

4   One and a half *hywysc'* at *Colom* are mentioned instead. See above, *s.n. Culum*. Because Uffculme is apparently not named in The Great Cartulary's text of Æthelwulf's Decimation (S.303), but only in the narrative version in the *De antiquitate*, Sawyer has given Æthelwulf's grant of *Offaculum* a separate number (S.1697) rather than including it (as a variant) in S.303: *De antiquitate*, §§53 and 69 (ed. & transl. Scott, pp. 112 and 142); *Cronica*, §§16 and 56 (edd. & transl. Carley & Townsend, pp. 40 and 108). *Colom* in the cartulary's text, however, may be the same as *Offaculum* in the *De antiquitate*, and the latter's hidage for the estate (twenty-four hides) may be an interpolation. See below, pp. 239–40. In his translation of Æthelwulf's grants in the *De antiquitate*, Scott printed 'Culmstock' for *Offaculum*, an identification rejected by Hazel Hudson and Frances Neale, whose objection was noted by Carley (*The Chronicle*, edd. & transl. Carley & Townsend, p. 289, n. 205). On the Decimation charter, see above, *s.n. Brannocmynstre* and Monk Okehampton, and below, pp. 322–4.

5   Domesday Book, I, 111vb (Devon, 23.9).

6   'Note of the alienated land of *Offeculum* and how it was subsequently restored': *The Great Chartulary*, ed. Watkin, I.126–8 (no. 172).

7   Discussed at length by Finberg *apud* Hoskins & Finberg, *Devonshire Studies*, pp. 59–77.

8   Leofric, consecrated in A.D. 1046, became bishop of Exeter in A.D. 1050; Earl God-wine, another witness, was in exile for a year from October 1051 and died in A.D. 1053. For a tripartite chirograph with a different aim, see Keynes, 'Royal government', pp. 254–5.

conditions under which his wife held the land and acknowledged that it belonged to St Mary, that is, to the church of Glastonbury. When Eadgifu died, however, Walter broke the agreement. His severing of the tenurial connexion with Glastonbury seems to have been formalised (or at least advertised) by his absence from the church on the feast of Mary's Nativity. Walter was punished for this wickedness, however, and fell ill. Believing himself near death, he repented of his sin and sent a glove to Glastonbury with his steward and members of his family, as a token of his intention to return the land to the monks; one of the community, meanwhile, was despatched to Uffculme to re-establish Glastonbury's authority. Walter's brother returned the glove to him, and, still *in extremis*, Walter sent two golden reliquaries (which had been promised by his late wife) and begged to be allowed to become a monk. The monks came to his sickbed, tonsured him, and clothed him in the monastic habit. Unfortunately (as far as Glastonbury's interests were concerned), Walter revived overnight, before he had been taken to the monastic infirmary, and his family ejected the monks who had remained with him, and dressed him again in his secular clothes. Having been saved by his kin from the temptations of repentance, Walter presumably did not succumb again, for in Domesday Book he is recorded as the independent holder of Uffculme in 1086.[9] The monks had kept the clippings of Walter's hair as tokens of his good intention, but these – and the tripartite charter, and Eadgifu's sixteen sureties – were nevertheless insufficient to stop Uffculme from becoming permanently attached to the landed property of Walter's heirs.[10]

This story sheds much light on what is otherwise a most obscure subject. Eadgifu's tripartite charter (if genuine) is of great interest:[11] it could, perhaps, have been a grant by the king with reversion to Glastonbury (as we have seen at Damerham in S.513) but, as it is said to have been granted by the abbot, it appears, rather, to have been an abbatial lease.[12] Land held from Glastonbury by lease is very poorly attested. Only S.509 for North Wootton in Edmund's reign offers any information on conditions of leasehold tenure, and (if genuine) its uniqueness among the abbey's tenth-century documents means that we cannot tell how common – or how unusual – its arrangements were; only this example at Uffculme offers substantial evidence from the mid-eleventh century of a lease of Glastonbury's land.[13] The *memoriale*, therefore, is a rare source of detailed information. It reveals that (as apparently in the case of S.509 in the mid-tenth century)

---

9   Domesday Book, I, 111vb (Devon, 23.9).
10 Uffculme was restored to Glastonbury by King Stephen in A.D. 1136 and confirmed by the Empress Matilda *ca* A.D. 1141, but it reverted to Walter's heirs not long thereafter: *The Great Chartulary*, ed. Watkin, I.126 (no. 171), *Regesta regum Anglo-Normannorum*, edd. Davis *et al.*, III.129–31 (nos 341 and 343). Finberg (Hoskins & Finberg, *Devonshire Studies*, pp. 68–77) discussed in detail the history of the estate in the twelfth century.
11 We have only the testimony of the *memoriale* that the charter was indeed a product of the mid-eleventh century; it could have been concocted in the twelfth century to bolster Glastonbury's case against Walter's heirs.
12 The opening of the *memoriale* seems to preserve the wording of this lost document.
13 There is a small amount of evidence for leases in 1066 in Glastonbury's entries in Domesday Book. See below, pp. 305–9.

a part was played in the administration of the lease by the king; in the case of Uffculme the bishop and ealdorman of the region were also involved. It tells us, too, the going rate in the mid-eleventh century for a one-life lease (seven marks); it may indicate – by the importance given to Walter's non-appearance at some sort of formal gathering (otherwise unattested) on 8 September – that payment was made on that day, which was also perhaps the occasion for either a literal or a merely symbolic reaffirmation of dependence on the abbot by his many tenants. The disappearance of the three charters should remind us that much may have been lost from the documentary record, especially where impermanent arrangements such as leases were concerned. The survival of the *memoriale*, apparently a record prepared as evidence in a dispute, should encourage us to remember that, although the evidence is rarely preserved at Glastonbury, seizures and appropriations did not go unchallenged. The precautions taken by the monks to ensure that the land return to the community seem inviolable, but they failed in their purpose. Churches across the country experienced similar difficulties in maintaining possession of lands which they leased to laypeople: Symeon of Durham noted the failure of the church of Durham to recover estates leased to the ealdormen of Northumbria by Bishop Aldhun (A.D. 990–1018).[14]

The post-Conquest history of Uffculme indicates that (though eventually unsuccessful) the monks did not give up the land without a fight. There is some uncertainty about events in the Conqueror's reign. The cartulary's scribe, presumably taking his information from a privilege granted to Glastonbury by Pope Innocent II in A.D. 1137, stated that the estate had been seized by William the Conqueror before its restoration by Stephen.[15] Perhaps the reference was to an intervention by the king to attempt to resolve the dispute between Walter and the monks. Perhaps, as Finberg suggested, William had issued a writ in support of Walter;[16] William certainly rewarded him well elsewhere for his service.[17] C. and F. Thorn have also proposed that the land had actually been confirmed to Walter by King William.[18] If that were true, it probably occurred before 1086; the *memoriale* is undated, and whether Walter's crisis took place before or after this hypothetical royal confirmation is uncertain. It seems less likely, however, that a Norman knight would suffer an access of guilt if he possessed a writ from his king. This would place Walter's illness, the near-return of the land, and the possible royal writ firmly before 1086.[19]

What is perhaps most important for our purposes is the crucial fact that none

---

[14] *Historia Dunelmensis ecclesie*, Book III, §4 (*Opera*, ed. Arnold, I.83–4). For several examples from Worcester, see Barlow, *The English Church 1000–1066*, pp. 174–5.

[15] *The Great Chartulary*, ed. Watkin, I.125–6 (no. 170). Watkin originally judged that the scribe had misunderstood or contradicted his documents on this point (I.126, n. 1), but he changed his mind to agree with Finberg that the Conqueror had intervened (Hoskins & Finberg, *Devonshire Studies*, where Watkin's revised opinion is cited on p. 66, n. 1).

[16] *Ibid.*, pp. 65–6.

[17] *Ibid.*, pp. 62–3.

[18] *Devon (Part Two)*, edd. & transl. Thorn & Thorn, 23.9 (note).

[19] Watkin dated Walter's crisis *ca* A.D. 1080 but the *memoriale* gives no date. Finberg considered that it '[could] not be much later than 1086' (*The Great Chartulary*, ed. Watkin, I.liv; Hoskins & Finberg, *Devonshire Studies*, p. 66, n. 2).

of this – not Eadgifu's tenure by lease, nor Walter's illicit appropriation of the land, nor a (putative) seizure by William, nor a (hypothetical) writ of confirmation – appears in Glastonbury's archive, nor in the entry for Uffculme in Domesday Book, which simply lists Walter as a lay tenant-in-chief and Eadgifu as his predecessor. There is no hint in Domesday Book of Glastonbury's claim on the land in 1066 or 1086. No marginal sign identifies Uffculme as a manor seized from or claimed by the abbey.[20] Nor does Uffculme appear in the expected places (where losses are habitually recorded): it is not on the list of *Terrae occupatae* in the *Liber Exoniensis* or at the end of the entry for the abbey in the Exchequer's text (where, at least in the returns for Somerset, Glastonbury's lost estates were grouped together). The silence of Domesday Book over Glastonbury's rightful ownership of Uffculme suggests that there may be other – perhaps many other – eleventh-century disputes disguised by omissions such as this, as well as many other overlords left off the record in favour of men or women whose dependent relationship is disguised.[21] Finberg went so far as to suspect that the Domesday Book jurors sometimes 'contented themselves with registering the name of a sitting tenant'.[22] It should be remembered, however, that the *memoriale* provides only Glastonbury's side of the story and no doubt omitted whatever would have prejudiced the abbey's case. A document granting the land to Walter could have been suppressed, for example; it would hardly have helped the monks' cause. Domesday Book itself can be convicted of gross distortion of reality in this instance only if we are certain that no such writ of King William existed.

The size of the estate may or may not be a problem: Æthelwulf's twenty-four hides in the *De antiquitate* may be a scribal error for fourteen, which is the total given in Domesday Book. That Æthelwulf's grant is attested nowhere but in the *De antiquitate* makes it open to interpretation. If genuine, it could have been issued as a quite separate grant, unconnected with that king's Decimation charter (S.303) and therefore naturally not included in its text. In that case another diploma must have existed, a document presumably seen by the author of the *De antiquitate* but now lost. In view of the dispute over Uffculme, some suspicion must attach to this hypothetical document, as it could have been produced to act as evidence of Glastonbury's ancient title to the estate. On the other hand, it is not found on any of the abbey's documentary lists, and it may never have existed. Another possibility is that a separate charter (also now lost) was created for Uffculme from the Decimation Charter itself (with place-name and hidage updated).[23] A com-

---

[20] The text of Domesday Book is sprinkled with these signs marking losses and/or disputes.

[21] This point has recently been the subject of debate: see Sawyer, '1066–1086', Fleming, 'Domesday Book and the tenurial revolution', and *Kings and Lords*, especially pp. 107–44, and Roffe, 'From thegnage to barony'.

[22] Hoskins & Finberg, *Devonshire Studies*, p. 64. See also Paul Hyams's argument that disputes were deliberately edited from the record (' "No register of title" ', pp. 133–41) and the discussion below, p. 308. Finberg hesitantly concluded that the silence of Domesday Book on the subject meant that Eadgifu was still alive in 1086, but the naming of Walter as the TRW tenant seems to contradict this.

[23] A possible parallel is S.313, from Winchester, an eleventh-century chirograph which seems to have been produced for the purpose of emphasising the Old Minster's historic

parison of the Great Cartulary's text of the Decimation charter and the description of Æthelwulf's grants in the *De antiquitate* appears to suggest that *Offaculum*'s twenty-four hides in the latter are themselves a substitution, replacing one and a half *hiwiscs* at *Colom* – which appear only in the charter's cartulary-text. This itself seems to suggest that *Offaculum* and *Colom* were the same place – or at least were thought to have been so at the time of the adjustment of the documents. The dispute over Uffculme (which carried on into the twelfth century) provides a clear context for the interpolation of an increased hidage and a different, probably more current, form of the place-name. The hidage may not literally have increased, however: *Colom*'s one and a half hides in the Decimation charter may be taken as representing only a fraction of the contemporary estate. It may be that Æthelwulf's grant applied to only part of the ninth-century estate which Glastonbury held (as has been suggested in other, similar, instances).[24]

If the identification of *Colom* with Uffculme were correct, it would potentially push the history of Glastonbury's ownership of Uffculme back into the mid-eighth century, when eleven hides at *Culum* were reputedly granted to the abbey. Three hides at *Cumbe* were apparently acquired at the same time. But, as we have seen,[25] exactly where this land lay is uncertain. Two identifications have been proposed for *Culum*: Culmstock (a few miles upriver from Uffculme)[26] and Uffculme. If we prefer the former identification, Glastonbury's eighth-century bequest was apparently lost by the mid-eleventh century, if not before, when the bishop of Exeter owned the five-hide estate at Culmstock; the circumstances of the subsequent history of *Cumbe* (possibly Culm Davy, further upriver) are obscure.[27] If we prefer the identification of *Culum* with Uffculme (and its eleven hides, added to *Cumbe*'s three, reproduce Uffculme's total in Domesday Book), there is no need to find an explanation for the difference in hidage between *Culum* (eleven) and Culmstock (five). The putative connexion could also provide some support for Æthelwulf's Decimation charter (or *vice versa*). Elsewhere, the charter appears to dispose of land which seems already to have belonged to the abbey – at Pennard, and *Sowy*, and *Lodegaresberghe*, for example; it has been interpreted as a grant not of land but of different privileges or exemptions from burdens on land already in the recipients' hands.[28] The appearance of *Colom* in S.303 may suggest, therefore, that Uffculme too may already have belonged to the community in the mid-ninth century, which would support its identity with *Culum* (granted in the eighth). But at this distance from the original transactions – and without the assistance of boundary-descriptions – it is not possible to distinguish with certainty between these estates in the Culm Valley, nor to trace the connexion between them and the later settlements which took their names from the river.

The date of Uffculme's acquisition, therefore, is uncertain, but its loss is

---

right to one property allegedly granted by Æthelwulf at the time of his Decimation. I am grateful to Susan Kelly for bringing this charter to my attention.

24 See above, *s.n. Brannocmynstre* or Monk Okehampton, and below, pp. 322–4.
25 See above, *s.n. Culum.*
26 *Devon (Part Two)*, edd. & transl. Thorn & Thorn, 2.12 (note); Finberg, *The Early Charters of Devon and Cornwall*, p. 8.
27 See above, *s.n. Culum* and *Cumbe.*
28 See below, pp. 322–4.

recorded in unique detail; save for the survival of the *memoriale*, Glastonbury's ownership of Uffculme itself would have been unknown,[29] and the abbey's continued presence in the Culm Valley after the mid-ninth century would have seemed unlikely.

Unidentified Five Hides #1 (Somerset)

At the end of Glastonbury's Somerset entries in Domesday Book, it is recorded that the father of Roger of Courseulles exchanged five hides which he held from Glastonbury for the estate of Limington (near Ilchester).[30] No clue to the location of these five hides or the identity of their new holder seems to survive, and they remain unidentified (though probably in Somerset, as they are recorded in that county's returns).

Unidentified Five Hides #2

The identity of another five-hide estate without a name may be easier to determine. The entry 'Cynewlfus de .u. hidis. G.' occurs in the contents-list of the *Liber terrarum* (LT27). As the gift by King Cynewulf of five hides at *Wudetone* in A.D. 760 is recorded in the *De antiquitate*,[31] it is probable that the scribe of the contents-list omitted this place-name by mistake. On the other hand, Cynewulf's (hideless) grant of *Huneresberg* on the River Parrett – also mentioned in the *De antiquitate* – has no record in the *Liber terrarum*, and it may be an alternative candidate for the entry.[32]

Upavon (Wiltshire)

According to an entry in the *Liber terrarum* contents-list, Edmund granted *Uppauene* to Ælfswith (S.1720; LT127). No other record of this grant survives, apart from the unreliable notice of *Huppauene* among the *alia [maneria] data Glastonie* in §70 of the *De antiquitate*.[33] Ælfswith was the recipient of a number of charters noticed in Glastonbury's archive, and her documents may have come to the church as a group, whether or not the community also received all the land in question.[34] Most of the estates which she received were nonetheless held by Glastonbury in 1066. However, two and a half hides at *Oppaurene* and the church to which they belonged were held in 1086 by the church of Saint-Wandrille; as this entry appears in Domesday Book's catalogue of the *terra regis*, it might be assumed that the king retained some control over the estate.[35] No holder TRE is named.

---

[29] Apart from the questionable reference in the *De antiquitate*'s abridged account of Æthelwulf's Decimation (see above, p. 236).

[30] Domesday Book, I, 91ra (Somerset, 8.41).

[31] *De antiquitate*, §§48 and 69 (ed. & transl. Scott, pp. 106 and 142); *Cronica*, §§16 and 54 (edd. & transl. Carley & Townsend, pp. 40 and 106). See above, *s.n.* North Wootton.

[32] *Ibid*. See above, *s.n.* Houndsborough.

[33] *De antiquitate*, §70 (ed. & transl. Scott, p. 144); see above, pp. 24–6.

[34] Unless more than one person of this name was involved, she was probably the wife of Ealdorman Ælfheah. See above, *s.n.* Idmiston. On Ælfheah's family and connexions, see Williams, '*Princeps Merciorum gentis*', especially pp. 147–54.

[35] Domesday Book, I, 65va (Wiltshire, 1.23 [g]).

Glastonbury's tenure of Upavon is therefore uncertain. If it did receive the land from Ælfswith or her heirs, even the *De antiquitate* failed to record the transfer, although Ælfswith's charter remained in the archive. This wealthy estate – situated on two converging branches of the River Avon, about forty-five miles north-east of Glastonbury at some distance from its other Wiltshire holdings – seems to have been in other hands, at least at the end of the Anglo-Saxon period and thereafter. Whether the abbey had held it between the mid-tenth century and the mid-eleventh cannot be determined on the present evidence.

Uplyme (Devon)
See *Lim.*

Ure
See *Ora.*

Walton (Somerset)
Walton was an estate assessed at twenty hides in Domesday Book.[1] No Anglo-Saxon documentation survives for Walton by name, but its pre-Conquest history probably belongs with that of the ancient estate of *Pouelt* (*q.v.*), of which it may have been a part; *Pouelt* has been discussed in detail above.

Wedmore (Somerset)
Glastonbury's claim to Wedmore – based on lost documents in the name of Bishop Wilfrid and King Centwine – has been discussed above under Clewer, an estate about which similar claims were made.

Westbury
Two entries on the contents-list of the *Liber terrarum* apply to land at Westbury. Grants by King Eadwig and King Edgar, both to Ælfhere, are recorded (S.1747 and S.1760; LT89 and LT90). These charters reappear nowhere else in the documentary record. Neither of these royal grants is explicitly mentioned in the *De antiquitate*, but we are told there that Ealdorman Ælfhere gave forty hides at Westbury (and five at Orchardleigh) to Glastonbury and that King Edgar confirmed the grant.[2] The text appears to quote from a charter (or an endorsement) in Ælfhere's name commending *cartula haec . . . hereditatis* to Glastonbury.[3]
    Westbury is not an uncommon name. Finberg identified the object of Glastonbury's charters as Westbury-on-Severn (Gloucestershire), where the king held a thirty-hide estate in 1066.[4] This land lay on the west bank of the River Severn,

---

1 Domesday Book, I, 90rb (Somerset, 8.11).
2 *De antiquitate*, §§62 and 69 (ed. & transl. Scott, pp. 130 and 144); *Cronica*, §§16 and 73 (edd. & transl. Carley & Townsend, pp. 42 and 138). For other grants in Glastonbury's archive involving Ealdorman Ælfhere, see *s.n. Bocland* and Orchardleigh. See also Williams, '*Princeps Merciorum gentis*', especially pp. 155–72.
3 Finberg (*The Early Charters of the West Midlands*, p. 57) suggested that this quotation might have come from an endorsement on Edgar's charter. If genuine, it could also have come from a separate charter for Orchardleigh.
4 *Ibid.*, pp. 54 and 57; Domesday Book, I, 163ra (Gloucestershire, 1.11).

about ten miles southwest of Gloucester and sixty miles northeast of Glastonbury. Finberg probably chose this Westbury in part because it was close enough to Glastonbury to make a connexion feasible but mainly because no other pre-Conquest documentation is explicitly associated with it. Other places called West-bury may be considered, however. A Westbury was confirmed to Wells in a charter of King Edward the Confessor (S.1042; A.D. 1065).[5] From the context, this must have been Westbury-sub-Mendip, just a few miles northeast of Wells and in 1066 a six-hide estate held by the bishop of Wells.[6] No earlier documentation for this Westbury is extant. Westbury-on-Trym, now a suburb of Bristol and about thirty miles from Glastonbury, has a more extensively documented Anglo-Saxon history, which points to a steady connexion with the church of Worcester from at least the reign of Offa until A.D. 824.[7] It was apparently the site of a community in the 960s,[8] and fifty hides there were recorded in Domesday Book as held by Worcester.[9]

None of these Westburys had the same hidage as Glastonbury's, but none is accounted for in the mid-tenth century, the period of the abbey's association. Westbury-sub-Mendip is by far the closest candidate (in distance), but its low hidage and its location – among a concentration of Wells's estates – count against it. Westbury-on-Trym's association with Worcester is not continuously attested and it may arguably have been interrupted by a period under Glastonbury's lordship (although there is no evidence of this at Worcester); and Ealdorman Ælfhere (the recipient of Glastonbury's Westbury) had close connexions with that see.[10] Westbury-on-Severn's royal status in 1066 might make it a more credible candidate, on the assumption that a royal gift to Ælfhere could have reverted to the Crown by the succeeding century; but this qualification might recommend yet another Westbury even more strongly. Westbury in Wiltshire (on the border with Somerset and about twenty-five miles northeast of Glastonbury) was held by Queen Edith in 1066 and assessed at forty hides (though constituting an entire

---

5 Keynes has argued convincingly against accepted opinion and in favour of the authenticity of this charter; see 'Regenbald', pp. 200–5.

6 Domesday Book, I, 89va (Somerset, 6.11).

7 A lost charter of Æthelbald, king of Mercia, reputedly granted sixty hides at *Westbyrig* to Eanulf (Finberg, *The Early Charters of the West Midlands*, p. 34). This transaction was cited in an extant charter in Offa's name which confirmed the reversion of the sixty hides to the church of Worcester (S.146). An original single sheet also survives, granting fifty hides at Westbury 'near the River Avon' to the thegn Æthelmund (S.139; A.D. 793x796). A charter of A.D. 804 in which the layman Æthelric (probably Æthelmund's son) indicated his intention to bequeath land at *Westmynster* (considered to be Westbury) to his mother for life, with reversion to Worcester (S.1187), is followed by the record of a dispute in A.D. 824 over *Westburgh* between Heahberht, bishop of Worcester, and the *familia* of Berkeley (S.1433), who had usurped the land against Æthelric's intentions. This dispute was discussed by Wormald in 'Charters, law and the settlement of disputes', pp. 152–7, and by Sims-Williams, *Religion and Literature*, pp. 174–6.

8 *The Heads of Religious Houses*, edd. Knowles *et al.*, p. 97.

9 Domesday Book, I, 164vb (Gloucestershire, 3.1).

10 See Williams, '*Princeps Merciorum gentis*', especially p. 157.

hundred).[11] This is another Westbury for which no pre-Conquest documentation survives, and this circumstance, as well as its hidage and its royal owner, may make it the most likely candidate for Edgar's grant to Ælfhere (as does its proximity to Orchardleigh, also said to have been granted to Ælfhere by the king, which is only a few miles to the west across the Somerset border). There is no particular objection to the ealdorman of Mercia holding a hundred in Wessex, particularly as Ælfhere may have been in an official position there as well as in Mercia, especially during Edgar's reign.[12] Glastonbury's difficulties in Wiltshire and its losses there in the mid-eleventh century are recorded (in passing) in the *De antiquitate*.[13] If Ælfhere had held it and passed it on to the monks, this Westbury could have left the abbey's hands at that time.

Why two grants of Westbury were made is unknown. The first may not have taken effect, or it may have transferred only part of the land to Ælfhere, the remainder coming to him during the next king's reign. Alternatively, Edgar's may simply have been a confirmation of Eadwig's grant. Without the texts, it is impossible to say. Whether the land was in turn transferred to Glastonbury is also uncertain: Ælfhere's gift to the community is recorded only in the *De antiquitate*, but the credibility of its statements on the subject is, as usual, open to question: a charter (with an endorsement) may have been the source of the information, but it may not have been genuine; alternatively, the author of the *De antiquitate* may have assumed (as he did routinely and sometimes mistakenly) that the existence of charters for laymen could always be taken to mean that the recipients had passed the land on to Glastonbury. No record of the Wiltshire Westbury between the reign of Edgar and 1066 is extant to indicate who held the land. Ealdorman Ælfhere was buried at Glastonbury, and part of his collection of charters (but not necessarily the lands documented therein) may have come to rest there with his body.[14] If, however, he did give Westbury to Glastonbury, and if the monks *were* forced to give it up, the loss of this very rich estate (valued at £100 in 1066)[15] must have been a blow.

---

11 Domesday Book, I, 65rb (Wiltshire, 1.16); Darlington, 'Introduction to the Domesday survey', p. 62. Stacy, too, has associated Ælfhere's grant with the Westbury in Wiltshire ('The estates', p. 14, n. 7).

12 Williams, '*Princeps Merciorum gentis*', p. 158. For Ælfhere's possible role in the murder of King Edward the Martyr in A.D. 978 and the anti-monastic reaction early in Æthelred's reign, see Fisher, 'The anti-monastic reaction', pp. 269–70, and Keynes, *The Diplomas of King Æthelred*, pp. 169 and 172–3. Keynes has described him as 'the most powerful layman in the kingdom'.

13 *De antiquitate*, §68 (ed. & transl. Scott, p. 138); *Cronica*, §79 (edd. & transl. Carley & Townsend, p. 150).

14 Ælfhere appears on an obit-list in a thirteenth-century manuscript from Glastonbury (London, British Library, Add. MS. 17450, 5v). His burial at Glastonbury is mentioned in an early chapter of the *De antiquitate* which is not to be found in William of Malmesbury's *Gesta regum Anglorum* (*De antiquitate*, §31; ed. & transl. Scott, p. 84) – if, that is, he is the *dux Alfari* whose tomb, according to the *De antiquitate*, was still to be seen in the church. Scott seems to be mistaken in rendering this name 'Ælfheah'. See Blows, 'A Glastonbury obit-list', p. 262, n. 30, and p. 267.

15 Domesday Book, I, 65rb (Wiltshire, 1.16).

Westcombe (Somerset)

Seven hides and three virgates at Westcombe were part of Glastonbury's twenty-hide estate of Batcombe in 1066,[16] and were presumably a sub-unit of its twenty hides when they were granted by King Edmund in a charter dated 940. For a discussion of this charter and the history of the estate, see above, under Batcombe.

Westhay (Somerset)

Westhay is named – in the *Cronica* alone – as one of the two *paruae insulae* granted in A.D. 670 to Glastonbury by King Cenwealh with land at *Ferramere*.[17] It has been discussed above, under Meare.

West Monkton (Somerset)

See *Cantucuudu* and *Crycbeorh*.

Westone

An entry in the contents-list of the *Liber terrarum* records the grant by King Æthelstan of *Westone uel Foxcote* to Æthelstan, who gave it to Glastonbury (S.1711; LT55). No text or other notice of this grant survives apart from that in the *De antiquitate* which states that 'Westone que nunc Foxcote dicitur' consisted of five hides, adding that the layman's bequest was confirmed by King Æthelstan; it also identifies the recipient-donor as Ealdorman Æthelstan, the Half-King, who became a monk at Glastonbury and left other estates to the community.[18] In 1066, an estate of five hides at *Fuscote* was in lay hands.[19] This was Forscote (also spelled Foxcote), east of Radstock, about twenty miles northeast of Glastonbury.

The identification of Æthelstan's *Westone* with Forscote is not necessarily earlier than the Trinity manuscript's text of the *De antiquitate* and the contents-list of the *Liber terrarum*, and should be treated with the usual caution. Weston and Foxcote/Forscote are reasonably common place-names, and even if the identification were contemporary with Æthelstan's grant it would not necessarily mean that the *Fuscote* in Domesday Book was the land in question. Whether or not Æthelstan's grant was of the estate later recorded in Domesday Book, we cannot be certain that Glastonbury ever held the land (although if the *Liber terrarum* did indeed testify to that effect, its evidence would have been more credible than that of the *De antiquitate).* If the latter's claim of a confirmation by King Æthelstan is to be credited, the gift would have to have been made (or an intention declared) well before Æthelstan Half-King's retirement to Glastonbury in A.D. 957. If

---

[16] Domesday Book, I, 90va (Somerset, 8.24).

[17] *Cronica*, §42 (edd. & transl. Carley & Townsend, p. 88).

[18] *De antiquitate*, §§54 and 69 (ed. & transl. Scott, pp. 112 and 142); *Cronica*, §§16 and 60 (edd. & transl. Carley & Townsend, pp. 40 and 112). See Hart, 'Athelstan "Half King" ', especially pp. 125–8. The pre-eminent layman of his time, he retired from Eadwig's court to Glastonbury, where he became a monk, probably in A.D. 957 after the division of the kingdom. (I should like to thank Simon Keynes, who derived this new date from his *Atlas of Attestations in Anglo-Saxon Charters*. See also Keynes, 'The "Dunstan B" charters', p. 191, n. 108.) On Æthelstan's gifts to Glastonbury, see above, *s.n. Brentefordlond*, and the list cited there; of these, confirmations by King Æthelstan are also claimed at *Lim* and Wrington (*q.v.*).

[19] Domesday Book, I, 88va (Somerset, 5.42).

Westone did come into the possession of the community (and if it is the Forscote in Domesday Book), it appears to have been lost before the Conquest. On the other hand, it may have been incorporated into another estate or may be disguised in the record under another name (other than *Foxcote*).

Westwere (Somerset)
See Parrett (River, Fishery on).

Whatley (Somerset)
A charter of King Edmund cited on the contents-list of the *Liber terrarum* apparently recorded a grant of *Wetheleage* to Glastonbury (S.1726; LT57). This charter is now lost, and no other notice of the transaction survives, apart from that in the *De antiquitate*, where there is evidence of some confusion over the number of hides.[20] Either the number ten found in some of the references to this grant is incorrect, or the estate was diminished in size or assessment before the mid-eleventh century; Glastonbury held four hides at *Watelei* in 1066.[21] Without a surviving text to analyse, it is impossible to determine Whatley's size at the time of Edmund's putative grant, or indeed to evaluate the genuineness of Glastonbury's claim to have acquired it from that king.

Whatley is adjacent to Mells (also the subject of a charter of the 940s), fewer than twenty miles northeast of Glastonbury.

Wheathill (Somerset)
A charter apparently entered in the *Liber terrarum* but now lost recorded a grant by King Edgar of *Wethehyl* to Glastonbury (S.1770; LT86). This charter, too, is unnoticed elsewhere, apart from in the *De antiquitate*; we discover there that the land at *Wetehulle* consisted of three hides.[22] Three hides at *Watehelle* were apparently held by Glastonbury in 1066, although this information is found only among the returns of Serlo de Burcy (the holder in 1086).[23] Wheathill does not appear among the *Terrae occupatae* in the *Liber Exoniensis* or at the end of Glastonbury's returns for Somerset, where the abbey's lost lands are listed. Stacy has suggested that this indicated that Glastonbury had acknowledged the loss without dispute.[24] But since the land was subsequently held by the monks, the testimony of Domesday Book may be misleading on this score and Glastonbury may have retained the land with no – or only temporary – interruption.[25]

---

20 *De antiquitate*, §§55 and 69 (ed. & transl. Scott, pp. 114 and 142); *Cronica*, §§16 and 64 (edd. & transl. Carley & Townsend, pp. 40 and 120). The main entry in the Trinity manuscript of the *De antiquitate* mentions ten hides, with *iiii* interlined above; other manuscripts note four hides. The summary of grants has ten. The *Cronica* likewise mentions ten hides in its summary but four in the main entry.

21 Domesday Book, I, 90va (Somerset, 8.26). The figure in the *Liber Exoniensis*, however, is five hides (E 168b1).

22 *De antiquitate*, §§62 and 69 (ed. & transl. Scott, pp. 128 and 144); *Cronica*, §§16 and 73 (edd. & transl. Carley & Townsend, pp. 42 and 138).

23 Domesday Book, I, 98ra (Somerset, 37.9 and note).

24 'The estates', p. 50. Against this argument is the presence of a marginal marker beside the entry. These usually denote land lost or in dispute.

25 Cf. above, *s.n.* Uffculme; and see below, p. 308.

Wheathill is located east of Lydford, about ten miles southeast of Glastonbury. As in the case of Whatley, the loss of the charter makes it impossible to judge whether the community did indeed acquire the land in the tenth century as it later claimed.

Wilton (Wiltshire)

The contents-list of the *Liber terrarum* records the existence of a document in Æthelred's name, now lost, 'de quodam predio in Wiltone dat' G.' (S.1774; LT133). The same document was listed on the *Index chartarum*, among charters for land granted directly to Glastonbury but no longer held by the community (IC C10). According to the *De antiquitate*, King Æthelred in A.D. 984 gave Glastonbury one *mansa* at Wilton for forty gold mancuses.[26] Although burgesses in Wilton are recorded in Domesday Book among the returns of several manors held by different lords, there is no detailed entry for the borough of Wilton itself and no indication of whether a *predium* there was still in Glastonbury's hands in 1066.[27] It is possible that Glastonbury did have a holding at Wilton shortly after the Conquest (if not before), as Abbot Herluin (A.D. 1100–1118) apparently paid sixty marks to redeem *quaedam terra* at Wilton which Geoffrey de Mandeville had seized.[28] The lost charter in Æthelred's name may have been concocted to help Glastonbury's case at the time of this seizure. It could, on the other hand, have been genuine.[29] Some presence on Glastonbury's part in the towns of the region – where the holders of property benefited from advantageous trading rights – is to be expected, but very little evidence survives.[30]

Winchester (Hampshire)

The text of a charter, dated 988, in the name of King Æthelred which granted a *curtis* in Winchester is extant in the *Secretum domini* (but not the Great Cartulary) (S.871).[31] The recipients of the charter are said to have been Æthelsige, bishop of Sherborne (A.D. 978/9–991x993), and a thegn, Æthelmær, and the *curtis* is said to have previously been held by *Edgeard*. This charter is not noticed elsewhere in Glastonbury's archive.

The rubric of S.871 in the cartulary reads 'Carta regis Athelredi confirmatoria eiusdem quo supra'.[32] The *supra* refers to a document (of *ca* A.D. 1137) issued by

---

[26] *De antiquitate*, §§63 and 69 (ed. & transl. Scott, pp. 130 and 144); *Cronica*, §§16 and 74 (edd. & transl. Carley & Townsend, pp. 42 and 142) (forty gold *markis* in the *Cronica*'s §74). On the Anglo-Saxon land market, see Campbell, 'The sale of land'.

[27] Domesday Book, I, 64va (Wiltshire, B.1). For references to borough-properties in Domesday Book, see above, *s.n.* Malmesbury.

[28] *Cronica*, §87 (edd. & transl. Carley & Townsend, p. 162).

[29] Compare, for example, S.870, a diploma of King Æthelred for a thegn, Æthelnoth, granting a *curtis* in Wilton (cf. Keynes, *The Diplomas of King Æthelred*, pp. 91–2 and 248–9), and S.871 (see below, *s.n.* Winchester).

[30] See *s.n.* Malmesbury and Winchester.

[31] This is one of only two charters which appear in the *Secretum* but not in the Great Cartulary; the other is S.253 for *Pouelt* (*q.v.*). The position of S.871 (but not that of S.253) could imply that it was a late addition to the collection.

[32] MS. Wood empt. 1, 253v.

Abbot Henry of Blois, informing the Glastonbury brethren of their need for a *hospicium* (guest-house) in Winchester and of the purchase of land formerly belonging to Conan *fenerator*.[33] Perhaps S.871 was manufactured to give retroactive authority to Glastonbury's (or another holder's) ownership by association with King Æthelred, but it may represent an authentic pre-Conquest transaction, perhaps an earlier title-deed for the property purchased by Abbot Henry. S.870 (also A.D. 988), with which S.871 has much in common diplomatically, is a grant of a *curtis* in Wilton to a thegn, Æthelnoth, and S.888 (for St Albans) and S.889 (for the Old Minster, Winchester) (both A.D. 996) are also diplomas for urban estates.[34] As I have mentioned above (in the discussion of Malmesbury and Wilton), Glastonbury's pre-Conquest presence in centres such as these would not be surprising, but the documentary evidence is largely lacking. S.871's demonstrable association with Glastonbury is limited to its appearance in one of its fourteenth-century cartularies, and there is no proof that any land in Winchester belonged to Glastonbury Abbey before the early twelfth century.

Winscombe (Somerset)
The contents-list of the *Liber terrarum* records a grant of *Wynescumbe* by King Edgar to Ælfswith (S.1762; LT114). This charter appears on List C of the *Index chartarum* (IC C9), although the accompanying note (*seruienti*) suggests that it ought properly to have been on List D (charters for lands given to laypeople, as opposed to lands given directly to Glastonbury). The text does not survive, but in the *De antiquitate* we are offered the information that 'Queen' Ælfswith gave Glastonbury fifteen hides at *Winescumbe*, a transaction confirmed by King Edgar.[35] In 1066 Glastonbury held fifteen hides there, according to Domesday Book, although one hide (probably at Winterhead) was lost before 1086 to the bishop of Coutances.[36]

As with Ælfswith's other grants,[37] there is no proof outside the testimony of the *De antiquitate* that it was she who passed the lands on to Glastonbury. The charters of which she was the recipient may have had notes to this effect written on their dorses, but no single sheets have survived to prove that the information was not an original contribution by the author of the *De antiquitate*. If we credit the *De antiquitate*, however, Winscombe may have been in Glastonbury's hands from Edgar's reign until the Norman Conquest (barring temporary, undocumented, seizure).

33 *The Great Chartulary*, ed. Watkin, III.703 (no. 1302).
34 See Keynes, *The Diplomas of King Æthelred*, pp. 91–2, 102–3, 248–9, and 254.
35 *De antiquitate*, §§62 and 69 (ed. & transl. Scott, pp. 130 and 144); *Cronica*, §§16 and 73 (edd. & transl. Carley & Townsend, pp. 42 and 138). There is no support for Ælfswith's status as queen. The Ælfswith who received S.866 (for *Kyngton, q.v.*) from King Æthelred was the wife of Ealdorman Ælfheah. If there was only one person involved, this Ælfswith was associated with a number of other grants of land which were recorded in Glastonbury's archive. Several (if not all) of these estates were acquired by Glastonbury, and in most cases were still held by the abbey in 1066. See above, *s.n.* Idmiston.
36 Domesday Book, I, 90ra and 88ra (Somerset, 8.2 and 5.12). See below, *s.n. Wintreth.*
37 See *s.n. Andersey*, Idmiston, *Kyngton*, *Streton*, and Tintinhull.

Winscombe was one of those manors appropriated by Wells during the protracted but ultimately unsuccessful attempt to annex the monastery to the see which was begun by Bishop Savaric (A.D. 1191–1205) and diligently pursued by Bishop Jocelin (A.D. 1206–1242). Litigation throughout the thirteenth century culminated in the loss of Blackford, Cranmore, Pucklechurch, and Winscombe to Wells.[38] It is curious that, although Pucklechurch's single-sheet charter (S.553) went to Wells – apparently when Glastonbury's case was finally lost – no other pre-Conquest diplomas for these four estates are known to have survived in the cathedral's archives.

Winscombe is on the edge of the Mendips, fewer than twenty miles northwest of Glastonbury.

Winterborne

Two diplomas granting land at *Winterborne* survive in the fourteenth-century cartularies. The first is a grant (with bounds) of twenty-five hides by Æthelred, king of Wessex, to his *princeps* Wulfhere in A.D. 969 (*recte* 869) (S.341). The second is a grant (also with bounds) by King Æthelstan in A.D. 928 of *bis binas quina* (that is, 2x2x5 = 20) hides to Ælfflæd (S.399).[39] Æthelred's charter was apparently copied into the *Liber terrarum* and was also listed in the *Index chartarum* and MS. 39a (LT115; IC B10; L42) (with the benefactor mistakenly represented as 'Eddred' in the first and last source).[40] In the *De antiquitate*, we are told that Wulfhere subsequently gave the land to Glastonbury.[41] Æthelstan's charter too was apparently copied into the *Liber terrarum* and was also noticed in the *Index chartarum* and MS. 39a (LT102; IC B4; L41).[42] In MS. 39a, Ælfflæd's unconfirmed status as King Edward's queen (awarded to her by the *De antiquitate*),[43] was further confused ('carta Athelstani regis facta Elfethe uxori sue').

Five other pre-Conquest charters preserved in the archives of Shaftesbury,

[38] See above, p. 12.

[39] For *bis* and *binas*, see *Aldhelmi Opera*, ed. Ehwald, p. 568. This hermeneutic expression may be an argument in favour of the authenticity of S.399.

[40] The rubric and witness-list of the text in the cartulary make the same error, while in the dispositive section the king's name is given as *Ethered*. It is nevertheless considered to be a diploma of King Æthelred of Wessex (see Keynes, 'Regenbald', p. 186, n. 4).

[41] *De antiquitate*, §53 (ed. & transl. Scott, p. 112). Omitted from the summary and from the *Cronica*.

[42] For a diplomatic analysis of this charter, one of the 'Athelstan-A' group, see Keynes, *The Diplomas of King Æthelred*, pp. 43–4, 'Regenbald', p. 186, and 'King Æthelstan's books', pp. 156–9. It bears a close relation to S.400 and was probably drawn up at the same time.

[43] *De antiquitate*, §§54 and 69 (ed. & transl. Scott, pp. 112 and 142); *Cronica*, §§16 and 60 (edd. & transl. Carley & Townsend, pp. 40 and 112). As I have mentioned, the *De antiquitate* also identifies the Ælfflæd who received Buckland Newton, *Hammedone*, and Okeford Fitzpaine (and reputedly gave them to Glastonbury) as the widow of Edward the Elder. William of Malmesbury (*Gesta regum Anglorum*, §126; ed. Stubbs, I.136–7) is the sole authority for her status as queen; see above, *s.n.* Okeford Fitzpaine. Meyer ('Women and the tenth century English monastic reform', pp. 46–7) has discussed the confusion over Edward's marriages and Ælfflæd's supposed interest in the reform movement.

Wilton, the Old and New Minsters at Winchester, and Cerne relate to land at *Winterburnan*. S.485 is a grant by King Edmund of two hides to the nun Wynflæd in A.D. 942. S.543 is a grant of one hide from King Eadred to his goldsmith and silversmith Ælfsige in A.D. 949. S.668, a charter of King Edgar dated 922 (*recte* 972?), granted ten hides to his thegn Eadric. S.746 is a charter dated 966 in King Edgar's name which includes the bequest to the New Minster of two hides at *Winterburna*, to which separate vernacular bounds (S.1589) probably applied. S.1217 is a foundation charter for Cerne Abbey established by the layman Æthelmær, which includes in the endowment ten hides at *Winceburnan* (A.D. 987).

The hidage alone of these grants potentially dissociates them from Glaston-bury's charters for Winterbourne.[44] This is only the beginning of the problem, however. If we look in Domesday Book we discover an alarming number of holdings called Winterbourne: at least thirty-five in Dorset and twenty-three in Wiltshire are named.[45] The modern map reveals a lesser, but still impressive, number. Gover *et al.* explained this profusion of Winterbournes by suggesting that the name had once applied to the entire upper part of the River Kennett, as well as to the River Bourne.[46] These two areas, which are both in Wiltshire but separated by twenty to thirty miles, are distinguished by a multiplicity of Winterbournes. In addition, a succession of settlements on the River Winterborne (*sic*) in Dorset, from its source to its junction with the River Stour, took their names from the river.[47] According to Domesday Book, Glastonbury held two of the Wiltshire Winterbournes in 1066: one estate of twenty-five hides at Winterbourne Monkton (on the upper reaches of the Kennett, in the Marlborough Downs, about fifty

44 For the identification of the places granted in S.485, see Forsberg, *A Contribution*, p. 204; for the places granted in S.543, see Grundy, 'The Saxon land charters of Wilt-shire', *Archaeological Journal* 77 (1920), pp. 22–3, Finberg, *The Early Charters of Wessex*, p. 90, and Gover *et al.*, *The Place-names of Wiltshire*, p. xli; for the Winter-bourne of S.668, see Grundy, *op. cit.*, pp. 24–5, and Hart, *The Early Charters of Eastern England*, pp. 253–4; for the Winterbourne of S.746, see Finberg, *The Early Charters of Wessex*, p. 95; for that of S.1217, see Finberg, *ibid.*, p. 174; and for S.1589, Grundy, *op. cit.*, p. 25, and Finberg, *op. cit.*, p. 95. Although Grundy's analyses proved inconclusive, he definitely rejected Birch's identification of the land granted in S.668 and S.1589 with Winterbourne Monkton (*Cartularium Saxonicum*, ed. Birch, III.395 and 468 [nos 1145 and 1192]).
45 For Dorset, see Domesday Book, I, 75rb, 77rb (x2), 78ra, 78rb, 79ra, 79rb (x3), 79va (x5), 79vb, 82ra, 82rb (x2), 83va (x6), 83vb (x2), 84ra, 84rb (x3), 84vb (x3), and 85ra (x2) (Dorset, 1.6, 5.1–2, 11.11, 12.11, 22.1, 26.13, 26.18–19, 26.30–1, 26.33–4, 26.36, 26.48, 36.3, 39.1, 40.4, 55.1, 55.7, 55.9, 55.11–12, 55.17, 55.27–8, 56.6, 56.10, 56.26, 56.28, 56.60, 57.3, 57.6, 57.10, and 58.2). For Wiltshire, see Domesday Book, I, 65rb, 66rb, 66va, 66vb, 68va, 69rb, 69vb (x2), 70rb (x2), 71ra, 72vb, 73rb (x3), 73vb (x2), and 74rb (Wiltshire, 1.17, 5.7, 7.8, 7.15, 16.6, 24.7–10, 24.35, 24.41, 25.24, 26.6, 27.18, 48.1–2, 63.1, 65.1–2, 67.36, 67.39, and 67.95).
46 Gover *et al.*, *The Place-names of Wiltshire*, pp. 309 and 384.
47 C. and F. Thorn have distinguished individual places as much as possible; see *Dorset*, Index of Places 1, *s.n.* River Winterborne, and *Wiltshire*, Index of Places, *s.n.* Winter-bourne. They have commented on the Wiltshire Winterbournes in their 'Note on place name identifications', *Wiltshire*, n.p.

miles northeast of Glastonbury) and one of five hides, which C. and F. Thorn have identified only as lying on the River Bourne, but which post-Conquest evidence seems to locate more specifically at Gomeldon (bordering on the abbey's estate at Idmiston).[48] What remains to be definitely determined is how these holdings related to the pre-Conquest charters which have survived.

S.341 and S.399 are to be found in the fourteenth-century cartularies at the beginning of the section headed *Winterborne*. Because the hidage of S.341 is the same as that of Winterbourne Monkton's assessment in Domesday Book, the two estates have been equated.[49] The bounds ought to help illuminate the question, but Grundy's examination of them was not very enlightening. He noted Birch's identification of the land granted in S.341 as one of the Wiltshire Winterbournes, but suspected rather that it applied to another estate, possibly in a different county, which he could not identify.[50] One relative certainty which emerged from his analysis, however, was that the two charters were not, in his opinion, for the same land. The bounds of S.399 nevertheless proved just as difficult to locate as those of S.341: Birch had suggested somewhere in Dorset, an identification which Grundy rejected, again offering no alternative.[51]

It should be remembered that the bounds might not be contemporary with the grants. Grundy dated the extant copy of S.399 to *ca* A.D. 1250.[52] If they were added after the grant was made, the argument that the charters related to separate estates would rest only on the difference in hidage and on Glastonbury's possession of two Winterbournes in different parts of the county in 1066.

Whether one or two estates were involved in the two charters, it is probable that the twenty-five hides of Æthelred's grant returned to the king not long after they were granted: if the recipient was the Ealdorman Wulfhere who, according to a charter preserved in Winchester's archive (S.362; A.D. 901), forfeited his lands for the crime of desertion, Wulfhere's Winterbourne would have to have been taken from him during King Alfred's reign; if he had turned his estate over to the abbey before his outlawry, however, its possession may have been secure, although it may be more likely that the land would have reverted to the king.[53] If the Winterbourne granted to Wulfhere by King Æthelred (in S.341) does relate to the twenty-five-hide estate held by the abbey in 1066, Glastonbury must have

---

[48] Domesday Book, I, 66va and 66vb (Wiltshire, 7.8 and 7.15 [and note]). Jones, *Domesday for Wiltshire*, p. 242; *A Feodary*, ed. Weaver, p. xxvi; Wiltshire, 7.14–15 (notes); Morland, 'The Glastonbury manors', p. 85. The later parishes of Winterbourne Dauntsey, Winterbourne Gunner, and Winterbourne Earls lie south of Idmiston.

[49] Darlington, 'Introduction to the Wiltshire Domesday', p. 96.

[50] *Cartularium Saxonicum*, ed. Birch, III.42 (no. 886). Grundy, 'The Saxon land charters of Wiltshire', *Archaeological Journal* 77 (1920), p. 23.

[51] *Cartularium Saxonicum*, ed. Birch, II.342 (no. 664); Grundy, 'Saxon charters of Dorset', *Proceedings of the Dorset Natural History and Archaeological Society* 60 (1938), p. 69.

[52] *Ibid.* Kitson, however, apparently accepted the description as contemporary (in his unpublished work on charter-bounds).

[53] See *English Historical Documents*, transl. Whitelock, pp. 541–2 (no. 100). In S.362 there is an account of Wulfhere's forfeiture of land by the River Wylye; Wulfhere's charters are said specifically to be void ('sit proscriptum et nil ultra prevaleant').

acquired (or re-acquired) it by the latter date, but there is no indication of when. As for the second charter (S.399), M.A. Meyer misunderstood the number of hides granted (he assumed twenty-five, not twenty), omitted to consider the second estate named in Domesday Book, and concluded from the existence of two charters for Winterbourne that they granted the same land, which he interpreted as Winterbourne Monkton. He ignored the problem raised by the existence of a previous grant, and he judged that, in the absence of evidence postdating Ælf-flæd's charter, it was likely that she had bequeathed the land to Glastonbury on her death in the mid-tenth century, adding that the 'Monkton' epithet in Domesday Book indicated lengthy monastic ownership.[54] This epithet was not necessarily attached to the land until the early thirteenth century, however.[55] Ælfflæd's charter, for twenty hides, cannot be directly identified with Glastonbury's estate on the River Bourne where the abbey held five hides in 1066, unless a dramatic reduction in hidage had occurred or three-quarters of the land had been lost. According to W.H. Jones this five-hide estate was Gomeldon, attached by the fourteenth century to Idmiston (another abbatial estate, also on the River Bourne);[56] the connexion is established by a *uetusta cedula* (of the bounds of Winterbourne and Idmiston) which was extant in the fifteenth century, listed in MS. 39a among the charters for Idmiston (L33). There are enough Winterbournes, however, for the neat equation – two pre-Conquest charters equals two Domesday estates – to be treated with suspicion. Further study of the bounds (their dates as well as their locations) might help to unravel these tangles.[57]

Winterbourne Monkton (Wiltshire)
See *Winterborne*.

Winterhead (Somerset)
See *Wintreth*.

Wintreth (Somerset)
According to Domesday Book, Glastonbury had held one hide at *Wintreth* in 1066, but the land had been lost by 1086 to the bishop of Coutances.[58] *Wintreth* is mentioned only in the bishop's entries, not in Glastonbury's or among the *Terrae occupatae* or in the lists of lost estates. This seeming omission would be explicable if the land could be found in another entry, and it has indeed been identified with an unnamed hide at Winscombe, held in 1066 by Glastonbury but said to have been lost thereafter to the bishop of Coutances.[59] A place called Winterhead is adjacent to Winscombe, and this land on the edge of the Mendips may be the land in question; no record of a *Wintreth* survives before this first appearance in

---

54 Meyer, 'Women and the tenth century monastic reform', p. 46.
55 Freeman, 'Winterbourne Monkton', p. 192.
56 Jones, *Domesday for Wiltshire*, p. 242.
57 Kitson (in his unpublished work on charter-bounds) has identified S.341 with Winterbourne Monkton, and S.399 with Winterbourne Gunner and Gomeldon.
58 Domesday Book, I, 88ra (Somerset, 5.12).
59 Domesday Book, I, 90ra (Somerset, 8.2 [note]).

Domesday Book, and it is possible that Glastonbury's *Wintreth* had long been part of Winscombe, sharing its history until separated from it between 1066 and 1086.[60] On the other hand, a different place altogether may have been involved.[61]

Witone

According to the corrupt confirmation-charter of William the Conqueror, a document for *Witone* was in the archive of the church of Glastonbury among other pre-Conquest grants.[62] William's charter should not be given undue credit,[63] but it may in this case indicate the existence of an otherwise unrecorded Anglo-Saxon estate. There is also the possibility, however, that the name is simply a corruption of *Wottone*, for North Wootton (*q.v.*).[64]

Woodyates (Dorset)

A charter of King Eadwig for land at *Widingete* was apparently in the *Liber terrarum*, according to the contents-list; the recipient, Brihthere, is said there to have given the land to Glastonbury (S.1753; LT35). No charter of Eadwig is mentioned in the *De antiquitate*, but the gift of *Widangete* to Glastonbury by Brihthere, with Eadwig's consent, is recorded there; in the summary of grants, Eadwig is said to have confirmed the gift.[65] The *Index chartarum*, however, preserves the record of a grant of *Widamgate* by King Edgar to a layman (S.1772; IC D20). No other notice of this grant survives. If it is not a mistake for Eadwig's charter (which does not itself appear in the *Index chartarum*) its existence might indicate that the land was back in the king's gift shortly after Brihthere received it from Eadwig. It is also possible that these charters were similar to S.509 for North Wootton, granted to laymen in the king's name but in actuality the record of temporary alienations of monastic property. If so, there is no record of its first acquisition.

Glastonbury held four hides at *Odiete* in 1066.[66] This was Woodyates, in Dorset, adjacent to the community's estates of Pentridge and Martin (part of Damerham), over fifty miles southeast of Glastonbury.[67] Finberg identified both the Anglo-Saxon grants with this place.[68]

---

[60] See above, *s.n.* Winscombe.

[61] Ekwall (*The Concise Oxford Dictionary of English Place-names*) gave no entry for Winterhead to help establish a connexion between it and *Wintreth*.

[62] *Regesta regum Anglo-Normannorum*, edd. Davis *et al.*, I.71 (no. 273); *De antiquitate*, §75 (ed. & transl. Scott, p. 154); *Cronica*, §83 (edd. & transl. Carley & Townsend, p. 154).

[63] See above, *s.n.* Berrow.

[64] Scott printed 'Wootton' in his English translation: *ibid.*, p. 155.

[65] *De antiquitate*, §§58 and 69 (ed. & transl. Scott, pp. 120 and 144); *Cronica*, §§16 and 67 (edd. & transl. Carley & Townsend, pp. 42 and 126) (no hides given).

[66] Domesday Book, I, 77va (Dorset, 8.4).

[67] The identification is established first by the position of *Odiete* in Domesday Book and secondly by the following sequence of names: *at Wdegeate, besuthan wudigan gæte, Odiete, Wudiete, Widiate* (Ekwall, *The Concise Oxford Dictionary of English Place-names*, p. 532, *s.n.* Woodyates).

[68] Finberg, *The Early Charters of Wessex*, pp. 172 and 173. The second identification carries a question-mark.

Woolavington (Somerset)
Woolavington was a sub-unit of Shapwick assessed at five hides in Domesday Book.[69] The history of Woolavington, on the edge of the Poldens, probably belongs to that of the ancient estate of *Pouelt*, which has been discussed in detail above.

Worstone
A charter in King Æthelstan's name granting land at *Worstone* to *Affe* was in the *Liber terrarum*, according to the contents-list (S.1710; LT54). No other record of this grant survives. *Korstone*, possibly the same place, appears in the *De antiquitate* only among the unreliable list of *alia [maneria] data Glastonie* of §70.[70] The land need not necessarily have come into Glastonbury's hands. It is untraceable in Domesday Book, unless it is *Corstune* (now Corston), between Bath and Keynsham, where the church of Bath held ten hides in 1066; another Corston, held by Malmesbury Abbey in 1066, lay a few miles north of Glastonbury's concentration of estates in northwest Wiltshire.[71] Both of these Corstons are mentioned in pre-Conquest charters from other archives.[72] Although Finberg and Sawyer identified *Worstone* as 'Worston' in Somerset, I have been unable to locate a place of that name in the county.[73] Morland has offered a further suggestion, that *Worstone* might be identified with Rolstone (in Banwell parish).[74]

Wrington (Somerset)
The text of a charter for twenty hides at *Wring'* is extant in the fourteenth-century cartularies (S.371). Dated 904, it records a transaction whereby King Edward the Elder, with Æthelred and Æthelflæd, at the request of Ealdorman Æthelfrith renewed a charter destroyed by fire.[75] According to the charter, Edward granted Wrington to Æthelfrith in perpetual heredity; a postscript adds that *Ethered*'s (a mistake for Æthelfrith's) son, Ealdorman Æthelstan Half-King, gave the land to

[69] Domesday Book, I, 90ra (Somerset, 8.5).
[70] *De antiquitate*, §70 (ed. & transl. Scott, p. 144); see above, pp. 24–6.
[71] Domesday Book, I, 89vb and 67ra (Somerset, 7.13, and Wiltshire, 8.6). A place recorded in Domesday Book with a name of similar form and also held by Glastonbury (*Coristone*: Domesday Book, I, 90va; Somerset, 8.20) has been identified with Croscombe.
[72] For the Somerset Corston, see S.476 (King Edmund to Æthelnoth), S.593 (King Eadwig to Ælfswith), and S.785 (King Edgar to Bath Abbey) (all preserved in the Bath cartulary). For the Wiltshire estate, see S.243 (King Ine to Malmesbury), S.305 (Æthelwulf's Decimation charter for Malmesbury), and S.1038 (a confirmation by King Edward for Malmesbury). The Malmesbury documentation is very doubtful.
[73] Finberg, *The Early Charters of Wessex*, p. 129; Sawyer, *Anglo-Saxon Charters*, p. 461.
[74] Morland, 'The Glastonbury manors', p. 98. He did not begin to explain how a gift of Rolstone by Æthelstan to a thegn and preserved at Glastonbury could have fitted into Banwell's complicated history (see S.373, S.806, and S.1042).
[75] A similar request by the same man is found in a tenth-century single sheet, dated 903, possibly from Christ Church, Canterbury (S.367). On the group of such charters from Edward the Elder's reign, see Stenton, *The Latin Charters*, p. 52; see also Robinson, *The Times of St Dunstan*, pp. 45–6, and Keynes, 'A charter of King Edward the Elder', pp. 307–8.

Glastonbury with the permission of King Æthelstan. This statement is repeated in the contents-list of the *Liber terrarum* (LT41). It was probably this charter which was noted in MS. 39a, although if so the king's name was copied incorrectly: 'Copia carte Eddredi regis de prima donacio manerii cum copiam bunde manerii' (L22).[76] Edward's grant makes no appearance in the *De antiquitate*; instead, we are told there that when Æthelstan became a monk he gave Glastonbury twenty hides at Wrington which King Æthelstan had given him; the summary of grants adds that King Æthelstan confirmed the ealdorman's gift.[77] There may be a hint of another charter for this transaction, from Æthelstan to Æthelstan, once in the *Liber terrarum*: that at least is one interpretation of an obscure reference ('Quedam carta de Wringtone'; LT 132). But there is another transaction involving Wrington mentioned in the *De antiquitate*, which this *carta* may have recorded instead. King Edmund, it is said there, restored Wrington to Glastonbury.[78] The status of this transaction is uncertain and questionable: if King Æthelstan granted the estate to Æthelstan Half-King, who brought it with him to Glastonbury on his retirement there in A.D. 957, a restoration by King Edmund to the abbey in the interval is difficult to explain. Without the text of the charter, its authenticity obviously cannot be judged; perhaps it is the transfer of the land to Glastonbury by Æthelstan Half-King which we should distrust (not to mention King Æthelstan's apparently redundant charter). In any event, Glastonbury still held twenty hides at *Weritone* in 1066.[79]

Wring was the old name of the River Yeo,[80] on which river Wrington is located,

---

[76] *Eddredi* seems to have been written over an erasure (MS. 39a, 42r).

[77] *De antiquitate*, §§54 and 69 (ed. & transl. Scott, pp. 112 and 142); *Cronica*, §§16 and 60 (edd. & transl. Carley & Townsend, pp. 40 and 112). If taken literally, the chronology of events is impossible: Æthelstan Half-King's gift, if made on his retirement to Glastonbury in A.D. 957, could not have been confirmed at that time by King Æthelstan (who died in A.D. 939). Æthelstan Half-King does attest charters as ealdorman in Æthelstan's reign (for example, S.422; A.D. 933). Perhaps an intention to give the land was declared before King Æthelstan's death. See Hart, 'Athelstan "Half King"', especially pp. 125–8. The pre-eminent layman of his time, he retired from Eadwig's court to Glastonbury, where he became a monk, probably in A.D. 957 after the division of the kingdom. (I should like to thank Simon Keynes, who derived this new date from his *Atlas of Attestations in Anglo-Saxon Charters*. See also Keynes, 'The "Dunstan B" charters', p. 191, n. 108.) See above, *s.n.* Brentefordlond, Foxcote, Lim, Mells, and Westone for other grants associated with Æthelstan Half-King. He is said – in the contents-list of the *Liber terrarum*, the fourteenth-century cartularies, or the (even less reliable) *De antiquitate* – to have granted all these (except *Brentefordlond*) to Glastonbury; it is not always possible to support this conclusion, which could have been drawn simply from the presence of his title-deeds in the archive. Only *Lim*, *Mells*, and *Wrington* were in the abbey's hands in 1066.

[78] *De antiquitate*, §§55 and 69 (ed. & transl. Scott, pp. 114 and 142); *Cronica*, §§16 and 64 (edd. & transl. Carley & Townsend, pp. 40 and 120). The summary chapters state that the gift was of twenty hides, but the main entries give the figure as twenty-one hides.

[79] Domesday Book, I, 90vb (Somerset, 8.27).

[80] Ekwall, *The Concise Oxford Dictionary of English Place-names*, p. 539, *s.n.* Wrington; the identification of Wrington is established by Ekwall from the following sequence of forms: *at Wring'*, *Weritone*, *Wringetone*.

about twenty miles north of Glastonbury. Grundy judged the bounds attached to S.371 to have included all of the later parishes of Wrington and Burrington.[81] He found no indications of a pre-Conquest original in the boundary-description, however, and the date of Burrington's attachment to Wrington is therefore uncertain. Its non-appearance by name in Domesday Book might suggest that its inclusion in Wrington's twenty hides was already established in 1066, and therefore, by implication, at the time of the extant charters (unless the hidage remained unaltered despite the addition of land). Some post-Conquest threat to Burrington may be hinted at by its confirmation to Glastonbury in the charter of William the Conqueror quoted in the *De antiquitate*; Wrington itself is not mentioned in that (corrupt) text.[82]

Wydancumbe

According to the contents-list of the *Liber terrarum*, King Eadwig granted *Wydancumbe* to a layman, Æthelric (S.1751; LT78). No other documentary record of this transaction exists; in the *De antiquitate*, however, it is said that *Ezericus* gave Glastonbury six hides at *Widecumbe*, with Eadwig's assent.[83] If Æthelric or his heirs did pass the land on to the monks, they do not appear to have held it securely (unless it was absorbed into an estate with a different name). I have found it nowhere else in Glastonbury's pre-Conquest record, nor in Domesday Book. It is possibly to be identified with Widcombe, now a suburb of Bath.[84]

Yarlington (Somerset)

An entry on the contents-list of the *Liber terrarum* records a grant of *Gyrdlingatone* by King Edmund to Wulfric, probably Dunstan's brother (S.1731; LT66).[1] The contents-list specifies that Wulfric afterwards gave the land to Glastonbury. No other documentary record of this transaction survives, but in the *De antiquitate* a gift of ten hides at *Girdlingetone* by 'Wilfrid' is mentioned (as is Edmund's consent to the gift).[2] Many (but not all) of the estates granted to Wulfric did indeed make their way into Glastonbury's endowment, both directly and indirectly.[3] If Wulfric did transfer the land to Glastonbury, the monks no longer held it

---

81 Grundy, *The Saxon Charters*, pp. 171–8.
82 *De antiquitate*, §75 (ed. & transl. Scott, p. 154); *Cronica*, §83 (edd. & transl. Carley & Townsend, p. 154). See above, *s.n.* Berrow.
83 *De antiquitate*, §§58 and 69 (ed. & transl. Scott, pp. 120 and 144); *Cronica*, §§16 and 67 (edd. & transl. Carley & Townsend, pp. 42 and 126).
84 A suggestion by Watkin, cited by Carley in the *Cronica* (edd. & transl. Carley & Townsend, p. 292 [n. 282]); see also Ekwall, *The Concise Oxford Dictionary of English Place-names*, p. 517, *s.n.* Widcombe, where only the post-Domesday forms *Widecume* and *Widecumbe* are cited.
1 On Wulfric, see Brooks, 'The career', pp. 8–11, and Hart, *The Early Charters of Northern England*, pp. 371–2; for details of Wulfric's extensive holdings, see above, *s.n.* Grittleton.
2 *De antiquitate*, §§55 and 69 (ed. & transl. Scott, pp. 114 and 142); *Cronica*, §§16 and 64 (edd. & transl. Carley & Townsend, pp. 40 and 122).
3 See above, *s.n.* Grittleton, Horton, Idmiston, *Kyngton*, Nettleton, Merton, Tintinhull, and Turnworth.

in 1066, when seven hides at *Gerlintune* were in lay hands;[4] according to Morland, the neighbouring holding at Woolston made up the remaining hides.[5] Yarlington and Woolston are near Wincanton (and Glastonbury's estates of Blackford, Holton, and Lattiford), about fifteen miles southeast of Glastonbury.

Neil Stacy has proposed that Yarlington was a member of Ditcheat; seven (unnamed) hides of the same value as Yarlington's were held at Ditcheat by a thegn in 1066 and by the count of Mortain in 1086.[6] Stacy did not discuss how (or when) Yarlington might have been incorporated into Ditcheat's thirty hides without changing the latter's assessment, nor how its history related to that estate.[7]

Yeovilton (Somerset)

A charter listed in the *Index chartarum* recorded a grant by King Edward the Elder of *Giffeltone* to a layman (S.1708; IC D8). No other reference to this grant appears in any of the abbey's sources. A second charter for *Gilfeltone* (sic), this time in the name of King Eadwig for the layman Brihtric, was apparently in the *Liber terrarum*: it is said on the contents-list that Brihtric gave the land to Glastonbury with his body (S.1754; LT118). No other documentary record of this charter survives, but Brihtric's bequest is mentioned – and seemingly quoted from – in the *De antiquitate*, where the grant is said to have been of five hides and made with the king's consent; the summary adds that Eadwig confirmed the gift.[8] Glastonbury did not hold Yeovilton in 1066, however; Domesday Book records eight hides there in lay hands.[9]

The charter of King Edward may have been held by Brihtric as a title-deed for Yeovilton. Morland, however, has suggested that in the reference in the *Index chartarum* Edward had been confused with Eadwig, and that the two charters cited in the *Index* and the *Liber terrarum* contents-list were actually one (Eadwig's).[10] In view of the apparent survival at Glastonbury of Brihtric's title-deeds for Camel and Henstridge, this explanation may be unnecessary. Brihtric's transfer of the estate to Glastonbury is not necessarily certain; the reliability of the testimony of the contents-list is a matter of opinion. Unfortunately, the evidence that Glastonbury ever held the land at Camel (not far from Yeovilton) and Henstridge, whose charters were also in the archive, is as inconclusive as it is for Yeovilton.[11] A document from Winchester (S.1512) may throw some light on the

---

4 Domesday Book, I, 92va–b (Somerset, 19.54–5).

5 Morland, 'Some Domesday manors', p. 41, and 'The Glastonbury manors', p. 98. Woolston, however, is assessed at three hides and one and a half virgates; so the correspondence is not exact.

6 Stacy, 'The estates', p. 31; Domesday Book, I, 90vb (Somerset, 8.30).

7 Morland has preferred to identify Ditcheat's lost hides with Stone. See above, *s.n.* Ditcheat.

8 *De antiquitate*, §§58 and 69 (ed. & transl. Scott, pp. 120 and 144); *Cronica*, §§16 and 67 (edd. & transl. Carley & Townsend, pp. 42 and 126). As in the cases referred to elsewhere – at Clutton and Westbury, for example – the quotation may be from an endorsement on the king's charter.

9 Domesday Book, I, 96rb (Somerset, 26.3). No TRE holder is explicitly identified.

10 Morland, 'The Glastonbury manors', p. 99.

11 See above, *s.n.* Camel and Henstridge.

question: a bequest by Brihtric to the Old Minster was copied into the *Codex Wintoniensis* after the text of a grant which he received from King Eadred (S.571).[12] There Brihtric announced his intention to give the land concerned (Rimpton) to the Old Minster at his death; in the meantime he gave his charter (and an earlier grant of the estate by King Æthelstan) to the community. He may have wished similarly to grant Yeovilton to Glastonbury and consequently deposited his two charters there to record his intention. If Brihtric's wish was fulfilled, Glastonbury lost the land before 1066; it is possible, however, that his intention was not realised, and that this one (or all three) of the estates recorded in Glastonbury's archive was never received by the abbey.

Yeovilton is between Ilchester and Glastonbury's estate at Podimore Milton, fewer than fifteen miles southeast of the abbey.

---

12 *Anglo-Saxon Wills*, ed. & transl. Whitelock, pp. 18 and 117–18 (no. 7). The document is dated A.D. 964x980. It was said to have been witnessed by the two Winchester communities and that of Glastonbury.

THE ENDOWMENT: SUMMARY-LIST OF SOURCES

The following is a summary-list of primary sources consulted and references cited in the preceding survey and analysis of Glastonbury's estates. The abbreviations and symbols used are listed below in the order in which they occur in the summaries. For details of the sources used, see above, pp. 10–41. A fully comprehensive list, including all references potentially relating to each place, would have been even more unwieldy than the summary provided. What follows is intended primarily as a guide to those sources where the place-name is found. For the fuller picture, the reader must consult the estate-histories themselves.

B   Berkshire

D   Devon

Do   Dorset

G   Gloucestershire

H   Hampshire

So   Somerset

S   Surrey

W   Wiltshire

S.   number in Sawyer's *Anglo-Saxon Charters*

GC   number in the Great Cartulary (Longleat House, Marquess of Bath, MS. 39; document number [of additional material] in Watkin's edition)

LT   number in the *Liber terrarum* (according to the contents-list)

IC   number in the *Index chartarum*

L   number in Longleat House, Marquess of Bath, MS. 39a

DB   reference in Domesday Book (to county volumes, gen. ed. J. Morris)

DA   *De antiquitate Glastonie ecclesie* (§ number in Scott's edition)

JG   John of Glastonbury's *Cronica siue antiquitates Glastoniensis ecclesie* (§ number in Carley's edition)

Historiola   *Historiola de primordiis episcopatus Somersetensis*, in *Ecclesiastical Documents*, ed. Hunter

*   not from Glastonbury's archive/not among Glastonbury's entries in Domesday Book for lands held TRE

^   a sub-unit in Domesday Book

Abbotsbury (Do) (LT99; *DB 13.1; DA §§55, 69; JG §§16, 64)

Aldamtone (Alhampton in Ditcheat?) (So) (IC D1; ^DB 8.30; DA §70)

Andersey (Nyland, in Glastonbury) (So) (S.250, 783; LT111; ^DB 8.1; DA §§36, 42, 60, 62, 69x2, 72, 73; JG §§2, 3, 16x2, 42, 49, 71, 73, 88, 95)

Ashbury (B) (S.288, 524, *1179; LT107, 108; IC A13; L45; DB 8.1; DA §§62, 69, as *Esseburi*; JG §§16x2, 73)

Ashcott (in Walton) (So) (^DB 8.11 and 8.14; JG §88)

Aust Cliff (G) (*S.77, *137, *401; GC, I, 205; IC C13; *DB 3.1; DA §§63, 69; JG §§16, 74)

Axe (1 h. + fishing rights) (So) (DA §§40, 69; JG §§16, 48)

Badbury (W) (GC, I, 203; S.568; DB 7.6; LT67; L43–4; DA §§57, 69; JG §§16, 66)

Baltonsborough (So) (S.1410; LT17; IC A19; L7; DB 8.22; DA §§46, 69; JG §§16, 52)

Batcombe (So) (S.462, *1485; LT106; DB 8.24; DA §§55, 62, 69x2, 72, 73; JG §§16x2, 64, 73)

Beckery (So) (S.250, 783; DA §§12, 36, 42, 60, 69, 73; JG §§16, 28, 42, 49, 71, 95)

Berrow (So) (S.793; IC D21; L21; DA §75; JG §83)

Binegar (So) (*S.1042; LT93; DA §§53, 69; JG §§16, 56)

Blackford (So) (LT53, LT81; IC C7; DB 8.9, *36.8; DA §§58, 62, 69x2, 75, 79; JG §§16x2, 67, 73, 83, 87)

Bleadney (So) (S.1253, 250, *1042; LT11; IC A18; L3; DA §§40, 42, 69, 72; JG §§3, 16, 47, 49)

Bodesleghe (So) (DB 8.12)

Bradley (LT22, 94; DA §§46, 69; JG §§16, 52)

Brannocmynstre (Braunton?) (D) (S.303, 791; LT19; *DB 1.5, *13a.3; DA §§53 x2, 69x2; JG §§16x2, 56, 57)

Brent (So) (S.238, 250; LT20; IC A4; L19; DB 8.33; DA §§32, 34, 39, 42x2, 69x2; JG §§14, 16x2, 33, 45, 49x2, 93)

Brentefordlond (Brampford Speke?) (D) (S.498; IC D15; L20; *DB 3.67, *16.123, *16.129, *24.2; DA §70)

Bristol (So) (MS. R.5.33, 81v)

Brompton (Ralph) (So) (LT16; DB 25.7; DA §§44, ?52, 69; JG §§16, 52)

Brunham (DA §52)

Buckland Denham (So) (S.555; LT116; L27; *DB 47.19)

Buckland Newton (Do) (S.303, 474, 742; LT50; L26, 28; DB 8.3; DA §§53, 55, 69x2; JG §§16x2, 56, 64)

Burrington (So) (DA §75; JG §83)

Butleigh (So) (S.250, 270a, 783; LT38; L6; DB 8.12?, 8.18, 8.19, 8.40; DA §§42, 52, 60, 69, 73; JG §§4, 16, 49, 55, 71, 95)

Byrhtulfingtun becocer (LT125; DA §70)

Camel (So) (*S.884; LT59–60, 119; *DB 1.22, 9.7; DA §70)

Camerton (So) (LT121–2; *DB 8.31; DA §§57, 69; JG §§16, 66, 88)

Cantucuudu / Caric / Crycbeorh (So) (S.237, *345; LT8; L47; DB 8.28, *1.18; DA §§37, 69; JG §§16, 43)

Catcott (in Shapwick) (So) (^DB 8.5)

Cecce (DA §69)

Cedern (DA §§48, 69; JG §§16, 54)

Ceollamwirthe (Chelworth/Chelwood) (W/So) (LT45; ?*S.356, ?*1205, ?*1797, ?*1485, ?*1038, ?*1579; ?*DBW 68.30, ?*8.7; ?DBSo *17.5, *?34.1; DA §70)

Cerawycombe = *Scearamtone*? (S.303, *373, *806; ?*DBSo 19.7; ??DA §§ 53, 69; JG §§16, 56)

Cetenesfelda (*Occenefeld*?) (S.303; ?DA §§ 53, 69; JG §§16, 56)

Charlton (in Doulting) (So) (^DB 8.23)

Chilton (Polden) (in Shapwick) (So) (^DB 8.5)

Christian Malford (W) (S.466; IC A10; L40; DB 7.4, 7.5; DA §§55, 69; JG §§16, 64)

Clatworthy (So) (DB 25.8)

Cleeve (So) (LT70; *DB 1.13; DA §§62, 69; JG §§16, 73)

Clewer (So) (LT10; IC A17, A20; L47a; *DB 5.19; DA §§40, 69; JG §§16, 47)

Clutton (So) (LT40; IC D12; *DB 5.14; DA §§53, 69; JG §§16, 56)

Compton Beauchamp (B) (*S.564; LT109; *DB 22.11)

Compton Dundon (in Walton) (So) (GC, I, 202; LT39; IC A8; L5; ^DB 8.11, ?8.13; DA §§48, 54, ?62, ?69x2, 79; JG §§16, 54, ?73, 87)

Cossington (So) (S.253 [boundary]; DB 8.7)

Cranmore (So) (LT69; DB 8.32; DA §§58, 62, 69x2, 79; JG §§16x2, 67, 73, 87)

Croscombe (in Pilton) (So) (?S.247–8; ^DB 8.20; DA §40; JG §47)

Culum (D) (S.303, ?*386; LT24, 26; IC D2; ?*DB 2.12, ?*23.9; DA §§48, ?53, 69 (x2?); JG §§16, 54)

Cumbe iuxta Culum (D) (LT25, ?126; *DB 36.18; DA §§48, 69; JG §§16, 54)

Cympanhamme (IC D14; DA §70)

Cynemersforda (IC D3; DA §70)

Damerham (W/H) (S.513, *1494, *1515; LT37; IC A9; DBW 7.1, *11.2; DA §§55, 69; JG §§16, 64, 88)

Deuerel (W) (?*S.766; LT51, LT52; L46; DB 7.3, 7.16, *17.1, *19.1, *24.18, *48.8; DA §§54x2, 69x2; JG §§16x2, 60x2)

Dinnington (So) (DB 8.36)

Ditcheat (So) (S.292; LT91; L13; DB 8.30; DA §§53, 69; JG §§16, 56, 95)

Doulting (So) (?S.247–8, 250; LT32; IC A5; L9; DB 8.23; DA §§40, 42, 53, 57, 69x3; JG §§16x2, 47, 49, 56)

Draycott (So) (DB 8.39, 19.12; DA §72)

Dulwich (S) (S.747; ?LT113; IC B7; DA §70)

Dundon (So) (DB 8.13; DA §§62, 69; JG §§16, 73)

Duneafd (= Downhead, So?) (DB 8.35; DA §§53, 69; JG §§16, 56)

Durborough (So) (LT71; DB 8.8; DA §§62, 69; JG, §§16, 73)

Easetenetone (LT130; DA §70)

Eatumberesder (IC D13; DA §70)

Edington (in Shapwick) (So) (^DB 8.5)

Edingworth (*Iodenwrthe*) (So) (DB 8.34)

Elborough (So) (LT31; IC D4; DB *5.11, 8.38; DA §§48, 57, 69x2; JG §§16x2, 54, 66)

Elosaneg (LT4; DA §70)

Escford (LT58; DA §§40, 55, 69; JG §§16, 47, 64)

Estun (*DBSo 5.34; DA §§63, 69; JG §§16, 75)

Eswirht (= *Inesuuyrth*?) (DA §§48, 69; JG §§16, 55)

Fiswere (IC A16; DA §§63, 69; JG §§16, 75)

Foxcote (So?) (LT55; *DB 5.42; DA §§54, 69; JG §§ 16, 60)

Fulebroc (DA §75; JG §83)

Gassig (*Iecesig*) (LT22, LT94; DA §§46, 69; JG §§16, 52)

Glastonbury (So) (LT1; DB 8.1; DA §37; JG §43)

Godney (So) (S.250, 783, ?227; DA §§36, 42, 60, 69, 73; JG §§4, 16, 42, 49, 71, 95)

Greinton (in Walton) (So) (DB ^8.15; DA §42)

Grittleton (W) (S.472; LT43; L36; DB 7.10; DA §§55, 62, 69; JG §§16, 64, 73)

Ham (So) (S.791; LT83; L15, 16; DB 8.17; DA §§62, 69; JG §§16, 73)

Hamanstane (LT134; IC D9)

Hannington (*Hammedone*) (W) (LT73, 74; IC C14; DB 7.2; DA §§55, 62, 63, 69x3; JG §§16x3, 64, 73, 75)

Henstridge (So) (LT95–7; *S.570; *DB 1.25, *14.1, *18.4; DA §70)

Hetsecome (So) (DB 8.38, 5.3)

Holton (So) (*S.1538; LT80; *DB 45.4; DA §§62, 69; JG §§16, 73)

Hornblotton (in Ditcheat) (So) (LT92; ^DB 8.30; DA §§53, 69; JG §§16, 56)

Horton (LT46–7; *DBG 46.2, DBDo *14.1; DA §§57, 69; JG §§16, 66)

Houndsborough (So) (?*DB 19.81; DA §§48, 69; JG §§16, 54)

Hunespulle = Huntspill (So) ? (LT28; *DB 24.28, *24.34; DA §§48, 69; JG §§16, 55)

Hutton (So) (DB 8.38)

Idmiston (W) (S.530, 541, 775; LT103–5; IC B3; L31–3; DB 7.14; DA §§62, 69; JG §§16, 73)

Iecesig (*Gassic* / *Sceacesceg*?) (LT22, LT94; DA §§46, 69; JG §§16, 52)

Ilchester (St Andrew's) (So) (DB 8.37, 15.1)

Inesuuyrth (LT28; DA §§48, 69; JG §§16, 55)

Kingstone (So) (DB 19.10; DA §§55, 69; JG §§16, 64)

Kington (W) (S.426, 866; LT85; IC B2; L37, 38; DB ?7.11, 41.8; DA §§55x2, 69x2?; JG §§16, 64x2?)

Korston = *Worston*?

Kulmeton (*Historiola*, p. 19; ?*DBSo 37.7)

Lamyatt (in Ditcheat) (So) (LT88; ^DB 8.30; DA §70)

Langford (W) (S.580, *612, *1811; LT61, 62; IC D11, D16; DB 7.12, 7.13, *13.13, 24.42; DA §§55, 69; JG §§16, 64)

Langley (W) (S.473; LT85; L39; DB 7.11, ?*24.31)

Lattiford (in Butleigh) (*Lodreford*) (So) (DB ^8.19)

Leigh-in-Street (*Lantokay*) (So) (S.1249, 250, 783; LT5, 6; IC A3; L1; DB 8.16?; DA §§38, 42, 69; JG §§16, 43, 49)

Linig (DA §§40, 69; JG §16)

Lennucmere (IC D5; DA §70)

Lim (D&Do) (S.442, 644; LT42; IC B9; L23, 24; DBD 4.1, DBDo 8.6, *DBDo 57.14, *2.5 ; DA §§54, 69, 75, 79; JG §§16, 60, 83, 87, 106)

Litlenye (S.1253)

Littleton Drew (W) (IC D10; L36; DB 5.6, 7.5; ?DA §70)

Lodegaresberghe (Montacute) (So) (S.303; LT33; *DB 19.86; DA §§32, 38, 53, 69x2; JG §§16x2, 43, 56, 82)

Lottisham (So) (S.1410, 292; LT91; L13; DA §§53, 69; JG §§16, 56)

Luccombe (So) (LT72; *DB 32.2, 38.1; DA §§62, 69; JG §§16, 73)

Lutramtone (= Littleton Drew)

Lydford (So) (S.1410; DB 8.4, *47.21)

Lydney (G) (*S.786; LT87; *DB 1.55, *32.11; DA §70)

Lyme Regis (Do) (=*Lim*)

Malmesbury (W) (DB M.4)

Marchey (St Martin's church) (So) (S.1253, 250, 783; DA §§36, 42, 60, 69, 72, 73; JG §§16, 42, 49, 71, 95)

Marksbury (So) (S.431; GC, I, 202; LT128; IC B5; L23; DB 8.29; DA §§54, 62, 69x2; JG §§16x2, 60, 73)

Martin (W/H) (S.513; LT37; IC A9; ?IC B1; L29, ?30; ?*DBW 7.1, *67.83, *68.10, *68.13; DA §§55, 69; JG §64)

Meare (So) (S.227, 250, 1249, 783; LT3; IC A3; L1, 4; ^DB 8.1; DA §§13, 33, 36, 42, 60, 69, 72, 73; JG §§16, 42, 49, 71, 95)

Mells (So) (S.481; LT101; IC B12; L10; DB 8.25; DA §§55, 69, 79; JG §§16, 64, 87, 88)

Mendip (land at foot of) (So) (IC A6)

Merton (S) (S.551, 747; LT112–13; ?IC B1, B7; L29, ?30; *DB 1.5)

Middeltone (So) (S.743; LT82; L14; DB 8.3; DA §§62, 69, 75; JG §§16, 73, 83)

Mildenhall (W) (*S.1263; LT84; DB 7.7; DA §§62, 69; JG §§16, 73)

Millescote (So) (DB 5.50, ?8.25)

Monk Okehampton (D) (S.303, *Birch 1245; LT23; ?*DB 16.3, ?*16.17; DA §§53, 69, 70; JG §§16, 56)

Monkton (Over) Deverill (W) (see *Deuerel*)

Moorlinch (So) (S.250, 783; DA §§42, 60; JG §§49, 71, 88, 95)

Nettleton (W) (S.504, 625; LT44; IC A15; L34, 35; DB 7.9; DA §§55, 62, 69; JG §§16, 64, 73)

Newetone Kastel (see Sturminster Newton)

North Wootton (So) (S.509; LT?27, 64, 131; IC A11; L8; ^DB 8.20; DA §§48, 55, 69x2, 72, ?75; JG §§16x2, 54, 64)

Nunney (So) (LT32; *DB 25.54; DA §§57, 69; JG §§16, 66)

Nyland (see *Andersey*)

Ocmund (see Monk Okehampton)

Occenefeld (= *Cetenesfelda*?)

Okeford Fitzpaine (Do) (?*S.764; LT49; IC A12; DB 8.2, ?*1.7, ?*54.6, ?*26.4; DA §§55, 69; JG §§16, 64)

Ora (?*S.391; LT12; ?DBH *11.1; DA §§40, 69; JG §§16, 48)

Orchardleigh (So) (LT117; *DB 5.52; DA §§62, 69, 70; JG §§16, 73)

Othery (So) (?IC B6; ?L18)

Ottery St Mary (D) (S.721, *1033; IC B6; ?L18; *DB 10.1)

Overleigh (So) (DB 8.16)

Ower (H) (DB 11.1)

Panborough (So) (S.626, 783; LT76; IC A14; L2; ^DB 8.1; DA §§58, 60, 69, 73; JG §§4, 16, 67, 71, 95)

Parrett (fishing rights) (So) (LT13; IC A2; DA §§38, 69; JG §§16, 43)

Peasucmere (LT77; DA §70)

Pedrithe (= Parrett)

Pedwell (in Walton) (So) (^DB 8.11; JG §88)
Pendescliue (LT110; IC D18; DA §70)
Pennard (West) (So) (S.236, 250, 303; LT7; IC A1, ?B8; L11, ?12; DA §§38, 42, 53, 69x2, 73; JG §§4, 16x2, 43, 49, 56)
Pennard (East = Pennardminster) (So) (S.563; LT68; IC ?B8, D17; ?L12; DB 8.21; DA §69; JG §16)
Pentridge (Do) (S.513; LT37; IC A9; DB 8.5; DA §§55, 69; JG §§16, 64)
Pidelan (LT124; ?DBDo *3.15, *3.16, *9.1, *12.5, *13.2, *26.20, *26.21, *26.22, *19.14, *48.1, *55.16, *56.48; DA §70)
Pilsdon (Do) (IC D6; *DB 56.46; DA §70)
Pilton (So) (S.247, 248, 250; LT9; DB 8.20; DA §§40, 42x3, 69, 72, 73; JG §§3, 4, 16, 47, 49x3, 93, 95)
Plush (Do) (S.347, 474; IC B11; L26, 28; DA §§55, 69; JG §§16, 64)
Podimore Milton (see *Middeltone*)
Portbury (So) (IC D7, D22; *DB 5.33; DA §70)
Pouelt (So) (S.248, 250, 251 [boundary], 253; LT15, 63; DA §§40, 42x2, 44, 47, 69x3, 72, 73; JG §§16x3, 47, 49x2, 52, 53)
Poweldune (So) (DA §§69, 72, 73; JG §§16, 34)
Pucklechurch (G) (S.553; GC, I, 205; LT98, 100; IC C6, C11; DB 8.1, ?*6.5, ?*42.3; DA §§55, 57, 63, 69x2, 79; JG §§16x2, 64, 74, 87, 88)
Puriton (So) (S.303; *DB 11.1; DA §§53, 69; JG §§16, 56)
Pylle (in Pilton) (So) (^DB 8.20)
Quantock Wood (land near) (So) (see *Cantucuudu*)
Raddington (So) (S.347; *DB 22.13)
Rowberrow (So) (LT65; DA §70)
St Andrew's church, Ilchester (see Ilchester)
Scearamtone (= *Cerawycombe*?) (S.303; DA §§53, 69; JG §§16, 56)
Scobbanwirht (*uel Sabewrtha*) (So) (S.292 [boundary], 1410; DB *47.22?; DA §§46, 69; JG §§16, 52)
Seacesceg (= *Iecesig*?) (LT22)
Sethebeorge (IC C12; DA §§63, 69; JG §§16, 74)
Shapwick (So) (S.250, 253, 783; DB 8.5; DA §§42, 60; JG §§49, 71, 95)
Sharpham (So) (LT123; DA §§72, 73; JG, §§3, 4)
Shepton Mallet (in Pilton) (So) (?S.247–8; ^DB 8.20)
Sowy (So) (S.250, 251, 303; LT14; IC A7; L17; DB 8.6; DA §§40, 42x2, 53, 60, 69x2, 79; JG §§16, 47, 49x2, 56, 71, 87, 95)
Stane (So) (LT56; IC C3; DB 8.39; DA §§55, 69; JG §§16, 64)
Stawell (So) (?LT120; IC C5; DB 8.10; DA §§57, 69; JG §§16, 66)
Stoke (So) (LT36, LT79; DB 8.39x2; DA §§54, 69, 72x2; JG §§16, 60)
Stourton (W) (LT129: *DB 36.2; DA §§58, 69; JG §§16, 67)
Street (So) (S.250, 783; DA §§42, 60; JG §§49, 71, 95)
Streton (So) (LT111; DB 5.43, 8.38; DA §§62, 69; JG §§16, 73)
Sturminster Newton (*Newetone Kastel*) (Do) (S.764; GC, I, 205; IC C8; L25, ?25a; DB 8.1; DA §§62, 64, 69x2; JG §§16x2, 73, 77)
Sutton (Mallet) (in Shapwick) (So) (^DB 8.5)
Tarnock (So) (*S.1042; LT120; IC C5; *DB 24.12–13; DA §§57, 69; JG §§16, 66)
Tintinhull (So) (LT34; DB 8.31, 19.9; DA §§55, 62, 69; JG §§16, 64, 73, 82)

Tone (20 h. on R.) (So) (S.248; DA §§40, 69; JG §§16, 47)

Torridge (land on R.) (D) (GC, I, 201; LT29–30; DA §§44, 52, 69x2; JG §§16x2, 52, 55)

Turnworth (Do) (LT48; *DB 45.1; DA §§55, 69; JG §§16, 64)

Twynam (Christchurch) (H) (*S.391; LT75; IC C4; *DB 1.28, *17.1; DA §§57, 69; JG §§16, 66)

Ubley (*Hubbanleghe*) (So) (IC D19; *DB 42.2; DA §70)

Uffculme (D) (see also *Culum*) (?S.303; IC C15; GC, I, 172; *DB 23.9; DA §§53, 69; JG §§16, 56, 88)

Unidentified 5 hides #1 (So) (DB 8.41)

Unidentified 5 hides #2 (LT27)

Upavon (W) (LT127; *DB 1.23g; DA §70)

Uplyme (D) (= *Lim*)

Ure (LT18; DA §§46, 69; JG §§16, 52)

Walton (So) (DB 8.11)

Wedmore (So) (S.*1042, *1115, *1507; IC C1, C2; DB *1.2, *6.15; DA §§40, 69; JG §§16, 47)

Westbury (?*S.1042; LT89–90; *DBG 1.11, *DBG 3.1, *DBSo 6.11, *DBW 1.16; DA §§62, 69; JG §§16, 73)

Westcombe (in Batcombe) (So) (^DB 8.24)

Westhay (So) (?S.227; JG §§16, 42)

West Monkton (So) (see *Cantucuudu*)

Westone (LT55; DA §§54, 69; JG §§16, 60)

Westwere (with fishing rights on Parrett) (So) (DA §69; JG §16)

Whatley (So) (LT57; DB 8.26; DA §§55, 69; JG §§16, 64)

Wheathill (So) (LT86; DB 37.9; DA §§62, 69; JG §§16, 73)

Wilton (*predium* there) (W) (LT133; IC C10; DA §§63, 69; JG §§16, 74, 87)

Winchester (H) (*curtis* in) (S.871)

Winscombe (So) (LT114; IC C9; DB 8.2, ?5.12; DA §§62, 69; JG §§16, 73)

Winterborne (S.341, 399, ?*485, ?*543, ?*668, ?*746, ?*1217, ?*1589; LT102, 115; IC B4, B10; L41, 42; DBW 7.8, 7.15; DA §§53, 54, 69; JG §§16, 60) (see Winterbourne entry in chapter III for further possibilities in Domesday Book)

Winterhead (= *Wintreth*) (So) (DB 5.12)

Witone (DA §75; JG §83)

Woodyates (Do) (LT35; IC D20; DB 8.4; DA §§58, 69; JG §§16, 67)

Woolavington (in Shapwick) (So) (^DB 8.5)

Worstone (LT54; DA §70)

Wrington (So) (S.371; LT41, 132; L22; DB 8.27; DA §§54, 55, 69x2; JG §§16x2, 60, 64)

Wydancumbe (LT78; DA §§58, 69; JG §§16, 67)

Yarlington (So) (LT66; *DB 19.54; DA §§55, 69; JG §§16, 64)

Yeovilton (So) (LT118; IC D8; *DB 26.3; DA §§58, 69; JG §§16, 67)

IV

ESTATE-MANAGEMENT, TENURE, AND
THE EVIDENCE OF DOMESDAY BOOK

The preceding survey concentrates on the component parts of the abbey's endowment, its estates, to the extent that their histories can be documented from the
surviving record. The diplomas (with some ambiguity) name donor, recipient, and
estate, giving details of hidage and, sometimes, a description of boundaries; but
they offer very little indeed on the subject of how the land was exploited and
administered, and as a result the ways in which the parts of the church's endowment were linked to the centre remain obscure. The estate-histories above therefore have been largely concerned with the apparent movement of property in and
out of Glastonbury's hands, rather than on habits of land-management or conditions of tenure. On these subjects there is a dearth of information which pertains
not just at Glastonbury but largely throughout the country.

THE PROBLEM OF MANAGEMENT

We know very little about the administration of estates in Anglo-Saxon England,
and most of what we know is very late in date. Some of the practicalities of life on
a great estate are illustrated in two principal texts: the *Rectitudines singularum
personarum*, an account of agrarian conditions probably from the reign of Edward
the Confessor, and the contemporary text known as *Gerefa*, a description of the
duties of a reeve.[1] A few late and fragmentary surveys from religious houses offer
additional material.[2] We can probably assume that in many ways great ecclesiastical and secular estates resembled one another. A system of estate-management
had to be established which would ensure that the estates ran smoothly, that the

---

[1] *Die Gesetze*, ed. Liebermann, I.444–55; *English Historical Documents*, transl. Douglas
& Greenaway, pp. 875–9 (no. 172) (*Rectitudines* only). See also Maitland, *Domesday
Book and Beyond*, pp. 327–30; Loyn, *Anglo-Saxon England and the Norman Conquest*,
pp. 196–202; and Harvey, 'Rectitudines'.

[2] Examples include the survey of Tidenham (Gloucestershire), which was leased by the
abbot of Bath to Archbishop Stigand A.D. 1061x1065 (S.1555; *Anglo-Saxon Charters*,
ed. & transl. Robertson, pp. 204–7 [no. 109]; also in *English Historical Documents*,
transl. Douglas & Greenaway, pp. 879–80 [no. 174]). A record of the services and dues
rendered at the bishop of Winchester's estate of Hurstbourne Priors, Hampshire, also
survives (attached to S.359; *Anglo-Saxon Charters*, ed. & transl. Robertson, pp. 206–7

abbot-landlord's interests were served – his rents and services rendered – without requiring the constant direct intervention of the abbot himself. There is little surviving information which can illuminate the everyday, secular side of an Anglo-Saxon monastery before the tenth (or indeed eleventh) century,[3] but it appears that, at least after the Benedictine reform, direct participation by monks in the exploitation of their estates was officially frowned upon. The proem of the *Regularis Concordia* states that the brethren should not visit the properties of the monastery unless either great necessity or reasonable discretion required it.[4] In B's Life of St Dunstan, which may have been written by a cleric who had actually been resident at Glastonbury in the mid-tenth century, we hear of Dunstan's brother, Wulfric, whom Dunstan had appointed with full authority to see to the outside business of his *uillae*, in order to ensure that neither Dunstan himself nor any monk should have to go out and concern himself with such worldly affairs.[5] This essential need to devolve responsibility (admittedly not unique to ecclesiastical estates) led to a number of different solutions, including the development of a network of estate-officials and the creation of leases and other subtenancies. Glastonbury's pre-Conquest charters are almost silent on this subject: not until 1066 and Domesday Book's testimony do we have enough information to begin to discern strategies of management and tenurial arrangements. That we then find priests and monks as tenants should alert us to the difference between ideology and reality (not to mention the difference between A.D. 970 and 1066).

Some of the needs of the monastic community would have been different from those of a secular lord. Although the number of monks no doubt varied, their basic régime did not, and their requirements of food and clothing were known and fixed. As Edward Miller has observed, 'it was merely a matter of subdividing this burden amongst manors, the productive capacities of which in crops or cash were also known'.[6] Different solutions were, of course, found at different places.[7] During the reign of King Æthelred, the *uilla* of Hickling in Nottinghamshire was expected to render every year to Ramsey Abbey ten *mittae* of malt, five of mash or

---

[no. 110]; *English Historical Documents*, transl. Douglas & Greenaway, p. 879 [no. 173]).

3   Foot, 'Anglo-Saxon minsters A.D. 597–*ca* 900', has summarised the material for the early period.

4   'Villarum autem circuitus, nisi necessitas magna compulerit et necessariae rationis discretio hoc dictauerit, uagando nequaquam frequentent' (*Consuetudinum*, ed. Hallinger, proem, §12 [p. 77]; *Regularis Concordia*, ed. & transl. Symons, proem, §11 [p. 8]).

5   'Quem sibi forinsecus in uillarum suarum negotiis potentem praepositum, ne uel ipse uel quispiam ex monastica professione foris uagaretur, inepta rei saecularis discursione, constituit' (B, *Vita S. Dunstani*, §18; *Memorials*, ed. Stubbs, p. 28). On Wulfric, and the lands which he held, see Brooks, 'The career', pp. 8–10, and Hart, *The Early Charters of Northern England*, pp. 371–2; see also above, chapter III, *s.n.* Grittleton.

6   Miller, *The Abbey*, p. 42.

7   For the arrangements at the episcopal community of Christ Church, Canterbury, and the establishment in the ninth century of a separate endowment for the communal needs of the clergy, see Brooks, *The Early History*, pp. 157–60; see also more generally John, 'The division'.

grout, ten of wheat flour, eight *pernae* (hams or sides of bacon), sixteen cheeses, two fat cows, and eight salmon.[8] At Peterborough and Abingdon in the later Anglo-Saxon period, cash-rents were allocated to specific purposes from particular estates.[9] At Ely, from the time of Abbot Leofsige (A.D. 1029–1035), all demesne manors rendered a farm (in food or money) to supply the community's needs.[10] At Bury St Edmunds, the year's requirement was divided into twelve monthly portions, and a list of the places responsible for one month's *feorm* survives, probably from the time of Abbot Leofstan (A.D. 1045–1065).[11] The system of farms employed by the great ecclesiastical establishments has been described by Reginald Lennard as 'a common feature of monastic estate management before the Norman Conquest',[12] but its roots lie far back, in secular arrangements.[13] We know that food-farms were rendered in Somerset to other ecclesiastical landlords as early as *ca* A.D. 900 (to the bishop of Winchester from Ruishton, for example),[14] but, as will be seen below, there is little explicit evidence of a system of food-farms at pre-Conquest Glastonbury,[15] nor is any income in cash or kind earmarked *de uictu* in its Domesday Book entries, as is found, for example, in those of St Mary's, Worcester.[16] Some system must nevertheless have been in place in order to provide for the needs of the community. One of these needs may have been cash, and some of the estates probably paid cash-rents to the abbey.[17]

Many factors must have been involved in the evolution of Glastonbury's system of estate-management. Distance from the abbey, the nature of the land, the type of husbandry, the size of the estate, the period and circumstances of its acquisition, and the nature of the system already in place when the estate was granted to the church must have combined to determine the conditions of its operation. In the absence of convincing evidence it would, I think, be dangerous to assume that before the Norman overhaul of monastic life, and even before the refoundations of the tenth-century reform, a kind of benign neglect had charac-

---

8 '.x. mittas de brasio, et .u. de grut, et .x. mittas farinae triticae, et .uiii. pernas, et .xui. caseos, et duas uaccas pingues, ...uiii. isicos'; S.1493 (A.D. 978x1016) (*Codex Diplomaticus*, ed. Kemble, IV.303 [no. 971]).

9 For example, £20 *ad uestitum monachorum* from Fisherton: *Chronicon Petroburgense*, ed. Stapleton, p. 164; Raftis, *The Estates of Ramsey Abbey*, p. 10.

10 Miller, *The Abbey*, pp. 36–7.

11 *Anglo-Saxon Charters*, ed. & transl. Robertson, pp. 192–201 (no. 104); *English Historical Documents*, transl. Douglas & Greenaway, pp. 880–4 (no. 175).

12 Lennard, *Rural England*, p. 133.

13 For the renders required by King Ine on ten hides of land in the late seventh century, see his laws (§70.1): *Die Gesetze*, ed. Liebermann, I.118–21 (*English Historical Documents*, transl. Whitelock, p. 406 [no. 32]).

14 S.1819. See Turner, 'Some Old English passages', p. 123.

15 Food-renders from North Wootton in A.D. 946 are attested in S.509 (see chapter III, *s.n.* North Wootton).

16 For example, at Daylesford and Evenlode, Blackwell, Sedgeberrow, Knightwick, and Himbleton: Domesday Book, I, 173rb, 173va, and 173vb (three entries) (Worcestershire, 2.44, 2.46, 2.63, 2.67, and 2.70).

17 Raftis, *The Estates of Ramsey Abbey*, pp. 10–11.

terised the endowments of Anglo-Saxon religious houses.[18] It is equally possible that the abbots of these houses were lords of estates organised to supply with efficiency their churches' needs, which went well beyond bread, fish, and ale to include costly items such as gold and silver reliquaries, precious vestments, and books.[19] From the ninth century, too, there were increasing quantities of tribute to pay.[20] Nor were the communities required to feed and furnish themselves alone: exactions by the king and other obligations could be a considerable expense and a drain on resources.[21] How the estates were organised to meet these burdens in the early Anglo-Saxon period is largely a matter for speculation, however; very little evidence survives and any picture we construct is based on fragments of information only. Supported by the hagiographical descriptions of Dunstan's building-works as abbot, for example, Neil Stacy has envisaged a pre-reform *familia* of *clerici* living in cells in the abbey-precinct at Glastonbury, each *clericus* supported by a holding of the church's endowment. The rest of the land, he hypothesised,

---

[18] For the view that the abbey found it 'unnecessary . . . to worry overmuch about the exploitation of its estates', see Costen, 'Dunstan, Glastonbury and the economy', pp. 33–7, especially p. 37. Compare Brooks's comments on Archbishop Wulfred's 'clear-sighted territorial policy' and his analysis of the archbishop's manipulation of the 'consolidated and well-administered' lands of Christ Church, Canterbury, in the early ninth century; see *The Early History*, pp. 132–42 and 157–60, especially p. 139. The issue of intensity of exploitation hinges to a large degree on the question of the extent to which there was a market for agricultural products; see Dyer, *Lords and Peasants*, p. 30. Costen's argument – that the abbey did not have the motivation and possibly also lacked the expertise to exploit its estates fully – seems to conflict with the image (which he has presented in another context) of Glastonbury and the other reformed monastic houses as innovators responsible for the radical replanning of the landscape in the tenth century ('Some evidence for new settlements', especially pp. 48–50, and 'The late Saxon landscape', p. 43).

[19] On the importance of treasures to churches, see Campbell, 'The sale of land', especially pp. 33–7.

[20] See Sawyer, 'The wealth of England'.

[21] Such burdens were lamented by Abbess Bugga in letters to Boniface: *Die Briefe*, ed. Tangl, pp. 21–8 (nos 14 and 15). The earliest authentic grant of immunity which survives in England was made by King Wihtred who in A.D. 699 freed the Kentish minsters from 'every exaction of public tribute' ('ab omni exactione publici tributi'; S.20). Similar terms were apparently extended to the churches of Wessex by King Ine (in S.245 and S.246, the latter especially adapted for Glastonbury). Wihtred's grant of immunity from *gafol* in return for prayers and 'honour' is recorded in his laws (§1): *The Laws*, ed. & transl. Attenborough, pp. 24–5. Nevertheless, Church land in the ninth century was still burdened by obligations, some of which are revealed by a series of Mercian privileges granted to relieve the ecclesiastical recipient from what were apparently onerous secular services. See, for example, S.172 (A.D. 814), in which the bishop of Worcester's church and all the other minsters in his diocese were exempted from the obligation of hospitality for twelve men attached to the *burh* at Worcester, and S.215 (A.D. 875), which exempted the Worcester diocese from the responsibility of feeding the king's horses. Exemptions such as these were worth paying for handsomely. Not all dues were owed to the king: Minster-in-Thanet owed rents of food, money, and clothing ('in pastu et pecunia uestimentisque') as well as *omnis obedientia* to Christ Church, Canterbury, in the 820s (S.1436; A.D. 825).

was leased to provide income.[22] According to this interpretation, the monastic reform would have occasioned a 'communalisation' of the endowment, and, as Æthelwold did at Ely and Oswald at Worcester and Ramsey,[23] Dunstan may have reorganised the estates of his house in order to support this new structure: we have seen the evidence of a possible tenth-century change in the pattern of the landscape and of potentially more intensive exploitation reflected in the acquisition of lands in Wiltshire;[24] but the documents are largely silent on these developments. The case of *Brunham*, where in A.D. 824 Abbot Guthlac reputedly sold land to a layman for a payment of 200s. for the abbot and 300s. for the monks, seems conversely to indicate the existence of such a communalisation at an early date; the record of this transaction, however, may not be trustworthy and may have been concocted – or at least corrupted – at a later date.[25] Furthermore, arrangements may have been restructured several times between the community's foundation and its reform by Dunstan.

If the abbot retained a direct interest in the exploitation of an estate, a network of officials would have been required to oversee the demesne (Old English *inland*). If he did not, responsibility must have fallen on a more independent group. References to estate-officials at Glastonbury are few, apart from B's report of Dunstan's brother, Wulfric, whom he described as *praepositus*. Another *praepositus*, Ceolwine, visited Dunstan in Bath on monastic business.[26] A *praepositus* clearly did not run Glastonbury's vast holdings alone, however. Large-scale demesne-agriculture, as attested on Glastonbury's estates in 1086,[27] would have required an extensive network of active personnel – or, as Sally Harvey has put it, 'the use of powerful estate officials'[28] – but the development of this group at Glastonbury in

---

22 Stacy, 'The estates', p. 42.
23 See the *Libellus Æthelwoldi* for a detailed history of Æthelwold's activities (*Liber Eliensis*, ed. Blake, pp. 63–117 and 395–9; *Anglo-Saxon Ely*, edd. & transl. Keynes & Kennedy). For Oswald, see the *Chronicon Abbatiae Rameseiensis*, ed. Macray, and the forthcoming publication by Nicholas Brooks and Catherine Cubitt of papers from the 1992 conference which marked the anniversary of his death. On the 'division of the *mensa*' in the early period, see John, 'The division', and Brooks, *The Early History*, pp. 157–60.
24 For example, see above, chapter III, *s.n. Pouelt*, for the former and *s.n.* Damerham and Grittleton (and map 7) for the latter.
25 See above, chapter III, *s.n.* Brompton Ralph.
26 *Vita S. Dunstani*, §34 (*Memorials*, ed. Stubbs, p. 47). Stacy ('The estates', p. 43) has called Ceolwine Wulfric's successor, but there is nothing in the source to validate this assumption. More than one *praepositus* at a time is not impossible. Although in B's Life Wulfric is directly associated with the running of the community's estates, the word *praepositus* does not itself necessarily point to an exclusively agricultural role for someone so named, and Ceolwine could have had other responsibilities – the monastic household, for example. Campbell has pointed out that *praepositus* ('reeve') 'is a pretty general sort of word'. On the responsibilities of a reeve in the mid-eleventh century, see 'Gerefa' (*Die Gesetze*, ed. Liebermann, I.453–5), Loyn, *Anglo-Saxon England and the Norman Conquest*, pp. 200–1, and Campbell, 'Some agents and agencies', especially pp. 205–8.
27 For the debate on the post-Conquest fate of Glastonbury's demesnes, see the literature cited below, p. 272, n. 38.
28 Harvey, 'The extent and profitability', p. 58.

the pre-Conquest period is hard to detect. A reference in Domesday Book to the abbot's reeve at Brent dimly reflects such an arrangement, while the presence of a number of tenants who were monks or priests may perhaps indicate direct involvement by monastic personnel.[29] It is also possible that the holders in 1066 of abbatial thegnlands – probably to be defined as land held from Glastonbury by tenants who could not alienate it[30] – represented this (otherwise missing) class of officials. Sally Harvey has proposed that on many ecclesiastical estates, administrative requirements led to an increase in 'ministerial tenures', subtenancies which provided a class of estate-managers.[31] Glastonbury had in the mid- to late eleventh century a significant proportion of its land in the hands of subtenants (named in Domesday Book).[32] But as we shall see, the conditions of tenure remain obscure, due to the lack of pre-Conquest evidence and the opaque quality of the testimony of Domesday Book.

There is a hint in the twelfth-century *Liber Henrici de Soliaco* that a system of hereditary servants settled on administrative tenures had been introduced at Glastonbury in the tenth century: David *Cocus* is said to hold 'misterium suum hereditarie ex tempore sancti Dunstani'.[33] The reliability of a late twelfth-century source as evidence for the tenth century is, of course, open to question, and the date of the institution of this system providing for the support of those who ran the monastic household cannot be fixed on the evidence available. Barbara Harvey has proposed that at Westminster an obedientiary system was a relatively late development, beginning to take shape 'within a generation of the foundation of the Confessor's church'.[34]

The seemingly best evidence of a hereditary tenure at Glastonbury before 1066 occurs in S.509, a diploma of King Edmund in which North Wootton was granted to a layman (the thegn Æthelnoth) *in eternam hereditatem*, as long as Æthelnoth paid the specified food-renders and other dues.[35] This charter, however, includes unique features, as we have seen, and is difficult to interpret. Another possible reference to hereditary tenure is arguably post-Conquest: in the *Scriptura Henrici* (an account of the abbey's lands made by Henry of Blois in the early twelfth century and later recorded by Adam of Damerham), Godwine the son of Eadwine is said to have held Nyland *iure hereditario*, but this was in 1086; in 1066 Nyland, according to the *Liber Exoniensis*, had been held by an unnamed thegn who

---

[29] In 1066 Vlgar *monachus* held land at Whatley and Downhead, two monks at Compton Dundon, Winegod *presbiter* at *Bodesleghe*, Alnodus *monachus* at Pilton, Goduuinus *presbiter* at Brent, and (according to the *Liber Exoniensis*) Wluuoldus *presbiter* at Stratton-on-the-Fosse. However, some ecclesiastical tenants (such as Spirites at Lamyatt) were clearly indistinguishable from secular landholders. On Spirites, see below, p. 288, n. 99.

[30] The meaning of the term 'thegnland' will be discussed below.

[31] Harvey, 'The extent and profitability', pp. 62–3.

[32] Tenants held lands accounting for approximately forty per cent of the gross value of the abbey's endowment (and forty-three per cent of its hides).

[33] *Sic*; *leg.* ministerium: *Liber Henrici*, ed. Jackson, p. 12.

[34] Harvey, *Westminster Abbey*, p. 85.

[35] See above, chapter III, *s.n.* North Wootton.

'could not be separated from Glastonbury'.[36] North Wootton and Nyland both appear in Domesday Book simply as portions of larger estates (Pilton and Glastonbury, respectively) and there is no hint in Domesday Book's entries of the possibly hereditary nature of these or any other of Glastonbury's subtenures.

DOMESDAY BOOK: GLASTONBURY'S HOLDINGS

In the absence of direct information in pre-Conquest sources on methods of estate-management at Glastonbury in the Anglo-Saxon period, we must turn to Domesday Book for a glimpse of the situation in 1066. The evidence provided by Domesday Book is not directed to this purpose, however: it is specific and specialised, geared to the presentation of the abbey as an economic and fiscal entity. Domesday Book tells us how much land Glastonbury held, and the value of that land; it records what proportion was farmed directly and what was held from the abbot by a variety of men and women (all of whom, for convenience, I shall call tenants); it gives us figures from which we can estimate the population of each estate, with some indication not just of the status of those recorded, but also of the type of labour which they performed; it records a variety of features of the agricultural landscape, such as woodland, pasture, meadow, and vineyards, and other manorial appurtenances, such as fisheries, mills, and churches – all elements of the economic identity of the estate. Thanks to the additional information provided in the *Liber Exoniensis*, which represents an earlier, fuller, stage of the material presented to the commissioners for Somerset, Devon, Cornwall, and part of Dorset,[37] the economic picture of Glastonbury's lands can be drawn in even greater detail, distinguishing the villagers' hides from the abbot's or tenant's in demesne, and counting even the pigs and cattle and sheep on most of the abbey's manors.

The economic data in Domesday Book have already provided the basis for a debate on Glastonbury's demesne-farming in the eleventh and twelfth centuries, and Stacy's study of the abbey's demesnes likewise relied heavily on its evidence.[38] Much more can be done in this direction. My aim here, however, is not to portray the economic state of affairs in 1066 and 1086. Nor do I intend to identify the tenants who held from Glastonbury in 1066 and trace the descent of their

---

36 *Adami de Domerham*, ed. Hearne, II.315. The meaning of the description 'could not be separated' will be discussed below.

37 The *Liber Exoniensis* was published in a facsimile-edition by the Record Commissioners in 1816 (*Libri*, ed. Ellis, I.1–494 and I.589–614). For a detailed description and analysis, see Finn, *Domesday Studies: the Liber Exoniensis*; see also Loud, 'An introduction to the Somerset Domesday', pp. 4–8. Its Dorset surveys do not include returns for Glastonbury, but some summary-statistics for the abbey's Wiltshire holdings are provided (E 527 b1).

38 Postan, *Essays*, pp. 259–77, and 'The Glastonbury estates: a restatement', Lennard, 'The demesnes', and 'The Glastonbury estates: a rejoinder'; Stacy, 'The estates', chapters 3 and 4.

property.[39] When we get to Domesday Book we have available to us for the first time evidence bearing on matters about which pre-Conquest sources have been largely silent. One aspect of this evidence has not received full analysis, and my examination here will focus on this one aspect only: the nature of the relationship between Glastonbury Abbey and its holdings.[40] This is not a simple matter, nor is the evidence notably revelatory. Tenurial relationships are rarely articulated in Domesday Book in a way we can fully understand.[41] Neither Domesday Book nor the *Liber Exoniensis* – which adds detail to the evidence of the Exchequer's text, naming more names and recording information on tenants in 1066 more consistently – is an easy witness. Much that would be illuminating is lacking, and what is there often proves obscure. But, thanks to Domesday Book, Glastonbury's tenants move from obscurity into, not the limelight, but at least the foreground. We can discover how much of each abbatial estate was held directly by the church itself and how much was in the hands of others. Especially for Somerset, where the evidence is the most detailed, we can discover how large the tenants' portions were (although there are no measures of area, as such, in Domesday Book), and their value. In addition (albeit dimly) we can perceive something of the nature of the tenurial link between the abbot and the men and women who held from him. A summary of this evidence for Glastonbury's estates in 1066 will be set out here, followed by a discussion of the data in Domesday Book relating to tenurial conditions and how they resist conclusive analysis.

I shall deal exclusively with hides (the assessment for tax purposes) and annual values (how much each manor was valued at [*ualet*] in 1066 and 1086).[42] A case could be made for comparing ploughland statistics, but in view of the disagreements over the meaning of ploughland – and, in particular, over the date of the situation represented by its assessment – I have restricted myself to the hidage totals.[43] Values offer other complications. The sums are clearly conventional. The

---

39 See Fleming's studies in general; for Somerset, see Loud, 'An introduction to the Somerset Domesday'.

40 For a different approach, see Stacy's discussion of Glastonbury's tenures ('The estates', chapters 1 and 2).

41 See, however, Roffe's observations that differences in status are emphasised by variations in diplomatic, and that layout was used to complement vocabulary in signalling dependence ('From thegnage to barony', p. 162).

42 There are hints in the *Liber Exoniensis* that (possibly only some of) the past values quoted are those which applied when the first Norman abbot, Thurstan, took office, probably in A.D. 1077 or 1078, rather than the values of 1066. If these later values differed from those at the time of the Conquest, we cannot tell. Most of the entries use the convention 'die qua rex E. f. u. & m.' ('the day on which King Edward was alive and dead'), but others state the value as 'qn. T. abb. recep.' ('when Abbot Thurstan received it'). Loud has interpreted all past values as representing the situation when Abbot Thurstan took office, assuming that the pre-Conquest income was the same ('An introduction to the Somerset Domesday', p. 16).

43 Some students of Domesday Book have seen the ploughland statistics as indicating the number of ploughs at work in 1066, and others have interpreted them as representations of the potential arable land. For a discussion of the problem and a collection of the evidence, see Darby, *Domesday England*, pp. 95–136. More recently Sally Harvey has proposed instead that the ploughland figures are fiscal assessments, revised in

process of their derivation is obscure and their actual significance a contentious issue.[44] John McDonald and G.D. Snooks have defined them as a record of the income of landholders, either in the form of rents received from the tenants who actually held the land or of revenue gained from the direct exploitation of the estate's resources.[45] The figures have provided economic historians with a means of examining the nature and degree of exploitation of agricultural resources – on different parts of one ecclesiastical estate, for example.[46] I shall use them here simply to provide a measure of the relative value of the holdings of Glastonbury's tenants, as opposed to the estates and portions of estates under the direct control of the abbot.

A chart of summary-statistics has been included at the end of this chapter to illustrate the data: the total number of hides held by Glastonbury in each county, the number of these held by tenants, their values, and the equivalent details for lands lost by 1086 are shown.[47] All sums calculated from data in Domesday Book are to some extent inevitably imprecise, as decisions about how the information should be used have regularly to be made, affecting the totals quite substantially. The additional data from the *Liber Exoniensis*, as we shall see, makes the manipulation of the figures even more discretionary. For this reason, all totals are tentative, approximate, and subjective.[48] Even the tally of estates is approximate, for (at least) two reasons: it is not always clear from the evidence in Domesday Book whether a named place was an estate in its own right or a sub-unit of another; and between 1066 and 1086, such relationships occasionally changed, a sub-unit becoming an independent manor, or one estate being assessed as two (or *vice versa*).

Glastonbury Abbey is recorded in Domesday Book as holding land in seven counties. The greatest concentration was in Somerset, in which over half of its lands lay, and where it ranked second only to the king in the size of its holding. The abbey also held substantial lands in Wiltshire, with a more modest number of

---

1085–1086, and representing a calculation for the future rather than a record of the past ('Domesday Book and Anglo-Norman governance', pp. 186–91, and 'Taxation and the ploughland'); but see Higham, 'Settlement, land-use, and Domesday ploughlands'.

[44] A consideration of the values recorded in Domesday Book led Maitland to admit to being 'baffled by the make-believe of ancient finance' (*Domesday Book and Beyond*, p. 473); Darby (*Domesday England*, pp. 201–31) reopened debate, but continued to reject values as an indication of geographical reality; recent scholarship, on the other hand, has tended to take the figures more seriously as economic indicators. In particular, McDonald and Snooks (*Domesday Economy*, pp. 78–96) have argued persuasively for a relationship between the stated values and manorial resources.

[45] *Ibid.*, pp. 77–8.

[46] For such a study of Worcester, see Hamshere, 'The structure and exploitation', which contrasts the circumstances on the bishop's, monks', and tenants' lands.

[47] See below, pp. 316–17.

[48] Loud's total of Glastonbury's lands in Somerset, for example, is different from mine; see 'An introduction to the Somerset Domesday', p. 15. See also Costen's figures ('Dunstan, Glastonbury and the economy', p. 37, and *The Origins*, p. 121). For 1086, there is at the back of the *Liber Exoniensis* (527v–528r) a tally of Glastonbury's manors in the counties of Wiltshire, Dorset, Devon, and Somerset.

estates in Dorset, and a single manor recorded in each of Berkshire, Devon, Gloucestershire, and Hampshire.[49]

Berkshire, Devon, Gloucestershire, and Hampshire

I shall begin with the counties in which Glastonbury had only one holding in Domesday Book. The land at Ashbury (in Berkshire) was caught in 1086 at a moment of change, a circumstance which produces some uncertainty. In 1066 Ashbury answered for forty hides, which by 1086 had been reduced to sixteen hides and two and a half virgates. Like so many of Glastonbury's estates, Ashbury was divided into portions which were recorded separately in Domesday Book: in addition to the abbot's land, three units totalling nine and a half hides were held by three tenants in 1086. Unlike the entries for estates in Somerset, a breakdown of the values of the tenants' portions at Ashbury is not given. No predecessors are named for these tenants, two of whose English names (rendered Aluuinus and Eduuardus)[50], however, may indicate continuity of tenure. Although Domesday Book shows that tenants held over half the revised number of hides at Ashbury in 1086, it is unclear what proportion of the estate they held in 1066 – if any. In my calculations I have counted tenants as holding the same number of hides in 1066 and 1086, but this is simply an assumption based on the observation that, although there was a great deal of change in personnel among Glastonbury's tenants on all its estates between the two dates, there is little evidence of change in the units of land themselves and in their tenurial status.[51] The fact that only a value TRW is given for what the men held, whereas the value TRE is for the entire estate,[52] could conversely indicate that in 1066 the abbot held everything. It would be particularly interesting to know what the situation was in 1066, for there was a church at Ashbury (with a priest holding one hide) included with the land of the post-Conquest tenants. This is one of the few churches on Glastonbury's estates to appear in Domesday Book, and an indication of whether it was held directly by the abbot or indirectly, by a secular tenant (as at Ilchester),[53] would have been welcome.

Glastonbury's single estate recorded in Domesday Book's returns for Devon was at Uplyme, which was held directly and entirely by the abbey. This was not the full extent of the abbey's eleventh-century possessions in Devon, however, as we have seen from the history of Uffculme.[54] Although Abbot Æthelweard (*ca* A.D. 1024–1053) had reputedly produced a tripartite lifetime lease for Uffculme

---

[49] For full references to the entries for each estate in Domesday Book, the *Liber Exoniensis*, and the Phillimore county-editions, see the list of estates provided at the end of this chapter, pp. 313–15. For the earlier evidence relating to each estate, see above, chapter III.

[50] Personal names are generally given here as they appear in Domesday Book.

[51] Hamshere observed the same combination of stability and change at Worcester; see 'The structure and exploitation', p. 43.

[52] The conventional abbreviations – TRE (*tempore regis Edwardi*) and TRW (*tempore regis Willelmi*) will be used here for convenience.

[53] See below, p. 282.

[54] See above, chapter III, *s.n.* Uffculme.

with a tenant, Eadgifu, at some time between A.D. 1046 and 1053, Eadgifu was dead by 1086 and her husband, Walter of Douai, had appropriated the land. In Domesday Book, Uffculme is listed among Walter's lands, with Eadgifu named as the holder in 1066. There is no mention of Glastonbury as her – or Walter's – landlord. No hint of a link with the abbey appears elsewhere in the Domesday record, either in Glastonbury's own entry or among the *Terrae occupatae*, the list in the *Liber Exoniensis* of disputed and reorganised lands.[55] This may support the suggestion that Walter held Uffculme on the authority of a writ (no longer extant) from King William. In any event, Glastonbury had lost the land by 1086, although it regained possession for some time in the first half of the twelfth century. The citation of Eadgifu as the tenant TRE tends to suggest that she was still alive in 1066, and therefore that Glastonbury's control over the land had not yet been challenged. Uffculme's fourteen hides may therefore be added tentatively to Glastonbury's other estate in Devon and to the total value of the abbey's holdings in 1066. This example should serve as a caution: had the unique document (which may have been prepared for legal proceedings) recording the lease and dispute not been copied into a cartulary which has survived, Glastonbury's possession of Uffculme in the eleventh century (and specifically, by inference, in 1066) would not have been known.[56] As modern study has increasingly shown, Domesday Book, so ostentatiously informative, is not all-inclusive.

Glastonbury held a single large estate in Gloucestershire – twenty hides at Pucklechurch – directly and entirely. Its single estate in Hampshire, Ower, was only a modest holding of one hide. It was held by a different tenant TRE and TRW. A rare elaboration in the record offers a glimpse of tenurial arrangements: the TRE tenant who held Ower, Elsi, could not go where he wished ('non potuit ire quo uoluit'), but always paid *gablum* to the abbot. This, as will be seen below,[57] could perhaps represent land held by lease or at farm.

Dorset

Glastonbury held six estates in Dorset in 1066, one of which (and one portion of another) the abbey had lost by 1086. The estates at Buckland Newton, Lyme Regis, Okeford Fitzpaine, Pentridge, Sturminster Newton, and Woodyates totalled fifty-eight hides, to which must be added twenty-two ploughlands not assessed for geld. The six-hide estate at Pentridge and four of the hides at Sturminster Newton were lost to the king, leaving the abbey with forty-eight assessed hides in the county in 1086.[58]

Apparently none of Glastonbury's estates in Dorset was held directly and entirely by the abbot, without tenants. Two – Sturminster Newton and Buckland

55 *Liber Exoniensis*, 495r–525r.
56 See further, below, p. 308.
57 See below, pp. 309–10.
58 In the case of Buckland Newton, Pentridge, Lyme Regis, and one portion of Sturminster Newton, no separate value is given for 1066, and consequently I have had to take the stated value to apply to both dates. Pentridge, though said to have been lost to the king, does not appear among the *terrae regis* in Domesday Book.

Newton – were divided, each with two tenants' portions TRW in addition to the abbot's holding.[59] No TRE names are given for the hides held by the tenants on these two estates in 1086, and it is again only an assumption that the tenancies already existed in 1066. The value of one of the Sturminster portions – the four hides lost to the king – is, however, given not just for 1086, but also for an unspecified past time,[60] thereby suggesting that the other portions also predated 1086, but with identical values at both dates. As will be seen, Domesday Book tends to expand somewhat on its usually concise entries when estates had been lost to another lord between 1066 and 1086.

A further twenty-one hides in Dorset – composed of the estates at Okeford Fitzpaine, Woodyates, Pentridge, and Lyme Regis – were held entirely by tenants in 1066, with no abbot's land. In 1066, tenants therefore held forty-two hides and one and a half virgates of Glastonbury's fifty-eight taxed hides in Dorset, a substantial proportion (over seventy per cent), but worth only £42 10s. of the £92 10s. total value of Glastonbury's holdings in the county (less than half); the demesne-holding was evidently very valuable, the tenants' land less so. Okeford Fitzpaine had been held by four thegns (*taini*), unnamed, who were replaced by four *milites* (one of them a woman). Woodyates, Pentridge, and Lyme Regis each had only one tenant TRW. Woodyates's tenant in 1086 is unnamed, and no information is given for 1066. At that date, Pentridge was held by Vluuardus, probably Wulfweard the White; that Glastonbury was apparently the landlord and Wulfweard only a tenant seems to have been ignored by William the Conqueror, who appears to have treated Pentridge as he did Wulfweard's other estates (which Wulfweard had probably held from Queen Edith).[61] According to Domesday Book, Wulfweard 'could not be separated from the church'.[62] No such statement is made about any of the other tenancies in Dorset. Vluiet, the tenant at Lyme Regis, *tenuit et tenet* the land from the abbey, an example (uncommon among Glastonbury's entries) of an overtly stated continuity of tenancy from 1066 to 1086.

In Dorset, therefore, despite the heavy concentration of tenancies, the only TRE tenants whom we know by name are Vluiet, who still held in 1086, and Wulfweard, whose land had just left Glastonbury's possession by that date. This contrasts greatly with Somerset where, as we shall see, the Exchequer's text – as well as the more complete entries in the *Liber Exoniensis* – records details about TRE tenants and tenures much more frequently.

---

[59] Sturminster Newton could have been divided into four, not two, tenants' portions, as four names are given; but three of these are grouped together, and the information given on values and hides seems to apply in that case to one piece of land held jointly. In Somerset, where more detailed information is available thanks to the *Liber Exoniensis*, it is clear that many sub-units of Glastonbury's estates were held jointly by several men.

[60] These four hides likewise do not appear among the *terrae regis* in Domesday Book.

[61] Wulfweard was closely connected with Queen Edith and seems to have been protected by her: this may explain why he maintained much of his property after the Conquest. When he died shortly before 1086, a significant proportion of his lands (particularly those in Somerset) went to the king; Loud has suggested that this could indicate that they had in fact been held from the queen and thus returned at Wulfweard's death to the royal demesne ('An introduction to the Somerset Domesday', p. 17).

[62] The meaning of this phrase will be discussed below.

Wiltshire

Glastonbury held fifteen estates in Wiltshire in 1066, a total of 260 hides and 2 virgates, with ten additional acres of meadow. Although by 1086 the monks had lost Kington St Michael and parts of four other estates – Littleton Drew (part of Grittleton), Langford, Winterbourne Monkton, and Christian Malford (two parts) (altogether seven hides and three virgates, and ten acres of meadow) – the value of their estates in Wiltshire rose dramatically between the two assessments: from £171 10s. to £218 (or £202).[63] Of these 260 hides and 2 virgates, only a small proportion – forty-one hides and one virgate (and eighteen acres), or about sixteen per cent – was in tenants' hands in 1066, in contrast with Dorset and Somerset; the figure in 1086 was forty hides, three virgates (plus eight acres), despite the loss of seven and a half tenants' hides (and ten acres), largely because ten valuable hides at Mildenhall changed from abbot's land to tenants' land. The value of the land held by tenants in the county rose accordingly: from £28 15s. to £38 15s.; but these figures do not represent the full value of tenants' holdings at either date, as in many cases the value of the tenant's portion was not recorded in the entries for estates in Wiltshire, only the total value being given.

In 1066, only three of Glastonbury's estates in Wiltshire – Badbury, Nettleton, and Mildenhall – were held directly and entirely by the abbot. Winterbourne may also belong in this category, if the one virgate lost to Waleran in 1086, which (according to 'the thegns') belonged to the church, and which the abbot claimed, was not tenant's land gone astray.[64]

Of the other eleven estates in Wiltshire, only two – Langford and Kington St Michael – were held entirely by tenants in 1066; in 1086 Glastonbury failed to retain the latter (though it was subsequently recovered) and part of the former. One hide at Langford, described as *tainlande* (whose TRE tenant was called Azor), was lost; but the abbey kept two other hides there, held from it TRE by two thegns and TRW by Edward of Salisbury. The lost hide at Langford appears twice, under both Glastonbury's and Edward's lands, and in both places the abbey's claim is expressed.[65] Kington St Michael, held TRE from the abbot by Aluuinus, appears in Domesday Book among the lands of Ralph of Mortimer. Its tenant in

---

63 I shall use the higher number, for the sake of effect only. The difference lies in the assessment of Damerham in 1086: the estate 'reddit £61, sed ab hominibus non appreciantur plusque £45, propter confusionem terrae et propter firmam que nimis est alta' (*sic*) ('renders £61, but is not assessed by the men at more than £45 on account of the confusion of the land and because of the rent which is too high'). Stacy has suggested ('The estates', p. 105) that the confusion resulted from appropriations by the canons of Damerham. They were ejected by Abbot Henry of Blois.

64 'Quam testificantur taini ad ecclesiam debere pertinere' (Domesday Book, I, 66vb; Wiltshire, 7.15). Certainly no information on this single virgate is given for 1066, unlike the lost hide at Langford, below.

65 'Taini diratiocinantur hanc terram ecclesiae Glastingeberie' ('the thegns adjudge this land to the church of Glastonbury') (Domesday Book, I, 69vb [Wiltshire, 24.42]); also '.i. hid' quae iure pertinet abbatiae ad tainlande' ('one hide which pertains by right to the thegnland of the abbey') (Domesday Book, I, 66rb [Wiltshire, 7.13]).

1066 could not be separated from Glastonbury and 'rendered service to the abbot'.[66]

Nine estates in Wiltshire in 1066 were divided into portions of abbot's land and tenants' land: Damerham, Hannington, Deverill, Christian Malford, Winterbourne Monkton, Grittleton, Kington Langley, Idmiston, and Monkton Deverill. With some exceptions, the tenants' portions formed quite a small proportion of the estate's total.

The difficulty of Damerham's revised hidage has already been mentioned.[67] Part of the problem was that the *firma* (Old English *feorm*, 'rent') was too high, according to Domesday Book, but no details are given. We can probably assume from the entry that, as there were three portions in 1086, tenants (who could not be separated from Glastonbury) held a similar number in 1066: their land was still called *terra tainorum* in 1086. At Hannington, it appears that in 1066 only three hides of the fifteen-hide estate were held by a tenant: the abbot had sold three hides to a thegn for three lives, but the term of the lease had obviously expired by 1086, for the three hides had returned to the demesne and were now with the other twelve.[68] The fact that one tenant held all fifteen hides together from the abbot in 1086 could suggest either that the other twelve hides had previously also been the subject of leases, or that they had been held directly by the abbot; the latter interpretation would suggest that by 1086 there had been a change in the status of the estate, which had been taken over as one unit by a tenant.[69]

One of Glastonbury's holdings in Deverill included, in addition to the abbot's land, one portion held by a tenant;[70] the tenant was the same TRE and TRW (an unnamed thegn) and his land could not be separated from the church at either date. One portion of Christian Malford was held by two tenants TRW; this was described as thegnland and seems to have been very small (assessed at only three virgates), but, as no separate values are given for the tenants' portions of many of the estates in Wiltshire, its value is impossible to judge. The estate at Christian Malford also included two detached portions of meadow (six acres in Stanton St Quintin and four in Littleton Drew) which had been leased to Brictric and Aluuardus TRE. This meadow was held TRW by the bishop of Coutances, although the acres 'deberent iacere in Cristemalford'.[71] No value is given for the acres of meadow; the economic significance of their loss therefore cannot be calculated.

Winterbourne Monkton included a single tenant's portion which could not be separated from Glastonbury and which was held TRE by Orgar. At Grittleton, two tenants' portions are recorded (whose tenants in 1066 likewise could not be separated from the church), but they are not named. One of them, however, can

---

[66] 'Inde seruiebat abbati' (Domesday Book, I, 72va; Wiltshire, 41.8).
[67] See above, p. 278, n. 63.
[68] 'De hac eadem terra .iii. hidas uendiderat abbas cuidam taino TRE ad aetatem trium hominum et ipse abbas habebat inde seruitium; et postea debebant redire ad dominium et modo cum aliis .xii. hidis sunt.': Domesday Book, I, 66va (Wiltshire, 7.2).
[69] I have chosen this interpretation for the purpose of my calculations.
[70] For the identification of Glastonbury's two Deverills, see above, chapter III, *s.n. Deuerel*.
[71] 'Should lie in Christian Malford'; Domesday Book, I, 66va (Wiltshire, 7.5).

probably be identified with Littleton Drew,[72] held TRE from the abbot by Aluuardus and also inseparable from the abbey at that date, which was lost to Geoffrey, bishop of Coutances.[73] At Kington Langley there were three tenants' portions, in addition to that of the abbot. TRE the holders – unnamed – could not be separated from Glastonbury. At Idmiston there was one tenant's holding in addition to the abbot's land, and the TRE holder, unnamed, bore the same restriction. Similarly, at Monkton Deverill there was one tenant, and the TRE holder – who in this case is named (Eisi) – likewise could not be separated from the church.

In Wiltshire, as in Dorset, the information about tenants is thus generally sketchy, contrasting, as we shall see, with the fuller details given for Somerset. TRE holders in Wiltshire are rarely named, except where land had been lost, in which case the holder in 1066 is always mentioned. No separate value is given in respect of the tenants' portions of most estates (although there are exceptions – Idmiston, for example). As has been observed, this makes it impossible to calculate what proportion of the value of the abbey's lands in the county was invested in tenants' lands, although as we have seen above, the hidage represented a relatively small proportion. For all of the nine estates with portions held by tenants (except Hannington, with its unusual reference to a three-life lease) and for all the estates held entirely by tenants (except two hides at Langford), the information that the holders could not be separated from the church is repeated. Only a small portion of land at Christian Malford and the lost hide at Langford are, however, called thegnland. The significance of this terminology will be discussed below.[74]

The great rise in values exhibited by several of the estates in Wiltshire (Damerham £36 to £45 or £61, Mildenhall £12 to £18, Winterbourne £12 to £20, Nettleton £8 to £13, Kington Langley £13 to £19 10s.) does not appear to follow a pattern with any tenurial significance, as different conditions apparently applied at the estates exhibiting the greatest increase.

Somerset

Glastonbury's largest holding was naturally in the county of Somerset. In 1066 the abbey held at least forty-seven estates, totalling 417 hides and 1 virgate of taxed land, to which must be added twenty-six hides and one virgate, forty ploughlands, and sixty-six acres which did not pay tax. I have calculated the value to be £363 16s. 6d. Although Glastonbury lost fifteen estates and seven portions

---

[72] I have followed Morland and C. and F. Thorn in identifying Littleton Drew with the portion of Grittleton held by the bishop: Morland, 'The Glastonbury manors', p. 85; *Wiltshire*, 5.6 (note). See above, chapter III, *s.n.* Grittleton.

[73] Geoffrey Mowbray, bishop of Coutances, belonged to the Conqueror's inner circle; in A.D. 1069 he played a leading part in the suppression of rebellion in the southwest. He was rewarded for services thus rendered by large grants of land, much of it in the region. See Douglas, *William the Conqueror*, p. 269, and Fleming, *Kings and Lords*, pp. 192 and 217–31. See also below, p. 283.

[74] See pp. 289–311.

of estates between 1066 and 1086 (totalling seventy-four hides and worth over £71 15s.)[75] and suffered a disadvantageous exchange, the total value of its lands in the county, like those in Wiltshire, nevertheless rose to £438 13s. 8d. in 1086. Of the total hidage in 1066, about fifty-eight per cent (244 hides and 1 virgate, plus 2 hides and 2 virgates untaxed) was held by tenants; their lands were worth more than £184 15s. 8d.,[76] just over half the total value of Glastonbury's holdings in Somerset. Approximately twenty-seven per cent of the tenants' hides (35% in value) were lost between 1066 and 1086.

In 1066 and 1086, the abbot held only three estates in Somerset directly and entirely: Podimore Milton, *Sowi*, and Baltonsborough (totalling twenty-three hides).

On the other hand, over half of Glastonbury's estates in Somerset were held entirely by tenants: East Lydford, Cossington, Durborough, Blackford, Stawell, *Bodesleghe*, Dundon, Whatley, Cranmore, Edingworth, Downhead, Ilchester, Hutton (two estates in 1066), Elborough, *Hetsecome*, Stratton-on-the-Fosse, Kingstone, two estates at Stoke-sub-Hamdon, Draycott, Brompton Ralph, Clatworthy, Winterhead, Wheathill, and an unidentified estate of five hides: twenty-six in all, totalling eighty-eight hides and one virgate, of which fifteen estates (forty-five hides) were lost between 1066 and 1086. All but two or three of these twenty-six (*Hetsecome* and Stoke-sub-Hamdon, and perhaps Kingstone),[77] had been held by a single, named, person in 1066. This is where the bulk of the immediately post-Conquest losses seems to have occurred.

Of the twenty-six estates held entirely by tenants, Glastonbury retained only eleven in 1086 (East Lydford, Cossington, Durborough, Blackford, Stawell, *Bodesleghe*, Dundon, Whatley, Cranmore, Edingworth, and Downhead). In 1066 East Lydford had been held by Aluuardus (who could not be separated from Glastonbury), Cossington by Aluuinus Pic, and Durborough by Oswald. Alnod had held Blackford, and *Bodesleghe* was held TRE by a priest, Winegod. Algar held Dundon, and Cranmore was held TRE and TRW by a single tenant, Harding, whose land could not be separated from Glastonbury. At Whatley the TRE tenant was another ecclesiastic, this time a monk, Vlgar, who could not be separated from Glastonbury.[78] He held the adjoining land at Dinnington, which, according

---

[75] The values given for Glastonbury's lost estates in Somerset differ in the Exchequer's text and the *Liber Exoniensis*, with the latter possibly representing a more accurate level of information. Further, composite values quoted in the Exchequer's text for lost lands are not to be trusted: four estates lost to the bishop of Coutances, for example, are said to be worth 100s. *et amplius* TRW (Domesday Book, I, 91ra [Somerset, 8.38]); the individual values for all four estates, in both 1066 and 1086, however, show totals of 230s. and 240s., respectively. The four estates taken by the count of Mortain, said to be worth £13 together, have individual values adding up to £15. I have used the latter values in my calculations.

[76] The values of two tenants' holdings are not recorded (one hide at Overleigh and five unidentified hides).

[77] There is no information about a TRE tenant at Kingstone. We can deduce that there was at least one, however, by the statement that in 1086 'ecclesia seruitium non habet', a phrase which elsewhere indicates land previously held by tenants but which Glastonbury had lost.

[78] According to Domesday Book, Walter Hussey held the four hides of Whatley in 1086,

to the *Liber Exoniensis*, bore the same restriction. Dinnington was probably not an estate in its own right: in 1086 Glastonbury's holding there appears to have been only a portion of the manor (of the same name) which was held TRE by Edmer Ator and TRW by Siuuardus. No TRE tenant is mentioned in either Domesday Book or the *Liber Exoniensis*, but in the latter under the heading *Terrae occupatae* it is stated that TRE the three virgates could not be separated from Glastonbury.[79] Morland has interpreted them as part of Kingstone, an estate which Glastonbury lost between 1066 and 1086, which lacked three virgates from its total in 1086.[80]

In 1086 Glastonbury had lost fifteen of the twenty-six estates which had been held entirely by tenants in 1066: Ilchester, Hutton (two estates), Elborough, *Hetsecome*, Stratton-on-the-Fosse, Kingstone, Stoke-sub-Hamdon (two estates), Draycott, Brompton Ralph, Clatworthy, Winterhead, Wheathill, and one unnamed estate. Eleven of these properties appear at the end of the abbot's entries on folio 91 of the Exchequer's text of Domesday Book (folio 172 of the *Liber Exoniensis*), grouped together by the name of the Norman lord who held them in 1086. Further details can be found in the entries under these men's names. Four other manors lost by 1086 whose tenants had held from Glastonbury in 1066 appear only under the entries for the men who held them TRW, not under those of Glastonbury as well. Almost all lost lands – or at least, all those which are mentioned in Domesday Book – are listed together in the *Liber Exoniensis* under the heading *Terrae occupatae* as well as in the main entries. Only occasionally does the information conflict.

The church of St Andrew's, Ilchester (with three hides) heads the list of lost lands which is found at the end of the abbey's entries. Brictric, who could not be separated from Glastonbury, held this church from the abbey in 1066. St Andrew's is the only case among Glastonbury's estates where the church itself is recorded as constituting the holding, rather than being simply an appurtenance of an estate (although that too is rare enough among Glastonbury's returns in Domesday Book). This may reflect a distinction between an ecclesiastical community and a proprietary church.[81] Brictric and Glastonbury lost St Andrew's to Maurice, bishop of London, who is said to have held in 1086 from the king.

The entry for Ilchester is followed by a list of four estates – Hutton, Elborough, *Hetsecome*, and Stratton-on-the-Fosse – lost to the bishop of Coutances, who is said to have held them from the king in 1086. Their values are given as a

---

and John (the Usher) held one hide of this manor from the abbot (Domesday Book, I, 90va [Somerset, 8.26]). The information in the *Liber Exoniensis* that Whatley paid tax for five hides allows us to add John's hide to Walter's rather than subtracting it (E 168 b1). There is nothing to confirm that this hide also was held by a tenant in 1066.

79   E 524 a6. Although these three virgates appear among the *Terrae occupatae*, where lost or reorganised lands are normally cited, the entry clearly states that they were still held from the church of Glastonbury. They may be there because they had moved from one estate to another. See above, chapter III, *s.n.* Dinnington and *Stane*.

80   Morland, 'The Glastonbury manors', pp. 71 and 74.

81   See Blair, 'Secular minsters in Domesday Book', and 'Local churches in Domesday Book', pp. 275–8, for general discussion and comparison across the country.

combined total only and all four are said to have been thegnland which could not be separated from Glastonbury (which had lost the service from them). Entries under the lands of the bishop of Coutances and in the *Liber Exoniensis* under the *Terrae occupatae* provide further information. Hutton, for example, was held by two thegns in 1066 as two manors, although the data given are not broken down into two parts. Elborough was held by Aluuardus, and *Hetsecome* by four un-named thegns. There is some uncertainty about the TRE tenant of Stratton-on-the-Fosse; in Domesday Book he is called Aluuoldus and it is said that he could not be separated from Glastonbury; the entries in the account of the *Terrae occupatae* call Stratton thegnland which could not be separated from Glastonbury, and name the TRE holder as Wuluold the priest.

Another estate, Winterhead, should have been included with these four proper-ties, as it too was lost to the bishop of Coutances, but it seems simply to have been left off the list. It appears nonetheless in the bishop's entries after Hutton and Elborough, with the information that Brictric had held it and that, like the other two, in 1066 it had been held from Glastonbury and could not be separated from the church.

A second group of lost estates follows, of land held by the count of Mortain from the king in 1086,[82] which had been Glastonbury's thegnlands TRE (King-stone, two Stokes, and Draycott). These too are given only a collective value, and further information on values, hidage, and previous tenants must likewise be sought in the entries for the count of Mortain's lands and in the list of *Terrae occupatae* in the *Liber Exoniensis*. All four are called thegnlands and are said in the list of *Terrae occupatae* to have been inseparable from Glastonbury; but only Kingstone is marked and described in the count's entries as previously belonging to Glastonbury. No TRE tenant for Kingstone is mentioned but there probably was one, as Glastonbury is said to have lost the service from the estate. To complicate the accounting of the count's seizures from the abbey, he held three manors called Stoke, whereas Glastonbury appears to have lost only two; fortunately one of the count's Stokes can be ruled out (as one of Glastonbury's losses) because the value is too high.[83] One of the abbey's two Stokes was held TRE by Aluuinus, and the other by three unnamed thegns. Draycott had been held by Uluui. Added to this account of manors lost to the Count was woodland in Butleigh which Glastonbury had held TRE, but no value is given for it.

The final entry for Glastonbury in Domesday Book concerns the loss of five hides which the father of Roger of Courseulles had given – to whom, it is not clear – in exchange for the manor of Limington. These hides, which have no name in

---

[82] Robert of Mortain was the Conqueror's half-brother, and although he held land in twenty counties, his power was concentrated in east Sussex and the southwest. On his career and property – particularly the seizure of land from twenty-four English monas-tic houses – see Golding, 'Robert of Mortain', especially pp. 139–41.

[83] In the list of *Terrae occupatae* (E 524 a4), two places called Stoke are said to have been worth 40s. (presumably 40s. each, as shown in the count's own entries, with a third Stoke assessed at £7). The accounting in the *Terrae occupatae* apparently mistakenly took each estate's separate value to apply to them both together. See also above, chapter III, *s.n. Stoke*.

Domesday Book or the *Liber Exoniensis* (neither in the main text nor in the list of *Terrae occupatae*), could not be separated from Glastonbury in 1066; but the abbey had lost the service from them in 1086.

Three more of Glastonbury's estates in Somerset held by tenants had been lost but somehow failed to be written in at the end of the abbey's entries, unlike those discussed above. At Brompton Ralph, Brictric had been the tenant TRE; William de Mohun held it in 1086. A cross marks the entry among William's lands; the holding is said to have been part of Glastonbury and inseparable from it in 1066, a statement repeated in the list of *Terrae occupatae*. The main entry in the *Liber Exoniensis* adds that it was thegnland. Clatworthy also was lost to William de Mohun; Aluiet was the TRE tenant on this thegnland, which could not be separated from Glastonbury. Clatworthy does not appear among the *Terrae occupatae*. The last of the estates lost by Glastonbury was Wheathill, held TRE by Serlo de Burcy. It too fails to appear among the entries for Glastonbury or in the list of *Terrae occupatae*, but the entry for Wheathill among Serlo's other holdings is marked with a cross and states clearly that Elmer had held the estate TRE from Glastonbury, from which church he could not be separated. Stacy has suggested that the absence of Brompton Ralph, Clatworthy, and Wheathill from the abbot's entries indicates that Glastonbury had accepted its loss of these estates, but, as the crosses appear consistently in the Exchequer's text, and Glastonbury's rightful ownership is mentioned in every case, and in the same terms as for those other estates which are listed as lost, it seems just as likely that their absence can be ascribed to error – either the return was not complete or the scribes failed to copy the final entries on the list.

A further eighteen estates in Somerset were divided into portions in 1066, held partly by the abbot and partly by a tenant or tenants: Glastonbury, Winscombe, Shapwick, Walton, Overleigh, Ham, Butleigh, Pilton, Pennard, Doulting, Batcombe, Mells, Wrington, West Monkton, Marksbury, Ditcheat, Tintinhull,[84] and Brent. Five of these experienced loss of land and Tintinhull was lost in an exchange. The exchange may not have been voluntary, for Tintinhull is marked in Domesday Book with a cross, as lands taken from their TRE holders were marked, and the transaction certainly does not appear advantageous to the abbey.[85] Fewer of the tenants TRE on these shared estates are mentioned by name than in cases where the estates were held entirely by tenants in 1066: of a total of

---

[84] Tintinhull, lost in an exchange with the count of Mortain, is recorded only in the count's entry, where Drogo is said to hold one virgate from the count; this virgate was held *pariter* by a tenant in 1066, according to the *Liber Exoniensis*.

[85] Tintinhull paid geld for only five hides although there were seven hides and one virgate there. It was worth £10 and £16 (TRE and TRW), to which the value of the virgate (one silver mark) should be added. It had a mill, meadow, pasture, and woodland. It was exchanged for Camerton, which may have been held by Glastonbury in the late tenth century (see above, chapter III, *s.n.* Camerton) and which paid geld for ten hides but was worth only £6 10s. and £7 10s. in 1066 and 1086 respectively. According to the *Liber Exoniensis*, a tenant held one hide of thegnland at Camerton from the abbot in 1086, just as a thegn had held it TRE from its landlord, from whom it could not be separated.

at least fifty portions held by tenants on these divided estates,[86] only fifteen have TRE owners ascribed by name to them in the Exchequer's text (although a further twelve can be identified from the *Liber Exoniensis*). The estates divided into portions varied considerably: in some, the abbot held a relatively small amount, whereas in others the tenant held only a tiny portion. They will all be treated together here, however.

Glastonbury itself consisted of twelve hides which did not pay geld and three attached 'islands', one of which, *Andersey*, was held by a tenant in 1086 (and possibly 1066 as well, as the tenant's Anglo-Saxon name, Godwine, might suggest). According to the *Liber Exoniensis*, this Godwine was a thegn who could not be separated from the abbey; the twelfth-century *Scriptura Henrici* provides the additional information that Godwine held *iure hereditario*.[87] At Winscombe, of the four portions held by Glastonbury's tenants in 1066, one had been lost to the bishop of Coutances, who held it from the king in 1086; its TRE tenant (Brictric) is the only one named of the four, and only about him is it said that he could not be separated from Glastonbury. At Shapwick, the abbot had a tenant (Warmund) in 1086 on half a hide of the land which did not pay tax (which in the *Liber Exoniensis* is called thegnland), and two tenants holding five other (taxed) portions. Unusually, the names of these portions are given, but not the names of their holders in 1066. (This is hardly surprising, however, as fourteen thegns who could not be separated from Glastonbury held four of these portions. In the *Liber Exoniensis* these are divided further, so that we know how many held each of the units of land; in addition, Alwi Bannesona – the only single holder of a portion – is named as the TRE holder of the fifth unit.) Five sub-units of Walton are also named, in addition to the abbot's land, but no holders are identified for 1066, except at Greinton (Vlmer) and Ashcott (Almerus).[88] As with Shapwick, the information in the *Liber Exoniensis* expands somewhat on that of the Exchequer's text, stating that the holders of the remaining sub-units could not be separated from Glastonbury: there we discover that there were five of them, only one, Algar, named (perhaps because he too was the only single tenant), but two, interestingly, identified as monks.[89] Overleigh appears to have had one hide of thegnland in 1066 (said to be *in dominio* of the church) which could not be separated from Glastonbury and which by 1086 had returned to the abbot's demesne. At Ham, there were three portions as well as the abbot's land, and the three TRE tenants were named as Leuric, Aluuold, and Almar. According to the *Liber Exoniensis*, one of these portions was thegnland. Butleigh had four tenants' portions in 1066; in the *Liber Exoniensis* it is stated that three thegns held the first portion (the Exchequer's text implies one only), and Sheerwold is named as the holder of the

---

[86] Domesday Book does not always indicate if the tenant of 1086 had a predecessor; therefore, a larger number of portions than has been identified may have been held by tenants in 1066.

[87] *Adami de Domerham*, ed. Hearne, II.315.

[88] Ashcott and Greinton, given their own entries in the Phillimore edition (Somerset, 8.14 and 8.15), were in fact part of Walton.

[89] See p. 271, n. 29, for other ecclesiastics holding tenancies.

second unit and Alstan of the third.[90] Lattiford, which belonged to Butleigh, was held TRE by Aluric, who could not be separated from Glastonbury, but TRW it was held from the king by Humphrey the Chamberlain. In the list of *Terrae occupatae* Lattiford is called a manor; it was apparently not independent in 1066,[91] however, but was upgraded after being detached from Butleigh and lost to the abbey.

Pilton was another estate with named constituent parts in Domesday Book – six in all (five named), none of which could be separated from Glastonbury. TRE tenants (Vluert and Elmer) are identified for only two of the portions in Domesday Book, but names for another three are supplied in the *Liber Exoniensis* (Elmer held a further two, and Sheerwold one). In addition, in 1086 Alnodus *monachus* held one hide of the abbot's land for twenty ploughs which did not pay geld – this hide is referred to as thegnland, which could not be separated from Glastonbury.[92] At East Pennard, only one hide of the large estate was held TRE by a tenant, Ailmarus; in the *Liber Exoniensis* it is said that this hide was thegnland. Two tenants' portions at Doulting are attributed (in the *Liber Exoniensis* only) to Ulmarus and Aluuardus. Batcombe had two tenants' portions in addition to the abbot's land. These were held respectively by Vluui and Alfhilla (the mother of the last Anglo-Saxon abbot, Æthelnoth). Neither TRE tenant could be separated from Glastonbury, but only Alfhilla's demesne-hides are called thegnland, the rest of her portion being called *terra uillanorum*. Mells likewise appears to have had two tenants' portions in addition to the abbot's demesne: Godeue held one hide in 1086 which her husband had held in 1066, and this could not be separated from Glastonbury. The other portion (of five and a half hides) was held by two unnamed thegns in 1066 and was lost to the bishop of Coutances, who is said to hold from the king. An estate at *Millescote* – held by the bishop of Coutances TRW and by two unnamed thegns in 1066 – could not be separated from Glastonbury and was, according to the *Liber Exoniensis*, thegnland. This *Millescote* has been identified with the lost portion at Mells.[93] Their hidage is identical and they were both held TRE by two tenants and TRW by the bishop of Coutances. But the values are quite different: 25s. TRE and TRW for the Mells portion and 40s. TRE and £4 TRW for *Millescote*. The former is mentioned in the list of *Terrae occupatae* as having been removed from the twenty-hide manor of Mells; the latter occurs in Domesday Book among the lands of the bishop of Coutances and in the list of *Terrae occupatae*; in that list *Millescota* is called a manor.[94] Morland identified both of these as a single lost holding, and I have chosen to count the two portions as one in my statistics. With such different values (and two entries on

---

90 The *Liber Exoniensis* makes it clear that Alstan held TRE and Alwardus TRW; the Exchequer's text may therefore have been in error when it identified Alstan as the holder in 1086.

91 The breakdown of hides at Butleigh in 1066 adds up to eighteen; Lattiford's two hides are required to make up the twenty-hide total of the estate.

92 He held it freely from the abbot with the consent of the king ('liberaliter de abbate concessu regis') (Domesday Book, I, 90rb [Somerset, 8.20]).

93 See above, chapter III, *s.n.* Mells and *Millescote*.

94 E 520 a1 (*Mulla*) and E 519 b3 (*Millescota*).

the list of *Terrae occupatae*) two separate units of land may, however, be involved, although the values may be incorrect, deriving from confusion in the record.

Wrington had two portions held by tenants in addition to the abbot's land there. Neither could be separated from Glastonbury. Only one tenant is named, Saulf, and he held the land TRE and TRW. At West Monkton, it was the demesne rather than the tenant's portion which the abbot found difficult to hold, an extremely rare circumstance for Glastonbury. According to Domesday Book, Bishop Walkelin (of Winchester) held the abbot's portion: 'modo tenet hanc episcopus Walchelinus de abbate; hec erat de dominicatu abbatis', in the version of the *Liber Exoniensis*.[95] Although the bishop held it *de abbate*, the £7 at which it was valued were explicitly 'for Walkelin's use'. Two tenants' portions which could not be separated from Glastonbury are also noted at West Monkton; the tenants in 1066 are not named, although the *Liber Exoniensis* reveals that three thegns held the first portion. Marksbury had one unit of land held TRE by a tenant, Osuualdus, who could not be separated from Glastonbury. Unusually, the tenant TRW is not named; he is simply called *tainus*. If this signifies a different, Anglo-Saxon, thegn, it would make Marksbury's portion one of very few subtenures held in 1086 by new Anglo-Saxon tenants, ones who had not already held those lands in 1066.

Ditcheat is another of the few estates with named constituent parts: there were five portions held by tenants, in addition to the abbot's land. As at Shapwick and Walton (whose portions are also named), no TRE tenants are identified in the Exchequer's text, although the *Liber Exoniensis* provides a breakdown of numbers and names one tenant, Spirites the priest, as the holder of Lamyatt (which was lost). All of the holders in 1066 are said to have been inseparable from Glastonbury. Three portions of Ditcheat were lost by 1086: seven hides without a given name were held by the count of Mortain from the king, and one unspecified hide held by two men, Alfric and Eurardus, at least one with an Anglo-Saxon name (held by an unnamed thegn in 1066).[96] There is some confusion over the final portion of Ditcheat – five and a half hides at Lamyatt – which Domesday Book records as held from Glastonbury TRW by Nigel. In the *Liber Exoniensis* and in its list of *Terrae occupatae*, however, Lamyatt appears as held in 1086 by Nigel (*medicus*) from the king, not the abbey.[97] This is a rare case of land recorded as lost in the *Liber Exoniensis* not being marked or described (or both) as such in the Exchequer's text of Domesday Book.[98] Stacy has suggested that Glastonbury's

---

[95] C. and F. Thorn have suggested that these demesne-hides were adjacent to the bishop of Winchester's lands at Taunton (*Somerset*, p. 356). By A.D. 1135 West Monkton was back in Glastonbury's demesne. Stacy has suggested that it may have been returned after Abbot Henry of Blois became bishop of Winchester in A.D. 1129 ('The estates', p. 53).

[96] This may be the otherwise unidentified hide (also held in 1086 by Aluric and Eurardus, also worth 20s., also inseparable from Glastonbury but now lost) referred to amongst the *Terrae occupatae* in the *Liber Exoniensis* (E 522 a4).

[97] The removal of *manerium uocatur Lamigeta* from Ditcheat is mentioned in the list of *Terrae occupatae*.

[98] This could mean that the scribes knew the information to be wrong and omitted it

hold on Lamyatt had been loosened when its Anglo-Saxon tenant, Spirites, was exiled by Edward the Confessor.[99]

Brent was an extremely valuable estate. Four tenants (including Godwine the priest) held portions in addition to the abbot's land there in 1086; the pre-Conquest tenants are not named, except for one, Ælfric the abbot's reeve, who was replaced in 1086 by another Ælfric, son of Everwacer. None of the tenants could be separated from the abbot TRE.

Thanks to Domesday Book, therefore, we can at least assemble some data on the men and women who held land from the abbey at the end of the Anglo-Saxon period and calculate the proportion of Glastonbury's total holdings which this land formed, both in hides and in value. The profile varies from county to county, as we have seen, with Dorset showing a very high proportion of land held by tenants, Wiltshire a very low proportion, and Somerset closer to half and half. Overall, tenancies formed a substantial part of the abbey's holdings (approximately forty per cent of the abbey's gross value and forty-three per cent of its hides).[100] The figures compare with those for Worcester, where thirty-nine per cent of the gross value of the church's estate (forty-seven per cent of its hides) was held by tenants.[101] In contrast, Barbara Harvey has estimated that the lands of the church of Westminster's tenants accounted for about seventeen per cent of the gross value of its fee in Domesday Book. She has pointed out that tenants were markedly more common on those estates which Westminster had acquired relatively late; where the monks had held the land securely for years, there seemed to be 'a marked hostility to subtenancies'.[102] This does not seem to have been the case at Glastonbury, where some of the apparently most ancient possessions of the abbey (such as Brent, Pilton, and Shapwick) were divided into portions which were held by the abbot and several tenants; but the difficulty of ascertaining exactly when in every case Glastonbury acquired the estates which made up its endowment in Domesday Book makes it difficult to draw conclusions to match Harvey's. In addition, conditions of tenure on the two abbeys' tenancies may have differed sufficiently to make any such comparison unhelpful.

Although many tenants holding from Glastonbury in 1066 are not identified, it is possible nonetheless to compile a list of thirty-four names, five of whom were ecclesiastics. With a few exceptions, the remaining twenty-nine had modest holdings only, usually consisting of one or two of Glastonbury's estates or portions of

---

deliberately, or that they left it out by mistake. There may also have been a dispute under way, not yet settled when the later record was compiled.

99 Stacy, 'The estates', p. 39. Spirites was a favourite of King Harold Harefoot and King Harthacnut as well as a *clericus regis* of King Edward. He held a large complex of estates until his exile, probably in A.D. 1065; see Barlow, *The English Church 1000–1066*, pp. 132, 135, and 156. His exile is noted by Hemming (*Hemingi Chartularium*, ed. Hearne, I.254) and in the returns for St Mary's, Bromfield (Domesday Book, I, 252vb [Shropshire, 3d.7]).

100 The omission of the values of most tenants' land in Wiltshire (and two in Somerset) must skew this result somewhat.

101 Hamshere, 'The structure and exploitation', p. 48. These figures show a greater discrepancy between value and hidage than is apparent at Glastonbury.

102 Harvey, *Westminster Abbey*, pp. 71–4. For more general (national) figures, see Ayton & Davis, 'Ecclesiastical wealth', especially pp. 52–8.

estates (although some also held other land elsewhere). Only four men are identi-fied as the tenant of more than two of the abbey's estates or sub-units: Brictric (five), Aluuardus (five), Aluuin Pic (three), and Almer (seven); but with so many tenants unidentified for 1066, the real number of estates held by any individual is impossible to calculate. The overall impression, however, is that a relatively large number of men and women held land from Glastonbury, and that most of the tenancies were not concentrated in the hands of a small élite.[103]

It appears that the land held by tenants – especially single, not joint, holders – was the most vulnerable to loss at the Conquest.[104] All but seven hides and three virgates of the total 105 hides and 3 virgates lost consisted of land in tenants' hands. Glastonbury after 1066 lost lands consisting of about fourteen per cent in value (thirteen per cent in hides) of its overall immediately pre-Conquest hold-ings; this represented a loss of about thirty-three per cent of its tenants' land in value (twenty-eight per cent in hides).[105] This circumstance must reflect not just the obvious change in English political fortunes, which must have meant the loss of status (if not of life) for many of the abbey's landholders as a result of Harold's defeat in October 1066; it must tell us something, too, of the nature of the link between the abbot and the tenants' estates. The loss of so many of these suggests that the land in the hands of tenants was the least firmly attached to Glastonbury, or at least the easiest to detach. Unfortunately, there is very little indeed in Domesday Book to illuminate the abbot-tenant link and clarify this phenomenon. Domesday Book's information is based, it seems, on a body of underlying as-sumptions which are nowhere spelled out to enlighten the modern reader. The nature of the ties between the abbey and its dependants is far from clear, although an examination of the terminology of Domesday Book – enigmatic though it no doubt is – can at least reveal something of their possible complexity.

DOMESDAY BOOK: CONDITIONS OF TENURE AND
THE PROBLEM OF TERMINOLOGY

The formulae in Domesday Book which express the tie between lord and man and the conditions by which land was held vary from circuit to circuit.[106] Conversely, terms occurring in all circuits, such as *seruitium*, undoubtedly did not bear the

---

103 At Worcester, the vast majority of tenants were also men of modest means, who held a single holding (occasionally a few). Hamshere has considered it likely that these men were resident on their tenancies; see 'The structure and exploitation', pp. 48–9.

104 Of lost tenants' land, only *Hetsecome*, Mells, and *Stoke* are identified as having had more than one holder. The two newcomers who benefited the most were the bishop of Coutances (twenty-six hides and one virgate, with ten additional acres) and the count of Mortain (twenty-one hides and unassessed woodland). Eleven other Normans held only modest amounts of property seized from Glastonbury (apart from Walter of Douai's substantial fourteen hides at Uffculme). Only nine hides of the appropriated land was said to have been held by the king in 1086.

105 Not all these losses were permanent.

106 Most of Glastonbury's estates were covered in circuit two (Wiltshire, Dorset, Somer-

same meaning in different parts of the country. For this reason, among others, the relationship between Glastonbury's abbot and those who held abbatial estates is difficult to define. At Glastonbury, by contrast with the more loquacious entries for the churches of Ely or Worcester, for example, the Domesday returns are terse and strikingly repetitive, with very few amplifications. Some data regularly appear (such as the information that the holder 'non potuit separari ab ecclesia'), but there is little to parallel the comparative wealth of detail on tenurial conditions to be found elsewhere. In synthetic discussions of late Anglo-Saxon tenure, these details are often imported from one county to another, and conclusions drawn about one place on the basis of information about somewhere else. In my analysis I have attempted to avoid using Domesday Book primarily as a quarry for examples; although where relevant I cite possible parallels in the entries for other, better documented, houses, I have chosen also to focus closely on Glastonbury's returns and examine them as a complete text, to see whether a close reading can be enlightening and reveal something of local tenurial circumstances. Although the spareness of Glastonbury's returns in Domesday Book may avoid the difficulties engendered by the use in other counties of a variety of obscure terms, close examination exposes problems of interpretation even with the few terms and phrases regularly employed. An additional complication – that these terms may have been an attempt to represent in consistent language a set of inconsistent circumstances – must not be forgotten. The ambiguity and vagueness which we find in the terminology may be just the tip of an iceberg of diversity and irregular custom. But we can deal only with what we have.

In general, it is inadvisable to take the data of Domesday Book and subject them to analysis as if they were complete; it is equally unwise to assume that all omissions are significant. Although most of Glastonbury's manors fell within the same circuit in 1086, it is clear that the treatment nevertheless differed from county to county within that circuit. Different information mattered – or was available – to different collectors of that information. Unfortunately, only for Somerset and Devon (and not the five other counties in which the abbey held land) do we have the earlier returns and fuller data of the *Liber Exoniensis*; as a result, we cannot properly compare Glastonbury's Somerset holdings with those in Dorset and Wiltshire, except in the final, edited, version of Domesday Book.

The existence of the same text in two forms may seem to be a boon, but duplication of material is not always a straightforward advantage. In some ways it makes interpretation of the evidence, which can be complicated by disagreements between the two versions, more difficult. It also makes the 'authorised', Exchequer, version of Domesday Book less authoritative, raising doubts not just about its reliability, but about the meanings of terms and the significance of their inclusion in or exclusion from the texts. A few examples should suffice to illustrate the differences between the two versions and the problems which these raise.

Most straightforward are cases where information in the *Liber Exoniensis* has been omitted from the Exchequer's version. Downhead and one portion of Doulting, for example, could not be separated from Glastonbury, according to the

set, Devon, and Cornwall). For the Domesday circuits, see Finn, *An Introduction*, pp. 38–40; for a chart of the possible stages of the returns of circuit two, see Barlow, 'Domesday Book: an introduction', p. 16.

Liber Exoniensis, but the Exchequer's text leaves out this information. We might conclude that these were copying errors, and therefore use the theoretically superior information of the earlier text to include the two lands in the list of those to which this restriction applied. More difficult are cases where the *later* text seems to be adding, rather than subtracting, detail. For example, in describing four of the five tenants' portions at Pilton, the *Liber Exoniensis* states that they could not be separated from Glastonbury, but it says nothing on that subject about the fifth portion. According to the Exchequer's version, *all* who held from the abbot on those estates could not be separated. This information is conveyed in the Exchequer's text in a general statement about the estate, rather than in a portion-by-portion description, as in the *Liber Exoniensis*. There are several possible interpretations. The collective statements in the Exchequer's version, which simplified the entries in the *Liber Exoniensis* and omitted their detail, by avoiding the repetition involved in describing the portions separately may have accidentally ignored peculiar differences (differences which might or might not have had any real significance); thus in this case the *Liber Exoniensis* may be more accurate and the Exchequer's scribe may have incorrectly attributed to one of Pilton's tenants a restriction which he did not actually bear. Alternatively, the information on the fifth tenant may simply have been left out of the *Liber Exoniensis* by mistake, an error which the Exchequer's scribe may have deliberately corrected. The same thing can be seen at Brent and Walton, where similar collective statements in the Exchequer's version, that none of the portions could be separated from Glastonbury, include some places about which this is not said in the *Liber Exoniensis*. Does this matter?

The answer to that question depends on whether an apparent omission by the author or scribe of the *Liber Exoniensis* has any significance. This is not simply a technical question, with the goal of determining a correct text; the greater aim is rather to decide what the information means, and inclusion or exclusion of detail is significant because it affects the shape of the data on which interpretation is based. If we knew whether the exclusion of information was meaningful, that is to say, whether those who are said to be inseparable from Glastonbury actually held their land on terms different from those of tenants about whom no such thing is said, we could analyse the cases in the two groups and draw further conclusions. If we were to decide that the exclusion was accidental, the two groups would merge instantly into one.

The same situation obtains with the references to thegnland. The Exchequer's text frequently omits the information (provided in the *Liber Exoniensis*) that a piece of land was thegnland (at, for example, Brompton Ralph, Camerton, Pennard, and Shapwick). Conversely, three places are identified in the later text as thegnland, but not in the *Liber Exoniensis*. Hutton and Elborough appear in the Exchequer's version in a list of four estates, collectively called thegnlands, although in the *Liber Exoniensis* only the other two on the list are given the title. Did the Exchequer's version just rationalise, and call them *all* thegnlands, in error? Or was the *Liber Exoniensis* in error to omit the term for these two? Would their status as thegnlands have been so obvious that the omission had no significance, leading the Exchequer's scribes to supply it automatically? A third example may help to enlighten us. Stratton, on the same list as the two mentioned above, is, like them, called thegnland in the Exchequer's text but not in the main entry for the estate in the *Liber Exoniensis*; in the list of *Terrae occupatae* in the *Liber Exoniensis*, however, Stratton is also called thegnland. This would tend to support the interpretation that the omission from the main entry in the *Liber Exoniensis* lacks significance; but, as J.H. Round warned, 'it is neither safe nor legitimate to make general inferences from a single entry' in Domesday Book,[107] and we must avoid drawing conclusions which rest on the very shaky foundation of a lone example from these complex texts.

Despite this uncertainty about their application, the meaning of the phrase 'non potuit ab ecclesia separari' and of the term *tainlande* must be examined, if we are to learn anything from Domesday Book about the conditions of tenure on Glastonbury's estates in 1066. To begin with, what can be said about Glastonbury's thegnlands? The evidence suggests that, in general, the grant of land as thegnland did not constitute anything like an enfeoffment: it appears to have been only a temporary alienation of the church's property. It seems too to have been a category of land which could be manipulated. At Overleigh, one hide which had been thegnland TRE was apparently back in the abbot's demesne TRW. On at least two estates, thegnland consisted of land which did not pay tax.[108] Among Glastonbury's returns at least, it was a category which seems to have applied most commonly to entire holdings, not portions. Several of the estates which the abbey had lost by 1086 are called thegnland, including Brompton Ralph, which is described thus in the *Liber Exoniensis*: 'haec mansura fuit teglanda de ecclesia Glastingesberie et non potuit ab ecclesia separare [*sic*]'.

There is little here on which to base an interpretation, nor is there elsewhere an explicit source which can illuminate the genesis of thegnland and provide a definition for us today. Specifically, scholars have been unable satisfactorily to distinguish thegnland from other types of non-demesne-land (or even, in some cases, to recognise a potential need for such a distinction). It has been suggested by Finn that in some cases thegnland was granted to 'those who served ecclesiastical organizations . . . in an official capacity'.[109] It is indeed clear that in addition to renders and/or cash, holders of thegnland owed services, but the process of accumulation of these responsibilities (and their nature) is obscure. One possible explanation of thegnland rests specifically on the responsibility of monastic establishments for the standard public burdens, described, for example, in a lease issued by Brihthelm, bishop of Winchester, as 'þæs woruldweorces þe a eal folc weorcean sceal' (S.693; A.D. 961);[110] most grants to Church and laypeople alike were specifically not exempt from these obligations.[111] The means by which they were met has not been fully discovered, but it may be that land was specifically

---

107 Round, *Feudal England*, p. 30.
108 Half a hide at Shapwick and a hide at Pilton.
109 Finn, *An Introduction*, p. 138.
110 'The secular service which must be performed by the whole nation': *Anglo-Saxon Charters*, ed. & transl. Robertson, pp. 62–3 (no. 33).
111 For example, S.431 (from Glastonbury's archive), specifies 'sit predicta terra libera in omnibus mundialibus causis preter pontis et arcis construccione expeditionisque adiuuamine in cunctis successoribus' ('let the aforementioned land for all successors be free from all worldly claims, except for bridge-building, fortress-building, and military service').

set aside, and that the land earmarked for these purposes 'retained a permanent distinction from the demesne and the *terra uillanorum*', as Stacy has suggested.[112] Some have associated a five-hide unit more strictly with the performance of the military element of these duties.[113] Stacy has found sufficient trace of the organisation of Glastonbury's endowment in five-hide units to conclude that the 'disposition of Glastonbury's estates had seemingly been made with the performance of the *trimoda necessitas* in mind'.[114] Glastonbury's Domesday thegnlands could be the descendants of such units; the editors of Wiltshire's Domesday Book returns have in fact defined thegnland as 'land reserved by a lord, commonly a church, for the maintenance of a thane, armed and mounted'.[115] Nevertheless, the fact that Domesday Book apparently catches at least one thegnland in movement throws some doubt on the permanence of the arrangement. The fact, too, that some thegnland clearly was on the abbot's demesne (as at Overleigh, where of two demesne-hides, one was thegnland)[116] and some on ungelded land points to a complexity which has not always been fully appreciated.

Other motives for the creation of thegnland can be suggested but not demonstrated. Although it was ideologically unsound, abbots, like the king, needed to provide for family-members:[117] Abbot Æthelnoth's mother, for example, was a tenant on thegnland at Batcombe in 1066. Ecclesiastical houses must also have sought support and patronage from important laymen: a few of Glastonbury's tenants who are recorded in Domesday Book were men of national stature,[118] and it is possible to envisage the abbey allowing them to hold the land on superior terms, perhaps without services, with the aim of soliciting their goodwill.[119] In some cases kings may have used monastic land rather than their own demesne for the same purpose. S.513, for example, a grant by King Edmund, provided for land to be given to his queen, Æthelflæd, for her lifetime, after which Glastonbury would take possession of the three places mentioned. At least one of the estates which it granted (Pentridge) was in 1066 in the hands of a subtenant with important connexions with King Edward's consort, Edith, thereby suggesting the continued association of this estate with the queen; in 1086 it was held by King William.[120] The ideal of the inalienability of Church lands, however, and the

---

112 Stacy, 'The estates', p. 34.
113 For example, Hollings, 'The survival', and Hollister, *Anglo-Saxon Military Institutions*, especially pp. 38–58.
114 Stacy, 'The estates', p. 38. See also Stevenson, 'Trinoda necessitas'; Stenton, 'The thriving', pp. 388–9; John, *Orbis Britanniae*, pp. 144–5; and Abels, *Lordship and Military Obligations*, pp. 54–7 and 125–31.
115 *Wiltshire*, edd. & transl. Thorn & Thorn, 1.3 (note); see also Finn, *An Introduction*, pp. 138–40.
116 'In dominio .ii. hidae una ex his fuit teinland.'
117 The giving of land to family (or other secular people) was expressly criticised in the Old English account of the establishment of the reformed monasteries: *Leechdoms*, ed. & transl. Cockayne, III.442–4; *English Historical Documents*, transl. Whitelock, pp. 920–3, at 922 (no. 238).
118 Such as Wulfweard the White, Harding of Wilton (Queen Edith's chamberlain), and Spirites the priest (a royal clerk).
119 Stacy ('The estates', p. 23) has also suggested this.
120 See above, chapter III, *s.n.* Damerham, and p. 277; there is some suggestion that

strong lordship of the ecclesiastical landlord would presumably have led to the development of specialised forms of subtenancy which would have offered the least risk to the integrity of the endowment. Different means – services, payments, commendation, rituals – would have been established to preserve the link between the monastic lord and the holder of thegnland (or indeed any sort of tenant) so that, when he or she died or the land otherwise came to be reabsorbed into the demesne, the church's title was as inviolate as possible. This, at least, would have been the desired goal.

Miller proposed that thegnland was not necessarily created from above, that is to say, granted out from the abbey's demesne; some thegnland in Domesday Book, he argued, could represent land given over by modest individuals eager to put themselves under the abbot's protection.[121] This appears to assume the identity of thegnland with any land held from the abbot by a layperson; it also blurs the distinction between types of lordship. Relationships involving property-rights and obligations were of (at least) three sorts, of varying strength, and although they could overlap it seems best to preserve at least a conceptual distinction here. The strongest involved the interest which actual tenure gave to a landlord – articulated by the terms *terra* or *consuetudines*. Additionally there was *soca* – rights of jurisdiction. Thirdly there was commendation, the weakest tie.[122] The nature of the connexion between thegnland and one or all of these is obscure. We are seriously hampered by the paucity of evidence on the subject, and Glastonbury's record is particularly spare. Domesday Book is our principal witness, and I shall now return to the task of defining the term thegnland from the evidence of that source.

The minimalist explanation – that thegnland could simply mean land held by thegns[123] – does little to advance our understanding of the tenurial relationship behind the name. Besides, at Glastonbury's estate of Batcombe, a tenant held a seven-hide portion, but only the five hides in demesne are called thegnland (the rest being identified as *terra uillanorum*). It was J.H. Round in his influential study, *Feudal England*, who defined thegnland as land which could not legally be alienated from the church which owned it.[124] Round compared the returns for Ely in the Exchequer's version with those preserved in two other texts – the *Inquisitio Eliensis* and the *Inquisitio Comitatus Cantabrigiensis* – and distinguished be-

Wulfweard the White, the holder until his death before or in 1086, had been one of the queen's thegns and had held his other estates from her.

121 Miller, *The Abbey*, p. 52; also Finn, *An Introduction*, p. 138.

122 Roffe has argued that *terra* constituted the essential identity of the manor. When the rights entailed in tenure of *terra* (which involved the payment of dues by the tenant) were combined with rights of jurisdiction (*soca*), the holder enjoyed full rights, a concept expressed by the term *saca et soca* (although not in East Anglia): 'From thegnage to barony', pp. 163–6; see also Reynolds, 'Bookland, folkland, and fiefs', p. 222.

123 Stephenson, 'Commendation', p. 297; Williams, 'Introduction to the Dorset Domesday', pp. 39-40.

124 Although thegnland existed on royal manors (South Petherton, for example [Domesday Book, I, 86rb; Somerset, 1.4]), it was found – if Domesday Book is to be taken literally – principally on ecclesiastical estates.

tween two types of tenure: sokeland could be alienated by its holder, but the holder of thegnland 'non potuit dare nec uendere' without the abbot's permission.[125] Tenants holding by both types of tenure could be found on different portions of the same estate: at Meldreth and Melbourne (Cambridgeshire), for example, there were eight tenants who could alienate their land and one who could not, the former holding *de soca* and the latter holding *thainlande*.[126] A writ of William the Conqueror distinguished likewise between those who held thegnlands and those who held *soca et saca*.[127] Although the holder *de soca abbatiae* could dispose of his or her land, 'saca et soca et commendatio et seruitium semper remanebat ecclesia de Ely'.[128]

On Ely's lands, therefore, the distinction between holders of thegnland and holders simply of *soca* is explicit; are there parallels at Glastonbury for this distinction? There is certainly no reference to anything like sokeland; no tenant of the abbot is said to be able to sell or leave his land. The tenants are not, however, prohibited from doing so in the same terms as at Ely (non potuit uendere, recedere, dare, ire): apart from two entries from counties other than Somerset,[129] the one repeated restriction applied to Glastonbury's tenants is the unfortunately more ambiguous 'non potuit ab ecclesia separari'.[130] The majority of Glastonbury's estates or portions of estates in Somerset and Wiltshire held by tenants were said to be subject to this restriction; but in some cases it is not mentioned. Does this prohibition have the same implications concerning inalienability of land as those at Ely, or might different forms of separation possibly be at issue? A much smaller proportion of Glastonbury's estates are called thegnland. Is this another way of saying the same thing? The simplest solution would be to assume so.

There is a slight possibility, however, that the term 'thegnland' and the phrase *non potuit ab ecclesia separari* are not synonymous in Glastonbury's entries in Domesday Book; at least, sufficient doubt exists to discourage us from immediately assuming them to mean the same thing. If the two are not synonymous, the prohibition of separation may not equal the inalienability of land, an equation laid out for us at Ely but not at Glastonbury. The question is at least worth examining, although it rests on an interpretation of textual inconsistencies which (as above) may not be significant. It might be unwise to ignore such evidence, however, in view of the oft-cited entry for Hinton in Dorset, where a priest who held one hide of thegnland 'poterat cum ea ire quo uolebat'.[131]

---

[125] Round, *Feudal England*, pp. 19–40, especially p. 36; see also Finn, *An Introduction*, p. 138, and Miller, *The Abbey*, pp. 50–1 and 63. On sokeland in the northern Danelaw, see Stenton, 'Types of manorial structure', pp. 7–55.

[126] Round, *Feudal England*, p. 36.

[127] *Ibid.*, p. 35.

[128] *Ibid.*, p. 36 ('*sac*, soke, commendation, and service always remained with the church of Ely').

[129] Idmiston, in Wiltshire, where Glastonbury's tenant 'qui tenebat TRE non poterat ab ecclesia diuerti', and Ower, in Hampshire, where 'tenuit de abbate et non potuit ire quo uoluit'.

[130] With one type of variation: at Marksbury, for example, the *Liber Exoniensis* substitutes *abbate* for *ecclesia*.

[131] Domesday Book, I, 76ra (Dorset, 1.31).

Coming back to Glastonbury's data, we face again the problem of inconsistencies in the two versions of the abbey's entries: at Ham, for example, three portions are said to be inseparable from the church, but only one of them is called thegnland, and that only in the *Liber Exoniensis*. Were the other two portions *not* thegnland, or are we simply to interpret them as thegnland without being told specifically that they are? Conversely, at Pennard one hide is called thegnland in the *Liber Exoniensis*, but nothing is said in either text about its being inseparable. Are we to assume that it was inseparable, or is the omission significant? Other entries, such as that for one hide in Camerton or three-quarters of a hide in Christian Malford, could be variously interpreted. When we read in Domesday Book that 'haec terra teinlande non potuit ab ecclesia separari', we could take the second half of the statement as a definition of the term or as an additional condition. It is ambiguous as it stands. A few further cases complicate the issue. At Overleigh, one of the two hides in the abbot's demesne 'fuit teinland, non tamen poterat ab ecclesia separari'.[132] This is not the only example in which thegnland appears to be *opposed* to the inability to alienate: at Clatworthy, likewise, 'haec terra non poterat separari ab ecclesia Glast., sed erat ibi tainlande TRE',[133] according to the Exchequer's text. The entry in the *Liber Exoniensis* for this estate adds to the confusion: 'haec mansura fuit teglanda de ecclesia Glast. ita quod non potuit ab ecclesia separari'.[134]

One circumstance tends to undermine any significance placed on the appearance or non-appearance of the 'thegnland' label. It seems to have been more diligently applied in cases where exceptional circumstances of at least two (observable) sorts pertained. First, it is quite consistently attached to those lands which Glastonbury had lost between 1066 and 1086. In the entry for the three-hide estate of Langford in Wiltshire, for example, two hides are stated without elaboration to be held in 1086 from the abbot, but the hide 'quae iure pertinet abbatiae ad tainlande' had been lost to the king. The presence of the term is even more striking in the section at the end of the abbot's Somerset returns, where most of the lost estates are listed: almost all are called thegnland. It appears that the 'thegnland' label was more consistently included in Domesday Book if the land had left Glastonbury's possession.

Secondly, although thegnland seems in most cases to be a pre-Conquest category and is usually mentioned in the past tense, there are a few exceptions, where the present tense is applied. Portions *de teglanda*[135] at Ham, Camerton, Pennard, and Shapwick are said in the *Liber Exoniensis* to be held by Norman tenants in 1086. This could perhaps be the result of scribal sloppiness, thanks to which the

132 'One of the hides was thegnland; nevertheless it was not separable from the church.' This is the Exchequer's version; the phrasing in the *Liber Exoniensis* differs slightly but maintains the adversative force of the Exchequer's *tamen*: 'una ex istis fuit teglanda TRE et quidam tegnus tenuit TRE sed non potuit ab ecclesia separari'.
133 'This land was not separable from the church of Glastonbury but it was thegnland there TRE.'
134 'This manor was thegnland of the church of Glastonbury to the extent that [with the result that?] it was not separable from the church.'
135 Old English *land* is neuter, but *tainland*, *teglanda*, and similar forms in Domesday Book appear to be Latin feminine nouns (perhaps drawing their gender from *terra*).

term had been attached by mistake to the Norman rather than the Anglo-Saxon context. Arguing against this are two examples from a later section of the Exchequer's text for Somerset, under the lands of the king's servants, where a part of Dulverton and one of Withypool about which there had been some dispute or confusion 'modo diratiocinata est in tainland' and 'modo diiudicata est esse tainland'.[136] Thegnland, then, seems to have been an active category still in 1086, despite the fact that the overwhelming majority of estates or portions are so described only with reference to 1066. It is impossible with the slight evidence available to us to determine whether this means that some land remained thegnland and some did not; in view of one body of recent opinion, that the Norman Conquest did not significantly alter ideas about the rights and obligations of property in England,[137] thegnland may not have disappeared as a concept in 1066; but Glastonbury's entries in Domesday Book do (mostly) give it the appearance of belonging to a dead order. Perhaps, however, it was just the majority of its Anglo-Saxon holders who were dead in 1086.

The occasional references in the present tense to a tenant's inseparability may further the question slightly. They too contrast with the overwhelming number of references in the past tense, applied to the TRE tenants only. Cranmore's tenant, however, who held TRE and TRW, was not separable ('non potest separari') in both the *Liber Exoniensis* and the Exchequer's text. This could be interpreted as an error and disregarded, but the case of Deverill makes it clear that we should be unwise to do so, for there the reference to the present is undeniable: 'nec potuit neque potest ab ecclesia haec terra separari'.[138] Tenants who had managed to maintain their holdings between 1066 and 1086 are therefore explicitly bound by the same tenurial restriction. Whatever equation we might have been tempted to make between post-1066 thegnland and land which continued to be inseparable at that date is confused by the following entry (if it is not a scribal blunder) for one of the portions of Pilton: 'Haec tainland fuit et nec potest ab ecclesia separari.'[139]

The present tense in the references to inseparability appears to apply only to continuing tenants,[140] although not all are so treated.[141] The present tense could indicate that the conditions of tenure of that particular tenant were explicitly the same before and after the Conquest, although, if we draw that conclusion, we raise the interesting question of just how everyone else's had changed. Another (more likely?) possibility is that such a restriction needed to be specified only for continuing tenants. If so, why was it necessary to spell it out for surviving

---

[136] 'Is now judged to be thegnland': Domesday Book, I, 98va (Somerset, 46.2–3).

[137] Reynolds, 'Bookland, folkland and fiefs', p. 224; see also Roffe, 'From thegnage to barony'.

[138] There is a similar reference in an entry for Cerne Abbey: 'Brictuinus . . . tenuit similiter TRE et non potuit recedere ab ecclesia nec potest' (Domesday Book, I, 77vb [Dorset, 11.1]). Brictwin too held TRE and TRW.

[139] That is the Exchequer's version; the wording of the *Liber Exoniensis* keeps the same sense ('tenet Alnodus monachus . . . – haec erat teglanda – de abbate et non potest separari ecclesia').

[140] At Pilton it is impossible to tell, as the TRE holder is not named (although the TRW tenant had an Anglo-Saxon name).

[141] Saulf, who held a portion of Wrington, is one exception.

Anglo-Saxons but not for new, Norman, tenants? The references to thegnland in the present tense show a different pattern, as the term was applied in all TRW cases to land held by Norman newcomers in 1086.[142] The difficulty could, of course, be argued away by citing scribal incompetence or inattention,[143] but this is not a very satisfactory solution.

If there is some doubt about the equation of the *non potuit separari* prohibition and thegnland, and about the relation of the first term to restrictions on the alienability of land, alternative explanations must be sought. According to Stephenson, Round in his later work suggested that freedom to depart meant not the freedom to dispose of land but the freedom to seek a new lord.[144] This raises the question of commendation, a subject which has generated much confusion and controversy.[145] At Ely, as has been seen above, and at other East Anglian houses (Bury St Edmunds, for example), the tenants who could leave their land were still attached to the abbey by the ties of soke and commendation and service – what Barbara Dodwell called 'seigneurial rights' – ties which also bound the holders of thegnland, who, lacking in addition the power of alienation, were subject to 'full ownership rights'.[146] Peter Sawyer has pointed out that simple commendation – the acknowledgement of a lord – was a relatively weak bond, which did not legally confer title.[147] Dodwell admitted that in relation to these eastern houses 'the exact nature of this seigneurial tie is obscure. It clearly included commendation, but was probably a compound rather than a simple bond. The whole trend of the evidence points to a tie that embraced more than commendation, for commendation, custom, and service all play their part'.[148] According to Dodwell, the relationship was inherent in the land, not the individual, that is to say, it was 'territorial not personal'. 'So frequently was the tenant of [temporarily alienated demesne] commended to the head of the church concerned that there would appear to be a definite connection between this dependent tenure and commendation.'[149]

---

[142] As it was in similar references outside Glastonbury's estates: cf. Nettlecombe (Dorset) where 'unus miles francigena habet duas hidas de teinland' (E 38 a1).

[143] Especially in view of the kind of blunder visible in the Mells entry, where the formula of the *Liber Exoniensis*, 'et non potuit separari', became 'sed non potuit separari' in the Exchequer's version; errors of this kind do not appear to be common, however.

[144] Stephenson, 'Commendation', p. 293; Eric John and Ann Williams have also subscribed to this view (*Land Tenure*, p. 138; 'How land was held', p. 38).

[145] For a variety of approaches, see Maitland, *Domesday Book and Beyond*, pp. 67–75; Miller, *The Abbey*, pp. 58–65; Stephenson, 'Commendation'; Dodwell, 'East Anglian commendation'; and Reynolds, 'Bookland, folkland and fiefs', pp. 222–3.

[146] Dodwell, 'East Anglian commendation', p. 293.

[147] Sawyer, '1066–1086', pp. 80–1; see also Roffe, 'From thegnage to barony', pp. 163–4. Fleming, however, has drawn attention to examples of post-Conquest disputes involving Norman claims to land through the 'personal' bonds (of commendation) as well as the tenurial rights of their Anglo-Saxon *antecessores*: *Kings and Lords*, pp. 126–30.

[148] Dodwell, 'East Anglian commendation', p. 304.

[149] There has been much discussion of this issue; cf. Maitland, *Domesday Book and Beyond*, pp. 69-75, Stephenson, 'Commendation', especially p. 306, n. 1, and Dodwell, 'East Anglian commendation', p. 299. The quotation is from Dodwell, pp. 293–4.

It was possible to work out this distinction between the possession of full ownership rights and of jurisdictional and/or so-called seigneurial rights in East Anglia, where the Exchequer's returns and the satellite-texts are rich in detail relevant to the question. But there appears to be no evidence in Domesday Book for the separate exercise of these seigneurial rights by Glastonbury Abbey. Service does indeed appear in its returns, and will be discussed below.[150] But I can find no suggestion of judicial *soca* in any of the abbey's entries (although an incident recounted in the *De antiquitate* may imply it,[151] and the privileges in the names of King Edmund and King Edgar claim a variety of legal rights).[152] Likewise, nowhere in Glastonbury's returns in Domesday Book is there any explicit notice of dependence, and commendation does not appear by name;[153] one phrase may imply it, but analysis of the question is bedevilled by the problem, discussed above, of the significance of omission of detail and of variation in terminology.[154]

The phrase in question is *de abbate*, as in 'Gerardus tenet de abbate Graintone'. Does this imply a seigneurial tie, as it did at Ely, where the more important holders of land were recorded, not explicitly as commended to the abbot, but as holding *de abbate* or *sub abbate*, terms which are synonymous in the Exchequer's text, the *Inquisitio Eliensis*, and the *Inquisitio Comitatus Cantabrigiensis* with the identification *homo abbatiae de Ely*?[155] Or rather, does the absence of the phrase from a substantial number of the entries for Glastonbury's estates imply the absence of the tie? A comparison of the entries in the Exchequer's version and the *Liber Exoniensis* should help to illuminate this question. Although the information on this matter is in most instances identical in the two sources, in a substantial number of cases an estate is said in the Exchequer's text to have been held *de abbate*, whereas the *Liber Exoniensis* is silent; the fact that the reverse is also true (with a number of other, different, lands identified in the *Liber Exoniensis* as held *de abbate*) suggests that the inclusion or exclusion of the term is not meaning-ful.[156] *De abbate* can, therefore, probably be taken as read in those entries which omit it.[157] But it seems impossible to determine what exact significance the phrase had for the Somerset commissioners and the Domesday Book clerks; it

---

150 See pp. 301–5.
151 A confrontation between Abbot Thurstan and the abbots of Muchelney and Athelney (*De antiquitate*, §76; ed. & transl. Scott, pp. 154–6) suggests that in the late eleventh century the abbot of Glastonbury had legal jurisdiction over these neighbouring abbots and legal independence in 'Glastonbury' (the territorial extent of which is uncertain).
152 S.499 and S.783. Neither of these survives in its original form and the texts may consequently have been altered after they were composed.
153 According to Sawyer, it is mentioned regularly only in circuits three and seven ('1066–1086', p. 83).
154 See pp. 291–2.
155 Dodwell, 'East Anglian commendation', pp. 293–4. Roffe ('From thegnage to barony', pp. 171–2) has noted that in Nottinghamshire, there is a distinction between Anglo-Saxons, who are said to 'have their land under' or to 'hold from', and foreigners, who are called 'men of' the tenants-in-chief.
156 See the entries for Walton, which illustrate omissions and inclusions in both directions.
157 By far the greatest number of the references to tenants holding *de abbate* occurs in relation to TRW rather than TRE tenants (but not all: see Brent, for example).

may perhaps have been synonymous with 'non potuit separari ab ecclesia', as the most noticeable omissions of that phrase occur in two blocks of entries, all of which concerning lands held *de abbate*.[158] It may have meant (as Ann Williams has suggested) land held by lease.[159] Certainly its absence should not be used as evidence of a type of tenure in which the tenant was not subject to the abbot. Whether at Glastonbury *de abbate* bore the specific meaning of commendation which it did at Ely is uncertain. Whether there were additionally bonds of commendation between the abbey and a group of free dependants is equally uncertain, but as these dependants are singularly invisible at Glastonbury the question may be otiose. If laymen did enter into a contract of commendation with Glastonbury without turning their land over to the abbey, we apparently have no record of it. If a lord undertook such a contract *and* surrendered his land, we have evidence only of the final result – Glastonbury's acquisition of the property – but not the conditions established by the transfer or its means.[160]

The rare references to 'free tenure' should be considered here. This is an uncommon term in Glastonbury's entries in Domesday Book,[161] and, as usual, its meaning is obscure. For example, Brictric held a hide at Winscombe in 1066 freely, though he could not separate from Glastonbury ('libere tenuit TRE, sed non potuit ab ecclesia separari'). This rather contradicts Paul Vinogradoff's description of free tenure as having nothing to do with status or condition, but as relating to the disposal of property (if 'separating' did indeed involve the latter).[162] Likewise there are four references to estates or portions of estates held *pariter*, which Stephenson defined as 'not an exact equivalent of *libere*, . . . but merely one variety of Anglo-Saxon free tenure which regularly implied liberty of alienation for a group of co-heirs'.[163] Three of Glastonbury's estates described thus (at Hutton, Stoke, and Alhampton in Ditcheat) could not be separated from the abbot.[164] Sawyer has interpreted references of this sort as indicating a tenant who could transfer his rights and obligations to someone else but could not put the land under another lord.[165] Roffe has upheld a connexion between 'holding freely (*libere*)' and freedom of commendation.[166] Given the invisibility of com-

---

[158] The entries are for Cossington, Durborough, Blackford, and Stawell (TRE and TRW); at *Bodesleghe*, Dundon, Ashcott, and Greinton *de abbate* is used in relation to the TRW tenants only.

[159] Williams, 'How land was held', p. 38; on leases, see further below (pp. 305–9).

[160] The statements in the contents-list of the *Liber terrarum* – that Wulfric's *successor commendauit* two estates (Horton and Nettleton; LT44 and LT46) to Glastonbury – may appear suggestive, but as the man in question brought the land with him on becoming a monk, *commendauit* may be more likely in this case simply to signify 'transfer' rather any element of commendation.

[161] In four places in the entry in the *Liber Exoniensis* for Shapwick there is a space left blank where the word *libere* (or *pariter*) would have been appropriate. In the Exchequer's version these words do not appear, nor do any blank spaces.

[162] Vinogradoff, *English Society in the Eleventh Century*, p. 406.

[163] Stephenson, 'Commendation', p. 295, n. 2.

[164] These three tenures (and the fourth, Tintinhull) are not described as held *pariter* in the Exchequer's text, but in the *Liber Exoniensis* only.

[165] Sawyer, '1066–1086', p. 80.

[166] Roffe, 'From thegnage to barony', p. 163.

mended men on Glastonbury's estates, and assuming the prohibition clause to mean inalienability of land, the second interpretation seems more suitable in the context of late Anglo-Saxon Glastonbury, though there is no evidence to prove it.

The second case of free tenure is that of a monk who held one hide of the land at Pilton in 1086 'liberaliter per consensu regis – haec erat teglanda – de abbate et non potest separari ab ecclesia'. If the freedom referred to the choice of lord, it would at least explain how thegnland, otherwise a dependent and inalienable tenure (if we know nothing else about it), could be free. There are other possible interpretations, however.[167] Sawyer's remarks are appropriate here: 'The suspicion that freedom in Domesday Book had a special meaning is encouraged by the fact that many people who clearly enjoyed the greatest freedom, the bishops, earls, and leading thegns, are normally never described as free. . . . The implication is that people described as free in fact normally had some limitation on their freedom.'[168]

One certain aspect of thegnland tenure on Glastonbury's estates is that it involved service. The evidence for service appears mainly in cases where it had been lost, along with the land, between 1066 and 1086. From the Somerset thegnlands of Hutton, Elborough, *Hetsecome*, and Stratton 'ecclesia seruitium inde non habet'; a similar phrase follows the entries for Kingstone and an unidentified five hides in both Domesday-texts.[169] In the *Liber Exoniensis* only, Glastonbury is said to have lost the service from three other thegnlands in Somerset which had been seized, two at Stoke and one at Draycott. In Wiltshire, Kington St Michael is not called thegnland, but the situation appears to be identical: 'Aluuinus tenebat hanc terram de ecclesia Glastingeberie, et non poterat ab ea separari, et inde seruiebat abbati.' Typically, we are in the dark as to not just the nature of these services, but their derivation. Dodwell suggested (and rejected) an identification of *seruitium* in East Anglia with 'a sum of money in recognition of the bond of commendation';[170] Glastonbury's entries are too terse to allow such speculation.[171]

If nothing else is clear from these references to the service due from thegnland, it is that J.E.A. Jolliffe's argument against the existence of a 'tenure of thegnage' ignored examples such as are found at Glastonbury. Jolliffe saw 'the land-right of thegns as a right of property void of condition, and their service as a *ministerium*

---

[167] The king's consent may have sanctioned the removal of secular burdens, leaving the tenant holding *liberaliter*, i.e., free of these obligations. 'Haec erat teglanda', then, could either mean that this freedom (with the king's consent) was what defined thegnland or, alternatively, that because it was thegnland, the king's permission was needed for the burdens to be lifted. It is also possible that the holder's monastic status was what made permission necessary.

[168] Sawyer, '1066–1086', p. 79.

[169] The latter is not called thegnland, but it is said to have been inseparable from Glastonbury.

[170] Dodwell, 'East Anglian commendation', pp. 299–300.

[171] It is interesting to note, however, that in the contents-list of the *Liber terrarum* and the rubrics of the *Index chartarum* all laymen who reputedly transferred land to Glastonbury are referred to as *seruientes*.

by personal undertaking not by tenurial condition'.[172] Not all thegnland was held by thegns, nor did all thegns hold thegnland, but when thegns did hold thegnland they were subject to services which formed part of the conditions of tenure. It is possible, in fact, that the kind of service rendered is what gave the land its name. The example of Durnford in Wiltshire (an estate of St Mary's, Wilton) is highly suggestive: it was held TRE by three Englishmen who could not be separated from the church. Two of them paid (*reddebant*) 5s. and the third *seruiebat sicut tainus*.[173] If we compare this with comments found in the entries for several estates of St Peter's, Westminster (at Naunton, Worcestershire, for example), that 'qui has terras tenebant sicut alii liberi homines seruiebant',[174] it appears that service could be defined by the tenant's status (or *vice versa*). Likewise, at Huddington (Worcestershire), an estate of St Mary's, Worcester, 'Wulfric tenuit, sicut rusticus seruiens'.[175] It appears, at least from the example of Batcombe, cited above, that a tenant did not necessarily owe thegnly services on the entirety of his or her estate, however, but only on the demesne-hides: only five hides of a larger tenancy there were called thegnland, the remainder being *terra uillanorum*.

Unfortunately, the services required from Glastonbury's estates were in all instances either self-evident, flexible, or extremely complicated (or all of the above); in any event, there is no surviving record, even in the entries in Domesday Book for those of Glastonbury's estates said to owe *seruitium*.[176] We must look elsewhere for possible parallels. Owing to the unsystematic use of the term thegnland and the possibility that it could describe different conditions in different parts of the country, such a comparative exercise has limited value, but it does at least introduce a range of options.

The *Rectitudines singularum personarum* specifies that on a thegn's bookland, in addition to the duty of bridge-work, fortress-work, and armed service, further service for the king could arise 'connected with the deer fence at the king's residence, and equipping a guard ship, and guarding the coast, and guarding the lord, and military watch, almsgiving and church dues and many other various things'.[177] Ecclesiastical lords no doubt had their own lists of special require-

---

172 Jolliffe, 'Alod and fee', p. 233. In contrast, see Campbell, 'Some agents and agencies'. A letter from Bishop Oswald to King Edgar *ca* A.D. 964 specifies that Worcester's tenants were subject to the authority of the bishop on account of the benefice leased to them (*beneficium prestitum*), according to the amount of land each one possessed (S.1368; translated in Brown, *Origins*, pp. 133–5).

173 'Rendered service like a thegn' (Domesday Book, I, 67vb [Wiltshire, 13.3]). Hollister has used this example to support his arguments about military service (*Anglo-Saxon Military Institutions*, pp. 79-80).

174 'Those who held these estates gave service just like other free men' (Domesday Book, I, 175ra [Worcestershire, 8.16]) (also Piddle [8.15]).

175 'Wulfric held it, rendering service like a peasant' (Domesday Book, I, 173va [Worcestershire, 2.57]).

176 Stacy ('The estates', p. 212) stated that one free tenement was claimed in the *Liber Henrici* of A.D. 1189 to have been held since Abbot Æthelnoth's day for *gafol* and riding service; this service could, however, have been imposed after 1066. I have been unable to find Stacy's example in the text of the *Liber Henrici*.

177 *Die Gesetze*, ed. Liebermann, I.444–5; *English Historical Documents*, transl. Douglas & Greenaway, p. 875 (no. 172).

ments. During the reign of King Edward, the abbot of St Alban's granted land to three men in return for the service (among others) of protecting the monastery from the wild beasts and robbers of the western region of the Chilterns.[178] James Campbell has emphasised how 'the control and exploitation of such rural empires' as were found throughout eleventh-century England depended on the service of men who maintained the link between the centre and the parts of these huge estates.[179] Bishop Oswald's letter to King Edgar, in which he spelled out the conditions of the leases which he had issued at Worcester, specified that the recipients should 'fulfil the whole law of riding as riding men should',[180] and should 'hold themselves available to supply all the needs of the bishop; they shall lend horses, they shall ride themselves, and, moreover, be ready to build bridges and do all that is necessary in burning lime for the work of the church. They shall be prepared to make deer hedges for the bishop's hunting, and they must send their own hunting spears to the chase whenever the lord bishop wishes.' The service required from tenants on Ely's lands who could not grant or sell their land is occasionally specified, showing a range of obligations, including riding service (as at Blot, where the tenant had to 'seruire cum propriis equis in omnibus necessitatibus' of the abbot)[181] and *auera* and *inguardus* (cartage and escort) (West Wratting and Balsham, Cambridgeshire).[182] Dodwell argued that on Ely's estates, *seruitium* was 'synonymous with labour obligations',[183] which included ploughing. Other agricultural services are spelled out in some detail, especially in East Anglia.[184] These most frequently apply to the tasks required of the labouring classes on their lords' land, rather than the obligations which tenants owed to their lords by virtue of their tenancy.[185] Labour services which thegns were apparently obliged to perform on lands they had leased are also occasionally specified.[186] Agricultural services also made up part of the category of *consuetudines*, 'customs',[187] which Glastonbury's entries typically fail to elaborate. Such customary

---

[178] *Gesta Abbatum*, ed. Riley, I.39–40.

[179] Campbell, 'Some agents and agencies', pp. 213–14.

[180] 'Ut omnis equitandi lex ab eis impleatur, que ad equites pertinet' (S.1368; *ca* A.D. 964); transl. Brown, *Origins*, pp. 133–5.

[181] 'Serve in all necessities with his own horses': Round, *Feudal England*, p. 39.

[182] Domesday Book, I, 190vb (Cambridgeshire, 5.4M, 5.5, 5.6M, and 5.7).

[183] Dodwell, 'East Anglian commendation', pp. 299–300.

[184] For example, *Inquisitio Comitatus Cantabrigiensis*, ed. Hamilton, pp. 194–5.

[185] See the renders and services of the peasants (*ceorlas*) at Hurstbourne Priors *ca* A.D. 1050 (added to S.359: *Anglo-Saxon Charters*, ed. & transl. Robertson, p. 206 [no. 110]) and the labour services specified for the *geneat* and the *gebur* at Tidenham *ca* A.D. 1060 (S.1555; *ibid.*, p. 205 [no. 109]) (also in *English Historical Documents*, transl. Douglas & Greenaway, pp. 879–80 [nos 173–4]).

[186] See S.1305 (A.D. 963), a lease granted by Bishop Oswald to his thegn Æthelstan, who was required 'to [work] with all his might twice a year, once at haymaking and the other time at harvest'; *Anglo-Saxon Charters*, ed. & transl. Robertson, pp. 66–7 (no. 36).

[187] See, for example, the entry for the Worcestershire estate of Eckington, where Dunning and Brictric 'secabant in pratis domini sui per consuetudinem unam diem' ('reaped for one day in the meadows of their lord according to custom'): Domesday Book, I, 174va (Worcestershire, 8.7).

dues also consisted of renders or payments.[188] The opening entry in Domesday Book for the church of Worcester seems to specify that these customary dues were for the sustenance of the household –'omnes consuetudines inibi pertinentes ad dominicum uictum' – and that they were distinct from the *seruitium* due to the king and the bishop.[189]

It may be that service was a matter for negotiation. For example, at Worcester's estate of Cropthorne, 'Keneuuard et Godric tenuerunt et deseruiebant sicut ab episcopo deprecari poterant'.[190] As Miller has commented, all tenants probably owed it, but, because of the spectrum of landholders, 'there can hardly have been any specialised form of service. The terms on which the obligation of thegnland were conceived must have been wide enough to comprehend whatever honourable service a king's thegn or abbot's steward would perform and that of a tiny sokeman, whose burdens are likely at least to have been peasant burdens and may well have been near to servile.'[191] Glastonbury had, of course, no sokemen of the East Anglian kind, and tenants below the rank of thegn are hard to identify. Nevertheless, there must have been distinctions in the service owed by the man who held a minster with its attached three hides (St Andrew's, Ilchester) and that of the five thegns who shared a five-hide portion of the estate at Shapwick. Queen Edith's chamberlain, Harding of Wilton, no doubt rendered a different type of service – if he rendered any at all – from that owed by Ælfric son of Everwacer.

It is of course worth remembering that the conditions of service may not have been determined by Glastonbury Abbey. Any functioning estate would have had its own system in place and, when estates were granted to Glastonbury by lay lords, it is possible that their terms of service and their 'management-structure' were retained.[192] Agricultural services, in particular, and other *consuetudines* must have been very variable and probably were determined at the local level. The author of the *Rectitudines* was concerned to emphasise the variety of *landlaga* ('estate-law'), 'because not all customs about estates are alike'.[193]

As for military service, there is nothing in the evidence at Glastonbury which advances the debate on military obligations in late Anglo-Saxon England.[194] At

---

188 As at the royal estate of Seaborough in Somerset, where twelve sheep and one bloom of iron were paid *per consuetudinem* by each free man (Domesday Book, I, 87vb [Somerset, 3.1]). The ninety *massae ferri* paid to Glastonbury from Pucklechurch probably represent a similar customary due. Stenton argued that in origin *consuetudines* were almost certainly commuted food-rents or farm ('Types of manorial structure', pp. 37–8).

189 Domesday Book, I, 172va (Worcestershire, 2.1).

190 'On the terms which they could seek from the bishop' (Domesday Book, I, 174ra [Worcestershire, 2.73]). Similarly, a nun held Cudley 'sic deprecari poterat' (Domesday Book, I, 173va [Worcestershire, 2.54]).

191 Miller, *The Abbey*, p. 53.

192 Stacy, 'The estates', pp. 39–40.

193 *Die Gesetze*, ed. Liebermann, I.452–3; *English Historical Documents*, transl. Douglas & Greenaway, pp. 876–7 (no. 172).

194 See, *inter alia*, Vinogradoff, *English Society in the Eleventh Century*, pp. 85–8; Hollister, *Anglo-Saxon Military Institutions*; Dyer, *Lords and Peasants*, pp. 40–3; Abels, *Lordship and Military Obligations*; and Campbell, 'Some agents and agencies'.

Worcester, where discussion is frequently focussed thanks to the survival of relatively full evidence, there is a problem in distinguishing between the service owed to the bishop by tenants on his lands and the public obligations of service in the *fyrd*. Vinogradoff thought thegnland to have been the subdivision of ecclesiastical property 'to which the defence of the sees as to *fyrd* was confided'. He concluded this because the estates of the thegns were so similar to the fees and fractions of ordinary (post-Conquest) knights 'that the passage from the one to the other was effected without any noticeable break'.[195] At Glastonbury, certainly, the land held by tenants in 1066 did not change its tenurial condition dramatically, in that it was still held by tenants in 1086, although the holdings had been consolidated and a smaller number of men held them.[196] Dyer too has suggested that a military role was envisaged for the tenants of the bishop of Worcester,[197] and we should at least consider that at Glastonbury, as Dyer has argued for Worcester, the very large number of knights of the post-Conquest *seruitium debitum* was fixed 'in the knowledge of [the house's] large number of existing dependent tenures'.[198] Certainly it was these tenants after 1086 whose duty it was to provide the *milites* for which Glastonbury was responsible.[199] There is no reference at Glastonbury to compare with the evidence for military service among the pre-Conquest tenants of the church of Worcester. There, it is quite specifically associated with leased land: when the Dane Simund seized the episcopal estate at Crowle and refused to return it and it was lost from the demesne of the monks (*a dominico uictu monachorum*), the military service was nonetheless retained by the ploy of granting the estate to Simund for one life on the condition that he serve the monastery on military expeditions and acknowledge the prior's lordship by annual renders of money or a horse.[200]

One final element remains to be added to this discussion of thegnland and land temporarily alienated from the demesne. Leases – temporary grants made by the holders of bookland, with reversion to the grantor after a specified period of time – were issued by monastic houses as early as the late seventh or early eighth century.[201] I have, so far, avoided making the association between leases and the

---

[195] Vinogradoff, *English Society in the Eleventh Century*, p. 87.

[196] The same pattern is also to be found at Worcester; see Hamshere, 'The structure and exploitation', p. 43, and Dyer, *Lords and Peasants*, p. 45.

[197] *Ibid.*, p. 43.

[198] *Ibid.*, p. 47. Both houses owed forty knights.

[199] Finn, *An Introduction*, p. 140.

[200] 'Ut pro ea ipse ad expeditionem terra marique – que tunc crebro agebatur – monasterio seruiret, pecuniaque placabili siue caballo ipsum priorem unoquoque anno recognosceret': *Hemingi Chartularium*, ed. Hearne, I.264-5. Earl Leofric had compelled Prior Æthelwine to grant the land.

[201] See S.1252 (A.D. 699x717) for a one-life lease by the bishop of Worcester and S.1254 (A.D. 718x745) for a two-life lease by the same church. Land held by lease (*læn*) and *lænland* frequently have been taken as synonymous (see Williams, 'How land was held', p. 38, for example), but this identification ignores some awkward complexities. Despite King Alfred's distinction between bookland and a lord's *læn* to his man (in his preface to his translation of Augustine's Soliloquies: *King Alfred's Version of St Augustine's 'Soliloquies'*, ed. Carnicelli, p. 48; *Alfred the Great*, transl. Keynes & Lapidge, p. 139), examples from Worcester show that land held by formal ecclesiasti-

lands held by Glastonbury's tenants which have been under discussion. This may be taking caution too far, but there appears to be some evidence to discourage us from assuming a simple equation between the two.[202]

There are only two explicit references in Domesday Book to leases of land belonging to Glastonbury. The entry for Hannington's fifteen hides (in Wiltshire) includes a rare expository statement on the recent history of the estate: 'De hac eadem terra .iii. hidas uendiderat abbas cuidam taino TRE ad aetatem trium hominum. Et ipse abbas habebat inde seruitium. Et postea debebat redire ad dominium. Et ita modo cum aliis .xii. hidis sunt.'[203] This conforms to the pattern familiar from the church of Worcester's leases; what is exceptional, however, is its context: it is unique among Glastonbury's returns in Domesday Book. None of the subtenures described as thegnland or as inseparable from the abbey is recorded in anything like these terms. The statement may not represent unusual circumstances, but its presence here is noticeably eccentric, in the context of the abbey's returns. Unfortunately, the only other reference in Domesday Book to a lease of Glastonbury's property is not particularly helpful in illuminating the circumstances at Hannington, for it concerns a piece of specialised land, not a subtenancy. It occurs at the end of the abbey's entries, where ten acres of meadow which the abbot had leased (*praestitit*) TRE to two men had been lost by the time of the survey. The ten leased acres, which the text says 'debent iacere in Cristemalford', are not called thegnland. Another portion of the same estate (Christian Malford), however, is so called. This apparent distinction between leased land and thegnland seems to find support in the entry in the *Liber Exoniensis* for the Somerset estate of Woolmersdon – an estate held by Alfred of Spain to which had been added one and a half virgates which had in 1066 been part of the royal manor of North Petherton: one virgate had been leased (*accommodata* in the *Liber Exoniensis* and *praestitit* in the Exchequer's text) TRE *de dominica mansura* and the other half-virgate *fuit teglanda*.[204] At Tatton in Dorset, an estate of Cerne Abbey, there may likewise be hints of a distinction: one portion was held by a thegn who could not be separated, and the other was held by two thegns *prestito* (presumably meaning 'by lease').[205]

cal lease could in fact be categorised as bookland. In S.1347 (A.D. 984), a single-sheet original issued by Bishop Oswald, for example, the Latin text is followed by a vernacular note which implies that the lease converted the estate in question from loanland to bookland. See also Maitland, *Domesday Book and Beyond*, pp. 313–18, and S.1334, S.1350, and S.1367. *Lænland* as such was presumably a temporary alienation of a different kind (probably not recorded in writing).

202 Unlike Finn (*An Introduction*, p. 139), who used the example of Hannington, the only one of Glastonbury's estates which was described in Domesday Book as leased, to illustrate his discussion of thegnland.

203 'The abbot sold three hides of this same land to a certain thegn TRE for three lives; and that abbot had the service from [the land]; and after it had to return to the demesne, and so now it is with the other twelve hides.'

204 E 508 b4. It is interesting that this distinction is obscured in the Exchequer's text (Domesday Book, I, 97ra [Somerset, 35.1]), where it is said that Aluui had leased (*praestitit*) the entire one and a half virgates.

205 Domesday Book, I, 83va and vb (Dorset, 49.10 and 55.23).

No church's surviving archive can match the series of leases from Worcester.[206] The overall theory behind the system and some details of its operation are laid out for us by Bishop Oswald in his letter to King Edgar and in the so-called *indiculum* prepared in 1086 for the Domesday commissioners.[207] The surviving leases themselves show that conditions of tenure varied considerably, although an annual rent of some sort was usually involved. Leases for much shorter terms than the usual one or, more frequently, three lives may have been far more common than the surviving documentation implies; inevitably, records of short-term arrangements (if kept) would have had little chance of survival. Many leases were written in the vernacular; Glastonbury's archive preserves almost no Old English documents, and information on any leases it might have issued is (perhaps for this reason) very slim. The one estate which from independent testimony we can identify as held by lease from Glastonbury in the mid-eleventh century (Uffculme) shows no hint in Domesday Book of being so; another estate (North Wootton), which the evidence of a mid-tenth-century Latin diploma might also indicate was leased land, likewise is not identifiable as such in Domesday Book.

Taking this latter case first, the charter for North Wootton (S.509, a grant by King Edmund in A.D. 946) has been discussed in detail above, where it was suggested that the system of food-renders and other dues it recorded as being owed to the abbey may have represented the terms of a lease of the abbey's land to the layman Æthelnoth.[208] The form of the charter differs from the church of Worcester's leases (in particular being issued in Latin by the king and not by the ecclesiastical head of the community), and the charter's grant of perpetual inheritance to Æthelnoth implies a hereditary tenure, rather than the usual term of one or three lives. Nevertheless the abbey's ultimate lordship was clearly stated: if Æthelnoth should default on his obligations, the land was to revert to Glastonbury (*in usum fratrum*), and if Æthelnoth should incur punishment for a crime, the land should not be forfeited to the king but returned to the abbey. In Domesday Book, North Wootton appears simply as a sub-unit of Pilton; it is recorded there that its holder could not be separated from the church in 1066. This might suggest that all other lands about which this was said in Domesday Book were held on the same conditions as those by which Æthelnoth had held North Wootton; but we should need more evidence to conclude from this that all the lands which 'non potuerunt ab ecclesia separari' were held by ecclesiastical lease. It is also possible that the lease represented in S.509 (if that is what it was) did not endure until 1066.

A more straightforward instance of a pre-Conquest lease of Glastonbury's

---

[206] See, *inter alia*, Maitland, *Domesday Book and Beyond*, pp. 301–18; Robinson, *St Oswald and the Church of Worcester*; Atkins, 'The church'; John, *Land Tenure*, pp. 113–39; Sawyer, 'Charters of the reform movement'; Dyer, *Lords and Peasants*, pp. 40–7; Barlow, *The English Church 1000–1066*, pp. 174–5; and Barrow, 'How the twelfth-century monks of Worcester perceived their past', pp. 55–7. For a continental comparison, see the grants *in precaria* by Cluny discussed by Bouchard in *Sword, Miter, and Cloister*, especially pp. 98–101 and 220–1, and Rosenwein, *To Be the Neighbor*, pp. 113–22.

[207] S.1368; *ca* A.D. 964 (*Origins*, transl. Brown, pp. 133–5); and *Hemingi Chartularium*, ed. Hearne, I.287–8 (*Origins*, transl. Brown, pp. 148–9).

[208] See above, chapter III, *s.n.* North Wootton.

land, at Uffculme (in Devon), has also been discussed in detail above.[209] We are told in a *memoriale* (probably a brief prepared for a lawsuit) that a tripartite document was written in the mid-eleventh century to record the lease of the estate to Eadgifu for one life and to underline Glastonbury's right to reclaim the land at her death. Uffculme was appropriated by her second husband, Walter, however, and he appears in Domesday Book as the holder TRW, without reference to the abbey. As we have seen, there is a possibility that Domesday Book's silence on the subject of Glastonbury's ultimate lordship is not as sinister as it might first appear, for a writ of William the Conqueror (now lost) might have formally transferred the land to Walter, cancelling (though perhaps only temporarily) Glastonbury's rights. If no such writ existed, however, the case of Uffculme should raise the possibility of serious deficiencies in Domesday Book's evidence, as the texts contain no hint of Glastonbury's claim, nor of any ongoing tenurial struggle for the land. The case of the Somerset estate of Winsham may provide a parallel: in a narrative source, the *Historiola de primordiis episcopatus Somersetensis*, we discover that in *ca* A.D. 1060 the bishop of Wells attempted to retrieve Winsham from a certain Alsie, who held the estate by lease but was not rendering service; Alsie resisted – by force – the bishop's attempt to retrieve the land.[210] Domesday Book betrays nothing of either the lease or the dispute: Alsie held TRE and Osmund TRW from the bishop.[211] At Uffculme, as at Winsham, no lease and no dispute are mentioned in Domesday Book. This should make us wonder what other lands Glastonbury may have been struggling – unrecorded – to retain in the eleventh century. Paul Hyams has argued that disputes were deliberately edited from the record where possible.[212] Finberg himself suspected that the Domesday commissioners sometimes 'contented themselves with registering the name of the sitting tenant', a course of action which would have left many rightful overlords unacknowledged and dependent relationships disguised.[213] Other estates which, in Domesday Book, Glastonbury was not recorded as holding but which had been granted to the abbey in the pre-Conquest period and which reappeared in the twelfth century as Glastonbury fees may be worth consideration in this regard.

Given the difficulty of identifying what land was held by lease from Glastonbury in 1066, the actual conditions of tenure on its leased land are inevitably very obscure. From the fact that the estate and the meadow specifically said to have been leased at Hannington and Christian Malford (respectively) were not called thegnland, and the fact that the thegnlands and lands which could not be separated from the abbot were not identified as leased, we must at least consider that different categories were involved and that different tenurial situations pertained.

---

[209] See above, chapter III, *s.n.* Uffculme.

[210] *Ecclesiastical Documents*, ed. Hunter, pp. 16–17.

[211] Domesday Book, I, 89va (Somerset, 6.12). Presumably the bishop's action was successful.

[212] Hyams, ' "No register of title" ', p. 139.

[213] Hoskins & Finberg, *Devonshire Studies*, p. 64. This has recently been the subject of debate and disagreement; see Sawyer, '1066–1086', and Fleming, 'Domesday Book and the tenurial revolution', and *Kings and Lords*, especially pp. 107–44.

But what could distinguish the two? At Hannington, the thegn who leased the land rendered *seruitium* to the abbot, as did tenants on thegnland. The tenure was for three lives and was thus, like thegnland, presumably not hereditary or alienable. Could the distinction be that on leased land the tenant became the legal lord of the estate (perhaps acquiring *soca*), whereas Glastonbury retained that position in relation to its thegnlands? Or could it be that the 'full ownership rights' which the abbey exercised applied not to its thegnlands but only to those estates held by lease? Perhaps, once leased, the estate opted out of the system evolved by the monastery to fulfil its public burdens (although the natural interpretation of the better documented situation at Worcester would argue against this). Different possibilities abound, but the evidence for Glastonbury is too sparse to direct us and we can only speculate.

The evidence for *firma* (Old English *feorm*, 'farm') paid to Glastonbury is so slight that very little can be deduced about the meaning of the term on the abbey's estates in the late Anglo-Saxon period.[214] Across the country, 'farming' seems to have involved renting out land for an agreed annual return or a lump sum (the farmer in turn receiving the dues and renders from the estate).[215] These arrangements may have been less frequently put into writing, as they could be very short-term: Hereward the Wake held land in Lincolnshire *ad firmam* from the abbot of Crowland on terms to be negotiated every year.[216] The only instance of the word among Glastonbury's returns occurs in the entry for Damerham, where the *firma* is said to be too high and where there were complications about the value of the estate. It is possible that thegnland and land held *ad firmam* were identical, but the evidence supplied by Domesday Book in this case offers no link. Similarly, land held *ad firmam* could have been land held by lease: Lennard made the connexion between the two, saying, however, that it was unclear whether the holder of land put out to farm was indeed a lessee.[217] From his study of Worcester, John Hamshere has concluded that ordinary subtenants stood in a different relationship to the lord than did the holders of 'farms', but just how this might have worked is uncertain,[218] and Glastonbury's entries offer no clue. Meanwhile, the single reference among Glastonbury's entries to *gablum* (Old English *gafol*, 'rent'),[219] which occurs in the return for Ower in Hampshire, would be more informative were it not unique. Elsi held Ower from the abbot and could not go

---

[214] For a full discussion of the subject nation-wide, see Lennard, *Rural England*, pp. 105–75.

[215] Williams, 'How land was held', p. 38. Benefactions to ecclesiastical houses could bear the requirement that the donor or his kinsman retain the land for his lifetime: at Ramsey Abbey, such a holder paid *census* and *feorm, uice firmarii* (see, for example, *Chronicon abbatiae Rameseiensis*, ed. Macray, p. 175).

[216] Domesday Book, I, 377rb–va (Lincolnshire, CK.48). Another short-term arrangement which was recorded (although the term *feorm* is not used) is the extant early eleventh-century agreement between the community of Worcester and Fulder, by which he held an estate for three years in return for a loan to the church of £3 (S.1421; *Anglo-Saxon Charters*, ed. & transl. Robertson, pp. 154–5 [no. 79]).

[217] Lennard, *Rural England*, p. 168.

[218] Hamshere, 'Domesday Book: estate structures', p. 157.

[219] On *gafol*, see Loyn, *Anglo-Saxon England and the Norman Conquest*, p. 193.

where he wished, 'sed semper reddidit gablum abbati'.[220] This could represent rent on a farmed or leased estate; it could be akin to the payment made *pro recognitione* to St Mary's, Pershore;[221] but in the absence of corroborating evidence little can be deduced from the reference.

The analysis may be summarised thus. Although the entries for Glastonbury's lands in Domesday Book do not define their terms, a comparison of the somewhat inconsistent use of those words and phrases having tenurial significance in both the available versions of Glastonbury's returns to the Domesday commissioners of 1086 leads me tentatively to conclude that none of the abbey's tenants could be 'separated' from the church and that, where this formula was left out, 'we can suspect accident rather than design'.[222] Stacy has taken this conclusion one step further: 'In all probability, thegnland would describe the majority of Glastonbury subtenures on the eve of the Conquest, for the Domesday Book clerks were to take the term as read, and generally only used it when special circumstances prevailed.'[223] This is possible, but close study has emphasised to me the opaqueness of the text and the dangers of generalisation. It does seem most likely, however, that Glastonbury had full ownership rights, including rights of jurisdiction and commendation, over all the lands which it is recorded as holding in Domesday Book, none of which could be alienated. Commendation was probably part of the thegnland package, intrinsic to the creation of subtenancies. Miller concluded that at Ely thegnland had the appearance of a new category of landholding, 'introduced into a society which had previously known only the dichotomy between *dominium* and *soca*'.[224] In contrast, such tenures seem well entrenched at Glastonbury, if only because the rights and conditions seemed not to need definition, nor even (in many cases) identification. A few exceptions aside, the monotonous repetitiveness and consistently uncommunicative quality of Glastonbury's entries in Domesday Book present a uniformity which contrasts sharply with the variety to be found in the returns for the properties of other houses – in the record of services due to Worcester, for example, which 'suggests that there was no uniform system of tenure',[225] or in the obviously more mixed composition of the tenants of East Anglian monasteries. Nevertheless, Glastonbury's apparent uniformity could be real or it could be textual; the few variations in Domesday Book's returns for land not held directly by the abbot seem – unless all the terms and idioms employed are synonymous – to offer a glimpse of variety. Quite different conditions of tenure could have existed on the abbey's estates, rationalised and disguised by the great book-keeping enterprise.

Almost all the land which Glastonbury lost between 1066 and 1086 was described as thegnland, and the rest was said to have been held by tenants, with

---

220 'But always paid rent to the abbot' (Domesday Book, I, 43ra [Hampshire, 11.1]).

221 Azor held land in Pershore and 'inde seruiebat ecclesie et pro recognitione dabat in anno monachis unam firmam aut .xx. solidos' ('he served the church from it, and he paid one *firma* or twenty shillings a year to the monks *pro recognitione* [in acknowledgement?]'): Domesday Book, I, 175rb (Worcestershire, 9.1b).

222 Stacy, 'The estates', p. 34.

223 *Ibid.*

224 Miller, *The Abbey*, p. 57.

225 Dyer, *Lords and Peasants*, p. 43.

the exception of the land seized from the demesne of West Monkton by the bishop of Winchester (which was returned in the twelfth century). Distance from the abbey as well as the nature of the tenurial link no doubt played a part: isolated estates, such as Brompton Ralph, Clatworthy, and Uffculme, presumably were particularly vulnerable to powerful Norman lords consolidating their holdings.[226] The detailed account of Uffculme's loss fleshes out the bare record of such appropriations. This was not merely a post-Conquest phenomenon, however, as a papal rebuke to Ealdorman Ælfric on Glastonbury's behalf, or the cautionary tale of the abbey's fickle benefactor Ælfwold (not to mention the records of other churches), make clear;[227] before 1066 Glastonbury may have had to struggle as a matter of routine against such depredations. But the Norman Conquest clearly provided the occasion for an escalation of the process of prising land away from the abbey; estates held directly were barely touched, but about a third of the land held by its tenants was seized.[228] The description of the majority of the lost estates as thegnland may indicate that if there were different forms of subtenure, thegnland was the most vulnerable.

Glastonbury's last Anglo-Saxon abbot, Æthelnoth, who was vilified in house-tradition for his own *dilapidaciones* (but of treasures, not lands),[229] was taken to Normandy in 1066, along with a group of other important Anglo-Saxons whom William the Conqueror considered needed watching; Æthelnoth was certainly back in England by 1072, if not by December 1067 when the king (and some of the other hostages) returned.[230] Despite his temporary exile, Æthelnoth exhibited impressive staying-power, as he was not deposed until 1077x1078.[231] His succes-

---

[226] Stacy, 'The estates', p. 52.

[227] *Memorials*, ed. Stubbs, pp. 396–7; William of Malmesbury, *Vita S. Dunstani*, §25; *ibid.*, pp. 313–14. See also below, pp. 329–30. For cases of the despoliation of Worcester's endowment, see *Hemingi Chartularium*, ed. Hearne, I.248–86. A good collection of examples involving other churches is given by Barlow in *The English Church 1000–1066* (pp. 174–5). Symeon of Durham's *Historia ecclesiae Dunelmensis* (Book III, §14) illustrates the same difficulties. Lands which Bishop Aldhun (A.D. 990–1018) had leased to the earls of Northumbria proved hard – in some cases impossible – to retrieve: *Symeonis Monachi Opera*, ed. Arnold, I.83–4.

[228] Approximately ninety-eight hides, valued at at least £93 17s. (about twenty-eight per cent of its tenants' hides and thirty-three per cent of tenants' recorded values).

[229] He was accused in the *De antiquitate* of plundering the abbey's treasure: §§66, 68, and 74 (ed. & transl. Scott, pp. 134, 138, and 152); *Cronica*, §§79 and 82 (edd. & transl. Carley & Townsend, pp. 150 and 154).

[230] Æthelnoth's excursion to Normandy is recorded in the Anglo-Saxon Chronicle (DE), *s.a.* 1066, and the return of the king and others of the hostages *s.a.* 1067. Æthelnoth witnessed the decisions of the council of Winchester in April 1072 (*Councils and Synods*, edd. Whitelock *et al.*, I.604).

[231] A charter of *Eylnotus abbas* by which he made provision for the poor is preserved in the Great Cartulary (ed. Watkin, III.701–2 [no. 1300]), dated April 1079. Watkin counselled against hasty assumptions of forgery. If the document is genuine, the date (at least) has presumably been altered. For Æthelnoth's deposition, probably at Whitsun 1078, see *Councils and Synods*, edd. Whitelock *et al.*, II.624–5; see also *Acta Lanfranci*, in *Two of the Saxon Chronicles*, ed. Plummer, I.289. According to Eadmer, he lived 'for a long time' thereafter in dignified confinement at Canterbury: see

sor, the first Norman abbot of Glastonbury, Thurstan, put down with violence a rebellion by the monks against his régime and consequently spent several years in disgrace in Normandy, although he, too, returned, perhaps even by 1086.[232] It is impossible to determine how the actions of these abbots influenced the relations of the king with their house, but it may be that Æthelnoth's appropriations of the abbey's treasures were made with the purpose of buying the Conqueror's favour – or, alternatively, supporting rebellion. Whatever the circumstances, Æthelnoth's star fell in 1077 or 1078, and his successor apparently failed fully to safeguard Glastonbury's lands. Perhaps Thurstan's own disgrace and at least temporary absence weakened his position with the king and thereby sealed the fate of a substantial proportion of his church's endowment.

We must remember, however, that the majority of Glastonbury's subtenancies do not appear to have been threatened by the Norman Conquest. At Ely, William the Conqueror ordered that the men who had seized Ely's thegnlands should hold them 'under' or 'of' the abbot and render him the customary service – in other words, that the pre-Conquest conditions of tenure should be resumed.[233] Although Glastonbury was not quite so lucky, it retained control of an extremely wealthy demesne and a very large amount of tenants' land, and after 1086 the abbey even regained some of the lands it had lost.

Memorials, ed. Stubbs, p. 420, and Sharpe, 'Eadmer's letter', pp. 213–14. See also the discussion by Harmer (*Anglo-Saxon Writs*, pp. 553–4). Whitelock described Æthelnoth as the only Anglo-Saxon abbot of those whose names are recorded who was still in office in A.D. 1077/8 (*Councils and Synods*, II.625), but there were others who were not deposed until the 1080s (Wulfketel, abbot of Crowland *ca* A.D. 1061/2–1085/6, for example).

232 After a clash between the monks and the abbot's men-at-arms left several of the former dead in the church, Thurstan was sent back to Caen in disgrace in A.D. 1083, though not formally deposed from his position (ASC 1083; *De antiquitate*, §78 [ed. & transl. Scott, pp. 156–8]; *Cronica*, §85 [edd. & transl. Carley & Townsend, pp. 156–8]). He apparently put his name to a record of Glastonbury's estates not paying geld which is at the end of the *Liber Exoniensis* ('Haec terra emmendata est in manu Turstini abbatis': E 528 a3) and witnessed an account of a trial held at Laycock *ca* A.D. 1086 (*Regesta regum Anglo-Normannorum*, edd. Davis *et al.*, I.127; *English Historical Documents*, transl. Douglas & Greenaway, pp. 485–6 [no. 52]). According to the *De antiquitate*, however, he redeemed the abbacy from William Rufus after the Conqueror's death, for the sum of five hundred pounds (§78 [ed. & transl. Scott, pp. 156–8]; *Cronica*, §86 [edd. & transl. Carley & Townsend, p. 158]).

233 Finn, *An Introduction*, p. 139.

ESTATES NAMED IN DOMESDAY BOOK AS BELONGING TO GLASTONBURY ABBEY

References beginning 'DB, I' refer to Domesday Book proper (the so-called 'Exchequer' text); 'E' refers to the *Liber Exoniensis*; and the final reference is to the relevant county volume of the Phillimore edition of Domesday Book (gen. ed. J. Morris).

Berkshire
Ashbury (DB I, 59va; 8.1)

Devon
Uffculme (DB, I, 111vb; E 346 b1; 23.9)
Uplyme (DB, I, 103va; E 161 a1; 4.1)

Dorset
Buckland Newton (DB, I, 77va; 8.3)
Lyme Regis (DB, I, 77va; 8.6)
Okeford Fitzpaine (DB, I, 77va; 8.2)
Pentridge (DB, I, 77va; 8.5)
Sturminster Newton (DB, I, 77va; 8.1)
Woodyates (DB, I, 77va; 8.4)

Gloucestershire
Pucklechurch (DB, I, 165rb; 8.1)

Hampshire
Ower (DB, I, 43ra; 11.1)

Somerset
Alhampton (see Ditcheat)
Andersey (see Glastonbury)
Ashcott (DB, I, 90rb; E 164 b1; 8.11 and 8.14)
Baltonsborough (DB, I, 90va; E 167 a1; 8.22)
Batcombe (DB, I, 90va; E 167 b1; 8.24)
Blackford (DB, I, 90ra; E 163 a2; 8.9)
Bodesleghe (DB, I, 90rb; E 164 a1; 8.12)
Brent (DB, I, 90vb; E 170 b2; 8.33)
Brompton Ralph (DB, I, 95va–b; E 357 a2 and E 509 b2; 25.7)
Butleigh (DB, I, 90rb; E 165 b1; 8.18)
Butleigh (woodland) (DB, I, 91ra; E 173 a1; 8.40)
Camerton (1086 only) (DB, I, 90vb; E 170 a5; 8.31)
Catcott (see Shapwick)
Charlton (see Doulting)
Chilton Polden (see Shapwick)
Clatworthy (DB, I, 95vb; E 357 a3; 25.8)

313

Compton Dundon (see Walton)

Cossington (DB, I, 90ra; E 162 b2; 8.7)

Cranmore (DB, I, 90vb; E 170 b1 and E527a; 8.32)

Croscombe (see Pilton)

Dinnington (DB, I, 90vb; E 172 b2 and E 524 a6; 8.36)

Ditcheat (DB, I, 90vb; E 169 b2–170 a4, E 519 a3, and E 522 a4; 8.30)

Doulting (DB, I, 90va; E 167 a2; 8.23)

Downhead (DB, I, 90vb; E 171 b2; 8.35)

Draycott (DB, I, 91ra; E 172 b5, E 267 a2, and E 524 a7; 8.39)

Dundon (DB, I, 90rb; E 164 a2; 8.13)

Durborough (DB, I, 90ra; E 163 a1; 8.8)

East Lydford (DB, I, 90ra; E 161 b2; 8.4)

East Pennard (DB, I, 90va; E 166 b1; 8.21)

Edington (see Shapwick)

Edingworth (DB, I, 90vb; E 171 a1; 8.34)

Elborough (DB, I, 88ra and 91ra; E 139 b3, E 172 b1, E 516 a4, and 524 a2; 5.12 and 8.38)

Glastonbury (DB, I, 90ra; E 172 a1; 8.1)

Greinton (DB, I, 90rb; E 164 b2; 8.15)

Ham (DB, I, 90rb; E 165 a1; 8.17)

Hetsecome (DB, I, 87vb and 91ra; E 137 a1, E 172 b6, and E 524 b1; 5.3 and 8.38)

Hornblotton (see Ditcheat)

Hutton (DB, I, 88ra and 91ra; E 139 b2, E 172 b1, E 516 a3, and E 524 a2; 5.10 and 8.38)

Ilchester (St Andrew's) (DB, I, 91ra and 91rb; E 171 b1, E 197 b2, and E 522 a1; 8.37 and 15.1)

Kingstone (DB, I, 91ra and 92ra; E 172 b3, E 266 b2, and E 524 a3; 8.39 and 19.10)

Lamyatt (see Ditcheat)

Lattiford (DB, I, 90rb; E 165 b2 and E 522 a5; 8.19)

Marksbury (DB, I, 90vb; E 169 b1; 8.29)

Meare (see Glastonbury)

Mells (DB, I, 90va; E 168 a1 and E 520 a1; 8.25)

Middlezoy (DB, I, 90ra; E 162 b1; 8.6)

Millescota (DB, I, 88vb; E 147 b1 and E 519 b3; 5.50)

North Wootton (see Pilton)

Overleigh (DB, I, 90rb; E 164 b2; 8.16)

Panborough (see Glastonbury)

Pedwell (see Walton)

Pilton (DB, I, 90rb; E 165 b2; 8.20)

Podimore Milton (DB, I, 90ra; E 161 b1; 8.3)

Pylle (see Pilton)

Shapwick (DB, I, 90ra; E 161 b3; 8.5)

Shepton Mallet (see Pilton)

Stawell (DB, I, 90ra; E 163 a3; 8.10)

Stoke-sub-Hamdon (DB, I, 91ra and 92ra; E 172 b4, E 267 a1, E 513 a1, and E 524 a4; 8.39 and 19.11)

Stoke-sub-Hamdon (2) (DB, I, 91ra and 92ra; E 172 b4, E 267 b2, E 513 a2, and E 524 a4; 8.39 and 19.14)
Stratton-on-the-Fosse (DB, I, 88va–b and 91ra; E 145 b2, E 172 b7, and E 524 b2; 5.43 and 8.38
Sutton Mallet (see Shapwick)
Tintinhull (1066 only) (DB, I, 91vb; E 266 b1; 19.9)
Unnamed (5h) (DB, I, 91ra; E 172 a2 and E 524 a1; 8.41)
Walton (DB, I, 90rb; E 163 b1; 8.11)
Westcombe (see Batcombe)
West Monkton (DB, I, 90vb; E 169 a2; 8.28)
Whatley (DB, I, 90va; E 168 b1; 8.26)
Wheathill (DB, I, 98ra; E 453 a4; 37.9)
Winscombe (DB, I, 90ra; E 161 a2; 8.2)
Winterhead (DB, I, 88ra; E 140 a1; 5.12)
Woolavington (see Shapwick)
Wrington (DB, I, 90vb; E 169 a1; 8.27)

Wiltshire
Badbury (DB, I, 66va; 7.6)
Christian Malford (DB, I, 66va; 7.4)
Damerham (DB, I, 66va; 7.1)
Deverill (DB, I, 66va; 7.3)
Grittleton (DB, I, 66va–b; 7.10)
Hannington (DB, I, 66va; 7.2)
Idmiston (DB, I, 66vb; 7.14)
Kington Langley (DB, I, 66vb; 7.11)
Kington St Michael (DB, I, 72va; 41.8)
Langford (DB, I, 66vb and 69vb; 7.12, 7.13, and 24.42)
Littleton Drew (DB, I, 66rb; 5.6) (meadow only: DB, I, 66va; 7.5)
Mildenhall (DB, I, 66va; 7.7)
Monkton Deverill (DB, I, 66vb; 7.16)
Nettleton (DB, I, 66va; 7.9)
Stanton St Quintin (meadow only) (DB, I, 66va; 7.5)
Winterbourne (DB, I, 66vb; 7.15)
Winterbourne Monkton (DB, I, 66va; 7.8)

County	No. of Estates Held by the Abbey		No. of Estates Held Entirely by Abbot		No. of Estates Held Entirely by Tenants		No. of Estates Divided between Abbot and Tenants		No. of Hides Held by the Abbey		Values	
	1066	1086	1066	1086	1066	1086	1066	1086	1066	1086	1066	108
Berkshire	1	1	0	0	0	0	1	1	40h.	16h. 2½v.	£35	£3
Devon	2	1	1	1	1	0	0	0	20h.	6h.	£14	£
Dorset	6	5	0	0	4	3	2	2 (−1pt)	58h. +22pl.	48h. +22pl.	£92 10s.	£75 1
Gloucestershire	1	1	1	1	0	0	0	0	20h.	20h.	£20	£3
Hampshire	1	1	0	0	1	1	0	0	1h.	1h.	20s.	20
Somerset	47+	32+	3	3	26	11	18	18 (−7pts)	417h. 1v. +26h. 1v. untaxed +40pl. +66 acres	348h. 2v. +24h. untaxed +40pl. +66 acres	£363 16s. 6d.	£438 13
Wiltshire	15	14	4	4 (−1pt)	2	1 (−1pt)	9	9 (−3pts)	260h. 2v. +10 acres	252h. 3v.	£171 10s.	£2
Totals	77+	58	9	9 (−1pt)	35	16 (−1pt)	29	30 (−11pts)	816h. 3v. +26h. 1v. untaxed +62pl. +76 acres	692h. 3½v. +24h. untaxed +62pl. +66 acres	£697 16s. 6d.	£811 3

h.	=	hides	* some values not recorded
v.	=	virgates	** most values not recorded
pl.	=	ploughlands	
pt	=	part	

No. of Hides in Tenants' Hands		Values of Tenants' Lands		No. of Estates Lost	Hidage of Lands Lost	Values of Lands Lost	
1066	1086	1066	1086			1066	1086
9½h.	9½h.	£12	£12	0	0	0	0
14	0	£10	–	1	14h.	£10	£12
2h. 1½v.	32h. 1½v.	£42 10s.	£30 10s.	1 (+1pt)	10h.	£10	£10
0	0	0	0	0	0	0	0
1h.	1h.	20s.	20s.	0	0	0	0
44h. 1v. +2h. 2v. untaxed	182h. 3v. +2h. 2v. untaxed	£184 15s. 8d.*	£141 4s. 8d.*	15 (+7pts)	74h.	£71 15s.	£77 11s.
41h. 1v. +18 acres	40h. 3v. +8 acres	£28 15s.**	£38 15s.	1 (+5pts)	7h. 3v. +10 acres	£9* 2s.	£9* 12s.
52h. 1½v. +2h. 2v. untaxed +18 acres	266h. 1½v. +8 acres	£279 0s. 8d.*	£235 9s. 8d.	18 (+13pts)	105h. 3v. +10 acres	£100* 17s.	£109 3s.

317

V

SOME ISSUES

Further material could doubtless be added to the Anglo-Saxon history of many of the places discussed in the preceding chapter, particularly if the scope were widened to include all the post-Conquest sources. Each addition modifies the story; new information might drastically change any one of the histories offered above. Diplomatic criticism of the corpus of Glastonbury's Anglo-Saxon charters will clarify some of the doubts (and probably raise new ones). Other studies will, I hope, make use of the copious and complex material relating to the estates documented in the charters to pursue different leads. An overall analysis of the donors of land to Glastonbury would clearly be of great interest, for example.[1] To my mind, however, the most striking issue raised by the process of the collection and criticism of the evidence, in particular the charter-material, has been the question of its interpretation. The effect of probing these documents has frequently been to make them less, rather than more, communicative. The strength of their testimony on the fundamental matter of the changing shape of Glastonbury's endowment is consequently difficult to assess.

But first, perhaps the most obvious question relating to the sources used in estate-histories is that of the authenticity of the charters. Glastonbury's Anglo-Saxon diplomas have been greeted with little enthusiasm by many historians: W.H. Stevenson was particularly dismissive, stating that the fourteenth-century cartularies 'abound[ed] in clumsy and impudent forgeries, so much so that the occurrence in them of a formula is of itself sufficient to cast suspicions upon its authenticity'.[2] At the other end of the spectrum of opinion, H.P.R. Finberg, while acknowledging Glastonbury's 'evil reputation', pointed out that it was nevertheless clearly a 'favoured community . . . which could produce [many] genuine charters in evidence of title'.[3] More recently, Heather Edwards likewise has been less severe in her judgments.[4] Until the entire archive has been subjected to diplomatic analysis, the charter-evidence is necessarily restricted in its application. But even when the diplomas have been criticised as a group, all questions will not have been answered: only tentative judgments for or against the authenticity of some of the extant diplomas will be possible, although others will be (and

---

[1] On two of Glastonbury's important patrons, see Hart, 'Athelstan Half King', and Williams, '*Princeps Merciorum gentis*'; more generally, see Loud, 'An introduction to the Somerset Domesday', and Blows, 'Studies', especially pp. 271–99 and 345–52.

[2] *Two Cartularies*, ed. Bates, pp. 36–7.

[3] Finberg, *The Early Charters of Wessex*, p. 14.

[4] Edwards, *The Charters*, especially pp. 77–8.

have been) relatively easy to identify as forgeries. The lost charters (over one hundred) are obviously beyond the reach of effective diplomatic criticism. The best evidence for judgments on their status will come from the estate-histories themselves, combined with an awareness of archival trends (which criticism of the extant texts will develop).

It is also important to remember that a forged document does not necessarily indicate a false claim. Charters can have been fabricated for a variety of reasons, not all of them dishonest; and their very manufacture is part of the evidence. The tenth century saw across the country the production of documents (some copies and some forgeries) recording transactions of the seventh, eighth, and ninth centuries. Glastonbury's single sheet in Baldred's name (S.236) is one example.[5] The production of this charter may have been prompted by some now invisible development on the land or, alternatively, by changes in archival practice necessitating a recopying or rewriting of the old single sheets. An eighth-century postscript added to a Shaftesbury charter of the 670s (S.1256 and S.1164) describes the difficulties which could arise, for example, when one estate of a multiple grant became separated from the others and required independent documentation. Glastonbury's S.247 in Ine's name may have derived from such a situation. Another motive for the creation of documentation could have been provided by disputes over possession.[6] A post-Conquest context for the fabrication of documentation for a dozen or so estates is offered by the lengthy struggle between Glastonbury and the bishopric of Wells which began with a take-over bid by Bishop Savaric (A.D. 1191–1205).[7] Other, now undocumented, disputes no doubt arose at other times and over other land, and forgeries could have been composed in the course of those disputes in support of the illicit claims. Glastonbury's extant single-sheet diploma of Eadred for Pucklechurch may have been concocted after the estate was granted to Wells.[8] Such activity was not confined to ecclesiastical landholders. Forgery by a layman is recorded by Henry of Blois, abbot of Glastonbury A.D. 1126–1171, in his description of a case involving a certain Odo, who had apparently received three manors from Henry's predecessor but refused to return them to the abbey and offered a *falsum cyrographum* in defence of his title.[9] His (incompetent) duplicity exposed, Odo lost. On the other hand, if Glastonbury did not have a good case when a dispute arose over one of its holdings – specifically if it had no suitable charter for the estate at issue – there was little to stop the abbot and monks from creating their own title-deed, a deception justified (as they no

---

5   See above, pp. 10–11, and chapter III, *s.n.* Pennard.
6   For the importance (and effectiveness) of the possession of written proof of title in the process of law, see Keynes, 'Royal government and the written word', pp. 248–51. Glastonbury's disputes are not well documented, as we have seen: Wormald has described the abbey as an 'absentee' from his list of recorded pre-Conquest lawsuits ('A handlist of Anglo-Saxon lawsuits', p. 272, n. 33) and cited only S.1705 and S.1777, lost restitutions of *Cumtone* and Pucklechurch. The *memoriale* on Uffculme (*q.v.*, chapter III above) was probably prepared for legal purposes.
7   See above, p. 12.
8   S.553 (A.D. 950). See above, chapter III, *s.n.* Pucklechurch, and Abrams, ' "Lucid intervals" '.
9   *Adami de Domerham Historia*, ed. Hearne, II.305–6.

doubt would have seen it) by their legal right to the land. Other, 'valid', reasons for forgery can be imagined. If land held from the abbey by a man convicted of a crime was seized along with the estates which he held in his own right,[10] for example, the church – wrongfully deprived – may have manufactured documentation to prove its case. That some fabricated documents may have been in support of legitimate claims complicates matters, but cannot be ignored. It emphasises the fact that whatever survives, including forgeries, is part of the evidence.

Other aspects of the charter-record which deserve further study can only be indicated, not pursued, here. The vernacular boundary-clauses attached to the pre-Conquest diplomas in Glastonbury's archive are in almost every case preserved (like the texts themselves) only in cartulary-copies. Although some are contemporary with the grant of the land, others could have been added to the text of the grant at any time between its original composition and the mid-fourteenth century. At Glastonbury (as elsewhere), there is evidence for the existence of boundary-descriptions as separate sheets, thereby illustrating how detached – literally – the perambulation of the estate could be from the original grant.[11] The bounds provide essential information, which I have used extensively in my discussion of the endowment, but, until their date of composition has been determined, the context of their evidence – pre- or post-Conquest, contemporary with or composed hundreds of years after the original grant – is uncertain. It has been assumed by many historians that the land described in an Anglo-Saxon charter's bounds is identical with the land granted in the first instance by the named grantor – a tempting assumption, but quite misleading in cases where the estate had expanded or contracted between the time of its grant and the date of the description preserved in the later mediaeval cartulary-copy. Linguistic analysis is badly needed to clarify individual cases.[12]

Before we leave the subject of boundary-clauses, another direction of profitable enquiry should be mentioned. The bounds offer material – not much, but often more than is available in other sources – which indicates something of the

---

10 For Æthelwold's objection to this practice, see his account of King Edgar's establishment of monasteries (*Leechdoms*, ed. & transl. Cockayne, III.432–45; *English Historical Documents*, transl. Whitelock, pp. 920–3 [no. 238]). See also chapter III above, *s.n. Winterborne*.

11 'Bunde de Wynterborne et Idemyston in uetusta cedula' were recorded as extant still in the fifteenth century (L33), as was a copy of a charter of King Edward the Elder for Wrington *cum copiam bunde manerii* (L22). In the case of the *copia bundarum de manerii de Niewtone* (L25a), also in MS. 39a, the bounds are not said to be attached to any particular charter. The statement at the end of the cartularies' text of a charter for Langford (S.580), that 'qualiter predicta terra giratur in libro qui dicitur Landeboke inuenitur' ('the way in which the aforementioned land is encircled can be found in the book called the Landbook') seems to indicate the presence of even more independent boundary-clauses copied into the *Liber terrarum*. Alternatively, it could mean that the fourteenth-century scribe was too lazy to copy out the full text of the Langford charter and referred the interested reader to a complete text in the *Liber terrarum* should his abbreviated copy be found inadequate. In MS. 39a, copies of Eadred's charter for Pennard and Edgar's for Ham are said to have been *excepte/exceptis limitibus* (L12 and L15).

12 Not that the expert philologists always agree: see chapter III, above, *s.n.* North Wootton and Pilton.

resources of the region at the time of the description's composition. A summary of this evidence, combined with that from the dispositive sections of the charters themselves and from Domesday Book, would provide a most interesting collection of data on fisheries, salt-production, minerals, and features of the natural and man-made landscape. This material may even offer hints of economic motives behind the transactions documented so tersely in the charter-record: Glastonbury's divestment of its holding at Braunton in Devon in A.D. 973, for example, may tie in with its having acquired another coastal fishery, at Twynham in Hampshire, in Eadred's reign. This type of data, combined with an analysis of the physical characteristics of each estate and its possible context in the region, could begin to suggest what role some of these places might have played in the economy of the Anglo-Saxon abbey. Domesday Book would naturally be of particular value in such a study.[13] Economic data of another sort can be gathered where charters specify a price paid for land.[14]

Place-names offer another line of enquiry. Eilert Ekwall's sequences of forms in his *Concise Oxford Dictionary of English Place-names* frequently omit the evidence offered by name-forms preserved in Glastonbury's documents, in particular, those found in the contents-list of the *Liber terrarum*, the *Index chartarum*, and MS. 39a. This is especially unfortunate because, although admittedly the contents-list and the *Index* were copied in the mid-thirteenth century, they may nevertheless preserve relatively closely the pre-Conquest name-forms of the single sheets; some names which appear to have been obsolete by A.D. 1066 (such as *Pouelt*) are recorded on these lists of A.D. 1247/8. The lists consequently provide the earliest forms of the names of many of the places discussed in this survey, which are commonly otherwise attested only in Domesday Book and later mediaeval sources. Not only would it be an advance in place-name studies to incorporate the data from the *Liber* and the *Index*, but it would establish more securely (or indeed discredit) some of the identifications (including my own), which are currently based perhaps a little too much on probability, apparent similarity, and location, rather than on the proper principles of place-name scholarship.

More than anything, the estate-histories above have emphasised – at least to me – our inadequate grasp of the subtleties of land tenure and of the practical import even of those documents which have been preserved intact. Many questions about the mechanics of land-conveyancing and landholding remain obscure. Difficulties of interpretation face us from the start, as they have faced historians at least since Maitland.[15] The question of what exactly a charter conveyed has frequently been asked. Is a formal diploma a record of a grant of land, a grant of rights, or a grant of exemption? Could it document a grant of permanent ownership of land already held on a short-term basis, that is to say, a conversion from

---

[13] Della Hooke has shown what can be done elsewhere (see bibliography); see also Darby, *The Domesday Geography*.

[14] Sales are recorded at Badbury, Baltonsborough, *Bocland*, *Bradanleag*, *Brentefordlond*, *Brunham*, *Iecesig*, *Kyngton*, Marksbury, Pennard, *Pouelt*, and Wilton; they range in date from A.D. 744 to 987. On the Anglo-Saxon land market, see Campbell, 'The sale of land'.

[15] *Domesday Book and Beyond*, especially pp. 226–44.

one form of tenure to another? The answer is probably that a royal charter could achieve all of these things; unfortunately, there may often be no way of distinguishing which was intended at any one time, since the solemn diploma expresses itself in sublimely general terms (with some exceptions), and is sufficiently formulaic to disguise (whether deliberately or accidentally) a variety of functions. Close study of estate-histories can produce the disquieting suspicion that the specific import even of surviving documents may at times be impenetrable. Glastonbury's estate-histories have revealed many examples of this uncertainty, all of which raise interesting questions and illustrate what a range of intentions might have existed on the part of the grantor.[16]

A charter of King Eadwig concerning Panborough, for example, has generally been thought to represent the original acquisition of land there by Glastonbury (S.626). I have pointed out above, however, that (if genuine) the diploma may instead have been granted in order to free from all secular obligations an estate which the abbey already held on different terms.[17] The obscurity of the document's intention effectively ties our hands with respect to determining Panborough's status before the grant in A.D. 956: because there is no other evidence, we can entertain several possibilities, ranging from the previous full possession of the estate (and subsequent loss) by the abbey, restricted possession (with secular burdens), temporary possession (with reversion to the king), or no former connexion at all. Different readings of the charter could support each of these options. If the statement of exemption is false, however, it is nevertheless noteworthy that it was considered realistic enough to claim; and we should ask when such a spurious concession could have been added (and whether it was effective).

Similar difficulties attach to the more specific case of King Æthelwulf's Decimation charter (S.303; A.D. 854), although in that instance other evidence can be brought to bear on the question. Æthelwulf, according to the Anglo-Saxon Chronicle (*s.a.* 855), 'conveyed by charter the tenth part of his land throughout all his kingdom to the praise of God and his own eternal salvation'.[18] This is usually taken to mean the creation and distribution of bookland. A reference in Asser's Life of King Alfred is more explicit: Æthelwulf 'freed the tenth part of his whole kingdom from every royal service and tribute . . . for the redemption of his soul and those of his predecessors'.[19] S.303 is one of a series of charters relating to Æthelwulf's Decimation which still survives and which has in the past failed to inspire scholars' confidence, with the exception of Finberg.[20] More recently,

---

16 For similar (and different) questions raised by the abbey of Cluny's tenth- and eleventh-century documents for its landed property, see Rosenwein, *To Be the Neighbor*, especially pp. 109–43.

17 See above, chapter III, *s.n.* Panborough.

18 '7 þy ilcan geare gebocude Æþelwulf cyning teoþan dæl his londes ofer al his rice Go[de] to lofe, 7 him selfum to ecere hælo.'

19 'Æthelwulfus praefatus uenerabilis rex decimam totius regni sui partem ab omni regali seruicio et tributo liberauit, in sempiternoque graphio in cruce Christi, pro redemptione animae suae et antecessorum suorum' (§11; *Asser's Life of King Alfred*, ed. Stevenson, pp. 8–9; *Alfred the Great*, transl. Keynes & Lapidge, pp. 69–70).

20 On the Decimation charters in general, see *Councils*, edd. Haddan & Stubbs,

Susan Kelly has argued in favour of these texts.[21] She has proposed that a standard Decimation text was issued at a meeting at Wilton at Easter 854; individual versions were then provided for different beneficiaries, with the addition of specific information on their own estates which were affected. Malmesbury Abbey's text (S.305) offers the closest parallels to Glastonbury's, which is itself the most detailed (up to eleven places are mentioned).[22] The dispositive section of S.303 specifies that the king is giving 'the tenth part of the lands throughout our kingdom not only to holy churches, but we have also made the same grant to our thegns established in them,[23] in such a way that the grant may remain fixed and immutable, free from every royal service and worldly burden'. Asser's comment helps us to see that although a straightforward gift of land in some cases may have been involved, a Decimation charter could be granted also to an existing holder of land, with the effect of relieving the recipient of the burdens (such as those of hospitality)[24] which the land would otherwise bear – burdens from which not even ecclesiastical land was automatically exempt. This ambiguity naturally complicates the attempt to determine the history of the estates involved, if the grant could represent either the conveyance of land into Glastonbury's ownership or the freeing from particular services and/or dues of lands already within the abbey's endowment. That there are records (rarely fully respectable, but not to be ignored) of prior ownership for four of the estates listed in Glastonbury's Decimation charter might suggest that some or even all of the lands affected were already held in A.D. 854. Pennard and *Culum*/Uffculme are thought-provoking examples, which might lead us to speculate that the list in S.303 represents a contemporary roll-call of the abbey's estates. On the other hand, even if we accept that the text of the Decimation charter may be respectable enough, the attached lists may not be contemporary: we have no way of knowing, as they survive only in later mediaeval cartulary-copies and could have undergone significant alteration.[25]

Glastonbury's Decimation charter offers one further puzzle which concerns us here. Five of the estates mentioned involve units of one and a half hides or less; yet other evidence may point to the estates named as being much larger.[26] This

---

III.636–45, Finberg, *The Early Charters of Wessex*, pp. 187–213, and *Alfred the Great*, transl. Keynes & Lapidge, pp. 232–4.

[21] I am grateful to Susan Kelly for allowing me to read her unpublished discussion of the Decimation charters, which has substantially broadened my understanding of the texts and the nature of the transaction; her analysis of the Decimation as a whole has helped to confirm several of my own observations drawn from the Glastonbury material alone.

[22] On the three extant versions of the list of Glastonbury's lands involved, see above, chapter III, *s.n. Brannocmynstre* or Monk Okehampton. For the other Decimation texts, see S.302, S.304, S.305, S.307, S.308, S.312, S.313, and S.315.

[23] S.303 has *in eisdem constitutis*, which allows this translation; S.305 has *in eodem*, which causes greater difficulty.

[24] Susan Kelly, in her unpublished paper, has suggested that the heavy burdens of providing hospitality for the king's or ealdorman's retinue may have been the target of these exemptions.

[25] Blows has argued for their antiquity, pointing to the forms of the place-names ('Studies', pp. 255–6).

[26] See above, chapter III, *s.n. Brannocmynstre* or Monk Okehampton.

might suggest that the sum cited in the charter was a fraction of the estate, a notional representation of the exemption from secular burdens of part of its profits. In other words, if these low numbers equalled one-tenth of the estate's assessment, we could have interpreted their appearance in the grant as a way of representing the dedication of one-tenth of the lands' profits to religious ends. But the numbers do not appear to work out at one-tenth; and in any event the other five or six estates listed seem to be represented *in toto*. Perhaps a clue lies in the rather obscure terms in which the king extended his Decimation not just to churches but to secular lords, a process which has not proved easy to understand; at least in Glastonbury's text, this concession seems to be extended specifically to royal thegns established on ecclesiastical lands: perhaps, therefore, the small units of *Cetenesfelda*, *Lodegaresbergh*, *Colom*, *Ocmund*, and *Branuc* were held from Glastonbury by king's thegns, and it was these portions of those estates which were at issue and which alone were granted exemption; if so, why the remainder of the estate would not be freed from burdens remains unexplained. Alternatively, the answer may lie in later manipulation of the lists of estates.

Other, equally impenetrable, circumstances can lie behind other, seemingly more straightforward, documents. At Ashdown, for example, land apparently granted by charter from the king to a layperson seems instead to have been given to that layman by his brother (according to the latter's will). Why a royal diploma came into play is unclear, but it might have served to confirm the existing holder's possession, perhaps in the absence of other documentation.[27] King Edmund's grant of North Wootton to the thegn Æthelnoth has been discussed at length above:[28] the charter (S.509) has in some respects the appearance of an hereditary grant to a layman by the king, but the monks evidently held North Wootton as theirs at the time and granted it out to Æthelnoth with expectation of return. The dues from the land were paid to the abbot, not the king; and North Wootton appears in Domesday Book as an ordinary holding of the abbey. Another diploma of Edmund (S.513, for Damerham) clearly granted an estate to his queen for a fixed term, with its reversion thereafter to Glastonbury spelled out. Whether this land too was already in the abbey's hands at the time is unclear.[29] The question of the king's relationship to the community (or rather, specifically to its land) must be considered here: if Glastonbury was indeed (still) a possession of the house of Wessex at this date (A.D. 944x946, at the dawn of reform), the attempt to distinguish between royal land and abbatial land might be misconceived. This hypothetical royal lordship might account for the king's apparent habit of granting abbatial land (and his seeming disinclination, for so many years, to grant charters in the abbey's favour).[30] In any event, it seems that the blanket equation of a grant with a conveyance of land – and of a 'book' with bookright and hereditary tenure – is

---

27 See above, chapter III, *s.n.* Ashbury. S.525 for Washington (in Abingdon's archive) is an exact parallel. The brothers' title-deeds may have been destroyed in the fire which is known to have consumed other charters belonging to their father, Ealdorman Æthelfrith; see Keynes, 'A charter of King Edward the Elder', pp. 307–8.

28 See above, chapter III, *s.n.* North Wootton.

29 See above, chapter III, *s.n.* Damerham.

30 See below, pp. 337–41.

unsound.[31] The former existence of three consecutive charters for land at Camel (issued by Edmund, Eadwig, and Edgar to laymen and recorded in the contents-list of the *Liber terrarum*) may indicate that the documents were grants for one lifetime only. It is also possible that they were not 'repeat' grants of temporary tenure at all, but rather confirmations by the king of the successive holders' permanent possession of the estate.[32] Alternatively, they could have imposed different conditions of tenure on each recipient, perhaps reducing the secular burdens on the estate, or granting rights of alienation, or converting the land to hereditary possession; or – another line of argument altogether – perhaps we should not always think in terms of land-transfers or tax-exemptions or hereditary rights, but of something more abstract, involving relationships such as commendation.[33] If the intentions of the grantor are obscure to us where the documents survive, how much more elusive must they be in cases such as Camel, where documents have been lost, or where transactions are completely unrecorded.

Other explanations can be offered, however, for the existence of apparent regrants of the same land: we have seen that two charters granting Idmiston to Wulfric in consecutive years probably reflect a splitting of the estate, which was then conveyed to the same recipient in two equal parts.[34] Unfortunately, without additional information (such as the hidage of the transaction compared with the total hidage of the estate), the grant of an entire estate and the grant of only a portion will look the same in the record, even when the texts survive. When dealing with an archive such as Glastonbury's, where so many charter-texts have been catalogued and then lost, this difficulty is additionally acute. The gift of the estate of Nunney by King Eadred to Glastonbury which is recorded on the contents-list of the *Liber terrarum* actually involved (according to the *De antiquitate*) only part of the land; the other part is apparently unrecorded. Similarly, we can tell that two surviving charters for *Lim* applied to two places, not one, thanks to the appearance of two *Lims* with corresponding hidages among Glastonbury's returns in Domesday Book.[35] In this period, place-names usually give no hint if they apply to more than one estate: epithets employed with the aim of distinguish-

---

[31] The import of bookright is encapsulated in, for example, Alfred's preface to his version of St Augustine's Soliloquies: 'ac ælcne man lyst, siððan he ænig cotlyf on his hlafordes læne myd his fultume getimbred hæfð, þæt he hine mote hwilum þaron gerestan, and huntigan, and fuglian, and fiscian, and his on gehwilce wisan to lænan tilian, ægþær ge on se ge on lande, oð þone fyrst þe he bocland and æce yrfe þurh his hlafordes miltse geearnige' (*King Alfred's Version of St. Augustine's 'Soliloquies'*, ed. Carnicelli, p. 48) ('every man, when he has built a hamlet on land leased to him by his lord and with his lord's help, likes to stay there some time, and go hunting, fowling and fishing; and to employ himself in every way on that leased land, both on sea and land, until the time when he shall deserve bookland and a perpetual inheritance through his lord's kindness': *Alfred the Great*, transl. Keynes & Lapidge, p. 139).

[32] See above, chapter III, *s.n.* Camel. Other cases – that of Horton, for example (*q.v.*) – might suggest that if reconfirmations were required, this was a development of the tenth century.

[33] See above, pp. 298–300.

[34] See above, chapter III, *s.n.* Idmiston.

[35] See above, chapter III, *s.n. Lim*.

ing different places of the same name seem not to be found in the Anglo-Saxon written record. The two units of *Lim*, for example (one on either side of the Devon-Dorset border), are indistinguishable (by name) in the documents. The many estates which took their names from rivers can cause particular confusion, as in the case of the multiple Winterbournes.[36] It is consequently very difficult to determine exactly what a name referred to: not only could several different estates have exactly the same name, but a name could also change its frame of reference and not represent the same territory each time it appeared in the record. 'Pilton', for example, seems to have meant different things at different times.[37] Some names became obsolete when the large areas they stood for acquired smaller identities (such as *Pouelt*, *q.v.*); conversely, place-names doubtless could also be lost if the land they represented amalgamated with or was absorbed into another land-unit, whose name was then applied to the whole.

An associated concern is that of hidage. Hidage is difficult to interpret. Originally a notional area, a hide came to be a unit of assessment, although an approximate area of 120 acres was also associated with it by the time of the later Anglo-Saxon period.[38] Without specific information, it is hard to tell the difference between changes in assessment and changes in actual area. Simply put, an estate said to have consisted of twenty hides in A.D. 700 and ten hides in A.D. 950 could have lost half its territory or could instead have had its assessment revised. Conversely, an estate which seems to have been static, comprising thirty hides in A.D. 850 and A.D. 1066, could have changed in size though not in hidage. Stephen Morland has frequently exploited the related principles of reduced assessment or 'beneficial hidation' (where an estate's hidage was lowered) and boundary-extension (where an estate gained territory but its hidage remained the same),[39] but proof of these processes – which undoubtedly occurred – is elusive in the pre-Conquest period,[40] especially at Glastonbury. There, only the late

---

36 See above, chapter III, *s.n. Winterborne*.

37 See above, chapter III, *s.n.* Pilton.

38 In the seventh and eighth centuries it was conceived of as the area of land adequate to support one household or family (*locum unius familiae* or *terra unius familiae* in Bede, for example: *Historia ecclesiastica gentis Anglorum*, Book IV, §23; *Bede's Ecclesiastical History*, edd. & transl. Colgrave & Mynors, p. 406); its actual area on the ground must have varied considerably, however. See also Maitland, *Domesday Book and Beyond*, pp. 357–62 and 386–95; Charles-Edwards, 'Kinship, status, and the origin of the hide'; and the entry from Henry Spelman's *Archæologus in Modum Glossarii*, pp. 352–3, reproduced by Dumville in 'The tribal hidage: an introduction', pp. 228–9.

39 Morland, 'Hidation'.

40 Few documents are as explicit as a lease from Worcester (S.1409; A.D. 1051x1055) which ends with the statement that 'at the king's summons, the holder shall discharge the obligations on these one and a half hides at the rate of one, for three lives'; *Anglo-Saxon Charters*, ed. & transl. Robertson, pp. 208–9 (no. 111). For Chilcomb, where King Alfred and King Æthelred are said to have renewed a reduction from one hundred hides to one which had been granted by the earliest Christian kings, see S.1812 (A.D. 871x899) and S.946 (A.D. 984x1001); see also *Anglo-Saxon Writs*, ed. & transl. Harmer, pp. 373–80 and the literature cited there. The case of Pyrford, Surrey, where in 1086 'the men of the hundred [had] never seen or heard of a writ on the king's behalf

testimony of Domesday Book offers explicit evidence.[41] Loud, while admitting that the evidence was largely invisible, has assumed a substantial degree of beneficial hidation on the abbey's estates before the Conquest.[42] On the basis of the available evidence, however, it is difficult to assess the degree of stability of hidage (or area) on Glastonbury's estates. According to Dyer, at Worcester (where the documentation is more lavish) the hidages given in the extensive series of pre-Conquest leases coincide in only twenty cases out of seventy with the figures for the same estates in later documents.[43] Beneficial hidation was a most desirable perk, reducing the tax-burden on the land. But without explicit statements such as we find in Domesday Book, reduced assessment cannot necessarily be preferred, as an interpretation, over the simple possibility that the estate lost territory. Boundary-extension is particularly difficult to chart – more frequent (and better dated) descriptions of the bounds would help. Manipulation of the hidage was clearly a feature of Anglo-Saxon landholding, but we must beware of introducing it as the only solution when information is missing or when the surviving data conflict. When other answers fail, it is tempting to fall back on hidage-fiddling, but explanations based on incomplete information about these unreal realities are very doubtful.

As if this were not bad enough, it is clear that hidage-figures may have been tampered with and rendered up-to-date by later scribes: the grant of six hides at Pennard in the cartularies' text of S.236 should be compared with the twelve hides of the non-contemporary single-sheet copy, the latter figure possibly tying in with the twelve hides attributed to ancient Glastonbury.[44] The scribes of the cartularies themselves may have made numerical adjustments in the charters which they copied, taking their cue from later figures, those in Domesday Book in particular. Details of Glastonbury's holdings in A.D. 1066 were readily available in the later mediaeval archive, no doubt in several copies; one still survives in MS. R.5.33.[45] It would not have been difficult to make the hidage of the title-deed agree with the contemporary assessment of an estate; however, as long as the document which mattered (for legal purposes) continued to be the single sheet (original or copy) rather than the cartulary-text, the substitution of more attractive numbers in the copying of the latter would have made little sense.

which placed it at that value' (Domesday Book, I, 32vb [Surrey, 6.5]) suggests that revisions in hidage in the mid-eleventh century were routinely effected by royal writ.

[41] Several cases of beneficial hidation can be found among Glastonbury's entries in Domesday Book: Ashbury, for example, was assessed at forty hides TRE, reduced to sixteen hides, two and a half virgates TRW (Domesday Book, I, 59va [Berkshire, 8.1]). Ten hides at East Pennard were subject to tax in 1066, 'although there are twenty hides there' (Domesday Book, I, 90va [Somerset, 8.21]). Elsewhere, cases of more than one change of hidage between 1066 and 1086 are recorded in Domesday Book: at Pyrford, for example, the estate was assessed at twenty-seven hides before Harold held it, sixteen hides while he held it, and eight hides *modo* (the latter written in the margin) (Domesday Book, I, 32vb [Surrey, 6.5]).

[42] Loud, 'An introduction to the Somerset Domesday', p. 16.

[43] Dyer, *Lords and Peasants*, p. 45.

[44] See above, chapter III, *s.n.* Glastonbury and Pennard.

[45] MS. R.5.33, 131r–137ra (lacking the abbey's Gloucestershire and Hampshire estates).

A few other complications enlivening the evidence of the charters must be mentioned. In particular, as we have seen, the existence of a diploma in the archive need not have signified that the abbey possessed the land it granted at that – or any other – time. Documents could have been in the archive due to circumstances unconnected with the ownership of the land. Diplomatic reasons, for example, may lie behind the presence in the archive of two charters of King Eadred which seem to have been duplicates of charters preserved in other archives; these are of the 'Dunstan B' type, which may have been produced at Glastonbury, originally under Dunstan's guidance, from the 940s to the 970s.[46] King Eadred stored some of his *rurales cartulae* at Glastonbury for a while,[47] and other laypeople might also have used the abbey simply as a repository for their documents,[48] or might have consigned all their charters to the archive at their death, including some for lands with which the church had no connexion. There is a possibility that in the reign of King Æthelred the Unready the abbots of Ely, Glastonbury, and St Augustine's were assigned (in rotation) the office of chancellor; this could mean, as Frank Barlow has suggested, that the three monasteries were thereby appointed official centres for the issue of diplomas.[49] Glastonbury could therefore have held documents for lands far removed from its own endowment. Nor, as we have seen, does the presence in the archive of a charter granting possession to a layman in the reign of King Alfred, for example, mean that the property in question reached the abbey at that time; the charter may have been preserved by the holder of the land as his deed of title, and the estate and the document – or simply the latter – may not have been acquired by the church for several generations.[50] Equally, charters could have been out of date. Just as

---

46 LT 97 and LT 109: cf. a grant of Henstridge to Brihtric, preserved in the cartulary of Shaftesbury Abbey (S.570), and a grant of *Cumtone* to Ælfheah, preserved at Abingdon (S.564). See above, chapter III, *s.n.* Henstridge and Compton Beauchamp. See Hart, *The Early Charters of Northern England*, pp. 19–22, on the possible connexion of both 'Dunstan A' and 'Dunstan B' diplomas with Glastonbury; on the latter particularly, see Keynes, 'The "Dunstan B" charters'. I am grateful to Simon Keynes for allowing me to see his study of these charters in advance of publication and for discussing them with me.

47 B, *Vita S. Dunstani*, §19 (*Memorials*, ed. Stubbs, p. 29).

48 Churches may not have been the safest places for laymen to store their charters. The variety of formulae found in forgeries (which seem to draw on different house-styles and a range of archival characteristics) may indicate plundering from such deposited documents, which could have offered a supplementary source in addition to the church's own documentary holdings. Although the theory that Anglo-Saxon laymen routinely deposited their charters in monastic archives for safekeeping has long been a commonplace (see Stenton, *The Early History*, pp. 43–4), it is striking that there appears to be no incontrovertible evidence for the practice. Stenton's example – drawn from an incident at Abingdon in the 1320s – is far removed from an Anglo-Saxon context (Salter, 'A chronicle roll of the abbots of Abingdon', pp. 732–3).

49 For the statement that the three houses held the *cancellarii dignitas* in the late tenth and eleventh centuries, see *Liber Eliensis*, §78 (ed. Blake, pp. 146–7). There is no confirmation in other sources for this claim. For its significance, see Barlow, *The English Church 1000–1066*, pp. 125–7.

50 See above, chapter III, *s.n.* Hannington, for example.

churches allowed land out of their grasp for a fixed term, so laypeople's gifts to religious communities could themselves be temporary and restricted,[51] although there is no explicit evidence of this at Glastonbury. Conversely, estates temporarily leased to laypeople by the abbey for a price might not have been returned, as at Uffculme.[52] Other archives also demonstrate that charters could be annulled;[53] their later value as title, therefore, would have been nil. Such annulments frequently involved the seizure of estates from men who had committed crimes and whose lands were forfeited to the king.[54] If estates which these men had given to ecclesiastical houses were confiscated, their charters – no longer valid – could nevertheless have remained with the church.

It is also possible that some of the documents which have been preserved could have been ineffective. Some bequests, for example, though recorded, may never have taken effect.[55] Some of the charters deposited in Glastonbury's archive by men who were or intended to be buried there (and bequeathed land to the church as their soul-scot)[56] might fall into this category, if the donor changed his mind or the family resisted the abbey's attempt to take charge of the property. Yeovilton may be such a case.[57] And benefactors could change their minds. The brief moment of repentance and munificence experienced by Walter, Glastonbury's tenant at Uffculme, has been discussed in detail above.[58] William of Malmes-

51 A certain Alfred granted land to Christ Church, Canterbury, probably in A.D. 871, but his daughter was to have it back if she wanted it (and could get it): *Select English Historical Documents*, ed. & transl. Harmer, pp. 11–12, 46, and 87 (no. 8) (S.1202).
52 See above, chapter III, *s.n.* Uffculme. The neighbouring community of Muchelney Abbey also had difficulties recovering an estate loaned for three lives: S.884 (A.D. 995) tells how the lessees actually obtained a grant of bookland before their crime was exposed and the diploma annulled.
53 In a diploma of A.D. 997, King Æthelred annulled the charters he had granted to other beneficiaries and restored land at Downton to the Old Minster (S.891). The charter obtained by fraud which was cited and condemned in S.884 (see n. 52 above) was annulled by the bishops, ealdormen, and principal laymen. If the document they revoked was a royal diploma (as seems to have been the case) this is a most interesting and significant incident.
54 See S.362 (A.D. 901) whereby King Edward the Elder officially cancelled the charters for an estate previously held by Ealdorman Wulfhere, who had been exiled by King Alfred (*English Historical Documents*, transl. Whitelock, pp. 541–2 [no. 100]); in S.937 (A.D. 990x1006, probably 999), King Æthelred denounced any title-deeds surviving from a number of estates, including three forfeited by Ælfric *cild* when he was outlawed for treason (*ibid.*, pp. 582–4 [no. 123]).
55 For example, David Dumville has argued this for the will of King Eadred (S.1515; A.D. 951x955) in a paper which he has kindly allowed me to read in advance of publication.
56 On soul-scot (from Old English *sawlsceattas*), see Godfrey, *The Church in Anglo-Saxon England*, p. 324; see also *Die Gesetze*, ed. Liebermann, I.146.
57 See above, chapter III, *s.n.* Yeovilton. Reputedly granted to Brihtric, he is said to have given it to Glastonbury 'with his body'; there is no further record of Yeovilton until it appears in Domesday Book in lay hands. A document in Brihtric's name preserved in the *Codex Wintoniensis* (S.1512; A.D. 964x980) reveals that during his lifetime he deposited at the Old Minster charters for an estate which he planned to give to the church after his death (*Anglo-Saxon Wills*, ed. & transl. Whitelock, p. 18 [no. 7]).
58 See above, chapter III, *s.n.* Uffculme.

bury's Life of St Dunstan introduces another cautionary tale, concerning a certain Ælfwold (*opulentus*) who, stricken with an illness, became a monk at Glastonbury. He gave some holdings (*possessiunculae*) to the abbey but came to regret this decision and attempted unsuccessfully to retrieve his lands by various means (including bribing the king).[59] Land was also seized from the abbey by force: an ealdorman Ælfric who in the late tenth century appropriated lands belonging to Glastonbury received a papal letter in rebuke.[60] Glastonbury's appeal to Rome on the matter (unfortunately, only the reply is extant) may reflect a failure by the king to protect the abbey's proprietary rights in this case. Regrettably, the pope did not specify the identities of the *praedia* and *uillae* seized by Ælfric; nor was the land necessarily returned. Abbots may themselves have been guilty of appropriating their community's estates; Æthelweard, the penultimate Anglo-Saxon abbot of Glastonbury (A.D. 1027–1053), is accused of this in the *De antiquitate*.[61] When the abbot faced financial difficulties (and the late tenth and early eleventh centuries must regularly have presented him with these), the endowment of his church had to be harnessed to the cause. Information provided in the *De antiquitate* – that Brihtwold, bishop of Ramsbury (A.D. 1005–1045), redeemed all the monks' lands in Wiltshire, which had been yielded to the royal treasury as a mortgage at the time of the Danes – reveals yet another way in which land might leave the endowment (although in this case it returned).[62] In the difficult days of Danegeld and *heregeld*, if payment was not made by a certain day, anyone who was able to discharge the obligation could do so and receive the land from which the payment was due. Hemming alleged that some despoilers of the church of Worcester acquired its estates by paying the taxes on them, although the church or tenant who held them was actually willing to pay.[63] It is unlikely that Worcester surren-

---

[59] William of Malmesbury, *Vita S. Dunstani*, §25 (*Memorials*, ed. Stubbs, pp. 313–14). Punishment and retribution for this crime were accomplished quickly and effectively; thanks to Dunstan's prayers, Ælfwold was eaten by foxes.

[60] *Memorials*, ed. Stubbs, pp. 396–7; see Keynes, *The Diplomas of King Æthelred*, p. 182, n. 104, on the two possible identities of this Ælfric (either the ealdorman of Mercia banished in A.D. 985 or the ealdorman of Hampshire who flourished between A.D. 983 and 1009). The former reputedly seized lands from a certain widow, Eadflæd; see S.937.

[61] *De antiquitate*, §66 (ed. & transl. Scott, p. 134); *Cronica*, §82 (edd. & transl. Carley & Townsend, p. 154). The accusation may be false, of course. See below, pp. 348–9.

[62] 'Omnes illas terras ab antiquo fuisse Glastonie sed tempore Danorum, cum inportabiles pensiones regnum grauarent, fisco regio uel alias pignori addictas, sed ab episcopo redemptas et redditas': *De antiquitate*, §68 (ed. & transl. Scott, pp. 138–40; *Cronica*, §79 (edd. & transl. Carley & Townsend, pp. 150–2). The bishop had apparently been a monk of Glastonbury. Similar sacrifices were made across the country, whether for payments to the king or directly to the raiding armies. In A.D. 994 or 995 Archbishop Sigeric was forced to borrow ninety pounds of silver and two hundred mancuses of gold from the bishop of Dorchester to prevent raiders from burning down Canterbury Cathedral. In return the bishop received an estate in Buckinghamshire (see S.882). In that case the archbishop is said to have given the original title-deed to the new holder. For other examples, primarily from the reign of Cnut, see Lawson, *Cnut*, pp. 191–4.

[63] *Hemingi Chartularium*, ed. Hearne, I.277–8; see also Barlow, *The English Church 1000–1066*, p. 173. Brooks has pointed out that when crises required such sacrifices,

dered its documents on such occasions. Charters in the archive, therefore, did not necessarily mean that the land concerned was safely in the community's hands.

A number of factors, therefore, could account for the presence in an ecclesiastical archive of charters for lands which the church had never held; and many more factors could conspire to remove land from the abbey's endowment, possibly leaving charters behind. Estates could have been appropriated by the king, appropriated by someone else (perhaps after being leased, when the link between the community and the land was potentially most fragile), exchanged, or reclaimed by a lay donor after a bequest. On the other hand, land which was lost could also be retrieved. Furthermore, even if a holding remained an unchallenged part of the endowment, it need not have been static; estates were split, amalgamated, renamed, reassessed (and their terms of tenure reclassified). These events may have left their mark on the documentary record, but on the other hand they may be wholly (or partly) invisible. This is to be remembered if all that survives is a seventh-century charter and an entry for the land in Domesday Book or, alternatively, a single grant by a tenth-century king. Some developments may never have been recorded and this, combined with the loss of documents, creates an appearance of stability which may conceal substantial activity. The record is so fragmentary that change – even significant change – can easily have gone unsignalled. Meanwhile, the evidence for the estates for which we have the most documentation proves perversely to be the most difficult to use. The earlier the evidence, the more complex the story, which can become impenetrable from the point of view of following the history of the land and the relationship of its various parts.[64] Close study of the estate-histories exposes these complexities, which may seem to make interpretation impossible; but I would argue that their analysis deepens our understanding of the life-cycle of an estate, creating a greater appreciation of the hidden possibilities when we are faced, as we so often are, with large gaps in the evidence.

Invisible transactions aside, the way in which we understand the charter-evidence will determine what use we can make of it. In particular, any judgments to be made about patterns of growth and loss must rest on our interpretations of the grants' terms. Does a charter in the archive mean that land really first came physically and legally into the abbey's possession in the transaction which it represents, as is so often assumed? And does the regrant of the land to Glastonbury fifty years later mean that it had slipped out of the abbey's hands in the interval? It could have been appropriated by the king – perhaps to endow members of his court – and returned to the abbey whenever the abbot could claim it; alternatively, the land may not have been lost, but simply leased, with a new charter issued to mark its reversion to its ecclesiastical lord; it is also possible that succeeding kings could have issued charters merely to confirm and support the

---

Christ Church, Canterbury, may have sold many estates to the king or other buyers, and that unless the estates were recovered at a later date (and charters written describing their history), their alienation would have left no trace in Canterbury's archives (*The Early History*, p. 283).

[64] See, for example, chapter III, *s.n.* Ditcheat.

holder's continued and interrupted possession.[65] We cannot be certain of the meaning of these documents, but our interpretation of the endowment hangs on these questions, and very different impressions follow, depending on how we answer them. At Glastonbury, for example, it makes the difference between a picture on the one hand of landed resources constantly in a state of flux or, on the other, of a quite stable collection of properties, increasing with remarkable suddenness in Edmund's reign. As we shall see, this is the crux of the problem involved in drawing conclusions about periods of growth, as we cannot be certain that land recorded as in the abbey's hands in A.D. 842 and 1066 was also its property in (say) A.D. 900. Other questions complicate the issue. Does the scarcity of ninth-century charters for Glastonbury simply represent another calamity for which vikings can be blamed? Even if monastic discipline collapsed, was the site utterly *desolatus*?[66] Could the scarcity (or absence)[67] of direct grants to the abbey by Kings Æthelbald, Æthelberht, Æthelred, Alfred, Edward the Elder, and Æthelstan (that is, from A.D. 855 to 939) signify not a period of complete corporate dissolution (and the consequent suspension of landownership) but rather reflect other, more impenetrable, circumstances? Was the dramatic increase in the number of diplomas in Edmund's name a real expansion of the abbey's lands, or does it represent simply an explosion of charter-writing (or charter-forging,[68] or charter-preservation)? What do the twenty-four grants by Edmund to lay recipients which are preserved in Glastonbury's archive have to do with the abbey?

I shall begin with this last question, which raises the specific problem of grants to laypeople and the subsequent fate of the estates involved. There are far more of these grants to lay recipients by tenth-century kings recorded at Glastonbury than there are direct royal grants of land to the abbey;[69] this feature of the archive has, in fact, been taken as a sign of its good faith, on the assumption that no monk-forger would have produced a charter in favour of a lay recipient.[70] Laypeople could have had charters fabricated, however (witness the enterprising Odo),[71] and, moreover, even if their single sheets had been authentic the corresponding cartulary-texts might have been contaminated. Laypeople's charters, therefore, cannot be entirely above suspicion. Even when the recipients (and donors) were no longer alive, the documents were valuable proof of title: the case of Horton, for example, or Mildenhall, where an eighth-century charter may have been given to Glastonbury as a title-deed when the land was granted to the abbey in the mid-tenth century, appears to show that charters for estates in lay hands could survive

---

65 But note the case of Horton (*q.v.*, chapter III), which seems to have come to Glastonbury with an eighth-century deed and a diploma of Eadred (but nothing in between).

66 See below, pp. 337–41.

67 Those extant may be forgeries.

68 Edmund's association with Dunstan and the early reform of Glastonbury may have made him the preferred choice of forgers.

69 See the charts below, pp. 350–2.

70 For the archival approach to the criticism of diplomas, see Keynes, *The Diplomas of King Æthelred*, pp. 9–10. Edwards particularly has argued on principle in favour of the authenticity of charters to lay beneficiaries (*The Charters*, *passim*).

71 See above, p. 319.

for very long periods of time.[72] It is axiomatic that Glastonbury's possession of these title-deeds need not mean that it held the land at the time of the grants documented therein – or indeed, as we have seen above, at any other time. The evidence for the acquisition by Glastonbury of the lands named in the charters to laypeople is, in fact, frequently not very sound. Glastonbury's archive offers no parallel to S.1182 (A.D. 762), one of the earliest recorded gifts by an ordinary layman to a religious house.[73] This Latin charter in the name of Dunwald, a thegn of Æthelberht II, king of Kent, transferred to St Augustine's, Canterbury, land which Dunwald had been given by the king. Other archives also preserve vernacular documents, such as S.1512 (A.D. 964x980), in which Brihtric bequeathed the title-deeds (in the name of Æthelstan and Eadred) for his estate of Rimpton and promised the estate to the Old Minster, Winchester, on his death.[74] At Glastonbury, as we have seen, notes to the effect that the land was given to the abbey by the recipient of the charter (or someone else) may have been made on the single sheets (perhaps as endorsements);[75] a few of these notes seem to have survived because they were copied in the extant cartularies, and briefer versions of the information – which appear on the contents-list of the *Liber terrarum* – may have had the same origin. In many other cases, however, only in the *De antiquitate* is it claimed that the lay recipients of diplomas turned the land granted to them over to the abbey; it is not at all clear whether these statements in the *De antiquitate* derive from information now lost (provided, say, by the hypothetical endorsements), or whether the author(s) had a habit of assuming that all archivally documented lands granted to laypeople must have been handed over to Glastonbury by their recipients.[76] If Glastonbury owned the land in 1066 (and in over half the cases it did), we might find the testimony of the *De antiquitate* compelling; but if it did not, there is an increased temptation (not necessarily justifiable) to

---

[72] It also raises the unpleasant question of whether we can tell the difference between one transaction – the transfer of old title-deeds, with the land, in the tenth century – and two – an eighth-century conveyance (which lapsed) followed by another transfer in the tenth century.

[73] The only text of a grant by an individual other than a king or a bishop which is preserved among Glastonbury's documents is that by Lulla *ancilla Christi* in A.D. 744 (S.1410; LT17). The one vernacular document noted on the contents-list of the *Liber terrarum* (LT23) may have been a private charter, but it has since been lost. LT26 for *Culum*, also now lost, appears to have been another private document.

[74] *Anglo-Saxon Wills*, ed. & transl. Whitelock, p. 18 (no. 7).

[75] The endorsements on the four surviving single sheets from Glastonbury's archive give no such information; but three of the four are grants directly to the abbey. For examples of these possible endorsements, see chapter III, *s.n.* Grittleton and Wrington. For endorsements recording changes of ownership on extant single sheets from other archives, see S.106 (A.D. 764 for 767) and S.287 (A.D. 839). See also Kelly, 'Anglo-Saxon lay society', pp. 44–5.

[76] Batcombe seems to offer a mistaken assumption of this sort, with the *De antiquitate* perhaps incorrectly taking an earlier title-deed belonging to a certain Ælfsige as evidence of his grant of Batcombe to the abbey, whereas according to Ealdorman Ælfheah's will, it was Ælfheah who bequeathed the land to Glastonbury after the death of his wife. See above, chapter III, *s.n.* Batcombe.

doubt.[77] The substantial number of grants to laymen of lands which Glastonbury did not own at the Conquest (according to the evidence of Domesday Book) or in 1247/8 (according to List D of the *Index chartarum*) causes particular difficulty. The following interpretations are possible: Glastonbury had indeed received the property from the charter's recipient or his or her heir, but lost it before 1066; alternatively, an intention to grant was somehow blocked; or, Glastonbury never had an interest in the land but simply preserved the charter of its grant. To this must be added the possibility that the charters were not permanent conveyances of land but something else – a lease, for example, as the document for North Wootton seems to be, or some other temporary arrangement which had lapsed by 1066. Perhaps the apparent transfer of land to the abbey by these people was simply the reversion to the abbey of estates which it had leased out.[78] In addition, we must not forget that Domesday Book's record may be incomplete, despite its seeming comprehensiveness, and that Glastonbury's real status as holder of certain estates in 1066 may be disguised by the failure of the commissioners to record its title.[79] A further possibility, that the designation of the place granted in the charter changed and is not recognisable in Domesday Book, is another complicating factor, as is the fact that some land not named in Domesday Book was probably silently assessed in the entry for another estate. All these considerations act as a check on general conclusions about lay benefactions and, therefore, about the composition of Glastonbury's endowment in the second half of the tenth century, when grants to laypeople appear in radically larger numbers among the abbey's documents. If the majority of these grants did apply to land in which the abbey had no interest – the charters for which were preserved for diplomatic reasons, as has been argued[80] – the reinterpretation of these grants as benefactions to the abbey would have involved a significant deception, effected (apparently) by the time the *Liber terrarum* was compiled.

It is a moot point whether, after so many ambiguities have been exposed in the evidence, any conclusions about the changing shape of Glastonbury's endowment

---

[77] There are about thirty places for which a document or a notice of a grant to an individual beneficiary survives in Glastonbury's pre-Conquest archive but which did not belong to the abbey in 1066, according to Domesday Book. The number is difficult to calculate exactly, however, and may be misleadingly low. An additional twenty or so places granted to laypeople have not been counted in the total because they are unidentified; identified places recorded in pre-Conquest charters but not named at all in Domesday Book confuse the issue further. At least some of these probably were not held by Glastonbury in 1066 and could be added to the conservative total of thirty. By comparison, approximately thirty-nine estates granted to private or religious individuals appear as Glastonbury's in Domesday Book. The remainder of the unidentified estates would belong here. See the lists below, pp. 353–4. A significant number of these grants predate A.D. 940.

[78] See above, *s.n.* North Wootton.

[79] Paul Hyams's general arguments to this effect can be found in ' "No register of title" '. Uffculme is an obvious example from among Glastonbury's estates, though perhaps not as simple a case as it seems (see above, chapter III, *s.n.* Uffculme). See also Clutton and Clewer, above (chapter III), for the possible invisibility in Domesday Book of a relationship between Glastonbury and the ostensibly independent holder in 1066.

[80] Blows, 'Studies', pp. 338–45.

can be drawn. We cannot be certain what percentage of the charters granted has survived, nor how many of them are genuine. Yet, leaving aside these doubts (and all those questions which have so far occupied discussion here), it does seems that in the mid-tenth century a striking change came over the charter-record and, arguably, the lands it represented. Some speculation on the nature of this change is irresistible.

I have attached to the end of this discussion four lists of grants recorded in Glastonbury's archive: royal grants of land to the abbey (by reign), charters in favour of Glastonbury from ecclesiastical donors, royal grants to recipients other than the abbey, and lastly grants of privilege and exemption. Striking patterns emerge when the grants are separated out in this way. Before the tenth century, for example, we are dealing most commonly with grants directly to Glastonbury. Bearing in mind the reservation that royal grants could have had a particular appeal for forgers seeking to uphold an otherwise shaky title to property, almost every reign from the late seventh century is represented. Beginning with grants by Cenwealh, Baldred, Centwine, and Ine – whose various claims to be the first benefactor of the house have been discussed above[81] – there is a particularly large number of charters in Ine's name granting land directly to the abbey (possibly as many as ten),[82] more than are attributed to any other Anglo-Saxon king; a degree of inflation in these figures is likely to have been caused by Ine's reputation as the builder of the abbey-church and his later association with the foundation of the house, which may have recommended him to forgers. No grants by the sub-king Æscwine, Cædwalla (although he is said to have confirmed a grant by Bishop Hædde[83]), or Brihtric are recorded. Grants by Æthelheard (with Frithugyth), Cuthred, Sigeberht, Cynewulf, Ecgberht, Æthelwulf, and Æthelbald – between one and three each – show a relatively regular pattern, though seemingly less bountiful from Brihtric's accession. Comparing this with charters granted nation-wide, Glastonbury first falls short of and then greatly exceeds the curve on two counts: Cædwalla's eight known grants ignore Glastonbury, but its charters in Ine's name represent over half of his total surviving output. Up to and including the reign of Æthelbald (d. A.D. 860), these are the two principal points where Glastonbury's figures oppose the norm. Whether this apparently consistent recognition by the West Saxon kings was dynastic or personal, however, is uncertain. Most of their burial sites are unrecorded (though Glastonbury later claimed Centwine's).

Before proceeding to the next phase, the evidence of grants to Glastonbury by eighth- and early ninth-century Mercian kings must be considered. The context of these transactions must be sought in the (unfortunately now ambiguous) relations between the two kingdoms. King Æthelbald is said to have sold two estates to Glastonbury and had disposal of two others; King Offa reputedly also sold an

---

[81] See above, chapter III, *s.n.* Glastonbury.

[82] Or as few as seven. The doubt about the number arises from the multiplication of versions of S.248 (S.247 and possibly S.1672 and IC A5) (see above, chapter III, *s.n.* Doulting and Pilton).

[83] The grant of *Lantocai* (mentioned in the *De antiquitate*, §39 [ed. & transl. Scott, p. 92] and in S.250). Cædwalla is also mentioned as a supporter of the abbey in the privileges in Ine's and Cuthred's names (S.250 and S.257).

estate to the abbot of Glastonbury and granted another to a layman who gave it to the abbey with Offa's permission.[84] Stacy interpreted this activity as 'the beginning of a reorientation of the abbey's interests', heralding a determined attempt 'to remove Glastonbury permanently from Wessex to Mercia'.[85] Transactions attributable to the Mercian king Cenwulf are difficult to identify if only notices survive, as they can be confused with those of Cynewulf, king of Wessex. Much depends on the analysis of several documents preserved exclusively in the *De antiquitate* and cited nowhere else. A papal and a royal privilege (in the name of Pope Leo III and King Cenwulf, respectively) profess to grant, apparently to Cenwulf's son, Kenelm, personal possession of the religious community of Glastonbury.[86] Finberg cited these privileges to demonstrate that Cenwulf 'with the acquiescence of the feeble king Beorhtric, contrived to turn Glastonbury into a private family possession'.[87] The earlier activities by Cenwulf's predecessors (and the preservation of their charters at the abbey) do appear to indicate both a freedom of action in Wessex on the part of the Mercian kings and a connexion with the community at Glastonbury, and Offa's designs on Bath Abbey offer a precedent for a (successful) takeover bid.[88] Whether the privileges contain sufficient genuine material to bear the weight of interpretation they have been given,[89] however, is questionable. Even their twelfth-century redactor had doubts about them, and if not spurious they are far removed from their original form.[90] Not

---

84 See above, chapter III, *s.n. Bradanleag, Iecesig*, Lydford, *Inesuuyrth*, and *Hunespulle*. A confirmation by Æthelbald is also claimed for Lulla's grant of Baltonsborough (*q.v.*); the *Athelbaldus rex* who appears in an alleged later confirmation of the seventh-century grant of Brent (S.238) is so out of context that the reference – whose significance would in any event be obscure – could be to either the Mercian or the West Saxon king of that name. See also *s.n. Fiswere* for a slight suggestion of an even earlier Mercian grant to Glastonbury (A.D. 712x716).

85 Stacy, 'The estates', p. 11.

86 *De antiquitate*, §§49–51 (ed. & transl. Scott, pp. 106–10); the king's privilege is S.152 (A.D. 797).

87 Finberg, *The Formation of England*, pp. 105–6.

88 The dispute over Bath between King Offa and Heathored, bishop of Worcester, at the synod of Brentford is summarised in S.1257 (A.D. 781) (*English Historical Documents*, transl. Whitelock, pp. 505–7 [no. 77]). Offa claimed Bath as the inheritance of his kinsman, King Æthelbald, and the bishop surrendered it. As part of the transaction Offa purchased land on the West Saxon side of the Avon from King Cynewulf. Bath's strategic position on the border between the two kingdoms clearly recommended it to Offa, and his claim to hold it by proprietary right was accepted by the Church; see Sims-Williams, *Religion and Learning*, pp. 159–61. That Cenwulf may have planned or achieved a similar takeover further into West Saxon territory is not impossible.

89 See Edwards, *The Charters*, pp. 52–5, at p. 55: 'It may well be that . . . Beorhtric ceded Glastonbury to Mercia as part of a treaty'; Blows, 'Studies', pp. 193–225, at p. 199: 'In establishing his son in possession of Glastonbury . . . Cenwulf was making a pointed political gesture, . . . striking at the West Saxon genealogy through the West Saxon patrimony'. See also Robinson, *Somerset*, p. 38, n. 3.

90 *De antiquitate*, §51 (ed. & transl. Scott, p. 110). They survive as twelfth-century Latin translations of vernacular versions of Latin originals. The attribution to Glastonbury in A.D. 797 of holdings of eight hundred hides is particularly worrisome (this being the approximate total of the abbey's endowment recorded in Domesday Book).

long after Cenwulf's reign, however, there is evidence of another Mercian king, Burgred, granting land in Somerset (to a Somerset man) and land in Mercia to (perhaps) a member of the West Saxon royal house,[91] both transactions being recorded at Glastonbury. Burgred married the daughter of Æthelwulf, king of Wessex, and their joint venture against the West Welsh is mentioned in the Anglo-Saxon Chronicle (*s.a.* 853). Whether the grants recorded in Glastonbury's archive represent Mercian control continuing to extend into Somerset in the mid-ninth century or instead mirror an alliance between two equal kingdoms is a matter for debate. It is, however, striking that – apart from Cædwalla and Æscwine – the only West Saxon king before A.D. 860 who is not portrayed as a benefactor to Glastonbury is Brihtric, Offa's son-in-law and Cenwulf's contemporary. In addition, Brihtric's successor, Ecgberht, Cenwulf's later contemporary, is poorly represented in Glastonbury's archive.[92] Whatever Glastonbury's relationship with this succession of Mercian kings had been, as Mercian political power waned in the ninth century it must have been desirable to re-establish the close connexion with the royal house of Wessex through Ecgberht's descendants.

The subsequent development is quite striking, however: there are no known charters directly in favour of Glastonbury from four of the next five kings of Wessex after Æthelbald (Æthelberht, Æthelred, Alfred, and Æthelstan), and Edward the Elder is represented by only one grant. Despite a general slowing-down of charter-production, which has been interpreted as an after-effect of viking disruptions, other houses preserve a sufficient number of diplomas in the names of these kings to prevent us from attributing Glastonbury's long fallow period to a cessation of charter-writing. Furthermore, these kings all chose other churches for their burial. This apparent eclipse – which may or may not reach back to Brihtric's reign – lasts from at least A.D. 860 until the reign of Edmund.

The most common explanation for the absence of grants to Glastonbury – at least in the first part of this period – is that, as a result of viking depradations, it ceased to exist: that it was *desolatus*, as William of Malmesbury described it in his *Gesta pontificum Anglorum*.[93] Asser's well known critical assessment of the state of the monastic life among the English during Alfred's reign does not actually confirm that the site of Glastonbury was abandoned; in fact, Asser says that although they no longer maintained the *uita monastica*, a number of *monasteria* remained in the region of Alfred's foundation of Athelney (a dozen miles from Glastonbury).[94] Charters, lists, and the *De antiquitate*, though imprecise and unreliable testimony, may nonetheless preserve a record of a number of abbots who flourished in the later ninth and early tenth centuries; in addition, obits

---

[91] See above, *s.n.* Binegar and Lydney.

[92] One grant to the abbey in his name is lost (LT 30), and Edwards has argued that the other, a grant to a layman by *Edbirtus rex Occidentalium Saxonum* (S.270a), may instead be a charter in the name of Brihtric's queen, Eadburh (*The Charters*, pp. 56–7).

[93] 'Desolatus, aliquantis annis notos desiderauit incolas' ('deserted and for many years without known inhabitants'): §91; ed. Hamilton, p. 196. For a discussion of the fate of ecclesiastical communities during the First Viking Age, see Dumville, *Wessex and England*, pp. 29–54, especially pp. 31–3.

[94] *Life of King Alfred*, §93; ed. Stevenson, pp. 80–1; *Alfred the Great*, transl. Keynes & Lapidge, p. 103.

observed for the years 836, 842, and 876, possibly from a set of annals or a chronicle which has not survived, may be taken to indicate a community functioning at that time and able to preserve traditions in the succeeding years.[95] The preservation of charters of the seventh, eighth, and first half of the ninth century seems similarly to argue for institutional continuity. Rather than being destroyed, it seems more likely that the community continued to exist, perhaps in a debased or secularised form which later earned it the contempt of the Benedictine propagandists and distorted the accounts of its reform in the tenth century. That Alfred apparently ignored Glastonbury (later records attribute to him only the gift of a cross)[96] has been taken as a powerful argument against the abbey's continued existence, but other explanations can be proposed. Perhaps at Glastonbury the vernacular replaced Latin for business-documents in the late ninth century,[97] but only Latin diplomas were subsequently preserved in the cartularies which survive.[98] Blows, on the other hand, has offered a political explanation, arguing that Alfred did not favour the abbey because it was associated with the ringleaders of a plot against his father, King Æthelwulf.[99] It is noteworthy, however, that the

---

95   See Foot, 'Glastonbury's early abbots', pp. 176–9. A list of abbots thought to have been compiled in the second half of the tenth century (preserved in London, British Library, MS. Cotton Tiberius B.v, part 1, at 23va) does not ascribe dates to the men named and consequently no abbots can be securely placed in the ninth century. On the obits, see *De antiquitate*, §67 (ed. & transl. Scott, pp. 136–8), and Blows, 'A Glastonbury obit-list', p. 258, and 'Studies', pp. 408–13. Tunberht, bishop of Winchester, who had been a monk of Glastonbury, apparently died in A.D. 878x879 not 876 as recorded at Glastonbury (*Handbook of British Chronology*, edd. Fryde *et al.*; O'Donovan, 'An interim revision: part II', pp. 108–9). Blows ('Studies', pp. 411–12) has suggested that as this would probably have postdated Edington, it indicates that the abbey survived the wars of the 870s.

96   'Huic successit filius eius Aluredus qui ad hoc ut ecclesias ditaret non thessauro non patrimonio, non sumptibus, non redditibus parcendum putauit' ('His son Alfred succeeded him and he refrained from enriching the churches with treasure or patrimony or properties or revenues'), with the exception of a miraculous cross (*The Great Chartulary*, ed. Watkin, I.144 [after no. 202]); in the *De antiquitate* it is claimed that Alfred's gift was a fragment of the true cross (§53; ed. & transl. Scott, p. 112).

97   Compare Nicholas Brooks's analysis of the late ninth-century archive at Christ Church, Canterbury: *The Early History*, pp. 167–74 and 359–62.

98   It may be unlikely, but the present lack of Old English wills and charters among Glastonbury's documents may suggest that Latin and vernacular records were filed – and perhaps subsequently copied – separately. If there was a collection of vernacular documents, it seems to have been ignored or deliberately jettisoned by the abbey's cartularists. Notice is preserved of only two vernacular documents (one in the *Liber terrarum* [LT23] and one in MS. 39a [L16]), but neither of these is preserved. Apart from S.152, the privilege in the name of Cenwulf, king of Mercia, and the associated privilege of Pope Leo (both in the *De antiquitate*), there seems to be no evidence of Latin translations of vernacular originals (*De antiquitate*, §§49–51; ed. & transl. Scott, pp. 106–10; these privileges do not appear in the *Cronica*). For Latin translations of Anglo-Saxon wills in other archives, see Sheehan, *The Will in Medieval England*, pp. 54–5.

99   Alfred's brother Æthelbald and Ealdorman Eanwulf were both patrons of Glastonbury; 'Studies', pp. 276–83. For their conspiracy to depose Æthelwulf, see Asser's

apparent neglect by Alfred is not a feature exclusive to his reign but is consistent with the pattern that seems to characterise the years from the mid-ninth century (or earlier) to A.D. 940.

If Glastonbury was not destroyed, the fate of its endowment must be considered. I would suggest that it is possible that an enduring community retained its holdings and even, perhaps, its corporate identity.[100] Certainly a substantial number of estates which the abbey claimed it had been granted in the seventh, eighth, and ninth centuries were held in A.D. 1066, without any documentation surviving to record a regrant or a restitution in the interval.[101] Even estates at some distance which had been given to the abbey before the First Viking Age were apparently still held after A.D. 900: Glastonbury exchanged Braunton, reputedly received from King Æthelbald, for another estate in A.D. 973.[102] The case of Braunton also illustrates that estates granted to Glastonbury before the later ninth century which did not belong to the abbey in A.D. 1066 need not have been lost during a pre-reform hiatus, as Costen has assumed:[103] opportunities for loss between the mid-tenth century and the mid-eleventh would not have been lacking. The absence of evidence for restitutions is nevertheless not a firm foundation on which to rest an argument for continuous landholding, especially in the light of possible documentary losses and the other, more abstruse, inadequacies of the charter-record which I have been emphasising. Without an inventory deriving from a survey such as that recorded in Domesday Book, it is impossible to tell exactly what lands (of what value) Glastonbury held at any one date.

Possibilities other than continuity must therefore be considered. Fleming has argued that Alfred and Edward the Elder absorbed the lands of defunct monaster-

---

Life, §§12–13 (ed. Stevenson, pp. 9–12 and 195–9); *Alfred the Great*, transl. Keynes & Lapidge, pp. 70–1 and 234–5, n. 26. For Eanwulf's burial at Glastonbury, see *Chronicon Æthelweardi*, Book IV, §2 (*The Chronicle of Æthelweard*, ed. & transl. Campbell, p. 36), and for his gifts to Glastonbury see above, chapter III, *s.n.* Ditcheat.

[100] For an opposing opinion on the retention of the abbey's lands, see Costen, 'Dunstan, Glastonbury and the economy', pp. 26–9. Costen has argued that 'without monks to use the vast estates indicated in the early charters, it would have been impossible to have kept a hold on them. Large areas of land which provided an income would have been of little use to a few priests.' I would question this view.

[101] This would include estates such as Baltonsborough, Bleadney, Brent, Butleigh, Godney, Leigh-in-Street, Lottisham, East and West Lydford, Marchey, Meare, West Pennard, Pilton, *Pouelt* (comprising the estates on the Poldens), and *Sowy*. A number of other early grants to the abbey – such as those of *Crycbeorh* or *Culum* and *Cumbe*, for example – may also have been followed by unbroken possession (if the lands involved are to be identified with West Monkton and Uffculme). No attempt has been made to make a comprehensive list, due to the complexities involved in identifying some of the estates granted in early charters. The total could conceivably be swelled by places such as *Pedrithe* and the *terra ad pedem Munedup* (allegedly the gifts of seventh-century kings): continued possession of these unidentified places could be disguised by changes of name. See above, pp. 325–6. Only a handful of restitutions of early possessions are formally recorded: see IC A8 in the name of Edward the Elder (for *Cumtone*) and LT 32 in Eadred's name (for Doulting).

[102] S.1695 (LT 19)and S.791; see above, chapter III, *s.n. Brannocmynstre*.

[103] Costen, 'Dunstan, Glastonbury, and the economy', p. 29.

ies into the *terra regis* or used them to endow royal officials.[104] This process is visible at Abingdon and at Ely, where, according to Wulfstan of Winchester, part of the former monastery's endowment had been appropriated by the king and the latter's taken into the royal treasury after the abandonment of the religious house.[105] Evesham's lands were apparently given *ca* A.D. 940 to a *nefandissimus princeps*, possibly Ealdorman Ealhhelm, and at his death passed to another layman, Wulfric, and Oswulf, bishop of Ramsbury, before being retrieved at a reform-synod in A.D. 969.[106] The geographical position of these houses – in the Danelaw or near the border – distinguishes them from Glastonbury, and the parallel may not, therefore, be exact. If the testimony of later writers can be credited, however, Glastonbury also belonged to the king in the early tenth century: Osbern described it as incorporated into the royal *stipendium*, and to B it was *insula regalis*.[107] It may be, therefore, that royal lordship kept the endowment together; but whether such a state of affairs was a response to the crises of the Scandinavian wars or an ancient and traditional condition of patronage is uncertain. Furthermore, continued integrity of the endowment would not necessarily have meant that the lands continued to support a religious community; on the other hand, royal lordship need not have ruled out enduring ecclesiastical life. The young Dunstan was tonsured at Glastonbury, and Irish *peregrini* flocked there in his youth, drawn by its cult of St Patrick.[108] Religious life at the abbey in Dunstan's early days probably had been stimulated by the aftermath of Alfred's programme for religious revival,[109] but whether there was a significant change in the identity of the abbey's endowment – and particularly in its status in relation to the king – is obscure.[110]

There can be no doubt about the existence of a religious community on the site in Æthelstan's reign, and yet direct royal grants to the abbey continue to be conspicuously absent from the record. It may be that Glastonbury's relationship

---

104 Fleming, 'Monastic lands'. But see Dumville, *Wessex and England*, pp. 29–54.

105 Abingdon, *monasteriolum neglectum ac destitutum*, retained an endowment of only forty hides, while another hundred were *subiectae regali dominio*; these were restored to Æthelwold by King Eadred. Ely, *locus destitutus et regali fisco deditus*, was bought by Æthelwold from King Edgar (*Vita Æthelwoldi*, §§11 and 23; *Wulfstan of Winchester*, edd. & transl. Lapidge & Winterbottom, pp. 18–21 and 38).

106 The acquisition by Ealhhelm was described in ideological terms in the Evesham house-history, being presented there as a seizure and the secularisation of a continuing monastic community: *Chronicon Abbatiae de Evesham*, ed. Macray, pp. 77–8; Williams, '*Princeps Merciorum gentis*', pp. 145–6.

107 'Ea tempestate Glestonia regalibus stipendiis addicta, monasticae religionis penitus erat ignara': Osbern, *Vita S. Dunstani*, §6; *Memorials*, ed. Stubbs, p. 74; B, *Vita S. Dunstani*, §3, *ibid.*, pp. 6–7.

108 B, *Vita S. Dunstani*, §5; *Memorials*, ed. Stubbs, pp. 10–11. See also Abrams, 'St Patrick and Glastonbury', pp. 233–6.

109 On the impact of Alfred's ecclesiastical reforms, see Dumville, *Wessex and England*, pp. 185–205.

110 Blows has argued that Glastonbury 'was treated as a royal monastery from its foundation' ('Studies', p. 280). Costen, on the other hand, saw a fundamental difference between 'the Glastonbury of Dunstan's childhood and the monastery of his maturity' ('Dunstan, Glastonbury and the economy', p. 26).

with the house of Wessex offers one approach to the apparent drought which seems to have begun in the early or mid-ninth century, but it is not a simple matter to explain. If a house were a royal holding, perhaps the king would not grant it land in a way which would be visible in the charter-record. Æthelstan did not neglect Glastonbury in other ways: like many churches, it received relics and royal visits.[111] In addition, the abbot of Glastonbury may have been particularly prominent in Æthelstan's charters in the early 930s,[112] and, despite the absence of extant direct royal gifts of land, in the *De antiquitate* a total of eighty-six hides is said to have been granted to the abbey by Æthelstan's thegns, which 'testifies to his pious affection for Glastonbury, for [the thegns'] devotion is frequently offered to the place which they see their master's heart burning for'.[113]

Grants by private individuals to the abbey must therefore be drawn into the discussion; but, as we have seen, these leave a most ambiguous trace in the record. Although the archive routinely preserves grants to individuals by the king, the interpretation of this class of document is not clear-cut. Among the complications is the difficulty of rigorously distinguishing title-deeds, whose recipients had no connexion with Glastonbury, from those grants to men and women who transferred the land in question to the abbey. This is not exclusively a tenth-century problem. Early grants to individual recipients are recorded in Glastonbury's archive, but in the name of only one king (Centwine) before the reign of Cynewulf. Relative antiquity might explain a differential survival of the documents, with a larger number of pre-tenth-century diplomas for laypeople being lost, but a more important reason for the modest number may be sought in charter-granting habits. In the earliest period, grants to individuals seem to have been relatively rare throughout the country, except in cases where the land was given to a religious person or used to found a community. Not until the third quarter of the eighth century does the national distribution change and the number of royal grants to laypeople increase; Glastonbury reflects that change nicely with its eight grants by Cynewulf.[114] Thereafter, numbers range from none (Brihtric and Æthelberht)

---

[111] On Æthelstan's relics, see Robinson, *The Times*, pp. 71–80. His gifts of relics to Glastonbury were recorded *in texto sancti Dunstani* (now lost); *De antiquitate* §54 (ed. & transl. Scott, p. 114). The pious lady, Æthelflæd, whom he visited at Glastonbury was said to be a relative (*Vita S. Dunstani*, §10; *Memorials*, ed. Stubbs, pp. 17–18).

[112] An Abbot Ælfric witnessed first in the series of charters between A.D. 931 and 934 which preserve a number of abbots' attestations. Ælfric appears after Dunstan on the list of Glastonbury's abbots in Tiberius B.v, but in the *De antiquitate* he is said to have been appointed in A.D. 927 and to have been in office for fourteen years (§§54 and 71; ed. & transl. Scott, pp. 112–14 and 146); see Foot, 'Glastonbury's early abbots', p. 182, and Dumville, 'The Anglian collection', p. 42. Winchester had an abbot of the same name at this time, however (see S.412), and it may have been this man who witnessed the extant diplomas. No abbots' attestations are preserved for the last five years of Æthelstan's reign.

[113] 'Predicta igitur omnia per ministros regis Ethelstani Glastonie collata eiusdem regis ascribuntur munificencie et pium eius in Glastoniam affectum famulorum loquitur liberalitas, quorum deuocio frequenter inclinatur quo dominorum animum uiderint inardescere' (*De antiquitate*, §54; ed. & transl. Scott, p. 114).

[114] As has been noted above, some of the grants attributed to King Cynewulf (of Wessex) known only from notices may have been issued by King Cenwulf (of Mercia); it is

to one (Offa, Ecgberht, and Æthelred of Wessex), two (Burgred and Alfred), three (Æthelbald), and four (Æthelwulf and Edward the Elder).

With Æthelstan's reign there is a dramatic change: fourteen grants to individual recipients are attributed to him, followed by a remarkable twenty-four grants from Edmund during his seven years in power.[115] The charters of Eadred, Eadwig, and Edgar continue this trend, though less spectacularly: seventeen, fourteen, and sixteen grants, respectively. Eadwig's figures, though high, are not as impressive as those of the other kings when seen against the background of the total number of grants to individuals which he is known to have made (Glastonbury's record accounts for fourteen of about seventy-five, as opposed to Edmund's twenty-four of approximately sixty). The drop in Æthelred the Unready's reign in the number of grants to laypeople recorded at the abbey (only three) appears to signal another change in the pattern; and there are no further grants of land to other individual recipients by the remaining, eleventh-century, kings.

Whether or not we allow that these charters are representative of genuine transactions, and whether or not differential survival can account for some of the early gaps, and even whether or not we understand quite what they meant to convey, there was clearly something different happening in this second phase which found a reflexion in the written record. Can any sense be made of these figures?

The increase in the number of recorded charters for individual, usually lay, recipients undoubtedly has a practical aspect. Because more and more laypeople turned their land over to religious communities in the tenth century, their charters – and those of previous holders of the land – appear in increasing numbers in ecclesiastical archives; the majority of the documents of their ancestors, on the other hand, for land which remained in lay possession, would have perished without record.[116] It has been suggested above that some at least of the tenth-century documents were leases, not gifts of land, but it may be difficult to interpret them all in this way. Alternatively, if the charters do indeed represent the conveyance of land, there must have been some motivation encouraging laypeople to grant property to Glastonbury which would help to account for the extraordinary number of their charters recorded there, compared with the earlier phase of the endowment. That the incidences of such generosity seem to increase significantly in the reign of Æthelstan may reflect something of the ideology and influence of that pious king, who was responsible for the 'consolidation of local ecclesiastical revival'.[117] The increase in aristocratic lay piety known from the second quarter of the century must have influenced the disposal of property

---

sometimes difficult to tell the difference between the two names. A large number of grants by the king of Mercia is unlikely, however; and, even if we subtract a few grants in order to allow for some confusion in the record, Cynewulf's total is still substantially higher than that of the other early kings.

115 Æthelstan was a favourite of mediaeval forgers, however; and I have already identified Edmund as an attractive choice at Glastonbury (see above, p. 332), in view of his association with Dunstan and the early years of reform.

116 Although charters for land in lay hands seem in some cases to have survived for centuries; see above, p. 332.

117 Dumville, *Wessex and England*, pp. 141–71, especially p. 167.

among the landed class,[118] and it is presumably this development – a change in the pattern of patronage – which is reflected in the archive.

It is interesting to note that this phenomenon apparently predates the formal reform of Glastonbury – whatever that might have entailed. It is likely, however, that when Edmund and Dunstan established there the first reformed monastery in England – according to Æthelwold[119] – the endowment of the house reflected the change in further and significant ways. The nature of property-holding at Glastonbury is obscure throughout its history, and the moment or moments of transition to communal landholding are difficult to identify. It may be that before reform each member of a family of *clerici* was supported by a holding of the church; if so, the 'communalisation' of the endowment would have entailed significant restructuring.[120] From the point of view of direct royal gifts, Edmund's seven grants mark a revival of visible royal generosity, continued throughout the reform-period by Eadred and Edgar. Glastonbury may have been especially favoured thanks to Dunstan's close relationship with the royal house. The gift by Edmund of the large estate at Damerham could be interpreted as one means of financing the changes required by reform (and in the process perhaps regularising a royal monastery which offended against reform-ideals).[121] It has also been suggested that reform revolutionised the character of Glastonbury's use of its landed resources. Stacy first observed the eastward movement of the endowment, especially into Wiltshire, which began in the mid-tenth century, a development which may have been motivated by the desire to exploit better-draining soils.[122] Dunstan's brother, Wulfric, a *praepositus* of the abbey according to B, received charters for some of these lands and may have played an important role in this extension of the house's endowment. On the other hand, grants of Dundon and Ham may represent the intensification of land-use nearer the abbey. Michael Costen has proposed that a reorganisation of the landscape into nucleated, planned, settlements also began at this time;[123] as specialised and linked land-

---

[118] On grants to 'religious' women as an index of this increase in lay piety, see *The Historia Brittonum*, ed. Dumville, III.14–15, and Dumville, *Wessex and England*, pp. 177–8.

[119] *Leechdoms*, ed. & transl. Cockayne, III.438; *English Historical Documents*, transl. Whitelock, pp. 920–3, at 921 (no. 238).

[120] Arrangements may have been restructured several times between the community's foundation and its reform in the tenth century. On the 'division of the *mensa*' in the early Anglo-Saxon Church, see John, 'The division', and Brooks, *The Early History*, pp. 157–60. See also above, pp. 268–70.

[121] See above, chapter III, *s.n.* Damerham.

[122] Stacy, 'The estates', pp. 2–3.

[123] Costen, 'Some evidence for new settlements', and 'Dunstan, Glastonbury, and the economy'. In recent years there has been a wealth of studies on the phenomenon of nucleation; see especially Fox, 'Approaches to the adoption of the midland system'. For the application of the problem in Somerset, see Aston, 'Rural settlement in Somerset'. Archaeologists have found nucleation difficult to date: despite forty years of excavation at the site of the deserted village of Wharram Percy in Yorkshire, no definite chronological context for its nucleation has been established. Dates ranging from the tenth to the twelfth century have been suggested: see Beresford & Hurst, *The English Heritage Book of Wharram Percy*, pp. 79–84.

units – characteristic of early estate-organisation – were severed from the larger whole, new, more independent estates developed and new communities were established. It is possible that – if they are genuine – the large number of grants by Edmund to laymen which are recorded in Glastonbury's archive may reflect an aspect of this development. Edmund may have set about building up Glastonbury's landed resources, not just by direct gifts, but by granting to individual recipients estates which they would be encouraged to transfer to the abbey. The reorganisation of Glastonbury's endowment may in fact have been effected by the lay subtenants who received land from the king for this purpose.[124] It is perhaps unlikely that Edmund directed the fate of his grants of bookland in this way, however, and the king may not have intended the recipients of his largesse here or elsewhere to transfer the land in turn to a religious house; some more complex and untraceable process with this end result may be envisaged, whereby laypeople began by commending themselves to the abbey, which gradually extended its lordship, reduced them to tenants, and acquired their land. Piety and imitation may, on the other hand, be the most relevant considerations of all; as the comment in the *De antiquitate* suggests, royal attachment to the house might have provoked a sustained outburst of *imitatio regis*,[125] and if a layman wished to gain royal approval, a grant to the king's favourite religious community may have been a politic gesture. Brooks has credited Dunstan with inspiring 'a massive transfer of landed resources from the secular aristocracy to the religious aristocracy', a process with significant consequences for the life of the Anglo-Saxon Church in the later tenth century.[126] It was also a development which eventually necessitated – and may even have immediately produced – major changes in record-keeping practices.[127] At Glastonbury, the presence of royal burials,[128] and continuing strong connexions with pre-eminent aristocratic families,[129] probably also attracted donations.

124 We could speculate that these grants to laypeople represented a change in administrative practice necessitated by the physical restructuring of the land; rather than grants of bookland, they could have been temporary alienations of abbatial property, like the grant to Æthelnoth of North Wootton (*q.v.*).

125 See above, p. 341.

126 Brooks, 'The career', p. 23.

127 Blows ('Studies', pp. 26–31) has suggested that the *Liber terrarum* was compiled at this time to establish the identity of the abbey's patrons.

128 King Edmund, King Edgar, and King Edmund Ironside were buried there; *De antiquitate*, §§55, 62, and 64 (ed. & transl. Scott, pp. 116, 130, and 132). King Eadred may have wished to be: see Keynes, 'The "Dunstan B" charters', p. 188, n. 99.

129 The anniversaries of several important men and women are noted in a list of obits from Glastonbury preserved in London, British Library, MS. Add. 17450 (s. xiii). See Blows, 'A Glastonbury obit-list'. Laymen thus commemorated include Æthelstan Half-King, reputedly a generous benefactor of the house (see above, chapter III, *s.n. Brentefordlond*), who retired to Glastonbury in A.D. 957, possibly at the division of the kingdom. (I am indebted to Simon Keynes, whose *Atlas of Attestations in Anglo-Saxon Charters* has allowed him to arrive at this new date; see 'The "Dunstan B" charters', p. 191, n. 108.) Æthelstan's senior position among Edgar's lay supporters was taken at that time by Ealdorman Ælfhere, whom Keynes has described as the most powerful layman in the kingdom (*The Diplomas of King Æthelred*, p. 170); he and his brother

The chronology of these transfers is more tenuous than it first appears. We must remember that grants made to laypeople in Æthelstan's or Edmund's reign did not necessarily reach Glastonbury immediately, even if the recipient of the charter himself bequeathed the land to the abbey. A time-lag of perhaps twenty years might be credible, in which case Glastonbury may have experienced a surge of gifts beginning in the late 940s and continuing even into Æthelred's reign, although as I have pointed out above, not all the lands granted to lay beneficiaries necessarily made their way into the abbey's endowment.

Dunstan and Glastonbury continued to be especially favoured after Edmund's death. Eadred gave land directly to the abbey and also continued to endow lay-people, seventeen of whose charters are recorded in Glastonbury's archive. During the early years of his reign the rise in order of precedence of Dunstan's brother Wulfric can be charted in attestations.[130] Eadred is said to have preferred Dunstan above most of his chief men and to have deposited at the abbey 'all the best of his goods, namely many title-deeds and the ancient treasures of preceding kings, as well as various precious things he had acquired himself'.[131] Responsibility for royal diplomas seems to have rested at Glastonbury when the king – who was troubled with ill health – was unable to see to business himself. As we have seen, a series of royal grants with a distinctive diplomatic, the so-called 'Dunstan B' charters, has been identified as a type developed by Abbot Dunstan at Glastonbury.[132] One of their striking characteristics is the consistent absence of the king's attestation, and it has been suggested that 'the affairs of the realm were conducted in the king's absence by persons who had been empowered to act in his name', that Dunstan was among the persons in question, and that his powers extended to the production of royal diplomas.[133] Although the earliest extant charter of this type is dated 951 (S.555), several diplomas in Edmund's name from the 940s seem to anticipate the style and to underline the association with Dunstan and Glastonbury.

On Eadwig's accession, Dunstan fell into disfavour and was forced to flee the country. The effect at Glastonbury of this reverse is uncertain. B's Life gives no information on Dunstan's replacement: the shadowy 'pseudo-abbot' Ælfsige may

Ælfheah, ealdorman of central Wessex, seem to have been especially associated with Glastonbury. They too (and Ælfheah's wife, Ælfswith) appear on the obit-list and are said to have granted many estates to the abbey. According to John of Worcester, Ælfheah was buried at Glastonbury (*Chronicon, s.a.* 971; *Monumenta Historica Britannica*, edd. Petrie & Sharpe, p. 577). The abbey's claim to be Ælfhere's burial-place is relatively weak in comparison (occurring only in an interpolated chapter of the *De antiquitate* [§31; ed. & transl. Scott, p. 84]); see Blows, 'A Glastonbury obit-list', p. 267. Ælfswith reputedly retired there on the death of her husband. On the estates said to have been given by these three, see above, chapter III, *s.n. Bocland* and Idmiston.

130 Brooks, 'The career', p. 13.
131 'Optima queque suorum suppellectilium, quamplures scilicet rurales cartulas, etiam ueteres precedentium regum thesauros, necnon et diuersas proprie adeptionis sue gazas, sub munimine monasterii sui fideliter custodiendum': B, *Vita S. Dunstani*, §19; *Memorials*, ed. Stubbs, p. 29.
132 See above, p. 328.
133 Keynes, 'The "Dunstan B" charters', pp. 185–6.

have been a layman intruded by the king or a respectably elected monk.[134] Eadwig was later accused by Æthelwold of distributing the 'lands of the holy churches to rapacious strangers'.[135] In A.D. 956 he embarked on a remarkable programme of grants across the country, the recipients being (apparently) new favourites who may have dispossessed the old: Wulfric's estate at Nettleton may have been caught up in these developments.[136] The obscurity of the charter-record does not allow us to distinguish 'rapacious strangers' from less objectionable recipients among those charters preserved at Glastonbury. Nevertheless, the number of grants to individual laypeople in Eadwig's name is low in relation to his total output, and this may suggest that Glastonbury did not suffer unduly. It could, on the other hand, simply reflect an eclipse of status. Keynes has pointed out that few – if any – of Eadwig's diplomas are of the 'Dunstan B' type, and that the king is therefore unlikely to have continued to rely on the abbey's diplomatic services as his predecessors seem to have done.[137] Keynes has pursued the point by drawing attention to the three surviving charters issued in Edgar's name as king of the Mercians in A.D. 957 – all of the 'Dunstan B' type and all without Edgar's attestation – and has suggested that while Eadwig may have shunned the abbey as a centre of production for charters, Edgar (or his counsellors), even before the union of the kingdom, did not. The retirement at Glastonbury in A.D. 957 of Æthelstan Half-King,[138] who had had responsibility for Edgar's upbringing, may further reflect that the abbey's and Eadwig's interests had not always run together.

Glastonbury's position was retrieved by Dunstan in Edgar's reign. While most of Edgar's diplomas have been attributed to the activities of a royal secretariat, 'Dunstan B' charters continued to be produced throughout his reign, even after Dunstan's elevation to Canterbury.[139] In Glastonbury's archive, the eight direct grants in Edgar's name and the unbroken flow of lay bequests (sixteen) seem to reflect the continuing royal attachment to Glastonbury. Edgar chose the house for his burial, as did important members of the secular aristocracy.[140]

No charters survive at Glastonbury in the name of Edward the Martyr, and the effect that Dunstan's support of that king might have had on his old house is uncertain. Ælfhere, ealdorman of Mercia and a patron of the abbey, who was

---

134 In the *De antiquitate*, the *pseudo abbas* Ælfsige is described as having been thrust on the community by the king, but this retroactive judgment may be coloured by the later triumph of the reformers (§58; ed. & transl. Scott, p. 120). On Ælfsige's appearance in the charter-record, see above, chapter III, *s.n.* Nettleton and Panborough.

135 *Leechdoms*, ed. Cockayne, III.432; *English Historical Documents*, transl. Whitelock, p. 920 (no. 238).

136 See above, chapter III, *s.n.* Nettleton.

137 Keynes, 'The "Dunstan B" charters', p. 170.

138 See above, p. 344, n. 129.

139 S.802 (A.D. 975) was said to have been granted at the request of the Glastonbury monk Ælfwine and to have been written at the abbey. Keynes tentatively has associated the later production of 'Dunstan B' charters at Glastonbury more generally with Ælfwine, who was the *successor* of Dunstan's brother Wulfric and a kinsman of the king (*ibid.*, pp. 191–3).

140 See above, p. 344, nn. 128–9.

described in Byrhtferth's Life of Oswald as a destroyer of monasteries in this period, is not accused of any 'anti-monastic' activities at Glastonbury. Elsewhere his actions probably had more to do with limiting the secular powers of monastic houses in his ealdordom than with any anti-ecclesiastical feeling.[141] During Æthelred the Unready's reign Glastonbury's position may be indicated by the prominence of its abbot in charter-attestations: Ælfweard (A.D. ?975–?1009) heads the list of abbots in a significant number of charters between A.D. 988 and 1009,[142] indicating a regular presence at court and an apparently senior status there. The unsubstantiated assertion in the *Liber Eliensis* mentioned above – that Glastonbury was one of three monasteries in the country with the status of a kind of chancery during the reign of Æthelred the Unready – might support this impression of importance.[143] Otherwise, Glastonbury's relations with Æthelred are not especially well documented. The reputed mortgaging of Glastonbury's estates in Wiltshire to the royal treasury for Danegeld or heregeld need not signify a withdrawal of royal favour:[144] times were desperate, and Glastonbury was not alone in suffering from the burdens of taxation. Archbishop Sigeric's sacrifice of at least one estate to protect his church from attack by vikings has already been mentioned.[145] Æthelred's seven direct grants to Glastonbury are topped only by Ine's, although, like Ine's, they need not all be genuine. While Æthelred's generosity to the house seems to continue the pattern of his predecessors, in his reign the number of grants to lay recipients recorded in the archive drops off dramatically.

After Æthelred's reign, only one royal grant to Glastonbury is recorded. Edmund Ironside allegedly granted an estate to the abbey 'with his body';[146] after this the series ends completely. No grants of land to Glastonbury by Cnut, Harald Harefoot, Harthacnut, or Edward the Confessor are known. This tailing-off of royal gifts in the eleventh century and the absence of any diplomas of the later Anglo-Saxon kings may be attributable to the general decline of monastic influence at court after its reform-period peak.[147] Alternatively, the apparent inactivity

---

[141] Ælfhere, '*sumens munera enorm[i]a*' ('appropriating enormous revenues'), ejected monks from a number of monasteries in Mercia; *Vita Oswaldi archiepiscopi Eboracensis*, in *The Historians of the Church of York*, ed. Raine, I.443–4; *English Historical Documents*, transl. Whitelock, pp. 912–17, at 912–13 (no. 236); see also Williams, '*Princeps Merciorum gentis*', especially pp. 166–70.

[142] Ælfweard attested thirty-six extant charters, twenty-four of them in first place. It is interesting to note that his attestations seem to begin at Dunstan's death, not at the start of his abbacy.

[143] See above, p. 328, n. 49.

[144] *De antiquitate*, §68 (ed. & transl. Scott, pp. 138–40). The philanthropy *tempore Danorum* by Brihtwold, bishop of Ramsbury (A.D. 1005–1045) and once a monk of Glastonbury, who bought them back, is not precisely dated. It could presumably apply to a need for cash experienced by the abbey in either Æthelred's or Cnut's reign.

[145] S.882 (A.D. 995). See above, p. 330, n. 62.

[146] *De antiquitate*, §64 (ed. & transl. Scott, p. 132).

[147] Simon Keynes has noted that cartularies in the archives of other churches show a similar scarcity of diplomas for the later Anglo-Saxon period: 'Studies', I.167. See also Fisher, 'The anti-monastic reaction'.

could be a result of archival losses, but as so many other, earlier, charters are preserved, this explanation is not satisfactory. It is perhaps possible that the absence of grants from the reign of Cnut onwards represents the eclipse of Glastonbury's royal connexions more specifically and the cooling of the special relationship, although later kings continued to give gifts of vestments and ornaments to the abbey, and a surviving privilege in Cnut's name may have an authentic basis.[148] Cnut in particular may have had ambiguous feelings about Glastonbury, associated as it was with the dynasty which he had displaced: the visit which he made to the tomb of Edmund Ironside at the abbey (perhaps in A.D. 1032)[149] may have been undertaken to make the point that his kingship rested at least in part on a treaty with that king, whom he honoured as a brother.[150] Such a display might have been engineered by Cnut to ingratiate himself with the members of the West Saxon aristocracy who were associated with the community. He may have thought that an affirmation of his brotherhood with the kings of Wessex would diminish the degree to which he was perceived as an outsider and usurper; overall, he took care to stress the continuity between his reign and what had gone before, and honouring Glastonbury may have been one step along that road.[151] But because Æthelred's sons were alive and well in Normandy and the West Saxon monarchy was not yet a thing of the past, feelings at Glastonbury might not have been very warm towards Cnut. M.K. Lawson has argued that the Anglo-Saxon æthelings 'were forgotten least in [the] house with which their forebears were closely associated', and that this may be reflected in the account of a dream in which Brihtwold, bishop of Ramsbury, had a vision of Edward the Confessor crowned king. This dream was said to have occurred at Glastonbury *tempore regis Cnutonis*.[152] Whether or not Cnut's relations with Glastonbury were delicate and involved a balancing of conflicting attitudes, he nevertheless does not appear to have been a benefactor in any significant way, but directed his attention elsewhere. If there was an estrangement in Cnut's day, it did not seem to have had too adverse an effect on the abbey's resources, although such a judgment can only be made from the comfortable distance of 1066, when the community's great wealth, if threatened earlier in the century, had been restored. In fact, during Cnut's reign, it is likely that the richest monastery in the land must have faced one of the biggest tax bills, as Lawson has pointed out,[153] and despite its wealth Glastonbury may have felt the financial squeeze. The reputed alienation of abbatial lands by the penultimate Anglo-Saxon abbot, Æthelweard (*ca* A.D. 1024–1053), represented as sheer rapaciousness and bad behaviour, may have been connected with

---

148 S.966 (A.D. 1032); Cnut reputedly gave a pall for Edmund Ironside's tomb, and Harthacnut gave a shrine or reliquary (*De antiquitate*, §§64 and 66 [ed. & transl. Scott, pp. 132 and 134]).

149 The privilege in his name (S.966) is ascribed to that year (in one of Glastonbury's cartularies; A.D. 1030 in the other); Lawson, *Cnut*, p. 138.

150 'Pia querela fraternos manes honorans': *De antiquitate*, §64 (ed. & transl. Scott, p. 132); Lawson, *Cnut*, p. 138.

151 *Ibid.*, pp. 138–9.

152 *Vita Edwardi*; *The Life of King Edward the Confessor* (ed. & transl. Barlow, pp. 85 and 8–9); *De antiquitate*, §68 (ed. & transl. Scott, p. 140); Lawson, *Cnut*, pp. 155–6.

153 *Ibid.*, p. 193.

financial pressures and the need for ready cash. Losses are difficult to date, but a substantial proportion of those lands granted to Glastonbury or to its alleged benefactors in the mid- and late tenth century were not among the abbey's holdings in Domesday Book, and it may be that they were lost during the reigns of Æthelred and Cnut, signalling not so much a withdrawal of royal protection or a weakening of the power of abbatial lordship but rather a response to the financial burdens which even such a rich abbey must have struggled to withstand.[154] If the *Liber terrarum* was a pre-Conquest production, as some have argued,[155] its compilation could have been linked to a concern to establish title and protect against losses at a time when the endowment was experiencing pressure from without, and documentation affirming the abbey's ownership and securing its lands as closely as possible to the house would have been especially desirable. Such difficulties seem to be largely a thing of the past by the 1060s, however; the accusation that Abbot Æthelnoth (A.D. 1053–1077/8) despoiled the house of its treasures may relate to other, political, exigencies which required cash.[156] In any event, the community could not legitimately cry poor in 1066, with an endowment of over eight hundred hides across seven counties.

As a landowner, Glastonbury Abbey clearly experienced many changes between the endowment of the religious house in the late seventh century and its enjoyment in the mid-eleventh of the healthy portfolio of property revealed by Domesday Book. Attempting to chart these changes is a risky enterprise. The extant documents may not even approximately reflect the ebb and flow of the abbey's landholding over these many centuries; if that is the case, my attempt to extrapolate from the surviving written evidence some observations on charter-production, charter-transmission, and royal and aristocratic patronage may have led to phantom conclusions. If so, I would hope that the elaboration of the questions has nevertheless exposed at least the dimensions of the problems involved, even if solutions remain elusive.

---

[154] As Domesday Book provides the only record of pre-Conquest non-ownership, so to speak – that is to say, because at no time other than 1066 do we have any record not only of what the abbey held but of what it did *not* hold – losses cannot be pinpointed at any time before the Conquest. However, a substantial proportion of the grants after A.D. 940 were for estates apparently not in the abbey's hands in 1066 (see the lists below, pp. 353–4); if we credit the idea that some of these grants to laypeople made by Edmund and his successors were indeed granted to the abbey, and that the land took some time to reach the church's endowment, which lost it some time thereafter, a greater degree of loss in the eleventh century (rather than the tenth) might be likely.

[155] See above, pp. 14–17.

[156] It has been suggested above (pp. 311–12) that Æthelnoth's interesting career offered scope for the kind of political manoeuvring which is accomplished with money. Alternatively, a rebellious west country may have looked to Glastonbury for leadership and financial support.

(2) King Cenwealh (A.D. 642–672): S.227 (LT3), DA §36
(0) King Æscwine (A.D. 674–676)
(3) King Baldred (A.D. 676x685): S.236 (LT7), S.1665 (LT13), DA §38
(2) King Centwine (A.D. 676–685): S.237 (LT8), S.1666 (LT1)
(0) King Cædwalla (A.D. 685–688)
(7?) King Ine (A.D. 688–726): S.238 [=S.1671?] (LT20), S.248 [=S.247 =S.1672?=IC A5?] (LT9), S.251 (LT14), S.1670 (IC A6), S.1673 (LT12), DA §40 (*ECW* 373), DA §40 (*ECW* 377)
(2) King Æthelheard (A.D. 726–?740): S.253 (LT15), S.1676 (LT29)
(1) Queen Frithugyth (?A.D. 729x739): S.1677 (LT16)
(1) King Cuthred (A.D. 740–756): S.1678 (LT18)
(1+?1) King Æthelbald (Mercia) (A.D. 716–757): S.1679 (LT94), *S.1410 (LT17) (two estates of multiple grant by laywoman placed at his disposal)
(2) King Sigeberht (A.D. 756–757): S.1680 (LT63), DA §40
(3) King Cynewulf (A.D. 757–786) or King Cenwulf (Mercia) (A.D. 796–821):[158] S.1684 (LT27), S.1685 (LT39), DA §48
(1) King Offa (Mercia) (A.D. 757–796): DA §48
(0) King Brihtric (A.D. 786–802)
(1) King Ecgberht (A.D. 802–839): S.1693 (LT30)
(1+?1) King Æthelwulf (A.D. 839–858): DA §53 and S.303 (LT 136)
(1) King Æthelbald (A.D. 855–860): S.1695 (LT19)
(0) King Athelberht (A.D. 860–865)
(0) King Æthelred (A.D. 865–871)
(0) King Alfred (A.D. 871–899)
(1) King Edward the Elder (A.D. 899–924): S.1705 (IC A8)
(0) King Æthelstan (A.D. 924–939)
(7) King Edmund (A.D. 939–946): S.466 (IC A10), S.1723 (LT58), S.1724 (LT100), S.1725 (LT56), S.1726 (LT57), IC A12, DA §55
(6) King Eadred (A.D. 946–955): S.553 (IC C6), S.568 (LT67), S.1741 (LT75), S.1742 (LT32), IC A13, IC C5
(3) King Eadwig (A.D. 955–959): S.625 (IC A15), S.626 (LT76), S.1757 (LT53)
(8) King Edgar (A.D. 959–975): S.743 (LT82), S.764 (IC C8), S.791 [?=S.1773] (LT83), S.1768 (LT81), S.1769 (LT72), S.1770 (LT86), DA §62 (*ECW* 505 and 506)

---

157 Transactions are cited by Sawyer-number and *Liber terrarum*-number, if they appear in Sawyer's handlist and in the contents-list of the *Liber*; if not in the latter, the relevant number in the *Index chartarum* is given; if the charter is not listed there, the number in MS. 39a is given. Chapter-numbers in the *De antiquitate* are given only if that source is the sole witness to the grant; if two grants by one king occur in the same chapter, they are distinguished by their numbers in Finberg's *The Early Charters of Wessex*. Grants of privilege are given on a separate list, below. The total omits possible duplicate reference, which are indicated by square brackets on the list.

158 There is some difficulty in distinguishing between Cynewulf of Wessex and Cenwulf of Mercia where only a notice of a grant survives.

(0) King Edward the Martyr (A.D. 975–978)
(7) King Æthelred (A.D. 978–1016): S.866 (L37), S.1774 (LT133), S.1775 (IC A16), S.1776 (IC C14), S.1777 (IC C11), S.1778 (IC C12), S.1780 (IC C13)
(1) King Edmund Ironside (A.D. 1016): DA §64
(0) King Cnut (A.D. 1016–1035)
(0) King Harald Harefoot (A.D. 1035/6–1040)
(0) King Harthacnut (A.D. 1040–1042)
(0) King Edward the Confessor (A.D. 1042–1066)

GRANTS BY BISHOPS AND RELIGIOUS WOMEN TO GLASTONBURY ABBEY (8)

(2) Bishop Wilfrid (A.D. 680s?): S.1674 (IC C2), S.1675 (LT10)
(2) Hædde, bishop of the West Saxons (A.D. 680/1): S.1249 (LT5), LT6 (with consent of Kings Centwine and Baldred and confirmation by Cædwalla)
(1) Forthhere, bishop of Sherborne (A.D. 712): S.1253 (LT11)
(1) Lulla (*ancilla Christi*) (A.D. 744): S.1410 (LT17) (confirmed by King Æthelbald and King Cuthred)
(1) Sulca (*ancilla Christi*) (A.D. 757x786): DA §48
(1) Tunberht, bishop of Winchester (A.D. 871x879): S.1703 (LT33)

ROYAL GRANTS TO OTHER RECIPIENTS (117)

(0) King Cenwealh (A.D. 642–672)
(0) King Baldred (A.D. 676x685)
(3) King Centwine (A.D. 676–685): S.1667 (IC C1), S.1668 (IC A17), S.1669 (LT4)
(0) King Cædwalla (A.D. 685–688)
(0) King Ine (A.D. 688–726)
(0) King Æthelheard (A.D. 726–?740)
(0) King Cuthred (A.D. 740–756)
(0) King Sigeberht (A.D. 756–757)
(8) King Cynewulf (Wessex, A.D. 757–786) or King Cenwulf (Mercia, A.D. 796–821): S.1681 (LT31), S.1682 (LT84), S.1683 (LT25), S.1686 (IC D1), S.1687 (LT24), S.1688 (IC D3), S.1689 (LT47), S.1690 (IC B1)
(1) King Offa (Mercia, A.D. 757–796): S.1692 (LT28)
(0) King Brihtric (A.D. 786–802)
(1) King Ecgberht (A.D. 802–839): S.270a (LT38)
(4) King Æthelwulf (A.D. 839–858): S.288 (LT107), S.292 (LT91), S.1694 (LT40), S.1698 (IC D5)
(2) King Burgred (Mercia, A.D. ?852–873/4): S.1701 (LT93), S.1702 (LT87)
(3) King Æthelbald (A.D. 855–860): S.1699 (LT92), S.1700 (LT64), LT22
(0) King Æthelberht (A.D. 860–865)
(1) King Æthelred (A.D. 865–871): S.341 (LT115)
(2) King Alfred (A.D. 871–899): S.347 (IC B11), S.1704 (LT73)

351

(4) King Edward the Elder (*et al.*) (A.D. 899–924): S.371 (LT41), S.1706 (IC D6), S.1707 (IC D7), S.1708 (IC D8)

(14) King Æthelstan (A.D. 924–939): S.399 (LT102), S.426 (IC B2), S.431 (LT128), S.442 (LT42), S.1709 (LT125), S.1710 (LT54), S.1711 (LT55), S.1712 (LT95), S.1713 (LT52), S.1714 (LT51), S.1715 (LT134), S.1716 (IC B3), S.1717 (LT36), IC B12

(24) King Edmund (A.D. 939–946): S.462 (LT106), S.472 (LT43), S.473 (LT85), S.474 (LT50), S.481 (LT101), S.498 (IC D15), S.504 (LT44), S.509 (LT131), S.513 (LT37), S.1718 (LT59), S.1719 (LT49), S.1720 (LT127), S.1721 (LT45), S.1722 (LT65), S.1727 (LT99), S.1728 (LT34), S.1729 (LT48), S.1730 (LT124), S.1731 (LT66), S.1732 (IC D12), S.1733 (IC D14), S.1734 (IC D13), S.1735 (IC D10), LT61

(17) King Eadred (A.D. 946–955): S.524 (LT108), S.530 (LT104), S.541 (LT105), S.551 (LT112), S.555 [?=S.1737] (LT116), S.563 (LT68), S.580 (LT62), S.1736 (LT96), S.1738 (LT122), S.1739 (LT121), S.1740 (LT120), S.1743 (LT46), S.1744 (LT98), S.1745 (LT126), LT97, LT109, IC B8

(14) King Eadwig (A.D. 955–959): S.644 (IC B9), S.1746 (LT69), S.1747 (LT89), S.1748 (LT110), S.1749 (LT129), S.1750 (LT77), S.1751 (LT78), S.1752 (LT123), S.1753 (LT35), S.1754 (LT118), S.1755 (LT60), S.1756 (LT88), S.1758 (LT130), IC C7

(16) King Edgar (A.D. 959–975): S.721 (IC B6), S.742 (L26), S.747 (LT113), S.775 (LT103), S.793 (IC D21), S.1759 (LT117), S.1760 (LT90), S.1761 (LT111), S.1762 (LT114), S.1763 (LT74), S.1764 (LT119), S.1765 (LT80), S.1766 (LT70), S.1767 (LT71), S.1771 (IC D19), S.1772 (IC D20)

(0) King Edward the Martyr (A.D. 975–978)
(3) King Æthelred (A.D. 978–1016): S.871, S.1779 (LT79), S.1781 (IC D22)
(0) King Edmund Ironside (A.D. 1016)
(0) King Cnut (A.D. 1016–1035)
(0) King Harald Harefoot (A.D. 1035/6–1040)
(0) King Harthacnut (A.D. 1040–1042)
(0) King Edward the Confessor (A.D. 1042–1066)

ROYAL GRANTS OF PRIVILEGES

A.D. 704 King Ine (LT 2 and LT 135 [=S.245?]; S.246)
A.D. 725 King Ine (S.250)
A.D. 745 King Cuthred (S.257; LT21)
A.D. 797 Cenwulf, king of Mercia (S.152)
A.D. 854 King Æthelwulf (S.303; LT136) (Decimation)
A.D. 944 King Edmund (S.499)
A.D. 971 King Edgar (S.783)
A.D. 1032 King Cnut (S.966)

ESTATES GRANTED TO INDIVIDUAL RECIPIENTS
WHICH WERE NOT HELD BY GLASTONBURY ABBEY IN 1066
(according to Domesday Book)

The following is a list of identifiable places for which pre-Conquest grants to individual recipients are recorded in Glastonbury's archive but which do not appear (with these names) among the abbey's holdings in Domesday Book. Those marked with an asterisk do not appear at all in Domesday Book's returns; the remainder are recorded there as held by other lords. In most cases, the estate in question was claimed as part of Glastonbury's pre-Conquest endowment, but the authority of this claim is not always strong. For details, see the entries in chapter III. The first list overleaf comprises lands granted to lay recipients which are mentioned in Glastonbury's record (again, usually as gifts to the abbey) but which are unidentified; their holders in 1066 therefore are unknown. The last list consists of places granted to individual recipients which Glastonbury is recorded as holding in 1066. These lists perforce disregard difficulties of authenticity and identification and ignore the subtleties which complicate the estate-histories and obscure the question of possession and transfer; they are nonetheless offered here as a rough and ready guide for comparative purposes. See the discussion above, especially, pp. 332–4 and 340–6.

Abbotsbury (Do)	Merton (S)*
Berrow (So)*	Orchardleigh (So)
Binegar (So)*	Ottery St Mary (D)
Brentefordlond (Brampford Speke) (D)	Pilsdon (Do)
Buckland Denham (So)	Plush (Do)*
Camel (So)	Portbury (So)
Camerton (So)	Raddington (So)
Cleeve (So)	Rowberrow (So)*
Clutton (So)	Stourton (W)
Compton Beauchamp (B)	Tarnock (So)
Dulwich (S)*	Turnworth (Do)
Foxcote (So)	Ubley (So)
Henstridge (So)	Upavon (W)
Holton (So)	Wedmore (So)
Horton (So)	Westbury (W?)
Huntspill (So)	Winchester *curtis* (H)
Lydney (G)	Yarlington (So)
Martin (W/H)	Yeovilton (So)

ESTATES NAMED IN OTHER RECORDS AS GRANTED TO LAY RECIPIENTS BUT NOW UNIDENTIFIED

Aldamtone
Bradanleag
Byrhtulfington becocer
Ceollamwirthe
Cympanhamme
Cynemersforda
Easetenetone
Eatumberesder
Elosaneg
Hamanstane
Hunespulle

Iecesig
Inesuuyrth
Lennucmere
Lutramtone
Peasucmere
Pendescliue
Pidelan
Westone
Worstone
Wydancumbe

ESTATES GRANTED TO INDIVIDUAL RECIPIENTS WHICH GLASTONBURY ABBEY HELD IN 1066
(according to Domesday Book)

Andersey (So)
Ashbury (B)
Batcombe (So)
Buckland Newton (Do)
Butleigh (So)
Cranmore (So)
Culum and *Cumbe* (?Uffculme, D)
Damerham (W/H)
Deuerel (W)
Ditcheat (So)
Durborough (So)
Elborough (So)
Grittleton (W)
Hannington (W)
Holton (So)
Hornblotton (So)
Idmiston (W)
Kington Langley (W)
Lamyatt (So)
Langford (W)

Lottisham (So)
Lyme Regis (Do)
Marksbury (So)
Mells (So)
Mildenhall (W)
Nettleton (W)
North Wootton (So)
Okeford Fitzpaine (Do)
East Pennard (So)
Pentridge (Do)
Pucklechurch (G)
Stoke (So)
Stratton (So)
Tintinhull (So)
Uplyme (D)
Winscombe (So)
Winterbourne (W)
Woodyates (Do)
Wrington (So)

BIBLIOGRAPHY

ABELS, R.P. 'Bookland and fyrd service in late Saxon England', *Anglo-Norman Studies* 7 (1984) 1–25

ABELS, Richard P. *Lordship and Military Obligations in Anglo-Saxon England* (Berkeley, CA 1988)

ABRAMS, L.[J.] 'A single-sheet facsimile of a diploma of King Ine for Glastonbury', in *The Archaeology and History of Glastonbury Abbey*, edd. L. Abrams & J.P. Carley (Woodbridge 1991), pp. 97–133

ABRAMS, L.[J.] ' "Lucid intervals": a rediscovered Anglo-Saxon diploma from Glastonbury Abbey', *Journal of the Society of Archivists* 10 (1989) 43–56

ABRAMS, L.[J.] 'St Patrick and Glastonbury Abbey: *nihil ex nihilo fit?*', apud D.N. Dumville *et al.*, *Saint Patrick, A.D. 493–1993* (Woodbridge 1993), pp. 233–42

ABRAMS, L.[J.] & CARLEY, J.P. (edd.) *The Archaeology and History of Glastonbury Abbey. Essays in Honour of the Ninetieth Birthday of C.A. Ralegh Radford* (Woodbridge 1991)

ABRAMS, Lesley Jane 'The Pre-Conquest Endowment of Glastonbury Abbey: the Growth of an Anglo-Saxon Church' (unpublished Ph.D. dissertation, University of Toronto 1991)

ANDERSON, O.S. *The English Hundred Names: the South West Counties* (Lund 1939)

ANON. 'First annual meeting', *Proceedings of the Somerset Archaeological and Natural History Society* 1 (1849/50) 3–26

ANON. *Fourth Report of the Historical Manuscripts Commission* (London 1874)

ARNOLD, Thomas (ed.) *Symeonis Monachi Opera Omnia* (2 vols, London 1882/5)

ASHE, Geoffrey (ed.) *The Quest for Arthur's Britain* (2nd edn, London 1971)

ASTON, M.A. (ed.) *Aspects of the Medieval Landscape of Somerset. Contributions to the Landscape History of the County* (Taunton 1988)

ASTON, M.A. & LEECH, R. (edd.) *Historic Towns in Somerset. Archaeology and Planning* (Bristol 1977)

ASTON, M.A. *Interpreting the Landscape. Landscape Archaeology in Local Studies* (London 1985)

ASTON, M.A. (ed.) *Medieval Fish, Fisheries and Fishponds in England* (Oxford 1988)

ASTON, M.A. 'Rural settlement in Somerset: some preliminary thoughts', in *Medieval Villages*, ed. D. Hooke (Oxford 1985), pp. 81–100

ASTON, M.A. & ILES, R. (edd.) *The Archaeology of Avon. A Review from the Neolithic to the Middle Ages* (Bristol [1986])

ASTON, M.A. & BURROW, I. (edd.) *The Archaeology of Somerset. A Review to 1500 AD* ([Taunton] 1982)

ASTON, M.A. & LEWIS, C. (edd.) *The Medieval Landscape of Wessex* (Oxford 1994)

ASTON, M.A., *et al.* (edd.) *The Shapwick Project. A Topographical and Historical Study 1989 (2nd) Report* (Bristol 1990)

ASTON, M.A. & COSTEN, M.D. (edd.) *The Shapwick Project. A Topographical and Historical Study. The Third Report* (Bristol 1992)

ASTON, M.A. & COSTEN, M.D. (edd.) *The Shapwick Project. A Topographical and Historical Study. The Fourth Report* (Bristol 1993)

ASTON, M.A. & COSTEN, M.D. (edd.) *The Shapwick Project. A Topographical and Historical Study. The Fifth Report* (Bristol 1994)

ASTON, T.H., *et al.* (edd.) *Social Relations and Ideas. Essays in Honour of R.H. Hilton* (Cambridge 1983)

ATKINS, I. 'The church of Worcester from the eighth to the twelfth century', *Antiquaries' Journal* 17 (1937) 371–91 *and* 20 (1940) 203–29

ATTENBOROUGH, F.L. (ed. & transl.) *The Laws of the Earliest English Kings* (Cambridge 1922)

AYTON, A. & DAVIS, V. 'Ecclesiastical wealth in England in 1086', in *The Church and Wealth*, edd. W.J. Sheils & Diana Wood (Oxford 1987), pp. 47–60

BARING-GOULD, S. & FISHER, J. *Lives of the British Saints* (4 vols, London 1907–13)

BARKER, K. 'The early history of Sherborne', in *The Early Church in Western Britain and Ireland*, ed. S. Pearce (Oxford 1982), pp. 77–116

BARLOW, F. 'Domesday Book: an introduction', in *Domesday Essays*, ed. C. Holdsworth (Exeter 1986), pp. 16–28

BARLOW, Frank *The English Church 1000–1066. A History of the Later Anglo-Saxon Church* (2nd edn, London 1979)

BARLOW, Frank (ed. & transl.) *The Life of King Edward the Confessor who Rests at Westminster* (2nd edn, Oxford 1992)

BARRACLOUGH, Geoffrey (ed.) *Mediaeval Germany 911–1250: Essays by German Historians* (2 vols, Oxford 1938)

BARROW, J. 'How the twelfth-century monks of Worcester perceived their past', in *The Perception of the Past in Twelfth-Century Europe*, ed. P. Magdalino (London 1992), pp. 53–74

BASSETT, Steven (ed.) *The Origins of Anglo-Saxon Kingdoms* (London 1989)

BATELY, J.M. (ed.) *The Anglo-Saxon Chronicle. MS A, The Anglo-Saxon Chronicle: a Collaborative Edition* (Cambridge 1986)

BATES, E.H. (transl.) 'Text of the Somerset Domesday', in *The Victoria History of the County of Somerset*, I, ed. E.H. Bates (London 1906), pp. 434–526

BATES, E.H. 'The five-hide unit in the Somerset Domesday', *Proceedings of the Somerset Archaeological and Natural History Society* 45 (1899) 51–107

BATES, E.H. (ed.) *Two Cartularies of the Benedictine Abbeys of Muchelney and Athelney in the County of Somerset* (1899)

BELL, Martin, *et al.* *Brean Down Excavations 1983–7* (London 1990)

BERESFORD, M. & HURST, J. *The English Heritage Book of Wharram Percy Deserted Medieval Village* (London 1990)

[BERNARD, Edward] *Catalogi Librorum Manuscriptorum Anglie et Hibernie* (Oxford 1697)

BETTEY, J.H. *The Suppression of the Monasteries in the West Country* (Gloucester 1989)

BIRCH, Walter de Gray (ed.) *Cartularium Saxonicum: a Collection of Charters Relating to Anglo-Saxon History* (3 vols, London 1885–93)

[BIRD, W.H.B.] *Calendar of the Manuscripts of the Dean and Chapter of Wells* (2 vols, London 1907–14)

BLAIR, J. 'Local churches in Domesday Book and before', in *Domesday Studies*, ed. J.C. Holt (Woodbridge 1987), pp. 265–78

BLAIR, J. 'Secular minster churches in Domesday Book', in *Domesday Book*, ed. P.H. Sawyer (London 1985), pp. 104–42

BLAKE, E.O. (ed.) *Liber Eliensis* (London 1962)

BLOWS, M. (ed.) 'A Glastonbury obit-list', in *The Archaeology and History of Glastonbury Abbey*, edd. L. Abrams & J.P. Carley (Woodbridge 1991), pp. 257–69

BLOWS, Matthew 'Studies in the Pre-Conquest History of Glastonbury Abbey' (unpublished Ph.D. dissertation, University of London 1991)

BOND, F.B. 'Glastonbury Abbey excavations. Tenth annual report', *Proceedings of the Somerset Archaeological and Natural History Society* 72 (1926) 13–19

BOND, F.B. 'Glastonbury Abbey. Report on discoveries made during the excavations of 1908', *Proceedings of the Somerset Archaeological and Natural History Society* 54 (1908) 107–30

BOND, F. Bligh *The Gate of Remembrance* (Oxford 1918)

BOUCHARD, Constance Brittain *Sword, Miter, and Cloister. Nobility and the Church in Burgundy, 980–1198* (Ithaca, NY 1987)

BRETT, C. (ed. & transl.) 'A Breton pilgrim in England in the reign of King Æthelstan', in *France and the British Isles in the Middle Ages and Renaissance*, edd. G. Jondorf & D.N. Dumville (Woodbridge 1991), pp. 43–70

BROOKS, N. 'Anglo-Saxon charters: the work of the last twenty years', *Anglo-Saxon England* 3 (1974) 211–31

BROOKS, N. 'England in the ninth century: the crucible of defeat', *Transactions of the Royal Historical Society*, 5th S., 29 (1979) 1–20

BROOKS, N. 'The career of St Dunstan', in *St Dunstan*, edd. N. Ramsay *et al.* (Woodbridge 1992), pp. 1–23

BROOKS, N. 'The development of military obligations in eighth- and ninth-century England', in *England before the Conquest*, edd. P. Clemoes & K. Hughes (Cambridge 1971), pp. 69–84

BROOKS, Nicholas *The Early History of the Church of Canterbury. Christ Church from 597 to 1066* (Leicester 1984)

BROWN, R.A. *Origins of English Feudalism* (London 1973)

BURROW, Ian *Hillfort and Hilltop Settlement in Somerset in the First to Eighth Centuries A.D.* (Oxford 1981)

BUSH, R.J.E. 'Clatworthy', in *A History of the County of Somerset*, V, ed. R.W. Dunning (London 1985), pp. 31–8

CALTHROP, M.M.C. 'Abbey of Abbotsbury', in *The Victoria History of the County of Dorset*, II, ed. W. Page (London 1908), pp. 48–53

CAMPBELL, A. *Old English Grammar* (Oxford 1959; rev. imp., 1962)

CAMPBELL, A. (ed. & transl.) *The Chronicle of Æthelweard* (Edinburgh 1962)

CAMPBELL, J. 'Some agents and agencies of the late Anglo-Saxon state', in *Domesday Studies*, ed. J.C. Holt (Woodbridge 1987), pp. 201–18

CAMPBELL, J. 'The debt of the early English Church to Ireland', in *Ireland and Christendom*, edd. P. Ní Chatháin & M. Richter (Stuttgart 1987), pp. 332–46

CAMPBELL, J. 'The sale of land and the economics of power in early England: problems and possibilities', *Haskins Society Journal* 1 (1989) 23–37

CARLEY, J.P. 'An identification of John of Glastonbury and a new dating of his Chronicle', *Mediaeval Studies* 40 (1978) 478–83

CARLEY, James P. *Glastonbury Abbey. The Holy House at the Head of the Moors Adventurous* (Woodbridge 1988)

CARLEY, James P. & TOWNSEND, D. (edd. & transl.) *The Chronicle of Glastonbury Abbey. An Edition, Translation and Study of John of Glastonbury's 'Cronica sive Antiquitates Glastoniensis Ecclesiae'* (Woodbridge 1981)

CARNICELLI, T.A. (ed.) *King Alfred's Version of St. Augustine's 'Soliloquies'* (Cambridge, Mass. 1969)

CARVER, Martin (ed.) *In Search of Cult. Archaeological Investigations in Honour of Philip Rahtz* (Woodbridge 1993)

CASH, J.O. 'The Saxon church at Glastonbury. St Dunstan's tower', *Notes and Queries for Somerset and Dorset* 20 (1930–2) 193–7

CHAPLAIS, Pierre (ed.) *Essays in Medieval Diplomacy and Administration* (London 1981)

CHAPLAIS, P. 'Some early Anglo-Saxon diplomas on single sheets: originals or copies?', *Journal of the Society of Archivists* 3 (1965–9) 315–36; reprinted in revised form in *Prisca Munimenta*, ed. F. Ranger (London 1973), pp. 63–87

CHAPLAIS, P. 'The Anglo-Saxon chancery: from the diploma to the writ', *Journal of the Society of Archivists* 3 (1965–9) 160–76; reprinted in revised form in *Prisca Munimenta*, ed. F. Ranger (London 1973), pp. 43–62

CHAPLAIS, P. 'The authenticity of the royal Anglo-Saxon diplomas of Exeter', *Essays in Medieval Diplomacy and Administration*, ed. Pierre Chaplais (London 1981), XV

CHAPLAIS, P. 'The origin and authenticity of the royal Anglo-Saxon diploma', *Journal of the Society of Archivists* 3 (1965–9), 48–61; reprinted in revised form in *Prisca Munimenta*, ed. F. Ranger (London 1973), pp. 28–42

CHAPLAIS, P. 'Who introduced charters into England? The case for Augustine', *Journal of the Society of Archivists* 3 (1965–9) 526–42; reprinted in revised form in *Prisca Munimenta*, ed. F. Ranger (London 1973), pp. 88–107

CHARLES-EDWARDS, T. 'Kinship, status, and the origin of the hide', *Past and Present* 56 (1972) 3–33

CLARKE, H.B. 'The Domesday satellites', in *Domesday Book*, ed. P. Sawyer (London 1985), pp. 50–70

CLEMOES, Peter & HUGHES, K. (edd.) *England before the Conquest. Studies in Primary Sources presented to Dorothy Whitelock* (Cambridge 1971)

COCKAYNE, O. (ed. & transl.) *Leechdoms, Wortcunning, and Starcraft of Early England* (3 vols, London 1864–6)

COKER, J. *A Survey of Dorsetshire* (London 1732)

COLGRAVE, Bertram & MYNORS, R.A.B. (edd. & transl.) *Bede's Ecclesiastical History of the English People* (Oxford 1969)

COLGRAVE, Bertram (ed. & transl.) *The Life of Bishop Wilfrid by Eddius Stephanus* (Cambridge 1927)

COLLINSON, J. *The History and Antiquities of the County of Somerset* (3 vols, Bath 1791)

CORCOS, N.J. 'Early estates on the Poldens and the origin of the settlement at Shapwick', *Proceedings of the Somerset Archaeological and Natural History Society* 127 (1983) 47–54

COSTEN, M. 'Dunstan, Glastonbury and the economy of Somerset in the tenth century', in *St Dunstan*, edd. N. Ramsay *et al.* (Woodbridge 1992), pp. 25–44

COSTEN, M. 'Huish and Worth: Old English survivals in a later landscape', in *Anglo-Saxon Studies in Archaeology and History* 5, edd. W. Filmer-Sankey *et al.* (1992), pp. 65–94

COSTEN, M. 'Settlement in Wessex in the tenth century: the charter evidence', in *The Medieval Landscape of Wessex*, edd. M.A. Aston & C. Lewis (Oxford 1994), pp. 97–107

COSTEN, M. 'Some evidence for new settlements and field systems in late Anglo-Saxon Somerset', in *The Archaeology and History of Glastonbury Abbey*, edd. L. Abrams & J.P. Carley (Woodbridge 1991), pp. 39–56

COSTEN, M. 'The late Saxon landscape. The evidence from charters and place-names', in *Aspects of the Mediaeval Landscape of Somerset*, ed. M.A. Aston (Taunton 1988), pp. 32–47

COSTEN, Michael *The Origins of Somerset* (Manchester 1992)

CRAMP, R. *Anglo-Saxon Connections* (Durham 1989)

CRAMP, R. 'Monastic sites', in *The Archaeology of Anglo-Saxon England*, ed. D. Wilson (London 1976), pp. 201–52

CRICK, J. 'The marshalling of antiquity: Glastonbury's historical dossier', in *The Archaeology and History of Glastonbury Abbey*, edd. L. Abrams & J.P. Carley (Woodbridge 1991), pp. 217–43

CROWLEY, D.A. (ed.) *A History of Wiltshire*, XII (London 1983)

DARBY, H.C. *Domesday England* (Cambridge 1977)

DARBY, H.C. & FINN, R.W. *The Domesday Geography of South-West England* (Cambridge 1967)

DARLINGTON, R.R. 'Introduction to the Wiltshire Domesday', in *A History of Wiltshire*, II, edd. R.B. Pugh & E. Crittall (London 1955), pp. 42–112

DARLINGTON, R.R. (ed. & transl.) 'Text and translation of the Wiltshire geld rolls', in *A History of Wiltshire*, II, edd. R.B. Pugh & E. Crittall (London 1955), pp. 178–217

DARLINGTON, R.R. (transl.) 'Translation of the text of the Wiltshire Domesday', in *A History of Wiltshire*, II, edd. R.B. Pugh & E. Crittall (London 1955), pp. 113–68

DAVIDSON, J.B. 'On some Anglo-Saxon charters at Exeter', *Journal of the British Archaeological Association* 39 (1883) 259–303

DAVIDSON, J.B. 'On the charters of King Ine', *Proceedings of the Somerset Archaeological and Natural History Society* 30 (1884) 1–31

DAVIES, W. 'The Celtic Church', *Journal of Religious History* 8 (1974/5) 406–11

DAVIES, W. 'The Latin charter-tradition in Western Britain, Brittany, and Ireland in the early mediaeval period', in *Ireland in Early Mediaeval Europe*, edd. D. Whitelock *et al.* (Cambridge 1982), pp. 258–80

DAVIES, Wendy & FOURACRE, P. (edd.) *The Settlement of Disputes in Early Medieval Europe* (Cambridge 1986)

DAVIS, G.R.C. *Medieval Cartularies of Great Britain. A Short Catalogue* (London 1958)

DAVIS, H.W.C., *et al.* (edd.) *Regesta Regum Anglo-Normannorum, 1066–1154* (4 vols, Oxford 1913–69)

DICKINSON, F.H. 'West Monkton charter', *Proceedings of the Somerset Archaeological and Natural History Society* 28 (1882) 89–98

DOBLE, G.H. *Four Saints of the Fal* (Exeter 1929)

DODWELL, B. 'East Anglian commendation', *English Historical Review* 63 (1948) 289–306

DOEHAERD, Renée *Le Haut moyen âge occidental. Économies et sociétés* (Paris 1971)

DOUGLAS, David C. & GREENAWAY, George W. (edd.) *English Historical Documents 1042–1189* (2nd edn, London 1981)

DOUGLAS, David C. *William the Conqueror. The Norman Impact upon England* (London 1964)

DUMVILLE, David N. *Britons and Anglo-Saxons in the Early Middle Ages* (Aldershot 1993)

DUMVILLE, D.N. 'English Square minuscule script: the background and earliest phases', *Anglo-Saxon England* 16 (1987) 147–79

DUMVILLE, David N. *Histories and Pseudo-histories of the Insular Middle Ages* (Aldershot 1990)

DUMVILLE, David N. *Liturgy and the Ecclesiastical History of Late Anglo-Saxon England: Four Studies* (Woodbridge 1992)

DUMVILLE, David N., *et al.* *Saint Patrick, A.D. 493–1993* (Woodbridge 1993)

DUMVILLE, D.N. (ed.) 'The Anglian collection of royal genealogies and regnal lists', *Anglo-Saxon England* 5 (1976) 23–50

DUMVILLE, David [N.] & KEYNES, S. (gen. edd.) *The Anglo-Saxon Chronicle: A Collaborative Edition* (23 vols, Cambridge 1983–)

DUMVILLE, David N. (ed.) *The Historia Brittonum* (10 vols, Cambridge 1985–)

DUMVILLE, D.N. 'The Tribal Hidage: an introduction to its texts and their history', in *The Origins of Anglo-Saxon Kingdoms*, ed. S. Bassett (London 1989), pp. 225–30 *and* 286–7

DUMVILLE, D.N. 'The West Saxon Genealogical Regnal List and the chronology of early Wessex', *Peritia: Journal of the Medieval Academy of Ireland* 4 (1985) 21–66

DUMVILLE, David N. *Wessex and England from Alfred to Edgar. Six Essays on Political, Cultural, and Ecclesiastical Revival* (Woodbridge 1992)

DUNNING, R.W. (ed.) *A History of the County of Somerset*, III, IV, V, VI (London 1974–92)

DUNNING, R.W. 'Dinnington', in *A History of the County of Somerset*, IV, ed. R.W. Dunning (London 1978), pp. 147–50

DUNNING, R.W. 'Ilchester', in *A History of the County of Somerset*, III, ed. R.W. Dunning (London 1974), pp. 179–203

DUNNING, R.W. 'Ilchester: a study in continuity', *Proceedings of the Somerset Archaeological and Natural History Society* 119 (1974/5) 44–50

DUNNING, R.W. 'Kingstone', in *A History of the County of Somerset*, III, ed. R.W. Dunning (London 1974), pp. 203–9

DUNNING, R.W. 'Montacute', in *A History of the County of Somerset*, III, ed. R.W. Dunning (London 1974), pp. 210–43

DUNNING, R.W. 'Northover', in *A History of the County of Somerset*, III, ed. R.W. Dunning (London 1974), pp. 224–9

DUNNING, R.W. 'Stoke sub Hamdon', in *A History of the County of Somerset*, III, ed. R.W. Dunning (London 1974), pp. 235–49

DUNNING, R.W. 'Tintinhull', in *A History of the County of Somerset*, III, ed. R.W. Dunning (London, 1974), pp. 255–65

DUSSART, F. (ed.) *L'Habitat et les paysages ruraux d'Europe* (Liège 1971)

DYER, Christopher *Lords and Peasants in a Changing Society: the Estates of the Bishopric of Worcester 680–1540* (Cambridge 1980)

EDWARDS, Heather *The Charters of the Early West Saxon Kingdom* (Oxford 1988)

EDWARDS, Heather 'Two Documents from Aldhelm's Malmesbury', *Historical Research* 59 (1986) 1–19

EHWALD, R. (ed.) *Aldhelmi Opera Omnia* (Berlin 1913–19)

EKWALL, Eilert *The Concise Oxford Dictionary of English Place-names* (4th edn, Oxford 1960)

ELLIS, H. (ed.) *Libri Censualis Uocati Domesday Book Additamenta ex Codicis Antiquissimis* (2 vols, London 1816)

ELLIS, P. 'Excavations in Glastonbury 1978 and 1979', *Proceedings of the Somerset Archaeological and Natural History Society* 126 (1981/2) 33–42

ELLIS, P. 'Excavations at Silver Street, Glastonbury, 1978', *Proceedings of the Somerset Archaeological and Natural History Society* 126 (1981/2) 17–31

ELLISON, Ann *Medieval Villages in South-East Somerset: a Survey of the Archaeological Implications of Development within 93 Surviving Medieval Villages in South-East Somerset (Yeovil District)* (Bristol 1983)

ELLISON, Ann *Villages Survey. Interim Report* (Bristol 1976)

ERSKINE, R.W.H. & WILLIAMS, A. (edd.) *Domesday Book. Studies* (London 1987)

ERSKINE, R.W.H. (gen. ed.) *Great Domesday. Facsimile* (6 boxes, London 1986–92)

ERSKINE, R.W.H. & WILLIAMS, A. (edd.) *Great Domesday. Somerset* (London 1989)

EYTON, R.W. *Domesday Studies: an Analysis and Digest of the Somerset Survey* (2 vols, London 1880)

FARAL, E. *La Légende arthurienne; études et documents* (3 vols, Paris 1929)

FARLEY, A. (ed.) *Domesday Book, seu Liber Censualis Willelmi Primi Regis Angliae* (2 vols, London 1783)

FAULL, Margaret L. (ed.) *Studies in Late Anglo-Saxon Settlement* (Oxford 1984)

FINBERG, H.P.R. (ed.) *Gloucestershire Studies* (Leicester 1957)

FINBERG, H.P.R. *Lucerna. Studies of Some Problems in the Early History of England* (London 1964)

FINBERG, H.P.R. 'Some early Gloucestershire estates', in *Gloucestershire Studies*, ed. H.P.R. Finberg (Leicester 1957), pp. 1–16

FINBERG, H.P.R. 'Supplement to The Early Charters of Devon and Cornwall', *apud* W.G. Hoskins, *The Westward Expansion of Wessex* (Leicester 1960), pp. 23–33

FINBERG, H.P.R. 'The abbots of Tavistock', *Devon and Cornwall Notes and Queries* 22 (1942–6) 159–62

FINBERG, H.P.R. *The Early Charters of Devon and Cornwall* (Leicester 1953)

FINBERG, H.P.R. *The Early Charters of the West Midlands* (2nd edn, Leicester 1972)

FINBERG, H.P.R. *The Early Charters of Wessex* (Leicester 1964)

FINBERG, H.P.R. *The Formation of England 550–1042* (London 1976)

FINBERG, H.P.R. *West-Country Historical Studies* (Newton Abbot 1969)

FINN, R. Welldon *An Introduction to Domesday Book* (London 1963)

FINN, R. Welldon *Domesday Studies: the Liber Exoniensis* (London 1964)

FINN, R.W. 'The making of the Somerset Domesdays', *Proceedings of the Somerset Archaeological and Natural History Society* 99/100 (1954/5) 21–37

FISHER, D.J.V. 'The anti-monastic reaction in the reign of Edward the Martyr', *Cambridge Historical Journal* 10 (1950–2) 254–70

FLEMING, R. 'Domesday Book and the tenurial revolution', *Anglo-Norman Studies* 9 (1986) 87–101

FLEMING, Robin *Kings and Lords in Conquest England* (Cambridge 1991)

FLEMING, R. 'Monastic lands and England's defence in the Viking Age', *English Historical Review* 100 (1985) 247–65

FLEURIOT, Léon *Dictionnaire des gloses en Vieux-Breton* (Paris 1964)

FOOT, Sarah Rosamund Irvine 'Anglo-Saxon Minsters A.D. 597–*ca* 900: the Religious Life in England before the Benedictine Reform' (unpublished Ph.D. dissertation, University of Cambridge 1989)

FOOT, S.[R.I.] 'Glastonbury's early abbots', in *The Archaeology and History of Glastonbury Abbey*, edd. L. Abrams & J.P. Carley (Woodbridge 1991), pp. 163–89

FORSBERG, R. *A Contribution to a Dictionary of Old English Place-names* (Uppsala 1950)

FORSBERG, R. 'Topographical notes on some Anglo-Saxon charters', *Namn och Bygd* 30 (1942) 150–8

FOSTER, S. 'A gazetteer of the Anglo-Saxon sculpture in historic Somerset', *Proceedings of the Somerset Archaeological and Natural History Society* 131 (1987) 49–80

FOX, H.S.A. 'Approaches to the adoption of the midland system', in *The Origins of Open-Field Agriculture*, ed. T. Rowley (London 1981), pp. 64–111

FOX, H.S.A. 'The alleged transformation from two-field to three-field systems in medieval England', *Economic History Review*, 2nd S., 39 (1986) 526–48

FOX, H.S.A. 'The boundary of Uplyme', *Report and Transactions of the Devonshire Association* 102 (1970) 35–47

[FOX, H.S.A. (ed.)] *The Origins of the Midland Village* (Leicester 1992)

FREEMAN, J. 'Winterbourne Monkton', in *A History of Wiltshire*, XII, ed. D.A. Crowley (London 1983), pp. 192–8

FRYDE, E.B., *et al.* (edd.) *Handbook of British Chronology* (3rd edn, London 1986)

FYFE, T. 'Glastonbury excavations, 1926', *Proceedings of the Somerset Archaeological and Natural History Society* 72 (1926) 20–2

FYFE, T. 'Glastonbury excavations, 1927', *Proceedings of the Somerset Archaeological and Natural History Society* 73 (1927) 86–7

GALBRAITH, V.H. *Domesday Book. Its Place in Administrative History* (Oxford 1974)

GARBETT, H.L.E. & ALEXANDER, N. 'Compton Beauchamp', in *The Victoria History of the County of Berkshire*, IV, edd. W. Page & P.H. Ditchfield (London 1972), pp. 523–7

GELLING, Margaret *Signposts to the Past* (London 1978)

GELLING, Margaret *The Early Charters of the Thames Valley* (Leicester 1979)

GELLING, Margaret *The Place-names of Berkshire* (3 vols, Cambridge 1971–4)

GODBOLD, S. & TURNER, R.C. 'Medieval fishtraps in the Severn estuary', *Medieval Archaeology* 38 (1994) 19–54

GODFREY, John *The Church in Anglo-Saxon England* (Cambridge 1962)

GOLDING, B. 'Robert of Mortain', *Anglo-Norman Studies* 13 (1990) 119–44

GOOD, G.L., *et al.* (edd.) *Waterfront Archaeology. Proceedings of the Third International Conference on Waterfront Archaeology Held at Bristol 23–26 September 1988* (London 1991)

GOODCHILD, W. 'St Boniface and Somerset', *Notes and Queries for Somerset and Dorset* 11 (1908/9) 172–3

GORDON, D.J. (ed.) *Fritz Saxl 1890–1948. A Volume of Memorial Essays from his Friends in England* (Edinburgh 1957)

GOVER, J.E.B., *et al.* *The Place-names of Devon* (2 vols, Cambridge 1931–2)

GOVER, J.E.B., *et al.* *The Place-names of Surrey* (Cambridge 1934)

GOVER, J.E.B., *et al.* *The Place-names of Wiltshire* (Cambridge 1939)

GRANSDEN, A. 'The growth of the Glastonbury traditions and legends in the twelfth century', *Journal of Ecclesiastical History* 27 (1976) 337–58

GRESWELL, W. 'King Ina's grant of Brent to Glastonbury', *Notes and Queries for Somerset and Dorset* 7 (1901) 255

GRUNDY, G.B. 'Saxon charters of Dorset', *Proceedings of the Dorset Natural History and Archaeological Society* 55 (1933) 239–68; 60 (1938) 75–89; 61 (1939) 60–78

GRUNDY, G.B. *The Saxon Charters and Field Names of Gloucestershire* (Bristol 1935–6)

GRUNDY, G.B. *The Saxon Charters and Field Names of Somerset* (Taunton 1935); also published in eight parts with consecutive pagination in *Proceedings of the Somerset Archaeological and Natural History Society* 73–80 (1927–34)

GRUNDY, G.B. 'The Saxon land charters of Hampshire with notes on place and field names', *Archaeological Journal* 81 (1924) 31–126

GRUNDY, G.B. 'The Saxon land charters of Wiltshire', *Archaeological Journal* 76 (1919) 143–301, *and* 77 (1920) 8–126

GRUNDY, G.B. 'West Monkton. Revised notes of its charter', *Proceedings of the Somerset Archaeological and Natural History Society* 84 (1938) 104–6

HADDAN, Arthur West & STUBBS, W. (edd.) *Councils and Ecclesiastical Documents relating to Great Britain and Ireland* (3 vols, Oxford 1869–78)

HALLINGER, Kassius (ed.) *Consuetudinum Saeculi X/XI/XII Monumenta Non-Cluniacensia* (Siegburg 1984)

HAMILTON, N.E.S.A. (ed.) *Inquisitio Comitatus Cantabrigiensis* (London 1876)

HAMILTON, N.E.S.A. (ed.) *Willelmi Malmesbiriensis Monachi de Gestis Pontificum Anglorum Libri Quinque* (London 1870)

HAMSHERE, J.D. 'Domesday Book: estate structures in the West Midlands', in *Domesday Studies*, ed. J.C. Holt (Woodbridge 1987), pp. 155–82

HAMSHERE, J.D. 'The structure and exploitation of the Domesday Book estate of the Church of Worcester', *Landscape History* 7 (1985) 41–52

HARMER, F.E. (ed. & transl.) *Anglo-Saxon Writs* (2nd edn, Stamford 1989)

HARMER, F.E. (ed. & transl.) *Select English Historical Documents of the Ninth and Tenth Centuries* (Cambridge 1914)

HARRIS, Kate & SMITH, William *Glastonbury Abbey Records at Longleat House: a Summary List* (Taunton 1991)

HART, C.[R.] 'Athelstan "Half King" and his family', *Anglo-Saxon England* 2 (1973) 115–44 (revised in *The Danelaw* [London 1992], pp. 569–604)

HART, C.R. 'Some Dorset charter boundaries', *Proceedings of the Dorset Natural History and Archaeological Society* 86 (1964) 158–63

HART, C.R. *The Danelaw* (London 1992)

HART, C.R. *The Early Charters of Eastern England* (Leicester 1966)

HART, C.R. *The Early Charters of Northern England and the North Midlands* (Leicester 1975)

HART, W.H. (ed.) *Historia et Cartularium Monasterii S. Petri Gloucestriae* (3 vols, London 1863–7)

HARVEY, Barbara *Westminster Abbey and its Estates in the Middle Ages* (Oxford 1977)

HARVEY, P.D.A. '*Rectitudines singularum personarum* and *Gerefa*', *English Historical Review* 108 (1993) 1–22

HARVEY, S.P.J. 'Domesday Book and Anglo-Norman governance', *Transactions of the Royal Historical Society*, 5th S., 25 (1975) 175–93

HARVEY, S.P.J. 'Recent Domesday studies', *English Historical Review* 95 (1980) 121–33

HARVEY, S.P.J. 'Taxation and the ploughland in Domesday Book', in *Domesday Book*, ed. P. Sawyer (London 1985), pp. 86–103

HARVEY, S.P.J. 'The extent and profitability of demesne agriculture in England in the later eleventh century', in *Social Relations and Ideas*, edd. T.H. Aston *et al.* (Cambridge 1983), pp. 45–72

HAVINDEN, Michael *The Somerset Landscape* (London 1981)

HEARNE, Thomas (ed.) *Adami de Domerham Historia de Rebus Gestis Glastoniensibus* (2 vols, Oxford 1727)

HEARNE, Thomas (ed.) *Hemingi Chartularium Ecclesiæ Wigorniensis* (2 vols, Oxford 1723)

HEARNE, Thomas (ed.) *Johannis Confratris et Monachi Glastoniensis Chronica sive Historia de Rebus Glastoniensibus* (2 vols, Oxford 1726)

HICKES, George *Linguarum Veterum Septentrionalium Thesaurus Grammatico-Criticus et Archaeologicus* (2 vols, Oxford 1703/5)

HIGHAM, N. 'Settlement, land-use and Domesday ploughlands', *Landscape History* 12 (1990) 33–44

HILL, D. 'The Anglo-Saxons 700–1066 AD', in *The Archaeology of Somerset*, edd. M.A. Aston & I. Burrow ([Taunton] 1982), pp. 109–17

HOARE, R.C. (ed.) *Registrum Wiltunense* (London 1827)

HOLDSWORTH, Christopher (ed.) *Domesday Essays* (Exeter 1986)

HOLDSWORTH, C. 'The Church at Domesday', in *Domesday Essays*, ed. C. Holdsworth (Exeter 1986), pp. 51–64

HOLLINGS, M. 'The survival of the five hide unit in the western Midlands', *English Historical Review* 63 (1948) 453–87

HOLLINRAKE, C. & HOLLINRAKE, N. 'The abbey enclosure ditch and a late-Saxon canal: rescue excavations at Glastonbury, 1984–88', *Proceedings of the Somerset Archaeological and Natural History Society* 136 (1992) 73–94

HOLLISTER, C.W. *Anglo-Saxon Military Institutions on the Eve of the Norman Conquest* (Oxford 1962)

HOLT, J.C. (ed.) *Domesday Studies* (Woodbridge, 1987)

HOOKE, Della *Anglo-Saxon Landscapes of the West Midlands: the Charter Evidence* (Oxford 1981)

HOOKE, Della (ed.) *Anglo-Saxon Settlements* (Oxford 1988)

HOOKE, Della 'Charters and the landscape', *Nomina* 15 (1991/2) 75–96

HOOKE, Della (ed.) *Medieval Villages. A Review of Current Work* (Oxford 1985)

HOOKE, Della *Pre-Conquest Charter-Bounds of Devon and Cornwall* (Woodbridge 1994)

HOOKE, Della *Worcestershire Anglo-Saxon Charter-Bounds* (Woodbridge 1990)

HORNE, E. 'The Edgar Chapel apse, Glastonbury Abbey', *Notes and Queries for Somerset and Dorset* 22 (1936–8) 242–4

HOSKINS, W.G. & FINBERG, H.P.R. *Devonshire Studies* (London 1952)

HOSKINS, W.G. *The Westward Expansion of Wessex* (Leicester 1960)

HUDSON, H. & NEALE, F. 'The Panborough Saxon charter, A.D. 956', *Proceedings of the Somerset Archaeological and Natural History Society* 127 (1983) 55–68

HUDSON, H. 'Wedmore', *Proceedings of the Somerset Archaeological and Natural History Society* 129 (1985) 11–12

HUGHES, Kathleen *Church and Society in Ireland, A.D. 400–1200* (London 1987)

HUGHES, K. 'Evidence for contacts between the Churches of the Irish and English from the synod of Whitby', *England before the Conquest*, edd. P. Clemoes & K. Hughes (Cambridge 1971), pp. 49–67

HUGHES, K. 'The Celtic Church: is this a valid concept?', *Cambridge Medieval Celtic Studies* 1 (1981) 1–20

HUNT, R.W. 'Manuscript evidence for knowledge of the poems of Venantius Fortunatus in late Anglo-Saxon England', *Anglo-Saxon England* 8 (1979) 279–95

HUNT, W. (ed.) *Two Chartularies of the Priory of St Peter at Bath* (1893)

HUNTER, J. (ed.) *Ecclesiastical Documents* (London 1840)

HYAMS, P. ' "No register of title": the Domesday inquest and land adjudication', *Anglo-Norman Studies* 9 (1986) 127–41

JACKSON, J.E. 'Kington St Michael', *Wiltshire Archaeological and Natural History Magazine* 4 (1858) 36–124

JACKSON, J.E. (ed.) *Liber Henrici de Soliaco, Abbatis Glaston* (London 1882)

JAMES, M.R. *The Western Manuscripts in the Library of Trinity College, Cambridge. A Descriptive Catalogue* (4 vols, Cambridge 1900–4)

JENKINS, D. & OWEN, M.E. 'The Welsh marginalia in the Lichfield Gospels', *Cambridge Medieval Celtic Studies* 5 (1983) 37–66 *and* 7 (1984) 91–120

JOHN, Eric *Land Tenure in Early England. A Discussion of Some Problems* (Leicester 1960; rev. imp., 1964)

JOHN, Eric *Orbis Britanniae and Other Studies* (Leicester 1966)

JOHN, E. 'The church of Worcester and the tenth-century reformation', *Bulletin of the John Rylands Library* 47 (1964/5) 404–29

JOHN, E. 'The division of the mensa in early English monasteries', *Journal of Ecclesiastical History* 6 (1955) 143–55

JOLLIFFE, J.E.A. 'Alod and fee', *Cambridge Historical Journal* 5 (1935–7) 225–34

JONDORF, Gillian & DUMVILLE, D.N. (edd.) *France and the British Isles in the Middle Ages and Renaissance. Essays by Members of Girton College, Cambridge, in Memory of Ruth Morgan* (Woodbridge 1991)

JONES, G.R.J. 'Continuity despite calamity: the heritage of Celtic territorial organization in England', *Journal of Celtic Studies* 3 (1981/2) 1–30

JONES, G.R.J. 'Multiple estates and early settlement', in *Medieval Settlement*, ed. P.[H.] Sawyer (London 1976), pp. 15–40

JONES, G.R.J. 'Multiple estates perceived', *Journal of Historical Geography* 11 (1985) 352–63

JONES, G.R.J. 'The multiple estate as a model framework for tracing early stages in the evolution of rural settlement', in *L'Habitat et les paysages ruraux d'Europe*, ed. F. Dussart (Liège 1971), pp. 251–67

JONES, W.H. *Domesday for Wiltshire* (Bath 1865)

KELLY, S. 'Anglo-Saxon lay society and the written word', in *The Uses of Literacy in Early Mediaeval Europe*, ed. R. McKitterick (Cambridge 1990), pp. 36–62

KEMBLE, J.M. (ed.) *Codex Diplomaticus Aevi Saxonici* (6 vols, London 1839–48)

KENAWELL, William *The Quest at Glastonbury. A Biographical Study of Frederick Bligh Bond* (New York 1965)

KER, N.R. *Books, Collectors, and Libraries. Studies in the Medieval Heritage* (London 1985)

KER, N.R. 'Hemming's Cartulary: a description of the two Worcester cartularies in Cotton Tiberius A. xiii', in *Books, Collectors, and Libraries*, ed. N.R. Ker (London 1985), pp. 31–59

KEYNES, S. 'A charter of King Edward the Elder for Islington', *Historical Research* 66 (1993) 303–16

KEYNES, Simon & LAPIDGE, M. (transl.) *Alfred the Great. Asser's Life of King Alfred and Other Contemporary Sources* (Harmondsworth 1983)

KEYNES, Simon *An Atlas of Attestations in Anglo-Saxon Charters, c. 670–1066* (Cambridge 1993)

KEYNES, Simon & KENNEDY, A. (edd. & transl.) *Anglo-Saxon Ely: Records of Ely* (Woodbridge, forthcoming)

KEYNES, S. 'England 900–1016', in *The New Cambridge Medieval History*, III, ed. T. Reuter (Cambridge, forthcoming)

KEYNES, S. 'King Æthelstan's books', in *Learning and Literature in Anglo-Saxon England*, edd. M. Lapidge & H. Gneuss (Cambridge 1985), pp. 143–201

KEYNES, S. 'Regenbald the chancellor (*sic*)', *Anglo-Norman Studies* 10 (1987) 185–222

KEYNES, S. 'Royal government and the written word in late Anglo-Saxon England', in *The Uses of Literacy in Early Mediaeval Europe*, ed. R. McKitterick (Cambridge 1990), pp. 226–57

KEYNES, Simon 'Studies on Anglo-Saxon Royal Diplomas' (2 vols, unpublished Fellowship dissertation, Trinity College, Cambridge 1976)

KEYNES, Simon *The Diplomas of King Æthelred 'the Unready', 978–1016. A Study in their Use as Historical Evidence* (Cambridge 1980)

KEYNES, S. 'The "Dunstan B" charters', *Anglo-Saxon England* 23 (1994) 165–93

KEYNES, S. 'The Fonthill letter', in *Words, Texts and Manuscripts*, edd. M. Korhammer *et al.* (Cambridge 1992), pp. 53–97

KEYNES, S. 'The lost cartulary of Abbotsbury', *Anglo-Saxon England* 18 (1989) 207–43

KING, Margot H. & STEVENS, W. (edd.)   *Saints, Scholars and Heroes. Studies in Medieval Culture in Honour of Charles W. Jones* (2 vols, Collegeville, MI 1979)

KIRBY, D.P.   'Problems of early West Saxon history', *English Historical Review* 80 (1965) 10–29

KNOWLES, David & HADCOCK, R.N.   *Medieval Religious Houses. England and Wales* (2nd edn, London 1971)

KNOWLES, David, *et al.*   *The Heads of Religious Houses. England and Wales, 940–1216* (Cambridge 1972)

KNOWLES, David   *The Monastic Order in England* (2nd edn, Cambridge 1963)

KORHAMMER, Michael, *et al.* (edd.)   *Words, Texts and Manuscript. Studies in Anglo-Saxon Culture presented to Helmut Gneuss on the Occasion of his Sixty-fifth Birthday* (Cambridge 1992)

LANE POOLE, E.H.   *Damerham and Martin. A Study in Local History* (Tisbury 1976)

LAPIDGE, Michael & ROSIER, J.L. (transl.)   *Aldhelm. The Poetic Works* (Cambridge 1985)

LAPIDGE, Michael   *Anglo-Latin Literature 900–1066* (London 1993)

LAPIDGE, M.   'B. and the *Vita S. Dunstani*', in *St Dunstan*, edd. N. Ramsay *et al.* (Woodbridge 1992), pp. 247–59

LAPIDGE, Michael & GNEUSS, H. (edd.)   *Learning and Literature in Anglo-Saxon England. Studies presented to Peter Clemoes on the Occasion of his Sixty-fifth Birthday* (Cambridge 1985)

LAPIDGE, M.   'The cult of St Indract at Glastonbury', in *Ireland in Early Mediaeval Europe*, edd. D. Whitelock *et al.* (Cambridge 1982), pp. 179–212

LAPIDGE, Michael & WINTERBOTTOM, M. (edd. & transl.)   *Wulfstan of Winchester. The Life of St Æthelwold* (Oxford 1991)

LARSON, Lawrence Marcellus   *Canute the Great* (New York 1912)

LAWSON, M.K.   *Cnut. The Danes in England in the Early Eleventh Century* (London 1993)

LEACH, P. & ELLIS, P.   'The medieval precinct of Glastonbury Abbey – some new evidence', in *In Search of Cult*, ed. M. Carver (Woodbridge 1993), pp. 119–24

LENNARD, R.   *Rural England 1086–1135. A Study of Social and Agrarian Conditions* (Oxford 1959)

LENNARD, R.   'The demesnes of Glastonbury Abbey in the eleventh and twelfth centuries', *Economic History Review*, 2nd S., 8 (1956) 355–63

LENNARD, R.   'The Glastonbury estates: a rejoinder', *Economic History Review*, 2nd S., 28 (1975) 517–23

LIEBERMANN, F. (ed. & transl.)   *Die Gesetze der Angelsachsen* (3 vols, Halle a. S. 1898–1916)

LOMAX, Frank (transl.)   *The Antiquities of Glastonbury* (London 1908)

LOUD, G.   'An introduction to the Somerset Domesday', in *Great Domesday. Somerset*, edd. R.W.H. Erskine & A. Williams (London 1989), pp. 1–31

LOYN, Henry   *Anglo-Saxon England and the Norman Conquest* (2nd edn, London 1979)

MACDONALD, J. & SNOOKS, G.D.   *Domesday Economy: a New Approach to Anglo-Norman History* (Oxford 1986)

McKITTERICK, Rosamond (ed.)   *The Uses of Literacy in Early Mediaeval Europe* (Cambridge 1990)

MACRAY, W.D.   *Annals of the Bodleian Library, Oxford* (2nd edn, Oxford 1890)

MACRAY, W.D. (ed.)   *Chronicon Abbatiæ de Evesham ad Annum 1418* (London 1863)

MACRAY, W. Dunn (ed.) *Chronicon Abbatiæ Rameseiensis, a sæc .X. usque ad an. circiter 1200: in quatuor partibus* (London 1886)

MAGDALINO, Paul (ed.) *The Perception of the Past in Twelfth-Century Europe* (London 1992)

MAITLAND, F.W. *Domesday Book and Beyond. Three Essays in the Early History of England* (Cambridge 1897)

MAWER, A. & STENTON, F.M. *The Place-names of Worcestershire* (Cambridge 1927)

MEYER, M.A. 'Women and the tenth century English monastic reform', *Revue bénédictine* 87 (1977) 34–61

MILLER, E. *The Abbey and Bishopric of Ely. The Social History of an Ecclesiastical Estate from the Tenth Century to the Early Fourteenth Century* (Cambridge 1951)

MITCHELL, Bruce *Old English Syntax* (2 vols, Oxford 1985)

MOORE, John S. (ed.) *Domesday Book. Gloucestershire*, gen. ed. J. Morris (Chichester 1982)

MORGAN, F.W. 'Domesday geography of Somerset', *Proceedings of the Somerset Archaeological and Natural History Society* 84 (1938) 139–55

MORGAN, Philip (ed.) *Domesday Book. Berkshire*, gen. ed. J. Morris (Chichester 1979)

MORGAN, Philip & THORN, C. (edd.) *Domesday Book. Lincolnshire*, gen. ed. J. Morris (2 vols, Chichester 1986)

MORLAND, J. 'St Bridget's Chapel, Beckery', *Proceedings of the Somerset Archaeological and Natural History Society* 35 (1889) 121–6

MORLAND, J. 'The Brue at Glastonbury', *Proceedings of the Somerset Archaeological and Natural History Society* 68 (1922) 64–86

MORLAND, S.C. 'Further notes on Somerset Domesday', *Proceedings of the Somerset Archaeological and Natural History Society* 108 (1963/4) 94–8, reprinted in *Glastonbury, Domesday and Related Studies* (Glastonbury 1991), pp. 23–7

MORLAND, S.C. 'Glaston Twelve Hides', *Proceedings of the Somerset Archaeological and Natural History Society* 128 (1984) 35–54, reprinted (with footnotes) in *Glastonbury, Domesday and Related Studies* (Glastonbury 1991), pp. 61–84

MORLAND, Stephen C. *Glastonbury, Domesday and Related Studies* (Glastonbury 1991)

MORLAND, S..C. 'Hidation on the Glastonbury estates. A study in tax evasion', *Proceedings of the Somerset Archaeological and Natural History Society* 114 (1970) 74–90, reprinted in *Glastonbury, Domesday and Related Studies* (Glastonbury 1991), pp. 31–47

MORLAND, S.C. [review of C. Thorn & F. Thorn (edd.), *Domesday Book: Somerset* (1980)] *Proceedings of the Somerset Archaeological and Natural History Society* 125 (1980/1) 137–40, reprinted in *Glastonbury, Domesday and Related Studies* (Glastonbury 1991), pp. 49–53

MORLAND, S.C. 'Some Domesday manors', *Proceedings of the Somerset Archaeological and Natural History Society* 99/100 (1954/5) 38–48, reprinted in *Glastonbury, Domesday and Related Studies* (Glastonbury 1991), pp. 11–21

MORLAND, S.C. 'The Glastonbury manors and their Saxon charters', *Proceedings of the Somerset Archaeological and Natural History Society* 130 (1986) 61–105, reprinted in *Glastonbury, Domesday and Related Studies* (Glastonbury 1991), pp. 87–132

MORLAND, S.C. 'The Saxon charters for Sowy and Pouholt and the course of the River Cary', *Notes and Queries for Somerset and Dorset* 31 (1982) 233–5, reprinted in *Glastonbury, Domesday and Related Studies* (Glastonbury 1991), pp. 55–7

MORLAND, S.C. 'The Somerset hundreds in the Geld Inquest and their Domesday manors', *Proceedings of the Somerset Archaeological and Natural History Society* 134 (1990) 95–140

MORRIS, John (gen. ed.) *Domesday Book. A Survey of the Counties of England* (38 vols in 43, Chichester 1975–92)

MORRIS, John & WOOD, S. (edd.) *Domesday Book. Surrey* (Chichester 1975)

MUNBY, Julian (ed.) *Domesday Book. Hampshire*, gen. ed. John Morris (Chichester 1982)

NAPIER, A.S. & STEVENSON, W.H. (edd.) *The Crawford Collection of Early Charters and Documents now in the Bodleian Library* (Oxford 1895)

NEWELL, W.W. 'William of Malmesbury on the antiquity of Glastonbury', *Publications of the Modern Language Association of America* 18 (1903) 459–512

NÍ CHATHÁIN, Próinséas & RICHTER, M. (edd.) *Ireland and Christendom: the Bible and the Missions* (Stuttgart 1987)

O'DONOVAN, M.A. 'An interim revision of episcopal dates for the province of Canterbury, 850–950', *Anglo-Saxon England* 1 (1972) *and* 2 (1973) 91–113

O'DONOVAN, M.A. (ed.) *Charters of Sherborne* (London 1988)

PADEL, O.J. *Cornish Place-name Elements* (Nottingham 1985)

PADEL, O.J. 'Glastonbury's Cornish connections', in *The Archaeology and History of Glastonbury Abbey*, edd. L. Abrams & J.P. Carley (Woodbridge 1991), pp. 245–56

PARSONS, David (ed.) *Tenth-century Studies. Essays in Commemoration of the Millennium of the Council of Winchester and Regularis Concordia* (Chichester 1975)

PEARCE, S. 'Estates and church sites in Dorset and Gloucestershire: the emergence of a Christian society', in *The Early Church in Western Britain and Ireland* (Oxford 1982), pp. 117–38

PEARCE, S. 'The early Church in the landscape: the evidence from North Devon', *Archaeological Journal* 142 (1985) 255–75

PEARCE, Susan (ed.) *The Early Church in Western Britain and Ireland. Studies Presented to C.A. Ralegh Radford* (Oxford 1982)

PEARCE, Susan *The Kingdom of Dumnonia. Studies in History and Tradition in South-western Britain A.D. 350–1150* (Padstow 1978)

PEERS, C.R., *et al.* 'Glastonbury Abbey excavations, 1928', *Proceedings of the Somerset Archaeological and Natural History Society* 74 (1928) 1–9

PEERS, C.R., *et al.* 'Glastonbury Abbey excavations, 1929', *Proceedings of the Somerset Archaeological and Natural History Society* 75 (1929) 26–33

PEERS, C.R., *et al.* 'Glastonbury Abbey excavations, 1930–31', *Proceedings of the Somerset Archaeological and Natural History Society* 77 (1931) 83–5

PEERS, C.R., *et al.* 'Glastonbury Abbey excavations, 1932', *Proceedings of the Somerset Archaeological and Natural History Society* 78 (1932) 109–110

PEERS, C.R., *et al.* 'Glastonbury Abbey excavations, 1933', *Proceedings of the Somerset Archaeological and Natural History Society* 79 (1933) 30

PEERS, C.R., *et al.* 'Glastonbury Abbey excavations, 1934', *Proceedings of the Somerset Archaeological and Natural History Society* 80 (1934) 32–5

PEERS, C.R., *et al.* 'Glastonbury Abbey excavations, 1935', *Proceedings of the Somerset Archaeological and Natural History Society* 81 (1935) 258

PEERS, C.R., *et al.* 'Glastonbury Abbey excavations, 1937', *Proceedings of the Somerset Archaeological and Natural History Society* 83 (1937) 153–4

PEERS, C.R., *et al.* 'Glastonbury Abbey excavations, 1938', *Proceedings of the Somerset Archaeological and Natural History Society* 84 (1938) 134–6

Bibliography

PETRIE, Henry & SHARPE, J. (edd.) *Monumenta Historica Britannica* (London 1848)

PLUMMER, Charles (ed.) *Two of the Saxon Chronicles Parallel, with Supplementary Extracts from the Others* (2 vols, Oxford 1892/9; rev. imp., by D. Whitelock, 1952)

PORTER, H.M. *The Celtic Church in Somerset* (Bath 1971)

POSTAN, M.M. *Essays on Medieval Agriculture and General Problems of the Medieval Economy* (Cambridge 1973)

POSTAN, M.M. 'The Glastonbury estates: a restatement', *Economic History Review*, 2nd S., 28 (1975) 524–7

PUGH, R.B. & CRITTALL, E. (edd.) *A History of Wiltshire*, II (London 1955)

RADFORD, C.A.R. 'Excavations at Glastonbury Abbey 1962' *and* 'Glastonbury Abbey excavations, 1963–4', *Notes and Queries for Somerset and Dorset* 28 (1961–7) 114–17 *and* 235–6

RADFORD, C.A.R. 'Glastonbury Abbey', in *The Quest for Arthur's Britain*, ed. G. Ashe (2nd edn, London 1971), pp. 97–110

RADFORD, C.A.R. 'Glastonbury Abbey before 1184: interim report on the excavations, 1908–64', in *Medieval Art and Architecture at Wells and Glastonbury* [ed. L. Colchester] (1981), pp. 110–34

RADFORD, C.A.R. 'The Church in Somerset down to 1100', *Proceedings of the Somerset Archaeological and Natural History Society* 106 (1961/2) 28–45

RADFORD, C.A.R. 'The excavations at Glastonbury Abbey 1951–4', 'The excavations at Glastonbury Abbey 1955', 'The excavations at Glastonbury Abbey 1956–7', 'The excavations at Glastonbury Abbey, 1959', *Notes and Queries for Somerset and Dorset* 27 (1955–60) 21–4, 68–73, 165–9, *and* 251–5

RADFORD, C.A.R. 'The pre-Conquest Church and the old minsters in Devon', *Devon Historian* 11 (1975) 2–11

RAFTIS, J.A. *The Estates of Ramsey Abbey: a Study in Economic Growth and Organization* (Toronto 1957)

RAHTZ, P. & HIRST, S. *Beckery Chapel 1967–8* (Glastonbury 1974)

RAHTZ, Philip *English Heritage Book of Glastonbury* (London 1993)

RAHTZ, P.A. 'Excavations on Glastonbury Tor, Somerset, 1964–6', *Archaeological Journal* 127 (1971) 1–81

RAHTZ, P.A. 'Pagan and Christian by the Severn Sea', in *The Archaeology and History of Glastonbury Abbey*, edd. L. Abrams & J.P. Carley (Woodbridge 1991), pp. 3–37

RAHTZ, Philip, *et al.* *The Saxon and Medieval Palaces at Cheddar. Excavations 1960–62* (Oxford 1979)

RAINE, J. (ed.) *The Historians of the Church of York and its Archbishops* (3 vols, London 1879–84)

RAMSAY, Nigel, *et al.* (edd.) *St Dunstan: His Life, Times and Cult* (Woodbridge 1992)

RANDS, S. 'West Pennard's Saxon charter', *Notes & Queries for Somerset and Dorset* 33 (1992) 117–21

RANGER, Felicity (ed.) *Prisca Munimenta. Studies in Archival & Administrative History presented to Dr A.E.J. Hollander* (London 1973)

RAVENHILL, W. 'The geography of Exeter Domesday: Cornwall and Devon', in *Domesday Essays*, ed. C. Holdsworth (Exeter 1986), pp. 29–49

RENDELL, I.M. 'Blackford (Wedmore), "The Bishop's Palace"', *Proceedings of the Somerset Archaeological and Natural History Society* 107 (1962/3) 72–8

REYNOLDS, S. 'Bookland, folkland and fiefs', *Anglo-Norman Studies* 14 (1991) 211–27

REYNOLDS, S. 'Towns in Domesday Book', in *Domesday Studies*, ed. J.C. Holt (Woodbridge 1987), pp 295–309

RILEY, H.T. (ed.) *Gesta Abbatum Monasterii Sancti Albani* (2 vols, London 1867)

RIPPON, Stephen 'Landscape Evolution and Wetland Reclamation around the Severn Estuary' (unpublished Ph.D. dissertation, University of Reading 1993)

ROBERTSON, A.J. (ed. & transl.) *Anglo-Saxon Charters* (2nd edn, Cambridge 1956)

ROBINSON, J.A. 'Andresey, or Nyland', *Notes and Queries for Somerset and Dorset* 18 (1924–6) 74–9

ROBINSON, J.A. ' "Crucan" or "Cructan" ', *Notes and Queries for Somerset and Dorset* 17 (1921–3) 43–4

ROBINSON, J.A. 'Memories of St Dunstan in Somerset', *Proceedings of the Somerset Archaeological and Natural History Society* 62 (1916) 1–25

ROBINSON, J. Armitage *Somerset Historical Essays* (London 1921)

ROBINSON, J. Armitage *St Oswald and the Church of Worcester* (London [1919])

ROBINSON, J.A. 'The historical evidence as to the Saxon church at Glastonbury', *Proceedings of the Somerset Archaeological and Natural History Society* 73 (1927) 40–9

ROBINSON, J. Armitage *The Times of St Dunstan* (Oxford 1923)

ROBINSON, J. Armitage *Two Glastonbury Legends: King Arthur and St Joseph of Arimathea* (Cambridge 1926)

ROBINSON, J.L. 'St Brigid and Glastonbury', *Journal of the Royal Society of Antiquaries of Ireland* 83 (1953) 97–9

RODWELL, W. 'Churches in the landscape: aspects of topography and planning', in *Studies in Late Anglo-Saxon Settlement*, ed. M.L. Faull (Oxford 1984), pp. 1–23

ROFFE, D. 'From thegnage to barony: sake and soke, title, and tenants-in-chief', *Anglo-Norman Studies* 12 (1989) 157–76

ROSENWEIN, Barbara H. *To Be the Neighbor of Saint Peter. The Social Meaning of Cluny's Property 909–1049* (Ithaca, NY 1989)

ROSE-TROUP, F. 'The Anglo-Saxon charter of Brentford (Bampford), Devon', *Report and Transactions of the Devonshire Association* 70 (1938) 253–75

ROSE-TROUP, F. 'The Anglo-Saxon charter of Ottery St. Mary', *Report and Transactions of the Devonshire Association* 71 (1939) 201–20

ROUND, J.H. *Feudal England. Historical Studies on the Eleventh and Twelfth Centuries* (London 1895)

ROWLEY, Trevor (ed.) *The Origins of Open-Field Agriculture* (London 1981)

RUMBLE, Alexander (ed.) *Domesday Book. Cambridgeshire*, gen. ed. J. Morris (Chichester 1981)

SALISBURY, C.R. 'Primitive British fishweirs', in *Waterfront Archaeology*, edd. G.L. Good *et al.* (London 1991), pp. 76–87

SALTER, H.E. (ed.) 'A chronicle roll of the abbots of Abingdon', *English Historical Review* 26 (1911) 727–38

SANDERS, W. Basevi (ed.) *Facsimiles of Anglo-Saxon Manuscripts* (3 vols, Southampton 1878–84)

SAWYER, P.H. *Anglo-Saxon Charters. An Annotated List and Bibliography* (London 1968)

SAWYER, P.H. 'Charters of the Reform movement: the Worcester archive', in *Tenth-century Studies*, ed. D. Parsons (Chichester 1975), pp. 84–93 *and* 228–30

SAWYER, Peter (ed.) *Domesday Book. A Reassessment* (London 1985)

SAWYER, P.H. *From Roman Britain to Norman England* (London 1978)

SAWYER, P. (ed.) *Medieval Settlement* (London 1976)

SAWYER, Peter '1066–1086: a tenurial revolution?', in *Domesday Book*, ed. P. Sawyer (London 1985), pp. 71–85

SAWYER, P. 'The wealth of England in the eleventh century', *Transactions of the Royal Historical Society*, 5th S., 15 (1965) 145–64

SCOTT, John (ed. & transl.) *The Early History of Glastonbury. An Edition, Translation and Study of William of Malmesbury's 'De Antiquitate Glastonie Ecclesie'* (Woodbridge 1981)

SHARPE, R. (transl.) 'Eadmer's letter to the monks of Glastonbury concerning St Dunstan's disputed remains', in *The Archaeology and History of Glastonbury Abbey*, edd. L. Abrams & J.P. Carley (Woodbridge 1991), pp. 205–15

SHEEHAN, M.M. *The Will in Medieval England*, (Toronto 1963)

SIMS-WILLIAMS, Patrick *Religion and Literature in Western England, 600–800* (Cambridge 1990)

SIMS-WILLIAMS, P. 'St Wilfrid and two charters dated AD 676 and 680', *Journal of Ecclesiastical History* 39 (1988) 163–83

SLOVER, Clark H. 'Glastonbury Abbey and the fusing of English literary culture', *Speculum* 10 (1935) 147–60

SMITH, A.H. *English Place-name Elements* (2 vols, Cambridge 1956)

SMITH, A.H. *The Place-names of Gloucestershire* (4 vols, Cambridge 1964–5)

SPELMAN, Henry *Archæologus in Modum Glossarii ad Rem Antiquam Posteriorem* (London 1626)

STACY, N.E. 'The Estates of Glastonbury Abbey c.1050–1200' (unpublished D.Phil. dissertation, University of Oxford 1971)

STAPLETON, T. (ed.) *Chronicon Petroburgense* (London 1849)

STENTON, F[rank] M[erry] *Anglo-Saxon England* (3rd edn, Oxford 1971)

STENTON, Frank Merry *Preparatory to 'Anglo-Saxon England'* (Oxford 1970)

STENTON, Frank M. *The Early History of the Abbey of Abingdon* (Reading 1913)

STENTON, F[rank] M. *The Latin Charters of the Anglo-Saxon Period* (Oxford 1955)

STENTON, F. 'Types of manorial structure in the Northern Danelaw', in *Oxford Studies in Social and Legal History*, ed. Paul Vinogradoff (9 vols, Oxford 1909–27), II.3–96

STEPHENSON, C. 'Commendation and related problems in Domesday', *English Historical Review* 59 (1944) 289–310

STEVENSON, William Henry (ed.) *Asser's Life of King Alfred* (Oxford 1904; rev. imp., by D. Whitelock, 1959)

STEVENSON, W.H. 'Trinoda necessitas', *English Historical Review* 29 (1914) 689–703

STUBBS, William (ed.) *Memorials of Saint Dunstan, Archbishop of Canterbury* (London 1874)

STUBBS, William (ed.) *The Foundation of Waltham Abbey* (Oxford 1861)

STUBBS, William (ed.) *Willelmi Malmesbiriensis Monachi de Gestis Regum Anglorum* (2 vols, London 1887–9)

STUTZ, U. 'The proprietary church as an element of mediaeval Germanic ecclesiastical law', in *Mediaeval Germany 911–1250*, ed. G. Barraclough (2 vols, Oxford 1938)

SYMONS, Thomas (ed. & transl.) *Regularis Concordia Anglicae Nationis Monachorum Sanctimonialiumque. The Monastic Agreement of the Monks and Nuns of the English Nation* (Edinburgh 1953)

TANGL, M. (ed.) *Die Briefe des heiligen Bonifatius und Lullus* (Berlin 1916)

TAYLOR, H.M. & TAYLOR, J. *Anglo-Saxon Architecture* (3 vols, Cambridge 1965–78)

371

THACKER, A. 'Æthelwold and Abingdon', in *Bishop Æthelwold*, ed. B. Yorke (Woodbridge 1988), pp. 43–64

THOMSON, Rodney *William of Malmesbury* (Woodbridge 1987)

THORN, C. & THORN, F. (edd.) *Domesday Book. Devon*, gen. ed. J. Morris (2 vols, Chichester 1985)

THORN, C. & THORN, F. (edd.) *Domesday Book. Dorset*, gen. ed. J. Morris (Chichester 1983)

THORN, C. & THORN, F. (edd.) *Domesday Book. Shropshire*, gen. ed. J. Morris (Chichester 1986)

THORN, C. & THORN, F. (edd.) *Domesday Book. Somerset*, gen. ed. J. Morris (Chichester 1980)

THORN, C. & THORN, F. (edd.) *Domesday Book. Wiltshire*, gen. ed. J. Morris (Chichester 1979)

THORN, F. & THORN, C., *et al.* (edd.) *Domesday Book. Worcestershire*, gen. ed. J. Morris (Chichester 1982)

TURNER, A.G.C. 'A further selection of Somerset place-names containing Celtic elements', *Bulletin of the Board of Celtic Studies* 15 (1952–4) 12–21

TURNER, A.G.C. 'A selection of North Somerset place-names', *Proceedings of the Somerset Archaeological and Natural History Society* 96 (1951) 152–9

TURNER, A.G.C. 'Notes on some Somerset place-names', *Proceedings of the Somerset Archaeological and Natural History Society* 95 (1950) 112–24

TURNER, A.G.C. 'Some aspects of Celtic survival in Somerset', *Proceedings of the Somerset Archaeological and Natural History Society* 97 (1953) 148–51

TURNER, A.G.C. 'Some Old English passages relating to the episcopal manor of Taunton', *Proceedings of the Somerset Archaeological and Natural History Society* 98 (1953) 118–26

TURNER, A.G.C. 'Some Somerset place-names containing Celtic elements', *Bulletin of the Board of Celtic Studies* 4 (1950–2) 113–19

VINOGRADOFF, P. *English Society in the Eleventh Century: Essays in English Medieval History* (Oxford 1908)

VINOGRADOFF, Paul (ed.) *Oxford Studies in Social and Legal History* (9 vols, Oxford 1909–27)

WALLACE-HADRILL, J.M. *Early Germanic Kingship in England and on the Continent* (Oxford 1971)

WALLACE-HADRILL, J.M. *The Frankish Church* (Oxford 1983)

WATKIN, A. 'The earliest Glastonbury seal', *Proceedings of the Somerset Archaeological Association* 94 (1948/9) 156–8

WATKIN, A. 'The Glastonbury "pyramids" and St. Patrick's companions', *Downside Review* 63 [N.S., 43] (1945) 30–41

WATKIN, Aelred (ed.) *The Great Chartulary of Glastonbury* (3 vols, 1947–56)

WEAVER, F.W. (ed.) *A Feodary of Glastonbury Abbey* (1910)

WEAVER, F.W. 'Glastonbury Abbey excavations', *Notes and Queries for Somerset and Dorset* 12 (1910/11) 114–16

WEAVER, F.W. & MAYO, C.H. (edd.) 'Index to Abbot Monington's "Secretum" ', *Notes and Queries for Somerset and Dorset* 12 (1910/11) 273–80, 321–8, 356–63, and 13 (1912/13) 41–8, 89–96, 136–44

WEBSTER, Leslie & BACKHOUSE, J. (edd.) *The Making of England. Anglo-Saxon Art and Culture AD 600–900* (London 1991)

WHITELOCK, Dorothy (ed. & transl.) *Anglo-Saxon Wills* (Cambridge 1930)

WHITELOCK, D[orothy], *et al.* (edd.) *Councils and Synods with Other Documents relating to the English Church, I, A.D. 871–1204* (2 parts, Oxford 1981)

WHITELOCK, Dorothy (transl.) *English Historical Documents c. 500–1042* (2nd edn, London 1979)

WHITELOCK, Dorothy, *et al.* (edd.) *Ireland in Early Mediaeval Europe. Studies in Memory of Kathleen Hughes* (Cambridge 1982)

WHITELOCK, Dorothy 'Some charters in the name of King Alfred', in *Saints, Scholars and Heroes*, edd. M.H. King & W. Stevens (2 vols, Collegeville, MI 1979), I.77–98

WHITELOCK, D. 'The authorship of the account of King Edgar's establishment of the monasteries', in *Philological Essays*, ed. J.L. Rosier (The Hague 1970), pp. 125–36

WILLIAMS, A. (ed.) 'How land was held before and after the Norman Conquest', in *Domesday Book. Studies*, edd. R.W.H. Erskine & A. Williams (London 1987), pp. 37–8

WILLIAMS, A. 'Introduction to the Dorset Domesday', in *A History of the County of Dorset*, III, ed. R.B. Pugh (London 1968), pp. 1–60

WILLIAMS, A. 'Introduction to the Dorset geld rolls', in *A History of the County of Dorset*, III, ed. R.B. Pugh (London 1968), pp. 115–23

WILLIAMS, A. '*Princeps Merciorum gentis*: the family, career, and connections of Ælfhere, ealdorman of Mercia, 956–83', *Anglo-Saxon England* 10 (1982) 143–72

WILLIAMS, A. (ed. & transl.) 'Text and translation of the Dorset geld rolls', in *A History of the County of Dorset*, III, ed. R.B. Pugh (London 1968), pp. 124–47

WILLIAMS, M. *The Draining of the Somerset Levels* (Cambridge 1970)

WILLIAMS, T.W. *Somerset Mediaeval Libraries* (Bristol 1897)

WILSON, A. & TUCKER, J. 'The Langley charter and its boundaries', *Wiltshire Archaeological and Natural History Magazine* 77 (1982) 67–70

WILSON, David M. (ed.) *The Archaeology of Anglo-Saxon England* (London 1976)

WORMALD, F. 'The Sherborne "chartulary" ', in *Fritz Saxl 1890–1948*, ed. D.J. Gordon (Edinburgh 1957), pp. 101–19

WORMALD, P. 'A handlist of Anglo-Saxon lawsuits', *Anglo-Saxon England* 17 (1989) 247–81

WORMALD, P. *Bede and the Conversion of England: the Charter Evidence* (Jarrow Lecture 1984)

WORMALD, P. 'Charters, law, and the settlement of disputes', *The Settlement of Disputes in Early Medieval Europe*, edd. W. Davies & P. Fouracre (Cambridge 1986), pp. 149–68

WORMALD, P. 'The uses of literacy in Anglo-Saxon England and its neighbours', *Transactions of the Royal Historical Society*, 5th S., 27 (1977) 95–114

WYNDHAM, K.S.H. 'In pursuit of Crown land: the initial recipients of Somerset property in the mid Tudor period', *Proceedings of the Somerset Archaeological and Natural History Society* 123 (1978/79) 65–73

YORKE, Barbara (ed.) *Bishop Æthelwold, his Career and Influence* (Woodbridge 1988)

ZIMMERMANN, H. (ed.) *Papsturkunden, 896–1046* (2 vols, Wien 1984/5)

INDEX OF MANUSCRIPTS

INDEX OF ANGLO–SAXON CHARTERS

Documents are cited by their number in Sawyer's *Anglo-Saxon Charters*; reference-numbers for the contents-list of the *Liber terrarum*, the *Index chartarum*, and MS. 39a (see pp. 31–7) are also given, where relevant.

DATE DUE

			Printed in USA

HIGHSMITH #45230